BRETT'S
HISTORY OF
PSYCHOLOGY

BRETT'S
HISTORY OF
PSYCHOLOGY

EDITED AND ABRIDGED
BY

R. S. PETERS

THE M.I.T. PRESS

MASSACHUSETTS INSTITUTE OF TECHNOLOGY
CAMBRIDGE, MASSACHUSETTS

VOL. I FIRST PUBLISHED IN 1912
VOL. II FIRST PUBLISHED IN 1921
VOL. III FIRST PUBLISHED IN 1921

ABRIDGED ONE-VOLUME EDITION PUBLISHED IN 1953
REVISED EDITION 1962

This revised edition © George Allen & Unwin Ltd. 1962

First M.I.T. Press Paperback Edition, February 1965
Second Paperback Printing, April 1967

Copyright © 1965
by The Massachusetts Institute of Technology
All rights reserved

Library of Congress Catalog Card Number: 65-15931
Printed in the United States of America

PREFACE

The late Professor Brett's *History of Psychology* in three volumes was
a classic. It combined an astonishing erudition about details of past
psychological systems with a catholicity of approach to what is now
called psychology. It tried to show not only the development of psychology from the earliest times to the present day—in itself a formidable
undertaking—but also to exhibit in general terms the influence of
medical, religious, and philosophical thought on theories about man.
There is thus a great deal of historical material in Brett's work which is
both important and interesting to the student of psychology and which
is not readily available in other histories of psychology.

There are, however, certain obvious defects in Brett's three volumes
if they are looked at from the point of view of the modern student. In
the first place they are unwieldy and contain too much material. In the
second place they do not carry the student much beyond the beginning
of the twentieth century, volume one having been published in 1912
and volume three in 1921. The decision was therefore taken to publish
a revised edition of Brett's history in one volume with a concluding
chapter bringing his history up to date.

The abridgement of another man's work is always a difficult task.
The editor decided not to re-write the text, but only to omit sections
and to add an introduction to the work as a whole, short introductions
to each section of the work, and a concluding chapter. It is thus always
clear both from the type used, as well as from the style, when the
student is reading Brett's own words and when he is reading the
editor's additions. A list of omissions from the text will be found at the
end. The concluding chapter presented great problems; for there are
many excellent modern histories of psychology and the editor did not
want to do again in a short compass what has been better done by
others at greater length. The final chapter therefore attempts to single
out the main trends of twentieth-century psychology, to summarize the
most important theories about man, and to show the ways in which
these trends and theories are continuations of or reactions against the
traditions of enquiry so ably depicted by the late Professor Brett. The
result, it is hoped, is that the revised work differs from other histories
available in containing a great deal of early material—e.g. on Greek,
Stoic, Patristic, Scholastic, and Cartesian psychology—which is either
omitted altogether or briefly summarized in other histories; it also
differs in the way in which the material as a whole, and especially the
twentieth-century material, is presented, which is meant to be comple-

mentary to rather than a substitute for other modern histories of psychology.

The abridgement of three volumes to the size of one involves not only difficult decisions about what ought to be omitted but also the devising of a framework for knitting together what is left. Brett was primarily a philosopher and it therefore seemed appropriate to knit together his material in a philosophical framework without doing violence to his historical approach. Now the modern philosopher's interest in psychology lies in its concepts and methodology. Therefore a methodological framework for Brett's historical material has been devised which is a way both of knitting together the material and of raising many points of methodological interest in connection with a variety of psychological enquiries. Of course the framework often creaks. Logical distinctions can never do justice to the complexities of historical growth. But it was thought worth-while to combine a framework, which is essential to the presentation of such a mass of material, with a methodological commentary which provides a unifying theme of interest to modern philosophically minded students of psychology.

In conclusion the editor must prepare the reader for a certain discrepancy in style and outlook between the main body of the work and his own contributions. No apologies are necessary for the philosophical theme and manner of presentation; for this also characterized Brett's own three volumes. But the philosophical temper of 1951 is very different from that of 1921. To many the revised edition will, perhaps, appear more like the Festival of Britain skylon sticking out of the Crystal Palace than the winning design for the reconstruction of Coventry Cathedral. This kind of criticism is inevitable with all revisions and reconstructions. The revision of Brett, however, has the advantage of avoiding all possibility of confusing the words of Brett with those of his reviser.

R. S. PETERS

BIRKBECK COLLEGE
UNIVERSITY OF LONDON
September 1951

PREFACE TO SECOND EDITION

In the second edition the basic structure of the first edition has been preserved. There are, however, some alterations and additions of a quite major character. For instance, three major sections of the original Brett (Ch. XII, Sec. 5, 'From Taine to Binet', and Ch. XIV, Sec. 6, 'Feeling and Emotion'), which were mistakenly omitted in the first edition, have been included. Also the editor has added expositions of his own of Aristotle and Hobbes because he considers that Brett's original exposition of the ideas of these thinkers was too brief in relation to their importance for modern philosophically minded students of psychology. The editor wishes to stress that this history is for philosophically minded students of the history of psychology, a point not grasped clearly enough by some critics of the first edition. Also the final chapter on 'Twentieth-Century Theories,' which has been altered and added to, was written with the needs and interests of British and American students predominantly in mind. No attempt has been made to take account of anything that has happened in psychology after about 1950. Thanks are due to many who have suggested improvements for the second edition, especially to Mr. Foss and Miss Veness, who contributed sections to the first edition, and to Prof. Oldfield and Prof. Zangwill for their help with minor corrections. Thanks are also due to Mrs. Phyllis Cope who compiled the Index for the second edition.

R. S. PETERS

BIRKBECK COLLEGE
UNIVERSITY OF LONDON
January 1961

CONTENTS

PREFACE

PART I

I. THEORY, POLICY, AND TECHNOLOGY

1. Introductory . . . . . page 25
2. Psychology and the myth of subject-matter . 25
3. Questions of theory 28
4. Questions of policy 30
5. Questions of technology 30
6. Philosophical and metaphysical questions . 32

II. PRE-SOCRATIC SPECULATION

A. *Introductory* 37
B. *Speculative*

1. The Ionians 40
2. Parmenides 41
3. Empedocles 42
4. Anaxagoras 45
5. Democritus 47
6. Pythagoras 51

C. *Ethico-religious*

1. The Pythagoreans 51

D. *Medical*

1. Alcmaeon 52
2. Hippocrates 54

III. THE SOPHISTS, SOCRATES, AND CONSCIOUSNESS OF METHOD

A. *Introductory* 60
B. *The Sophists*

1. Protagoras 62
2. Gorgias 63

C. *Socrates*

1. Relation to Sophists 64
2. Moral Psychology 65

D. *Aristippus*

1. Sensationalism 66
2. Cyrenaic theory of feeling 67

IV. PLATO AND THE START OF THE RATIONALIST TRADITION

A. Introductory . . . . . *page* 69
B. Speculative

1. The *Timaeus* account of man 71
2. Motion and the metaphysical picture of the soul 75
3. Sensation, memory, imagination . . . 76
4. Feeling 80

C. Ethico-religious

1. Orphic influence 83

D. Epistemological

1. The cognitive faculties of the soul . . . 85

E. Educational

1. Plato's conception of education . . . 89
2. The stages of the soul's education . . . 90
3. Education for the good life 91

V. ARISTOTLE'S MODIFICATION OF RATIONALISM

A. Introductory 94
B. Aristotle's conceptual contribution to psychology 96

1. 'Soul' co-extensive with life 96
2. The soul as the first actuality of a body furnished with organs 99
3. Soul as the source of movement but not itself moved 102
4. The levels of soul 104

C. Speculative

1. Aristotle's physiology 105
2. The special senses 106
3. The 'connatural spirits' 113

D. Epistemological

1. Sensation as assimilation 114
2. Common sense, memory, and dreams . . 115
3. Imagination 121
4. Reason 123

E. Ethical and religious

1. Practical reason and conation . . . 125
2. Active and passive reason . . . 134

PART II

VI. THE DEVELOPMENT OF THE ETHICO-RELIGIOUS TRADITION (Pre-Christian)

A. *Introductory* . . . . . *page* 143
B. *The Stoics*

1. Relation to previous doctrines . . . 146
2. First principles 147
3. The soul and its activities 148
4. Imagination and reason 151
5. Freedom 155

C. *The Epicureans*

1. General principles 158
2. Sensation 159
3. Reason, freedom, and pleasure . . . 161

D. *The fusion of the Greek and Hebrew traditions*

1. The Hebrew tradition 166
2. The Jews of Alexandria 169
3. Philo 171

VII. THE DEVELOPMENT OF THE ETHICO-RELIGIOUS TRADITION (Christian)

A. *The Early Christian Fathers*

1. St. Paul 181
2. Clement 184
3. Origen 191

B. *Medical Influences*

1. Asclepiades 195
2. Athenaeus 196
3. Galen 197

C. *Neo-Platonism*

1. Relationship to Platonic doctrine . . 204
2. Plotinus' account of the soul . . . 205
3. The activities of the soul 208

D. *The psychology of St. Augustine*

1. Revelation and introspection as methods 214
2. The soul and the body . . . 215
3. Sensation, memory, and self-knowledge . . 217
4. Imagination and reason 221
5. The ascent of the soul 223

VIII. THE REINTERPRETATION OF
AUTHORITIES

A. *Introductory* . . . . . *page* 226
B. *Plato, Aristotle, or Augustine?*
1. Intellect, will, affections 229
2. Alexander's treatment of Aristotle's Reason . 233
3. Porphyry on animal intelligence . . . 235
4. Proclus' Neo-Platonism 237

C. *Arabian adaptations*
1. The Arab mind. 241
2. Alkindi 244
3. Avicenna. 246
4. Alhazen 250
5. Averroes. 255

D. *Subjects of controversy in the schools*
1. The method of scholasticism . . . 257
2. The spirit and the body . . . 258
3. Sense-perception 259
4. Reason and will 260
5. Conscience 262
6. Self-knowledge 263
7. Universals and the soul . . . 264

E. *From Alcuin to Aquinas*
1. Alcuin and Eriugena 266
2. John of Salisbury and William of Conches . 269
3. Hugh of St. Victor 272
4. Alexander of Hales 278
5. Albert and Aquinas 280

IX. THE CHALLENGE TO AUTHORITY

A. *Introductory* 289
B. *Ethico-religious*
1. Bonaventura and Eckhart . . . 291
2. Duns Scotus and William of Ockham . 293
3. Buridan 296
4. St. Theresa 297

C. *Speculative*
1. Roger Bacon and Witelo . . . 300
2. The mysteries of nature . . . 303
3. Macchiavelli and Montaigne . . 306
4. Pomponazzi 311

D. *Medical*

1. Vesalius and Harvey . . . . *page* 315
2. Villanova and Paracelsus 316
3. Cardanus, Telesius, Campanella, and Scaliger . 318

E. *Educational*

1. Vives 323

PART III

X. THE GATEWAY OF METHOD

A. *Introductory* 335
B. *The influence of other sciences*

1. General 336
2. Astronomy and mathematics . . . 337
3. Optics 339
4. Mechanics and chemistry 341

C. *The observationalist method of induction* . . 349
D. *The rationalist method of deduction* . . . 354

XI. THE RATIONALIST TRADITION

A. *Descartes*

1. Physiology 359
2. The body as a machine 360
3. The senses 362
4. The mind 365
5. The passions 368
6. Descartes compared with Aristotle . . 370
7. Animals as machines 372

B. *Gassendi, Hobbes, and the reaction*

1. Gassendi 377
2. Hobbes 378
3. More and Cudworth 386

C. *The Occasionalists*

1. Geulincx 387
2. Malebranche 388

D. *Spinoza*

1. Organic unity 394
2. The passions: Spinoza's development of Descartes 396
3. The influence of reason 405

E. *Leibniz and Wolff*

1. Leibniz's background and importance . . 406
2. Continuity, activity, and representation . . 408
3. Wolff's systematization of Leibniz . . 413

XII. THE OBSERVATIONALIST TRADITION

A. *British empiricists and associationists*

1. Locke . . . . . . *page* 417
2. Berkeley 423
3. Hume 429
4. Hartley 436
5. Reid and Stewart 443
6. Brown and Hamilton 447
7. James Mill 449
8. Bain and J. S. Mill 456

B. *Continental empiricism and reactions against it*

1. The French enlightenment 465
2. Bonnet 478
3. Tetens 481
4. Maine de Biran and Cournot . . . 488
5. From Taine to Binet 494
6. Wundt 504
7. Mach and Avenarius 514
8. Ebbinghaus and Külpe 516

C. *The Beginning of Social and Animal Psychology*

1. Social psychology 519
2. Animal psychology 525

PART IV

XIII. PSYCHOLOGY BECOMES SELF-CONSCIOUS

A. *Introductory* 533
B. *Kant's critique of speculation*

1. The attack on rational psychology . . . 535
2. Kant's 'anthropology' 538
3. Kant's importance 541
4. Practical and theoretical reason . . . 543

C. *Herbart's mathematical psychology*

1. The soul and phenomena 545
2. Self-preservation and the principles of mental action 549
3. Classification of mental activities . . . 556
4. Beyond psychology 562

D. *Beneke's restatement of 'faculty' psychology*

1. Beneke and Herbart compared . . . 563
2. The 'prime faculties' and their development . 565

E. *Schopenhauer and Von Hartmann*

1. The sources of 'will' psychology . . *page* 574
2. Schopenhauer's reinstatement of the will . 575
3. Von Hartmann and the unconscious . . 578

F. *Fechner's experimental pan-psychism*

1. Fechner's inspiration 580
2. Psycho-physics 584

G. *Lotze's soul psychology*

1. Speculative philosophy 591
2. The details of Lotze's system . . . 593
3. Psychology without metaphysics? . . 599

H. *Brentano and Lipps*

1. Brentano's neo-scholasticism . . . 601
2. Lipps's psychology of 'force' . . . 604

XIV. THE INROADS OF PHYSIOLOGY AND BIOLOGY

A. *Introductory* 610

B. *The influence of physiology*

1. Eighteenth-century physiology . . 612
2. Problems of localization . . . 618
3. Problems of neurology . . . 625
4. Problems of sense-perception . . 630
5. Vision and hearing 639
6. Feeling and emotion . . . 646
7. Ziehen 655
8. Münsterberg 657

C. *The influence of biology*

1. Spencer 660
2. Lewes, Mill, and Darwin . . . 666

D. *New syntheses*

1. Ward 675
2. Stout 684
3. James 686

XV. TWENTIETH-CENTURY THEORIES

A. *Introductory* 691

B. *The observationalist tradition*

1. Introspectionism 692
2. Behaviourism and animal psychology . 694
3. Skinner's Operationism . . 699

C. *Reactions against the observationalist tradition*

1. Purposive psychology 702
2. Gestalt psychology 710

D. *The influence of technology*
1. Medicine and Freudian psychology . *page* 715
2. Child psychology and intelligence tests . . 731
E. *The influence of other sciences*
1. Biology and physiology 737
2. The social sciences 744
F. *Psychology as a theoretical science?* . . . 751
G. *Conclusion* 761

LIST OF MAJOR OMITTED SECTIONS   763

BIBLIOGRAPHY FOR STUDENTS   769

INDEX OF PROPER NAMES   773

ACKNOWLEDGMENTS

The Editor wishes to thank Mr. Brian Foss of Birkbeck College, University of London, for contributing the physiological section in Ch. XV, Miss Thelma Veness of Birkbeck College for contributing the section on recent developments in tests in Ch. XV, and Professor C. A. Mace of Birkbeck College for his advice on the general plan of the revised edition. He would also like to thank Professor Mace and Dr. R. L. Saw of Birkbeck College for their help with the bibliography, and Dr. Norbert Elias of the Department of Social Studies, Bedford College, University of London, for his constructive criticism of the first draft of the final chapter.   R. S. P.

January 1953.

PART

I

Chapter One

THEORY, POLICY, AND TECHNOLOGY

I. INTRODUCTORY

In his Preface to the first volume of his *History of Psychology* the late Professor Brett declared his intention of exhibiting 'the nature of man . . . as forming the centre of three great lines of interest, namely, the study of human activities as the psychologist sees them, the study of human life as the doctor looks at it, and the growth of systematic beliefs as reflected in philosophy and religion.' Emphasis was laid by him on what may be called 'psychological data in the strict sense; around these data are grouped such theories as diverge from the phenomena of consciousness to derivative doctrines of the soul's antecedents, environments, and future possibilities.' Before proceeding to the exposition of Brett's text the case must therefore be stated for retaining such a wealth of philosophical, religious, and medical material in this abridgement of his *History of Psychology* for modern students.

2. PSYCHOLOGY AND THE MYTH OF SUBJECT-MATTER

It is often supposed that it is possible to make distinctions between enquiries by reference to the subject-matter with which each is concerned. Many would say that we are now much clearer than Professor Brett was about what the proper subject-matter of psychology is and that we could therefore rule out a great deal of his material as irrelevant. If this were the case it would follow that a historian of psychology would only have to make a compilation of the various descriptions of and theories about the subject-matter in question in order to write his history; he would be able to dismiss as irrelevant many past enquiries in the same sort of way as a collector of coins can reject buttons. This superstition about science springs from a well-worn misunderstanding of enquiry, which is often referred to as the Book of Nature view. Ever since Francis Bacon people have supposed that knowledge is acquired by studiously collecting 'data,' storing them under a variety of headings, and then cautiously making generalizations which do not go beyond the data. There is, as it were, a Book of Nature which is being laboriously compiled with chapters set aside for different scientists to write. The material for each chapter is the 'subject-matter' of a special science.

This account is defective in at least two major respects. In the first place it omits to stress that no one starts afresh in the acquisition of knowledge. We all stand on the shoulders of our ancestors; we inherit a tradition. The very language we speak incorporates in a condensed form all kinds of assumptions about things, people, and situations. We take things for granted that our ancestors discovered by trial and error; we can neither avoid nor dispense with our social inheritance which is handed down in the form of countless traditional skills and assumptions. We also probably inherit certain innate patterns of response which are modified and made more subtle by our experience of things and situations. Bacon and his followers—especially Locke and Hume—seemed to picture the acquisition of knowledge as the building up of general assumptions after repeated contact with things and situations of a similar kind. They put the emphasis the wrong way round. In fact we start with assumptions which are very general. We learn by contact with particular things and situations to differentiate and to particularize. We are never without assumptions, never without knowledge, even if it is of a very primitive and undifferentiated kind. This is as true for the race as it is true for the individual. As we shall see, the enquiry which we now call psychology took about two thousand three hundred years to differentiate itself from a mass of very general speculations about everything and anything.

In the second place we have interests in and attitudes towards our environment as well as expectations of it. These, too, are partly innate and partly socially acquired. We notice what interests us; we remember what is of importance to us; we forget what we do not want to remember. We are never without interests in and attitudes towards our environment just as we are never without expectations of it and assumptions about it. Patient, passive, presuppositionless enquiry is a methodological myth. When our expectations are disappointed our interests lead us to ask further questions. Asking questions is a surrogate and less irrevocable form of that departure from routine behaviour by animals which we call problem-solving behaviour. We differ from most of them in being able to solve problems 'in our head' instead of committing ourselves irretrievably to action. Thinking is trial and error in imagination, not the cautious colligation of data. Just as problem-solving behaviour starts when routine activities are interrupted or break down, so we ask questions when one or other of our expectations is falsified or when traditional assumptions are no longer adequate to explain diversity of experience. In the falsification of our expectations by contact with our environment, in the challenge to traditional assumptions, we have the germ of scientific activity. This procedure is known technically as 'verifying hypotheses.' The so-called data or subject-matter come in at the point when we go to look in order to confirm or falsify some hypothesis. Just as when we walk into a room we notice what is of interest to us, so when we are engaged on an enquiry we collect the type of 'data' or make the kind of observations which are relevant to our interests and previous assumptions. Data can never be collected or observations made without interests and expectations. A person conducting an enquiry has questions to answer rather than a subject-matter to examine. So-called subject-matters are relative always to the interests and expectations of enquirers. Thus the only adequate way of differentiating the different sciences is to single out different traditions of enquiry. We cannot sit down and methodically sort out the different sciences by reference to their subject-matter.

No doubt there is a quite usual and harmless sense of the term 'subject-matter' in which, in any account of scientific method, petrologists, ornithologists, and astronomers can be said to have different subject-matters. There are traditions of enquiry concerned with certain classes of objects like rocks, rooks, and stars. And these are as different from each other as coins are from buttons. Speaking about subject-matters in this way is useful for practical and didactic purposes; it facilitates the setting of examinations, the organization of research, university departments, and other institutional devices for perpetuating traditions of enquiry. But this way of talking about subject-matter is useless for advanced sciences like physics and chemistry and in the case of psychology there are so many other sciences concerned with human beings that distinction by reference to objects of interest is not very helpful. What we call psychology is just an amalgam of different questions about human beings which have grown out of a variety of traditions of enquiry. If a psychologist wants to know why some people are habitually depressed he cannot rule out an answer in terms of glandular deficiency just because physiologists or biochemists study that sort of thing. A working scientist differs from a teacher preparing people for examinations; he cannot dismiss possible answers to questions because they are not on the syllabus.

The late Professor Brett was therefore on safe ground in exhibiting what we call psychology as arising from a variety of traditions of enquiry into the nature of man—religious, medical, philosophical, and many others which space prevented him from including. He was also wise in giving a prominent place to what he calls 'psychological data in the strict sense.' By this he meant introspective reports or reports by subjects themselves on their own doings and feelings. For, although nowadays we would not want to make a rigid distinction between these reports which other people can make about a person and those which he alone can make about himself, nevertheless if we were pressed to distinguish psychology from biology, physiology, and certain other sciences which overlap with psychology, we would probably have recourse firstly to certain types of question which have been traditionally asked about man and secondly to the use of introspective reports in answering such questions. For the biologist a dog, an ape, and a man are on a par in that reliance is not placed on introspective reports in confirming or falsifying assumptions about them. The psychologist, on the other hand, is like the doctor, the philosopher, and the religious writer in taking into account what people say about their own doings and feelings, their symptoms as well as their signs. Thus Brett is to be defended not only for showing psychology as an enquiry differentiating out of a variety of traditions, but also for singling out medical, religious, and philosophical traditions as those which are especially relevant. By implication he dismisses as absurd the common assumption, enshrined in so many introductory chapters to text-books of psychology, that there is a separate science of psychology which can be distinguished from other sciences by reference to its subject-matter.

We have therefore to trace the history of various traditions of enquiry, some of which have now been amalgamated under the general heading of psychology. Of some of these traditions we can *now* say that they were concerned mainly with religious questions, moral questions, scientific questions, technological questions, philosophical questions, or metaphysical questions. But this could not always have been said; in fact our interest in and ability to say this sort of thing, to sort out these different sorts of questions, are themselves the product of a tradition of enquiry which we now call critical philosophy. Historically speaking these logical distinctions were slow to emerge like the distinctions between custom, law, and morality. We, who inherit the tradition of Kant and Hume, find it difficult to realize how difficult it was for earlier thinkers to grasp distinctions which seem to us so obvious. As Brett's monument of erudition has been abridged and welded together by the editor in a manner which presupposes such later logical distinctions it is necessary, briefly, to indicate the type of criteria used.

3. QUESTIONS OF THEORY

Enquiry, it has been maintained, is the answering of questions. It represents the cross-fertilization of our expectations, attitudes, and interests with actual contact with our environment. Now certain sorts of statements are verbalizations of our expectations whereas others are verbalizations of our interests and attitudes. If a person says that iron expands when it is heated he is *describing* what he expects to observe, but if he says that swords ought to be beaten into pruning hooks he is expressing an attitude towards the use of iron, or *prescribing* a course of action. Descriptions are answers to questions of theory; prescriptions are answers to questions of policy. Questions of theory are answered in the end by some process of going to look. Often we cannot do this and have to rely on memory or testimony. Memory is a delayed and very fallible way of looking; testimony is reliance on other people's looking or memory. Those whose interest in going to look is the confirmation or falsification of general assumptions like 'iron expands when heated' are conveniently referred to as scientists; those whose interest lies in establishing descriptions of particular events or series of events like 'Plato finished writing the *Republic* in 370 B.C.' are conveniently referred to as historians. The scientist is interested in what was, is, and always will be the case; the historian is interested in what was the case or in what is now the case.

Scientific and historical enquiries both presuppose each other[1] as all knowledge is a cross-fertilization of general assumptions with particular observations. The difference between the two is a matter of emphasis only. To test a general assumption like 'iron expands when heated' it has to be combined with an initial condition statement describing a particular state of affairs like 'this is a case of iron being heated' to which the general assumption is relevant. A conclusion is then deduced from a combination of the general and the particular statement such as 'this piece of iron will expand.' The observation that the iron actually does expand is then a confirmation of the general assumption that iron expands when it is heated. Now doubt could be cast on whether this was in fact a piece of iron, whether it was in fact being heated, or whether it did in fact expand. In other words the initial condition statements or the observation statements could be treated as hypothetical instead of the general assumption. A historical enquiry would then begin to decide whether the particular events described by these statements actually occurred. In order to test the statement that it was in fact heated it would have to be combined with other general assumptions like 'heated iron smells acrid.' From this together with the initial condition statement that there was an acrid smell it could be deduced that the iron had been heated. Historians assume countless such generalizations in establishing their hypotheses about the past. These generalizations are often of such a trivial kind, so deeply embedded in common-sense knowledge of the world, that we tend to overlook them. But examples like these bring out the complementary character of science and history. Both types of question are termed 'theoretical' because they are answered by some process of going to look. Agreement can often be reached about the answers to such questions because, whatever a person's interests and attitudes may be, he will usually agree with another person if asked a simple question about what is before his eyes. A person who prefers swords to pruning hooks will usually agree with a person who prefers pruning hooks to swords when asked by the blacksmith whether the iron is changing shape on the anvil.

4. QUESTIONS OF POLICY

A great number of questions, however, are not about what is or was or will be the case but about what *ought* to be the case. Answers to such questions of policy are appraisals rather than assumptions, prescriptions rather than descriptions. They express our interests, attitudes, and demands rather than our expectations. They cannot be confirmed or falsified by simply looking at things or situations. The man who says that peace is better than war cannot be refuted by being made to look at swords as well as pruning hooks or by being taken from his husbandry to watch a battle. The wrongness of killing people is not revealed to us by simply watching a battle; we cannot put our ear to the ground and hear goodness steal by; the sacredness of a shrine is not made manifest to the nose of one who lingers there. Of course appraisals are seldom made, policies for living seldom recommended, without looking at things, people, or situations, or without memories of them or testimonies about them. But such appraisals and prescriptions are not statements of fact, neither can they be inferred from statements of fact. Assumptions are extremely *relevant* to appraisals, descriptions to prescriptions; but there is no valid inference from one to the other. Words like 'wrong,' 'good,' 'sacred' do not express our expectations so much as our interests in, demands of, and attitudes towards things, people, and situations. People can agree in their expectations of and assumptions about things, people, and situations, yet they can at the same time differ radically in their attitudes to, interests in, and demands of them. And if they disagree about such questions of policy there is no agreed procedure for settling the dispute; there is no procedure in answering questions of policy which has the same measure of agreement as going to look in answering questions of theory. That is why such questions, which are pre-eminently the concern of moralists like the Stoics and Epicureans or religious teachers like Jesus and St. Paul, are so notoriously difficult to settle.

5. QUESTIONS OF TECHNOLOGY

In addition to questions of theory and questions of policy there are what may be called questions of technology which are logical hybrids. They arise within a context of policy not clearly stated and involve questions of theory as well. They are, as it were, questions about our requirements. The old moral philosophers used to refer to these questions as questions of means which were to be handed over to scientists; they themselves conducted 'typically ethical enquiries' about questions of ends or 'intrinsic values.' This tendency to separate means from ends is doubly dangerous in that it not only encourages the illusion that there are final ends of human endeavour, but also leads people to suppose that questions of means do not involve any moral or policy considerations. But policy complications apart, technological problems are solved by *constructing* states of affairs describable in initial condition statements rather than by testing historical or scientific hypotheses. An engineer has to construct a bridge according to certain specifications. His problem is to devise a state of affairs in the various materials from a description of which, together with certain general assumptions about stresses, température, expansion, and so on, the specification can be deduced. Plato required an educational system which would produce a morally and intellectually élite class of rulers. He made various assumptions about human development and the ways in which children can be influenced at different ages. His educational proposals were a statement of his institutional requirements for attaining his ends, involving answers to both questions of theory and questions of policy.

The types of question which we have already distinguished enable us to identify some of the strands of enquiry in Brett's history. Many of the early writers were concerned predominantly with questions of policy and questions of technology. Their assumptions about and expectations of human nature were embedded in ethico-religious works which expressed, in the main, attitudes to life and requirements of character. Spinoza and St. Augustine, the Stoics and St. Thomas, all approached the material of human nature with ethico-religious interests. Yet they showed profound insight into the dispositions of men and the causes and consequences of certain types of behaviour. Any ethico-religious teacher who advocates a way of life or states his requirements of human nature must understand his material if he is to exert much influence. But it is not every saint or prophet who can make his understanding explicit in a form that can be preserved in a book. Not all good cooks write cookery books. In Spinoza's *Ethics*, however, or St. Augustine's *Confessions* we have examples of ethico-religious works with insight into human nature made explicit. Similarly Hippocrates and Galen, concerned mainly with technological problems of producing healthy bodies by regimen, diet, and medicines, wrote up their manuals in which they incorporated many useful and interesting assumptions about human nature, while educationalists like Locke and Vives made lasting contributions to our theoretical understanding of man. Of course these writers made no conscious attempts to test systematically the assumptions which they used. Had they done so they would have been scientists and not technologists. As a matter of fact what we have distinguished as theoretical science emerged very late in the history of psychology. But these early writers are not to be dismissed merely because they proposed policies for life and worked out their requirements for health and happiness. After all, most psychology even nowadays is technology rather than theoretical science. Whether a great number of interesting and important assumptions about human beings can ever be answered by the direct test of the theoretical scientist instead of by the roundabout, indirect tests of the technologist is a most important question which must be discussed in our final chapter.

6. PHILOSOPHICAL AND METAPHYSICAL QUESTIONS

We have still to deal with the philosophical and metaphysical strands in Brett's history. What we now call philosophical questions are alike in having a second-order character. They presuppose a certain degree of self-consciousness and sophistication about language, first-order activities, and rules of procedure. Scientists, moralists, and technologists are engaged on the first-order activities of testing hypotheses, recommending policies, and satisfying practical requirements. For the most part they just get on with their jobs without being troubled much about what they are doing. Philosophers, on the other hand, stand back from these activities and describe the rules of procedure involved. Often they propose alterations in procedure; they change the rules as well as try to understand them. The pre-occupation of philosophers with words is derivative from this second order character of philosophical enquiry. Scientists and moralists bother little about words; for them words are tools for dealing with things, people, and situations. Philosophers, who have often been referred to historically as 'spectators,' overhaul the tools of scientists, moralists, and others engaged on first-order activities, and critically review their procedures. If a moral philosopher attempts, like a moralist, to recommend a way of life or a new conception of society, he does so in a second-order manner by re-defining words like 'justice,' 'good,' and 'natural' or by concentrating on certain procedures for deciding on 'rightness' or 'wrongness' like looking at the consequences of actions or paying attention only to people's motives. Philosophers who are also moralists wave words instead of flags. Similarly epistemologists do not attempt often to discover new facts about the world; rather they examine the meanings of words like 'knowledge' and 'belief' and suggest relevant procedures for arriving at one rather than at the other. Those pre-occupied with scientific method do not confine themselves to doing experiments; they describe and make suggestions about the procedures of scientists and the concepts employed by them. It has often been said that people knew how to reason before Aristotle just as they knew how to behave morally before Hume. These philosophers attempted to make explicit what was implicit in the reasoning and morality of men, just as Kant tried to lay bare the presuppositions and procedures of science, morality, and aesthetic judgment. But they did not invent these activities or compete with the people who were actually engaged in them; practice usually precedes principles.

Philosophical enquiries are enormously important in the history of psychology. In the first place enquiries about man have been influenced by prevailing assumptions, usually derived from practice in other sciences, about knowledge and how to obtain it. The welding together of a mass of Brett's material under such headings as 'The Rationalist Tradition' and 'The Observationalist Tradition' is an attempt to exhibit this influence. Also quite a lot of material has been co-ordinated by tracing the influence of the concepts and methods of other sciences on psychology. For those who believe that success can be achieved in science by following some sort of recipe naturally tend to suppose that concepts and methods which have proved useful in one science will help the advance of another. In the second place a great number of apparently psychological discussions are really philosophical discussions in disguise. Because of their interest in the tools and methods of knowledge philosophers have been always extremely interested in the mind. But very often the conundrums they have posed about the various faculties of the mind like 'reason,' 'will,' 'desire,' 'conscience,' and so on, which many have treated as questions of introspective psychology to be settled by internal observation, are more properly to be regarded as questions about logical justification. The discussion, for instance, about the different parts of the soul, originating in Plato's classic case of the clash between reason and desire, is a pictorial way of distinguishing actions for which no reasons are given to oneself or others from actions preceded by giving reasons. The controversy about innate ideas was really a discussion about the status of assumptions for which, so it seemed, no factual reasons could be given, rather than a scientific wrangle about our pre-natal equipment. The celebrated dispute over abstract ideas was, in part at least, another example of logic masquerading as introspective psychology. Over and over again we find epistemological and logical questions about different classes of assumptions disguised as psychological questions about the equipment and workings of the mind. That is one reason why it is historically impossible, as the late Professor Brett saw so clearly, to separate the history of psychology from the history of philosophy.

Metaphysical questions are far harder to be clear about. Some of them are logical questions about the meanings of words like 'cause,' 'substance,' 'attribute,' 'mode,' and so on. Very often attempts are made to define these terms by reference to other such terms in order to give a very general description of anything and everything. The result may be an imposing verbal pattern culminating in the Absolute which it is very difficult to relate to our ordinary experience. There is, however, another kind of metaphysical activity which is very closely linked with scientific activity which can be described as the production of models. Models can be either limited to a particular range of facts for which an explanation is sought or extended to the whole universe. The latter sort of description is the metaphysical model par excellence. Models of the first sort are inseparable from scientific activity, though most tough-minded expositors of the history of science conveniently forget about them. Examples are the model of the planetary atom or the undulating ether. Kelvin is reputed to have said: 'When I have made a mechanical model I understand a process.'[1] These models, by producing in our imaginations a picture which resembles familiar phenomena like marbles revolving round billiard balls, waves, or mechanical devices, make us feel comfortable about the phenomena which we wish to explain. Strictly speaking they have no logical explanatory value; for, logically speaking, an explanation of a phenomenon consists in being able to deduce it from general assumptions combined with initial condition statements—e.g. the expansion of a piece of iron from the assumption that iron expands when it is heated together with the initial condition statement that this is a case of iron being heated. The history of psychology provides many illustrations of such models— Hume's model of the mind as a theatre on whose stage the players glide in and out or a commonwealth in which the members constantly change but are always related to each other by constant relationships of a hierarchical kind, Locke's picture of the mind as a sort of box or as a *tabula rasa*, Freud's picture of the mind as a miniature society some of whose members have formed themselves into a kind of underground movement, and the early picture of animal spirits coursing along tubes in the body

The metaphysical model par excellence is the extension of a picture drawn from a limited range of phenomena to make us feel comfortable about not just another limited range of phenomena but the universe as a whole. Spinoza's universe, based on his knowledge of mechanics and dynamics, was like a vast mechanical clock; Aristotle's, based on his interest in the pursuit of objects of satisfaction by living organisms, was a complicated teleological series of events which attain or seek to attain quiescence vividly portrayed by God's endless self-contemplative satisfaction; Leibniz's universe was a variegated system of animated

<hr />

[1] Quoted from W. George: *The Scientist in Action*, p. 331.

bodies of varying degrees of complexity such as his microscope had revealed to him on a smaller scale. All these very general descriptions can be seen to be extrapolations from a limited range of phenomena with which the metaphysicians were very familiar—mechanical systems, teleological behaviour patterns, and miscroscopic phenomena. Whitehead describes metaphysics as 'the science which seeks to discover the general ideas which are indispensably relevant to the analysis of everything that happens.'[1] It involves 'the utilization of specific notions, applying to a restricted group of facts, for the divination of the generic notions which apply to all facts.'[2]

Much of the material presented in Brett's early volumes is what would now be called metaphysical. Many would advocate its omission on these grounds. But it is all very well for us now to look back on the history of thought and to dub certain statements as metaphysical and certain others as scientific, meaning that the latter are empirically verifiable whereas the former are not. But, historically speaking, verifiable and unverifiable statements are jumbled together in the work of most writers up to the late nineteenth century. Also it is impossible at any given time in the history of thought to characterize statements as either scientific or as metaphysical. This is well illustrated by the modern position with regard to statements about the mind. We tend, in a rather tough-minded way, to say that statements about the mind are either statements about our dispositions to behave in certain ways in certain situations or they are metaphysical. Yet, if we examine statements about 'instincts' or about 'the unconscious' they cannot be fitted conveniently into either of the proposed baskets. Similarly, although we would be tempted to say that the mind is not an extra sort of thing describable by some metaphysical model like that of a box, a bundle, a theatre, a stream, or a miniature society, but a short-hand term for our various abilities, skills, and tendencies, when we consider the evidence for telepathy, telekinesis, and other paranormal phenomena, we are not at all sure which of these remarks about our various skills, abilities, and tendencies are metaphysical and which are not. The early writers about the mind or soul were in a similar position; but they differed, for the most part, in not having any explicit methodological rule like the verification principle by means of which they could rule out certain sorts of statement as undiscussable. For these reasons the word 'metaphysical' does not appear as a label for any of the late Professor Brett's material. Instead the word 'speculative' is occasionally used to remind us of the difficulty of distinguishing, either logically or historically, what is metaphysical from what is

---

[1] A. N. Whitehead: *Religion in the Making*, p. 84 (footnote).
[2] A. N. Whitehead: *Process and Reality*, p. 6.

scientific and to enable us to group together those enquiries which seem to be the product of speculative curiosity as distinct from those which are obviously subservient to policies for living or technological requirements. The general labels of 'policy' or 'technology' do not appear in the section headings either; instead these types of enquiry are particularized by sub-headings like 'ethico-religious' or 'medical' or 'educational.' Similarly the philosophical strands are particularized by sub-headings like 'epistemological' or by terms like 'rationalist' or 'observationalist' which denote a particular philosophical view about scientific method.

We have now outlined our logical apparatus for the presentation of Brett's historical material. Our ability to attempt such logical distinctions in no way invalidates Brett's attempt to show how psychology arose historically out of a mass of different traditions many of which were not much akin to that of theoretical science. Indeed if anyone attempted to write a history of psychology as a theoretical science he would have to begin with the nineteenth century—perhaps later. For conscious attempts to test assumptions about man did not emerge till Darwin had shattered the common belief in our supernatural origin. Psychologists, as it were, are nibbling at the very core of the forbidden fruit. But they should never forget that they inherit the tradition of a long line of philosophers, medical men, and ethico-religious writers who prepared the way for their entry into the garden.

Chapter Two

PRE-SOCRATIC SPECULATION

A. Introductory

We tend to think of science as a 'body of knowledge' which began to be accumulated when men hit upon 'scientific method.' This is a superstition. It is more in keeping with the history of thought to describe science as the myths about the world which have not yet been found to be wrong. Science had its roots partly in primitive pictures of the world and partly in primitive technology. There has been a great deal of discussion about the primacy of disinterested speculation or practical inventiveness in the early stages of science. Some maintain that those who said that the earth was made of air, or had an underlying mathematical structure, or was composed of atoms, were the originators of science; others uphold the claims of those who started measuring for irrigation schemes, or mixed tin with copper in order to make bronze, or guided their ships by the stars. Both parties are surely right; yet both fail to bring out the core of what we now call 'scientific method.' This began when men began consciously to challenge the stories that they were told and to produce counter-examples to support their contentions. Men may inherit stories from their parents; they may think them up on a cold winter's night in order to pass away the time; they may evolve them while trying to make better weapons or heal their wounds. This is a matter of history—often of personal biography—and is of little methodological interest. The crucial stage for the methodologist comes when conscious attempts are made to *test* the stories provided by tradition, speculative curiosity, or practical necessity.

Showing a man that his story is wrong usually involves producing a better story oneself. In argumentation, discussion, and the production of counter-examples drawn from memory, observation, and testimony, we have the core of what we now call science. Experimentation, measurement, and all the paraphernalia of the laboratory are but more precise ways of producing confirmations or counter-examples. Science consists in conscious attempts to refute other people's stories and in the production of better stories to supplant them. The history of science is the history of stories which have been shown to be false or only partially correct.

To those who think of psychology exclusively in terms of rats in mazes, neurotics in the consulting room, intelligence tests, and brass instruments, it cannot seem anything but odd to start the story of psychology with the early Greek cosmologists. Yet the theories of Heraclitus and Empedocles anticipate on a cosmic scale the struggle between love and hate particularized in the Freudian theory of ambivalence and the application of mathematical techniques to nature goes back to the Pythagoreans. The Greek cosmologists were important because they broke loose from the accepted religious traditions and produced what they considered to be better stories about the origin and stuff of the world. They speculated. In science it is better to have speculated and to have been found wrong than never to have speculated at all. Their speculative zeal and love of argumentation were not, however, matched by care in observation or ingenuity in experiment. It is true that some of them, especially the Ionians, blew up skins, put their ears to twanging strings, tasted water, and watched the stars. But they were regarded as impious, even as indecent by others who scorned such gross methods. The Greek aristocrats, in the main, regarded contact with the raw materials of nature as degrading. They handled men and symbols; the lesser breeds handled liquids and solids. This lack of contact with materials, which left a hiatus between mathematical techniques and empirical observation, was an unfortunate consequence of the social structure of the city states. There were also widespread religious scruples which retarded the observation of the heavenly bodies. The typically Greek contribution to the rise of science was therefore the speculative spirit and the love of argumentation. The love of argumentation was revived with the schoolmen of the Middle Ages without the speculative spirit. It was left to the physical scientists of the sixteenth and seventeenth centuries to combine the speculative spirit with the detailed observation of phenomena. They began almost where Democritus left off.

It is an interesting fact that detailed speculations about man were the last to emerge in the history of science. The heavenly bodies, the objects remotest from man, were the first objects of scientific interest. Speculation advanced slowly through the realms of the inorganic until, in the nineteenth century, detailed observation of animals paved the way for detailed and systematic observation of men. In the earliest stages of speculation theories about man were incorporated in and often deductions from wider speculations. The psychology of the Greeks was therefore crude, embryonic, and subservient to wider interests.

To the Greek thinker of the sixth century before Christ the human being appears to be a peculiar modification of certain universal principles. He is matter primarily, and as such is part of the material world. He exhibits modes of action which are, sometimes at least, initiated from within. Above all, he shares with other animate beings the peculiar quality of being alive. Now as regards the matter or stuff of which he is made, this must ultimately be the same as the matter which appears in other forms throughout the world; the same, in fact, as ultimate matter. What this ultimate matter is we do not at present inquire, and certainly do not oppose matter to spirit as though these two were by nature hostile. With a singular openness of mind the first inquirers were prepared to take into account all phenomena in their attempts to define the ultimate stuff of which things are made, and consequently include among those data what they conceived to be the qualities of the soul. There is therefore no hard and fast line of distinction between soul and not-soul. The popular analysis of nature as containing four primary qualifications or states, earth, air, fire, and water, provides a starting point. Either one of them is really prior to the others, or there is some other thing or condition of things prior to them.

The early philosophers, and especially the Ionian school, are frequently described in a way that lays far too much emphasis on the cosmological point of view. They were indeed 'physical' philosophers, but the title includes what we now assign to the students of physics, medicine, and of physiology. The decisive factor in the choice of a 'first matter' is frequently some biological observation. The world is the macrocosm; man is the microcosm, and the one explains the other. We know something of the medical teaching of the time, and the idea that man was the universe in miniature was clearly expressed; it is necessary also to recognize that the plastic substance of Thales or the air of Anaximenes were chosen by their advocates for reasons that refer primarily and directly to the life of man. If the historian of philosophy can afford to neglect these indications, the student of psychology must insist on the influence which is exerted upon the most comprehensive theories by those who study in a philosophic spirit the phenomena of daily existence. Man discovers that he is part of a universe; that his very nature and disposition are subject to laws and can be treated as universals; that training, dieting, and habituation make him master of himself. These discoveries produce, in reflective minds, the concept of a world which is the expression of laws, not abstract decrees but regular forms of action, principles involved from all eternity in the beginning of things. The word 'cosmic' tends to become vague in the mouth of mystic writers. For the Greek there was no vagueness in the idea of all-pervading order; the universality never dissipated the possibility of immediate practical application; on the contrary, the idea was a perpetual source of practical deductions. This is clearly seen if we pay sufficient attention to the spirit in which ideas, now very commonplace, were first put forward. To the student of human nature, apparently so spontaneous and original in its manifestations, it must at first have been a great revelation to realize that behind this complex being there was a world of elements, and that the very nature of man, his temperament, passions, and thoughts, could be controlled by those who knew the secrets of climate and food. It is not the specialist curing a disease that comes before us with these theories; it is rather the speculative mind attracted by the widest notions and capable of seeing man as a product of great forces; it is the philosopher who speaks of diet and regimen, believing that he finds in these the elements of good living, of bodily health, and spiritual purification. If we are to understand rightly the relation of psychology to philosophy we must take into account ideas as widely divergent as those of the Pythagorean philosopher and the practising physician. Only in this way shall we see how really complementary are the varying points of view. Climate and disposition, food and morals, the humours of the blood and errors of thought, these are the terms in which the relation between macrocosm and microcosm are continually stated and restated.

B. Speculative

The novelty introduced by the Greek cosmologists did not consist solely in the challenge to existing traditions and the production of better stories; it consisted also in their attempt to explain all things on the basis of one principle. The attempt was premature but it encouraged speculation and occasioned many competing theories about the stuff and structure of the world.

I. THE IONIANS

Thales set speculation in motion by maintaining that everything was made out of water. Anaximander preferred the 'Boundless' and Anaximenes the air. Heraclitus favoured fire. He distinguished grades of knowledge and supported his speculations by crude empirical observations. Everything, for him, is in constant flux. Thus sensation is made to depend upon motion; it is essentially a relation between man and objects and belongs exclusively to neither, a microscopic picture of the eternal transience. Reason, or sentience, similarly enters man from without like the air which he breathes; it depends upon the fiery element in the universe and is weighed down by the grosser matter of the body. It flashes in the body like lightning in the clouds.

The cosmological point of view furnishes the idea of a universal system which is, in respect of its substance fire and in respect of its activity or life, an embodied law. The existence of the individual is that of part within a whole; and as the elements in the whole are better and worse, so the individual is better or worse according as he has more or less of the better elements. The greater excellence belongs to the so-called Fire, and man's superiority consists in the entrance of this Fire into his composition. By it he becomes the reason which is in the universe; knower and known are assimilated one to the other and form a unity so that the activity of the part is in harmony with that of the whole to which it belongs, and the life of man is one with the life of the universe.

2. PARMENIDES

Parmenides had laid hold of thought and meditated on its nature, as Heraclitus had directed his attention to perception. Thought has a permanence which perception seems to lack; it has a stationary character in comparison with the qualitative changes of perception; it is more akin to Being, while perceptions are akin to Becoming.

These are metaphysical rather than physical notions, and their influence, as seen in the works of Plato, spent itself mainly upon theories of knowledge. Ideas about the constitution of man and of the soul are found in the fragments attributed to Parmenides, but their importance is somewhat discounted by the fact that they come in what is called by Parmenides the Way of Opinion. Parmenides selected those ideas from current teaching and did not regard them as demonstrable truths; they formed an appendix to his first principles, a manual of science for those who required 'facts' as well as principles. This part of the work is therefore of interest only when it seems possible to detect traces of principles in the selection of details.

The nature of man is described by Parmenides as a mixture ($\kappa\rho\hat{\alpha}\sigma\iota\varsigma$) of elementary qualities. Perception is due to likeness between the external object and the corresponding element in the individual. Mind is the product of the material composition of the body, and the activities of mind, the thoughts, vary in relation to the different constitutions of men. Sensibility is a fact, and therefore belongs to Being, or the totality of things that are; as such it cannot come and go, but must always be found where there is any reality or Being. For otherwise when it came it would come from nowhere, and when it went it would go nowhere. If we can venture to put an interpretation on the curious statement of Parmenides that even a corpse has sensations, it must be this, namely, that sensations cannot arise out of nothing, and therefore matter (even in its lowest forms) as such has sensibility; death is not the end of sensibility for matter but only the cessation of the individual's sensations. The evidence is too slender to justify speculation, but it is allowable to suggest that Parmenides here came upon a problem of great interest. The naturalists maintained that nothing came out of nothing; there is a physical antecedent for every physical event or effect. Parmenides maintained the same doctrine, but used it rather as a dialectical weapon. If nothing comes from nothing, that which is cannot have come from that which is not; sensibility certainly *is*, it is included in the sum of reality, and therefore it must have come from something. But can it come from something other than itself? If matter produces sensibility, has not something come out of nothing? The point was a problem to the atomist, even to Epicurus. It troubles materialism at all times; and the opposite is the assertion that sensibility is not a product of insensible matter, but that all matter is endowed with the power of sensation. This was probably the view of Parmenides, and it is interesting to see how the dialectic of his school arrived logically at a conclusion which is the forerunner of all theories in which consciousness is made to arise out of subconsciousness, or matter and mind are made coeval.

3. EMPEDOCLES

Empedocles occupied a unique position; he combined scientific with speculative inquiry, and the fact that he was interested in the cause and cure of diseases accounts for his attention to detail and for a psychology which is comparatively elaborate. He has, however, no idea of system, and is so far from making any consistent series of deductions from one or more first principles that he leaves his teaching a collection of disconnected statements.

In opposition to earlier physical philosophers he posits as his ultimate factors the four elements. These are unchanging forms of reality, and consequently satisfy the idea of real being which the Eleatic doctrine had made current. Individual existences are formed by the more or less temporary union of these elements. The quality of any particular compound depends on the mixture of these elements. Thus Empedocles laid the foundation for the important notion of temperaments or the idea that an individual's characteristics depend upon the mixture of elements in the body. Though rudimentary, the idea is in Empedocles what it has remained ever since, a broad physiological determination of those aspects of a man's nature which depend upon his bodily structure. The tendency to lay emphasis on physiological data is also shown in the assertion that the blood is the seat of intelligence, while the intelligence is not made distinct from the senses. How sensations are united in the perception of an object, or how the blood functions in the production of knowledge Empedocles does not explain. We may perhaps conjecture that his experience as a doctor inclined him to the view that the whole body is really the unit of activity and the power of thought stands in some relation to the condition of the body as a whole. This conjecture is supported by the fact that the decrease of consciousness which occurs in sleep is explained as a reduction of vitality, a symmetrical cooling of the blood.

Empedocles regards all action as requiring contact, and therefore regards sensation as an effect due to the contact of that which causes it. Every object that produces a sensible effect does so by means of effluxes or emanations; these enter the pores according to their suitability; for all cannot enter the same pores, and perception is due to the action of like upon like. This famous formula appears here in its most explicit statement. It involved several difficulties; such as the fact that it confined each sense organ to a separate department and prevented the possibility of the synthesis which knowledge requires. It seems, however, to have been necessary from the Greek point of view to establish a natural relation between the sense organ and the external object; this affinity was easily interpreted as identity of matter; only in Heraclitus and Anaxagoras is this standpoint abandoned and with it the formula, 'like is known by like.'

The general conditions required for the production of a sensible fact are two: first, a harmonious relation between the emanations and the receptive organ; second, likeness between that which perceives and that which is perceived.

The theory of 'effluxes' is obviously of paramount use in the explanation of vision. For reasons not easy to see, Empedocles practically passes over those sensations which are forms of touch, namely, touch itself and taste; he is more anxious to reduce the rest to this type than to explain the type itself, for all that we are told is merely the conditions required for sensation, not the actual causes; it is clear that *if* the effluxes do not fit the pores, and *if* the object and organ have not the community of nature which is called likeness, there will be no sensation; but, given these conditions, why should sensations arise? Why does not one stone feel another under these conditions? In brief, what is there beyond physical facts to explain the psychic result? In his failure to tell us we see how limited is the outlook of Empedocles; there is still no specific problem of consciousness.

The phenomena of smell affords the most suitable matter for the application of a theory of 'effluxes.' Smell, says Empedocles, is due to the reception of particles from the odorous bodies, and this naturally seems to receive support from the fact that odour is often associated with bodies wasting in decay. Sound affords a difficulty where it might least be expected. The exciting cause is the air, but instead of saying that we hear the moving air, Empedocles says that the current of air strikes on the cartilage within the ear, which rings like a gong; we therefore hear the sound thus produced. Before commenting on this we may first state the explanation of vision.

The eye, the organ of vision, is composed of the four elements; the interior is fire, next comes water, and outside the air and the earth. As 'like is known by like' we shall perceive fire by fire, water by water, and so on with the rest. The effluxes reaching the eye from without explain our ability to see objects at a distance from us, and reduce this also to a form of touch.

The application of the two general principles meets, so far, with no special difficulty, but in other respects problems arise which are almost insoluble. In the case of hearing we have a 'gong' within the ear; in the case of sight we have a fire in the eye. These appear to be exceptional cases of a similar kind, for while all the elements of the eye are percipient of their 'like element,' the light in the eye has some further functions. The evidence being scanty and obscure, explanation is difficult. We may assume, however, that the prominence of these two additional factors is due to the observation of (*a*) ringing sound in the ear, (*b*) the flashing of the eye.

It is not possible from the existing evidence to decide exactly how we are to explain the details of the theory of vision. Empedocles has combined a general principle with particular observations that do not harmonize with it; and any attempt to create an explanation of the detail can only be highly speculative. Similar inconsistencies are to be found in his theory of transmigration. Empedocles tried to explain desire, also, in terms of his general principle of like seeking like. Thought he regarded as a function of the composite organism. The discrepancy between his religious doctrine of transmigration and his materialistic explanation of thinking did not seem to trouble him at all. On this point he is the forerunner of mysticism.

4. ANAXAGORAS

The work of Anaxagoras marks an important epoch in the development of psychology. Strongly influenced by the Eleatic doctrines, he arrives at the conclusion that there are in the universe a number of primary 'things' or unchangeable forms of Being; it follows that all differences in things must be explained as differences in the elements whose mixture makes the thing. The philosopher's interest is accordingly centred on the principle of this mixture and its cause. He finds from observation that men attribute actions to reason, and this is sufficient to justify the assertion that reason is the starting-point of the activity which has put in order the chaotic mass of original matter. Reason in this way becomes an immanent force that makes for order, itself pure and unmixed, but the cause of all mixture, a power inherent in some things, and ruler or organizer of all.

The path of development from this idea to that of a universal Reason is obvious. Anaxagoras, so far as we know, made no advance that way. He looks at man only to find a principle of activity. Cognition he overlooks. Man remains a part of the universal Being, that which is always and everywhere; but the generalization applies only to activity and motion. Between mind or reason (νοῦς) and the soul of man, as sources of action, no distinction is made; and therefore the element which is specifically knowable to man, his self-consciousness, is not the element which appears as important. If importance had been attached to it, the Reason which orders the universe must have been described as acting intelligently; and we should then have had a concept of the world as governed by purpose and controlled by final causes. This idea, we are told, Anaxagoras failed to reach.

Passing from the general cosmical standpoint, we find in Anaxagoras some interesting remarks on purely psychological questions; but there is no evidence of systematic treatment, and in some cases the assertions made are merely deductions from general principles. Sensation and sense-perception are broadly characterized as changes in the organism. These changes are due to a relation of unlike to unlike. It was usual at this period to suppose that contact or impression was sufficient to produce the required change; but sensation seems to be in Anaxagoras the recognition of difference, and this requires a difference between the perceiving element and that which is perceived. No perception is impossible, because every part of every organism contains all possible differences of quality, and will therefore possess the opposite of any possible object of perception. This is the application to sensation of the doctrine that 'all things are in all.' Anaxagoras adds that perception is always painful; this he deduces from the fact that perception becomes painful in excess, e.g. when a light is too brilliant; but he seems unaware that there is any difficulty in asserting that a sensation is painful when the pain is not perceived; he speaks of sensation as a relation between objects with little or no reference to consciousness, except as a result attained in some cases through the relation. Particular sensations are treated consistently with these principles. In sight an image is reflected in the pupil of the eye, but only on that part which is of the opposite colour. Smell is due to particles of a contrary nature entering in the act of respiration; hearing is due to sound which passes through the ear to the brain; 'the bone which encloses [the brain] forms a cavity into which the sound rushes.'

Anaxagoras shows a tendency to treat psychology from a point of view which is best described as biological. A confusion between vital function and consciousness leads him to say that plants have reason and knowledge. Many writers, supplied with far more facts, have fallen into the same error and confused intelligible with intelligent action.

The doctrine that 'everything is in everything' does not apply to Nous; on the contrary, we are definitely told that there is a portion of everything in everything except Nous, 'while there are some things in which there is Nous also.' This is the way in which Anaxagoras 'laid down the distinction between animate and inanimate things.'[1] The question arises, What is the reason for the superiority of one creature over another if Nous is the same in all? The answer given by Anaxagoras appears to have been that the superiority depended on the organism; the 'reason' was the organism, and was therefore aided or hindered according as the organism is more or less developed. In that case reasoning would be analogous to running, an activity which is executed well or badly according as the structure of the organism is better or worse.

This view, if this interpretation is correct, would coincide with the saying of Parmenides which makes 'the thought of men depend entirely upon the constitution of their limbs,'[2] and fall in line with contemporary ideas about 'mixture' and the tendency of the body to obstruct thought under conditions of fatigue or disease. Being unmixed, Nous is always the same in kind; it is not like bone, a substance whose quality depends on the preponderance of one element over others in a mixture; but yet there is a definite ratio of more and less; larger animals are more sensitive, sensation being proportionate to the size of the organ.

5. DEMOCRITUS

Democritus definitely undertakes to explain all phenomena from a mechanical point of view. The universe is made out of atoms and all things that exist are compounds of atoms. In addition to the atoms we require only motion, and psychological phenomena will clearly come under the category of motion. Sensation in general is explained as the interaction of body on body. In the structure of the sensitive frame there are soul atoms inserted between the other atoms that make up the body. The action to which we have just referred is a special form of the general interaction of material bodies recognized by physics. Anything peculiar in the nature of soul-activity is due to the character of the soul-atoms, which differ in some respects from other atoms. The difference is, however, only a difference of

---

[1] Burnet, p. 297. [2] *Ibid.*, p. 298.

degree; soul atoms are more subtle and more rapid in motion; they are spherical in shape; but beyond these material differences there is no distinction of kind. We are, therefore, now in a purely mechanical world, and it only remains to indicate what psychological theory is involved in this point of view. We may first see how sensation can be explained in terms of motion.

All sensation is an affair of touch involving immediate contact. The impression produced at any one part spreads through the body and consequently may be felt everywhere. The atom is solid but not itself perceptible; the bodies which we perceive are complexes of atoms, and bodies differ because atoms differ in order, figure, and position.

These characters, which are purely geometrical or spatial, constitute the primary qualities which are perceived by touch. As before, we naturally ask for an explanation of this fundamental sense, and here, too, we find no psychological analysis. Democritus is content to reduce all sensation to forms of touch without explaining touch itself.

The objects which produce taste do so in accordance with their shapes; acid taste, for example, is produced by atoms that are 'angular, winding, small, and thin.' Smell may be explained in the same way, though Democritus himself neglects to give an account of it. In the case of sound we have first to overcome the difficulty which arises from the distance between the source of the sound and the hearer. Here we find a theory analogous to the 'emanations' of Empedocles; the source of sound throws off particles which, mingling with like elements in the air, stream into the ear and so come to the soul. There is no reason why these particles should strike only on the ear, and they do, in fact, strike upon the whole body; but the ear alone hears, because that organ is best adapted to receive and retain the air. Of vision Democritus gives a more elaborate account. Sight is like hearing, in that the original source of the sensation may be at a distance from the person; a medium for transmission is therefore required, and something must pass from the object to the 'soul' of the person. In Democritus the immediate object of seeing, as of hearing, is the air. The primary object, the thing, sends off 'images' which, acting on the air, mould it into the shape of the original object; thus the eye is touched, as it were, by an air-figure which is a copy of the distant object.

To this physical theory of perception by the eye Democritus adds a theory of colour. He considers that the primary colours are four—white, black, red, and green. A colour is an effect produced by atoms and is expressible in terms of the figure of the atoms in a manner analogous to that in which varieties of taste are explained by differences in the shapes of atoms. All other colours are formed by the mixture of these four.

Such is the explanation of different sensations and the way in which they are produced. We may now ask what theory of perception is involved in this. The immediacy of touch seems to guarantee the truth of sense-perceptions; but Democritus recognizes that where a medium is used, as in sight, that which immediately touches the organ (the air) may not be free from foreign elements or influences. In the case of sight especially, the configuration of the air may be so changed as not to represent the object faithfully. The senses are, therefore, sometimes inadequate and deceptive. Again, the qualities perceived are in all cases, except touch, secondary, and due to a relation between the object producing the perception and the organ. The condition of the organ varies, and with it the result, the perception, must vary. It is clear, therefore, that while sensations are true in so far as they are what they are, the perception may easily be different from the original object (in sight) or from the normal effect (e.g. in taste). To this extent the senses deceive us. In spite of the materialism of his physics, Democritus distinguishes 'true' from 'obscure' knowledge. These are divisions of knowledge according as it depends on sense or reason; the superiority of reason is consistent with the doctrine that the atom is knowable, but not an object of sense. If we inquire further into the value of this reason we find it interpreted in terms of motion: the material image of the object causes thought by its action on the material soul. In reducing the soul to a form of body, 'a body within the body,' Democritus develops one of the two elements which formed the complex idea of 'hylozoism,' the life-endowed matter of the 'physical philosophers.' Life, whether of body or of mind, is primarily motion; in a sense this is a return 'to the standpoint of the savage who, when he sees an animal move, is unable to explain the fact except by supposing that there is a little animal inside to move him';[1] but while the principle of thought is the

[1] R. D. Hicks, *Aristotle De Anima*, p. xxvi.

same in both cases, Democritus has nothing in common with primitive animism or the Homeric notion of the soul, and his attitude on the question of the soul's nature is obviously the result of viewing man only as an object. With this bias he naturally thinks primarily of the actions of the will, to the exclusion of knowledge, and volition seems to be a power of motion possessed by a 'body' as its own nature. The body in question is called soul on account of its distinctive features, namely, the spherical shape, fineness, and mobility of its parts.

Democritus accepts the canon 'like perceives like,' modifying its meaning by a new interpretation. In harmony with his other views he makes likeness a relation between substances of similar degrees of subtlety; the more subtle complexes of atoms escape the senses, but the soul is affected by them: they pass through the gross matter of the body without contact, but come into contact with the soul-atoms which have less void between them. We shall do no injustice to Democritus if we compare this process to that of straining a fluid: what slips through the larger mesh is caught in the smaller. It is possible then to give a meaning to the assertion that thought is superior to sense; it is by its nature conversant with objects not known to the senses. Democritus appears to have distinguished various faculties of the soul and to have assigned a seat to each in a different part of the body. We hear that he located thought in the brain, anger in the heart, and desire in the liver. The maintenance of our life is connected with the act of breathing. The soul being composed of atoms, and these atoms being exceedingly fine and easily moved, there is danger that the surrounding air should force them out of the body. The act of breathing introduces into the body fresh vital matter, and also as an incoming current checks the outgoing of those atoms already mingled in the body. This part of the doctrine recalls the position of Heraclitus. It involves the idea that there is a soul outside of the body distributed throughout the universe and imparted directly to the individual. Also there is a tendency in Democritus to interpret the constitution of the universe in a manner which does not cease to be materialistic, but none the less becomes Pantheistic in the sense in which the later Stoic doctrines are Pantheism. Democritus is the first to make a direct denial of immortality; the particular combination of atoms which makes the individual is broken up and dispersed at death, and on the same physical analogy we must regard the soul as sharing the dissolution of the body.

6. PYTHAGORAS

Pythagoras was brought up in the Ionian cosmology but introduced an innovation which was far reaching in its effects. Like his predecessors he did mathematics but he was unlike them in thinking that the universe had a fundamentally mathematical ground-plan. He suggested that qualitative differences were dependent on differences in the underlying mathematical structure of nature. This was a tremendous simplification on previous Ionian theories because it no longer mattered what the stuff of the universe was; all that mattered was that it was capable of receiving a variety of mathematical forms. This imaginative idea, which was later developed by Plato in his theory of forms and by the physical scientists like Copernicus and Kepler in their cosmological speculations, proved particularly successful in the sphere of acoustics. Pythagoras was able to show that qualitative differences between musical notes depend solely on the rates of vibration of the string—i.e. on the way in which a string takes up a series of geometrical shapes. If this holds for what we can hear why should it not also hold for what we can see? Why should not all appearances be dependent upon more fundamental geometrical structure? This amazingly fruitful speculation started at a time when empirical observation was not well developed. Instead, therefore, of developing into physical theories like those of Kepler, Copernicus, and Galileo, it passed into the mathematical mysticism of the Pythagoreans and Plato. If the structure of reality is geometrical the study of geometry will purify the soul for insight into and communion with reality. The injunction on Plato's Academy 'Let no one enter here who does not know geometry' proclaimed an initiation formula as well as a test of competence.

This fusion of mathematics with mysticism was not occasioned simply by the rather negative attitude towards sensory observation; there was also at hand positive encouragement from a religious tradition of purification. This was most influential on the development of theories about the soul and to this we must briefly turn.

C. Ethico-religious

I. THE PYTHAGOREANS

The speculations of the philosophers did not exhaust the opinions of mankind on questions concerning the soul. In the Orphic traditions there is evident trace of the preservation of popular ideas which had been steadily maintained and handed on from generation to generation, a legacy from the earlier days of the Homeric poems, or from the still earlier times which seem to be indicated in the poems of Hesiod. In this more popular substratum of opinions we find beliefs that have no scientific origin or support; they make no pretence of a theoretical justification, but represent the systematized ideas which developed out of superstitions and are maintained, with a continuous purification from grosser elements, by the priests and religious authorities. For reasons entirely outside the range of scientific observation, the Pythagoreans, adopting the Orphic tradition, maintained the transmigration of souls. The idea is significant in two ways; it definitely implies that the soul exists apart from the body, and it opens up the way to a rational psychology which gives independent value to the soul on the ground of metaphysical or ethical problems; for these appear to have no solution without the idea of a soul endowed with a life of its own. The doctrine involves a dualism, for the soul is a thing dwelling in the body, a captive in the garrison, or a prisoner in the dungeon. It follows that there is no organic relation between soul and body, and the naturalistic tendency which moved toward the idea of a soul which resulted from the constitution of the body was, under these influences, entirely checked. It is out of the belief in a future life that this dualism springs, and the mystical doctrine that the body is the tomb of the soul becomes, through Plato, the basis of all the psychology that admits another life, whether obtained by transmigration as in Orphism, or by resurrection as in Christianity.

D. Medical

I. ALCMAEON

The scientific character of the work done by Pythagoreans seems to have borne fruit in other directions by diffusing a spirit of exact inquiry. To Alcmaeon of Crotona we owe the first treatment of the human organism which is in any sense based on direct scientific work. How far his theories were guesses and his methods crude will be apparent from the account of them; but it will be no less apparent that he marks a great advance upon all previous theories in exactness and concentration. Alcmaeon belonged to the school of doctors established at Crotona. As a doctor his attention was naturally directed primarily to physiological and biological facts; and with Alcmaeon begins the long history of the influence which a study of the human organism has had on theories of the soul, sometimes for better and some-

times for worse. It was hardly probable that at such a time a speculative mind would be free from a tendency to false analogies. We
find these clearly indicated, and it is therefore all the more creditable to Alcmaeon that he made a direct study of causes, perhaps
even to the extent of practising dissection. From his observations of
the human organism he formulated theories of the structure and
functions of the sense organs; in the case of the eye observation
seems to have been attracted first by the presence in it of fire and
of water. The former is discovered through the sensation of light,
obtained by striking the eyeball, the so-called 'intra-ocular
light'; the latter is obvious to ordinary inspection. This intra-
ocular light was not considered to be in any sense a subjective
phenomenon; it was supposed to be the action of fire enclosed in
the eye which is surrounded by diaphanous sheaths that keep in
both fire and water. In order to give both these elements a function
vision is explained as a combined process of reflection and radiation; reflection gives an image of the object in the watery element
of the eye, while radiation is an activity of the fire directing a ray
outward to the image. Similarly in hearing we have a twofold
process: the moving air conveys the sound to the vacuum contained in the air. This vacuum, which is really a chamber filled
with air, mediates the passage of sound, for without it the air and
not the sound would be transmitted to the brain. Upon the other
senses—smell, taste, and touch—Alcmaeon has nothing to say
beyond what ordinary observation would suggest. It is interesting to observe that he explains sleep as due to the retirement
of the blood into the larger blood-vessels.

So far our results seem to be purely scientific, but there is
another side to the character of Alcmaeon's work. The tendency
to follow the lead of analogy is obvious in more than one instance.
An interesting example is afforded by Alcmaeon's assertion that
the young of birds are nourished by the white, not the yellow
part in the egg. This assertion was maintained against the contrary view current at the time, but the only reason assigned was
the likeness of the white of an egg to the milk with which mammals
nourish their young. It is doubtful whether Alcmaeon's assertion
that the brain is the centre of conscious life was due to scientific
knowledge or deductions from mystical notions. On the one
hand, the brain is in the centre for the senses; it is a meeting-place
for the channels of the senses; it acts in a way that causes the

motions of the sense-organs to come to rest. Alcmaeon also made a distinction between thought and sense. On the other hand, when we are told that the soul is self-moving, that it is on that account immortal, that it is divine in the sense that the sun is divine, we seem to have traces of early mysticism, added to the results of inductive observation. Here, as in some later theories, we must recognize a dualism of science and faith giving independent results which there is as yet hardly any conscious intention to unify.

2. HIPPOCRATES

Hippocrates represents the school of Cos, which in the fifth century B.C. was the flourishing rival of the school at Cnidus. The genius of Hippocrates seems to have secured the victory for Cos and the consequent decline of its rival. Medical knowledge was still hardly free from the bondage of superstition inherited from the days when the priest was also the medical man, and that combination formed the current idea of a doctor. The treatise "On the Supernatural Disease" is a lively discussion of the relations between magic and medicine; it exhibits a sturdy opposition to all occult causes, and is a philippic against any but scientific methods of treating diseases. There is a singularly modern touch in several of these treatises, and this one in particular is a criticism that might have been written by a modern physician to destroy a belief in the royal touch or in demoniac 'possessions.' The original lack of distinction between religion and medicine accounts for the general character of primitive medical treatment. The 'incubation' of the Aesculapian temples was faith-healing tempered by science. But by the end of the fifth century this phase of development had concluded. The Aesculapian traditions were mingled with the results of philosophical speculation. To both were added the practical knowledge and methods of the gymnastic trainer, in those days (no less than in these) an important authority on the strong man made perfect. How much had been done before their day is beyond accurate calculation, but it is enough to recall to the reader's mind the physiological theories of Alcmaeon, Philolaus, Empedocles, Anaximenes and Diogenes of Apollonia, Anaxagoras, or Democritus. In Hippocrates we study a culmination rather than a beginning; the tracts have to be regarded as a mirror of the age, and their contents are valued as a reflection of the most brilliant speculation of those times.

The treatise entitled 'On Regimen' is perhaps the most characteristic document in the whole collection. It contains the theory for which empirical medicine was waiting; practice had revealed a relation between food and health: an insight into the reason was wanted. It embodies a philosophical doctrine. The 'Sophists' laid stress on the dogma that the understanding of medicine depended on the understanding of man. This put the one before the many; it involved starting with an abstract idea of man and deducing from the nature of man its correct treatment. Medicine was suffering from a vicious method, and in opposition to this Hippocrates declares that the study of man must be concrete. Emphasis is now laid on climate, seasons, localities, winds—in fact, all the elements which make environment. It is the life and not the thing that should be studied: not man as a fixed quantity, but man as a sequence of states. For this view man *is* what he *breathes*; and the importance of that view was great. Plato was quick to see its meaning, and worked out its principles when he made education a nurturing of the soul in salubrious regions. Aristotle employs the idea continually; it became, in short, the accepted doctrine. Its very lack of originality made its discovery more effective: for in it people recognized what they had thought before, what every theory of 'air' had been inarticulately proclaiming.

This essay on the philosophy of health deserves at least a brief analysis to show its range and character. It begins with the declaration that the particular is only to be understood through the universal, the part through the whole. The question of diet must therefore be preceded by a disquisition on the nature and structure of man. There are certain elements in the composite body of man, and knowledge of good and bad health is simply a knowledge of the relation between these elements. Sometimes one predominates, sometimes another: activity and nutrition produce their effects by increasing and decreasing the power of any one element; on this analysis of the problem it seems clear that the whole science of health is simply a question of properly adjusting the relation between food and exercise.

These are indeed the causes which we can directly control. But there are also conditions: in reality, when the doctor gives his prescription he takes into account the heavens and the earth, the stars, the winds, the seasons, and the localities. The extreme cases are easily recognized. Excessive fatigue or excessive eating exhibit symptoms easily understood. Medical skill lies in detecting slight changes; for these produce little immediate effect, but are cumulative: to explain the full meaning of this the author states his first principles. Life is a continual process. Animal organisms are composed of two principles divergent in nature but convergent in function. These are fire which moves, and water which nourishes. Each strives against the other, but neither attains a final victory: when fire overcomes water it destroys its own source of nourishment; when water overcomes fire it loses its possibility of movement. In other words, nature requires a balance between extremes: the body must not become full of humours, nor must it dry up and be sapless. The language here is picturesque: in the manner of Heraclitus we are told that all things perpetually change; the opposition of the principles is likened to the action of two men working a saw—both must work, but they must work in opposite ways with equal and opposite reaction. The law of distribution, by which the nutritive substance is distributed over the body, is called a harmony. The formative element is the fire. To the action of fire is due the entire arrangement of the parts of the organism: in this the microcosm is a copy of the macrocosm. The finest kind of fire is invisible and intangible: it regulates everything and is the source of all the activities called vital or intellectual. The vital activities belong to the soul: this is weak in youth and in age; for it is wasted away in youth by the rapid growth of the body and grows weak in the period of decline; only in the mean or middle age is it complete. The ideal physical constitution is attained when the finest (i.e. most refined) forms of water and fire are combined. This is a middle condition which realizes an almost stable equilibrium. If the physical constitution is inclined to an extreme, either in respect of the water or the fire, the least addition derived from external circumstances will produce disease. Excess in the original constitution naturally makes the individual susceptible to those external conditions which emphasize his tendencies. For example, when the water-element is dense and the fire-element thin, the constitution is cold and humid; the winter season is naturally dangerous for such an one. By varying the respective quantities of the water and fire a formula can be attained for each constitution, and the medical direction is to counteract the excess and restore the ideal or balanced constitution. Similarly, men at different ages have different constitutions, for infancy is a condition in which the humid is in excess: the fire gradually attains and then gradually loses its supremacy. The same principles explain all the different degrees of intelligence, but the treatment hardly merits serious discussion: the author was clearly convinced that mental activity was directly dependent on physical states, but the dogma that a healthy body necessarily produces an intelligent soul is not successfully maintained. The contrary thesis, that physical derangements cause mental derangement, is more easily defended. An interesting point to notice is that certain dispositions are said to depend, not on the mixture of elements but on the condition of the pores (or paths) through which the soul passes. These dispositions are the quick-tempered, the idle, the crafty, the simple, the ill-natured, and the kindly. These seem to be regarded as ways in which the inner nature goes forth: dependent therefore on the paths of exit. The voice is also an outgoing activity, and its quality depends on the nature of the channels. In both cases the quality can be changed by a treatment which changes the physical states.

Such is the general outline of the first book of the essay on diet or mode of living. A few characteristic points from other works may be added. From the statement above it is clear that the fundamental requirements of life are spirits and humours. Considering first the physical structure, we find the basis is the four elements—air, fire, water, earth. To each of these substances corresponds a quality called dry, hot, moist, or cold; and again in correspondence with these a Humour, namely, blood (warm), phlegm (cold), yellow bile (dry), black bile (moist). Health is defined as the right mixture of these; disease is consequently a disturbance of the relations, usually expressed as a change of ratios. The body not only requires to maintain definite relations between its own elements, but also to stand in certain relations to the universe around it. Its nurture depends on three things—food, drink, and air. To the ancient mind the 'air' seems to have been a generic term for all causes of disease other than those of food and drink. The vascular system was divided between veins and arteries, and the opinion most widely accepted was that the arteries contained air while the veins contained blood. This extreme doctrine was afterwards modified, and the air and the blood were located together in the same vessels. To one who thinks of the body as irrigated throughout by air, who attributes the cause of pulsation to the shock of air meeting blood, who moreover feels dimly that man is in direct connection with the whole universe through the continuity of this air, the importance of this factor must have assumed the greatest proportions. Within the body the brain occupies the most important place. From it proceed all the veins of the body: they spring up from this root and grow downwards, branching out to the various parts of the body. Here is the seat of intelligence: into the brain lead the various passages of sense—eyes, nose, ears. It is from the brain that the eyes derive the humour that feeds the pupils; and all diseases begin from the brain because from it flow the humours that are found throughout the body. The close connection of physiology and psychology in these passages is liable to produce a false impression of the writer's attitude towards the brain and its functions. If the brain receives a shock, loss of speech, sight, or hearing may follow; from wounds on the brain paralysis and death ensue. The brain, then, is the seat of intelligence, but only because it is adapted to retain the air; it is no more than a medium by which the air communicates to us its nature. Some have made the diaphragm the seat of intelligence, others the heart. Both are wrong, because, while these are quick to respond to changes, the sensations felt in them are merely reflex actions due to the contraction of air-vessels. Thus the heart palpitates in fear; there is a diffused sensation in the body produced by excessive joy or sorrow; but these are secondary; the movements thus produced are 'reverberations' of the original encephalic motion. Thought can only arise in the absence of commotion; insanity arises from a humid condition of the brain which causes it to move perpetually and produces confusion of the senses. Here the author treats of the brain as the cause of all phenomena, normal or morbid; by it we think and by it we fail to think; fears and dreams are due to its changing states. But while we see with our eyes or hear with our ears, it is doubtful whether Hippocrates would say we think with the brain. The writers incline at least to say either the brain thinks, or the air thinks and communicates the thought to the brain.

The subject of dreams is treated in a short essay which is in the main disappointing. The author clearly thinks some dreams belong to a special class that can only be understood by the interpreters who have a science of their own. He remarks that prayer is an excellent thing, but it does not remove the need for self-help; and then proceeds to enumerate types of dreams with their appropriate antidotes when they indicate morbid conditions. In the dream state, according to this writer, the soul acts freely; it is no longer disturbed by sensations, for the body sleeps. In other words, the waking state is that in which the soul is passive and the sense-organs preponderantly active; the dream state is one of activity, for the soul then produces impressions instead of receiving them. Underlying the descriptive part of this essay there seems to be the idea that the soul discovers in sleep what in the waking state goes unnoticed. This amounts almost to the idea that a latent consciousness comes to the surface in dreams, but the author naturally does not make that notion very clear, and all that is said is of this kind: 'When the stars appear [in the dream] to wander this way and that with no necessity, the dream indicates disturbance of the soul due to worry.' The antidote is to turn the mind towards light subjects that produce laughter. Such advice would be good still. But the proposition 'black objects seen in a dream foreshow danger and disease' proves that the author was not always equally sure in his touch. On the whole, this essay shows a very wild use of analogy and no accurate study of the causes of dreams. It serves, however, to show that in this period there was a recognized distinction between those dreams that were supernatural signs and those which stood in a close relation to bodily conditions, and could be used as prognostics of health or disease.

Chapter Three

THE SOPHISTS, SOCRATES, AND CONSCIOUSNESS OF METHOD

A. Introductory

With the Sophists a new era begins in the history of psychology. Though we may not speak of the Sophists as a school, or indeed as having a definite body of doctrine common to them, there is one aspect of Sophistic teaching which deserves to be regarded as a common characteristic. For the Sophists interpret their age in trying to restore the individual and assert his rights, and this element, common to all enlightenments, seems to furnish the peculiar flavour of their work.

The importance of this direction of thought is first clearly seen in Socrates. But Socrates is the culmination of the tendency; for what was accomplished before him the Sophists deserve credit; if Socrates set before all things the concept of the self as a fully developed union of moral and intellectual powers, it is to the Sophists we owe that emancipation of the intellect which makes possible the idea of a self-determining agent.

.The Sophists are usually credited with the dissolution of old traditions and destructive criticism of religion: but this is a view which hardly does justice to each and all. In Protagoras at any rate we have a type of thinker concerned to do more than run a tilt against traditions. The fact seems to be that men had now arrived far enough on the road of development to demand some scientific explanation of knowledge. Hitherto they had asked little more than explanations of the known systematic classification of objects guided by one or other of the available hypotheses. Mankind has only a limited power of speculating on the basis of accepted hypotheses: the multiplication of theories generates weariness of the flesh, and the spirit cries out to be released from the eternal circling of thought round the apparently unknowable. It is in their recognition of this temper that the greater Sophists agree: their claim to serious consideration lies in the fact that they took the new demands seriously. From the physical and metaphysical they retire to experience, and the motto of Protagoras is simply 'back to man.'

The critical attitude of Socrates and of some of the Sophists towards unbridled speculation and arrogant claims to knowledge ushered in the spirit of the scientific tradition without its later techniques and apparatus. The questions 'How do you know?' and 'What do you mean?' became the stock-in-trade of the critical philosopher and of all inquirers who demanded rational grounds for belief. If we consider the history of thought from the Greeks to the present day these two questions, when persistently asked, have had two main effects, one beneficial and the other detrimental. On the whole the beneficial effect far outweighs the detrimental.

The beneficial effect has been to stop people from talking nonsense by insisting on a criterion for what is to count as sense. Protagoras' view was that we cease to talk sense when the statements we make cannot be checked by the experience of human beings. Socrates' passionate endeavour was to make people say what they have to say clearly and to produce supporting reasons for it. Without rules of evidence and clarity of expression there is no way of telling whether one person's story is a better one than somebody else's. Argumentation thus degenerates into verbal hairsplitting and oratorical legerdemain. This insistence on verifiability and clarity is inseparable from what we now call the scientific spirit.

The detrimental effect was to make people think that methodology was the gateway to knowledge. Protagoras set the fashion for a whole succession of inquirers who thought that they had to present their epistemological credentials before they got on with the job of discovery, and that *bona fide* credentials would assure them of success. When later psychologists like Locke and Hume prefaced their inquiries into human nature by trying to decide on the limits, certainty, and extent of human knowledge, or when modern psychologists write tiresome preliminary chapters extolling the methodological purity of their inquiry, they unwittingly follow in the footsteps of Protagoras. Similarly others, following Socrates, have thought that precise definition of scientific terms is the key necessary to unlock the secrets of Nature. The truth seems to be that there are no methodological recipes for being a successful scientist. At best people like Protagoras and Socrates prevent their more imaginative colleagues from talking nonsense; at worse they prevent them from talking at all. There is thus something of a paradox about this increasing awareness of method. Science without speculation is sterile; yet speculation without a certain degree of methodological sophistication is abortive. But preoccupation with methodology tends to dry up the imagination. Socrates, significantly enough, got decreasingly interested in physical science as he got increasingly interested in definitions; yet without his critical spirit science would be indistinguishable from mythology. The speculative spirit must somehow be chained to earth by the questions 'How do you know?' and 'What do you mean?' But these questions must not be permitted to incarcerate it.

B. The Sophists

1. PROTAGORAS

In Protagoras we have the elements of a science of man, the groundwork of Socrates and Plato, and he rightly makes an empirical type of psychology the ground of his general conclusions. His aim requires that he should first show in what sense knowledge and experience are identical in their limits. That about which we talk must be, not the hypothetically knowable, but the actually known: in other words the actually experienced. He thus founds a psychological method of speculation.

In the process of experience the fundamental fact is the relation which the object bears to the subject. In order that I may have knowledge of an object it must affect me in some way. The interpretation of the process as given by Protagoras is based upon the idea of Heraclitus that all being is activity, and activity means in plain language perpetual transition from one state to another. The essential feature of the world of objects is therefore movement ($K\acute{\iota}\nu\eta\sigma\iota s$), and the relations between any two or more things can always be expressed in terms of motion. An experience, then, is primarily an impression; two things, previously independent of each other, come into such a relation that the movement of the one is affected by the movement of the other. It is not to be supposed that things are movement; on the contrary, the movement belongs to the thing as its essential attribute. Since movements can vary, being quicker or slower as the case may be, we have as many qualities in things as there are actual modes of motion. A quality of an object is not a permanent possession of that object; it is merely a mode of its movement, a phase of its existence, and as the relation of the object to me is really a relation of contact between the thing and my organism, both the thing and the organism are affected in the process of perception. Thus, for example, when I see this orange there are two realities and two processes. The orange is one thing, the eye is another; the relation between them qualifies both, giving to the orange the quality of colour, and to the eye the condition which is called perception of the orange.

This simple and straightforward account of perception must

have been in the main what Protagoras taught. From it we can get a correct understanding of the famous saying, 'Man is the measure of all things: of that which is that it is, and of that which is not that it is not.' It is unfortunate that usually only the first clause is quoted, for the second is the really significant element. As a whole it enunciates the doctrine that reality is not wider than the sum of all experiences, past, present, and to come. It was a prescription for the purgation of knowledge and the elimination of pseudo-sciences. And it was all the more valuable for the additional declaration that all knowledge is of the class sensation. We cannot say that Protagoras denied all knowledge that was not sense-knowledge; he was only interested to declare that the higher knowledge must be, like sensation, a definite activity of a human kind. It is against the world of objects which man cannot know that he protests; they must be either knowable—that is, capable of producing a real inner activity of the human mind—or be nothing at all.

Protagoras gives us nothing that can be called a system of psychology. His universal term movement ($K\iota\nu\eta\sigma\iota\varsigma$) covers all affections of the individual, both perceptions and emotions; and he is not interested enough in psychology as such to classify or distinguish these affections. It is, however, clear that Protagoras holds a theory which implies a definitely psychological method. He is, in his time, what Locke was in later days and Kant still later. He requires knowledge to be tested and limited by the appeal to 'impressions,' and he is prepared to assert that where experience ends the knowable ceases.

2. GORGIAS

From our point of view none of the Sophists is so important as Protagoras. The same spirit of criticism is shown, however, in Gorgias, and his third canon reflects another phase of psychological inquiry. Granted, says Gorgias, that we know anything, we still cannot impart that knowledge. The relation of one consciousness to another is such that it seems impossible to transfer a state or condition from one to the other. This is a genuine problem, and hardly soluble at this stage. If my state of mind when I know something is an activity of my mind, and that activity produces a physical result, sound, the hearer's state of mind is an effect of that effect; in short, a movement of his mind:

and these two movements, of my mind and the hearer's mind, are co-existing facts. They cannot be one and the same, and if they are different it seems to follow that each mind must exist in isolation. As the condition of an object cannot be at the same time a condition of the perceiving or knowing subject, we can know nothing; as the condition of the speaker cannot be at the same time the condition of the hearer, we can impart nothing. For the solution, theoretically, of this problem, Gorgias required a mass of material not at that time available; consequently he succeeded only in stating a problem, but the mere statement was itself a considerable advance upon all theories that rested upon such doctrines as 'like knows like.' Psychology progresses in Gorgias towards a recognition of the significance of consciousness, and the gulf which lies between the material object and the thinking subject.

C. Socrates

I. RELATION TO SOPHISTS

In a history of philosophy Socrates and the Sophists can hardly be placed in one class. In a history of psychology Socrates can be regarded as an appendage to the line of Sophists, as one who worked in their spirit with new aims and with purposes that tended to check the development of psychology. It is in his grasp of the concept of the individual that Socrates breathes the spirit of the Sophists; not merely in reference to morals, but in every respect. It is inaccurate to distinguish Socrates as one absorbed in ethical questions only: it is equally inaccurate to assert that he believed in the reality of knowledge, while the Sophists did not. The first statement is inaccurate because Socrates makes no abstraction of action from knowledge; he looks upon man as a whole, and merely emphasizes the function of knowlege in the scheme of life. The second is inaccurate because the Sophists cannot be taken as a school whose teaching implied that there could be no real knowledge. We may rather say that Socrates was like the Sophists in directing all attention upon the individual, but Socrates is peculiar in regarding the individual from a less scientific or theoretic standpoint than did the Sophists; for Socrates the individual means the person. The Sophists of whom we have spoken were content to show the relation of the individual to his world. Socrates desires to teach the individual his relation to himself. Self-development, self-consistency, and self-knowledge are the key words of his teaching. From this standpoint he takes up the question of method and diverges from psychology. Influenced by the Sophists, he adopts a psychological standpoint without elaborating any psychological theory; in place of the analysis of psychic life we have a dialectic of concepts.

2. MORAL PSYCHOLOGY

Incidentally Socrates contributes to what may be called the psychology of Ethics. Man has by nature a tendency to strive after happiness, and this natural conation is the root of all desire. Satisfaction of desire is only found in the good, so that all desire is really the will to be happy, which is the same ultimately as the will to be good. But while this appears to be a psychological analysis, it is in reality a metaphysical doctrine made explicit only in part. For we require to know why the object of desire is the same as the good, and the answer cannot be given from any merely psychological standpoint. As Socrates failed to distinguish the desirable, i.e. the good in psychological terms, from the true end of man, i.e. the good in metaphysical terms, so he fails to make clear the reason why the will always acts in accordance with clear knowledge. Both these defects are due to one source, namely, a defective analysis of emotion. In trying to present man as a unity, Socrates gives inadequate attention to the obvious effects in the way of conduct which show the dualism of human nature. Being chiefly interested in the concept of man he distinctly works upon the basis of an ideal concept of man, and the theory finds its true conclusion in the concept of an ideal wise man, such as the Stoics elaborated.

It follows from this that will is either nothing at all or simply the reason when it is in action, practical reason. The analysis of human nature gives us only reason and the passions, and the passions cannot overcome reason. This conclusion is due to the idea that man has faculties which are essentially distinct and therefore do not affect each other. Man cannot have passions in the rational part, nor reason in the emotional part; the parts co-exist, but beyond that are not related; the psychology of motive resolves itself into the question which among the elements is the stronger when there is conflict between the opposing elements. The doctrine is therefore rightly called 'rational determinism,' since it gives the first place to reason as a faculty and recognizes no quality in actions except such as are due to excellence or defect of knowledge. In one respect this analysis must have seemed defective to Socrates himself. His method was primarily introspective, and his ideas of the source of action were derived from reflection. In his declaration that he was guided by a daemon (δαιμόνιον) we have the recognition of an element in the self not capable of analysis. The psychology of Socrates was too simple to explain all the facts, and of this he was conscious in his own experiences. The reason for action in many cases was too obscure to be definitely assigned to a rational insight or a clear desire. Action of the highest kind is often in its origin due to instincts, and these are reactions of the self as a whole, showing us that the self as a whole is something more than the parts which we have in an analysis, something therefore that appears to be relatively transcendental. Whatever Socrates really meant by this term 'daemon,' he certainly regarded it in this way as a factor in conduct which by its very nature defied further explanation; and there is no doubt, from the way in which he trusts it, that he considers it in some sense divine, belonging therefore to that undercurrent of individual life which is the universal and the divine element in all beings.

D. Aristippus

I. SENSATIONALISM

The development of psychology which Socrates arrests is distinctly assisted by Aristippus, who is superior to Socrates in logical precision just as he is inferior in breadth of vision and grasp of human nature. Starting from the position of Protagoras that knowledge is primarily perception and perception is inner movement, Aristippus develops the sensationalism which is obviously latent in the doctrine.

In the sphere of cognition he recognizes only the subjective state, the inner movement of which we are conscious and from that deduces the proposition that all knowledge is subjective, the thing remaining unknown and only the effects of its action being perceived. This seems clear from the fact that things appear differently to different people or to the same people at different times. Thus the doctrine of Protagoras was perverted into complete phenomenalism, and likewise the third tenet of Gorgias was joined with it in the assertion that one man cannot know the feelings of another, so that words as used in common language cannot be known to be means of communicating knowledge. In the sphere of action this uncertainty makes it rational for every man to aim at the production of the one thing which he can certainly know to exist, that is, his own state of feeling.

2. CYRENAIC THEORY OF FEELING

Aristippus must be allowed the credit of grasping one psychological truth which is too often obscured; he saw clearly that feelings as feelings have in themselves no distinctions of better and worse. This he formulates in language natural to a time when psychology and anthropology, psychics and physics, are hardly distinguished. Feelings or perceptions are for him movements either smooth or rough (λέια, τραχεῖα, κίνησις), and from the point of view of feeling pleasant or painful. Pleasure or pain must accordingly be an experience and a quality of existing time, or the present; the past and future should not be considered. The object of pleasure is not identical with its quality; all pleasure as such is good, even if derived from unworthy objects or disreputable actions, and all pain is bad. The only differences recognized are those of quantity, of greater and less intensity.

In its historical context, this clear exposition of psychological truths deserves credit. One further point was added which showed its limitations. For objects physically identical produce different effects. 'The sight, for instance, of the sufferings of others, if they are real, gives a painful impression; if only seen on the stage, a pleasurable one';[1] and from this it follows that experience cannot be analysed as merely a physical impression on a physical object. It is this which compels the Cyrenaic to allow the existence of something more than sense-impressions, which in fact sooner or later compels the recognition of a self reacting to impressions and interpreting them through a system of ideas; but for this, with all its implications, man was not ready, and the only result of the admission for the Cyrenaics is a slow but sure change in their teachings. The later Cyrenaics followed the ethical trend of thought and proclaimed the superiority of rational pleasures and

[1] Zeller, *Socrates*, E.T., p. 359.

the need of a well-balanced judgment of pleasures. For this they had no psychological basis, and expounded their doctrine rightly but not consistently. If we may venture to generalize from the character of Aristippus and the tone of his whole teaching, it would perhaps be right to say that it lapsed into a feeble doctrine of faculties. For the superiority to feeling and necessity of being master of the passions which is claimed by Cyrenaics as much as Cynics, implies that the rational part can stand aloof from the desires and choose deliberately which it will admit and which should be rejected.

Chapter Four

PLATO AND THE START OF THE RATIONALIST TRADITION

A. *Introductory*

Plato is an important figure in the history of psychology for two main reasons. In the first place many details of his psychological descriptions were revived again and again by later writers—for instance, the division of the soul of man into reason, spirit, and appetite, and the separation between the divine rational part and the more earthly irrational part. In the second place his more general assumptions about method, or the proper way to obtain knowledge rather than mere opinion, exercised a profound influence on many later theorists.

Plato carried on the epistemological tradition of the Sophists and Socrates and gave it a twist with which they would have had little sympathy. He believed, like they did, that inquiry needed a prior epistemological justification; we cannot safely set about trying to answer questions about the nature of man or the state until we have assured ourselves that our method of inquiry is infallible. He differed, however, from Protagoras and his later followers like Locke and Hume in the recipe for inquiry which he advocated. To start from observations, to check our assumptions by experiment could never take us out of the realm of mere opinion; knowledge proper could only come to those who used the peerless instrument of reason rather than the shoddy tool of sense. Like Descartes, who followed him, he saw in the procedure of mathematics the key to knowledge. In this assumption he was strongly influenced by the Pythagoreans who believed that the physical universe had an underlying mathematical structure, a sort of ground-plan that mathematics alone could reveal. Plato generalized this imaginative speculation and thought that even abstract conceptions like justice had underlying formal properties. His tripartite theory of the soul was probably an application of Pythagorean harmonics to the immaterial realm—when reason, spirit, and appetite combined together at the right pitch then justice or harmony resulted. From his exaltation of mathematics followed his attitude to experiment and observation and many details of his psychology like the separation between reason and sense. The psychology of most philosophers is epistemology in disguise.

In mathematics, so Plato assumed, we have certain knowledge and deal with a special class of objects, like the geometer's triangle, that are not deceptive and which do not change. He therefore maintained that any inquiry in which this sort of certainty is not attainable cannot terminate in knowledge. If we consider the claims of observation and experiment, as put forward, for instance, by Protagoras, we find that we are dealing with a Heraclitean flux of deceptive appearances. We can always make mistakes about what we perceive. Perception, therefore, cannot give us knowledge, for, by definition, knowledge is of unchanging objects, and when we really know we can't be wrong. Thus, in a famous passage,[1] he dismisses as frivolous those who experiment with strings in harmonic inquiries. They should rather study the perfect consonances revealed by reason. What we call science is therefore the systematization of uncertain opinions. Here Plato was quite right. Science is hypothetical. To admit that we may be mistaken is the beginning of science, and, as Socrates saw, the beginning of wisdom. Plato used the word 'knowledge' in such a way that we can only have knowledge of essences or underlying formal patterns not revealed to sense. Whether there are such patterns or whether the certainty of mathematics is a consequence only of following our own rules for the use of certain symbols has been a matter of dispute for centuries between rationalists and empiricists. Certainly what Plato called 'knowledge' is of no concern to modern scientists who have long since freed themselves from the epistemological neurosis of countless philosophers —the search for certainty about the world. But Plato's conception of how to attain true knowledge had a great influence on scientists and methodologists up to the seventeenth century. He was the first systematic rationalist.

Plato's psychology was not dictated solely by his epistemological preoccupation. Aesthetic and religious considerations also entered into it and possibly political interests as well. Scholars debate about the extent to which his tripartite division of the soul was a way of reinforcing his demand for a three class state composed of rulers, warriors, and workers, rather than a blend of Pythagorean harmonics and the Pythagorean characterization of the three types of life as exemplified by the model of the spectators, combatants, and buyers and sellers at the games. But few would query the religious source of his doctrine of reminiscence or the aesthetic source of his view that reason inhabits the head because the head is the roundest part of the body and that which is nearest the heavens.

Thus Plato's dominant interests were aesthetic, religious, and epistemological. There are certain parts of his psychology which seem more purely speculative—e.g. some of his theories about motion and sensation—but these are few and far between. His descriptions are characterized by that love of symmetry and harmony which were the dominant Greek categories of thought. It is this fascination with form which provides the link between the aesthetic satisfaction with circularity, the exaltation of mathematics as the key to reality, and the worship of reason as the source of orderliness and symmetry. The views that the planets must move in circles because circular motion is

---

[1] *Republic*, Book VII.

the only perfect form of motion, that the reason inhabits the head because the head is nearly circular, that justice is a tripartite harmony of the soul or the state, that there is a cosmic number by means of which cyclic changes can be explained, are all of a piece. Mathematics was the key to the underlying harmony of nature. The true, the beautiful, and the good were different facets of this ground-plan. Reason, which exists in a different way from sense or appetite, was both the source of this harmony and the means by which it was revealed. Method masqueraded as metaphysics.

B. Speculative

1. THE 'TIMAEUS' ACCOUNT OF MAN

In the *Timaeus* we find an elaborate description of the creation and structure of the body. The first and most important part is the marrow, of which one portion is the brain, made to be enclosed in the skull; the other is the spinal cord in its bony sheath. The brain, as the most perfect part and designed to receive the divine seed, is made in the perfect figure and is round; similarly the head is described as a globe. The spinal cord is both round and elongated. These two are the conductors of vital force, for on them the soul acts: the rational part of the soul acts on the brain, the other on the marrow. The vertebral column and the general structure, sinews, and flesh are next considered. Flesh is regarded by Plato as obstructing sensation: consequently all the more sensitive parts were made with a comparatively slight covering of flesh, excepting the tongue. The flesh is only a medium for the transmission of the external impression to the conscious centre, and the less there is to traverse the better; the tongue is an exception because its flesh is especially endowed with powers of discrimination. After describing the creation of hairs and nails, Plato tells us the Creators 'divided the veins about the head and interlaced them about each other in order that they might form an additional link between the head and the body, and that the sensations from both sides might be diffused throughout the body.' The whole structure is an organism continually at work assimilating new matter and giving off waste material; these activities may be called processes of repletion and depletion, corresponding by general analogy to the activities of inspiration and expiration.

Such is the general structure of the body; we may now pass to the functions which it performs. These are of particular interest because it is here that we meet the fundamental concept motion. It will be shown later that the act of perception, as a relation to the external world, is interpreted through the idea of motion which as a property common to the object in the act of impressing, and to the subject as a recipient of impressions, forms the constructive link between man and his sensible world. Before discussing that point we must deal with the physiological activities, the motions of the body and of the nutritive soul.

We have stated briefly the material structure of man. If we turn now to the composite organism, the united soul and body, we find its specific difference consists in vitality, in the possession of a vital principle or soul. The fundamental activity which all other activities presuppose is that of nutrition; we have therefore, as logically first, the principle of desire, which leads to nutrition. The soul of man is from the first dual; the rational soul created by God and placed in the head; the demiourgoi create the irrational soul which is placed in the body. The irrational soul comprises a better and a worse part: the better part is that which inhabits the heart and functions in such manifestations of life as energy, courage, and ambition; the worse part is placed below the diaphragm and functions in desire and appetite and nutrition.

This description is in Plato thoroughly subordinate to irrelevant purposes. If it were merely psychological the estimate of values could hardly be thus set forth; there are no possible reasons within the limits of science for thus degrading the nutritive functions; only from an ethical or metaphysical standpoint is this subordination of one soul to another justified. Plato's psychology in the *Republic* is a kind of phrenology on a large scale; in the *Timaeus* it is the leaven of fact in the myth; in neither is it free from influences that prevent a purely scientific treatment. The inductive and deductive methods are employed with little or no distinction, and conclusions are reached from empirical or rational premises with equal facility. Reason is assigned to the brain probably on purely deductive grounds, that being the part nearest the heavens and man, being, as it were, an inverted plant, 'for the divine power suspended the head and root of us from that place where the generation of the soul first began'; the heart was probably chosen as the seat of courage from the observation of the feelings attending fear, anger, and the like; while the desires and passions could be relegated to the lowest parts not only to banish them as far as possible from the head, but also as a result of observing the processes of nature and the automatic production of such states of desire as hunger or thirst.

These 'souls' may be distinguished according to the quality of their movements. From the ethical point of view we speak of self-control: Plato describes this as self-originated and regular motion. The perfect and self-sufficient motion, the circular, is confined to the head. The lowest part does not share in self-originated motion at all; it preserves only a chaotic state of disturbance analogous to the general chaos of irrational motion in the first stage of existence; it is akin to the life-principle of trees and plants, the purely passive existences. But though by nature and production the spirit of life which inhabits these lower regions of the organism is thus a 'plant-soul,' Plato seems to recognize that its co-existence with other soul-faculties involves some degree of co-operation unless man is to fall asunder into two distinct parts. Means are therefore devised for keeping the extremities in communication. As the desires arising in the lowest soul are known to and can disturb the highest soul, so the movements of the highest soul can produce effects in the lowest. This is the explanation of that most surprising part of Plato's psychology, the teleological theory of the liver. The liver, we are told, acts as a mirror for thought; hard by it is the spleen, which acts as a sponge to keep it clean. The first obvious intention is to explain the control which reason must be capable of exerting on this lower part; being itself wholly irrational the lower soul must receive direction in the way of perception—perception itself being ultimately motion. When we are told that the liver reflects thought as a mirror reflects an image, we are really being told that the liver has a power of reaction which is controlled by the law 'like perceives like.' The power of thought is like the acid element in the liver: it is therefore capable of commanding sympathetic activity in the liver; and this explains why some people not only *know* a thing to be bad, but also have a positive disgust for it, a *feeling* of its badness.

Here Plato is constructing his theory in reference to the composite nature of man, and his ideas are mainly those of the medical writers. The body is directly affected by the soul on account of the 'sympathy' between them, so that the bodily states are reflections of the states which would now be called mental.

Closely connected with this subject are the views of Plato on sleep and dreams. The characteristic of sleep is the cutting off of the soul from external influences. As the eye is cut off in sleep from the light, so the soul is shut up in itself and its motions subside in the hours of darkness. But a certain amount of agitation sometimes remains: 'If the quiet is profound, sleep with few dreams falls on us: but if some of the stronger motions are left, according to their nature and the places where they remain, they engender visions corresponding in number and kind.' On the meaning of dreams Plato speaks a little uncertainly. He regards them sometimes as an activity of the desiring part of the soul, and in the *Republic* a remarkable passage on the moral character of dreams shows that he considered them the expression of desires which are usually suppressed. The duty of the good man is to prevent the rebellious activity of the desires; he neither starves nor surfeits this part of himself, and so his sleep is not troubled by its sorrows or joys. Similarly, he will put to rest the spirited element and so free the reason from all disturbances. So far Plato gives a very 'scientific' account of dreams; he is following the example of the doctors who had already begun to restrict the belief in divination. In the *Timaeus* Plato speaks as though all these states, dreams, inspiration and possession alike, were merely abnormal conditions, or at best a dim expression of desires that might indicate some reaching out after the final objects of desire and so be, as it were, intimations of things eternal. In the *Republic*, on the contrary, he seems to favour the idea that in sleep the rational soul, if it is not troubled by the irrational parts, can attain truths not otherwise revealed. We must conclude, therefore, that Plato on this point was equally affected by the traditions of the supernaturalists and the criticisms of the naturalistic schools. In this we see the beginning of such a theory as that which Philo was content to put forth, a compromise between religion and science which was not altogether an irrational course for those who held that soul and body were distinct in essence. For on such a basis it is natural to see in a physical explanation of dreams a theory that might well be true of all cases in which the soul was hindered by the body, and yet be quite irrelevant in regard to the separate activities of the Reason. This is hardly the place to discuss Plato's reasons for making the liver the organ of divination. The passage (*Tim.*, 71) is a mixture of satire and

sense: the sense is in the explanation of forebodings as dependent
on organic states; this is the divination in life given 'to the foolishness of man': 'after death the liver becomes blind,' says Plato,
thereby denying the utility of that divination which was actually
practised with the liver of victims, and which probably suggested
the whole line of thought elaborated in these sections of the
Timaeus.

2. MOTION AND THE METAPHYSICAL
PICTURE OF THE SOUL

We have observed already that the superiority and inferiority of
parts of the soul can be expressed in terms of motion, the circular
self-originated motion being characteristic of the noblest, the
impressed lineal motion of the lowest. The history of the soul is
the history of a gradual establishment of self-dependence and
equilibrium out of a state of chaos never quite superseded. In
the beginning there is a chaos of movement, all possible forms of
external movement taking effect on the body which aimlessly yields
to every force. This state can never be quite superseded in the life
of a human being, because he is always in intimate connection
with the outer world; he continually takes in and sends out air;
he absorbs matter as nutriment and again gives it back; last, but
not least, he remains subject to the impressions called sensations.

In this sketch of the beginning of soul-life, Plato attains a
breadth of treatment nowhere surpassed. For his basis he has the
fact more explicitly stated by Aristotle that the young live by
sensation and emotion; time brings with it a less impressionable
condition and more control by the central organ, to say nothing
of habit which, as it implies less plasticity, eliminates the possibility of some movements. On this basis he builds the magnificent
structure of imagination and sees with poetic intuition the relation
of part to whole. Bound down in its prison the body, the soul is
literally in touch with the whole universe, and no movement
thrills that universe without its sympathetic tremor in the
mortal body; reason asserting itself as a power brings order into
the smaller cosmos of the human soul, and so attunes it to the
harmony of the world's Soul and of God. Thus the structure of
the theory can be built up from below, on the foundations of
motion, and so reach to the heavens of reason. This we must

leave for a while in order to consider the lower functions of the psychic organism.

3. SENSATION, MEMORY, IMAGINATION

In the treatment of sensation Plato relies on his conception of the human body as capable of receiving impression from without and responding with an inner motion. Sensation is not coeval with life; for at first the soul is without sensation on account of the chaotic condition of the whole organism. Sensation emerges as soon as some degree of order is established; then the organs of sense begin to act according to their distinctive nature and separate sensations arise. Thus Plato explains discrimination as primarily a result of physical or psychological distinctions: in other words, he bases discrimination of perceptions on difference of motions, the inner on the outer, the particular on the general, the individual on the cosmic.

All sensation is a mode of perceiving external force; perception is fundamentally reaction; some parts of the body are subject to shock, but do not themselves respond with any inner movement, such as the hair and nails: these are moved but not movent, receive but do not transmit motion; they are non-conducting. The sentient parts have the peculiarity of being easily moved and of transmitting the motion, which thus spreads over the whole organism and so reaches the soul. This is the general principle of which we have special examples in the special organs.

The eye was created full of gentle fire which does not burn, but is what we call light. This light is homogeneous with that in the outer world. Sight occurs when the light within joins with the light outside the eye; for then a continuous substance is formed and motion can be transmitted along the ray which is qualitatively identical everywhere and literally continuous. At night the connection is broken: cut off from the outer motion the inner fire ceases to move: rest is then induced and sleep; though sometimes the motion persists and then dreams occur.

The 'affections peculiar to the tongue' are caused by particles which either contract or relax the vessels ($\phi\lambda\acute{\epsilon}\beta\epsilon\varsigma$) of that organ. The objects of taste are either (a) bitter, or (b) salt, or (c) acid, or (d) sweet. According to their composition these different kinds of bodies produce the corresponding tastes.

Smells do not admit distinctions of kind. The sensations of this class are produced through the veins about the nose which are too fine to admit particles of earth and water and too wide to be excited by those of fire and air. Smell, therefore, is produced by vapours or 'half-formed substances,' that is, substances in an intermediate condition such as mist or smoke, derived respectively from water and solid bodies. The region affected by smells lies between the head and the navel, and the effect is produced by the nature of the physical contact; rough particles are irritating or painful and smaller particles soothing or pleasant.

Hearing is described on the same general principles, as the result of impression or shock. For speech is a kind of blow transmitted through the ears, by means of the air in the cavities of the body, to the blood and the brain and so reaching the soul. For character of the sound as to pleasantness or unpleasantness depends on the character of the motion, which may be swift and violent, or even and smooth.

All sensations in Plato are produced by specific action on the special sense organ, and consist of a motion, more or less diffused through the organism, which has variations of quality. Such sensations as those of the eye are neither pleasurable nor painful, and in that case the motion is unrestrained and unimpeded: pleasure arises when the motion is produced by particles that suit the organs they enter, and pain is the effect of unsuitable particles. We may also say that the character of the motion, its violence or smoothness, affects the character of the sensation; but the statements of Plato on this point are not very clear, and the subject can be left until we discuss his theory of pain and pleasure.

From one point of view man is an organism in contact with the world around him, and he must therefore be studied as an object among objects; from another, he is the centre of a world which may or may not have its objective counterpart, a world of ideas which must in some degree be subjective. In discussing perceptions we take up the cognitive aspect of man's life and all that we should now call subjective, in a sense hardly appreciated by Plato. The difference between the ancient and modern use of the term 'subjective' is not expressible in a phrase, it must be understood through a study of the whole of the Greek theories of man's rational life.

Hitherto we have dealt only with what are called 'affections' (παθήματα). In the *Theatetus* Plato clearly shows that the life of the soul is more than the passive existence implied by the term 'affections': this we are forced to acknowledge if we consider sensations themselves, for we cannot abstract sensations from memory or knowledge without practically denying sensations themselves. If any creature is merely sensitive it is not a man but an animal; for example, an oyster or a tadpole. There is also a fallacy in the popular habit of speaking as though the organs of sensation were independent of one another and of the whole; on the contrary, man is not a mechanical structure like a Trojan horse, made up of disconnected parts, but rather an organic and functional unity. The correct way to describe sensations is to say that we perceive this or that *through* the appropriate organ. Plato is not at this stage prepared to commit himself to the statement that the *soul* is that which actually perceives; it is sufficient for the present purpose to establish the idea of a central unity which functions through the organs of sense. This introduces us to the inner mechanism of the rational being: we now cross the threshold and study the operations of the mind when it thinks.

Knowledge, we are told, consists not in 'affections,' but in the activity of the mind which thinks them. This activity is not in all cases pure; there is a region of intermediate activities about which Plato says little, but which are nevertheless recognized by him as important. The functions in question are those of memory, mental association, imagination, and emotion.

Memory is defined as the preservation of a sensation. A slight ambiguity attached to the Greek word for oblivion (λήθη) leads Plato to make an interesting distinction. The opposite of remembering is forgetting, and that which is forgotten is, for the soul, non-existent. The power of memory seems to require some persistent condition of the ideas that can be recalled: it is necessary therefore to distinguish between those affections of the body which can and those which cannot be recalled. Some affections of the organism are 'quenched' and never reach the soul: of these there is no memory; they form a part of the universe of motion but not a part of our conscious life. It seems scarcely correct to call these states subconscious; for Plato, that which is not in consciousness is outside of it, and his psychology does not include any states of mind that are beneath the threshold of consciousness. The wide extent of the term soul makes it possible to regard some processes of the soul as external to the conscious self; motions arise within the psychic organism which have no effects upon the mental life. It is necessary, then, to distinguish three things: first, the impression from without which never arrives in consciousness or, in Platonic language, reaches the soul; secondly, the conscious state or idea which has lapsed into oblivion; thirdly, the potentialities which are developed in learning and make possible that remembering which is not conditioned by our previous life on earth. Here we have again the Platonic division which recognizes three types of existence: that of the body, that of soul and body, and that of the soul alone.

In its primary form memory is for Plato practically consciousness: if the sensation once establishes itself in the conscious life it persists either as a potential thought or as an actual idea. Oblivion in this second sense of temporary forgetfulness is the nearest approach which Plato makes to the notion of subconscious states. The transition from potential to actual is effected by the active effort of recollection. While memory is no more than the retention of sensuous impressions, recollection is a distinct act involving principles of connection between ideas.

In the *Lysis* Plato speaks of liking a person or thing for the sake of some other person or thing; he recognizes there the transference of affection, and speaks of 'association' in the popular sense in which anyone may say nowadays that he values a thing 'for its associations.' In the *Phaedo* the principle of association is definitely stated as the explanation of the way in which, for example, the lyre might remind me of its player or a picture remind me either of the person represented or his friend. Plato also says that the association can be based on likeness or unlikeness: it is clear, therefore, that he had observed and roughly analysed this class of mental phenomena. The activity of mind in thus supplying the counterpart of any given experience is called anamnesis, recollection; of its transcendental significance we must speak later.

Imagination is a mental activity in a sensuous form; sensation, memory, and opinion are all accompanied by an imagination. The word phantasy ($\phi a \nu \tau a \sigma i a$) in Plato suggests the unreal as opposed to the real; the art of phantastic ($\dot{\eta}$ $\phi a \nu \tau a \sigma \tau \iota \kappa \dot{\eta}$) is the art of producing appearances; so, being concerned more with the cognitive value of mental processes than their intrinsic characteristics, Plato pays little attention to this power of producing unreal appearances. There is a science of imitations called 'representation' (ἡ ἐιγαστιγη) which aims at truth more than the art of phantastic: to this the preference is given, and among the cognitive faculties we shall find conjectural representation (ἐιγασία) included. The emotions we leave for consideration later; with the passing remark that Plato at one time regards them as belonging to the body and at another as belonging pertaining to the soul.

4. FEELING

These are the conclusions at which Plato arrives when he considers the soul in relation to the world and in itself. There still remain the phenomena which are due to the composite nature of man, the feelings. To understand these we must consider man as a whole, a composite unity. The theory of feeling is closely associated with doctrines of sensation and of desire. Sensations, as we have seen, are explained on the basis of motion; the question of feeling is primarily a question of the relation between sensation and feeling; for feelings differ from sensations, and some explanation of this difference is required.

In the earliest doctrine of the Cyrenaics the difference between sensation and feeling had been expressed as a difference in the quality of movement. Sensation, they said, is a movement: it acquires the quality of pleasure or pain from being either gentle or violent. It is possible to conceive also a third state, in which the motion is imperceptible; there are therefore three possible conditions:

(a) Imperceptible movement: absence of pleasure and pain.
(b) Perceptible gentle movement: pleasure.
(c) Perceptible violent movement: pain.

Starting from this position, Plato finds in it two objectionable features. First, it is a doctrine of relativity. Any attempt to reduce the world to mere relations was opposed by Plato; he asserts continually that there must be something positive and real, things as well as relations between things. Secondly, it is a mechanical doctrine, resting entirely on fact and disregarding significance. The mere statement that pleasure is a quantity of motion cannot be accepted by Plato, because it implies no teleological estimate of the facts.

As revised by Plato, the theory appears in the following form. Sensation is attended by emotion when it passes from a slight and imperceptible to a more violent degree of motion. The quality of being pleasant or painful is due to the direction of the movement according as that is natural or unnatural. Thus quality is added to quantity as interpreted as conformity or want of conformity to nature. If we add that 'natural' means productive of the Good and this good is an object outside the range of the Becoming (an Idea), the teleological character will be obvious.

A like result is obtained if desire is made the starting point of the inquiry. All desire is a movement of the soul from a state of want to a state of completeness. In some cases it rests on experience, and the desire is an inclination toward an object or state given in a previous experience. In addition to this type of desire, there is also that which is usually called 'instinct,' the natural striving of the soul after its natural or real fulfilment. Here again we find the teleological view predominant. There are certain desires and objects of desire such that their adaptation one to another is a part of the order of the universe. Thirst, for example, is a natural desire and drink is its natural complement. The actual idea of the object is usually more complex: for example, the object is thought of as 'warm drink,' and an element is thus added which is a product of experience. Desires may therefore be distinguished as primary and secondary, or as innate and acquired.

The unity of conscious life is never overlooked by Plato, and involves a close connection between sensation, memory, desire, and judgment. All emotions belong to the soul, for they are conscious states, and therefore in some way connected with knowledge. The body never has knowledge, however indispensable an instrument it may be to the attainment of knowledge in some cases; and therefore naturally the body is not the seat of desires or emotions. The soul when affected by desire is in a condition essentially painful; for desire is consciousness of incompleteness. But there is no desire totally devoid of pleasure; for desire is a tendency to greater perfection, and that in itself is pleasant.

The want is a definite feeling due to a condition of the body. Co-existent with this is the desire for that which satisfies the want. The satisfaction is the opposite of the want: it is absent when want is present. Since the body is occupied by the want, that which is concerned with the fulfilment must be the soul. Desire, then, is a non-corporeal function; it belongs to the soul and involves memory.

The soul knows itself and knows also the body. Pains and pleasures arise from both sources, though as known the affections are in the soul. Since the source is twofold, affections can be classified according as they belong to body or to soul or to both at once. Again, pleasures are distinguished as mixed or unmixed. The mixed pleasures are found in each of the former classes. In affections of the body there is a mixture, for example, of the pain due to cold and the pleasure of growing warm. In affections of the soul, fear, regret, lamentation, love, and jealousy, there is mixed feeling; in tragedies and comedies pain and pleasure are felt at once; tragedy arouses a 'pleasing horror,' and comedy presents the ridiculous and therefore arouses pity and laughter. In the case where body and soul are both affected another type of complexity occurs: the body may be in pain while the soul has pleasure, e.g. the pain of hunger combined with pleasure of expectation, or body and soul may both be in pain as when pain of the body is joined with despair of relief. The unmixed pleasures belong to the soul. They are such as arise from colours, figures, sounds, or smells, and are in general pleasures that are not preceded by pain; the intellectual pleasures are to be reckoned with these.

These we may call the psychological determinations of pleasure and pain. In the *Philebus* they are somewhat confused with ethical considerations of value. It is obvious that Plato's surrender of the original dualism of body and soul is only partial; the consciousness which is required for feelings admits an inner dualism, an opposition of reason and feeling identical with the opposition of good and bad. The opposition of mind and body remains; mind is superior as cause and origin of motion; pleasure is always inferior, for it is an effect of that which moves or causes and the highest activity of mind being the apprehension of the Ideas and its own specific self-motion, all perceptions of pleasure are inferior. Pleasure is therefore not the final good: it is the quality of a process and disappears in the conclusion of the process; the process is the restoration of a natural state whose quality is neither pleasant nor painful but neutral.

Plato declined to accept that form of relativity which reduces pleasure to a mere negation, the negation of pain; but he recognizes relativity in the other sense, and bases on it his argument against the Heraclitean dogma that no state can be permanent. From the view of life as perpetual change it seems to follow that no pleasure could persist for an appreciable time; there would always be a process of Becoming, the passage from one condition to another, but never a persistent state, a Being. The argument is analogous to that which reduces time to a transition from future to past and ignores the present. Plato's reply is based on the idea of imperceptible increments: it is not any change but a great change that produces pleasure or pain. Small changes are subconscious and do not necessarily amount to a perceptible difference of feeling. Thus pain and pleasure do not overlap; there is between them, as it were, an area of neutral ground within which man may abide.

In the theory of feelings expounded in the *Philebus* we see the origin of the moral struggle. To the soul in itself belong pleasures that are not preceded by want; to man as a mixed being belongs the dual consciousness of want and of possible satisfaction. As pleasures are known to be good or bad, there arises from this a moral struggle. We see from the *Republic* (Book IV) that this is a conflict between desire and the spirit, ἐπιθυμία and θυμός. It is possible to yield to desire, and in so doing be angry with oneself: man is thus to some extent divided against himself when he does what is evil knowing that it is evil.

C. Ethico-religious

I. ORPHIC INFLUENCE

Plato does not review, as does Aristotle, the psychological work of earlier thinkers. It is, however, obvious from such references as he gives and from the nature of his work as a whole, that he is strongly influenced by previous theories. The account we have given of his psychology so far recalls many points of earlier doctrine; but from Thales to Democritus we look in vain for any adequate treatment of cognition, of the psychical as distinct from the physical. Plato is alive to the importance of purely psychic phenomena, and proposes to describe and account for them. In so far as he describes them we have an analytic theory of the soul; when he attempts further to account for them, difficulties arise;

the border between analysis and hypothesis is crossed; and his theory of the soul, becoming transcendental, absorbs the speculations of Orphism and Pythagorism. The term 'psychology' in its strict sense does not include these speculations, but it is not possible to explain Plato's views without these metaphysical and theological notions.

The Orphic idea of a soul which has reality apart from the body was primarily formulated in relation to the idea of successive existences. Its value is entirely relative to the purpose which it serves, the possibility of salvation by works in successive incarnations. All theories that reduce soul to one or more modes of motion run counter to this; and the idea, which appeals strongly to Plato, will have to be sacrificed if no reason can be given beyond what Orphic or Pythagorean enthusiasts can adduce. But support is at once found for the notion in the very fact that physical theories leave unexplained the phenomena of the rational life. The explanation of true knowledge thus requires and supports a new doctrine of soul; the fact of knowledge is the verification of what we can deduce from this concept of soul, and the explanation of knowledge leads upward from sense to an eternal reason.

Hitherto the psychology of cognition has been concerned only with things. Reflection shows us that we have also knowledge of relations and ideals of goodness and beauty; in the abstract sciences we deal with notions which may be referred to sensible objects but cannot have been derived from them. Even so common a notion as that of the straight line is a notion to which nothing in the sensible world corresponds. We are thus brought face to face with facts that compel us to look for some source of knowledge other than the senses. A clue to the right solution is given by memory. An experience frequently recalls a former experience, and we are perfectly aware that we revive the former experience by an act of mind. But in some cases that which is remembered has never been experienced in this life; the remembrance must therefore be the revival by the soul of experiences that belong to the soul itself. That which we thus recollect is truth independent of the present time, in its nature eternal; and therefore our own thought, properly understood, proves that the soul has an existence of its own, an activity independent of all sensation, and a life which is at least not limited to the span of a bodily existence.

This theory, commonly called the theory of Reminiscence (ἀνάμνησις), is Plato's proof of thought as an independent reality. Motion, the predominating factor in earlier thought, has received due recognition; beside it Plato puts Consciousness as something irreducible. But this argument does not prove more than two facts, the reality of the soul as that which thinks and the reality of its activity as unique. As the soul has commerce with the eternal and immutable, the Ideas which are represented in its concepts, there is a presumption that it is itself no less eternal. The soul might, however, have a life longer than the life of the body, yet ultimately perish. We need, therefore, some further proof of immortality which Plato supplies from metaphysical reasoning. We can only say of this that Plato succeeds in supporting his belief with arguments from the essential simplicity and unity of the soul; the point remains to the last a matter of belief.

D. Epistemological

I. THE COGNITIVE FACULTIES OF THE SOUL

Having thus established the reality of the soul, Plato is able to develop a theory of cognition. The soul is capable of three states —knowledge, opinion, and ignorance. These are the names of the way in which the soul can be related to objects; with respect to the real, it has knowledge; with respect to the contingent, opinion; and with respect to the non-existent, ignorance. This classification is obviously derived from logic; from the point of view of psychology we must describe knowledge as the pure activity of mind, opinion as a mixed activity, and ignorance as either the privation of action, a condition of darkness when the soul is not kindled, or perverse activity. When Plato formulates these distinctions in terms of psychology we find four faculties mentioned—thinking, understanding, belief, and conjecture. These distinctions, then, form a scale from the best to the worst, from the pure activities of soul to those most impeded by sense. But the idea is always the same: soul is imprisoned in body: the body hinders the soul and hence the differences in our forms of knowledge. Psychologically the dualism to which Plato commits himself has no solution: the world of reason never even comes into contact with the world of sense; percept and concept remain unconnected. This is the natural result of beginning from the basis of motion to explain sensation and from thought to explain reason. Whether Plato succeeded in restoring unity to the world of man is a question that does not come into psychology.

These faculties are not to be confused with the parts of the soul mentioned above. When Plato divides the soul into its parts he is dividing one from another the distinct aspects of life and assigning to each a definite principle in a definite place. The faculties are not thus distinct; they are not manifestations of different principles, but activities of reason dependent upon objects which call the activity into being. The primary difference is that between the pure activity of intellect (νόησις) and the activities conditioned by the body (δόξα). The pure activity may be either knowledge (ἐπίστημη) or understanding (διάνοια), according as the object is an idea (a pure unity), or a scientific concept (a unity given in a multiplicity). The activity which is conditioned by the body (δόξα) comprises belief (πίστις), a practical but unscientific knowledge of the use of things, and conjecture (ἐιγασία), which apprehends objects as they are presented, but takes no thought of their significance. The criterion of excellence in the case of the thinking soul is the degree to which it is capable of thinking over the given data. Plato's distinctions are based on this idea: the lowest form of thinking is the bare recognition of the object; the highest is the comprehensive intuition of the man who sees all things as part of a system (ὁ συνοπτικός), realizes that each part has its being in the whole, and brings that system to bear upon each thing.

It is not difficult to describe knowledge in general terms, but a scientific definition can only be obtained by a long process of discrimination and logical analysis. In the *Theatetus* Plato undertook that task, and from that dialogue chiefly we gather his views on the different operations of the mind when it thinks. There is no doubt that the foundation of our thought is laid in sense-perception, and Plato finds it convenient to arrange his argument in the form of a refutation of the doctrine 'sensation is knowledge.' The indefinite character of the term 'sensation' (ἄισθησις) must be remembered; the crucial point of the discussion lies in the fact that a man who knows something *feels* sure of it; knowledge is therefore psychologically a kind of feeling and it is true that knowledge is felt certainty. The ordinary man can thus reasonably maintain that knowledge is feeling, and that when he knows he also feels that he knows: does it follow that feeling is knowledge? The attack on the problem must begin by explaining more accurately what is involved in sensation. Life is activity, and the life of the soul is sustained and preserved by activity. We do not look, therefore, for permanent and changeless conditions of the soul, but for processes caused by action and reaction. A simple example of sense-perception, such as perception of colour, can be analysed and shown to involve two factors— agent and patient; while the colour is itself neither of these but the product of both. The real in these cases is in one sense no more than appearance. For the product varies with variation in the factors concerned. Relativity enters into our perceptions in a double sense: the object which appears large at one time will appear small at another if put beside a greater; that which tastes sweet to a man in health may seem bitter to the same man under other conditions of the body.

From this it becomes clear that there are two distinct mental conditions: one is the immediate recognition of an impression, while the other is the reference of that impression to a system of ideas which is recognized as existing before and after the present moment of feeling. While feeling is the psychological core of the mental state that forms judgments, it is not the whole mental state; knowledge is more than feeling. The first point at which Plato finds sensationalism weak is that of time; if past and future are to be taken into account the present must be transcended: but sensation does not carry us beyond its own limits of time. It is possible to prove that sensation is only a part of the mental state; we have a sensation when we see the letters of a language though we say we do not know the language; we have knowledge of an object when we remember it, though we say that we have at the time no perception of it by the senses. These cases establish a difference between sensation and other functions of the mind; they also prove that knowledge is more complex than direct sense-perception.

The idioms of everyday speech preserve the fallacies of un- critical thought. The Greek could parallel an Englishman's way of saying 'I see your point,' or 'I feel the truth of your remark.' The pioneer of psychology and logic has to treat these phrases as crystallized theories and show their truth or falsity. Plato succeeds in showing that there is a kind of sight that is not of the eye and a kind of feeling that is not a sensation of the same kind as sensations of heat or colour. It might, however, still be true that knowledge was a feeling; if not of these kinds yet of another kind; and none the less feeling. This raises the crucial question, Is a man always right when he feels that he is right? If so, it will be necessary to admit that the feeling is its own guarantee, which was the essence of the original individualistic maxim of Protagoras. This point can only be decided by an inquiry into the nature of error. At this point Plato's inquiry divides into the two allied subjects of psychology and logic: the logical aspect must be omitted here and the psychological presented alone.

The argument has made it apparent that sensation implies an immediate relation to an external object: while the mind is capable of activities concerned with objects that are not sensibly present. This point is first made in connection with memory; when the mind remembers it recalls an object by means of an idea. The soul is likened to a block of wax on which objects impress their resemblances; retention of these impressions is memory, and memory makes possible the recall of past impressions and the co-existence of new and old impressions. When the mind is stored with these ideas derived from sensation, it conducts, as it were, an inner conversation, a dialogue with itself. This inner speech is the judgment which flows forth in the outer judgment, the spoken opinion. A man's opinions are his inner judgments; they consist in processes of thought by which the connection of one idea with another is asserted or denied.

The content of the mind has now expanded; it has not only sense-impressions and the memory of sense-given data, but also ideas for which there is no counterpart in the sense-world. While the objects exist in the outer world, their relations are the work of the mind; equality, difference, even Being itself is an object for the mind only. Abstracted from these relations the mere sensation becomes wholly irrational, meaningless, and empty of being; it has no share in knowledge, and is so far from being the substantial core of our understanding that it proves to be ultimately a meaningless abstraction. The fallacy of sensationalism lies in its persistent habit of constructing the history of the mind backward; it finds in sensation the last product of analysis, and then makes it the first element of construction. The truth rather is that sensations are the occasions for our mental activities. The mind develops, and its development is marked by an increasing complexity. In the idea of development is found the explanation of error. There is, as it were, a twilight of the mind, in which ideas are sorted and united incongruously. This stage, the stage of opinion, is liable to error; opinion may be right or wrong. If opinion were knowledge it would follow that in error we had knowledge and knew that we did not know; being only a stage on the road to knowledge, opinion is assent to judgments that unite ideas. Right opinion correctly unites ideas in its judgments; false opinion results from incorrect union of ideas; in both the ideas are known as ideas, but not understood as parts of a system of ideas.

The result of the argument is to show what knowledge is not. It shows two things: first that psychological and logical conviction are different; certainty is a subjective condition possible whether the opinion is right or wrong; secondly, that mental conditions have degrees of development. Even in knowledge itself Plato admits the difference between latent possession and active envisaging; it is possible to have knowledge and not bring it into the full light of consciousness.

E. Educational

I. PLATO'S CONCEPTION OF EDUCATION

In addition to his analysis of sense and intellect, Plato provides us with a psychology of education. He is not content with stating the nature of the ideal intellect, the mind of the man who views all things from the lofty standpoint of speculative insight; he indicates the way in which such an intellect may be formed. For Plato the true life of the soul is a continuation of that process by which at first order rose out of chaos; education is information, not the mere acquisition of knowledge, but the formation of mind, the process by which form is attained. Knowledge cannot be thrust into the soul from without nor attached to it as an ornament may be attached to the body; knowledge is activity, and the wise man is he who has acquired through training perfection in the exercise of his faculties. Education thus understood is a theory of life and sums up all the sciences that are concerned only with departments of life: it includes all that makes the soul more perfect and all that makes the body less a hindrance. For the discipline of the body athletic exercises are prescribed; for the discipline of mind intellectual pursuits are needed.

2. THE STAGES OF THE SOUL'S EDUCATION

Plato does not forget that the nature of man is tripartite, nor that life is more than the single purpose which a man may consciously keep before him. As there are in man reason, spirit, and desire, each of these must be affected by the training; for the whole is made of the parts and can only be reached through them. Hence the formation of the soul begins with the indirect influence of beauty in the surroundings: upon this beauty the soul feeds and becomes like to that which it thus assimilates. In a more advanced stage direct instruction begins, not with the unemotional detail of science, but in the concrete ideals of sage and hero; the memory for fact is still weak, but the young mind is impressionable and easily roused; the spirit ($\theta\upsilon\mu\acute{o}\varsigma$) glows and the zeal of emulation is awakened; it is enough that this ambition be for the attainment of the good, that the mind has received its bent. When at last the irrational self has reached its years of discretion and the right spirit has been evolved, the intellect can be trained so that, passing through the realm of mathematical truths, it comes at last to the speculative vision of the Ideas and grasps the Idea of the Good. As there are in the world three natures—(1) the Ideas, or Limit, (2) the composite natures ($\tau\grave{\alpha}\ \mu\iota\kappa\tau\grave{\alpha}$), (3) the unlimited or matter—and as the soul is itself intermediary between Pure Forms and the Formless, so the process of development through which it goes is threefold: for there is first the process of moulding the material, irrational nature; then the intermediary stage in which concrete embodiments of law are studied; and finally the highest stage in which the laws of nature are made the subject of thought and the mind thinks over the last great law of all things, the Good in which they live and move and have their being. Plato was doubtless perfectly conscious of the latent mysticism of his doctrine; he saw that the soul in turning round from darkness to light comes finally to itself; above the unity which it contemplates in the world of things, a unity which it looks upon face to face, is the still higher unity in which it is itself included; but from the mysticism of later schools Plato is saved by the fact that he does not regard the existent as wholly dependent on consciousness; the Idea of the Good is like the sun in the heavens: it reveals the world of intelligible things to the mind as the sun reveals to the eye its world of objects; but there is no suggestion in Plato that the object is ever other than external to the mind; consciousness of truth is never merely consciousness of self, and the mind does not contain the intelligible objects any more than the eye contains the world of things visible.

At the most speculative heights of his doctrine Plato is never far from the concrete world of practice. From this theory of the ideal intellect he turns naturally to the discussion of character. In the theory of education there are obvious traces of the medical doctrine of humours. The physiologist tended to make the nature of man wholly dependent upon the mixture of the elements and describe each temperament as due to the excess of one element over others in the mixture. Plato rightly treats the subject with reference to psychology rather than physiology; man is not merely a mixture of elements, he is a mixture of natures, and the science of temperaments requires as its complement a science of characters. Character depends largely on the extent to which one or other of the natures is developed; a man may be characterized by excess of passion, or of spirit, or of intellect. As there is in all things one way which is right and many that are wrong, so here the right proportion is one that permits the rule of intellect. The study of man from this point of view involves a theory of conduct and brings us to the psychology of ethics.

3. EDUCATION FOR THE GOOD LIFE

For Plato life is essentially conduct. As it is not possible to say everything at once, so it is not possible to avoid treating life as though it were a collection of activities: but as the parts of the soul make one soul and the parts of the State one State, so the parts of our life make one life whose extension, so to speak, is conduct. In the theory of conduct Plato reaches the true goal of his exhaustive study of man. If we look at the soul from the point of view of its activity we find that its parts are knit together by the conative element, the Eros which is an impulse toward the attainment of a desired end. This reaching out after the unattained is the way in which life expresses itself: through it the being becomes conscious of its needs. Life then becomes a perpetual striving after the fulfilment of the need, whether it be for physical or spiritual satisfaction. To be able to fulfil the need adequately the creature must clearly understand what the need implies; the impulse must not be blind but work with its end in full view and clearly lighted. Hence true to the Socratic teaching, Plato realizes that the first and greatest condition of successful life is the knowledge of the end. There can be no stopping short of the end of ends, the universe itself, the all beyond which there is nothing; life must rest on truth that has no hypothesis. This is the reason why Plato spends so much time and trouble in expounding the nature of the intellect and its end; but the intellect is for him the light that lighteth every man, and while, in the process, we live that we may know, in the end we find that the knowledge has been the guide and master of our daily life.

It is unfortunate that Platonism is frequently regarded as 'intellectualism,' the term meaning (if anything) a theory of life as the passionless contemplation of truth, the primacy of the will to know. The foundation of this view will be seen if we consider Plato's actual position, which is ultimately a theory of the will to live.

Desire is a condition of the soul, and all desire is ultimately of one kind, the creature's recognition of incompleteness. Desire may be either physical or psychic in respect of its origin; but its satisfaction requires an idea of the object, and must therefore depend on the mind. The will (which in Plato is not expressly distinguished from the desire or impulse) depends upon the mind's grasp of an end; the creature acts in the way which it thinks best. All conduct is therefore in the first case merely doing what one thinks best. A theory of conduct involves reflection, and right conduct can only be achieved when that which is thought best is at the same time truly and really the best. Hence the impulse must come under the rule of the mind, and the mind must be trained to think rightly. In a sense therefore the will, in Plato, is not free; the result is an intellectual determinism. But for Plato the distinction would be meaningless: the control of impulse by reason is only the attainment of harmony within the individual who thus attains his true freedom.

Men act for ends which they approve; they live for that which they like, and their likings reflect their nature. The common element in all cases is the liking ($\phi\iota\lambda\acute{\iota}\alpha$); the distinction of characters depends upon the tendency of the likings, and this again depends upon the balance of the elements in the nature of man: evil likings arise from natures in which the evil elements predominate. Plato would not admit that the liking is neither good nor bad, but is made such by its object; he would not say that a good pleasure means a pleasure in that which is good. On the contrary, the liking is a quality of the nature, and its goodness or badness is an intrinsic quality exhibited in the choice of ends which are also independently good or bad. On the other hand, it is not correct to suppose that an evil nature is one in which the lower elements are active. There are degrees of goodness, and, while in man the parts of his soul are related as superior and inferior, so that the good of the higher part is better than that of the lower, there is none the less an excellence of each part. In the analogy between man and the State we find a distinctive excellence allotted to each part of the State, and, correspondingly, to each part of man. Reason has for its excellence (or virtue) wisdom; spirit has courage; desire has temperance; and the three are fused into one by a law of relations, that rule of co-operation which constitutes Justice. Evil, therefore, is not the possession of any one part, whether higher or lower; it consists entirely in the breach of proper relations between the parts. As the type is realized by a correct mixture, as the essence of the good is due proportion ($\mu\epsilon\tau\rho\iota\acute{o}\tau\eta s$), so that activity which is good rests upon and expresses a nature duly proportioned and balanced.

The theory of education thus elaborated is really a doctrine of development. The soul is situated between a worse and a better: it has the potency of good and a vague innate consciousness of an Absolute Good towards which it may strive. The Pythagorean strain in Platonism comes out in this: there is no substantial unity of soul and body but only a mode of co-existence; this is the state in which the soul is set to work out its own salvation, and the salvation is attained by purification, not the lustrations of magic ritual but the asceticism of reason. No part of Plato's teaching belongs so vitally to his thought as this idea of the ascent of man through discipline; no part of Platonism commanded more attention in later days; for by this ascent man becomes like God, and Christian writers found in that idea the real value of heathen philosophy.

Chapter Five

ARISTOTLE'S MODIFICATION OF RATIONALISM

A. Introductory

Aristotle is often extolled as the founder of scientific method. His claim to this title rests on a slight misconception of science which dies very hard—the view that science is a vast body of knowledge accumulated by a laborious and systematic process of classification and definition. This view may conceivably fit some sciences like botany and petrology—but even in these it is difficult to defend. It certainly does not fit astronomy, physics, or any of the more advanced sciences. Aristotle was director of a vast research organization at Athens called the Lyceum. This was a central clearing station where the findings of numerous research workers on a great number of topics ranging from marine biology to political science were catalogued and classified. Aristotle believed fervently in the virtues of observation, classification, and definition. Those who equate science with the compilation of a vast encyclopaedia or Book of Nature therefore see in Aristotle the originator of scientific method.

Few would dispute that, from a scientific point of view, Aristotle's work was a great improvement on Plato's. He was the son of a doctor and had not Plato's contempt for observation and contact with materials. His deficiencies as a scientist can be traced back to Plato's influence on him—to his retention in a disguised form of Plato's theory of essences and to his doctrine of final causes. Plato had maintained that there existed an idea or essence of everything in an eternal realm and that the world as it appears to us is a degeneration from the blending or intermingling of these ideal patterns. To explain anything for Plato was, therefore, to pierce by means of reason or intellectual intuition the veil which shrouded these ideal patterns from us. To have a vision of the essences was to see the reason why of things. True discourse, so he said, mirrored the blending of the essences. This feat of making our talk fit the forms could only be achieved with the help of intellect, not with the help of sense. Aristotle objected to the notion of a world of essences existing apart from the world as it appears to us. He believed that the essences were inseparable from the material in which they were embodied. The world is made up of form and matter, of natural kinds or infimae species all of which have a natural place. The essence of a thing, be it man or plant or sponge, exists always, if only in embryonic form, inseparable from its matter. Far from being an ideal pattern from which a thing has degenerated, an essence is the completed form which a thing will attain and towards which it will naturally develop.

If we want to know what the essence of a thing is it is not sufficient to sit down and think. We have to make observations and collect a number of things of this and similar species. We then sort out the essential properties of a thing from its accidental ones—man's rationality, for instance, from the colour of his hair. After repeating many instances of a thing the 'that' of sense leads on to the 'why' of intuition, when the essence of a thing is spotted. Thus a completed scientific text-book will consist in definitions of all forms or essences—i.e. names of infimae species like 'man' or 'horse' plus their defining formulae, guaranteed by intuition.

Explanation of the behaviour of a thing consists in referring to the essential properties of the natural kind or class of things to which it belongs, each class having its characteristic and invariant ways of behaving. Why do bodies fall or smoke rise? Because it is part of their essence to seek their natural places on the earth or in the heavens. Why do men make laws? Because rationality is part of their essence. Things do what they do because they are what they are. This is true but not very illuminating. Aristotle provided the paradigm for common-sense or low-level explanations—often, too, for circular explanations. He substituted the logic of classification for Pythagorean mathematics as the key to the ground-plan of nature. Qualitative distinctions were for him irreducible. Quality, not quantity, was the basic category of reality.

The objection to this type of explanation is its theoretical triviality. So few deductive consequences follow from saying that man is a rational animal because it is merely classificatory and incorporates no causal assumption. To say that man is rational is a shorthand device for indicating his tendency to make laws, to plan means to ends, to devise rules for conduct, and so on. If we answer the question 'Why do men make laws?' by saying 'Because men are rational' we are unpacking from our word 'rational' more or less what we have put into it in terms of dispositions to behave in certain ways in certain situations. Most people who ask the question 'Why do men make laws?' want an answer in causal terms; they do not want to be referred to a definition which is a shorthand device for summarizing what they already know about men. It is true that Aristotle distinguished four types of 'causes'—material, formal, efficient, and final. The material cause is the stuff out of which something is made, the formal cause the pattern or 'law of development' of a thing, the efficient cause is the internal or external agency which makes a thing move, and the final cause the end towards which a thing develops. When, however, we examine Aristotle's examples we find that the formal, final, and efficient causes are usually the essence in disguise—the essence 'flower' being, for instance, the formal, final, and efficient cause of the growth of flowers. The theoretical barrenness of this type of explanation was due to Aristotle's view of the universe as a collection of natural kinds all unwinding towards their appointed ends in their natural places and to his treatment of efficient causes mainly as internal agencies. It was not until the time of Galileo that final causes were consciously discarded as scientifically irrelevant and efficient causes conceived of as something other than inner agencies or entelechies. This paved the way for explanation in terms of the functional dependence of variables which had far greater deductive possibilities than Aristotelian explanation by recourse to qualitative classifications. But the Galilean revolution in physical science took centuries to exert a major influence on psychology, where such a revolution may well be out of place anyway. It might be argued, too, that though Aristotle made little empirical contribution to psychology, and though he had a limited conception of scientific method, he made a considerable *conceptual* contribution to psychology, which included a demonstration of why mechanical types of explanation will *never* be of much use in psychology. Ever since the seventeenth century thinkers have tried to explain the behaviour of men as if they were bodies in motion, animals, machines, or dynamic systems—with a singular lack of plausibility and success. Aristotle, in his natural science, generalized categories and concepts which had their natural home in the realms of life where, as a marine biologist, and the son of a doctor, he himself was particularly at home. It might well be the case, therefore, that what he said about living things was remarkably acute but that he made the mistake of generalizing these descriptions to wider fields. Psychologists since Hobbes might well have made the obverse mistake of thinking that what Aristotle said about men could be discounted because his mode of thought had little application in the physical sciences and that mechanical modes of thought should therefore be extended to the realm of life and mind. If Aristotle was metaphysical in extending categories appropriate to the realms of life to nature as a whole, mechanistic theorists have been equally metaphysical in extending their concepts to the realms of life and mind. Aristotle gave good reasons for showing why such an extension must be inappropriate.

His view, as put forward mainly in Books 1 and 2 of the *De Anima*, can be summarized in four main assumptions:

(a) That 'soul' is co-extensive with 'life.'
(b) That soul is the actuality of a body furnished with organs.
(c) That the movements of such a body are to be explained in terms of its soul, but that the soul itself is not moved.
(d) That there are levels of soul which form a kind of hierarchy, the lower being a necessary condition of the higher, but the higher transforming the lower.

B. *Aristotle's Conceptual Contribution to Psychology*

1. 'SOUL' CO-EXTENSIVE WITH LIFE

Aristotle insisted on the widest possible definition of 'soul' and returned to the old pre-Platonic, pre-rationalistic view that soul is virtually the principle of all life—οἷον ἀρχὴ τῶν ζώων. The natural expression for a living thing is ἔμψυχον σῶμα—'body with a soul,' where the adjective ἔμψυχον stands for the attribute that distinguishes living from non-living bodies. To a large extent Aristotle's account of the relationship between soul and body is an attempt to bring out what is implied in this common expression in everyday speech.

In early Homeric thought the word ψύχη had no connection with what later theorists considered to be the essential attributes of soul—feeling and thinking. ψύχη was simply the force that keeps a man alive, which leaves a man's body when he dies or loses consciousness. It was very closely connected with respiration and might leave the man's body through his mouth or through a wound. It was not connected in the thought of the Homeric Greeks with θύμος which is the generator of motion and which was usually connected with the limbs and with the emotions, or with νόος which was the cause of images and ideas. The concept of the soul as a whole and of the body as a whole emerged later, and the soul was thought of as an entity with the attributes of feeling and thinking which had previously been thought of as distinct. The soul, in this expanded form, was thought to leave the body at death. This manner of thinking reached its culmination, perhaps, in the doctrine of the Orphics and Pythagoreans, and Plato, of course, rationalized and made coherent the account of θύμος and νοῦς and the training of νοῦς for its departure from the tomb of the body. Aristotle, however, returned to the old tradition of ψύχη and enriched it with acute distinctions. He started from the linguistic point that some natural bodies are called ἔμψυχον or animate, whereas others are not, and asked what the criterion was by means of which the distinction is made. He said:

'We take, then, as our starting-point for discussion that it is life which distinguishes the animate from the inanimate. But the term "life" is used in different senses; and, if life is present in but a single one of these senses, we speak of a thing as living. Thus there is intellect, sensation, motion from place to place, and rest, the motion concerned with nutrition, and further, decay and growth. Hence it is that all plants are supposed to have life. For apparently they have *within themselves* a faculty and principle whereby they decay and grow in opposite directions; they grow equally in both directions, in fact in all directions, as many as are constantly nourished and therefore continue to live, so long as they are capable of absorbing nourishment.'

Plants have a soul because the explanation of their development seems to lie in themselves. Fire moves, but only upwards. Stones move, but only downwards. But plants grow in any direction where nutriment is to be found. They have a τέλος and their movement is to be explained by reference to their tendency to persist in any direction towards such a τέλος. It is in virtue of such self-originating tendencies that all living things move.

This power of self-nutrition can be isolated from all other powers, but not they from it. Animals have this power; but they also have sensation, especially touch which is the primary sense. And touch may exist apart from other senses as nutrition can exist apart from sensation. And, in a similar way, no animal which has a variety of senses is without the sense of touch. With sensation usually goes appetency— which includes desire, anger, and wish. For where there is sensation, there is pleasure and pain; there is therefore also desire which is appetite for that which is pleasurable. It is not clear whether animals have imagination, but some of them have also the power of locomotion, which is the movement by means of which desires are satisfied. And, of course, man has also reason, by means of which he imposes a plan or rule on his desires. The soul, therefore, is 'that whereby primarily we live, perceive, and have understanding: therefore it will be a species of notion or form, not a matter or subject.' Talk of 'soul' is a way of describing and explaining what bodies do that are different in most important respects from other bodies. It is not a way of referring to something *distinct* from bodies. This is indeed a far cry from the Pythagorean-Platonic notion of soul.

But what, it might well be asked, is the importance of this classicatory sort of move for psychological theory? Aristotle, it might be agreed, faced squarely the problem of what we *mean* when we talk of life and mind. Mind, he maintained, is a particular way in which bodies may be said to have life. There are some bodies in nature whose alterations and movements are self-produced, and to be explained in terms of direction towards certain ends or limits. This self-direction can be conducted with or without sensation and with or without what he called a rational formula. By 'mind' we mean self-direction in accordance with a rational formula. Very good, it might be argued; but how does this help psychology?

The answer is that the notion of classification in science as being just the separation of sciences from each other by reference to their 'subject-matter' is pretty unhelpful; for different sciences arise because different *problems* arise and different types of answers develop. We can treat a man as a body and explain his movements in terms of physical laws if all we wish to explain is why he falls to the ground at a certain rate; for in this respect he is no different from a stone. But we distinguish jumping off a cliff 'on purpose' from descending on the top of a landslide. Jumping is something we do, whereas being swept away by a land-slide is something that happens to us. The movements involved in jumping and in slipping require a different sort of explanation. That is why we do not say 'What was the point of descending on the top of a land-slide?' We might say, on the other hand, 'What made you slip?' just as we would say 'What made the cliff fall?' and expect the same sort of answer. Aristotle saw that in some respect men are what he called passive, just as physical things are passive; but men are not merely passive, and in so far as we distinguish the types of movement they make from those of inanimate things we do so by attributing to them soul or minds which are the source of these particular sorts of movements. Psychology, surely, began as a systematization of the things that people do as distinct from the things that just happen to them. And the things that they do are those which are self-originated.

Aristotle can be rightly criticized for attempting no systematic explanation of certain kinds of things that may well be self-originated but which a man does not do 'on purpose.' In Homer such things as dreams, visions, and mental aberrations were attributed to the intervention of the gods. This is one way of saying that these are not the sorts of things that men do on purpose. Indeed attention has often been drawn to the close connection between the gods of Euripides and the dark forces within man. Aristotle, it is true, spoke of the passions which he connected with specific bodily conditions. He appealed to them in the main to describe cases like madness, and brutish incontinence where there was a breakdown in rationality. But he had no systematic theory of what could be explained by reference to them. He pointed out that if our body is in a certain state we often find ourselves experiencing the feelings of a man in terror in the absence of any external cause. Therefore he said that passions, like anger, should be defined as a certain mode of movement of such and such a body by this or that cause and for this or that end. 'That is precisely why the study of the soul must fall within the science of Nature, at least in so far as in its affections it manifests this double character.' Anger can be the appetite of returning pain for pain, or the boiling of the blood or warm substance round the heart, depending on whether the dialectician or the physicist is looking at it. But although he therefore thought that reference to passion was an explanation in terms of 'soul' he never developed any systematic theory in this field. One suspects that the passions were a bit of an embarrassment to him. For a man is obviously suffering something rather than doing something in so far as what is going on is explained in terms of soul. It was left to Freud to describe and develop laws about the sort of directionality appropriate to the passions. Aristotle had the conceptual apparatus for developing these sorts of explanations but was fascinated either by plants or by rational action.

2. THE SOUL AS THE FIRST ACTUALITY OF A BODY FURNISHED WITH ORGANS

It has been remarked that Aristotle held that activities of soul were always accompanied by bodily motions and that there was always the physical as well as the psychological story to be told about the soul. How then did he envisage the relationship between the two?

He frequently went out of his way to criticize previous theorists for *naïveté* on the subject of the *body* as well as on the subject of the soul.

'They attach the soul to, and enclose it in, a body, without further determining why this happens and what is the condition of the body. And yet some such explanation would seem to be required, as it is owing to their relationship that the one acts, the other is acted upon, that the one is moved, and the other causes it to move; and between two things taken at random no such mutual relations exist. The supporters of such theories merely undertake to explain the nature of the soul. Of the body which is to receive it they have nothing more to say: just as if it were possible for any soul taken at random, according to the Pythagorean stories, to pass into any body. This is absurd, for each body appears to have a distinctive form or shape of its own. It is just like talking of a transmigration of carpentry into flutes: for the craft must employ the right tools and the soul the right body.'

This analogy is very good for the type of relationship that Aristotle had in mind, which derived from his general account of the relationship between matter and form and potentiality and actuality. Bodies are above all things held to be substances. But substances can be either matter which in itself is not this or that; shape or form, in virtue of which the term this or that is applied; and thirdly the whole made up of matter and form. Matter is identical with potentiality, form with actuality. But there are two meanings of actuality. It can mean either the power of acting or the activity itself. The possession of knowledge, says Aristotle, is different from the actual exercise of knowledge.

These distinctions apply admirably to the body and soul. The body is not an attribute of a subject. It stands rather as a subject of attributes —that is matter. The soul, therefore, must be substance in the second sense of form. It is the form of a natural body which has in it life as a capacity, or ἕξις. Such a substance is actuality in the first sense. Body is δύναμις or potentiality in relation to this capacity. The soul is therefore the first type of actuality of a natural body that has life in it as a capacity. A natural body which is possessed of *organs* answers to the required description. For even plants have very primitive organs. The soul is therefore 'the first actuality of a natural body furnished with organs.'

Aristotle used some other examples to bring out the sort of relationship which he had in mind. The best one is the eye. If the eye were an animal, eyesight would be its soul, this being the form or capacity of the eye. As the sensation of a part of the body is to that part, so sensation as a whole is to the whole sentient body as such. And just as the actual seeing is the actuality of the eye in the second sense of 'actuality,' so too is the waking state of the soul. The soul is therefore the actuality of the body in both senses—as a capacity to see and as the actual seeing.

This, Aristotle claims, is a good definition not simply because it sets out the facts in a clear manner, but because it contains and presents the cause of the phenomenon in question. It is 'cause' in the sense of efficient cause as the soul has to be referred to when one asks why motion originates. For instance, in the case of movement from place to place, there must be some reference to concepts like 'wish' and 'desire' which is part of what is meant by 'soul.' 'Soul' too is the cause of such movements as the formal cause. For movements towards an object are explained by regarding them as part of the exercise of a ἕξις or capacity. The notion of a final cause is also obviously indispensable. For the capacities in question, by reference to which we explain movements of the body in locomotion, are capacities implying directedness. The final cause is 'the reason for the sake of which'—if a more literal translation of the Greek is required. If movements are to be explained by reference to the rational soul, then a formula is imposed upon concepts like 'desire' and 'wish.' This is another way of saying that movements are now varied not only in relation to an end, but also in accordance with standards of what is efficient and correct. Plans and rules are imposed on desire.

Surely Aristotle here indicated the sorts of concepts which are absolutely indispensable for accounting for anything which we call a human action. An action is typically something done for the sake of something. To pick it out we have to discover that for the sake of which certain movements of the body take place. This counts as an explanation because we must assume a ἕξις or capacity to do things for the sake of such an end. Also, we often postulate a wish or desire, in the occurrent sense of 'wish' and 'desire,' as initiating such directed sequences, or as their efficient cause. If we speak merely of wishes or desires there is no implication about plans or rules in relation to the end. But when we speak of 'reasons' and 'intentions' such additional assumptions are implied. How can we dispense with an explanatory framework such as this if we are interested in accounting for human actions? For how else could we bring out the sort of actions with which we are confronted save in terms such as these? To discover the goals towards which men tend to direct their actions and the sorts of rules which they follow in their pursuit is surely the basic task of any science of human action, whether it is called psychology or social anthropology. There are, of course, further questions to be asked about such tendencies, and Aristotle was well aware of them. He had, for instance, in his theory of training, a lot of interesting assumptions about how such ἕξεις or dispositions are built up. Also, in his account of voluntariness and choice, he listed some of the conditions under which such habits break down. These very interesting matters are discussed in the *Nicomachean Ethics*.

It could also be said, too, that there is nothing much wrong with what he says about the body in general, though he obviously got some of the details wrong. He regarded the body, especially certain of its organs, as potentiality in relation to the actuality of soul. This is another way of saying that the physiological story can be viewed as a necessary condition of explanations in terms of 'soul' and not as a substitute for them, or as a series of assumptions from which psychological explanations could be deduced. His main reasons for regarding such a substitution or deduction as logically impossible are connected with what he says about the soul as the source of movement but not itself moved. So we can pass to his third assumption.

3. SOUL AS THE SOURCE OF MOVEMENT BUT NOT ITSELF MOVED

In this matter of movement Aristotle accused his.predecessors of the all-pervading mistake of concluding from the fact that the soul is the cause of movement, that it is itself moved. For Democritus and others had pictured the soul as moving the body on the analogy of quick-silver being poured into a wooden statue and drawing the soul after it by contact. But the soul, he maintained, moves the body 'by means of purpose of some sort, that is thought.' And thinking is not a sort of motion any more than desire or sensation are. 'Nor is it correct to speak of the soul as being itself moved, as in anger. It is even scarcely correct to say that the soul feels anger; for that would be like saying that the soul weaves or builds. We should rather not say that the soul pities or learns or thinks, but that the man does so with the soul; and this too not in the sense that the motion occurs in the soul, but in the sense that motion sometimes reaches to, sometimes starts from the soul.'

Aristotle gave many arguments for his views which are largely *ad hominem*—directed against Empedocles, Democritus, the Pythagoreans, and others. But the core of his criticism springs from his general claim that his predecessors had misunderstood the sort of concept that 'soul' was. How, for instance, can a capacity be moved? It is a concept that belongs to the wrong logical type. We can explain movements as exercises of a disposition. But a disposition is not the sort of thing that could itself move or be moved.

What then about the exercises of a disposition? Could not thinking as distinct from a capacity to think be regarded as a species of move-ment? Aristotle had many interesting suggestions to make under this head. He said, for instance, that motion involves movement in space, but a thought is not a whole in the sense in which we speak of a spatial magnitude as a whole. The parts 'have a serial unity like that of number, not a unity like that of spatial magnitude.' In practical thought the processes have a limit; they go on for the sake of something outside the process which gives them their unity. This is why we call them 'thoughts.' Theoretical processes 'come to a close in the same way as the phrases in speech which express processes and results of thinking . . . thinking has more resemblance to a coming to rest or arrest than to a movement; the same may be said of inferring.' Other mental activities have the end built into them in the same sort of way. We see and have seen; we learn, and have learnt; we infer and have inferred. The end or limit is, as it were, built into what we mean by the process. How could such a process ever be described in terms of mere move-ments? We, as it were, come to rest in the very performance of the activity. But the same is not true of activities which are not, as he calls them, complete in themselves. We do not build and have built. The movements lead up to the end-product of a house which is outside the process. But in both theoretical and practical processes the unity in virtue of which we call them types of 'thinking' or 'thoughts' cannot be described in terms appropriate to mere movements. There are movements, of course, which lead up to sensation—in the external object and in the medium, and some sort of alteration occurs in the sense-organ. It takes on the form of the external object without the matter in a process of assimilation. As he puts it, motion sometimes reaches to and sometimes starts from the soul. Sensation and reminiscence are different in this respect. But it is wrong to regard either sensation and reminiscence themselves as a form of movement or as themselves moved. And in this he was quite correct; for though motions may be necessary conditions of both sensation and remembering, reference to them is not involved in what we *mean* by these terms. When we say that we see or remember something we are reporting what Ryle later called an achievement. We are speaking of a standard (what Aristotle calls a 'limit') that has been attained. We are not making a report about movements in our mind or body. And such 'limits' or 'standards' do not characterize movements unless they are thought of as part of an action. Movements just happen; they are neither correct nor incorrect.

The same sort of analysis is eminently defensible in the sphere of what Aristotle called locomotion, or the gross movements of the body from place to place. To explain them in terms of desire or thought is to regard them as exercises of a ἕξις or capacity into which a τέλος or end is built as part of its meaning. We can simply indicate the τέλος as when we say that he moved across the room in order to pour out a drink or we can refer to 'thirst'—the propensity of the man without which the reference to the τέλος would not be explanatory. When reason is involved there is the additional suggestion that these movements are made according to plans and rules. Aristotle, in Book 17 of the *Metaphysics*, stressed the connection between acting with a rational formula and being capable of contrary effects. The hot is capable of heating only but the medical art is capable of producing both health and disease. The contrary is a privation or the removing of the positive term. What he seemed to mean by this is that rational activity is the sort of process which implies standards of correctness from which there can be a falling short. This is not the case with purely physical processes unless they are put to rational use in an art.

There are thus, I think, about three connected arguments which show that mechanical theories will not do in psychology. The first argument is to point to the logical characteristics of disposition terms like 'purpose' and 'knowledge.' It is significant that a mechanical theorist like Hobbes wanted to dispense altogether with the notion of the actualization of a potentiality. He tried to describe dispositions as actual movements of a minute sort. He went to the heroic lengths of suggesting that even habits are actual motions made more and more easy by perpetual endeavours. But this is to confuse a theory about how we came to acquire habits with what we mean by 'habits.' And Aristotle himself believed that some ἕξεις or capacities can be *built up* by the continual occurrence of types of movement.

The second argument would be concerned with the final rather than with the formal cause. It would show that movements are only regarded as part of an action if they lead up to an end and if they can be showr to vary concomitantly with the conditions necessary for the description of an end. Reference to an end is therefore necessary to explain the movements involved in locomotion. It is a conceptual tool necessary for distinguishing classes of movements, not itself an extra movement. The third argument is that, at the rational level of soul, locomotion proceeds according to schedules, plans, and rules, which we impose on our movements. This enables us to describe them as intelligent or stupid, correct or incorrect. And these sorts of description are inappropriate where mere movements are involved. That is one of the things which makes the description of the effects of heat different from those of an art which involves standards of efficiency and correctness. And, in the case of some activities of mind which are 'complete in themselves,' these standards are built into the meaning of the concepts— e.g. perceiving, inferring.

In brief, although what Aristotle said about the absurdity of thinking that the soul itself moves or could be moved, is, to a large extent, a series of *ad hominem* arguments, these arguments presuppose an acute insight into some of the logical characteristics of mental concepts. Some of his points can be generalized to show the logical inappropriateness of trying to translate psychological explanations into mechanical ones or of inaugurating a programme like that of Hobbes or Hull for deducing psychological descriptions from mechanical ones.

4. THE LEVELS OF SOUL

Aristotle maintained that the types of soul resemble the series of figures. 'For alike in figures and in things animate, the earlier form exists potentially in the later, as for instance, the triangle potentially in the quadrilateral, and the nutritive faculty in that which has sensation . . . There is no sensitive faculty apart from the nutritive: and yet the latter exists without the former in plants. Again none of the senses is found apart from touch; while touch is found apart from the others, many animals having neither sight nor hearing nor sense of smell.'

This inseparability of parts has two important implications in Aristotle's theory. The first is that the lower functions are necessary conditions for the possession of the higher. This would accord well with an evolutionary doctrine, although Aristotle had no such genetic assumption. The second is the obverse of this doctrine. For if a soul is rational as well as perceptive and nutritive the rational formula will affect the manner in which the lower functions are exercised. Men, because they are rational, perceive and feed in a manner which is different from that of animals and plants. He worked this assumption out in a most interesting manner in what he says about rational desire or desireful reason in the *Nicomachean Ethics*.

Aristotle finally recognizes no 'parts' of the soul, but he frequently adopts the language of other schools or of current opinion, and also fails to free himself entirely from the influence of those who had previously divided man, as with a hatchet, into rational and irrational natures. There are two modes of division: one is spatial separation of part from part, the other is logical distinction. The Platonists went too far in their talk about 'parts,' and laid themselves open to the charge of localizing different 'souls' in different parts of the body. This involves a second soul to unite these souls (for there must be unity) and so to infinity. The objections to such division are obvious, and Aristotle rejects both the tripartite division of Plato and the dual division of Xenocrates. The only true basis of division is that which starts from functions and classifies them; if such classification is natural it will put together those manifestations of soul-life that are most alike. In this way it is possible to make a working classification of functions as capacities of nutrition, sensation, thought, and motion, regarding the soul as the basis of all these. When speaking with a view to problems of conduct Aristotle employs the popular distinction of rational and irrational parts, subdividing the irrational into two parts, one of which is entirely beyond the reach of reason, while the other is amenable to the control of reason. No importance can be attached to this treatment, as it is obviously a mere convenience and not a theory. The fourfold classification given above is the nearest approach Aristotle makes to a definite theory of 'parts': it belongs essentially to the physical science of the soul; a much more serious division becomes apparent when we take the word soul in its widest possible sense and consider the relation of pure reason to the understanding.

C. Speculative

1. ARISTOTLE'S PHYSIOLOGY

Aristotle starts from a strictly psycho-physical standpoint, and is inclined to give a dual explanation of the phenomena of life according as the physical or psychic aspect is considered. It will be useful to summarize the main points in Aristotle's physiology which affect his exposition of psychic activities.

In respect to nutrition, Aristotle thought that food was transmitted to the stomach and there cooked by the animal heat. It is 'made liquid in the stomach and intestines, and this liquid *steams* up through the small vessels of the mesentery, which lead to the larger vessels, and thence to the heart: *there* it ceases to be ichor and becomes blood.' Of the vascular system Aristotle had not correct knowledge. The heart is the central seat of life, sensation, motion, and heat. These are intimately united: heat is a principle of expansion, while contraction is produced by the cold air which rushes into the space thus created; the heart is the place from which the tendons arise, and these tendons move the limbs.

This view, in itself groundless, makes easy the explanations of motions that result from feelings: the parts of animals are capable of changes and may become larger or smaller under the influence of heat or cold or imagination or even thought. Ideas, whether as images or as thoughts, are consequently kinaesthetic and automatically generate motion. The actual medium by which the soul produces motion in the body is the pneuma.

The brain is given an inferior position in the organism. One reason for this is its locality; the heart occupies the noblest position and has an *a priori* claim to be regarded as the seat of the noblest functions. The brain is cold, and its function is to counteract excessive heat of the heart. Nerves were unknown to Aristotle, and their place is taken, to some extent, by channels (πόροι), which contain the spirits. There is no adequate explanation of the way in which the heart assists sensation, for blood is not sensitive. The only argument in its favour is the actual observation that the brain is insensible: a fact which seemed to exclude that claimant and leave the field open for the *a priori* argument in favour of the heart.

2. THE SPECIAL SENSES

Aristotle's account of the special senses exhibits the working of his main principles. His writing on these topics shows a scientific spirit, free from harmful presuppositions and alive to the value of detailed observation. This attitude of mind is best expressed by saying that Aristotle gives prominence to biological valuations. Plato had formulated the idea of man as a 'political creature,' as a being formed in and for society, but the metaphysical consideration of first causes makes him rather halfhearted in the pursuit of that scientific knowledge which deals with second causes and admits but little insight into anything beyond. Aristotle has a more fully defined idea of the good life: within the life of the cosmos falls that of the state; within the state is the individual; and as the life of the citizen is the proximate universal by which we judge the standard of conduct or practice in the case of the individual, so the individual's life is a universal that comprehends many species. The psychological functions, embracing as they do the whole individual life, are valued according as they further its excellence more or less. On this basis Aristotle ranks the senses in the following order: touch and taste are most important for life; smelling, seeing, hearing are not only useful for life, but enter into the concept of the good life, the life that rises above the merely necessary to a state of culture. This notion of the relation of the senses to the general scheme of existence does not enter into psychology further. Another idea, that of the mean, is a distinct guiding principle in the actual development of the theories. Sensation is a discriminative faculty. The differences which it perceives are real differences between objects, qualities of the objects perceived; but they are also relative differences, for their perception depends upon a relation between object and sense. Hence in the sphere of any given sense-faculty we have a double scale. There are, on the one hand, the extremes and the middle states in respect of the object, and on the other the extremes and the middle states in respect of the subject. In some cases the objective scale overlaps the subjective, as when the objective cause of sound produces no perception from being too slight or is too great to admit of discrimination, sound becoming noise. The language of Aristotle distinguishes in each sense the activity from the cause. These are defined relatively; only that stimulus can be called a stimulus of hearing which is actually at some time heard. On its objective side the stimulus, when not realized in sensation, comes under the general head of motion. The world in which we live is a world of motions, all capable of being quantitatively related to each other, as more or less; and of these some are realized in relation to our organism and produce the qualitative change called sensation. For example: 'If we touch something and pronounce it hard, the hand itself must be soft as compared with what it touches; and similarly, if with the same hand we touch something else and pronounce it soft, the hand must be hard compared with what it now touches. The same hand, then, must be soft to the one thing, hard to the other, and we perceive in the first case the excess, and in the second, the defect of hardness, in the object as compared with the hand.'[1] From the excess and defect in this case we see that the mean belongs to the organ: it has its own state which serves as the norm and fixes the mean in any sensation; the sensation is knowledge of the difference, discrimination. The doctrine of the senses requires now a statement of three things: (i) the nature of the organ, (ii) its mode of relation to objects, (iii) the nature of the sensations.

(a) *Touch*.—We begin with touch as being the most important. In opposition to the popular view, Aristotle maintains that flesh (σάρξ) is not the organ, but only the medium. Touch is thus brought into line with the other sensations. The true organ of touch is something within, possibly the heart. Man is surrounded with flesh just as he is surrounded by air; the flesh covers him like a membrane, and when the object is touched or touches us, it pierces through the covering to the inner organ of sensation. The medium has in this case the peculiarity of being inseparable from us; unlike air or water it is essentially part of us; for which reason it has been overlooked in those previous theories which made touch merely contact of the object and the flesh. A faculty is defined by reference to its object. Touch is the sense of the tangible; but this sphere is not simple; it includes (i) the hot and the cold, (ii) the fluid and the solid. As these are not reducible to one we have to accept the conclusion that the sense of touch is not clearly explicable: it remains for us complex, and includes the senses of touch and of temperature.

(b) *Taste*.—Taste is analogous to touch in being a sense whose medium is a part of the organism. It differs from touch in so far as medium and organ are one, the tongue. In both cases the organ is connected with the heart, and that is the 'foundation of the senses.'

Touch and taste are both senses connected with nutrition. Aristotle rejects the reduction of all senses to touch, but he considers taste is a form of touch; the nutrient matter must come into actual contact. We now see why flesh is the *medium* but not the *organ* of touch. Contact as such is not a cause of sensation: mere juxtaposition is useless; all sensation requires for

[1] Hicks, *De Anima*, 424a 2 note.

its production some medium between the outer object and the organ.

(c) *Smell.*—The sense of smell comes midway between touch and taste on one side, and sight and hearing on the other, i.e. it comes between those that are forms of touch and those that require a medium capable of overcoming the difficulty of distance. The organ of smell is the nose (or its analogue, the olfactory passages in birds) in the case of animals that breathe: it is constituted of air and smelling occurs in inhalation. In the case of fish the process is the same, but gills and water are the organ and element respectively. The medium, then, is air (or water) conveyed into the channels of the nose (or gills), and then producing the sensation by means of the connatural spirit (σύμφυτον πνεῦμα). The stimulus thus reaches the heart.

The process by which we perceive odour is to be distinguished from a doctrine of emanation. Aristotle's meaning is that a motion is propagated by the object in the medium, and by the medium in the sense which transmits it to the heart.

Aristotle, in opposition to Plato, asserts that there are species of odours: some are pleasant accidentally, such, for example, as become pleasant through hunger when the animal is pleased by the smell of food; others are pleasant in themselves, as the smell of flowers. The pleasure in this case also has a biological significance; the pleasures in question are due to the fact that odours are light and ascend to the brain, making it healthy.

(d) *Hearing.*—The organ of hearing, the ear, is composed of air. The medium of sound is the external air. The process of which hearing is the result is a change in the medium produced by either (i) the collision of two sonant bodies, such as brass plates, or (ii) the purposive expulsion of air through the larynx. Aristotle here adds to Plato's vocal sound (φωνή) the more general object of hearing, noise (ψόφος). Great stress is laid on the function of the external ear and the intra-cranial cavities. The shape of the ear enables it to act like a funnel, conducting the moving medium to the point at which the spirits natural to animals are also in motion. Thus there is a complete chain of movement from the first impulse given by the object up to the 'soul,' the centre at which there is conscious realization of sensation. Hearing has the peculiarity of being a sense which mediates between minds—between teacher and pupil, for example. Sounds are divisible into classes, non-vocal and vocal; the vocal can be subdivided according as they are or are not significant. Intelligible sounds obviously have a new and, according to Aristotle, 'accidental' importance analogous to the symbolic value of some objects of sight, e.g. written letters. In one other respect hearing has importance: harmony has emotional quality, and music can be made a factor in the formation of the soul; for every musical mode has a character and tends to produce in the hearer a similar character.

(e) *Vision.*—The first attempts to frame a theory of vision started from the elements contained in the eye. These were supposed to be fire and water. The water acts as a mirror and explains the reflection on the surface of the eye, which is seen by one person looking into the eyes of another. The fire is an active power which seems to be sent out to the object, so that the eye might be said to illuminate its own object, as a lantern lights a road.

Alcmaeon treated vision as a problem of physiology: he stated the parts of the eye and added a theory of their functions. But he either failed to explain vision or his explanation has been lost. After him came Empedocles with a theory that was based on cosmological notions, vision being treated as a special case of the relations between man and the universe. It is clear that when Empedocles formed his theory common opinion was inclined to assume an active and passive element in vision. The active element or 'looking' was distinguished from the passive element or 'seeing,' and this distinction persists afterwards. Looking is an act and a cause; seeing is an effect and requires a cause. So in Empedocles we get the elaborate simile of the eye and the lantern. As a lantern illumines the object, so the eye sends out light and makes things visible. But the eye also receives impressions; emanations come into it and these are then perceived under the universal law that like perceives like. At this point our knowledge about Empedocles breaks down. We require to know whether the inner fire goes right out of the eye to the object, or only reaches to the outer surface of the eye. The point cannot be decided: there is some comfort in the reflection that Plato probably knew the theory and preserved the essence of it in his own explanation of vision.

The emphasis which Alcmaeon laid on the water in the eye,

and the assertion of Empedocles that the eye contains the elements earth, air, fire, and water, each of which perceives its 'like,' point to the significant conclusion that the image in the pupil was taken to be the real object of vision. This is a natural mistake to make: it was certainly made by Democritus, whose whole theory of vision is an attempt to show how that image gets into the eye. Empedocles spoke of 'emanations'; Democritus speaks of 'images.' The former are merely particles which come from the object to the organ of sense; the latter are floating pictures of objects which enter the eye as representations of things. This picture-theory is, if anything, retrograde. It was necessary to go back to the idea of vision as the effect of sense-stimulation without this idea of 'copies' of things. The Platonic theory is known as the doctrine of 'synaugeia' (συναυγέια), or 'union of rays.' According to this, the light or fire in the eye proceeds outward: it does not reach to the object but transforms the air, making it of a similar nature; thus eye and object are connected by a homogeneous medium. The object sets up a movement in this medium, which, because it is everywhere of the same kind, transmits that motion without interruption. The result is the sensation of sight.

In this theory Plato skilfully combines all the problems and finds a solution for them all. The solution is theoretical in the sense than an algebraic problem is theoretically solved; in other words, he resolves all the difficulties that exist in current theories with reference to everything except experience. This is characteristic of science when devoid of experiment. The difficulties and their solutions are these: first, the element of 'looking' is accounted for by retaining the ocular fire; secondly, the fact that we see only in the direction in which we look is explained by saying that the ocular ray transforms the surrounding air in the direction in which it goes, and *only* the transformed air is capable of transmitting the motion; thirdly, the part played by the object is recognized; fourthly, the image in the eye is ignored and the difficulties of reflection which it caused are removed. These are the qualities which made Plato's doctrine worthy of the attention which it afterwards received.

This sketch of preceding theories shows the problems and solutions which Aristotle had before him when he framed his own theory. He, no less than his predecessors, is concerned primarily with the explanation of the relation between eye and object, with the conditions of sight rather than the psychological fact of sight-perception. The first point, therefore, is to decide the medium of vision. This, as Plato had seen, must explain both how we see and why we do not see: it must explain the significance of light and darkness. Aristotle's persistent categories are those of potentiality and actuality; sight is an actualization of a medium which in darkness exists potentially. This medium cannot belong to the eye only—for we *look* in the dark but do not see; nor can it belong to the object, for that exists though it is not seen. It must therefore be something which, when actualized, makes actual the relation of object and eye. Aristotle thus deduces (for we must regard it as a deduction, not as an experimental discovery) the nature of the diaphanous (τὸ διαφανές). The object of vision, it must be remembered, is determined from the point of view of sight, and each sense has a specific object. It is not the same as the object of touch, for we touch in the dark what we do not see: it is not the 'thing' in general, but the visible thing, that is colour. If, then, colour is the object it is not also the medium, and the diaphanous is not colour; neither is the diaphanous air, for air has colour in so far as it is seen. Aristotle makes the nature of the diaphanous so completely a matter of deduction from the analysis of sight that the only way to describe it is to say that it is the objective condition of seeing, the universal possibility which in its actuality constitutes the indispensable condition of all seeing. The process then is as follows. The diaphanous becoming actual constitutes light; colour depends on light as light depends on the diaphanous; colour is that qualification of the light which is propagated through the diaphanous to the eye; it is therefore the true object of vision.

So far Aristotle has solved the problem of the relation between the eye and its object. The further question remains, How does the soul perceive what the eye sees? Aristotle maintains that the eye consists of water, for this is diaphanous, and thus the external and the internal media are alike. This water is supplied to the eye from the brain, the eye being in fact a 'focus' of the brain. Thus a movement proceeds from the object to the eye, and through that 'inwards' until it results in vision.

Looking back on this theory we see how much progress has been made. The idea of a fire from the eye is rejected. Plato had been compelled to explain our inability to see in the dark as due to the extinction of this fire by the darkness, which Aristotle condemns as nonsense. The image on the pupil is now clearly recognized as only one case of reflection, analogous to that in a mirror, and Aristotle realizes that if the image is the cause of vision there is no reason why the mirror should not see. On the other hand, the idea of Democritus that colour is purely subjective is corrected by making it dependent upon the object both for its production and its definite character. Aristotle has no conception of a world which exists only for mind; but he has the power of placing himself at a point of view from which he can distinguish the elements of an experience before they are fused in the experience.

3. THE 'CONNATURAL SPIRITS'

Throughout the psychology of Aristotle we meet with continual reference to the 'connatural spirits,' the σύμφυτόν πνεῦμα. This is a subject of great importance in later psychology, and it will be convenient here to sum up the doctrine of the pneuma as we have it before and in Aristotle.

The obvious relation of breath to life leads to the natural primitive view that air and the principle of life are either akin or identical. Life is activity, and this activity is exhibited as intaking and outgiving, notably in inspiration and expiration. For the physical philosopher attracted by the idea that man is the microcosm and the universe a corresponding macrocosm, this becomes part of a cosmological theory as we have it in Anaximenes or Diogenes of Apollonia. It is a fallacy to interpret these theories in terms of 'spirit' in any sense which that word acquires from later associations. The philosopher looked upon the air as the scientist of today might look upon the steam in the locomotive: its laws of expansion and contraction· were the explanation of life as a mechanical system of activities. The point of view is the same in the case of the medical men, though their interest is more directly centred upon living organisms and concerned with the principles of health and disease. Digestion and climate are with them the main objects of attention, and the inner heat of the body forms the centre of investigation. The body has a 'natural' fire or principle of heat, and this is nourished by the pneuma. Diogenes of Apollonia makes the air in the organism the medium by which all sense-affections are brought to consciousness. Thus air comes to be at once the inner principle of organic and rational life. In

Aristotle the connatural spirit contains the vital heat and is found in all things that have life (ζωή); it is the life-principle (ζωτική ἀρχή) which resides in the heart. Sensations are conveyed to the central seat of sensation, the heart, by that which fills the veins; and the veins are filled with blood and pneuma. Through the influence of the medical writers the inner pneuma has become distinct from the outer pneuma, i.e. the air which we breathe. The inner pneuma is a secretion resulting from processes going on in the body; it moves with the blood and is said to depend on the blood for existence (possibly because loss of blood reduces vitality). The active element is of the nature of fire (τὸ θερμόν), and this is the principle of fertility in seed: this heat is not distinguished from pneuma except in so far as the pneuma may lose its principle of heat and so become insufficient. There is apparently a definite ratio required in the composite substance consisting of blood and pneuma which fills the veins; excess of the blood-element reduces vitality, as in sleep; death may be due to exhaustion of heat, though excess of heat may also destroy the exact balance of elements which makes life possible.

The most interesting part of Aristotle's theory is the use of pneuma in all sense-experience. The organs of sense are in every case constructed to propagate the outer movements inward to the pneuma which they contain; this movement results in a further movement which the pneuma transmits through the blood to the centre, the heart. The pneuma is thus a sentient organism of a subtle nature spread through the body and acting as the universal medium of sensation. In later psychology this appears as a doctrine of 'animal spirits.'

D. Epistemological

I. SENSATION AS ASSIMILATION

The vegetative functions carried on by a soul-endowed body are of interest only when they come into consciousness. Although in order to proceed methodically the nutritive soul should be first considered, the primary importance of consciousness justifies us in beginning from sensation.

Sensation is primarily a faculty of discrimination. Its antecedent in the wider realm of physics is motion, for the perceptions of sense arise when a movement comes through the body to the soul.

But in its own nature sensation is unique: it is not a motion at all from the inner point of view; it is a form of knowledge, and knowledge is primarily the cognition of an object with respect to what is or is not. Discrimination is therefore the primary characteristic of sensation: the sense as such discriminates qualities as, e.g., black and white in vision, sweet and bitter in taste.

Another passage of the *De Anima* tells us that sense is receptive of form without matter. The object produces an impression, as the seal does on wax; as the object is in its activity such also is the sensation or activity of the sense-organ. The object of sensation does not transmit any material thing to the soul: the stone I see is not in my soul, nor are any particles or emanations lodged in my soul; the truth is rather, that objects condition the way in which the soul acts, dictate the form of that activity. If the sensation is true, the activity of the soul must correspond to the nature of the object, the common element, then, between perceiver and perceived is not a material thing but a form, and sense can be described as receptive of form. To prevent confusion, we must further remember that receptivity here implies passivity: what actually happens is that the sense changes from one form to another or from lack of form to form; in so far as sensation of something differs from no sensation there must have occurred a definite change relative to a definite object. A sense is receptive in so far as it admits changes which come from without.

The value of this definition of sense in terms of function is very great. It breaks away from those early ideas of transmission of particles which had never explained sensation at all: it succeeds in showing the significance of contact as the condition of sensation; and it settles the question whether perception demands a relation of like to like or unlike to unlike. The object is always unlike the sense-organ; its reality as perceptible consists in its power of affecting the organ: by that power it arouses an activity of the organ and, as that is the sensation, the object is assimilated by the organ in the act of sensation. An object that does not admit of this assimilation cannot be perceived: it is like food that cannot be digested.

2. COMMON SENSE, MEMORY, AND DREAMS

The doctrine of the special senses explains the relation of man as a psychic being to the world around him: it shows how he comes into contact with that world; not merely as body may be in contact with body, the physical relation of objects; but as sentient comes into relation with sensible so that each partner in the relation realizes itself in the unity of the relation. The unity of the senses themselves now calls for explanation.

The question of unity is naturally treated after discussion of the separate senses comprised in that unity. But there is no possibility of observing any one sense either in isolation from others or in abstraction from the unity which comprehends them all. Aristotle is therefore frequently somewhat obscure in his remarks, finding himself compelled to speak as though the individual senses had synthetic functions of their own. He repeatedly tells us that a single sense comprehends a class of objects. The class of sounds, for example, is the province of hearing, and includes all that is audible and inaudible. The inclusion of these negative terms will be understood if we remember (a) that the sensation is the realization of a stimulus; (b) that the stimuli actually realized fall between extremes not realizable; but these extremes themselves are not outside the class: if they ever were realized they would be realized in that class and no other.

The problem of a central sense arises from two considerations: (a) the ear does not see, but the man who hears is also the man who sees; (b) each sense has a specific object, a quality of things; but some qualities are given in more than one sensation, e.g. roundness along with sensations of sight or touch.

From (b) arises another problem: a sense has discrimination only of differences in its own sphere, of red and green, e.g. in the sphere of colour. How, then, can we discriminate between sensations that belong to different spheres—between sight and sound, for example? Clearly we have here a new grade of unity. The world of objects, reviewed as objects of sense, divides into groups or classes: the particular sensations are unified in their genera; and again, each genus is a species of a higher genus, the all-embracing consciousness. The problem then is that of consciousness, in respect of (a) its function as unity of particular sense-mediated states of consciousness; (b) its reflexive function, or consciousness of being conscious.

(a) A consideration of our actual experiences shows us that perceptions are complex. My perception of an object which I see includes in addition to the specific object of sight (colour) other elements, such as figure. The sense-faculty is capable of only one determination at one time: I cannot see red and green at the same time or in the same act. But I do see a 'round red' thing in one indivisible act. The necessary conclusion is that two faculties are employed in this act: the particular sense functions along with a sense which is not particular in that acceptation of the term: it is 'common'—that is, shared by all the senses. The proof of this is deductive: if the sense by which we perceive figure were identical with that by which we perceive colour, there would be two movements at the same time in the recipient organ and they would modify or even neutralize each other. Conversely, if I had a sense for figure over and above all other senses, I should be capable of appreciating figure alone: experience contradicts this.

Aristotle is here dealing with psychological data which belong to the border region between external and internal activities, and must employ introspection to determine his theory; but he does not abandon his main category, which, throughout his psychology, is motion. Motion includes local motion or movement from place to place, and change or movement from one condition to another. In all sensation an objective stimulus is the cause of a change which proceeds through a medium into consciousness. Viewed as motion (κίνησις), change gives rise to problems, such as the question, How can that which is one undergo at one and the same time two distinct changes? But if this physical standpoint is abandoned the difficulties appear to vanish; quantitatively two separate motions cannot coexist, but must fuse; qualitatively, plurality and unity can coexist. In this conclusion, namely that coexisting determinations are possible in consciousness, Aristotle seems to have rested. He enumerates the 'common sensibles' as motion, rest, magnitude, figure, number; he speaks of them as 'accidental,' though sometimes distinguishing them from the 'accidental' perception implied in recognition; and leaves these statements without further examination from the point of view of consciousness. The exact difficulty which Aristotle here meets is shown in this ambiguous use of 'accidental.' In the perception that this is black and sweet, the element of sweetness is accidental in so far as it is not the specific object of sight; it supervenes in the perception from another source: similarly, the complex perception of 'this object' may have, supervening upon it, elements not given as strict effects of the stimulus. If I say 'this white object is the son of Diares,' I imply a perception to which I add a significance possible only because it is *my* perception—dependent, that is, upon knowledge which I have and others may not have. Here the perception that this is the son of Diares is 'accidental'; but at the same time it is immediate for me: it is a reaction to a stimulus, a perception made possible by my possession of that particular knowledge in the same way that perception of 'the white' is made possible for me by my possession of that power of sensation. Upon this interesting topic Aristotle is not sufficiently explicit to make further statements possible. It is clear, however, that Aristotle saw exactly the significance of his own position. *All* sensation implies activity on the part of the sentient organ; and perception implies activity of the percipient person. A highly complex sensation is not ultimately distinguishable from a complex perception: and that again from an act of judgment. The only real point of distinction between the union of a particular sensation with a common sensible and the union of a particular sensation with an inferred fact is in the habits of the individual. No one has ever been in such a condition as not to unite figure with colour; such union is not a product of experience; but the perception of 'this' as 'the son of Diares' is a result of experience due to the nature of the percipient, though a 'second nature.' As we are talking of the mechanism of conscious life and really of motion, there is no objection from Aristotle's point of view to the idea of unconscious inference; and such a latent (mechanical) unity is indistinguishable from the activity by which we apprehend common sensibles along with special sensibles, though this is, of course, in no sense inference.

(*b*) The second point is summarily settled. If I do not perceive that I see, in one indivisible act, there will be that which sees and that which perceives, and these will require a third faculty to unite them. To cut short this infinite process we assert that the sense perceives itself. As this applies to all the senses, the consciousness of self-knowledge which accompanies all specific sensation must be a function of the 'common sense.' This point Aristotle does not further develop.

Having now crossed the line from outer to inner, from sensations of objects to consciousness; having, that is to say, explained the determination of inner motions or changes by outer stimuli, Aristotle proceeds to deal with inner motions as they persist after stimulation. He has all the time implied the existence of inner activity; the conscious being is always active, his passivity consisting only of determinations, changes in which he is passive in so far as he is not pure causality but shares in the causality. When the object is withdrawn, the activity expresses itself by re-stimulating the central sense and so reproducing the very effects, so far as form is concerned, which the sensible object produced. As the process of sensation actualizes or gives form to the sense-faculty, an image is primarily the effect of the external stimulus, and regarded in abstraction from its source may be called an image or presentation. Representation, or the reproduction of the image in the absence of the original stimulus, is imagination. By virtue of these inner movements, which are psychic, man is able to store up and reproduce many images, and one image may be the cause of another, or more correctly one movement may set up a movement which previously occurred in some relation with it. The possibility of storing up the movement is the condition of Memory; it is that retention without which memory is impossible. The term Memory is restricted by Aristotle in a manner peculiar to himself. It does not include mere retention: that is a condition, not a part, of memory. Memory is a condition in which an image present to the mind is known to be the copy of an object which had been present itself on some former occasion. In this way memory is an experience midway between mere passive retention and active recollection. The peculiar nature of memory is indicated in the formula, 'all memory involves time.' The further possibility of reviving an activity through its connection with an existing activity is the condition of Recollection. Aristotle is not able to explain this, but he gives a description of the facts which is adequate and presupposes only the laws of habit. Organisms always tend to create habits, and the soul has its 'habits' or sequences of ideas which follow each other in their order. The art of recollection consists in starting such a train of imagination. Recollection is the voluntary effort which by exciting an idea creates a stimulus for the whole chain of ideas. The laws of this process are the laws of association between psychic activities: the movement or change which we desire to initiate can be aroused by a present movement, which is either (a) like, i.e. identical with it, or (b) opposite, i.e. the negative counterpart, or (c) contiguous, i.e. part of a series which contains the object of search. Thus Aristotle formulates what have since been called Laws of Association, the laws of similarity, dissimilarity, and contiguity. Aristotle's own account is concerned with movements, psychic changes, thought of as analogous to physical movements, but differentiated by their power of self-origination. The phrase 'association of ideas' conveys a different meaning.

The 'common sense' is the basis also for the phenomena of sleep and dreams. Sleep is caused by fatigue, in which the 'common sense' loses vitality; it may also be caused by food in the stomach, for in the process of digestion gases ascend to the brain and then, descending to the heart, cause the heat of the body to collect around the heart. Sleep, whether caused by fatigue or by the process of digestion, involves a cessation of the activity of the senses: their images are, however, of the sensuous order, and therefore we may conclude that they depend upon the 'common sense.' Aristotle does not deny that dreams are more than mere imaginations; some elements of opinion are mingled in them, but the predominating characteristics unite closely with imagination, whether normal or abnormal.

Passing from this intermediate condition to the full light of wakefulness, we find Imagination is the basis of all thinking and a condition even of the highest rational activity. From the combination of many memories we attain our unitary experience. To understand this experience we must further analyse it, and, returning to the question of memory, consider the nature of our ordinary daily consciousness. Experience seems to be compounded of states of consciousness which are partly the immediate effects of present objects, partly revived impressions referred to past time, and partly anticipations. All of these must be, when actual, in the present; we are therefore compelled to explain the past (or future) character of a state which is itself present; in other words, we must explain the relations between memory, perception, and expectation. The difference of these states is a difference of time, not of actual time-relation but of time-quality. We are conscious in the case both of memory and expectation that there is a different time-reference. In the case of memory we can explain this: when we recognize a picture as a picture of someone, we hold apart in our minds the present picture and the absent person; similarly in memory we hold apart the present image and that of which it is an image. This is not a purposive act of intellect: it is a quality of the memory-image and possible in animals that have no intellect. This qualification is due to the co-operation of a time-sense with the faculty of imagination. Just as a memory of a particular sense-object, a white thing, can only be thought with the accompaniment of some figure, because the common sense functions in the representation, so any experience when revived is presented along with a sense of its time. This explains the time-reference in memory; and Aristotle applies the theory to expectation, presumably because he thinks of events as forming a series, a conclusion which does not follow from this explanation of a time-sense. If I have a series, a, b, c, and my present experience resembles b, it should recall a, b, and c as all past; whereas expectation implies that c is projected into a future. This certainly is a fact, but one that Aristotle can hardly be said to explain, if he implies it. The element of significance implied in such an activity carries us beyond the region of sense within which Aristotle undertakes to explain all the phenomena.

3. IMAGINATION

The sphere of the sensuous faculties terminates at the imagination. A crucial test of the nature of imagination would be furnished if we could know whether all animals possessed the faculty. As the animal is distinguished by the possession of sense without reason, it would follow that imagination depended on sense and not on reason. Our knowledge on that point being defective some uncertainty attaches to the description of imagination. It is sometimes associated with reason and will; sometimes it appears to be purely sensuous; sometimes it appears to be a kind of thought, at others no more than a decaying sense. Imagination can be clearly distinguished from both sense and thought: it is not sense, because we have the image when the sense is not acting (e.g. the image of an object no longer visible); it is not thought, because it involves no belief or reasoning. In brief, it is an intermediary faculty between sense and reason; as such it can be regarded from either point of view. If we take into consideration those functions of imagination which depend on voluntary activity we come at once to the act of thinking. The power of thought depends upon the power of retention; in the flux of sensations nothing would remain were it not that memory holds the universal element given in the particular sensation. Round this nucleus grows a cluster of memories; their differences excite comparison and discrimination, and reason begins its work. Henceforth it is reason that acts, but its action is directed to the images; without these images the discursive intellect never acts, and the voluntary manipulation of mental images is exactly what is meant by discursive reason.

For the psychologist the most interesting point is the character of the idea when it is present in the mind. The word idea suggests visual images just as phantasy suggests light, and it seems possible to have pictures presented to the mind in such a manner as to be entirely devoid of further significance. Such mental states might conceivably occur in reverie or in dreams. As a rule the image is not in this way 'pure fancy.' The image is accompanied by some distinctively rational activity: it is discriminated from some other image, it is made the object of a more or less developed judgment; it is attended by a conviction. Thus parallel with imagination stand opinion, belief, and conviction. The common basis for all these is sensation; from the senses comes the image as a natural product, and the image thus produced is the object of a second process of discrimination. When the images are thus handled by the mind there results an opinion ($\delta\acute{o}\xi\alpha$) or a belief ($\acute{v}\pi\acute{o}\lambda\eta\psi\iota\varsigma$); both these are mental states which combine the presentation of an image as representing an object with a definite attitude toward that object, a conviction with respect to it. Conviction being the work of reason it is clear that neither of these mental states is identical with pure imagination, for imagination as such does not involve reason. The decision of this point assumes considerable importance when previous theories are kept in mind. The relation of the image to the idea led the Pre-Socratic philosophers to blur the distinction between sensation and thought. Plato had paid little attention to imagination and left unanalysed the idea of appearance implied in the ambiguous phrase 'it appears to be,' 'it seems to be' ($\delta o\kappa\hat{\epsilon}\iota$, $\phi\acute{a}\iota\nu\epsilon\tau\alpha\iota$). The clear distinction of imagination and opinion ($\phi\alpha\nu\tau\alpha\sigma\acute{\iota}\alpha$, $\delta\acute{o}\xi\alpha$) was consequently the creation of a scientific distinction and a scientific terminology in place of previous vagueness and popular language. For Plato imagination remained a kind of judgment; the distinction between sense and knowledge was consequently less accurately defined by Plato than by Aristotle. On this hangs the important question raised in the *Theatetus* and the whole problem of universal knowledge; for if there is no distinction between what seems and what is thought, between the psychological image and the logical idea, the final victory must lie with the followers of Protagoras.

Though opinion is not far removed from sensation it is distinguished by involving judgment. Here, then, we pass from the region of sense to the region of thought. So soon as the sense-given data are united by the mind's activity, thinking may be said to have begun. This is primarily reflection, carrying with it the inevitable discrimination. The sensuous images no longer arrive in the mind and remain either unconnected or joined by automatic processes of association; on the contrary connections are looked for and asserted or denied, relations are established by an activity due to reason.

4. REASON

What, then, is the reason? It is clear that reason is something very different from sense: it is clear also that it is somehow higher and ranks above both sensation and the immediate results of sensation which seem to depend entirely on external stimulation. Reason is not the same thing as consciousness, for sensation is a form of consciousness; nor is it self-consciousness, for up to the present that idea has not been evolved. It is in its essential character the power of self-explanation; its beginning is found in the power of manipulating the products of sensation and giving an account of them: it goes beyond the mere consciousness of a given fact and adds to it a knowledge of causes. Reason belongs, of course, to the rational part of the soul; but if we divide the soul into rational and irrational 'parts' it is difficult to say where sensation comes; for sensation is not irrational in the sense that nutrition is. The fact is that the division of rational and irrational implies a false standpoint. Aristotle does not make his distinctions with reference only to the human intellect; his basis is the entire scale of Being from matter to form; and the point of particular interest is potentiality. Sensation is potentially reason because of its inherent power of discrimination and its tendency to extricate the universal from the particular. The same process of discrimination carries us on to still higher levels; sensation gives form without matter, and extricates from the multiplicity of sensations a preliminary universal; the forms thus precipitated by experience constitute a new plurality out of which a new unity can be evolved; and so the mind ascends to the highest generalizations. Beyond these are the axiomatic truths which do not come in this way from below, but are potentialities of the pure reason.

Within the region of sensation the effects are produced by external objects that come into relation with the senses. In the region of thought there is an active search for truth that implies some impelling force. It will be necessary first to explain the nature of this impulse; after that it will be possible to examine the doctrine of reason. For reason is with Aristotle, as with Plato, a light within: it guides the footsteps of man on the paths of daily life; it illumines the dark places of nature; in it is the birth of art, and it becomes at last divine and immortal.

The reason can be treated as sensation was treated: in both we have two correlated potentialities and an actuality. In the case of sensation there are the object, the sense-organ, and the actualized sensation. In the case of reason there are the object, potential reason, and actual reason. It is worthy of notice that the parallel is not exact: there is no organ of reason as there is an organ of sense; but the difference is slight because an organ of sense is properly such only when regarded as a potentiality of sensations. Another point of similarity between sensation and reason is due to the way in which the analysis is based on the objects. Reason is divisible from the point of view of its objects; these are either capable or incapable of change, either contingent or necessary. Whatever criticism may be passed on this view and its metaphysical implications, it is psychologically true that the mind assumes a different attitude towards objects that admit outward action and those that seem to exclude it. Toward the former man adopts an attitude distinctive of the practical reason or thought that implies action; toward the latter he adopts the attitude of a spectator, his reason is theoretical. The reason that is concerned with things that can be altered comprises two spheres, that of conduct or practice in the narrower sense and that of production.

E. Ethical and religious

I. PRACTICAL REASON AND CONATION

The objects of theoretical reason are immovable; the practical reason is concerned with all that is capable of being affected by human action. In order to understand this activity it is necessary to study the nature of that impulse which resides in all living creatures. Regarded universally, this impulse is a tendency towards a better state; it thus appears as a metaphysical principle, a universal law of progress which all created things fulfil. While it is true in this sense that all creation strives after a final good, the actual objects of individual effort are only aspects of this good or elements in it. Moreover there is no necessity for the creature to be conscious of the final good; it may fulfil the law without knowing it, and work the works of reason without definitely accounting for its actions in that way. When there is only sensation it is obvious that the end will be fulfilled instinctively rather than intentionally. In the case of natural appetites—hunger, thirst, and sexual passion—the good is sought instinctively and is realized through direct feelings. The creature strives only after food and drink: it fulfils through these the law of self-preservation. Thus there is seen to be a transcendent principle imbedded in the various activities of animate beings; the rational creature is conscious of the principle as well as of the impulse, and so becomes the subject of voluntary as well as impulsive actions.

There is no essential difference between impulse and will regarded as sources of action. In both cases the essential factor is that general principle of activity which we may call conation. This conation or striving is always a reaching out after some object; when the reason exerts control the act is voluntary. Man is so constituted as to stand between the animal and the divine natures; there are in him the desires of the beast united with a reason that is godlike: in the relation of these two are contained the problems of the psychology of conduct.

Conation acting in the irrational part of our nature depends on sensation for its direction. Sensations are always attended by pleasure or pain, and these again by Desire (ἐπιθυμία). As a generic term Desire includes all activities that either secure pleasure or avoid pain; it is the principle of action in relation to pleasures and pains.

Close to Desire Aristotle places Anger (θυμός). This is defended on psychological grounds: for desire and anger are both primary forms of conation and closely allied to sensation. The opposition between this and the Platonic view is intentional. The Platonic view is ethical; Aristotle is speaking in terms of psychology and physiology: he thinks therefore mainly of the two points in which desire and anger are akin. For they are both allied to sensation in that they depend on imagination as opposed to thought and are distinctively states of feeling.

Conation appears also in that part of the soul which conforms to reason. Here it appears as Wish, which is on the one hand akin to desire in being a form of striving after an apparent or real good, and on the other hand distinct from either desire or anger in being amenable to reason. This dual nature of Wish becomes an important element in the analysis of character.

The general idea of movement imparted to the organism belongs equally to sensation and conation. The capacity for receiving sensations must precede the formation of sense-images (φαντάσματα), and the sense-images are the exciting causes in the case of all conation. Thus movement of some sort is a common factor in sensation as a form of knowing, in desire as a form of inner change, and in local motion as the external expression of desire. Sensation is a movement that proceeds through the body to the soul. In Plato it covered much more than the activity of the five senses: it was, moreover, distinctively an affection of the soul, a suffering rather than a doing on the part of the soul, passivity and not activity. The characteristic of a passive state is that one condition gives place to another as a result of movement set up from without. This interpretation explains how sensation and conation come together under the head of movement, they are changes in which one condition arises out of another (ἀλλόιωσις); as subject to such processes of becoming the soul is passive. The term passive, however, has in Greek the same ambiguity that attaches to the word 'patient' or 'passion' in English; the word (πάθος) can also be used for conditions of disease and suffering. It was natural, therefore, to connect all the disturbances of the soul which appeared abnormal with the corresponding abnormal states of the body: in short, there are diseases of the mind as well as of the body, and the emotions are in many cases abnormal states of the psychophysical organism. Following the slow transition of terms and evolution of ideas we see how the soundness of mind and the soundness of body naturally came at first under the general idea of health; medical terms consequently proved useful in describing the pathology of the mind, and to some extent the associations of the terms guided the growth of ideas. The result is a diagnosis of psychic states with prescriptions for their treatment; we hear of this or that 'diathesis' and even of the 'kathartic' treatment of emotions.

The sensitive, conative, and affective states of the soul are closely allied, and, as we have seen, come together under the general idea of changes that occur in the life of the soul. The distinguishing characteristic of sensation is its cognitive aspect; in conation the active element is conspicuous; while in emotions or affections the passive side is most in evidence. All sensation is connected with pleasure and pain; conation is directed toward the removal of pain or attainment of pleasure, and ultimately becomes the progressive movement toward higher perfection, whether regarded physically as higher vitality or ethically as rationalized conduct: the affections are the changes of the soul upon which pain and pleasure attend. These affections are enumerated by Aristotle as desire, anger, fear, courage, envy, joy, benevolence, hatred, and pity. The list is not intended to be exhaustive, and there is no attempt to make an exact classification of emotions. Desire has an emotional quality because it begins in the pain of want and ends in the pleasure of satisfaction. Anger, fear, and courage are types of feelings which are allied to Temper or the spirit of resistance; anger arises from the sense of wrong and seeks after revenge; fear is consciousness of danger with prospect of ultimate disaster; while courage is the consciousness of danger accompanied by assurance of successful resistance. The remainder come under the general head of Wish, and are attitudes of mind accompanied by imaginations of good or evil whether for oneself or for others. As wish is concerned with good and evil, the presence of the images of good and evil (φαντασία κακοῦ, ἀγαθοῦ) in each of these states justifies their position under this head. As the passions belong to body and soul in union they may be described from both points of view either in respect of causes and motives or in respect of physical conditions and manifestations.

Movement may be analysed under four categories—place,

quantity, quality, and form. As a change of form it covers generation and decay; as a change of quantity, increase and decrease; as
change of quality such transitions as those of sensation. This last
is the only motion which the soul directly imparts to the body.
Motion in this wide sense of action is the basis of conduct, and it
is important in view of ethical aims to determine the psychology
of motion.

Motion in general requires three factors—that which moves,
that which is moved, and that which acts as a fixed point upon
which the moving force rests. All movement requires this motionless basis, else there is no stable element, nothing but a flux of
movements passing from point to point. In the case of the universe the final good is that which moves but is not moved; and in
the microcosm of the soul it is the good, real or apparent, that
forms the basis of motion. To make motion definite and not
infinite, progressive and real instead of endless and unreal, was
part of the opposition of both Plato and Aristotle to the influence
of Heraclitus. The metaphysic of motion does not concern us
here except in so far as it forms the presupposition of the psychological treatment. That presupposition is simply the belief that
motion always involves an end, and finally an end of ends. The
creature moves toward an end which is given by the sensuous
imagination in the case of animals, and by that or by reason in the
case of man. Here we return to conation (ὄρεξις), and explain
exactly how the end (τὸ ὀρεκτόν) is reached. That which moves
but is not moved, the point of rest or final cause of motion, is the
idea or image in the soul; the appetite is the efficient cause of
motion, being the resident activity which acts directly on the
body; while that which is moved is the body. Thus whatever the
starting point may be, the proximate cause of a movement is the
conative element in the soul (ὄρεξις). Conation always depends
on imagination (φαντασία), and the image may be either immediately due to sensation or due to a reasoning process ending in
the selection of an image previously acquired. A difference arises
within the sphere of motion according as we think of regulated or
unregulated motion. At its lowest level conation is the immediate
impulse to pursue or avoid. When this impulse is subjected to
deliberation it is raised to the level of choice; for choice is rationalized impulse or conation based on rational deliberation. Thus a
movement may be the outcome of two distinct processes according

as the ultimate imagination which gives a picture of the end is the result of sense-processes or of reasoning. When sensation is the only factor we have action only; when reason intervenes action is co-ordinated and becomes conduct or practice.

Thus far the explanation of movement has been no more than a description of the processes which end in conscious action. The question of the origin of movement is still left; and this question is important because Plato has assigned movement to the soul as an innate property, while Aristotle declares that the soul is in itself unmoved. In answer to Plato, Aristotle elaborates the mechanical view of motion; the soul supplies only the final cause, the efficient cause is found elsewhere. There is in the body a power of motion having its seat in the heart. As the seat of sensation is also in the heart, this forms, as it were, a junction for the psychic and the physical parts of motion. A change which on one side is a sensation is on the other a mechanical process of expansion or contraction; imagination belongs to the central sense and consequently to the heart, so that it also has the dual character and is both a psychic change and a physical movement. Sense and reason, in so far as they have this physical aspect, can excite and direct motion; but the speculative reason is excluded because it is concerned with immovable things that are not objects of our actions.

The consideration of actions that can be regulated and systematized introduces the problem of conduct and particularly that of will. The close union between imagination and movement leads to actions that follow immediately on the presentation of an idea. The formation of character is a process by which this impulsive action is checked and the power of rational choice developed. The will to act is, in its first or primitive form, a mere conation; conation is, in other words, the generic name, and will is a species of conation differentiated by the presence of deliberation. The perfect will is a conation completely rationalized; desire and wish and will are all harmonious in the complete character. This as an ethical ideal implies that the true good is the object of all. From the psychological standpoint the goodness or badness of the end is not of primary importance. The question which belongs to psychology is that of unity or co-ordination of impulses, not the question of the rightness of the intention. Here the important distinction is between greater and less degrees of control. The sphere of control is that of pains and pleasures, and control consists in the mastery over tendencies to excess. A man may lose control in the sense of forgetting himself and thus allowing the feeling to obscure his consciousness of propriety; such are the cases of incontinence in laughter or anger or in pursuit of gain and honour. These cases have not the same importance as others, because they are not so distinctively immoral; psychologically they are identical in kind with more serious lapses. For Aristotle will is ultimately reason; the life of feeling is a lower existence to which man only descends when he fails to maintain the dignity of his rational nature; the ideal character is that of the man who never loses his head, never fails to act from reasons or be able to defend his actions as properly calculated and adapted. In all things there is a mean; even in the emotions there is a mean, and reason dictates it.

The transition from action to conduct ($\pi\rho\hat{a}\xi\iota\varsigma$) is effected by reason. It is obvious that conduct must always retain the element of activity through which alone intentions can be carried out. It is therefore to conation that we look for the motive power; the natural conation for the good is the basis of a good character. But as the good may be an apparent and not a real good, there must be added to the conation and its imagination a rational power which attains truth. Thus to goodness as a natural striving after one's own good is added wisdom, the power of being right in one's calculations.

Wisdom, in this sense of practical wisdom, is a rational activity and therefore rooted in judgment. The relation of thought to action is well explained in the phrase 'affirmation and negation are to reason what pursuit and avoidance are to conation.' These are not interchangeable because there may be affirmation without pursuit, negation without avoidance; both elements are required for good action, namely, the will to do right ($\dot{o}\rho\theta\dot{\eta}$ $\ddot{o}\rho\epsilon\xi\iota\varsigma$) and a correct or true judgment ($\dot{a}\lambda\eta\theta\dot{\eta}\varsigma$ $\lambda\acute{o}\gamma o\varsigma$). For this reason the psychological terms used for the moral faculties must remain dual; moral choice, e.g., must be defined as a conation regulated by deliberation and the moral faculty as intellect fused with conation or conation fused with discursive reason.

The element called conation is common to all those states of the mind that have any connection with movement. The practical reason or intelligence required for conduct is concerned with things capable of change: for these are in some cases in our power and can be objects of deliberation. The practical reason therefore includes conation; this we can now leave aside and consider the negative aspect separately. The understanding in general (διάνοια) has many aspects, such as science, wisdom, empirical skill, practical wisdom, tact, and shrewdness. These popular terms can be reduced to two, wisdom (σοφία) and practical sense (φρόνησις); and finally the latter appears as subservient to the former, leaving wisdom supreme. The point of contact between these and the lower functions of intellect is found in conception (ὑπόληψις); for science is a right conception of universals in the sphere of the necessary, practical sense the right conception of the ends of action. The important point here is the correctness of the ideas; opinion is judgment but not necessarily right judgment; opinion and conception are much the same thing, but under some conditions the reason forms its conceptions with infallible accuracy; we then have those states of mind that attain ultimate truth. The explanation of this ultimate character of some conceptions is found in the simplicity of the objects apprehended; no process of judgment as a connection of ideas is then required; mediate thought passes into immediacy and the mind is in direct touch with its objects. This ultimate state is therefore an apprehension analogous to sense perception. It will be necessary to remember that for Aristotle the scale of knowledge has two limits: the lower limit is the immediate sense datum containing an implicit universal; the higher limit is the explicit universal upon which the mind lays its finger.

The characteristics of practical sense are to be discovered by studying the character of those who are wise in the matters of conduct. The essential is a correct apprehension of the universal in each case combined with a power of deliberation. Action is concerned with particulars, for a man must do a particular thing; no one is ever said to 'do' a universal. At the same time the truth belongs to the universal; there is in all conation a latent universal; as the individual creatures strive after particular good things they strive after final good which is the form of all actions; reason enters in as a power of bringing to consciousness this latent universal. The problem of the practical man is to keep together the given particular case of action and the universal to which it must belong. The nature of this connection between universal and particular can be seen more easily when the movement is possible in either direction, e.g. in the solution of mathematical problems when the general law is stated and the figure can be constructed. Here the mind works from a conclusion to a necessary starting-point; the construction of the figure really begins where the hypothetical process ends. In practice there is a similar process. He who deliberates says *if* the end is to be attained this course must be pursued; in other words, he works out the possible means to the end. Reason affirms the end, saying this should be done; conation furnishes the active desire to do it. The man whom we call practically wise is therefore one who grasps the end rightly, deliberates on the means correctly, and has the inclination to achieve the end. Here we have end of action, means, and motive power held together in one unity. This is the ideal which is, unfortunately, rarely attained.

It is obvious now that practical wisdom is an extremely concrete affair. The good man is not one who knows the right, but also one who acts on right principles. His character involves a definite kind of Wish which is really a certain kind of conation, a definite bent of character. The reason does not move and it cannot directly produce movement; teaching will not avail in this sphere unless there is also training. Goodness is a product which depends largely on habit, for it is only through habit that the tendency to movement can be directed into the required channels. There is such a thing as natural goodness; the creature may have a natural tendency in the right direction; but if this is to become stable it must be continuous and conscious. The continuity is secured by habit; for as time goes on the original power of movement in any direction becomes limited; plasticity decreases; instincts are inhibited, and those that have to be selected for cultivation pass from potentialities to fixed states. When this is achieved natural goodness has become moral goodness; nature has become second nature, and morality has penetrated to the innermost fibre of man.

The type is not always realized, and the study of man must include the varieties that arise from failure. The reasons for failure are to be found in natural defects. Individuals may start life maimed in respect of virtue; there may be some essential flaw in man's make-up, or disease may cause abnormal states. Aristotle's grasp of biological principles was sufficient to make

him alive to moral deformity as a natural phenomenon: wicked-
ness is not always viciousness; it is frequently a congenital defect
of will power. Where there is viciousness pure and simple the
condition approximates to that of the animal whose desires have
no controlling reason. It is an exaggeration to call a man a beast,
but as a descriptive term the word indicates a truth; desire may
be so perverse as to be inhuman. Bestiality is a phenomenon that
belongs to the sphere of natural science, and is to be explained
either as a failure of nature to produce the normal type or as a
decline from the normal state due to such accidental causes as
disease. The psychology of the normal self must be confined to
normal types which include certain degrees of perfection. The
perfect type involves a harmony of desire, wish, and will; variations arise when this harmony is not realized and the consciousness of the right coexists with tendencies in other directions.
Morality is concerned with pains and pleasures and vice is tendency to excess: a man may avoid pain too much or seek pleasure
too much, while it is his duty to pursue the mean in each case.
Assuming that he knows, and, in a sense, wills the good, what
conditions cause failure? The answer is an analysis of will showing
that in some cases desire rises into action before the process of
deliberation is complete. A modern psychologist would call this
an explosive will. In other cases the process of deliberation is
initiated by the strength of desire. The result is then a kind of
self-sophistication; the individual reasons to a conclusion which
he wants; the process as such is logically correct, but the wish is
father to the thought, the slave rules the master, and the whole
process is an unconscious parody of deliberation. This explanation
of moral failure is made more interesting by the fact that it opposes
the Platonic tradition according to which vice is ignorance.
Aristotle saw that it was possible to have a right conception and
yet fail in action; for the principle of action is not identical with
the principle of reason: man is not a creature ruled by knowledge,
he may have reason and yet not be wholly rational, he may lose
his reason and regain it as he may be drunk and become sober,
sleep and wake again. The physiological parallel is not a mere
analogy; the power of clear reasoning is not always at the same
degree of intensity. The drunkard ceases to realize vividly the
meaning of the precept he can quote, and in a similar way the
passions can reduce a man's realization of principle. It is not only

the young that suffer excess of emotion or become intoxicated with the wine of life. There is a connection between delirium, insanity, the torpor of great suffering, immoderate anger and overpowering lust which did not escape Aristotle, and to these observations he owed his insight into what is literally moral pathology.

2. ACTIVE AND PASSIVE REASON

The basis for Aristotle's division of intellectual functions is the character of the objects. These objects fall into two main classes, the changeless and the changeable: to which correspond theoretical and practical reason. The psychology of practice has been discussed and the minor topics present nothing of interest which is distinctively psychological. We pass now to the question of speculative reason. In the case of practical wisdom it was seen that the function of reason was to make explicit the universal latent in conation. Here we return again to the basis of sensation and follow the process by which the universal latent in sensation is made explicit for consciousness. The sense-processes leave in the mind certain forms, and imagination is the faculty of presenting the image which memory retains. Thus the mind becomes filled with forms and may be called the place of forms; when it is active it calls up by recollection the forms it requires and engages in active search for ideas connected with those present to it. The field of consciousness does not include all possible ideas; some· only are present to the mind ($\theta\epsilon\omega\rho\hat{\epsilon}\iota$) out of those which, in the wider sense, it possesses ($\check{\epsilon}\chi\epsilon\iota$). Thinking is therefore the actuality of ideas which otherwise exist potentially. Among the potential ideas are some that do not owe their origin to sensation; these are the first principles of knowledge. As in the case of practical so in theoretical knowledge a union is required between the particular and the universal, between the sense data and those highest principles which the mind knows intuitively. The connection is established by induction. The universals which constitute experience are produced as the automatic result of perception. From these first universals others may be evolved by comparison and abstraction and the wider generalizations of the sciences are reached in this way. The object of the mind is to reduce the world as far as possible to unity; a search for causes is the intermediary step, and induction is the process by which causes are learned.

The reason (νοῦς) is a fact of which there is no explanation; it comes from without in the sense that its cause cannot be indicated, perhaps because it is itself that which knows causes; it has its own objects, and by these we define it. The general principles which have guided us so far continue to be of use. Just as sensation is the actualization of two potential realities, that which can feel and that which can be felt, so the intellect is the realization of that which is able to understand and that which can be understood. In intellection as in sensation the two terms into which we can analyse the relation are, for our knowledge, mere abstractions. This fact is somewhat obscured in the case of objects of sensation; they appear to belong to an independent world because they have relations one with another: there is, for example, a relation of contact between bodies neither of which is called sensitive; but in the case of the objects of intellect we have no knowledge of them which indicates their Being as different from their being understood; their *esse* is *intelligi*. In this region of ultimate truth there can be no error; reason is infallible because in it alone truth has being; reason, as it were, lays its finger on its object and has an immediate knowledge just as we have immediate perception in sense. The difference between the relation which sense has to its objects and that which reason has to its objects is expressed by Aristotle in the statement that reason is not a mean between extremes; it does not deal with a foreign matter in which it realizes a mean; there is no defect or excess which falls outside its scope and makes for it a limit.

Taken as a whole, reason is divisible into form and matter. The matter is here, as always, passive in relation to the form; it is an aggregate capable of undergoing a change into a formed condition, for the term passive means ultimately capable of being raised to a higher level of organization. No matter is without form, because all perceptible matter has form in so far as it is perceived; but 'form' is a word with a significance that changes according to the context; the marble is matter in relation to the statue; the feelings are matter in relation to the life of reasonable conduct; and the chaos of perceptions is matter in relation to the intellect. The characteristic of the highest state of a rational being is the complete unification of his life. This he may achieve either in respect of ideas or in respect of actions. Intellectual development is a process from chaos to unity, but it is a process with well-defined steps. First comes the sensation which is itself a unity of differences, for under one sense, e.g. sight, come all the synthesis of sensations effected by the Common Sense; next comes the stage of Belief, which asserts a connection between experiences as a matter of experience; then the Understanding strengthens and establishes this belief, being the discursive reason. Thus a natural course of progressive unification lays the world of experience before the eye of the mind as a whole; man can see it all, there remains only the necessity of seeing into it, of looking through experience to the eternal truths of which it is the exponent. In all the intermediate processes there has been possibility of error: every partial act of unification is an opinion which we cannot refuse to form, an affirmation or negation which must be made and may be right or wrong. But at the last there is only pure truth; this is the mystery of the 'pure soul,' the unmixed intellect which is a faculty of universals and knows those truths which experience neither creates nor destroys.

The speculative knowledge in which all knowing culminates is essentially of universals. Aristotle provides a psychological basis for these universals in the first stages; they do not emerge from nothing, neither are they general statements spread out over a multitude of facts. On the contrary, all perception is of the universal; any given object is perceived as being of a certain sort: perception is therefore particular only in so far as it involves the activity of the sense-organ, which again involves the common sense and therewith the time and space sensations. Consequently, if we consider our knowledge of any given object from the point of view of its genesis, and remember that all our human thinking is conducted under conditions that involve the Imagination, we see that it is a complex of form and time and space. Any knowledge, Aristotle seems to say, is always a recognition of form, that being the representative of the thing; and in actual experience the time and the place are fused with this recognition of form in the concrete act of knowing. But the forms can be themselves organized in a higher unity; for the mind is an object to itself, thought being reflective. Consequently, though experience obviously gives us no chance of verifying the statement, it is *logically* conceivable that mind should ultimately be separate in existence; for its content, the forms, have independent universal reality, and they involve the activity which sustains them in actuality.

On the question of the active intellect, Aristotle's statements furnish an insoluble problem. From the historical point of view they are of primary importance, and our accounts of subsequent theories will best show their significance. It will be sufficient here to state exactly what Aristotle says.

Aristotle carries the distinction of activity and passivity through to the last. As there cannot be an infinite series of degrees it is natural and logical on the part of Aristotle to end with a Reason which is active and not passive, a culmination which Aristotle seems to have reached naturally and left as the point which thought reaches at last and beyond which thought cannot go. To others it has seemed a beginning rather than an end. Human curiosity is not content to see the barrier; it must needs look over it and if possible get over it to see what is beyond, firmly believing that there is something beyond. The idea of transcending experience haunts the human mind. Aristotle hinted at further problems, but he did no more than state them, while his successors have tried to solve them. This active intellect has formed a centre of speculations which trail through the centuries; an account of them would form too large a digression for this essay, and prove in the end irrelevant because Aristotle certainly meant little or nothing of what these later teachers found in his words. The cardinal passage is in Aristotle's treatise on the soul, and runs as follows: 'But since, as matter for each kind (and this is potentially all the members of the kind) there corresponds something else which is the cause or agent because it makes them all, the two being related to one another as art to its material, of necessity these differences must be found in the soul. And to the one intellect which answers to this description because it becomes all things, corresponds the other because it makes all things, like a sort of definite quality such as light. For in a manner light, too, converts colours which are potential into actual colours. And it is this intellect which is separable and impassive and unmixed, being in its essential nature an activity. For that which acts is always superior to that which is acted upon, the cause or principle to the matter. Now actual knowledge is identical with the thing known, but potential knowledge is prior in time in the individual: and yet not universally prior in time. But this intellect has no intermittence in its thought. It is, however, only when separated in time that it is its true self, and this, its essential nature, alone is immortal and eternal. But we do not remember because this is impassive, while the intellect which can be affected is perishable and without this does not think at all.'

The best interpretation of Aristotle's general position is that given by Rohde, who distinguishes sharply between the physical or naturalistic element in Aristotle's work and the speculative parts which to a large extent were simply the survival of traditions. This point of view seems amply justified, though it is necessary to remember that Aristotle may have retained the traditional doctrines on the basis of quite independent convictions. As a man of science Aristotle deals with the phenomena of life as they are given us in our consciousness and in the actions of others. But there is in Aristotle an element of mysticism, a vein of speculation more often seen in Plato. Behind the phenomena of mind he thinks there must be an agent, a power that thinks always, a thinking essence that comes into man from without and dwells in man. The dualism of Plato is to a great extent either rejected or refined away by Aristotle. Face to face with the greatest mystery of the soul he finds no new solution, but perpetuates in altered form the transcendental theory already taken by Plato from Orphism.

This explanation of Aristotle's affinities seems credible. While Aristotle's idea of God is not that of 'theology' in the modern sense of the term, he continually asserts that this active reason is 'divine,' 'godlike,' a thing that is unmixed and free from all affections, so that what he says of God he also says of the soul. His successors found his position unsatisfactory; the naturalism which treats reason as a function of the organism found support in some aspects of the master's teaching; others developed the latent possibilities of mystical dogmas. The only decisive point in Aristotle is the statement that the pure reason comes from without. That makes clear the belief of Aristotle that the soul is not a product of experience, not a mere outgrowth of sensations or a name for sensations and thoughts taken as a whole. If it does not arise in man as a product of organic life and does come from without, can it exist before or after this life? That was the problem which Aristotle did not solve; the very contradictions of his interpreters show that the text gives no final answer. It is possible to believe that a power of thought remains indestructibly the same under all conditions and yet maintain that it is only known under some conditions. In that case the agent is only known concretely, that is to say when united with the passive element; it may be conceivable and definable in abstraction, but not knowable in the full sense of the term. It is possible to frame a statement of what the active element would be if it existed out of its present relations, but not to assert that it actually does so exist. If the soul is likened to a sailor who guides and controls the boat while he is in it, we can ask what happens when the sailor steps out of the boat: but not every question can be answered. In brief, Aristotle's position on the question is really agnostic: as the history of psychology proceeds it will be evident that what is said on a future state is based on revelation; if we see in Aristotle a cautious mind knowing nothing of revelation, a Greek with all the clearness of thought and all the consciousness of mystery which characterized the best age of Greek thought, we shall understand his position.

PART

II

Chapter Six

THE DEVELOPMENT OF THE
ETHICO-RELIGIOUS TRADITION
(Pre-Christian)

A. Introductory

The death of Aristotle marked the end of an era. The speculative restlessness of the Greeks declined like their city-States. Their theories were welded into successive philosophies of life, just as their states were welded into successive empires. Speculation for its own sake gave way to symbolic pictures which served to reinforce ways of living. Policies for living rather than theories about life commanded the interest of philosophers.

The Stoics and Epicureans were preoccupied with the attainment of individual self-sufficiency as a substitute for the much lauded self-sufficiency of the old city-states. Life had become something to be endured rather than enjoyed; the problem was how to endure it best. How could the individual fortify himself against oppression, revolution, and social change? The Stoics advocated integrity of character, devotion to duty, humanity towards fellow-sufferers, and the rigorous discipline of the will; the Epicureans sought an escape from the hazards of life in cutting down the possible sources of misery. The Stoics and Epicureans are important only in the history of moral philosophy, not in the history of science. They put forward different forms of individualism one of which reached its culmination in Kant and the other in the English Utilitarians. Their interest to psychologists lies in their doctrine of the will and emotions, their general theory of the soul being mainly adapted from Plato and Aristotle.

The Christian adaptation of the ethico-religious tradition did not begin suddenly with the work of the early Christian fathers. The ground had been well prepared by the Jewish-Alexandrian school, especially by Philo, in whom we find a fusion of the religious fervour of the Hebrews and the conceptual interest of the Greeks. In psychology this led to an increased concern with introspective data, to the laying bare of the inward strivings of the soul, culminating in the work of St. Augustine.

Jesus himself had no speculative interests, his concern being primarily with the religious development of the individual. In his attitude to the learned he typified the practical man of simple faith and intuitive insight who trusts experience rather than a book and his heart rather than his head. He knew intuitively what to expect from people and the influences which shape their development of character. A brilliant diagnostician and curer of souls, he had little interest in formalizing or systematizing his assumptions. His injunctions and behaviour reveal psychological shrewdness and great ability in dealing with people, the sort of knowledge that appears in no textbooks of psychology. For him, just as for many modern psycho-therapists, psychology was an art and not a science.

The Christian theologians of the succeeding centuries shared Jesus' concern with personal salvation, but they embedded it in the sort of learned edifice that was anathema to his simple spirit. Their psychology was woven into a patch-work quilt of Jewish traditions, Platonic speculations, Stoic adaptations of the Greeks, and Pauline salvationism. Revelation vied with introspection as the source of psychological knowledge. In Augustine this dualism of method was epitomized in a combination of brilliant introspective penetration and religious reverence. The soul was the inner bastion of the believer; only certain speculations about it were discussable. What Augustine said about the soul is often of great interest and shows originality and insight. But it is what he did not say, the questions which he could not ask, which reveal, from the point of view of a modern scientist, the defects of his dualism of method. A scientist insists that everything is discussable. It does not matter to him whether an assumption is divinely inspired, handed down by tradition, or printed in a textbook. He is interested only in the inter-subjective evidence for it, not in its subjective origin.

The psychological speculations incorporated in the ethico-religious tradition are not to be disregarded solely because the men who made them were preoccupied mainly with questions of policy. The early builders of cathedrals built them to the glory of God; but in the process they discovered quite a lot about stresses and acoustics. Similarly a man who is preoccupied with building up a certain sort of character —a Stoic perhaps or a Christian teacher—may learn quite a lot in the process about himself and others. Usually such findings, as in the case of the Stoics or of Jesus, are neither systematized nor systematically tested. Logically speaking, the moulder of character is a technologist. His aim is to produce a character according to certain specifications— e.g. Stoic or Christian—in himself and others. In working upon his material—what he calls the human soul—he makes use of certain assumptions. Some of these do not work and are discarded; others work and he treats them as good enough for his purposes. He does not set out systematically to test them like a theoretical scientist. He is interested in men, not in man. In the works of prophets, preachers, and letter writers like Jesus, St. Paul, and Seneca there are quite a lot of interesting assumptions about human beings. Few of these find their way into histories of psychology which usually present the views of systematizers like Clement or Cicero. Most of the systematizers of this period reproduce the views of Plato or Aristotle with minor adaptations. The introspective data garnered in the struggle of scholarly souls for salvation were fitted into conceptual schemes deriving from the Greek and Hebrew traditions.

A modern parallel to the classical ethico-religious tradition represented by figures like Epicurus, Marcus Aurelius, Plotinus, and St.
Augustine, is the work of modern Existentialists like Sartre. Here, too,
we find a great number of psychological assumptions embedded rather
loosely in ethico-religious tracts. The laboratory and consulting room
are not the sole source of psychological inspiration. Many would put
the case even more strongly and assert that novelists, poets, and ethical
teachers know more about human beings than systematic psychologists.
They would say that Euripides and Thucydides tell us much more of
psychological interest than Aristotle; Horace, Juvenal, and Tacitus
much more than Plotinus or Clement; Proust and Graham Greene
much more than Stout and McDougall—and surely this attack on the
psychology of the textbook contains at least two important points. In the
first place it is often forgotten nowadays that there are diverse conditions
favourable to the production of hypotheses about human behaviour,
and the life of the novelist or politician may provide more such opportunities than the life of the academic psychologist. But nowadays these
hypotheses must be systematically tested in order to be scientifically
respectable. The laboratory and the consulting room provide the sort
of experimental situation where a beginning can be made with systematic tests. Such tests are not feasible in the Boulevards of Paris or
the lobbies of the House of Commons.

Secondly any scientific textbook is necessarily an abstract from
experience. In it are formalized certain assumptions describing what
is likely to happen under certain given conditions. It never contains a
complete description of a situation. Compared, therefore, with the
vivid and detailed descriptions of a novelist or of a man writing his
autobiography the textbook is bound to appear rather thin. But a
poet or a religious writer composing his confessions is no more *competing* with a theoretical psychologist than a man describing a sunset
is competing with an astronomer. It may well be that detailed descriptions are of interest to the theoretician in so far as they provide evidence
for or against certain general assumptions which he wishes to test.
But the undertakings are complementary, not antagonistic.

In the period with which we are dealing what we would now call theoretical science had scarcely begun since there were very few conscious
attempts to test general assumptions. What we find is little more than
repeated attempts to order introspective data and overt behaviour by
means of terms like 'reason,' 'will,' 'desire,' and so on, which were
really ways of trying to make explicit by means of shorthand terms a
host of detailed assumptions about human activities and their interrelations. Such primitive classifications were subordinate to ethical and
religious interests and contain a great deal of admonitory and confes-
sional material which would not now appear in textbooks. But often,
as in the case of St. Augustine especially, the introspective material is
so absorbing that it shines through the rather crude attempt to classify
it, and is of perennial interest.

B. The Stoics

I. RELATION TO PREVIOUS DOCTRINES

The history of psychology reached a significant climax in the work of Aristotle. In spite of the numerous differences Aristotle is closely connected with the Socratic and pre-Socratic traditions; in spite of a strong vein of empiricism and a regard for the natural sciences there is still left in Aristotle the speculative temper that verges on mysticism. To the last Aristotle is definitely one of the old school; but so complete was the work produced by this combination of speculative and empirical tendencies, that none of the later schools failed to find in it the starting point of their theories.

The characteristic of the Stoic and the Epicurean theories is the humanism of their interests. The change which comes over philosophy at this stage is produced solely by a change of interest; there are no new discoveries to subvert old theories; science contributed no fresh facts to undermine previous constructions; the times were retrograde rather than progressive. Only in the sphere of politics was there revolution and novelty producing a new atmosphere and a new environment. The vitality of the new thought was due to its origin; the struggle for existence under new conditions is the perennial source of great achievements, and the age of the Stoics and Epicureans was marked throughout by this character of strife. The actual outward form of this struggle, whether in the ebb of Alexander's conquest or the fresh tide of Roman imperialism, need not be described here; philosophy was the consolation of the spirit and the product of the deeper inward movement of reflection. When we look at the outward form of these systems it is most of all necessary to remember that they are like the temples wrought by hands; they are antiquated, unfinished, and strangely patched; but for those who will believe in order to understand they have something akin to the sanctity of religions nourished by the blood of martyrs.

The creed of the Stoic or Epicurean differs from the Platonic and Aristotelian in tone and character. It is misleading to say that the difference lies in the practical character of these later doctrines. Plato was essentially practical, and Aristotle recognized equally well that all sciences are instruments of the good life. Yet the

Stoic and Epicurean are in a sense more practical: they have a more vivid interest in human needs, and this vividness is due finally to the prominence given to feelings. Stoics and Epicureans alike are absorbed in the problems of the life of feeling: they acknowledge openly that man's whole being is concentrated in his passions, and their thought centres upon this fact, whether they preach restraint or justify indulgence. This is the new focus, the humanism of the new era. The interest which Stoic and Epicurean roused and maintained was due to this subtle innovation by which man's thoughts were turned again from the heavens to the earth, from the gods to themselves.

2. FIRST PRINCIPLES

The influence of Aristotle is obvious through all the succeeding schools. The Stoics took Aristotle's work as a basis and treated it to a somewhat drastic simplification. They reduced the categories to four; they cut down the four causes to two; the idea of development they reduced to a somewhat premature monism. In spite of their allegiance to Heraclitus the Stoics are never so far retrograde as to attempt to ignore Aristotle's work; the pre-Socratic elements which can be traced back to Heraclitus, no less than the Cynic elements, appear in Stoicism transformed by the influence of Aristotle. Above all, it was from Aristotle that they derived their method which combines analysis with development.

Turning first to the universe as an object of thought, we find the Stoics employ two categories or heads of classification, namely, action and passion. The world of things is consequently divisible into those that exert and those that submit to action. This classification does not imply any ultimate difference of nature; all things are real in so far as they are capable of acting or being acted upon; all things are therefore material, for this is the definition of matter. As the Stoic defines matter in terms of action there is no 'dead matter' and no opposition between matter and spirit. A pure monism results, apparent differences in the universe being ultimately differences of degree. The substance which is ultimately the Universe is called Fire, after the manner of Heraclitus. As cosmic it is the soul of the Universe, the all-pervading principle of activity; as regulative of all change it is the inherent law of the universe, its reason. The element in all things which gives form is of the nature of Fire and has different degrees in the different levels of being: in the inorganic it is a mere principle of cohesion (ἕξις), in plants it is a specific principle of growth (φύσις), in animals it is the higher principle of life (ψυχή), which is irrational or rational. Thus we have an ascending scale of existences forming a scheme of the universe based on the idea of development. The higher includes the lower in the way already taught by Aristotle.

From this scheme of the Universe it is obvious that the psychology of the Stoics is a natural history of reason. The active principle in all animate creatures is called 'soul,' and is the subtlest form of substance: it pervades the whole organism of the creature just as Reason pervades the universe. Thus the ancient analogy of macrocosm and microcosm is restored; with it is associated the idea of a participation in universal reason which leads to a theory of unconscious reason manifested in instincts. Mental activity as it is found in men is a developed and specialized form of the universal reason. Reason, as such, is to be regarded as a principle which is independent in its existence and activity. The creature who possesses reason is therefore only its vehicle, and is perhaps more correctly described as possessed by reason. From the physical point of view nature is filled with an active principle which moves by its own laws and fulfils its own ends. The first deduction from this premise is that nature and reason are synonymous; all the activities of uncorrupted nature must be rational in the primary and universal sense of rational; the animal will therefore be in many respects better than man, for the native tendency will often be more correct than the purposes of a sophisticated mind.

3. THE SOUL AND ITS ACTIVITIES

For the Stoic the real is always substance. The soul of a man is the most subtle form of that substance which is the stuff of the universe. The proof of this rests on the assertion that the power to act or be acted upon is the criterion of reality and also the essential attribute of matter. The Stoic therefore abolishes a spiritual world if by spiritual is meant that which falls outside the range of natural laws. Psychic phenomena are, accordingly, reduced to physical facts. The arguments brought forward to prove this position are not conclusive. The corporeal, they said, cannot be affected by anything that is not corporeal; the body is affected by the soul, and soul is therefore corporeal; mental characteristics are inherited no less than physical qualities, and must therefore be corporeal; for likeness and unlikeness cannot be predicated of anything that does not impress the beholder in a certain way and to convey impressions is to be active and material. In those arguments there are all the difficulties and defects which corrupt modern materialism: we may compare, for example, the way in which modern writers appeal to the conservation of energy as a proof that physical cannot be converted into psychic or psychic into physical movement, while the opponent replies that 'conservation of energy' is a formula that remains unaffected by a distinction of kind between psychic and physical energy. The fact is, that the Stoic was bent on maintaining a monism; terms are flexible and express little more than a point of view; the terms of the Stoic formulae were ultimately ways of stating the unity of the world and do not require further criticism. The main contentions, namely, that distinctions (such as soul and body) are not ultimately differences and that a living unity is necessarily a system of interactions, were valuable contributions to a scientific grasp of the world.

The ideas of unity and action arise naturally from a consideration of human life. The Stoic adopts these from previous writers, and shows no originality of treatment. The soul is a coherent material substance extended through the body. It can be described in any terms that satisfy the necessity of combining heat, mobility, and degrees of rarefaction. Heat is obviously a characteristic of the living creature; mobility is equally evident; while differences of character can be expressed in terms of finer or denser conditions of the soul-matter. The physical foundation of Stoic psychology is therefore the doctrine of spirits (spiritus, πνεύματα) already taught by more than one predecessor. This doctrine was gradually becoming more detailed; the details tended also to differ in different writers. Primarily the pneuma is the breath of life: it is a warm air closely associated with the blood; it is a *vital* principle transmitted in generation; it may be rarer or denser, and may be collected especially in one region of the body. The term pneuma is consequently used variably, being at one time equal to soul and at another time including more than is meant by soul (ψυχή). The Stoics persistently combined two lines of thought with no clear explanation of their relation. Taking man as an animal they described the soul as 'spirit,' a diffused air connected with the blood. This suffices for the vegetative functions; but a further stage is reached when, after birth, the creature breathes the air, while the last stage, the attainment of true rationality, is postponed until the fourteenth year. This attempt to describe the evolution of the individual soul is not intelligible. The evolutionary character of the doctrine, which makes the individual proceed through the stage of plant life into animal life, is interesting but undeveloped: the nature of the transition from the irrational to the rational condition remains obscure.

If the reader closes his eyes to these unfortunate gaps, it is possible to construct a general statement of the Stoic position. The soul is a fine material substance contained in the body and forming its bond of unity: it is liable to depletion and is nourished by vapours from the blood; it is one in nature with the external fire (or warm air) which pervades the Universe; and can therefore be described as a fragment of the Divine Fire or World Soul. Two physical dogmas are employed to support this theory. First, that of the 'mixture,' which explains the possibility of each part of the body being penetrated by the soul; secondly, that of tension (τόνος), according to which differences of various substances are explained as degrees of contraction, the same quantity of a given substance being capable of greater or less contraction without loss of coherence and unity. Difference of tension in the one original substance explains the difference of body from soul, and the soul itself may have differences of degree; the finest pneuma is in the left ventricle according to Chrysippus.

The majority of the Stoics refer to the breast as the seat of the soul; the main argument for this being the belief that the throat, the pathway of the Logos, comes up from the heart. As the soul is the bond of unity in man it has no parts, but it goes forth from its central position and its activity varies according to the differences of the organs employed. There are eight classes of activity, namely, the activities of the five senses, speech, generation, and reason. Of these the reason (τὸ ἡγεμονικόν) is considered supreme; its seat is the heart, and from this central fount run the different streams of the other senses; the multiplicity and unity thus co-exist, for the mind is one and it is one breath that lives in these different organs. The Stoics grasped this idea of unity from both the physical and psychic sides: the mind is not only one as one substance, but also as self-consciousness, a central ego.

From the nature and substance of the mind we pass to its activities. The soul has inherent activity and the Stoic lays stress on this aspect of mental life. The two main divisions of mental activity are those of knowing and feeling. In the former, knowing, there is a relation to the outer world and the soul begins with a power of action but with no actual endowment of knowledge. This is expressed in the statement that the soul is, at first, like a blank sheet of paper; the senses write upon it the elements of knowledge. The doctrine appears to have been stated at first without any qualification. Zeno speaks of impressions made upon the mind: Cleanthes defined the process as analogous to the impression produced by the seal on wax. Chrysippus revised this doctrine and declared that the result of sensation was not an impression but a modification of the mind. This was an important step, since it involved giving up the notion of an impression like the object and substituting for it an inner state of mind symbolic or representative of the object. The main point, that there is nothing in the mind which was not first in the senses, remained unchanged; but the difference in the theory, as a question of psychology, was considerable.

On the special senses the Stoics have little to say. They believed that sight depended on the emission of rays from the eye; these rays streamed forth in shape like a cone of which the base rested on the object and the point on the eye. All things being material, darkness must be considered an object which we see. Failure of sight occurs only when the pneuma of the eye is not active enough to reach the object or the object is too near; in the latter case, being near the point of the cone, the object is not covered by the rays, for they have not spread sufficiently to embrace it.

In the case of hearing, the sound actually heard is due to the wave of air which reaches the ear; a voice or any sonant object produces movement in the adjacent air, which in its turn sets in motion the air next to it, and this motion spreads like the ripples on a pool. Both sight and hearing, therefore, are mediated forms of touch. The other senses are similarly regarded.

4. IMAGINATION AND REASON

The Stoic psychology exhibits clearly the combination of analysis with the idea of development. In dealing with the mind of the individual the Stoics begin from the notion of the mind as devoid of all content, a white sheet on which the senses write their various characters. We have already seen that sensation was variously described as an impression or a change. The term impression implies pure passivity of the mind. But the Stoics were not inclined, as a whole, to support this doctrine. Their central thought is rather of co-operation; the object acts as a stimulus to the mind and the mind reacts to the stimulus. The Stoic arrived very nearly at the idea of forms of thought natural to the mind; but as nothing more than a bare activity is asserted, this idea remained a mere suggestion. The Stoic theory of mental development in the individual is interesting mainly for the concessions continually made to this innate activity.

At first we are to think of a mind devoid of content subjected to the action of an object. The result is an image of the object, a presentation as the modern psychologist says. For this the Stoic used the term Phantasy (φαντασία), which may be translated 'imagination,' if that term is taken in the strict sense of image-making. Phantasy is etymologically connected with light. The word idea also contains the notion of something seen (Cicero uses *visum* for this presentation). So that ideation will also represent this first stage of mental life. The phantasy is not unlike light in one respect; it shows the object to the mind and illuminates the mind; it is 'an affection occurring in the soul, revealing both itself and that which caused it.' In one and the same experience we know what whiteness is as a sensation, and also that this object before us is white.

The Stoic uses imagination where Aristotle would have written sensation. Apart from this difference the doctrine of Aristotle is closely followed. Experience is declared to be the result of presentations retained by the mind. A number of single sensations grow gradually into preconceptions or anticipations (προλήψεις). These are concepts which develop automatically in the mind of the individual. They are the work of the mind: not mere deposits or precipitates of experience, but actual products due to the activity of the soul. Here again we find in Stoicism a revision of Aristotle. Aristotle speaks of sensation as a critical faculty: the Stoic regards sensation as an activity of the central reason and the basis of an elaborate system of activities. The modes of mental activity are numbered and named; they are (1) incidence, (2) analogy, (3) transposition, (4) resemblance, (5) composition,

(6) opposition, (7) translation, (8) privation. For example, in composition the mind creates an idea of a centaur by putting together presentations given separately in actual experience; as a case of opposition there is the notion of death, framed as the opposite of life. Clearly we have in this list a tentative collection of forms of thought; they are almost forms of perception, for they are not on a level with categories of the understanding. Also, they appear to embody partly the principles of association of ideas which the Stoic may have wished to exhibit as activities of constructive reason.

The result of this process is a body of ideas common to all men. As reason is ultimately one, and all minds are parts of one Mind (or Fire), the Stoics logically assume that all minds come to similar states; in short, the content as well as the substance is similar in all. Hence we have the doctrine of a common reason or general disposition (*consuetudo* in Cicero). In later writers this is used as a test of truth; for what is universally believed is thus the ultimate exhibition of the reason diffused throughout the universe; universality is a mark of ultimate truth because it is a sign of the fact that in these beliefs the one Reason, the God in us, is manifest.

We have seen so far how the content of the mind arises naturally in the growth of experience. There are still some parts of this content which remain unexplained. In addition to the preconceptions already mentioned as arising spontaneously there are in the mind also ideas derived from instruction. Aristotle had already noted that the voice of the teacher is a Logos of a kind. The Stoic saw in the special sciences a kind of knowledge which could be attained as a rule only from a teacher. The reason of the individual therefore develops under the influence partly of a world of objects, partly of rational intercourse.

In addition to this genetic account of mental development there is also the question of the nature of mental activity. This element is called assent (συγκατάθεσις). The reaction of the mind to the presentations is a kind of affirmation or acceptance of the truth. This takes place at all stages and gives rise to the need for a criterion in each case. In the region of presentation (φαντασία) there is possibility of abnormal as well as normal action. In normal cases there is a real object (φανταστόν); in the abnormal cases there is presentation with no objective counterpart. These are called empty excitations, vain imaginings, having only a false appearance of objective truth (φανταστικόν). But how do we know the true from the false? Here the Stoics attempted to find a character in the object which was given also in the presentation. Conviction, they thought, being a mark of the inner state, must represent a quality of the object. They called such presentations cataleptic (φαντασία καταληπτική), and assigned this effect to a peculiar element (ἰδίωμά τι) in the object. Here the Stoics showed a complete misunderstanding of the real nature of psychological certainty. Instead of seeing that conviction may always exist where it is not justified, they kept before them the idea of the wise man who never errs. Excluding from such an ideal any possibility of abnormal states of mind, they felt safe in describing the ideal man's certainty as the natural product of the real object; for his judgments are never disturbed by subjective states, such as passion, and he must therefore have a final criterion of truth and falsity. In this, as in their ethical theory, the Stoics are hampered by the assumption of a pure reason which acts infallibly when free from disturbances. Error of conduct they refer to errors of judgment; and errors of judgment are due to diseased states of mind, the obliquities of passion, which cause assent to be wrongly given. Knowledge in the proper sense (ἐπιστήμη) is for the Stoic as it was for Plato, the unchangeable and unshakable grasp of reality. Such a theory implies the idea that reality is a fixed objective system producing its own effects in the mind; to which is added the idea that the mind is that reason within us which is by its own nature infallible. The emergence of this reason in man was ascribed to a process, and the creature becomes really rational in the fourteenth year. The central reason then dominates the whole being of the individual; reason can be said to develop in the sense that it comes to a knowledge of itself. From this the Stoic derived the idea of self-consciousness and of conscience (συνείδησις). The latter is merely self-consciousness in the sphere of rational choice, that is, of good and evil. The content which the individual's mind ultimately has is its own reason developed from a potential to an actual state. In this sense all knowledge is innate; but it should be noticed that the Stoics have no theory of innate ideas as definite notions always present in the mind. The Stoic rewrites the Platonic doctrine of reminiscence by the aid of Aristotle's doctrine of development. The origin of all knowledge as content of the mind is empirical, and the theory would be completely empirical if it were not for the fact that reason is not itself a product of experience. The Stoic could say (with Leibniz) that everything comes through the senses except the intellect itself. But that is a great reservation, and the Stoics were never quite clear how far knowledge was the product of experience, and how far it was the upcoming of a reason embedded in man's nature. This ambiguity shows itself even in the theory of sensation; for Stoic writings vacillate between the idea of sensation going inward to the central reason, and a central reason going out through sense-organs, which it used as its channels.

The reason (λόγος) has an inner activity and an outer activity. As inner reason (λόγος ἐνδιαθετός) it is the faculty of judgment and choice; as outer reason it is the power of speech (λόγος προφορικός). In this psychology of cognition the interesting feature is the emphasis laid on the individual's activity. While the presentation has the quality of being convincing, the actual assent is given by the individual and is his own independent action. Truth and error are therefore qualities of our judgment; the ideal of reason is a perfect judgment. This is for the Stoic a prologue to his central theme, the attainment of an infallible judgment. Reason in itself has no tendency to error; man has by nature the infallible reason; it follows that truth is natural, error unnatural; if men err it is through some depravity, and the supreme end of all science is the discovery of a cure for this depravity. The discussion of this corruption of nature forms the theory of emotions or mental disturbances which is the central portion of Stoic psychology, because it is most closely related to their practical interests.

5. FREEDOM

So long as the idea of universal reason prevailed the freedom of man could only be defended through the idea of concausation. Chrysippus appears to have explained freedom as the possibility of co-operating with the causality in the universe. Freedom is thus reduced to acquiescence; human action is destined but right action is the product of a state of mind in which the individual will is in harmony with the course of nature; on the other hand, purely rational action is in accordance with nature. The Stoic idea of harmony (*convenienter naturae vivere*) is thus at first a harmony of man with the universe in which freedom is the willing fulfilment of unchangeable laws.

The definition of emotions, or mental disturbances, attributed to Zeno is quoted in Diogenes Laertius as 'an irrational and unnatural movement of the soul or impulse in excess.' The basis of the definition is the idea of impulse which is a tendency of the soul to or from something. Impulse (ὁρμή) covers both appetite (ὁρμή) and aversion (ἀφορμή). These are obscure inclinations natural to creatures endowed with sensation, and are really subconscious workings of reason. As the creature attains a higher degree of reason impulse becomes rational (λογική) and becomes an element in conduct (πρακτική). In place of mere impulse we now have conscious adoption of ends of action (ὄρεξις κὰι ἔκκλισις). The will to attain or avoid is now a fully conscious assent; conversely assent is will; the distinction of intellect and will disappears and clear understanding in the sphere of practice is made identical with will. That mental disturbances are judgments was a dogma consistently held by Stoics of the early, middle, and late schools alike. The position involved rejecting the old antithesis of rational and irrational parts of the soul. The Stoics declare that virtue is knowledge; they do not agree that vice is ignorance; whether good or bad, the result is due to reason and the person is responsible. From the universal standpoint sheer fatalism seems the necessary corollary of the Stoic doctrine of reason. When, in later Stoicism, more attention is paid to the individual, the idea of harmony is rather that of harmony in the soul: every effect is the inevitable outcome of its cause, but man is not compelled to be irrational; by nature he is rational, and rational conduct is always possible as well as right. Truth, both speculative and practical, is a matter of judgment, dependent therefore on someone's judgment; it is the central reason which makes all our mental conditions to be what they are. Resting on the idea of self-conscious unity, the Stoic refuses to regard man as a thing acted upon by imaginations or impulses from without; as effective factors in life these are not impressions but rather expressions of the self. Man is not a slave to passions; there is no 'lower' self tyrannizing over a 'higher'; the affective side of our nature (τὸ παθητικόν) is not essentially distinct from the rational (τὸ λογιστικόν). The only valid distinction, then, is between right and wrong activities of the reason; the ideal is right reason, and with its attainment disappear all mental disturbances. The passions are diseases of reason; they are not (as the Peripatetics held) useful and good in some degree; a slight disease is not health, and a modified passion is not reason.

Stoicism underwent continual modification; its primary severity was not in accord with the varieties of human experience. Upon this point differences arose when it became apparent that error and vice are not identical in nature. A wrong opinion may be corrected when a vicious habit cannot be changed. The later Stoics consequently make allowance for habit and bent of character; they admit that vice becomes incorrigible and virtually adopt Aristotle's opinion that vice is in our power at first but may in time pass into a confirmed and unchangeable character, a second nature. A second source of modification arose from questions as to the causes of emotional excess. The early Stoics assign no cause but reason itself; the emotions are judgments and indicate a corruption of reason; but for this corruption no cause was assigned. The late Stoics, Epictetus and Marcus Aurelius, assign the cause to circumstances and influences, to things which are therefore to some extent beyond our power. In its analysis of conduct Stoicism became gradually more normal and assumed the saner positions of Aristotle. It continued to be obsessed by the idea of self-sufficiency; the self-sufficiency (ἀυταρκέια) of the Aristotelian ideal became an object of passionate and illogical devotion. The earliest teachers, Zeno and Chrysippus, paid more attention to general theories and concealed the fallacies of their position by avoiding details. The later Stoics are severely personal and self-conscious; they struggle with the problems of daily existence, and honestly strive to explain how a man can avoid folly and keep his temper. As we have seen the influence of circumstances was admitted; the wise man was not to be a rock that nothing could move; lapses were inevitable, and the mind no less than the body was subject to contagion and evil communications. But, if circumstances produce the mental disturbances, are we to rely on circumstances to effect the cure and restore the balance? The dignity of the Stoic here came to the rescue; he remained to the end convinced that the will of man was supreme over all external conditions. Into the morass of difficulties thus caused there is no need to plunge. Stoicism ended in moral fervour and logical bankruptcy. No one was able to cope with the antinomy of natural causality and moral freedom. The earlier Stoics were more scientific in temper; they lay emphasis on law and necessity, ending with fatalism. The later Stoics are more inclined to frame maxims and meditate on the uplifting of mankind; they grasped some of the principles of education and supplied in example what they lacked in theory; they failed to explain the possibility of freedom, but they succeeded in being free.

C. The Epicureans

1. GENERAL PRINCIPLES

The school of Epicurus has only one positive doctrine, that the end of life is Happiness. For the rest its tenets are negations; it denies immaterial reality, final causes, immortality of the soul, and universal ideas. These negations become intelligible if the relation of Epicurean to Stoic doctrine is remembered. The Stoic sank the temporal and the individual beneath the eternal and the universal. The Epicurean is an atomist in theory and practice; he believes in one life and that limited; he believes in his own reason and not in Universal Reason; he believes in his own purposes but not in Providence; in short, he is satisfied with a universe which is just that of the Stoics without their 'Reason.' If the Stoic could say that Nature and Reason are the same, the Epicurean could declare that our natures may be rational, but there is no real thing' which we can call Nature in general or Reason in general, and therefore the Stoic formulae were extravagances. The opposition on this point is far-reaching. The denial of Reason as defined by the Stoics carries with it the denial of final causes. The Epicurean has to write his history of the universe without the Stoic God, for he feels that he has no need of that hypothesis. The result is materialism. From the atoms all things arise under mechanical laws, and from the movement of atoms all occurrences can be explained. Physics may not suffer much from such a prejudiced treatment, but psychology is hopelessly maimed. A lengthy study of Epicureanism only reveals more and more clearly that its teaching, when not strictly ethical, was nothing but the provision of dogmas which filled out the traditional notion of a system. A brief summary will suffice for this part. The Epicurean doctrine asserts that the soul is corporeal, it is a body and part of body.

The doctrine of atoms reduces all the real to some form of body occupying space, the criterion of real existence being the power of receiving and producing impressions; the soul is asserted to be 'corporeal' with the implication that it is active and passive in relation to other bodies. Its genus, then, is that of the atoms; its specific difference is in the degree of its qualities, its superior mobility and lightness; in some respects it is similar to fire but is not by nature identical with fire; heat is a fundamental element in its nature and degrees of temperature constitute the peculiar qualities of individual souls. The soul has two parts, an irrational part diffused through the whole body (*anima* of Lucretius) and a rational part (*animus*) situated in the breast.

Thus conceived the soul is part of the world of nature and psychology a branch of physics. In a sense the theory is materialistic, but the materialism of this period involves little more than the idea of a real unity between soul and body; the opposition of mind and matter is a dualism not yet evolved, and the assertion that the soul is corporeal means only that it is capable of receiving impressions from bodies and producing motion in them. The given reality is the unity of body and soul; neither is known without the other; the dissolution of the partnership is the destruction of the self; in the hereafter there may still be matter and aggregates of matter, but the extinction of the individual self is the essence of death.

The soul, thus diffused like a subtle air through the body, gives life to every part; its presence all through the body accounts for the sympathy by which the whole feels the affections of each part; taken as an active substance contained by the body it explains all action. The soul is a mixture of four substances; of these three are like gases, one hot, one cold, and one similar to air; the fourth is nameless and is the seat of sensation. This last substance is self-moving, it is the soul of our soul; it moves itself and communicates its motion to the other substances and, as these move the body in which they are lodged, the motion thus begun spreads in widening circles outside to the world of objects.

2. SENSATION

The interests of Epicurus lead him to construct a psychology for the purpose of showing that a mechanical theory of life is possible. The rational part of the soul includes three faculties:

sensation, anticipation, and passion; of these the first two are concerned with knowledge and the last with action.

All our sensations are effects produced in the respective organs of sense by the effluxes from objects, the emanations or ἔιδωλα. Thus sight is due to the impact upon the eye of visible images, not to rays emanating from the eyes or change in a medium (as in Aristotle). A similar explanation can be given of every sensation. If we thus reduce all sensation to the action of external bodies on passive organs of sense, the differences in the quality of sensations must be explained by differences in the form or movement of the active bodies. Differences of colour are explained as due to the nature of the blow which the atoms give to the eye; the atoms themselves differ in figure, and their effect on the organs of sense varies accordingly. The atomic theory has the great advantage of simplicity; it reduces the external agency to its lowest possible terms; and thus it corrects incidentally errors which arose from undue multiplication of causes. Examples of this tendency to simplification are, first, the insistence on the fact that all qualities except extension, movement, and weight are secondary: sensation is a relation between object and subject which is realized when the atoms brought into contact with the organ of sense are adapted to its capacities. A second example of simplification is the assertion that the organ is the seat of sensation; we do not see with the eye in the sense that the soul looks through the eye as through a window; if that were so the soul would see best without the eye; on the contrary, it is the eye itself that sees.

The atoms given off by bodies come through the empty spaces or pores to the organ of sensation, and the impression converts the power of sensation into definite sensation. The term ἐπάισθημα seems to indicate a recognition of the fact that perception is the result of impressions produced on the sensitive organ; it is not the impression itself that we perceive, but the impression terminates in a perception of the object. The case of sight is treated in detail by Lucretius. Vision is the product of 'images' striking on the eye; the object appears to be distant when the atoms drive a large quantity of air before them, the amount of air being relative to the distance traversed; similarly one can see out of the dark because the light comes inward, but one cannot see out of the light into the dark because the dark air is then coming in and obstructs the organ. The sun blinds the eye because the fiery particles which make up its image are too strong for the eye to endure; angular objects appear round if they are distant because the atoms become displaced in transit, by the air; the corners of the 'image' are rubbed off. In a similar fashion all sensations are explained, atoms and motion being the only agents; the theory of Democritus is repeated with one variation, namely, omission of the air as a medium in sight and hearing. The omission of this medium is easily explained: the air for Epicurus is only a collection of atoms, and through its interstices the atoms from invisible bodies make their way. The air is therefore not required as a medium, though it may prove an obstruction to the transmission of '*idola*,' i.e. the atoms coming from the object to the sense-organ.

In its broad lines this method of explaining sensation was at the time anything but contemptible. It included the idea of motion; it explained quite simply the relation of objects to sense-organ; its hypotheses were few and it had all the simplicity which is so fatally attractive to those who think that 'common sense' is better than speculation. The failure of the method became more apparent when it was extended beyond the realm of sensation to that of reason. For Epicurus explained thought as he explained sensation. Atoms striking on the subtle matter of the thinking soul cause its ideas, just as the impact of atoms on the sense-organs cause sensations. In this way Epicurus explains our knowledge of imperceptible objects, what we should now call microscopic objects. The difference between sense and reason is clearly only one of degree; Epicurus did not believe in a distinct class of intelligible objects.

3. REASON, FREEDOM, AND PLEASURE

It is still possible to write a physiology of the senses which some people accept as an explanation of sensations. It was possible for Epicurus to write a physical theory of sensation which doubtless satisfied the uncritical. But neither a physiology nor a physical explanation of reason has ever proved more than an antidote to exaggerated mysticism. To see what Epicurus did toward the correction of Stoicism it will be necessary to pause and consider the nature of the soul's activities. In the most elementary function of the soul, namely sensation, there is nothing but a relation between the object and the sense-organ. Here there is no room for error. But the motion begun by the impression is carried inwards and another motion consequently arises within the mind itself. This inner movement constitutes opinion, the next higher function after sensation. At this point error becomes possible; for motion in the mind added to an impression constitutes judgment, and error is the addition of an irrelevant judgment or inner motion to the impression. Thus the Epicurean theory evolves a mechanical doctrine of thought. This is really the doctrine of association of ideas expanded to explain thought. Those ideas in us which are not directly injected by the objects are complex products due to the following processes: first, a notion may arise from many similar impressions, e.g. the general idea of man from the sight of many men; secondly, by change of proportions as the idea of giant or pigmy from that of normal men; thirdly, from similarity; fourthly, from combination as in the idea of a centaur. Thus the whole content of the mind is either impressions or complex products of impressions. A certain degree of mental activity is here admitted and attention is recognized as a condition of some perceptions. Imagination is explained by the Epicurean as different from sensation, but only because the atoms which penetrate to the mind are finer than those which affect the senses. The Epicurean analysis of the soul has one distinctive feature; it is at least a candid acknowledgment that sensation cannot be explained, for certainly no one could say that it is explained by asserting the existence of a part or quality whose only mark is the fact that we have sensations. But in spite of the inadequacy no more is attempted. Man has a power of sensation; out of his sensations come images; the images fuse into composite pictures which he uses as general ideas; this is his reason and his know-ledge. The theory follows the same line as those of the Stoic doctrine with a careful avoidance of real universals. For the Epicurean universal ideas are never more than complex products of particular ideas, ultimately of particular sensations. But with the Epicurean, as with the Stoic, mind is not purely passive; it has some activity and exercises discrimination. The Stoic looked at this from the point of view of psychology and called it 'assent.' Epicurus appears to have tried to express this in terms of physics; he spoke of an activity of the mind as though it threw itself into the stream of impressions and changed them, as a current of air breaks up a floating ring of smoke. The meaning of this is very obscure, but it seems to be a doctrine of error stated in terms of physical action. Epicurus was no fatalist: he believed in freedom of the will; he was probably well aware that, as Aristotle had said, a man cannot be free if he has no control over the contents of his mind (i.e. the imaginations); and he therefore made room for this degree of mental activity. Error can only be explained as our activity corrupting the natural union of impressions.

The idea of the soul's activity is intimately connected with another, namely, the question of freedom in choice. It is obvious that a theory of natural causation is liable to end in a doctrine of fatalism. Such a result would have wrecked all the aims of Epicurus. He avoided it by a legitimate handling of the atomic theory; though the argument fell into unmerited disgrace through the unintelligent criticisms of Cicero. This dialectical *tour de force* is known as the declination of the atom (clinamen, παρέγκλισις). It amounts to nothing more than the assertion that the atom never loses its original power of self-motion. Even in closely packed matter, e.g. a piece of iron, the atoms move incessantly. They are hindered and obstructed, but yet their activity is ceaseless. So in man the atom never ceases to exert itself; it fulfils the law of its being and co-operates with the other atoms to produce the effects we see. So long as the activity is resident in the atom its only law is its own nature. That, too, is the sense in which the mind is free; its power to throw itself one way or the other (the *injectus animi* of Lucretius) is the expression of its own nature and that is freedom. The point of the argument is its opposition to Stoic doctrines of fate. The Stoics introduced supernatural agencies (as the Epicurean would say). But naturalism has at all times prided itself on being immanent. Here Epicurus has succeeded in expounding the nature of immanent causality as opposed to transcendent control; it is the one piece of really strong argument in the whole theory, and its appearance is explained quite simply by the fact that in it Epicurus took a real interest. For physics, after all, mattered very little, and the only topic equal to this in importance is that of pleasure. Here, too, we have physical theory starting from the idea that affections are movements, psychic motions. The Cyrenaic had virtually maintained that pleasure is a form of excitement, a consciousness of being pleased. This Epicurus does not accept. He undertakes a fresh analysis of the relation between pleasure and sensation. As we have already seen, the ancients took motion as a generic term and counted both sensation and feeling as species of motion. Feelings, that is pleasure and pain, are therefore primarily motions, and the first point to decide is how the quality becomes attached to the motion. Aristippus cut the knot by classifying motion as smooth and rough, or gentle and violent. He admitted a possible state of motionless calm, but only the condition of gentle movement was called desirable. Plato added a teleological qualification and spoke of motion as in accord with or contrary to nature. Aristotle made pleasure a mark of perfection and not an end at all. Epicurus abandons Aristotle in so far as he still desires to make Pleasure the Good and say what it is, not merely what it does. Plato is rejected because all teleology is avoided, so we come back to Aristippus whom Epicurus follows because the Cyrenaic theory represents the view that pleasure is the good and all pleasure is really a state of bodily feeling: but Epicurus modifies the Cyrenaic doctrine in two important ways. In the first place, Aristippus recognized three terms: gentle motion, violent motion, absence of motion. This does not really help us, because either of the former terms is dual. We might have, e.g., a gentle pain or a violent pain, and unless some proof is given that mere gentleness of motion is pleasant, we still have to decide what makes the pleasantness of it. Plato had seen this, as Herbert Spencer saw that pleasure can only be an end if it is ultimately an increase of vitality or something more fundamental than mere pleasantness. Epicurus goes into the question more deeply than Aristippus, as indeed the work of Plato and Aristotle compelled him to do. Pleasure, he says, as a distinctive thing is a kind of excess, a reaction from pain. Life swings like a pendulum from extreme to extreme, pain is a motion and pleasure is a motion, but not to move is best. This seems like the Stoic doctrine, a theory of apathy or freedom from all affections; but from this it is rescued by an Aristotelian element. From Aristotle men had learned that there is an activity which is not perpetual change, a sort of equilibrium of motion, and Epicurus makes his Good a pleasure of this kind. This can be called freedom from disturbance (ataraxy), for it is a state of persistent equipoise, and ascribed to reason because reason is the regulating factor in life. The Stoic opposed reason to the senses and so tended to make the best state of man a state of reason devoid of sensation. The Epicurean could not see any meaning in this; he believed that a good digestion and pleasant sights and sounds really made up the pleasure that men wanted. Far too much has been made of the sensuous aspect of this statement. To understand it properly we must think of a modern parallel, such as the opposition between Kant and the Utilitarians. Kant was a Stoic in temperament and wished to exclude from the emotions which accompany our resolves all those which he called pathological elements. The Utilitarian is always Epicurean inasmuch as he would include in the idea of the Good all that makes for physical comfort, such as good health, good food, and a good income; while in the motives to good action he would admit the desire to make and to get happiness as a condition of general contentment. Epicurus gives us a dialectical defence of the position which is only a technical way of saying that the pleasures of the senses are transient. Reason alone can so guide and control men that they get the greatest possible amount of pleasure over the greatest length of time. Violent altercations, the interchange of 'paradise and the gutter' which the drunkard calls life, were wholly rejected by Epicurus. As this was only common sense worked up into a theory it was easily associated with the continuous cheerfulness (ἐνθυμία) which Democritus had already named. Epicurus associated with this a classification of desires as (a) necessary and natural, (b) natural but not necessary, (c) neither natural nor necessary. Of these the last should be overcome; the second moderated; the first alone require satisfaction. Thus contentment is easily obtained by the wise man. This is an ethical doctrine which has no further psychological significance.

A few stray points serve to show the limits of Epicureanism. The higher faculties are explained on mechanical principles. There are objects of the mind which the senses do not perceive; but these are not intelligible objects in the Platonic sense; they are merely realities of so fine a material texture that they escape the sense and can affect only the soul itself. In the same way dreams and apparitions are explained as the effects of material bodies extremely subtle in texture. The immortality of the soul is disproved: because the soul is a composite body made of atoms and death is the dispersion of its parts. Life as we know it seems dependent on the union of soul and body; the body is declared by Epicurus to be necessary for all sensation. Death ends this. But Epicurus might have declared in favour of immortality if he had considered the fact that the most subtle forms of matter are relatively least likely to disintegrate.

D. The fusion of the Greek and Hebrew traditions

1. THE HEBREW TRADITION

It has been well said that 'Scripture has no intention of giving a physiology of man; for this reason biblical psychology is not a natural philosophy of the soul of man.' The fact is that the Scriptures present only one side of human life, that which concerns the idea of salvation; for the rest the treatment of man is incidental and the language employed is popular. There is no use, therefore, in attempting to shape these scattered remarks into a definite theory; scientific results are not to be found, and the theosophic aspects, if any, will not be considered. Yet because of its peculiar tone and its great influence on later writings, chiefly through Jewish Alexandrian influences, some account of the Hebrew view of the soul must be given.

The body is uniformly regarded as that in which the soul exists. At times it is called a house, a tenement of clay; or it is a sheath. This expresses the relation of soul to body and agrees with the idea that life is a temporary condition; the exact nature of the relation is not explained. The soul simply embodies life and no dualism seems to be implied; the soul is not imprisoned in the body, and transmigration is not regarded as possible. The account of man's creation in Genesis II seems to indicate a belief that soul and body are a unity; when this is contradicted we have either uncritical metaphors or later Greek influences. Metaphor abounds whenever the soul is to be described; spirit and air, life and wind are commonly connected; while breath is associated with fire and so with animal life. The relation of the soul to vitality and vital processes is recognized; from this point of view soul and blood are commonly identified. There is no idea of a nervous system, but brain and marrow are mentioned and connected with sensation. As soul and blood are closely allied, the heart is naturally given the most important place: it is concerned with the bodily life, desire, will, sensation, and feeling. Whether the reference is to moral or intellectual life, to thoughts or purposes, it is the heart that is most frequently mentioned. The term seems, however, to have had a wide significance and to have stood for the whole of the inner parts of the chest. The Hebrew was most interested in feeling and his experiences were clearly of a type more common in the East than the West. For reasons not easy to define, the Eastern mind seems always strongly conscious of the organic states that accompany psychic activity. In the East the body is more easily affected and a feeling has more reverberation through the system. Consequently Eastern writers dwell more insistently on inner organic states: the heart understands, obeys, and rejoices; the organs below the diaphragm are said to feel love or sympathy; the liver is moved in the yearning of affection.

Spirit is distinct from soul. The spirit is not associated with the blood: it is superior to the soul which occupies a middle position between body and spirit. In the Old Testament the relation of body, soul, and spirit is not clear. The dualism that opposes the spiritual to the natural (body and soul) belongs to the New Testament; the Old Testament seems to imply a dualism of a different type, the crude opposition of flesh to spirit, soul or heart. This is an ethical dualism for which no strictly psychological explanation is given. Dreams are treated after the manner of all early animistic theories: they are activities of the soul, and follow the nature or bent of the individual's waking life. The law recognizes a degree of moral quality in dreams because of the continuity of life which makes the dreams of the good and bad differ according as the persons differ in the waking life. In the dream-state man is more vividly conscious of his inner nature and may therefore attain a recognition of truths that are not so clearly understood in the waking life. The peculiarly objective character of these visions suggests the idea that in them God directly speaks to man and some of the visions are described as revelations, God's direct communication with the soul. The latter are states of ecstasy and may occur when the subject is not asleep. There is thus a complex division: dreams may be either physical and illusory, false dreams, or psychic and genuine experiences of the self in a state of release from bodily influences; revelations are communications to the soul which may be received during waking ecstasy or the analogous ecstasy of deep sleep.

It is difficult to understand exactly what the Hebrews believed about ecstasy. The commentators are also frequently uncertain in their explanations; for example, some speak of a progressive development in the nature of these divine communications, but leave the reader in doubt as to whether there has been a real change in the nature of man or only an increase in knowledge by which cases of ecstasy have been proved to be mental derangements. There are two extreme views: one is the scientific view that all the recorded instances are cases of mental excitement due to natural causes; the other is the theosophic view more or less vaguely attempting to give a supernatural origin to the visions of ecstasy. For psychology the point of interest is the actual experience of the individuals; and there is no inherent difficulty in the supposition that mental exaltation is more easily attained by some than by others, and even at some periods of the world than at others. The writers of the books of the Bible represent many stages of civilization and differ in their points of view. They seem, however, to be agreed on the difference between morbid imagination and real insight. Diseases of the mind, such as the melancholy of Saul, are clearly recognized and described; but there is a strong tendency to allow the character of the result to influence judgment as to the cause. This error is shown in allowing the truth and falsity of visions to be a criterion of their origin; whether a dream comes true or not is a point that cannot be considered in a discussion of its origin. Modern views on hysteria and 'religious melancholy' make it difficult to say what was the real nature of ecstasy; for science goes too far when it takes the mystic's account of his experiences as a sort of unintentional diagnosis, while some of the accounts contain elements which may fairly be regarded as 'symptoms.' On the whole it seems fair to leave these more obscure points of subjective psychology out of our consideration, and let them be understood as best they may through the analogy of later records. It is to the statements of Philo or Plotinus that the inquirer must turn for guidance, and with that type of philosophy which 'would clip an angel's wings' must be united the records of great thinkers and poets who have left in later times testimony to the peculiar nature of strong mental exaltation. One point is worthy of mention: states of ecstasy produced by external agency, drugs, and the like, were well known to the ancient writers and were sharply distinguished from the true states of inspiration. Whether they were equally alive to the psychic effects of fasting or long meditation, and whether they appreciated the natural effects of the severe preparation which the body was sometimes made to undergo, may be doubted; an external agency would be more quickly recognized than such an internal source of abnormal mental intensity.

2. THE JEWS OF ALEXANDRIA

The beliefs which we found recorded in the Old Testament remained for a long period the heritage of generations. But just as Greek ideas changed during the age of expansion under Alexander, so the traditions of the Jews underwent considerable transformation in the very efforts of their champions to preserve them intact.

The first signs of change are seen in those writings which can be assigned to the beginning of the third century (300–250) B.C. The traditions of the Old Testament belong to the Jews of Palestine. The community called the Jews of Alexandria was a society sprung from the same stock, but deeply affected by the Hellenic life and culture with which they were in constant contact. The Jew has a singular vitality, and the history which is too briefly narrated in these pages exhibited the strength and character of that vitality. From first to last, there was no attempt to repudiate Hellenic thought; Judaism neither sank beneath the waves of Hellenism nor strove to keep out every drop of the encroaching waters. On the contrary, we find among the Alexandrian Jews that type of character which ultimately survives all dangers: the type that bends without breaking, absorbs without loss of individuality.

The Egyptian Jews appear to have formed a mixed society mainly Hellenic in manners and language, but still thoroughly Jewish in temper. For this community the Greek version of the Septuagint was made somewhere about the year 250 B.C. Into the disputes on the nature and authority of this translation, the version of the Septuagint, there is no need to enter: it is sufficient to remark that it was a version not wholly free from innovations. Even if there were no self-willed theorists among the translators and no direct intention to give the Scriptures a Stoic or Platonic colouring, there must still have been many an instance when the change from Hebrew to Greek words involved a change of atmosphere that amounted to change of doctrine. To the inevitable use of Greek scientific terms for the Hebrew originals can be traced the beginning of many allegories and many disputes. Thus the Septuagint forms a literary landmark of first importance, and next to it may be ranked the Book of Wisdom ascribed to Solomon. It appears from this work that Greek thought had struck root to an extent that some regarded as alarming; the Stoic fatalism and Epicurean advice which coloured the Words of the Preacher (Ecclesiastes) were an offence to the stricter sect and called forth an answer in the Book of Wisdom. Of the date of this book nothing is accurately known; it falls somewhere between 263 B.C. and A.D. 30; its author was not Solomon but a Greek Jew, and here it is taken as representing a stage of thought prior to the work of Philo. The points which are of interest for our present purpose may be briefly stated thus. The author appreciates to the full the exact requirement of his age: Judaism is inferior in some respects to Greek philosophy: it is none the less the one true religion, and only requires to be stated rightly and in language that can appeal to minds trained in Greek ways of thought. To meet this need it was necessary to find some common point at which Greek and Hebrew thought could unite. This seemed to be Wisdom. On the one hand the doctrines of matter, of the ideas, of the body as a hindrance and of wisdom as a cosmic power, could be drawn from Platonic and Stoic sources. On the other hand, from Sophia of the Greeks to the Wisdom of the Psalmist was an easy step for the uncritical mind of an enthusiastic Hebrew. Thus we obtain a type of the works that were to be only too common: a Greek substructure is covered with a Hebrew theory; wisdom, having run its course on earth, rises up to the heavens and becomes timeless, the coeval assistant of God, the source of all things good and of all the inner life of man whether it be inspired knowledge or the science of things earthly. A note altogether foreign to the Old Testament is struck in the repeated references to individual immortality; the idea is still in its infancy and the nature of this immortal life is vaguely outlined; but that man by eternal Wisdom attains eternal life seems certain to this writer.

The Jewish-Alexandrian school found its completest expression in Philo. The few traces of the development between 250 B.C. and Philo's lifetime show that he was part of an evolution that was nothing less than a national movement. The Jew was awake within the Hellenic sphere of influence, and here, as everywhere, he intended to proselytize.

3. PHILO

The work of Philo is not an isolated phenomenon: it is part of an intellectual movement of incalculable importance. In spite of the lofty aspirations of Plato and the equally lofty resignation of the Stoic, the literature of the West lacked something: no Greek could have named the deficiency of the *Phaedo* or put his finger on the weak spot in the armour of Chrysippus; it required a temper of a different make; it required a people whose God was jealous and whose faith was a flaming fire; in a word, the Greek had thought about himself until he was indifferent to all things and desperately sceptical; the Hebrew had still the fire of passion and the impetuosity of faith; with these he made life interesting and fused in one molten mass the attractive elements of every known doctrine. The result was pre-eminently unintelligible, but it was inspired. The strength of the new influence lay exactly in that strange fervour which must have seemed to the Greek a form of madness. And it was not only that fervour made all things possible; there remained the actual fact that psychology is lived as well as described; personal experiences go to make its history; to the mind that will strive and believe new worlds may be opened up, and if we find little enough in these writers on the senses or attention or such subjects, they are a mine of information on the life of the spirit. And here perhaps someone will ask, Is there a spirit? Is this more than words? The answer is in this record: a history of psychology is a history of two distinct things: first, the observation made by men upon one another; secondly, the observations which now and again the more powerful minds are able to make upon themselves. For many a long century after Philo we shall have to record the progress of psychology in both senses. It would be unwise to begin with any prejudices against those subjective data which are incapable of proof; they may seem at last to be the axioms of all psychology.

The works of Philo are lighted throughout by the strong reflection of personal aims and feelings. His peculiar method of exposition would be irritating beyond endurance if the reader were not continually sustained by a sense of the passionate earnestness which lies behind it and the ceaseless striving after an expression of deep feeling which pervades every page. This temper might be called spiritual fervour; but the term is inadequate, for religion and philosophy were combined in Philo and each limits the other. If we lay emphasis on the religious side, the scientific element in his work seems to be neglected; if the term 'philosophy' is used, the eccentricities of his allegorical explanation of Scripture seems to make the title ridiculous. It will be better, therefore, to avoid any attempt at a brief definition and leave Philo to state his aims and methods in his own language.

The first and leading feature of Philo's work is his religious interest. For him life is the restoration of the fallen soul: his doctrine is a theory of regeneration through wisdom. In his comment on the phrase 'all flesh had corrupted its way upon earth,' he writes thus: 'All flesh corrupted the perfect way of the everlasting and incorruptible being which conducts to God: and know that this way is wisdom: for the mind being guided by wisdom, while the road is straight and level and easy, proceeds along it to the end: and the end of this road is the knowledge and understanding of God.' Wisdom is the royal road by which man can return to perfection; in search of wisdom man should penetrate to the very boundaries of the world; for it is of more value than any merchandise. But it is in the world of thought that this exploration must be made, and in his appeal to his own soul to undertake this search Philo sums up the scope of his work: 'Do thou then, O my soul, travel through the land and through man, bringing, if you think fit, each individual man to a judgment of the things which concern him: as for instance, what the body is and under what influences, whether active or passive, it co-operates with the mind: what the external sense is and in what manner that assists the dominant mind: what speech is and of what it becomes the interpreter or has to contribute to virtue; what are pleasure and desire: what are pain and fear: and what art is capable of supplying a remedy for these things by the aid of which a man, when infected with these feelings, may easily escape or else, perhaps, may never be infected at all: what folly is: what intemperance: what committing unjustice: what the whole multitude of other desires which it is the nature of all destructive vice to engender, and also what are the means by which they can be averted.'

In addition to these statements of the purpose and the scope of his work we have also a defence of method: in commenting on the Confusion of Languages, Philo says: 'But they who follow only what is plain and easy think that what is here intended to be recorded is the origin of the languages of the Greeks and Barbarians, whom, without blaming them (for perhaps they also put a correct interpretation on the transaction), I would exhort not to be content with stopping at this point, but to proceed onward, to look at the passage in a figurative way, considering that the mere words of the Scriptures are, as it were, the shadows of bodies, and that the meanings which are apparent to investigation beneath them are the right things to be pondered upon.' This is only one of many explicit defences of the method. Philo is well aware that some will laugh at his method: perhaps more have laughed than he expected, but his method is not a mere form of exposition: it is one phase of the belief in a dual world. For the senses give us the outward show, the letter, but the mind penetrates to the inner meaning, the spirit that gives life. In all history there has been a mind at work: like is known by like and therefore this hidden truth can only be reached by mind. The significance of this will be more apparent later. For the present it is enough to indicate the general character of the work; we will now proceed to collect Philo's utterances on the general subject of Anthropology.

Regarding man from without we see that he occupies a middle position: he is in some respects akin to the animals, in others to such superior beings as stars or angels. His life, too, is divided between the life of the flesh and the life of the spirit, or between sense and reason. The explanation of this dual nature is to be found in the story of creation; for there we learn that man was created, as to his body, from the earth, and as to his soul, by God himself. Thus for Philo man is dual by nature primarily in the sense of the Hebrew theory which makes man two natures, united in one being. This line of thought makes the soul part of the Divine nature, the breath of God. Greek theories also speak of the Divine in man, and Philo continually employs both lines of thought, making the breath of God and the rational soul identical. From the Hebrew point of view the relation of soul to body is purely external: the soul is not dependent upon the physical organism, nor its product: it is a separate entity. This theory finds an ally in Pythagorism, hence Philo's further assertion that the air is full of spirits, some of which descend into human bodies, while others scorn to degrade themselves; which is a fine flight of fancy uniting three distinct ideas, namely, that of transmigration, of daemons, and of angels who are ministers of God. The proof of these beings is deductive: every element has its occupants, and therefore the air is occupied by spirits: the argument is not convincing in any case, and seems to overlook the previous statement that the birds occupied this region! But we shall not waste time seeking for consistency in Philo.

In this account of creation we are told that God created the animals in order of rank from the least sensitive, the fish, up to the highest, man. The distinguishing mark of the animate is sensation: this distinguishes animate from inanimate and also higher and lower classes of animate creatures. Taken as a principle of life, soul is thus common to all creatures: it has blood for its essence; it is transmitted from one generation to another. While the spirit is peculiar to man, the soul is a universal natural principle. From this point Philo develops the Stoic aspect of his doctrine. All things that exist have power of some kind: at its lowest level this is the power of self-conservation, called Habit, which is found in motionless objects such as stones. The next degree is the power of growth, which is a higher form of self-conservation, found in plants, for example. The third level is that of soul-life where we find perception, representation of ideas, and impulse. The common element in this scale is spirit in the sense of air. A vague scientific notion underlies this idea: when the lowest form of being is described as a 'spirit going forth from the centre to the periphery and returning upon itself,' we can only understand this as a doctrine of material cohesion, Stoic in its origin. Man, as last created, sums up all these forms: he has the various forms in his bones (analogous to the rocks of the earth), his hair and nails (analogous to the plants), and in the sensitive soul. Man is thus a microcosm: he has a material organism illuminated by the mind just as the macrocosm is a vast organism illuminated by the sun. The study of man and the study of the universe can be conducted on parallel lines, and to some extent the knowledge of man is a knowledge of God.

Of detailed physiology we find no trace in Philo; a casual reference makes it clear that he had no interest in the question whether the intellect was located in 'soul, membrane, or the heart.' The general tendency to regard the head as the main fountain of intellect is due to the fact that the organs of sight are located in the head: for the rest, Plato's *Timaeus* is clearly the accepted manual of physiology. From the same source comes the idea that man is regulated by the universal laws of motion, though Philo gives this a Biblical character by making the number seven express the law and connecting it with the Book of Genesis. Turning from structure to function we find a number of statements drawn from different sources and dictated by different standpoints. The soul is divided into two parts, rational and irrational. The irrational soul has seven parts—the five senses, the organ of speech, and the reproductive power. Sense is at first an inherent power of habit: at this stage it is said to be in a state of tranquillity. The object puts the sense in motion, e.g. colour sets in motion the sense of sight. In this way Philo restates the distinction of passivity and activity in sensation. The question then arises, What is the relation of the mind to the senses? The activity which the object arouses is not within our control: the outer sense is not subject to the will, and, in fact, hardly belongs to us: it is given to us only as being with us. There is, however, an inner sense which is closely allied with mind: the complete activity of the senses is a combination of both the senses in the act of perception. For reasons which are ultimately ethical, Philo here makes a distinction of considerable importance. He speaks frequently of the mind as irrigating the senses: it pours itself into the holes or channels of the senses and makes them fruitful. Thus intentional and unintentional actions, e.g. seeing and looking, can be distinguished. Though not apparently interested in the psychological question, Philo does in this way distinctly indicate the nature and function of innervation in the sense in which that term can be used to mean a control of animal spirits. The senses, he says, cannot be taught: they are in themselves neither good nor bad: for the moral life they are purely instruments. Regarded as instruments of knowledge the senses are inlets. Perception begins in the process by which something is put into the mind ($αἴσθησις=$ $ἔισθεσις$), the mind cannot know unless the material is thus furnished, but at the same time the material in itself is not knowledge: that which is inserted makes an impression on the mind as the seal does on the wax: the mind preserves this impression until forgetfulness smooths off its edges or erases it.

The first result of this sense-impression is an affection or appetite, which is the first motion of the soul. This is apparently the limit of the animal's life: the irrational creatures stay at this level; all their motions and changes are involuntary: they are, in short, purely passive and automatic. Sense and feeling and passive imagination include the entire psychic life of all creatures below the level of man.

Man is an animal to whom superior faculties have been granted. As an animal he lives the life which we have just described. To the senses belong pleasures which are, generically, motions: all pleasure is of the body and is hated by God. As man can be regarded from two points of view according as emphasis is laid on body or mind, so life may be regarded as developing in two directions. The downward movement is that which is outer, away from the inner light to outer darkness, away from reason to sense; the upward movement is the reverse. Philo sums up the condemnation of pleasure in a phrase: 'When that which is the better, namely, the mind, is united to that which is the worse, namely, the external sensation, it is then dissolved into the nature of flesh, which is worse, and into outward sensations, which is the cause of the passions.' This sentence is the meeting point of many contrasts: the senses are darkness, plurality, dissipation; the mind is light, unity, concentration. All the Platonic dislike of ignorance, the Stoic dislike of excitement that destroys reserve, the Eastern dread of unbridled passion, are concentrated in this sentence. The senses now stand condemned for three reasons. They are passive and inferior; they give no knowledge; they belong to that body which is our burden and may become the occasion of our ruin.

It is not possible to go far in a description of Philo's psychology without introducing the ethical values with which he confuses his treatment. The confusion is increased by the fact that the ethical valuation is itself twofold; for we may speak of the senses as sources of vice and so evil; or think of them as the means by which man learns about the world and so comes through nature to God; from this point of view we find them good in different degrees. Since Philo expressly says the senses are in themselves neutral, this distinction of uses involves no real contradiction. The neutrality is carried to an extreme: the senses are said to present bodies as they are without deceit; the senses of the wise man are good, of the fool, bad; memory is good or bad according as it retains the good or the bad. But considered as instruments the senses have relative values and sight ranks first. The three lowest are taste, smell, and touch; hearing and sight are to some degree philosophical, and of these sight is far superior. It is an exact image of the soul, for the eyes show every change of thought and feeling; by the eyes we know light: the eyes can survey all the earth; they can rise up to the heavens and raise our minds to the creator of all things.

With the subject of light we broach a theme which is an inexhaustible joy to Philo. In light he finds the objective emblem of mind and thought and God. 'As in the body the sight is the more important faculty, and in the universe the nature of light is the most pre-eminent thing in the same manner the part of us which is entitled to the highest rank is the mind.' This style of speech is repeated again and again; we will let this specimen suffice and state the doctrine of intellect without further embellishments.

Sense by itself is darkness: the mind is the light of man. The essence of mind is distinct: it is imperishable and it alone has freedom. Man alone has a voluntary self-moving intellect, and therefore he alone is free and responsible. As it controls itself under action, mind can, at will, go forth to the outer senses or withdraw into itself; from this follows the conclusion that thought and perception are in inverse ratio. In meditation we withdraw from the outer world. The nature of the intellect is variously described: it is an impression of the Divine nature, or a ray of Divine light, or a fragment of the Divine Being. Philo says nothing of the·differences implied in these phrases: for him they all mean one and the same thing.

The language of Philo is variable and inaccurate; there is, however, little reason to doubt his meaning. The first point to notice is that Philo admits no scientific knowledge of mind. In this he differs from the main trend of Greek thought: however much the Greeks exalted reason or believed that the world of sense and the world of reason were distinct they never advanced to the mystic standpoint of Philo, which practically makes man the vehicle of a supernatural consciousness. This position requires a disembodied reason which is, finally, a personal God: the Greek understood the meaning of universal law and universal reason, but the idea of a superhuman being in immediate contact with man was foreign to their nature. In brief, Greek thought moved between the opposite poles of scepticism and Pantheism. Hebrew thought tended to immanence without Pantheism; the attempt to maintain this position is itself a product of psychological conditions; the desire for a personal relation with a Divine Personality is the property of a distinct type of mind: it indicates a temper wholly distinct from that which leads to extreme rationalism; it belongs to the man who sets pity before pride, self-abasement before high-mindedness, feeling before thought. Our first duty, therefore, is to study the character of Philo, for this is more important than his scattered attempts to condense his ideas into words. He says: 'I am not ashamed to relate what has happened to me myself which I know from having experienced it ten thousand times. Sometimes when I have desired to come to my usual employment of writing on the doctrines of philosophy, though I have known accurately what it was proper to set down, I have found my mind barren and unproductive and have been completely unsuccessful in my object, being indignant at my mind for the uncertainty and vanity of its opinions and filled with amazement at the power of the Living God, by whom the womb of the soul is at times opened and at times closed up; and sometimes when I come to my work empty, I have suddenly become full, ideas being in an invisible manner showered upon me and implanted in me from on high; so that through the influence of Divine Inspiration I have become greatly excited, and have known neither the place in which I was nor those who were present, nor myself, nor what I was saying, nor what I was writing; for then I have been conscious of a richness of interpretation and enjoyment of light, a most penetrating sight, a most manifest energy in all that was to be done, having such an effect on my mind as the clearest ocular demonstration would have on the eyes.' This personal experience is made the ground of a definite instruction when he says: 'Therefore if any desire come upon thee, O soul, to be the inheritor of the good things of God, leave not only thy country, the body, and thy kindred, the outward sense, and thy father's house, that is speech, but also flee from thyself and depart out of thyself; being driven to frenzy and inspired by some prophetic inspiration. For while the mind is in a state of enthusiastic inspiration and while it is no longer mistress of itself but is agitated and thrown into frenzy by heavenly love and drawn upwards to that object, truth, removing all impediments out of its way and making everything before it plain that so it might advance by a level and easy road, its destiny is to inherit the things of God.'

In these two passages we have sufficient indication of a new view of knowledge: for real knowledge the mind must be the passive recipient of a Divine Illumination: wisdom is the light that lighteth, not every man, but every man that has been purified, and this is a light that knows itself. God has given every man an impulse toward salvation; this is primarily a purification from all the life of the senses: man departs from that in so far as he can abandon the belief in himself as capable of all knowledge; he comes through the life of the senses to a recognition that he knows nothing; this fits him for Divine wisdom which God alone can impart. In attaining this view Philo was doubtless helped by the Greek theory of the contemplative life and by current scepticism. The difference between his view and that of Plato, or Aristotle, is obvious; for the Greek contemplation was the last fruit of human wisdom; for Philo it is the first fruit of salvation. Similarly Philo cannot rightly be called a sceptic. Scepticism implies a belief in the impossibility of attaining absolute knowledge; Philo adopts scepticism merely as a phase of his belief that empirical knowledge is only a preliminary stage on the road to the great Illumination.

Life on this theory divides into two classes of experience: the one is the objective experience in which we come into relation with an inferior external world; the other is the subjective experience which wholly or partly dispenses with the inferior external relations, having in their place some kind of relation with superior external powers. The latter is sometimes called absolute; but a term which implies no relation is not accurate in this connection: man does not think himself, according to Philo, nor is he thought thinking itself: at his highest level he is in contact with a superior instead of an inferior world; in relation, therefore, to something not himself. We will now expound the doctrine from both points of view.

The idea that knowledge is attainable when the senses are inactive naturally brings into prominence the phenomena of dreams, trances, and prophetic vision. The phenomena of dreams are not regarded by Philo as unique: they are akin to the state of meditation, for both are conditions in which the mind abstracts itself from the senses. Intimations of immortality can, he says, be obtained even in the corporeal life under two conditions: first, in sleep when the mind discards all the imaginations derived from sense and is inspired by the truest divination; secondly, when in philosophic speculation the thinker shuts up the channels of the senses and forgets the outer world. From this passage it is clear that dreams are not after-effects of sensation; they are not movements set up from without, but activities of the mind moving itself: for even the imaginations are superfluous. In his treatise *On Dreams sent from God* Philo distinguishes three kinds. The first kind proceeds from God as Author of its motion and reveals what is known only to him; the second kind arises when our soul is set in motion simultaneously with the soul of the universe; the third is the kind that requires interpretation, but of its nature no further explanation is given. The second kind in this catalogue clearly indicates a theory of sympathy, and Philo explains the sense in which that doctrine might be accepted. Moses believed in the doctrine of sympathy, but not in a way that implied a world-soul; in other words, not in the Pantheistic sense. On the contrary, Moses 'teaches that this universe is held together by invisible powers which the Creator has spread from the extreme borders of the earth to heaven, making a beautiful provision to prevent what he has joined together from being dissolved; for the indissoluble chains which bind the universe are his powers.' A complete explanation of these powers could only be given in a treatise on Philo's religious and philosophical views. As this account is limited to his psychology nothing will be said beyond what is necessary for a comprehension of the rational life.

Chapter Seven

THE DEVELOPMENT OF THE ETHICO-RELIGIOUS TRADITION
(Christian)

A. *The Early Christian Fathers*

1. ST. PAUL

The psychology found in the writings of the Fathers has its root in the teaching of the New Testament, principally in that of St. Paul. The doctrine of St. Paul is itself a product of earlier speculation: it embodies older views and actually contributes little that is new. The characteristics of the new direction of thought are determined by the fact that rationalism gives way to spiritualism, the scientific to the religious standpoint. To say that Christian doctrine is primarily ethical is to say very little. Plato had used the ethical norms in a manner equally emphatic. The real difference between Platonism and Christianity is to be found in the difference between Hebraic and Greek temperaments, between the desire to feel strongly, to nourish lofty passions, and the (Greek) desire to subdue passion by reason. The Stoics interpreted the mixed mood of their age rightly when they declared that restraint was the essential element of goodness, and yet saw in rational joy the completion of life. The best introduction to patristic psychology is the ambiguous language of St. Paul; for here we are at the fountain-head of all the doctrines which treat the soul from the point of view of Christian Redemption, and which, therefore, find the questions of origin and destiny most important. The ideas of eternal life, of conquest over sin achieved partly by works and partly by grace, and of individual worth are the ideas that control discussion. The details are selected to suit these ends: at first science and tradition are neglected; but each succeeding writer adds new material, and as point after point is added the accumulated wisdom of previous ages is absorbed into the body of doctrine until the treatment becomes as comprehensive as we find it in Augustine or Thomas Aquinas.

With an abruptness that is a little startling St. Paul begins with the first man, Adam. Greek theories inclined rather to the thought of a first matter; or spoke of man as created along with other forms of being as a class. Whether the theory tended to creationism or to a form of development-theory, Man, for the Greeks, begins as a race: for St. Paul there is one historic individual, the first man.

For the creation of this first man St. Paul has accepted the Hebrew account (Gen. ii. 7), according to which the creation of man was the act of God. Before the living man, there existed God and Earth: God took of the earth, shaped it in the form of man, and then breathed into it the breath of life. Here we have three elements not far removed from the products of analysis in Greek philosophy: we have matter, form, and life.

In regard to the matter, little need be said: it is the terrestrial aspect of man and passes easily into the ethical notion of a lower nature which is of the earth earth-like. The form is primarily shape, and all organs are from the first created in their final completeness to serve the purpose which they now fulfil. So far man is but a perfect statue: the last great change is the miracle that makes the statue live. In opposition to all who make life dependent upon the organization of matter, St. Paul speaks of the life as something added to the formed matter. For the author of Genesis ii. 7 the soul plays no part in forming the body: it is not a vital principle inherent in matter; on the contrary, it is the first movement which is imparted to the inert mass. The essential notion seems to be the act of respiration; hence God's act of giving life is expressed as 'breathing into' the material form, that is, as the act which starts the breathing of the individual. St. Paul follows this account of creation but uses his term 'psyche' in a more developed sense; for him it is a principle of life imparted by God to man. At this point the Hebrew concept of 'breath' drops out of the significance of 'psyche' ($\psi v \chi \acute{\eta}$), and the Greek doctrine of the soul furnishes the guiding line for its description.

The vital principle to which we give the name 'soul' is, in the Pauline doctrine, common to man and the animals. If we now inquire into the life of the soul, we shall find the subject treated as a physical science—as a science of the natural man. The natural man or 'the flesh' has its thought, wish, desire, and reason. However high these faculties may rise, even though by reason we know

God, yet they remain earthly, natural, and not spiritual. Thus a dualism is created; man is natural and spiritual. Within the natural man we find all the organs of the sensitive, appetitive, and rational life; there is no opposition between matter and mind; man is simply a psychic creature (ψυχικός), and the Pauline view is monistic so far. To this principle is added an ethical or theological dualism. For it is not reason that constitutes the immortal soul: man as a creature is wholly mortal; reason does not outlive the bodily life. The immortal is spiritual (πνευματικός), another and a different principle wholly distinct from the psychic nature. In this use of spirit (πνεῦμα) the Pauline theology abandons the Greek line of development. The spirit is that part of man which enables him to draw near to God; but this is not to be achieved by knowledge, and the vision of God is no longer a reward for intellectual perfection, but a prize of that high calling which is ours by virtue of the moral nature. The spirit is thus primarily the divine element in man: its work is to mortify the flesh rather than to build up the body; it is not the natural principle of the Greek physical theories, but a unique principle that serves to explain the moral life of mankind and makes possible a mystic unity with God. The end of life is regeneration, and this is achieved by the entering into man of the spirit of God. The human spirit can be prepared for this spirituality by a moralization of the lower nature; the conquest of the flesh is a removal of obstructions, and the soul that realizes the truth of Christian doctrine is fit for the work of the Holy Ghost. As the first man's spirit came from God, so in this second birth of the spirit is an influence or inflowing from without, and what neither intellect nor will can attain is given to the pure in heart by the grace of God. This is the full stature of man, the final state of perfection which everyone is able to reach so long as sin does not prevent. Spiritual perfection is thus the crown of the psychic life. For its attainment man does not require a knowledge of things but rather a knowledge of himself. In the place of objective knowledge (ἐπιστήμη) St. Paul puts a subjective knowledge which is wisdom (σοφία) in the highest sense. To know oneself is for the Christian to realize the motives and intentions of the will, to have a conscience; the ideal is to have a conscience devoid of offence. Sin is thus made essentially a choice of evil accompanied by a knowledge of the good: when a man sins he sins against the light that is in him; a wrong

HISTORY OF PSYCHOLOGY

committed unknowingly is not a sin and is not imputed for sin; only when the law is revealed can there be sin against the law.

The position of St. Paul shows how the teaching of Christ influenced the study of mankind. In the main St. Paul abides by the Hebrew tradition. It would not be difficult to quote 'anticipations' of Christian doctrine from the Stoic writers or indicate points of affinity between Plato and St. Paul. But these common elements are details only; the Christian doctrine recasts all the material that it uses and stamps it with a new seal. Moral aims were common to Plato and St. Paul, to Stoic and Christian; but the personal view of God and the consequent strong realization of human personality were the property of Christian doctrine and its predecessor, the Hebrew Scriptures. The older Greek psychology abides within the limits of analysis and observation; Christian psychology is descriptive and introspective, more attached to faith and belief than to reason and sight. While the Greek required to base his belief upon evidence, the Christian could esteem those who having not seen have yet believed. The transposition of ideas was reflected in that later motto which to a Greek was foolishness, *credo ut intelligam*.

2. CLEMENT

The Christian schools of Alexandria were naturally led into the paths of eclecticism. The works of Philo showed a mixture of Greek philosophy and Hebrew tradition: Greek and Jew were united in that fervent and illogical faith, aptly described as a tendency rather than a system. As the Jewish-Alexandrian work presents one tendency, so the Christian-Alexandrian presents another. Their common qualities are indicated in the common title Alexandrian; their differences arise mainly from the different views they take of that Greek philosophy which both accept as true in part. Through the voluminous works of the commentators and allegorists runs a vein of consistent theory, varying in quality but never devoid of some rich metal; the task of eliminating what is valuable has not yet been accomplished, but it is sufficient for the present that the historical sequence can be shown with considerable clearness. Clement of Alexandria planned and perhaps wrote a book *On the Soul*. No trace of this now exists, and his opinions can only be reconstructed from the scattered statements found throughout his works. The ambiguity of the result is apparent from the different opinions of writers. Some regard him as Platonic; others emphasize the Stoicism of his attitude; to some he appears an amorphous collection of doctrines. The evidence seems to support none of these views; for while the language of Plato, the ideas of Stoic writers, and the vagaries of Philo jostle each other in every passage, there is an atmosphere of independence which rules them all. It is not with these or their phrases that Clement is concerned; he has the disregard of a true believer for the niceties of expression; his eagerness to state his belief seems to break out into each and all of the possible types of formulae; salvation and resurrection are the theme which makes the language of philosophy seem meagre and elementary. Amid the noise of dispute and the battle-cries of sects, it is easy to forget that though the old phrases are still used, the strife is waged under a fresh banner. Whether the phrase is Platonic or Stoic, it is used now by one who views those theories as plagiarisms, brilliant interpretations of a truth revealed primarily to Moses. The importance of phraseology dwindles immeasurably at the realization of that fact. Academic and Peripatetic, Stoic and Epicurean are distinctions that lose all value for one who sees in them only a channel for doctrines derived from a higher source and now again revealed more fully in those last days. Right across all the distinction of Greek schools falls the division of Christian and pagan; pagan philosophy collapses into a mass of subtleties uniform in character, a colourless sequence of attempts to fully understand the inspired wisdom of the Old Testament writers. The battle is set in array between orthodoxy and heresy.

The value set on Greek philosophy varied with different writers, but in the period and school of which we are speaking there was never a doubt of its subsidiary character. Clement defends and praises it only as the handmaid of wisdom: he is more the patron than the disciple of Plato: he is more inclined to excuse the shortcomings of the Greeks than lose himself in admiration of their achievements. Thus was the wedge inserted at the thin edge: the cleft widened rapidly. It was not possible to continue an elaboration of doctrines on divergent lines without a final split: problems arose and dogmatic solutions were demanded, forcing the learned to decide finally for Paul or Plato, for Stoic determinism or Christian freedom. The evolution of these problems will be apparent to the end of our subject. With Clement begins the serious development, and in him the student finds the first crude fusion of Christian and pagan speculation.

Clement's doctrine of the soul begins from the Biblical doctrine already described. The soul of man is a unity with a dual origin. It is in part rational or celestial, and in part irrational or terrestrial; and these 'parts' are distinctions rather than divisions. The rational soul (variously called ψυχή λογική or τὸ ἡγεμονικόν) is identical with that 'breath of God' mentioned in the Book of Genesis. It is either imparted by God to man or transmitted to man by the angelic powers, the creating spirits of Plato. Its essential character is that it is divine in origin and nature, a reason closely akin to divine reason, the ground and possibility of man's ascent to God. Sharply opposed to this rational soul is the irrational soul (ψυχή ἄλογος), which has a wholly different origin and is akin to the life-principle of animals. The details of this exposition are obscure, but such is the position in its broad outlines; in language and general conception the doctrine is strongly Platonic.

Turning to the question of the nature of man, Clement comes upon the problem of natural generation and the transmission of the soul which that involves. The central problem here is the question of the relation between the two souls. In the first man, Adam, the act of God creates one soul with two natures; henceforth the irrational or earthly soul is identical with the principle of life and is transmitted from parent to child. In its material aspect this is a fusion of the elements, of the world-matter in all its forms. This interprets the Biblical phrase, God created man from the dust of the earth; it also leads to an identification of the soul with blood and seed; the flesh is the dwelling-place of the irrational soul, within which again is the rational soul. There is thus an outer man and an inner man, and somewhat literally interpreted as dwelling one within the other. The strong influence of Greek theories here asserts itself and produces an innovation on the original Biblical doctrine. In Clement's analysis of the human mind there is a complexity and confusion beyond understanding. In his grasp of the psychic life there is the consistency of a clear purpose. The idea of spiritual progress is the ruling factor in his descriptive work, and the failure of his analysis is compensated by the success with which he completes his ethical doctrine. In addition to Platonic and Stoic ideas of the soul there is the doctrine of Wisdom (σοφία) already utilized by Philo. For Clement Wisdom is the First Mover, the source of movement for the soul; by Wisdom the soul is sown with the seed of the spirit and becomes spiritual in its nature. Since Wisdom, in this sense, is one with God, man also has through Wisdom the seed of a divine nature: he is capable thereby of rising up to the likeness of God. Thus the foundation is laid for a doctrine of redemption through Faith and Knowledge: before considering that doctrine in detail a few more remarks on the nature of the soul must be made.

When speaking of parts of the soul Clement employs either the Stoic division into eight or the Platonic division into three parts. In one passage the Stoic catalogue of eight parts is used as the basis for a complicated division into ten parts; elsewhere the Platonic tripartite division is quoted; the inconsistency is unimportant as Clement seems to have regarded the Stoic division as more exact, while the Platonic is more adapted to the doctrine of self-education. The process of self-education is a purification of the soul and a consequent return to a godlike nature: it bears a close resemblance to both Platonism and Stoicism in making reason superior to sense; it differs from both in the particular meaning given to reason by interpreting it as Wisdom.

The soul begins as a blank: the senses supply knowledge by way of impressions, and it is the irrational soul which, on account of its relation to the flesh, is capable of receiving the impressions. The irrational soul is easily moved and its receptivity is presupposed in conscious life; its movements are not, however, capable by themselves of giving knowledge. For this the co-operation of the rational part is required: a transition is then effected which amounts to self-consciousness and is the beginning of order in the whirl of motions. Here Clement reproduces the doctrine of the *Timaeus*, modified by the Stoic idea of a regulative reason; he is distinguishing the life of successive feelings from the life of ideas, and seems to grasp the necessity of introducing a principle of reason in order to convert impression into idea. The Stoic doctrine of activity harmonized with the Christian idea of personality and tended to make more explicit the assertion that knowledge is not a mere product of accumulated impressions but an outgoing activity of soul. Psychologically the result is a doctrine of apperception as well as perception, in which the development of Stoicism is apparent; for the perception is equated with the Stoic apprehension ($\kappa\alpha\tau\acute{\alpha}\lambda\eta\psi\iota\varsigma$), and the apperception with assent (συγκατάθεσις). The irrational soul serves as a mediator between the sense-objects and the rational faculty. Man differs from the animals in the possession of this rational faculty (λογική δύναμις), and through it he attains two powers, the impulse toward thought and the discrimination which makes him master and not slave of the sense-images. Following the Stoic line of thought, Clement regards reason as the power of finding a standard or criterion and thus attaining a judgment of value in respect to the world of sense-impressions.

The psychology of cognition in Clement is purely an introduction to the ethical teaching: it is a preliminary sketch of the human mind expressed in occasional summaries of previous systems. The psychology of conduct occupies a more important place, and, though drawn from various sources, is treated more elaborately as it leads to the ethical and theological conclusion of the whole scheme of Clement's work.

The human soul comprises two spirits (πνεύματα), the irrational or fleshly and the rational. In addition to its function in sensation the irrational spirit is the source of the passions, the sphere of desire, pleasure, and anger: it is, so to speak, the entrance for the passions and the exit for actions. The intentions which arise from thought and understanding pass through this intermediary into action. It follows that either the movements of the irrational soul overcome the rational, or the rational conquers: the aim of life is the attainment of that state in which reason is permanently superior. The activities of the lower and higher spirits are distinguished as desire and impulse; desire (ἐπιθυμία) belongs to the irrational part, while to the rational part belongs impulse (ὁρμή). Clement opposes the Gnostic 'heresy' that the body is essentially bad; he does not regard desires as wholly bad but rather as ethically indifferent; goodness and badness depend upon the end which they subserve, and this is a matter of will. When the will employs the (natural) desires for evil ends, they become evil. This distinction is important; it follows from the previous doctrine that all conscious distinctions belong to the ruling reason (τὸ ἡγεμονικόν), and this is the first clear recognition of the fact that good and evil are purely kinds of rational decision. From this arise important developments in the doctrine of will and freedom in choice.

The doctrine of Plato tended to make the irrational part of the soul evil in its own right: the Stoic theory tended to absorb will in reason; both drift helplessly toward rational determinism. The doctrine of redemption which figures in Hebrew and Christian theory required a theory of the will which admitted full responsibility. Sin is more than error: the position of Socrates could not be maintained by one who believed in the reality of sin. If, then, vice is voluntary, but the will is not inherently bad, it will be necessary to show exactly how the will is led into sin and how it may attain to righteousness.

Knowledge and action are so closely united in the doctrine of Clement that the solution of these questions must begin from a statement of the rational activities. The high reason ($\tau\grave{o}$ $\mathring{\eta}\gamma\epsilon\mu o\nu\iota\kappa\acute{o}\nu$) has power of choice ($\pi\rho o\alpha\iota\rho\epsilon\tau\iota\kappa\acute{\eta}$ $\delta\acute{\upsilon}\nu\alpha\mu\iota s$) on which depend the search for empirical facts, instruction and complete knowledge. Thus the progress of the soul is made dependent on the will to know. At the first there is complete ignorance, and the individual is placed in a world of desires and imaginations with no guiding light of reason. Hence the commission of sins. For want is natural to man; and from want arises desire which leads to sin; vain imaginations also lead astray. In both cases the moral guilt arises from the fact that the will gives assent; only by this act of will is sin constituted, and therefore it is just in the fact of sin that freedom is demonstrated. On the other hand, the will is not essentially sinful: it is from God and must be good; so that the cause of sin must looked for outside the will. Clement finds this cause in false images, snares, and delusions that mislead the soul. These are states of the soul; not external things but internal forces. With the facility common to his day and natural to a student of Philo, Clement makes these internal forces into spiritual influences, devils that possess men. Gnosticism here undoubtedly revenges itself by conquering the mind of its opponent for Clement admits a distinctly Gnostic doctrine. Sin is the triumph of darkness over light, of ignorance over knowledge. The way of salvation then can be only the way of knowledge.

From the flux of sensations man attains to a condition of partial stability by Faith. The soul has an impulse after knowledge, but its attainment is limited; before knowledge can be reached a degree of practical certainty must be accepted; it is necessary to believe when we cannot see, and the conscientious exercise of faith is the substitute for knowledge. There are natural limits to human attainment; men can be classified as material (ὑλικόι), psychic (ψυχικόι) and spiritual (πνευματικόι). To the last only belongs the possibility of complete knowledge (γνῶσις); for them the goal is a state of purity and rest. This is a state of vision (ἐποπτεία or θεωρία), and the idea clearly comes from Plato. But with it are mixed various elements. It is on the one hand a state of rest such as Philo described: it is a condition of apathy in effect, though not the Stoic apathy: it is immortality, the successful working out of the Aristotelian maxim, put on immortality; finally it is the perfect life of reason, faith made perfect through the vision of eternal truth. In its attainment man must have assistance against the evil spirits that assail him; and this is given by Christ the embodied Word.

The most important points in Clement's view of the soul can best be indicated by stating his views on the development of spirituality. The true end of life is likeness with God: this is attained when the soul realizes a harmony of all its parts. Harmony is one key word in Clement; it indicates the belief that the fully developed soul organizes will and knowledge and action in a perfect unity. Another key word is Faith. Faith is essentially an action, and is closely akin to the Stoic 'assent' (συγκατάθεσις). In human life every mental act involves belief or faith; in perception, for example, the individual accepts an indication and asserts an object; this is the primary form of Faith. In the beginning any isolated fact lacks proof; but man cannot refuse to accept everything; he must come to a halt and accept something. The liberation from doubt is accordingly an act of man, a will to believe; in this act man asserts his belief in some truth and so in truth itself and ultimately in God. In this sense it is true that 'there is no third term between a self-communication of the Divine and absolute scepticism.'

Clement, anticipating Augustine and Descartes, finds the starting-point of all our mental life in this assent to truth; all knowledge is only the elaboration and practice of belief. Belief is the active element in our knowledge; it supplements experience; and it furnishes a criterion of truth, for what we cannot believe we cannot accept as true. Here again the new doctrine transposes the Greek order: the motto is *credo ut intelligam*, and faith is the persistent element in all our mental progress.

Some rest in faith and ask no questions; others press on to the full understanding of all that is implied in faith, and these attain Gnosis, the perfection of human character. The education of the soul is carried out by means of action: nature cannot be forced but only developed: education, as in Plato, is a growth effected by right nourishment and right exercise. Virtue is knowledge in the sense that without knowledge virtue is impossible. This knowledge is not the mere acquisition of rules, but that inscribing of the law upon the heart which is due to right performance. Thus Clement grasps the important truth that character is a system of actions which have become natural. The crown of the discipline which leads to this end is love; at the last there is that perfect harmony which makes obedience to the law a service of love and, at the same time, a pure love of God. Self-love is really the root of evil: education overcomes this by making the self a harmony so that the will is no longer divided but wills the true good as its own object of desire. In this sense the will is free, because there is no conflict between law and desire but all desire aims to fulfil the law. The law is also reason, the Logos. There is in man the seed of the spirit (σπέρμα πνευματικόν): Wisdom (σοφία) is the Logos and the first-born of God; it is also the subjective knowledge which man may have imparted to him. Here Clement adapts Philo's teaching. The Logos as Wisdom is the wisdom of God; as going forth (λόγος προφορικός) it is the revealed wisdom, God made manifest in the Word that became flesh; as dwelling in man it is derivative wisdom or knowledge (γνῶσις). The upward progress of the soul is never more than a preparation: by it the soul is made fit to receive that communication of Divine wisdom which is the only source of absolute truth and knowledge. Man lives by faith and incomplete knowledge: his final reward is a spiritual vision for which there is required a light from above, the irradiation of the divine Reason.

3. ORIGEN

Our knowledge of Origen's views on the soul would have been more extensive and accurate if that voluminous writer had carried out his own programme; for he makes an elaborate statement of the problems awaiting solution, but never wrote the intended treatise. As it is, our information is scattered: the statement of the details in one consecutive account magnifies their importance; yet there are points of interest that deserve to be recorded. In the main Origen continues the work of Clement of Alexandria, but his method of exposition is that of a commentator or a controversialist: he seemed to require as a medium for his thoughts either a text to elucidate or an opponent to refute. What he says is therefore as a rule only that which is relevant to the occasion when another point is under consideration. It follows that omissions count for nothing: it can never be assumed that Origen disbelieved what he did not say; so long as the fact omitted is not in contradiction to his views it may be assumed that he did not reject it. This will not justify the attribution of anything to Origen over and above what he says; but it is useful to recollect that Origen worked on separate points and assumed a knowledge of current doctrine.

Origen makes all things dependent on God as their Creator. God, matter, and souls make up the totality of things; and God has united matter and souls in one world. Matter has various degrees, from worst to best; the soul too has degrees though it is one and the same in all. There is a soul in all animals, and its substratum is the blood, or, in creatures that have no blood, the vital fluid. Man has also the spirit imparted by God. The soul is Reason ($\nu o \hat{\upsilon} \varsigma$) fallen from its original glory and grown cold. How Origen proposed to reconcile these views of the soul cannot be discovered; for one theory says that soul is principle of life, the other that it is a degraded reason: Origen accepts both in spite of their opposition. So far as animals and men are concerned the difficulty might be overcome by supposing that Origen followed Plato in regarding the soul as living and giving life. But Origen's real difficulty is with the angels and daemons whom he also wishes to call souls. Some light may be obtained from the passage in the *De Principiis* where God is an ever-burning fire: the soul so long as it remains in God or with God is penetrated by this fire and is, so to speak, all fire. If the soul departs from God it loses this fire, grows cold and materializes. This seems to explain Origen's idea of cooling ($\psi \upsilon \chi \acute{\eta}$, $\psi \upsilon \chi \epsilon \hat{\iota} \nu$) and the position of the soul as intermediate between flesh and pure spirit.

The basis of Origen's speculations is Stoicism, the Stoicism of the Platonizing Stoics such as Posidonius. He adopts the dualism of nature and soul ($\phi \acute{\upsilon} \sigma \iota \varsigma$, $\psi \upsilon \chi \acute{\eta}$): he classes the functions of the soul as imaginative and impulsive ($\phi \alpha \nu \tau \alpha \sigma \tau \iota \kappa \acute{\eta}$, $\delta \rho \mu \eta \tau \iota \kappa \acute{\eta}$) in Stoic fashion: in the sphere of nature motion is confined to

organic activities while the soul moves by means of images acting
on imagination. In animals such as bees or spiders the imagination acts only in some one prescribed way: their instinct is simply
limited imagination. Reason is a fourth kind of movement; it
differs (1) from imparted motion such as inorganic things require,
(2) from the inner movement of plants or (3) of animals; it begins
and ends in itself. This distinction is obviously meant to prepare
the way for a doctrine of freedom: reason is not the slave of
imagination or appetite, and choice is not the mere supremacy of
the strongest motive; on the contrary, reason selects its line of
action with reference to, but not under, the control of the sensuous
experiences. The reason has a natural tendency to distinguish
good and bad, and adopts or rejects the imaginations accordingly.
Here the Stoic doctrine is abandoned in favour of freedom or
liberty of choice which with Origen is a postulate: without freedom of choice there would be no morality. This liberty is in
reality the Stoic 'assent' ($\sigma\upsilon\gamma\kappa\alpha\tau\acute{\alpha}\theta\epsilon\sigma\iota\varsigma$ in *De Principiis*, 3. 1. iv)
taken as the element contributed by the person to the action: the
mere presence of an object is not a reason for sin nor is it an
irresistible attraction: the assent of the mind converts the outer
conditions into inner causes of action, and therefore all action is,
to some extent, in our power. Here, as often, the Christian writer
avails himself of the doctrine of concausation, the $\sigma\upsilon\nu\alpha\acute{\iota}\tau\iota\upsilon\nu$,
which the Stoics had taken from Aristotle. This idea of co-oper-
ating causes was the one road out of fatalism which the Stoics
desired to use. The Christian finds it doubly useful. It explains
first the connection between temptation and sin: the temptation
is the circumstance or occasion, the sin is the act of using the
occasion; as there is no compulsion in an occasion, so virtue and
vice are free. It explains also the relation of God to man, for man
does not attain goodness by his own effort alone; his effort is
rather the occasion for the divine act by which he is assisted; God
co-operates with man to achieve what man cannot do unaided.
On this point of moral freedom Origen finds it convenient to
combine Aristotle's doctrine of responsibility with a Stoic version
of free movement; he is perhaps hardly aware that by freedom he
means more than responsibility, and the Stoic element explains
nothing beyond the mechanics of movement. Origen was aiming
at a theory of 'absolute' liberty; he failed to see that he had ended
in determinism, because for him reason and will are ultimately

the same. Origen calls the will 'rational desire' (λογικἠ ὅρεξις) and unites love and reason in it. With that he drops into the familiar line of Platonism, and its doctrine of Love (ἔρως), joined with Aristotle's conception of God as the final source of all upward striving.

The Stoicism which proved vain in face of moral problems returns to assist in the transcendental physics of the soul. Origen is an idealist; for him the soul is immaterial, a rational nature (φύσις νοερά) and in itself eternal. He finds the Greeks are in the main more akin to his thought than the Christians; for the Christians talked too much of the body and its resurrection, of physical torments for sin and sensuous enjoyments in heaven. But the Greeks make no provision for the resurrection of the body, not even for judgment and purgation in some cases; so Origen strives to work out a compromise, and it can hardly be a matter for surprise that the result was doubtful in respect of orthodoxy. As regards the resurrection Origen starts from the Pauline words 'sown in corruption.' Here the idea is that of seed, and the germinal reasons or seed-reasons are at hand in the Stoic doctrine. Nothing is required except to explain the soul as a principle of generation (seed) which embodies a law of production (reason or logos); it follows that as the seed dies in order to be quickened again, so the soul dies in order to live again; and in both cases death is not annihilation but only the cessation of one embodiment which can in due season be followed by another. This distinctly brilliant piece of controversial dialectic is matched by another. Origen employs the Stoic 'conflagration of the world' (ἐκπύρωσις) as a theory of purgation; this fire is like that which Moses saw, a fire that burns without destroying, a fire akin to the very nature of God, whose angels are as flames of fire. God is the fire that burns, but only the evil is destroyed in that fire; the pure are as the light that is not destroyed.

Origen believed in the pre-existence of the soul, but gives no explanation of the fact that in this life there is no memory of a former existence; he does not avail himself of the Platonic 'reminiscence,' but does maintain that the soul begins its life on earth burdened with sin.

This may seem to be far removed from psychology; but if the Christian views of materialism and immaterialism are to be understood these lines of development must be followed. It was not enough for Origen to assert immaterialism; he had to explain it; the other view can be seen in Tertullian. In his attempts to explain the materialistic phrases of the Bible Origen was distinctly an 'advanced' thinker; the medieval ideas of heaven and hell were not so refined as Origen's doctrine of eternal love and eternal remorse. With these contributions to the religious view of the soul may be joined the striking view of inspiration which Origen took. Inspiration is for him true or false, that is, normal or morbid. The morbid type belongs to imagination and is simply a diseased fancy. There is beside this a normal condition in which people may have visions and may prophesy. This normal state belongs solely to reason; it is a highly developed state of intellect; the true prophet does not fall into a fit or give oracles during a state of catalepsy, but remains conscious of his acts and remembers them afterwards. Inspiration is therefore not ecstasy, it is not possession by a spirit but the highest grade of self-possession. Origen is clearly not aware of the extent to which organic conditions give rise to inner states; the voice within seems to him to be always the voice of God speaking to the soul; reason withdrawing into itself has communion with divine reason. In this we trace the vein of mysticism common to the Platonizing Christians; it involves a second life within the sensuous life, and beyond the material world another world in which there are sights that the eye cannot see, sounds that the ear does not hear. But Origen is singularly free from excess; his mysticism amounts to little more than an able defence of the reality of an inner life, the reality that is of reflection and of the insight into the meaning of things which comes from the earnest striving after truths that outlive sensations. Origen is thus one of the greatest writers on the psychology of religious experiences.

B. Medical Influences

I. ASCLEPIADES

In the last century of the pre-Christian era the doctors who practised generally belonged to one of two schools, the dogmatists or the empiricists. Asclepiades stood in a class by himself; his disciples formed the school of Methodists. The greater doctors usually professed attachment to some school of philosophy; the majority were Stoics, but Asclepiades was an Epicurean. His

Epicureanism does not appear to have been strict. It amounts in the first place to making the pneuma a material substance composed of the finest atoms; secondly to an assertion of perpetual change, for his 'atoms' are in continual movement and are divisible. The corollary of this materialism is sensualism: the soul is really the activities of the senses taken collectively; reason is not a special faculty nor a specific part of the soul. If we remember that the orthodox view of the pneuma makes it a material substance extended through the body, and that the transmission of sensation from the periphery to the central reason (τὸ ἡγεμονικόν) was a standing difficulty, it will be clear that Asclepiades was not in fact far removed from the Stoic position, and created a type of eclectic doctrine mediating between Stoic and Epicurean. The most important school was that of the Pneumatists which arose in the time of Claudian. This school definitely attached itself to the Stoic theory and declared allegiance primarily to Chrysippus. The chief writer of this school was Athenaeus, and a review of his position will give an adequate idea of such parts of his doctrines as concern the present subject. He dealt with physiology, pathology, diaetetics, materia medica, and therapeutics: his physiology is of first importance in this connection.

2. ATHENAEUS

Athenaeus accepts the general position of the Stoics: only the corporeal is real and the pneuma is the active element. Matter is divided by the possession of qualities into four primary classes or elements, the warm, the cold, the moist, and the dry. These are not the elements, because Athenaeus will not presuppose elements, viz. earth, air, fire and water; nor are they mere qualities; they are substances whose characteristic is the quality in question. This position gave trouble to Galen, who does not appear to have understood it; it is a purely empirical standpoint which bases the division of elements on the apparent qualities instead of deducing qualities from the assumption of elements. For the science of medicine this was important. The living creature is made of these material elements, which can also be regarded as causes or powers (δύναμεις). The warm and cold were regarded as active, the wet and the dry as passive; all that occurs in the body is a process of taking in or giving out which involves the continual adjustment of the qualities. The problems of food which increases, of drugs which decrease internal heat; the use of baths and of exercise which lead to the escape of humours through the pores (διαπνοή); these and many other things are discussed on the basis of qualities whose material embodiments must be kept in equilibrium.

The organism is made into a living unity by the pneuma, which as merely animal life is the animal spirit (πνεῦμα ζωτικόν). This pneuma is not acquired but connate (σύμφυτον); from it develops the internal heat (ἔμφυτον θερμόν) and it also assimilates the outer pneuma which is taken in by breathing. The pneuma and the natural heat are centred in the heart; they are frequently regarded as almost identical. The pneuma has the three degrees assigned to it by the Stoics (ἕξις, φύσις, ψυχή); the ruling power of the soul is located in the heart. Upon the state of the pneuma depends the state of health; veins and arteries are filled with blood and pneuma; the only distinction is the proportions, the arteries having more pneuma. Physical condition is expressed in terms of the 'tone' of the pneuma (εὐτονία πνεύματος) in much the same way as modern druggists speak of 'tonics.' Distinct from this formula for health is the formula for constitutions. A good constitution (εὐκρασία) depends on the normal mixture of the elements; any abnormal increase of one or more elements disturbs the equilibrium and produces disease.

Many other points could be mentioned, but they are of interest only for a history of medicine. The peculiarities of age and sex, the importance of different seasons, the difference of youth and age—all these depend on mixture of qualities. Climate and district have to be considered, because the quality of the air man breathes greatly affects his health; the moon also exercises an influence on the air. These features show how the idea of the cosmos was kept in close contact with notions about human welfare; 'pantheism' as the Stoics understood it was capable of developing in cosmic views of body as well as cosmic views of mind.

3. GALEN

The development of the medical schools culminates in the combination of philosophy and medicine presented by Galen. As philosopher Galen is thoroughly eclectic; as physican he belongs to the Pneumatists. History repeats itself in Galen, for he appears as a second Hippocrates in character: his name has a similar significance in the history of medicine, he attained a reputation equally stupendous, and round his writings gathered a similar accretion of spurious works and pious additions. It is obvious that Galen was one of the many who know everything about something and something about everything. Medicine was his business and philosophy was his hobby; it is to his credit that he did not dogmatize on ultimate problems and realized the extent to which philosophical conclusions are, for the practical man, matters of taste. Galen the philosopher should not be taken too seriously; if we start with his working basis as a physician and see what he makes of the human being as the subject of diseases, the philosophy can be added as a tribute to the reflections of a cultured man of science. Galen belongs to no school; he may be called eclectic if that is a correct term for the unattached thinker; he is at times Peripatetic, frequently Platonic, still more often Stoic, moderately anti-sceptic and violently anti-Epicurean. This combination of views is easily understood; the Pneumatist theory draws Galen towards Stoicism; his divergences from Stoicism are theoretical and due to the influence of his Peripatetic teachers; his Platonism is innate.

The physician regards man as a psycho-physical being; the mind of man is closely related to his body, and mental states can be deranged or rearranged by treatment of the body. Consequently the study of man begins from the elements out of which he is made, and with Galen, as with his predecessors, these are the four qualities which determine temperaments. Against Athenaeus Galen maintains that qualities are not corporeal, but none the less treats them as bound up with matter, which was probably what Athenaeus meant. Galen struggles against the monism of the Stoics and prefers to support the doctrine of four elements. The point is really of little importance, for the emphasis falls in any case on the qualities. Here Galen follows the physicians of his school so far as the medical theory is concerned; his superiority lies in a wider treatment of the question. The Stoic philosophy influenced medical theory and medical theory reacted on Stoicism. There was consequently a growing tendency to think more of the body in its relation to the soul; the emotions afforded a middle ground, and the later Stoics formulate the control of reason over emotions as a science of control over the exciting causes; the passions and mental powers are seen to be closely connected with bodily states, and as passions are diseases of the soul that begin in physical causes, their cure lies partly in the treatment of bodily states. Galen completes the development in this line by taking mental, moral, and physical states as aspects of one life. Everything depends on attaining the normal temperament or that relation of qualities which constitutes the health of the creature. This is not one and absolute, but differs in different kinds of creatures and is the mean relative to the creature. According as one creature is better than another, e.g. man better than the animals, there is a relation of better and worse between temperaments. The normal temperament of the best creature is the ideal.

Before Galen's time the cardinal humours, blood, phlegm, black bile, and yellow bile, had been regarded as exhibiting specific mixtures of the elementary qualities. In Galen the combinations of the qualities were enumerated as forming thirteen types of temperament. A combination of the two positions produced at some later stage the popular doctrine of the Four Temperaments, which are distinguished according to the preponderance of one of the four humours. In this way the psychology of character was combined with the physiology of temperaments; anger, fear, and hope became effects of the material constitution of the body. This view of mental phenomena inclines strongly toward materialism. It is supported by the observed effects of wine and climate, and the fact that the Epicureans took note of these points is significant. Asclepiades had much in his favour, and Galen is anxious to show that the Epicurean is not the only explanation of things. Galen is not prepared to agree with Plato. If the soul is immaterial how can a physician explain the fact of drunkenness or madness? On the other hand, he will not accept the doctrines that make it material. He is consequently left in a sceptical position and declines to make a final statement on the question; he favours most a view of the soul which keeps close to the doctrine of temperaments and uses the idea of form. This theory runs somewhat as follows. If all things are to be classed as form or matter, Soul is form; but form is only a certain disposition of matter; and the soul must therefore be the mode of composition or the peculiar mixture of the corporeal elements. This interpretation of form completely destroys the substantiality of the soul as taught by Aristotle; form now becomes merely the relation between corporeal parts. The objections which are made against Aristotle by later writers show how this view became common and passed as Aristotelian; it differs but little from the view that the soul is a harmony or a name for the combined functions of the senses. As a form of immaterialism it was useless.

The physiology of this period recognizes three main organs of the body—brain, heart, and liver. The liver is the organ concerned in the production of blood from food and in it all the veins, i.e. blood-vessels, meet. The heart is the meeting-place of the arteries, i.e. vessels which convey animal spirits (πνεύματα). The brain is the source of the nerves: anatomy showed this, for when the body is dissected we find the spinal cord starting from the base of the brain and sending out nerves, like branches, to all parts. The brain is not, for Galen, an expansion of the spinal marrow; it is the origin or cause, not the effect. Brain and nerves can be further analysed into (a) the external membranes and (b) the inner substance, related to each other as are the bark and the pith of a reed. Of these the inner part is the true brain, the real seat of sensation and movement. The brain has, beside the outer rind and the inner substance, three parts, namely, the anterior ventricles, the middle section and the posterior ventricles. The last are most important, for these ventricles prepare and store up the animal spirits.

Galen continues the tradition which recognizes a connate pneuma and regards it as preparing the air introduced in breathing, so that all the acquired air is converted first into vital spirits (πνεῦμα ζωτικόν) and then by further refinement into psychic spirits (πνεῦμα ψυχικόν). The material thus refined is derived in part from the vapours of digested food; so that the production and the nature of the psychic pneuma depend on both the air and the food. Climate and diet therefore directly affect the rational powers, whether this pneuma is to be considered the soul itself or the organ of the soul.

The combination of physiology and pneumatology produces several points of doctrine. Each part has a particular constitution and a particular function. The distinctions of desire, temper, and intellect correspond to the physiological parts: desire pertains to the liver, being connected with nutrition principally; temper is vitality, and belongs to the spirits of the heart; intellect is connected with the brain. The nature of the individual depends on the relation of these three; and the character of each 'part' of the soul depends on the temperament of the part. Thus Plato's psychology is revived with additions.

The brain is partly soft and partly hard; the soft part is the cerebrum, the hard is the cerebellum; the nerves are similarly hard or soft according as they proceed from one or the other. Sensation is a matter of impression or passivity, movement demands activity; for these functions the soft and the hard substances are respectively adapted. Sensations may be either (1) accidental, arising from the inward parts and indicating their condition; (2) periodic, as of hunger or thirst; (3) effects of objects or the sensations by which we know external things. In this third class we have the sensations of the five organs of sense. In general, sense-perception is controlled by the condition that like is perceived by like. From the brain (or its extension the spinal cord) radiate the nerves which are adapted for sensation; they have a channel in which run the spirits derived from the brain. As the pneuma is one and flows out to all the sense-organs, it would seem as if any sensation might be obtained through any organ. The fact that this is not so is explained by saying that the pneuma is specifically different in each case. The eye-spirits (or pneuma of sight) are distinct from those of the organ of taste. The organ is in each case like the object (the eye-pneuma, e.g., is like light), and each sense-organ has in this way a 'specific energy.'

Following the lead of Chrysippus, Galen explains sensation as a dual process: first comes the impression which is a qualitative change in the organ; then the perception or consciousness of this change, which is the action of the brain. The nerves being extensions of the brain this perception arises in the nerves themselves: it is the reaction which the nerve, by virtue of its pneuma, makes in response to the stimulus. Here Galen directly opposes the older doctrine that sensation arises first in the central organ. The brain communicates its powers to the nerves which live with its life as the branches with the life of a tree. This is one of the most important effects produced by the recognition of nerves.

Of the special senses touch, taste, and hearing require no comment. Smell is due to a substance that is vaporous and between air and water; as this substance is distinct from the four elements it explains why men have five senses though there are only four elements. The sense of smell is not located in the nose but in the brain; we must draw in the breath or we smell nothing. As regards sight, Galen adopts the Platonic view with slight alterations. The luminous spirits stream down the optic nerve channels from the anterior ventricles of the brain. The outer air in its contact with the nerve is modified so as to become identical in nature with the nerve, a sort of prolongation of the organ of sight; the inner spirits communicate their nature to the outer air as the sun communicates its luminousness to the atmosphere around it. Thus the eye reaches out to the object by this medium and attains a sort of mediated contact. By habit men come to think that they see things outside the eye, so that when an object in the eye hinders the sight this also is thought to be outside, e.g. specks floating 'before' the eye or the illusions of delirium.

The nerves which serve for sensation are distinct from those that control movement. The former are soft and can receive impressions; the latter are hard. Galen makes a considerable contribution to science by distinguishing clearly nerve and muscle. The muscle has the power of contraction which is regulated by the nerve; for the nerve supplies the force. The brain is the source of movement, the nerve is the medium and the muscle the instrument. The distinction of hard and soft nerves is not, however, made absolute; some motor nerves are capable of sensation, and some sensory nerves grow hard and become capable of producing motion.

It is not surprising that Galen should prove most successful in the sphere of psycho-physics. On questions purely psychological he finds decision difficult; he strives in vain to look both ways at the same time, and cannot explain how the soul exists without the body or how it can be anything wholly dependent on body. Under the term Reason, Galen includes all functions that are not intuitive or automatic; imagination, memory, and reasoning are the divisions of the intellectual life, and in the manner of the Stoics Reason is made regulative. An acquaintance with Aristotle leads Galen to recognize an immediate certainty in sensation and in thought; a perfectly clear idea is true. At the same time Galen's 'reason' ($\nu o\hat{v}s$) is not generically distinct from sensation; the dividing line is not, as in Aristotle, drawn between sense and reason; there is no dividing line, and if imagination is called 'rational' nothing is meant beyond the fact that it is not a sensation. Galen chooses to follow Aristotle's hint that imagination must be partly rational (λογική), and improves on this by dropping out the sensuous species (αἰσθητική φαντασία). There is no ground for dogmatic statements about Galen's intentions in this matter but one point may be noted. After the Stoic developments, increasing stress is laid on mental activity; sensation is drawn closer to reason by laying more emphasis on the need of attention in order to convert a mere affection of the sense-organ into an actual perception. At the same time reason loses much of its transcendental significance when it is seen that its material must be derived from the senses. While reason may not be sensation, it appears to be little more than consciousness of sensations and of the relations between sensations. Thus self-consciousness as the permanent condition of experience attains recognition and usurps the place hitherto given to Reason by those who spoke of Reason as a unique and supernatural element in the human soul. With Galen the idea of self-consciousness is not fully developed, but in many respects its significance is understood. For example, consciousness of sense-affections is distinguished from the fact of sensation as mere affection of the organ. The complexity of some perceptions is analysed and shown to be due to rapid calculations added to the impression by the reasoning powers; in the perception of distance there is an element of habit which makes men think they see an object at a certain part of space; in the perception of movement there is a synthesis of perceptions, for the eye sees the object in a number of positions successively and thinks of it as moving. In both cases there is really a rapid inference which is necessarily a conscious process though not a process of which the individual is separately conscious. A modern writer might, with less accuracy, call it an unconscious influence.

Psychology here makes distinct progress though the ideas are not fully developed. A want of clearness diminishes the worth of suggestions that are none the less of considerable value. In the treatment of the will this want of clearness becomes more definitely a fault. Galen sees that voluntary and involuntary actions should be distinguished according to the presence or absence of intention. He classes as involuntary all natural movements, i.e. all activities that arise from sources with which reason is not concerned. These motions belong to nature (φύσις) as a non-rational power; such is, e.g., the beating of the heart. Such actions as are not thus purely natural are under our control and depend on the activity of the understanding. It may happen that the mind turns elsewhere and cannot afterwards remember that it purposed any one action. The fact remains that no motion could have occurred if there had not been some previous intention. It follows that some actions are due to purposes of which we are really unconscious, a contradiction which is perhaps due to the fact that Galen was ignorant of the nature of reflex action. In this division of actions as natural and voluntary he overlooked those that are involuntary and yet not natural in his sense of that term. The will is for Galen wholly dependent on the temperament and he is frankly fatalistic. He declares against the Stoics that all men are not alike, and believes that some are bad by nature. His ethical theory consequently has a practical trend, and he is able to agree with those Stoics who see in moral obliquity a proof of disease in the soul. For Galen the evil soul is a diseased soul, and as a patient requires a doctor so the vicious man must put himself in the hands of the good man for treatment and restoration to health. The source of evil is a disturbance of the condition of the organism. Desire and temper are the natural functions of the lower faculties and are not bad in themselves. Only in excess are desires bad, and excess is due to the abnormal condition of the organs. In this Galen declares for Aristotle and a mean state; but his idea of a mean is formed after the manner of a physician's idea of a normal temperament. We do not condemn the beating of the heart because it is sometimes out of order; neither should we condemn desire because desires sometimes run to excess.

C. Neo-Platonism

I. RELATIONSHIP TO PLATONIC DOCTRINE

Platonism is essentially an ethical doctrine and unites all its detail into a single theory of development toward perfection. Neo-Platonism starts with this idea, and its claim to be a revival of Platonism rests on the extent to which this ethical purpose is common to both. But while the outlines are similar the details are very different. The atmosphere of Neo-Platonism is at once more impersonal and more subjective. Plato diffuses an atmosphere of practical activity, and thinks chiefly of the good life as a system of human activities. Plotinus, the founder of Neo-Platonism, turns his eyes away from the world of change and action to the inner life of timeless meditation. For Plato the world that lies beyond the senses was a justification of human effort: it was primarily an answer to those who saw in life nothing but a ceaseless change that made effort vain and progress only a synonym for process. For Plotinus the supersensible is the spiritual world of the mystic. The years that intervene between Plato and Plotinus have slowly generated a distinction between the sensible and the supersensible world which is subtly different from that of Plato. The mysticism of Plato ends with an insight into the reality of life; the mysticism of Plotinus begins from that point, abstracts the reality from life and views existence as a state from which man strives to flee that he may depart from it and be with God. The change hinges upon the interpretation of Plato. If emphasis is laid on Plato's idea of the body as the tomb of the soul; if contemplation is valued before action; if the whole process of education is regarded exclusively as a liberation of the soul, the origin of Neo-Platonism can at once be seen. The divergence of Neo-Platonism from Platonism lies mainly in the metaphysical view of intellect as a cosmic reason. The Stoic doctrine of universal reason had been really a veiled materialism; nevertheless its 'pantheism' only required a fresh interpretation of reason to emerge as a theory of all-embracing intellect. If the pneuma of the Stoics is found to be an inadequate concept of the supreme unity, it is none the less true that it formulates an idea of unity, of passionless reason, and of pure rationality as the human ideal. Plotinus objects to many of the details of Stoic doctrine, as he objects also to Aristotle; but his metaphysical doctrine is strongly marked with Stoic characteristics and Aristotelian notions. This Neo-Platonism is therefore no mere reproduction of Platonic doctrine. It is to a large extent an independent construction by reason of the new standpoint adopted. Plotinus has a new idea of the rational life as something distinctively subjective. Out of this arise his virtues and his vices; for it leads to a deeper view of thought and at the same time makes impossible that trans-subjective use of thought on which he builds a metaphysic not unlike the vagaries of Gnosticism.

2. PLOTINUS' ACCOUNT OF THE SOUL

Man is a mixed form of being. This mixture is a divine mystery but none the less to be accepted; man is soul and body, one and many. The method to be pursued in psychology is the introspective method which analyses the forms of mental activity. The lowest of these is sensation which borders on mere plurality. For sensation a soul is required, and the exact nature of the soul must be defined. The doctrines of harmony (Aristoxenus) or entelechy (Aristotle) are rejected. The soul must be one and self-subsisting. As the soul is that which produces unity it cannot be itself the product of a mere aggregate, an argument which disposes of atomism. It is not possible for the inanimate to produce by mere combination an animated whole: the lifeless cannot produce life; consequently any attempt to generate a soul out of a complex of material elements necessarily fails. The doctrine of the Stoics is no better than that of Epicurus. If the soul is defined as pneuma or intellectual fire (πῦρ νοερόν) it must none the less be a pneuma of a particular kind or having a particular mode of being. Then the question arises what is the kind of pneuma which is specifically called soul, and what is that mode of the pneuma which makes it a soul as distinct from the species of pneuma which are not endowed with soul (πνεύματα ἄψυχα). The question itself shows that the mode is all-important; it is this that must be explained; and if the explanation of the mode (σχέσις, πῶς ἔχων) is the explanation of the soul the use of the term pneuma is invalid; the soul is but a species of pneuma, for, if it is pneuma at all, it is in essence wholly unlike any other pneuma. This somewhat formal refutation is in Plotinus secondary to the contention which really supports his conception of an immaterial soul. The soul in his view is the condition of our knowledge of all things material; to explain the nature of the soul as material is therefore to explain it through its idea of matter, through that which is itself dependent on the soul. If we consider the activities of the soul we see that its effects are not material, it has no quantitative changes, it produces unity in our perceptions and it can comprehend that which is not quantitative (e.g. justice). All these are functions which do not belong to matter, and justify us in regarding the soul as immaterial. Plotinus thus takes up a position strongly idealistic, and adopts a definite conception of psychology as a science of conscious life. In Plotinus, for the first time in its history, psychology becomes the science of the phenomena of consciousness, conceived as self-consciousness.

Of all the phenomena revealed in consciousness the most important is that of unity. This is exhibited in the first instance in man's physical unity; the affections of the different parts are known by the soul; they are therefore at one and the same time in the part and in the soul. This involves a difficulty. The body is extended and divisible; are we to say that the soul is equally extended and divisible? If so, it will have parts which are simply placed next each other, and the affection of one part will be known in that part only. As experience shows us that it is not the finger that feels pain but we feel the pain in the finger, it has been generally said that the feeling is transmitted to the central self. But what is this transmission? If the feeling is handed from part to part we must experience a feeling in each part and not one but innumerable feelings occur all along the line of transmission. As this is not the case, it is necessary to say that the soul is wholly in all parts. This relation of soul to body is the central mystery of our dual being; it is a necessary conclusion which is not further explicable: the composition and unity are unique and even the assertion that this is a 'mixture' is not accurate. Suppose we describe a line as white, can we call this a mixture? Can we say that the whiteness is straight? Obviously not; the elements are essentially different and have no predicates in common.

Thus Plotinus rejects the Stoic doctrine of pneuma and also the idea of a central reason (τὸ ἡγεμονοῦν). His own belief is that the soul is a reality belonging to a higher degree of Being than matter. The soul is that which has life in itself and gives life to the organism: it is immaterial and envelops the body; it is more correct to say that body is in soul than that soul is in body. The relation of soul to body is expressed by Plotinus as a form of collateral existence. Soul does not mix with body, but dwells beside it (πάρεστι) and either goes forth to it or withdraws from it. The One has descended, inexplicably, through soul to body; the soul consequently is a form of Being higher than that of body, and will move toward it or away from it according as it sinks or rises in the scale of Being.

To understand the position of the body in the scale of being we must revert to the metaphysics. The order of production is in a descending scale from the highest Unity, which is also the highest Being, to the last form of being, the lowest and the worst. The return which Nature strives to effect is a return of the lower to the higher, of the formless to the more formed, of the disconnected aggregate to the self-conscious Unity. At its lowest stage

form is expressed as a definite and persistent disposition of parts
(ἕξις). Nature thus begins her work in the inorganic; and, as all
form is of the nature of rational being, the inorganic partakes of
reason, i.e. order or rationality not conscious of itself as such.
The cause of all parts must ultimately be sought in the One
which (logically) precedes them and always comprehends them.
The secret power by which even the inorganic arrives at Form
proves that the Soul of the Universe is at work in it. The lowest
forms of being depend most on the Universal in which they live
and move; when matter attains a higher form in plant or animal
it acquires an independent power of production: the universal
soul creates within itself other productive agents. That form of
matter which has attained a sufficiently high level of being to
constitute a body receives a soul which coexists with it. Soul and
body are thus united substances, never mixed or fused, but always
remaining in a relation of 'assistance,' co-operating but not con-
substantial. It is extremely important here to observe that the
term body takes its meaning from the unity: it is matter that
precedes the unity; but, as we know it, body is matter endowed
with qualities which are the effects of its relation to soul. Motions
of the body are therefore describable as motions of matter; for
body is the soul's medium.

What has already been said about production and the scale of
being explains Plotinus' view that the soul's connection with the
body is a descent: its association with matter is a degradation even
though it is not wholly occupied in the mortal life. It cannot,
however, be placed in immediate contact with the body; its union
requires a mediating element, the Pneuma; in this the soul clothes
itself before putting on the garment of flesh. This aerial garb is
given to man by heaven and the stars, a body of the nature of fire
in which the soul dwells and through which it moves the body.

3. THE ACTIVITIES OF THE SOUL

Sensation is defined as the reception of forms in the matter
which accompanies soul. It is the process by which forms are
placed at the disposal of the soul (παραδοχή ἔιδους). Knowledge is
always an activity of the soul; sensation as such is not knowledge,
but a condition for the attainment of knowledge about material
things.

The independent character of the soul appears still more clearly in the sphere of knowledge. The soul uses the organs of sense as its instruments; it is itself unaffected; external impressions are made upon the sensitive soul by objects, but these impressions involve no self-recognition, no consciousness. The impressions are stored in the affective soul (τὸ παθητικόν) until the cognitive soul turns toward them and chooses to behold them. Plotinus here modifies the Aristotelian tradition. He deprives the senses of any function but that of transmitting forms which are the potential objects of cognition; the assimilation which Plotinus requires as the connecting link between the object and the thinking soul is represented as a modification of the passive sentient soul (the passive idea). All perception is itself an activity: the passivity implied in the soul's dependence on objects for its material results only in the deposit of forms in the receptive sensitive soul. When the soul exerts its activity and turns towards the things of sense it perceives (ἀντιλάμβανει, ἀντίληψις); this action may be described as facing toward the external world. The organs of sense are the means which the soul uses for this purpose. The soul is, in respect of its nature or substance, one, but in respect of its functions it is manifold. The body has parts, and to each part is assigned a different function, so that hearing can only take place by the ear, seeing by the eye; hence the soul is compelled to relate itself to different organs for the purpose of attaining what is given by each organ of sense. Though the soul is indivisible and therefore we say it is wholly in every part, this necessity produces a distinction if not a division, and creates the plurality of sense experience. The whole body is an instrument in the case of touch or movement, but the special organs of the other senses are the parts most adapted to the functions of sight, hearing, taste, and smell. The body also is the instrument of motion. The nerves, which begin from the brain, serve both for sensation and motion according as the soul uses them. Hence the brain is the most important part of the soul and reason has been placed in it, not because reason actually resides there, but because that is the point at which the immaterial reason comes into contact with the material organism and the sensuous soul. Plotinus here accepts the doctrine that desire is connected with the liver, spirit with the heart, and the deliberative reason with the head. This distinction of parts is analogous to that of the senses; it is a distinction of the instruments used for the various purposes, and only affects the soul in so far as it turns to one or the other to produce the effects required. Plotinus adopts Aristotle's doctrine of sensation as a faculty of discrimination, and of imagination as resulting from sensation. These belong to the calculative reason (τὸ λογιστικόν) and form a group of lower functions. Aristotle's description of imagination as partly a residuum of sensation and partly a rational function, serves for a transition from the lower to the higher activities of the soul. For memory is superior to sensation in the following way. Sensation is an activity common to soul and body; the soul is the agent which uses the body and in this case cannot perform its work without the body. Memory is not common to soul and body in the same way. As an example we might compare the soul to a weaver who cannot weave without instruments, but can think about weaving when the instruments are not at hand. The soul is independent in its actions, because even in sensation it has acted and not been merely passive. If the sensation left behind a definite impression, such as that of the seal on wax, these impressions would be required as material for the soul when it remembered anything. But this Plotinus denies. In the sensation the element of knowledge is due to an activity of the soul; hence that which remains, when the soul ceases to have an object before it, is the fact of having acted in a certain way. Memory then is simply the soul's power of knowing its own former activities. This seems to be proved by the fact that we have memories of activities which were not sensations, memories of thoughts themselves; and this could not be if memory was only a storehouse of impressions. Moreover, we remember that at a certain time something did not happen; how could this be if memory was always of sensible effects? Memory then depends on forms (τύποι), but forms are not impresses; they are modes of activity directed toward sensation rather than derived from it. Memory of that which did not happen is memory of an activity which failed to reach its object; clearly there could be no memory of an object that failed to reach the soul.

For Plotinus the subject of memory is a cardinal point. With the most penetrating insight he saw that all attempts to explain it as an after-effect of sensation were fundamentally wrong. Memory is simply consciousness viewed in extension: it is self-consciousness expanded into a time-series. All consciousness is in a sense self-consciousness: it is the self that makes unity, and unity is the essence of consciousness. Memory stems the flow of things, puts an end to the flux of the material world. It does this not because some one idea comes to a halt and survives the ebb of events, but because in it the soul is made manifest and the soul abides. Memory is the first clear proof that consciousness is not merely a complex sensation, an impression as temporary as the relation to which it is due.

Memory, then, is a state which may be described as an affection of the soul apart from the body. The body may assist or hinder the soul in its efforts, but the body does not itself remember in the proper sense of the term. Being a kind of thought and distinctively a mental activity it belongs to sensation rather than feeling. Feelings leave traces, and there is a certain cumulative tendency in feelings which amounts to a propensity; this is an obscure form of retention which occurs below the level of conscious unity. Even with sensation the bond is not close: people who have good memories for facts are often bad at recalling sense-experiences; and keen observers are not always good at remembering. Here the doctrine of imagination helps: it is the imagination that preserves the idea for a longer or a shorter time after the object is removed; it is accordingly the true condition of memory. Imagination has a twofold function: it preserves the forms which constitute sense-knowledge and it is the mirror of thought. The activity of the soul is involved in all actual perception. When the soul turns toward the material world it makes use of the images derived from sense-impressions. But the soul may also turn toward itself and its own content; it may make its own thoughts an object to itself and not only think but apprehend its own thoughts. This it does by means of the imagination, into which it projects its thought that it may make it the object of other thoughts.

Such is the nature of memory and such the uses of imagination. The doctrine of the dual imagination (sensitive and intellectual) leads up to an analysis of the process of thinking. The soul has three main types of activity: it may turn to that which is lower (matter and the senses) or toward the life within or toward that which is above it, Reason. In the first of these activities the soul performs the functions which do not involve reason (sensation and nutrition); in the second it produces discursive understanding which involves memory, ideation, and the lower forms of will and love; in the third it realizes unity with the divine in the forms of pure thought, in will and in love. In this Plotinus follows the lead of Aristotle with one significant change: Aristotle's list (nutritive, sensitive, rational) really duplicates the highest term and gives a dualism within the sphere of reason. Plato had also indicated a similar dualism. Plotinus thrusts sensation into the lowest part; classes understanding more closely with memory, and leaves the reason to form a separate and distinct class of activity. Another difference is to be found in the explicit recognition of a soul even in things inorganic, and by analogy a reason even in the (relatively) irrational part. This is a Stoic element woven into the web of Platonism and a necessary consequence of the doctrine of unity which abolishes any ultimate opposition of matter and form. Within the limits of psychology the three activities of soul are perception, reflection, and contemplation. The first is apprehension of effects produced by sensation, attention directed to the affections of the passive or irrational soul. Reflection or discursive thought is a kind of inner dualism, a spontaneous dividing of the conscious state into subject and object. In this the soul thinks and knows that it thinks. In the pure activity of thought there is no such dualism; the reason is then occupied with the eternal and changeless: the changeless has no before and after, consequently no time and no memory; for memory involves sequence. In this contemplation of the eternal the soul comes to rest and does not move out of itself as it does in reflection. Here, indeed, Plotinus seems to formulate the doctrine that to have the same state of consciousness continually is to be unconscious; but so far from admitting that this unconsciousness is a negation he makes it the most positive of all conditions: it is the highest and best state of the soul, its final and complete unity which is attained by pure contemplation of the One. This passionless contemplation being the ideal state toward which man strives, it is necessary to inquire into those disturbances of the soul which prevent its attainment. Thought in its highest form is passionless: it has certain refined forms of feeling such as pure love, but none of the motions which belong to the body can be transmitted to the rational soul; they reach only to the irrational or affective soul. For his physiology Plotinus relies partly on Plato, partly on medical writings. The vital functions he ascribes to the powers inherent in the blood which is contained in the veins: the veins start from the liver, which therefore has a direct connection with emotional states. For arguing, in the style of Plato, from the flushing of the face in anger and similar expressions of the emotions, Plotinus makes the liver the seat of the desires (τὸ ἐπιθυμητικόν), which include all impulses which lie at the root of the endeavour, whether for food or self-preservation. Plotinus thus practically identifies spirit and desire (τὸ θυμοειδές and τὸ ἐπθυμητικόν), regarding spirit as relative to the nature of the blood, since the quick-tempered are the 'hot blooded' people. With desire and fear are associated the movements of pursuit and aversion which imply a higher activity conscious of, but not disturbed by, the actual affections. The fact that pain or pleasure is a disturbance of the part affected, whereas right judgment about pleasure and pain demands an unmoved intellect, leads Plotinus to a rather striking analysis of emotions. The affections of the composite self may be divided according as they arise from without or from within, the former being due to external agency (as in receiving a blow), the latter to internal agency (the cravings of nature). In both cases there is a disposition of the animated whole. Since it is localized and we say the pain, e.g., is in the finger, the cognitive soul cannot be that which is affected, else we should say that the soul was in pain. Moreover, in a condition of pain or pleasure we determine upon a course of action; and this is not the function of the sensitive soul. The only possible conclusion, therefore, seems to be that the lower soul has the state or condition in question; the pain or pleasure is properly a knowledge of that condition, which coexists with the idea of some other condition better or worse. Thus there are really three elements in all pain or pleasure: there is the bodily disposition, the change which the body undergoes; there is the feeling in the sensitive soul which is pleasant or painful when the bodily change increases or decreases the unity between body and sensitive soul; while outside both, but co-existing with them, is the knowledge of these changes and their significances. Here as usual Plotinus has succeeded in working out an analysis in three terms, of which one is intermediary. All emotions (pain, pleasure, fear, anger, desire) belong to the unity which consists of body and sensitive soul, in other words, the animated body. But body never affects soul; the movement of which these are species is a movement produced by soul, never produced in it; so that all activity springs from the soul. The soul is not moved in the sense in which body is moved; so that ultimately the expression of the emotions is a corporeal movement produced by a motionless agent. As in the genesis of all lower from higher forms of being there is a going forth which neither affects nor detracts from the higher productive agent, so in the emotions all motion takes place in the material sphere and begins from higher states, such as opinion, which are themselves not states of motion. The typical case is that of blushing, which is a corporeal effect of the opinion that an act is shameful. Here Plotinus reaches, as a product of his introspective method, the first statement of the idea of self-consciousness. He has noted, too, that consciousness of self declines when the mind is most intent on its external object; while feeling and thought vary inversely. For Plotinus the stage of self-consciousness was not the ultimate goal: it may even be doubted whether he grasped the significance of the idea; for it is with him only an intermediary stage between consciousness of objects and the final unity which has no distinction of subject and object.

D. The psychology of St. Augustine

I. REVELATION AND INTROSPECTION AS METHODS

The work of St. Augustine is dominated by aims which partly assist and partly retard his inquiries. As a philosopher he seeks for truth, for knowledge that is without presuppositions and wholly certain, and this he finds only in inner experience. In the writings of Augustine we find a second influence, the theological bent, which employs revelation as the guarantee of truth. Knowledge is therefore divisible into two main classes according as it is derived from revelation or from introspection. In the sphere of metaphysics the nature of inner experience is made the starting-point for the construction of a metaphysic of knowledge, and this is Augustine's main interest. Subservient to this is the life of the self, the nature, origin, and faculties of the soul; which also attract the attention of Augustine for reasons both philosophical and theological. For the study of psychic life the power of accurate introspective observation is supremely valuable; throughout the work of Augustine we find this power exhibited in a remarkable degree.

Such inquiries as are associated with a taste for natural science do not fall within the scope of Augustine's genius: when he goes beyond the data of introspection he contents himself with the dogma of revelation; but within the circle of what may be called spiritual phenomena he moves with the assurance of a master. The supremacy of Augustine in the Church is easily understood: he combined with an exhaustive knowledge of theological doctrines an intellectual power capable of interpreting those doctrines luminously, and infusing into them a new life drawn from his own innermost being. The age was ripe for the originality which could contribute a deeper insight into the reality of the spiritual life, and this was the essence of Augustine's contribution to the progress of knowledge. The true keynote of his work is the dictum 'go not forth: withdraw into your own self: in the inward parts of man dwelleth truth.'

2. THE SOUL AND THE BODY

The world is, according to St. Augustine, created and sustained by God, who is the author of good. Man as a part of this world is a created being and our knowledge of his nature is based upon the account of his creation given in the Book of Genesis. All that Augustine has to say about the physical part of man is based on the revealed doctrine. As against the Manichaean doctrine that matter is created by the Devil, Augustine maintains that it is created by God. There is therefore no primary opposition of body and spirit from the cosmological point of view (such as Lactantius taught), and the dualism of mind and matter is not the same as the dualism of good and evil. The distinguishing mark of body is occupancy of space and the possibility of movement from place to place: a definition of matter or body which makes it, in the first instance, a particular kind of object. The mind does not know the nature of body, so the reality of matter can only be asserted on the ground of revelation; in other words, as matter is by definition an external objective reality it cannot be itself an experience, and therefore cannot be known in the full sense of knowing.

The world arises out of chaos by the creative act of God; man, as an organized creature, arises similarly by an act of creation out of pre-existing matter; the flesh was created out of damp earth. The history of creation is therefore continuous from the beginning up to the existence of the body. The question then arises, can we supply a natural history of the soul, that is, can we indicate a pre-existing material out of which it was formed? To this a negative answer is given; matter must always be that which has length, breadth, height, and spatial position; it must therefore be always distinct from soul, whether we speak of the four elements or that nameless fifth substance by which some have attempted to bridge the gulf between matter and mind.

The soul was created by God at the time when the body was created. Its creation and its birth are distinct events; as nothing was created after the six days of creation the soul must have been created then. The breath of God by which Adam became animated, or endowed with anima, was the act by which the soul was transmitted into the body. Augustine is careful to make his statements on these subjects very reserved; he is, however, sure upon certain points, which he sums up as follows: The soul is from God but not one with the substance of God: it is not corporeal; it was made by God, not in the sense that something of a different nature was made into soul (as earth was made into the physical man), but rather from nothing: it has a life which it cannot lose, and though mortal in the sense of being capable of change from better to worse, is indestructible, and so immortal.

Upon the subject of physiology, Augustine has little to say, and that little is of no great value. The body he regards as wholly dependent on soul so far as its life is concerned; its vegetative functions are not possible without soul, and the body itself has importance only as the medium of sensation and as that which the soul must rule. There is no intermediary substance between body and soul; but the elements which are most subtle, light and air, are most akin to soul, and are therefore those through which the soul acts in administering the body.

The will exercises rule of the body; the nerves are filled with air, which obeys the will, transmitting to the limbs the motions commanded by will. The elements of body recognized by the 'medici' include air which is contained in the lungs and diffused through the veins, and also fire. The fire is of two kinds: that which is hot, located in the liver, and that which is akin to light (luculentam qualitatem) which ascends up to the brain 'as it were the heaven of our body.' From the brain run channels (fistulae) to all the sense-organs, and from the neck and spine branch out countless minor channels over the whole body, thus making possible the sensations of touch common to all parts of the body. The mind sometimes turns in upon itself for the contemplation of truths that are known only by reason (reflection); at other times it receives messages from the nerves or institutes motion in the members. This motion is spontaneous, not due to external causes, but arising from the soul itself; it is peculiar to sentient creatures and spontaneity means the power of producing motion after the occurrence of sensation. Such movements as are involved in growth are not spontaneous: they do not imply a previous sensation on which they depend. The spontaneous movements depend on sense, not because sense produces them (for in that case all action would be reflex and automatic), but because sense is the awareness which conditions the activity of soul. Soul acts upon the body from its seat, the brain, which has three ventricles; the anterior is the nerve-centre, the posterior is the motor centre, and the middle ventricle is the seat of learning. The memory centre is required so that motions may be connected one with another, the past with the present. Such is the machinery of sensation and motion. Throughout Augustine is careful to assert that the physical and the psychic are distinct; the memory centre, e.g., is not itself memory. For their psychic functions all parts are dependent on the soul: it exerts an original activity (*intentio animi*) which produces motion and conditions all receptivity. If the soul is not intent the effects of external agents are unnoticed (latent). This is the first point at which we see how Augustine makes the Will the most important element in life. The simplest act of apprehension involves some degree of Will, for in it are compounded three elements; the mind is conscious of itself (*memoria*), aware of many possible objects of attention (*intelligentia*), and selects one with which it identifies itself (*voluntas*). The world for St. Augustine is the place of countless voices, voices of nature calling to the soul; but only those are distinctly heard toward which the soul exerts itself in the will to attend, and more than all these is the voice of God whose eternal presence is an eternal appeal to the human will.

3. SENSATION, MEMORY, AND SELF-KNOWLEDGE

The nature of the soul is, as we have seen, determined by St. Augustine on the basis of revelation. Its functions are all the manifestations of life, soul being a substance which partakes of reason and is suited to the task of ruling the body. This implies an action of soul on body which Augustine does not profess to explain: he shrinks from admitting the action of body on soul, and is careful at all points to make the affections of the soul follow or accompany rather than result from the corporeal affections; all emphasis is laid on the activity of soul; it produces all actions, and its actions always have some effect on the body. Sensation takes place through the five senses, and requires first an organic impression, upon which follows an affection of the soul. Sensation is therefore preceded by a physical change which is its condition though not its cause. When he gives a definition of sensation Augustine approaches it from the inner side, from the aspect of it as result. It is a form of awareness that is produced through the body. The significance of the phrase 'through the body' is explained thus: if we define sensation as merely awareness, it would include our awareness of such a physical process as growth, which we do not, in fact, feel; we know that our hair, e.g., grows, but we do not know this by feeling. It follows that we can be aware of events in two ways: by sensation and by reason; and the distinguishing characteristic of sensation is the actual feeling. This distinction we can discover by introspection, but the significance of the fact in so far as concerns the relation of mind to body is a mystery. In addition to the five senses we have the sixth sense, the traditional 'common sense,' by which we know that we have two or more sensations at a time. From the definition of sensation as awareness there follows the corollary that perception is always and only of our own modifications: the soul knows itself and its changes, and is limited to this knowledge.

The soul is regarded by St. Augustine as simple; and, following the Neo-Platonists, he says the soul is at the same time wholly present, not only in the entire mass of the body but also in every particle of it. The relation between soul and body as thus conceived is hardly explicable. It seems to be contradicted by the fact that some animals can be cut in two and yet continue to live in both parts, a fact which furnished a standing problem for philosophers. The only approach to an explanation is through analogy; the word is to the idea as body is to soul; and as the division of the word does not destroy the idea it expresses, so division of the body does not affect soul.

The 'simplicity' of the soul excludes the possibility of its containing different natures or essences; but not the co-existence of diverse 'parts,' which are really diverse functions. These are sometimes classified in the Aristotelian manner as nutritive, sensitive, and intellectual; but the division favoured by Augustine is that of Knowledge and Will or Love. Knowledge includes sensation, thought, memory, and imagination. The Will or Love is either of the world or of God.

We have seen in the case of sensation the emphasis laid by St. Augustine on the inner activity. To the soul itself he allows no knowledge, but asserts that the inner or central sense alone has knowledge. Memory he regards as a purely spiritual activity: the body may hinder it but can never help. From the assertion that the object of consciousness is always our own states, it follows that memory is always of ourselves and not of things. Memory may be either sensuous or intellectual. By the former we remember affections of the senses, and Augustine notes that this is the case for all the senses, i.e. we have a tactual memory, a visual memory, and so on. The memory is always spiritual; it is not a receptacle, and man cannot 'keep' an idea without thinking it or feeling it. It is not necessary that one should be always conscious of that which he knows; man, therefore, has knowledge as it were potentially, and memory is the act of restoring knowledge to consciousness. Augustine recognizes the conditions of a good memory and enumerates at different times what might be called Laws of Memory, viz. strength of the impressions, repetition, order, revision, and, above all, the exercise of the mind's activity in the first instance, the application of Will or attention. Memory is naturally connected with reminiscence or the art of reviving one idea by means of another. On this subject Augustine follows Plotinus. He totally disregards the physiological aspect of the process but recognizes the principles of association, agreement of one experience with another in respect to place, time, and manner, and resemblance of one object to another.

Thus far we have spoken of memory and reminiscence within the limits of sense-experience; if we turn now to the intellectual memory we shall find that for Augustine the true explanation of these mysteries lies in a metaphysical interpretation of life. Augustine accepts the position maintained by Plato in the doctrine of reminiscence (ἀνάμνησις), but with one important change, due perhaps to Neo-Platonic influences. This change is primarily the rejection of the idea that the soul forgets what it once knew. Plato's theory of reminiscence was also a theory of forgetting. Augustine refuses to accept the latter part, for he believes that all knowledge is really eternal, the living truth, in fact God; and our knowing is self-consciousness, the coming to consciousness of that eternal thought which is ours through the unity of our nature and God's being. This point of view dominates St. Augustine's writings and is expressed in many phrases of great depth and beauty. The soul, he says, always knows itself as thinking the absolute but is not always conscious of knowing; the soul's knowledge of itself is as it were a remembering of itself; the soul lives and moves in God and it is he, not its own former knowledge, that the soul recollects; the knowledge of God gives us when we attain it the feeling of ending our forgetfulness. Reminiscence is always the return into consciousness of that which has lapsed from consciousness; the Self is the exhaustless mine from which the jewels of thought are raised into the light: all that we find is found in our own minds. To learn, then, is to recollect and as all knowledge is innate, all learning is merely making explicit the innate. This we can only do for ourselves; it can only be effected by self-activity and only God can start it; human help is only the occasion, and the teacher cannot teach us but only enable us to learn. As we begin from God so all learning ends with God; growth of knowledge is the growing knowledge of God, and intellect ends with the comprehension of a verity which is God.

In this exposition we recognize Platonism penetrated by Christian mysticism. For Augustine the activity of the mind presents a mystery to be contemplated and studied but not to be solved. He realizes (after Plato) that the turning around of the soul is the essence of education; but he thinks it is not enough to face the light: the eye can see what it does not know, but the mind does not so much as see that which it is not fitted to see. If this is true of the mind, it is still more true of the spiritual eye. In the physical world seeing is believing; in the intellectual sphere belief is the condition of seeing. The soul cannot see before it is cured of its diseases, and therefore knowledge is impossible before the soul is in a fit condition. For knowledge is not like gold or silver: these we may know without having; knowledge we must have as part of our very being. The beginning of true knowledge then is not learning, but the will to learn, the disposition to exert the inner force, and so attain the true form of intellect, 'information' of the soul. This disposition is really given by the grace of God: it is a mystery; but Augustine indicates a way of attaining knowledge, namely, submission to authority by which he that would learn becomes fit to learn. This view of learning and of knowledge naturally terminates in an ideal of knowledge not unlike the Platonic.

4. IMAGINATION AND REASON

The imagination is for Augustine a faculty mediating between memory and understanding, not between sense and memory. Augustine regards imagination as a faculty or activity of the soul which has for its material the memory-images, just as sensation has the external objects for its material. He speaks of the imagination as working on its material, and consequently directly opposes any theory that inclines to describe it as a passive receptacle of images. That activity of the soul on which Augustine lays so much stress is manifested in the combination of memory-images, and goes so far in this way that imagination seems to absorb the work usually ascribed to reason. Augustine prevents us from supposing that imagination and reason are the same thing by pointing out that the work of imagination is limited to sense-images. The activity of the mind is seen also in thought, where its objects are of such a kind that imagination fails to be able to picture them; this is reason, a faculty of concepts as opposed to the faculty of images. Some of the most remarkable and penetrating observations of Augustine owe their origin to his careful study of the sense of rhythm. From this he came to a clearer perception of the subjective elements in experience. He observed that we are limited in our sense of rhythm; after a certain length we fail to grasp a piece of music as a whole; so that the grouping and unification of a series of experiences seems to be the work of the mind, and to vary with the power of the mind. Different minds have different degrees of capacity; animals have a sense of space and time which varies according to their kind and their relation to the universe. Time and space therefore represent the individual's mode of being: they are relative to it; the relation of the creature's body to the whole universe and of its duration to all time determines its perception in respect of space and time. The perception of time and space ends with life, being relative to our mode of existence.

Augustine believed in the immortality of the soul. Time, he said, is only the extensive measurement of experience, a *distentio animi*. The soul is not in time but time is rather the form in which the soul is presented to itself. There is consequently no difficulty in the idea of immortality, so far as time is concerned. The real problem is to find some reason for this continuous reality of the soul. Augustine finds it in the fact that reason is truth, and truth as such is not in a class of things to which change or corruption has any relevance. As we in fact say now, change is a category of the mind and not a category under which mind can be brought. In fact, all our ideas of things are forms of reason, and when true are eternal. The soul which has (or is) eternal truth must itself be eternal.

The distinctions made by St. Augustine are easy to understand if his general principles are understood. The mind strives always to see truth. In sensation it sees truth through the body, which is the only way of apprehending some truths. Reason is either a process or a state according as the term is used to mean reasoning or the result of reasoning. In other words, we may speak both of looking and of seeing in reference to the mind. The soul, when it reasons, looks for truth and when it has reason it sees truth, has the vision of truth. Knowledge is always of an object and seems to keep the object away from the observer; in perception there is an outer object, and science is no more than a system of such perceptions. But the perceptions themselves are not outside us: they are really ourself in action, and they illuminate themselves till the inner light increases and breaks up the darkness of ignorance. At that point men become conscious that the relation to outer objects is unsatisfactory. What a man knows truly he makes a part of himself: he grows with growing knowledge, not quantitatively but intensively, and so advances from scientific to philosophic knowledge, absorbing all 'facts' into one intuition of himself. After science with its delusion of externality, comes wisdom; here knowledge reaches its highest development, but the nature of man is still not wholly formed; so long as the reason is a dry light it is partly abstract, but when the will identifies itself with the known, when Love is added to Wisdom, every element in man's nature is fused into a unity, the unity is complete and the development is finished.

Augustine takes a strong line against scepticism. Truth is for him one and eternal and innate to every man, it is in fact a germinal Logos, it bears witness to itself, it is found even in error. What is doubt but belief in disguise, or thought questioning itself? Does not doubt involve all the functions that men profess to doubt? And what is error? If a man thinks that things are what they are not, can he know his error without at once knowing it as error, and so annihilating the essence of error? Error is, indeed, the purely irrational, that which has no reason and evades all reason. It might be said that error is a degree of knowledge or implies perfect knowledge. Augustine replies that knowledge has no degrees; a man either knows or does not know; doubt and hesitation are not degrees of knowledge, they are knowledge, and only appear to be a kind of ignorance because they imply a knowledge of limitation. To sum it all up: Augustine takes the terms self, knowledge, life as fundamentally one; we can only speak from experience and our negations are really affirmations about something: behind them all is consciousness, in which the self is one with itself and no man can get outside of that self or project himself out of the unitary experience, which is really the self viewed in extension. Psychology is based ultimately on metaphysics: its hypotheses are the axioms of life which are self-evident, unless they fail to be evident at all. It was just in this working back to the axioms of being that Augustine showed his power of thought and came so near to anticipating the use which Descartes made of these same axioms.

5. THE ASCENT OF THE SOUL

Such in brief outline is the psychology scattered through the works of Augustine. His thought terminates in a vision of life as a progress from God to God. Here there emerges the mystic element of his teaching. The soul has seven grades of being. First, there is soul simply as life, unifying and sustaining the organism; then the soul as sentient, the agent in perception to which belong habit and memory; third comes the soul which creates and supports the life of reason as practical faculty; fourthly, the soul turns from the world, values itself as better than body and seeks God in nature; the fifth condition is one of passive purity, a serene contemplation of truth; this leads to the sixth state, a state of activity on a higher plane exhibited in a craving for satisfaction of the mind; seventh and last is the vision of truth which is not a stage (*gradus*) but the goal, the final place of abiding (*mansio*). This last state is, of course, that ecstasy which has been already found in Plotinus. Augustine does not regard it in any way as a fanatical or abnormal condition. The foundation of the doctrine has been already laid in the earlier facts. For Augustine the soul goes forth in those activities which involve the outer world. The highest grade of these activities is science, which is a reasoned knowledge of things temporal. Above this is wisdom, the intellectual knowledge of things eternal. From such a beginning it is logical to assert that the higher activities of reason are self-centred, in them the soul discovers itself and its own nature, reveals itself to itself and understands that its content is no other than itself expanded. So we might suppose a man to know himself vaguely, then to see an image of himself in a glass, and finally to know himself through that image which revealed him to himself. The analogy has been used before Augustine's time and he could quote the words of the Apostle to support his belief that here we see as in a glass darkly. The state of true knowledge, the Gnosis of his predecessors, is for Augustine a state of ecstasy. He has described it and no words could be better than his own. 'And when our discourse was brought to that point,. that the very highest delight of the earthly senses, in the very purest material light, was, in respect of the sweetness of that life, not only not worthy of comparison, but not even of mention; we raising up ourselves with a more glowing affection toward the 'self-same' did by degrees pass through all things bodily, even the very heaven, whence sun and moon and stars shine upon the earth; yea, we were soaring higher yet, by inward musing, and discourse, and admiring of Thy works; and we came to our own minds and went beyond them, that we might arrive at the region of never-failing plenty, where Thou feedest Israel for ever with the food of truth' (*Conf.*, bk. ix, section 24, Pusey's transl.). Here we have clearly a state of feeling, the awakening of thoughts that lie too deep for words, vivid realization of limitless possibilities, and a condition charged with greater power than is found in the detached thinking of daily life. But there is in it nothing more than intensity verging on passionate self-abandonment to aspirations. These are conditions by no means uncommon in the history of genius; whether the vision is of gain or sacrifice, of empire or wealth, of earthly success or heavenly reward, life has its supreme moments of elevation for all who aspire. Whether we condemn them as illusions or explain them as pathological they remain undeniable psychological data. The interpretation put upon them is a different point. Augustine chooses to regard these exalted states as really highest and nearest the godlike. On the correctness of this nothing need be said here, and it is enough to remark that Augustine regards inspiration as the inflowing or inbreathing of transcendent superhuman powers; the artist, for example, has for the origin of his ideas a beauty which is transcendent, he does not see it in things, but looks through things to it. So in music, harmony is not a sequence of sounds but something over and above the sounds, some deep significance of eternal meaning which has taken upon itself this mode of appearance. Ultimately, indeed, all comes back to one phrase, God is all; the unity of all life's phases is found in oneself, a spiritual unity without quantity or diversity; and the unity of all spirits is likewise the one Spirit, God.

Augustine excels in his work because of the intense feeling which inspired it. No other philosopher ever wrote of the great mystery of being so as to show the agony of his thought in the way that Augustine wrote in the *Confessions*. There we have not only a theory but an autobiography of the soul, and the words come slowly as of one wrestling with his thoughts. The mind of Augustine seemed to take up all existent theories; flashes from Plotinus, Stoic writers, Clement and Origen light up this page or that; we seem to catch here and there a glimpse of familiar light shining from afar; but there is no denying that the brilliance of Augustine eclipses all those; he stands with the greatest, with Plato and Aristotle, and in one respect is superior to them. Psychology reaches a second great climax when its expositor can say that the foundation of the soul is continuous self-consciousness and thought is simply life reflected into itself.

Chapter Eight

THE REINTERPRETATION OF AUTHORITIES

A. Introductory

A great deal happened between the death of St. Augustine and the death of St. Thomas, but it cannot be seriously maintained that much happened which was of any great importance to the history of science in general and psychology in particular. The papacy emerged as a temporal power and heralded an age of politicians, administrators, and systematizers. The spirit of Gregory entered into the thought as well as into the action of the Church. Occasionally, as in the case of a St. Francis or an Abelard, the spirit of adventure or of criticism returned to challenge the institutions and learning now hallowed by tradition. But, in the main, it was an age of reinterpretation, adaptation, and 'endless wrangling over minor questions.'

Scholasticism has become a byword to designate quibbling over the details of a system whose basic assumptions are never seriously challenged. Gone was the bold speculation of the Greeks; gone, too, was the intense concern over ways of living which characterized the philosophy of the Stoics, Epicureans, and early Christians. For the Schoolmen or the Arabs wisdom lay in the past; Aristotle was the great philosopher. Averroes and Aquinas disagreed on many points, but their disagreements were mainly concerned with the correct interpretation of Aristotle. The task of the thinker resembled that of the administrator. Ideas, like the hierarchy of Church officials, had to be welded together into a secure and final system that would resist strains from within and corruption from without. Everything had to be sifted, cross-examined, and put in its appropriate place. Patient logic was applied to all the details; only the basic assumptions were logically unassailable because divinely revealed.

At the end of the period St. Thomas' *Summa* towers like the mediaeval cathedral—a massive expression of the mediaeval spirit, welding together the human and divine and lifting them up to God in a spire pointing towards finality and infinity. The patient, loving care of countless hands and brains, which, generation after generation, contributed to the building of these massive edifices of stone or ideas, astounds us; the extent and cohesion of their views over human affairs still leaves us breathless. We, whose climate of opinion is so different, would show a complete lack of historical imagination if we passed by without paying tribute to these magnificent monuments of the human spirit.

In its progress from Plato through Aristotle, the Stoics and the Christian Platonists, the doctrine of man underwent a continuous evolution. Parallel with this process there was also an evolution of religion, and on closer inspection it is obvious that the two processes interact. When the psychology becomes predominantly naturalistic it produces an antagonism toward the current theory of the gods: on the other hand, when it is either spiritualistic or rationalistic it forms an alliance with the supernaturalism of the period, and the two theories, of the gods and the souls, become mutually complementary. With the increased subjectivism of the third century in the Christian era this interaction of religion and psychology becomes so marked that the religion becomes psychological, and the psychology utilizes religion as a regulative standard. This phenomenon deserves a more detailed inspection both for its intrinsic importance and its historical significance.

The early history of human thought shows that level of reflection which has been called Animism. At that stage the world outside the individual is regarded as having life like that of man: the religion of nature was founded on this animistic view, but it was not a psychological religion: nature was regarded as having life and motion, but not consciousness. That view of the world passed away as man became more occupied with his own power of thought and learned to make a distinction between mind and matter. This new distinction was then itself projected: God for Plato was separated from the material world as the soul may be separated from the body. Instead of motion, conduct becomes at this stage the focus of attention, and a more definite form of anthropomorphism is evolved. The Stoics and Neoplatonists were clearly carrying on in the terms of their analysis of consciousness that anthropomorphism which had been at first elaborated in terms of the physical description of man. This was the main characteristic of the new thought which ran its course from Chrysippus to Plotinus, passed over into Christian Platonism, and so became the foundation of mediaeval thought. As the old religion was animistic, so the new religion was made psychological, and the latter is distinguished from the former only by the degree to which, in the interval, thought had become explicitly subjective.

A philosophy become religious and a religion waiting to become philosophical confronted each other in the second century of the

Christian era. The meeting-point of the two tendencies was Alexandria, and the question before the world was the possibility of uniting these two ultimate terms, philosophy and religion, in a further and final reduction. In Neoplatonism the senses received a partial condemnation: reason, the other half of the mental powers, was given a temporary superiority. By Christianity the feelings were again reinstated: love was proclaimed superior to pure thought and held a distinct place in the enumeration of the powers of the soul all through the Middle Ages.

During the second, third, and fourth centuries the science of the mind seems at first sight to have completely lapsed. That was not actually the case, but it is easy to get that impression because the subject becomes involved in the theological disputes of the period. As we noted above, at a certain stage in the development of thought the physical aspect of life is found less interesting than the psychical, and this was the case during the fourth century. The reconstruction of theology during this period was dominated by the received opinions on the soul and, conversely, the decisions reached act through the Middle Ages as the guiding lines for the development of all theories of the human soul. It is easy to lose sight of this fact because the language is now foreign to our ears: discussions about the nature of God, the humanity of Christ, or the original state of man seem far enough removed from the true sphere of psychology. Yet on consideration it is obvious that this is a very important stage in the history of psychological theory. When Augustine said 'I desire to know God and the soul' he was directly formulating the scope of psychology for many succeeding centuries. Though he may not have been fully aware of the fact, his own treatment both of God and the soul was a complete fusion of theology and psychology. It was the Augustinian influence that made the spiritualists of the nineteenth century speak of the powers of the soul as a copy of the Trinity; it was from Augustine that men acquired the habit of treating such problems as the origin of language in the form of discussion about the possible ways in which Adam may have named the animals. To pass over this period in silence would be to ignore the real beginning of many important inquiries, though that beginning was indeed obscure and veiled in curious terms.

B. *Plato, Aristotle, or Augustine?*

1. INTELLECT, WILL, AFFECTIONS

The results of the various disputes which affected the idea of the soul may be grouped under three heads, according as they are concerned with the intellect, the will, or the passions. With regard to the intellect, we have to notice that the Alexandrian tendency to lay emphasis on knowledge as the chief factor in spiritual development was checked and more importance attached to the will to believe. From the time of Clement of Alexandria there had been in the Church a growing opposition to the doctrine of Gnosis: this was thought likely to encourage the idea that salvation could be acquired by the individual's own gradual development without the need of faith in Christ. Against this Platonizing tendency the Fathers and the Councils set in opposition the doctrine of Faith, already begun by Paul and not really abandoned by the Alexandrian School. The outcome was a fresh analysis of the nature of religious experience which, at the hands of Augustine and other writers, became a singularly complete statement of what may be regarded as the essential nature of that aspect of mental life. At the time when this analysis was made it really supplied the place of a doctrine of the feelings. The eighteenth century evolved its idea of a threefold division of mental powers from the consideration of aesthetic feelings, which they saw could not be classed as forms either of intellect or will. Augustine was not far from the same standpoint, and his language at times suggests the same threefold division into knowing, feeling, and willing. Whenever after Augustine we find men breaking away from the current psychology of their day to develop the idea of Love as something which is neither wholly intellect nor wholly will, we must acknowledge that they are preparing the way for the final development of aesthetics and the consequent recognition of feelings as a specific class of psychological phenomena.

For Augustine the love of God was not only a feeling: it was also a duty. In the spirit of his age he failed to distinguish between the psychological nature of such mental stages and their ultimate value. Thus he was led to consider the love of God as in part an act of will necessary for salvation.

At this point the interest which had hitherto been directed

toward the intellect was directed to the will. It seemed as though the will could be regarded as equal in all men, so that, if there were differences in the intellectual endowments of individuals, there would yet be a common denominator in the will. There is, perhaps, no more persistent fallacy than this. To abstract the will from all other aspects of consciousness and assert that one can at least have good intentions, seems to be an inherent vice of human nature. The average mind of the twentieth century still harbours the belief that, however defective a person's general development may be, there is still no excuse for not having 'good intentions.' The dilemma which confronted Augustine is obvious. As the intellect cannot make men wholly like God, and yet it seems as though the prize of immortality should be given as a reward for effort and self-improvement, it was natural to say that the will was the means by which man qualified himself for God's forgiveness. But as the limitations of the intellect are inherent in it and no man makes his own intellect, so there is no logical reason why the will of the individual should not have its inherent limitations and by its very nature be incapable of some activities. From this point arose the Pelagian controversy. Pelagius maintained that man by his own will could choose the good; the act of grace was merely auxiliary, and redemption was obtained largely by the merit of the individual. Augustine opposed this theory. At an earlier stage of his teaching he had come to the conclusion that the essential factor in a moral life is the good will (*bona voluntas*). He had already laid down the principle that knowledge of God is impossible without faith, that is to say without a sympathetic reception of truth. Brought face to face with the problem of will, he realized more fully what his own doctrine implied, that it is impossible to get the good will if it is not given by nature or grace. Augustine seems to have realized that the will is really a function of the whole nature of man, and therefore dependent ultimately on that nature; the will expresses what we are, and we cannot will to be what we are not; conversion is not an act of will but a change of nature, preceding any possible change of will.

Thus the doctrine of predestination was formulated. Into its theological significance we need not diverge, but there are some other aspects of Augustine's teaching that should not be overlooked. In its psychological significance the doctrine of predestination is a restatement of Plato's description of the lie in the soul.

It involves the fundamental position that some mental states are of such a kind as to prevent the individual from grasping or realizing the moral significance of actions. Predestination is a doctrine which frankly and fully admits that some persons are devoid of the psychological factor called conscience. A modern psychologist would insist on predestination if he adopted the language of the Pelagian dispute. Augustine was eminently right both in admitting the fact of moral blindness and in reserving the possibility of reform 'through grace.' Whether his doctrine is repugnant to the Christian conception of divine benevolence is a question we do not profess to discuss. It was on experience and on psychology that Augustine based his doctrine; on that basis he was right in asserting that moral progress depends on the good will, and that if a man lacks that will there is no possibility of making so much as a beginning of moral development.

Thus the question under discussion involved great issues. It involved first of all the question of heredity, or, in the language of that age, the question of original sin. The breadth and depth of this problem was not fully grasped, but the higher plane on which the question is discussed raises the whole matter above a mere doctrine of responsibility. Aristotle could be content with the question of freedom in action; he could lay down rules for fixing responsibility and add a mere description of types of character. But here the question is that of responsibility for the character, a question that Plato had dealt with only through the medium of myth. Augustine sees the individual from the standpoint of eternity and understands that actions proceed from character and that the difference of character is an ultimate and insoluble mystery. It was the habit of his age to determine insoluble mysteries by dogmatic conclusions. From the transcendental standpoint the action of the evil nature is sin, and whether the evil nature is inherited or acquired, it remains sin. Here the Christian Father passes beyond the limits of Greek thought and of psychology. If the logic of predestination had always been clearly understood, later ages would never have lapsed into the psychological absurdity of supposing that sin is necessarily wilful or crime always a conscious rejection of the good.

Next to the intellect and the will come the affections. Here we must return again to the theological and Christological problems. The early Hebrew writers felt no difficulty in assigning to God the passions of anger, envy, and jealousy. The later writers refine the idea of God and admit, at most, righteous indignation, united with love in its most refined and elevated form. Christian writers speak of the wrath of God, and Lactantius wrote a treatise on that topic; but generally speaking God is removed beyond the sphere of affections and the interest formerly directed to that problem is now directed towards the affections of the God-Man. Some writers denied to Christ all feelings, particularly those who followed the Greek theology and the Eastern tendency to see in Christ only a Logos somewhat indefinitely related to a human form. But the main tendency was to assert complete humanity and therefore the power of feeling all human emotions. The language of the Gospels could be quoted to prove that Christ wept, hungered and felt fatigue. These human touches could be admitted because they satisfied the desire for an ideal that did not exclude sympathy. The deeper problem came later, when it was seen that full humanity involved also the tendencies regarded as specifically evil. It was characteristic of Augustine that he should include among these tendencies even concupiscence. This was felt to be contradictory to the whole mass of feeling which controlled the minds of those who formulated this ideal nature. The discussion produced the important decision that evil does not consist in feelings, but in the conscious adoption of feelings, a doctrine already involved in the Stoic theory of 'assent.' In spite of the problems raised by the curiosity of individuals, the ideal character was expressed in accordance with the fundamental feelings of mankind upon these questions, and therefore formed an abiding testimony to the character of human thought.

As Plato rightly points out, the life of the soul is to be regarded as the continuous expansion of a fundamental impulse ($\xi\rho\omega\varsigma$) which shows itself in many forms, chiefly in the impulse to act, to find satisfaction through relations with other kindred beings, to attain knowledge, and to satisfy the desire of continuity. This notion, which is more explicitly stated by later writers, is the fundamental idea that the basis of progress is self-expression. The highest form of this self-expression is seen in the way by which consciousness evolves more and more elaborate schemes of life and at the same time refines the details involved. When the level of conscious theorizing is attained and the individual becomes more distinctly aware of the relation between thought and action, those activities which seem to belong to him as an organic creature but do not proceed from his will are reckoned as outside his 'self' and therefore ultimately negligible. The automatic functions of the body are thus grouped together as 'lower functions'; they become dissociated from the self, which is increasingly thought of as limited to activities of the mind. The scientific attitude of Aristotle temporarily arrested this development, but it was continued by the Stoics in the most pronounced manner. Self-expression then became associated with self-repression; the wise man is capable of extending the range of his being by definitely overcoming all those elements of his composite nature which had been described as 'irrational' and therefore were to be regarded as the limit of the rational powers. Here we have, explicitly stated, the positive and negative movements of thought, namely self-expression as the realization of conscious control and the closely allied self-repression which is involved in the thought of self-sufficiency (αὐτάρκεια). The men who figure in history, and to whom alone a history of theory is able to make reference, are selected individuals above the average level, and have an exceptional consciousness of the relation between desire and restraint. Differences in circumstance and training lead to different ways of formulating this inner dualism, but in religion and philosophy the subjective factors are most obvious because in both there is a tendency to go beyond that objective control which seems to prevent science from being so distinctively personal in its results. One can hardly fail to see in the Stoic doctrine evidence of the tendencies described above. During the period of the Christian Fathers, from the Alexandrian School to Augustine, we find the results of Platonic and Stoic thought continuing to affect the structure of theories, largely because the individuals were continually driven back upon those very emotions and desires which produced the Stoic scheme of thought. Interest in the animal nature of man almost entirely dies out; there is no further attempt to study man as a physical organism, or even to allow considerations of that side of his nature to obstruct the flights of speculation.

2. ALEXANDER'S TREATMENT OF ARISTOTLE'S REASON

From this phase of our subject—human, all too human—we may turn to the dry light of scholarship. Next in importance to the corrupted Platonism of the fifth century was the work of the interpreters who claimed to present in their commentaries the real mind of Aristotle. First and greatest was Alexander, of the Carian town of Aphrodisias, a man skilled in medicine, competent to understand the master's interest in nature, yet at the same time not wholly free from the fascination of a cosmic philosophy.

The writings of these commentators are chiefly interesting to the student of classical scholarship. So far as concerns the substance of Aristotle's teaching, no fundamental changes were made, but the process of transmission changed the whole outlook gradually and subtly. The character of this change can be indicated in a few words. Alexander was conscious that the master's writings were somewhat behind the times; Aristotle had not the advantage of the discoveries made at Alexandria and used by the Neoplatonists; and Aristotle also had said too little about those parts of man's nature which ethics had since made prominent, namely independent individuality, subjective activity (the Stoic 'assent') and kindred points. Wherever the chance offers itself, Alexander touches up the Aristotelian dicta in that kind of improving spirit in which J. S. Mill edited his father's *Analysis of the Human Mind*. For the classical scholar the first problem is that of the relation between Alexander and Aristotle; for the student of history Alexander is an independent figure representing the Peripatetic school in its last phase.

While Neoplatonists studied Aristotle, the Peripatetics showed no tendency to adopt the Neoplatonic way of thought. The points common to Alexander and his contemporaries in the Neoplatonic circle are due in both cases to Stoicism.

His first contribution to the progress of ideas is the emphasis on activity. In the sphere of the senses we find him discussing the theories due to the progress of medicine after Aristotle, especially theories of vision; here his work is of little importance either in its character or its influence. The best known part of Alexander's comments is that which deals with the doctrine of Reason. Intrinsically this is subtle and not profitable; historically it is important for the part it played all through the Middle Ages, in the East and the West.

Aristotle distinguished the passive from the active reason, leaving no clear statement upon either the nature of these or their relations. Probably no more was meant than a distinction of content and activity; what a person thinks is dependent on his time, place and conditions in general; the power to think is thus presupposed, and must be defined as not similarly dependent on time and place. Taking the whole organism as the subject for analysis, the 'form' is the final cause, the life of reason for which man seems destined; the 'matter' is the progressive experience of sense, imagination and calculation, which Reason sets in order. Thus far Aristotle went, keeping close to his inductive basis yet unwilling to content himself with pure empiricism: whatever he thought Reason to be, it was not for him a 'transformed sensation'; it was rather the transforming agency.

Between the days of Aristotle and of Alexander the organism had been described more as a unity of distinct things, a coexistence of soul and body, as Plato regarded it. Alexander's attempt to revive the Peripatetic doctrine of form and matter was confused by this (Neoplatonic) line of thought. Alexander ended by applying his analysis to the mind alone and evolving within the limits of Aristotle's 'Form' a fresh distinction of matter and form. In consequence there are three 'Reasons,' the material ($νοῦς$ $ὑλικός$, hylicus, materialis, passivus), the acquired ($νοῦς$ $καθ'$ $ἕξιν$, $ἐπίκτητος$, in actu, habitualis) and the Pure Reason ($νοῦς$ $ποιητικός$, agens, actualis). Under these various names we shall meet these three degrees of the soul during the whole mediaeval period. The first is merely the power to acquire knowledge, an undetermined or blank capacity; the last is transcendental, variously explained; the second is the state of 'habit' which the soul attains through the action of the intellectus agens on the passivus.

3. PORPHYRY ON ANIMAL INTELLIGENCE

The spiritualistic or theological tendencies were not left in undisputed supremacy. As they were supported by dialectical arguments they were open to refutation by the same instruments. Porphyry undertook to do this, and the passages in his treatise on vegetarianism which deal with the proof that animals have souls are an interesting counterblast to some of the points mentioned above.

Porphyry's object is merely polemical, and we cannot treat his remarks on animal psychology as a serious contribution to the subject. As a Neoplatonist he has a quarrel with the Christian sects, and fastens on their habit of eating flesh as a proof of their moral depravity: they devour creatures that have souls like their own. The accusation requires to be supported with some proof that the said animals have souls in any sense like those of men and Christians. What are the alleged differences? Take first the question of Reason. This is either outgoing or indwelling. Clearly the animals have the former, for they understand each other: it is useless to say we Hellenists do not understand them, for neither do we understand the Scythians, whom no Christian would eat for all that. Further, some people *do* understand them— Apollonius of Tyana for example; and in any case we all acknowledge some degree of intelligibility in the sounds they make, for we distinguish signs of hunger, pugnacity, fear and so on. If, finally, this argument about speech is to be carried any further, what about the gods? Is their lack of speech a proof that they also lack intelligence, and why are they so little understood? Then as to the indwelling reason, this also must be conceded to animals. Animals seem to feel envy and engage in sexual rivalry: they have virtues after their kind, especially ants, bees, and storks, of which group the last is the most important because its peculiar virtue is piety. In respect of their senses animals are superior to man, and everybody knows that practical reason is an affair of the senses. If the animals have no written laws, neither had man at first. The soul cannot change its nature, and all that it achieves is regulated by its union with the body. If this union prevents the souls of animals from achieving some things, it may make possible other developments of which we have no conception. Men and animals have at least one more point in common: they are both liable to go mad.

This spirited statement of the case in favour of animal intelligence has two points of interest for us at this stage. The first is its easy dialectic, showing the facility with which the most unlikely conclusions can be drawn from plausible premises. The same thing was being done on the other side, but the results were more in accord with the wishes or prejudices of mankind and have therefore been handed on with more respect and care. The second is the fact that in this essay, perverse and polemical as it is, we have the required antithesis to that transcendental psychology which was described before. Porphyry has grasped the fact that, if an argument is going to be transcendental, it will not matter in what direction the transcendence is attempted. If animal intelligence is to be neglected or denied, why should so much be said about divine intelligence? The Neoplatonist had that advantage which he has held ever since: he was prepared to go up and down the scale of life indifferently. The prevailing religious tendency was to go up and not down, to discuss the relation of man to God or the gods and leave out of the system any reference to animals. If we now take in Porphyry, the scheme of the whole subject is completed. The central point is man, whose nature and activities are the real object of thought. This becomes more clearly defined on its inner side by the progressive discussion of the soul as a fragment or image of the divine mind, the latter being at the same time a moving image of changing ideas about the former. In respect of its outer side, the physical organism and the natural history of the mind, the reference to animals persists through the Middle Ages, but the whole subject lapses from official writings until the revival of the medical sciences. It is interesting to remember that Descartes, faced with the problem of adjusting the relations between animals, man, and God, chose to make reason divine, the passions human, and animals machines.

4. PROCLUS' NEOPLATONISM

The focus of interest during the fifth century was in questions that may justly be called religious. Whether we consider pagan or Christian teachers, the statement is equally true. In the case of pagan writers the tendency of thought is that which we call theosophical, and the main characteristics continue to be those of Plotinus. But, so far as concerns psychology, there is only a steady decline. The power of analysis shown by Plotinus does not reappear, but the latent possibilities of his system in the way of supernaturalism are developed beyond the limits of sane speculation. Omitting all the details of his teaching about metaphysical entities, we may notice that Proclus retained the doctrine of Plotinus that the soul occupies a position in the scale of Being between that which is divine and that which is sensuous (akin to matter). He also teaches, with Plotinus, that it has a power of free choice and may turn either toward the divine or toward the lower grades of being; and on this free choice depends the nature of its development. The one really significant fact in this teaching was its insistence upon the immaterial nature of the soul. This point was of some importance because, after the purely philosophical tendencies of the Christian Platonists, there had been signs of a reaction within the pale of Christianity. The Neoplatonists felt no inherent difficulty in asserting that the soul is essentially akin to that which they called divine. But for the Christian the nature of man seems to be infinitely distant from the nature of God, and this infinite difference leads to the rejection of a terminology that implies ultimate identity of substance. Gregory of Nyssa had gone so far in the doctrine of human spirituality as to incur the suspicion of heterodoxy. The reaction is seen in Hilary of Poitiers (A.D. 350), who asserts that, in distinction from God, all created things are material, including the soul of man. His position was maintained by others as late as the end of the fifth century, and its defenders could appeal to the authority of Tertullian. The reply to their arguments is found in Mamertus Claudianus.

At a later period we shall find the Arabian schools producing an Aristotelianism that is deeply affected by Neoplatonic theories. The point at which the required addition to Aristotle is possible comes in the question of the relation between the Passive Reason and that which Aristotle distinguished as Active Reason, and to understand the influences which produce the Arabian versions of Aristotle it is necessary to comprehend the last phase of Neoplatonism presented by Proclus (d. 485 A.D.). Proclus himself was not ignorant of Aristotle. His education began at Alexandria, where he seems to have studied Aristotle's *Logic*, and was continued at Athens under Plutarch, who wrote a commentary on Aristotle's *De Anima*. Marinus, the pupil of Proclus, describes his master as one who realized the ideal of Aristotle.

The Platonic doctrine that the Good is above and beyond Being forms for the Neoplatonist a new starting-point. The 'gnosis' of the Gnostics, the Christian Platonists, and the Neoplatonists, is that intellectual condition in which the soul apprehends the reality that transcends scientific knowledge. As distinct from the knowledge which depends upon the experience of the senses, this may be described as Faith or Belief. This development of Platonism, already made by the Christian Platonists, is adopted by Proclus, who puts Belief (πίστις) above knowledge; it is a form of thought which grasps realities that are not the objects of scientific thinking. Thus there are two distinct forms of Belief: that which is inferior to knowledge and that which is superior to it. The higher Belief then necessarily becomes the function of pure thought, a dialectic of Reason which acknowledges no restraints of experience, and which may therefore evolve systems of ideas that are really refined imaginations. That this was the actual result becomes obvious if we follow Proclus through his doctrine of emanations; but we shall limit ourselves to the points that affect the question of the relation between intellect and that higher realm with which it is connected. For ever since Plato wrote the *Timaeus* there had been a growing tendency to change the analogies and metaphors of the master into essential dogmas. Plato had spoken of the nutriment of the soul and pictured it as requiring nothing but truth for its daily food. The fatal step from analogy to dogma was taken by Augustine, among others, when he explained that the soul was immortal just because it had for its vital essence the immortal truths. Imagination and desire were already beginning to work upon the plastic material of Platonism, and theosophic ingenuity continued to explain, by way of mathematics and other forms of immutable truth, how the knowledge of God might be life eternal.

To achieve this ambition nothing is required except the construction of a scale of Being which shall correspond to a subjective scale of values. The lowest degree of Being is the body; above that comes the soul; in the soul the highest part is intellect; intellect constitutes another world, and as it is the highest when viewed from below, it is the lowest when viewed from above; for it is embodied Intelligence, on the borderline of that realm in which Intelligences and Intelligibles are grouped in ascending grades of purity up to the One. We are not surprised to find that this theory deals very extensively in the 'infinities'; but the highest powers are self-limiting, and the highest of all, the One, is rightly characterized as finite in so far as it is one and simple and indivisible, though in power it is infinite. Every kind of Being derived from the One is more limited in power than its source, and at the same time less limited in number. Thus the infinite plurality of things produced depends upon the infinite power of production in the One; while at the same time the fact that every effect has less power than its cause supports the view that the individuals lowest in the scale are most inferior in power. The pantheistic strain of Neoplatonism is not maintained in this doctrine; the One is not in all, but is a First Cause from which all forms of Being proceed and are thereby separated. The ethical development follows naturally; for the inferior strives continually to return to that higher level of power from which it has descended. As this may be actually achieved, the conclusion is a doctrine of reincarnation; the soul descends into the body and then regains a higher state, only to fall once more into the realm of body. Thus the individuals of our daily experience are eternal and imperishable souls that continually ascend and descend the scale of Being, dwelling for a time among the Gods and then again appearing for a time on the plane of matter.

The relation between Proclus and Plotinus requires to be carefully noted. The effect of Aristotle's teaching is seen in the argument that movement requires three terms: the First Cause as that which is itself unmoved but produces all motion; the intermediary which both moves and is moved; and, thirdly, that which is only subject to motion, the passive and inert substance. The soul belongs to the second type, for it has a principle of self-movement and is thus at once related by likeness to that which is superior to it, while it remains inferior to the First Cause because it is subject to motion. The peculiarity of the soul is its power of self-movement, which means its power of reflection. The self-movement is described as the power of turning back upon the self, and that is a power which belongs only to the incorporeal and is, in fact, nothing more than the idea of self-consciousness or reflection translated into terms of motion in order to give it a cosmic significance. The Aristotelian element in Proclus results in a separation of the One from that which the One produces. God therefore remains transcendent as a remote cause, not being identified with the immanent cause of motion in derivative beings. So in spite of much fanciful elaboration we have little more in this system than a re-statement of Aristotle's teaching. For the soul is primarily a principle of motion, as in Plato and Aristotle; it is constituted by the power of thought and is what it thinks; it is therefore immaterial in the sense that thoughts are immaterial; its activity proves it to be an independent reality; and, if we add to this the idea of separate existence, it may become a transcendent reality destined to live and move in transcendent regions of Being where there is neither space nor time. A doctrine so elaborate and so bold in its flights of constructive imagination was naturally destined to attract in all ages those who had the temperamental bias toward mysticism and aimed to construct some ontology of the intellect. For all work of that kind Proclus becomes the archetype. The importance of Proclus may be summarized under the following heads: he restated the doctrines of Plotinus in a manner eminently characteristic of his times (A.D. 411–485): he gives the functions of consciousness a peculiar place between matter and the transcendental forms of Being, a doctrine which later becomes a traditional dogma: he attempts to formulate a concept of consciousness, after the manner of Plotinus. Though the modern psychologist finds little occasion to quote Proclus, this last phase of ancient thought has influenced some modern writers. Hegel, as we know from his letters, felt a growing admiration for this writer, though it is doubtful whether that fact will enhance the reputation of either so far as psychology is concerned. It is interesting, however, to ask ourselves whether humanity has quite outgrown the doctrine that the food of the soul is truth. Is there any profound advance in many other forms of this doctrine of 'assimilation'? Are we any better off if we can solemnly endorse the statement that the 'food of the soul' is phosphorus, or that it lives on 'blood'? By touching these extremes thought finds its limits.

C. Arabian adaptations

1. THE ARAB MIND

The history of scientific thought during the Arab supremacy is mainly a record of transmission. Europe owes to the Arabs a debt of gratitude for the preservation of ancient documents; but there is little or no ground for any further enthusiasm. The reason for this will be made obvious as we proceed. First let us follow the path of our traditions from the near East to the further East.

The situation of Syria has already been noticed. Christianity took root in Syria at an early date; the doctrines were not very rigidly orthodox, but the general outline of Christian speculation may be determined as Monophysite and Nestorian. Judaism, the opponent of Christianity, had its stronghold upon the north-west of Arabia Felix, and from time to time emigrant Jews settled in Arabian territory. To the east lay Persia, and beyond Persia lay India, so that Arabia was, geographically, the meeting-point of the Byzantine Empire and the unconquered East. A careful study of the history of thought makes clear the fact that the seventh century is an epoch of prime importance. In the third century before Christ the Hellenistic world came to life through the conquests of Alexander. Much has been written about Alexandria and the fusion of East and West, of Greek and Jew, which took place there. The next great crisis in history is the awakening of Arabia, and in many respects this is a greater crisis than that of the third century B.C. When Greek and Jew met at Alexandria the result was inevitable: Greek thought was destined to gain little and lose much. When Arabia was filled with a new life there was a far more complex mass of material to be quickened: the Arab moved on from conquest to conquest and stretched his empire from India to Spain; he could command Greek, Hebrew, and Christian forces to aid his progress; he could boast a freedom unknown since the last days of Athens. Everything conspires to mark this epoch as the next great crisis in the history of Western culture after Alexander's conquests, an age more truly cosmopolitan than that of the Stoic or of early Christianity. Nothing seems to have been lacking except originality; every art and science was cultivated and disseminated; almost nothing was created.

The history of Arabian philosophy is mainly a record of translations and comments. This judgment, commonly passed on the philosophy as a whole, applies with still greater force to such topics as may be called psychological. The diversity of opinions and the dialectical disputes which belong more properly to the sphere of theology must be excluded from our narrative. On the other hand, there is no clear line of demarcation between the psychosophy which is allied to theology and those views of the soul which are more definitely scientific. We shall be compelled, under these circumstances, to keep in view the speculations which seemed to our Arab writers an essential part of the theory of the soul. In the union of psychosophy and psychology it is easy to see that most salient feature of Arabic traditions, the union of Neoplatonic and Peripatetic views. Plato and Aristotle are believed to be fundamentally identical; a view by no means so unjustified as some writers declare it, but not elaborated or defended by Arabs with much insight. The ideas attributed to Aristotle were often late additions to the Peripatetic doctrine: a strong infusion of Neoplatonism corrupted even the doctrines that were declared most distinctively Aristotelian. Yet in the main the part played by the Peripatetic and the Neoplatonic doctrines can be distinguished. The nature of man includes a natural and a supernatural part. For the natural part Aristotle is usually accepted, and the analysis repeats the familiar doctrine of his treatise *On the Soul*. For the supernatural part some version of Neoplatonism is the invariable basis. The Arabs, for the most part, show a keen interest in the metaphysics of the soul: their work tends to expend itself on the nature of the superhuman powers or intelligences, and bears a strong resemblance to the speculative thought of the last Greek and Christian schools. In this connection the Neoplatonic views of the One and of Reason served as a basis upon which the imagination could construct schemes of emanation. Aristotle's remarks about the 'active intellect' were so indefinite that it was possible to mount up through the teaching of the *De Anima* to a cloudy pinnacle of Neoplatonism. Thus we find a continual repetition of three groups of ideas. At the lowest level stands the life of the body and the senses, for which Aristotle, Galen, or some version of Aristotle, is the authoritative doctrine. Next comes the life of thought and the inner activities, for which also Aristotle is the main authority. Last comes the highest level of intuition or ecstasy, mainly Neoplatonic and closely connected with the general doctrines of the universe, the celestial spheres and the supreme Unity.

The Arab mind seems to have followed, by natural inclination, the ancient idea that man stands midway between a lower and a higher realm. The relation of the human soul to the lower realm is never seriously investigated: if it had been, we might have heard more of the animal nature of man and found in these writers a more valuable science of man. It is the higher realm that attracts their attention and so leads them to subordinate their psychology to their psychosophy. This fact would be evident from our narrative if we intended to describe the whole teaching of the Arab writers: it requires emphasis here because we have to select from the mass of material only those points that are of interest for the development of psychology. The time has now passed for dealing extensively with the mystical or theosophical speculations; what is worth saying on these subjects has been said in connection with Plotinus and his successors; for the future they will gradually cease to engage our attention. Yet before we leave that topic it may be as well to state how this side of the subject should be valued. The Neoplatonic line of thought is significant because it represents the idea of experience. In the Arab as in the Christian doctrines of the soul there is a painful lack of experiment; empirical tendencies only emerge occasionally and remain undeveloped; this was the weak point in the natural sciences, and psychology as a natural science was, in this respect, no exception. But experience shares with experiment the claim to be a source of knowledge about man, and the Neoplatonic line of thought cannot be dismissed altogether so long as it continues to represent that reflective study of the inner life from which new ideas might at any time be derived.

2. ALKINDI

The first name in the annals of Arabian philosophy is that of Abu Jaqub ibn Ishaq Al-Kindi, usually called Alkindi, one of the many who resorted to the University founded by Harun (A.D. 786–809) at Baghdad. He was reported to be a man of great learning, but so far as we know his genius was not in any way creative. Though he is described as an Aristotelian, his mode of thought is Neoplatonic, with some mixture of ideas derived from other sources. The human soul is regarded as an emanation from the soul of the world, united during life to a body, but in its essence independent of the body. It is a substance, uncompounded and immortal, which has descended into the world of the senses and retains the memory of its earlier state. In accordance with this view of its origin, the soul is regarded as acquiring knowledge either by the senses or by the reason: the senses apprehend the material forms, and the reason grasps the spiritual forms or the universals. The only work of Alkindi which is known is a brief work *On Intelligence*. This contains a doctrine of the degrees or kinds of Intelligence which reappears, with variations, in many subsequent Arab writers. There are four degrees in all, one external to the soul and three contained in it. The external Intelligence or Reason is an eternal cosmic essence or spirit. In the soul there is, first, that intellect which is called a potentiality, a latent power of understanding. Through the action of the external spirit this is raised to the higher degree of Habit, that is to say, an actual power of understanding (*intellectus in actu*). At this stage the individual is in possession of ideas, which he may, by his own activity, bring to a higher degree of perfection. This third and final stage is a full realization of intellectual principles and a power to use them.

The doctrine of the intellect, though difficult to comprehend, was so continually dwelt upon by the Arabs that it is necessary to understand at once what problem it was intended to solve. Ignoring the experimental side of the question, the Arabs plunged into speculations on the origin of human reason. Wisdom, to the Eastern mind, is always from above: knowledge may in some degree be the result of man's activity, but even so it requires a cause which is not itself. So the Arabs set themselves to explain how the intellect grows and becomes an independent reality in man. When the problem was formulated it proved to be by no means new. Plato was thought to have explained the universal factors in man's reason by reference to external causes, the world of Ideas: Aristotle had said that the Reason (Intelligence, *nous*) comes from without; the Gnostics had developed a more imposing theory, with a doctrine of intermediation calculated to satisfy the most scrupulous; in fact, all through the history of ancient Greek literature the 'masters' could be quoted to support the view that the intellect is not merely a function of the natural body. The views of Alkindi came probably from Alexander of Aphrodisias; but the Arab has his own reasons for his choice, and those reasons are emotional. As the race seems to be something eternal into which the individual enters at one particular point, so knowledge seemed to the Arab to be an eternal and abiding reality, everlasting and indivisible, which for a time reproduced itself in the individual.[1] There were, of course, degrees of realization; the fool and the wise man differed in the degrees of their intellectual illumination; and above the wise man stood the prophets, men whose intuitions surpassed both sense and reason, for in them the creative reason itself lived and moved.

This doctrine of the intellect has detained us a while because of its significance. The details can hardly be of interest any longer, but it is not difficult to see that, in spite of extravagances and a fatal loquacity, the Arab knew that the problem of consciousness was not to be solved by anatomy. If his metaphysical

---

[1] Philoponus is said to have introduced 'a realistic element by speaking of mankind as a collective thinker who is always thinking' (Bussell, *Religious Thought and Heresy in the Middle Ages*).

genesis of the intellect wearies our minds, let it be remembered that he does not weary us with fruitless discussions about the 'seat of the soul.' If we feel that his descriptions are the baseless fabric of imagination, let us remember that we know little of his thought, that he belonged to a people adapted by nature to subtle analysis and deep meditation; and that, in the absence of any scientific proof that body produces soul, he was justified in maintaining his belief that it does no such thing.

3. AVICENNA

Abu Ali Al-Hosain ibn Abdallah ibn Sina, the Avicenna of the Western mediaevalists, was a native of Bokhara, who lived A.D. 980–1037. Ibn Sina was an authority on medicine. His extensive, if not accurate, knowledge of Aristotle and of Galen accounts for his interest in the so-called lower faculties and for the care with which he reproduces what was regarded as the authoritative doctrine of the functions of the soul. His works form an encyclopaedia of what was then known about man; for in the *Canon* we learn all that was known at that time about the human body and the organs of sense; in the commentary on Aristotle's *De Anima* we have a definite statement of all the powers and faculties, from the senses to the pure intellect; and to this we may add, as a significant appendix, the poetical fragments which show that our author did not lack the hereditary mysticism of the Arab nature. Here, then, we have sufficient material for a systematic account of the whole subject.

Matter is for Ibn Sina eternal and uncreated, not an emanation from the first and cosmic Unity. The whole sum of existent reality is either material or spiritual; the former is the subject of physics and the latter of metaphysics. The soul comes midway between the corporeal and the spiritual worlds; its genesis is explained by the traditional doctrine of emanation, elaborately worked out on a plan derived from the Ptolemaic astronomy. Starting, as usual, from the First One, Ibn Sina describes the procession of the Spirits, namely the World-Spirit, the Spirits of the Planets, and finally the Active Intellect, the point at which Ibn Sina chooses to stop. As matter is not an emanation, this metaphysical doctrine only becomes interesting when we have to consider the relation of the soul to the active intellect. Before discussing that point we may start from the opposite end and reproduce Ibn Sina's account of the ascending scale of powers.

Ibn Sina begins with a proof that there are such things as powers of the soul; in other words, he undertakes to prove that there is a definite subject-matter for psychology. This proof, taken from Aristotle, consists in pointing out that voluntary movement and perception are not functions of matter; they can only be treated as the obvious manifestations of a spiritual reality. Granted that the soul is not to be reduced to matter and motion, psychology has for its sphere the classification and analysis of the soul's powers. From this point Ibn Sina proceeds to give an account of the soul which is essentially that of Aristotle. The powers are divided into three groups: the vegetative, animal, and rational. The vegetative powers are subdivided into three groups called generative, augmentative, and nutritive, according as they subserve the production, the growth, and the maintenance of the individual. This (Aristotelian) doctrine is an elaborate analysis of the purely physical side of life, combined with the assumption that the vital processes are not functions of matter, but of soul as united with matter. This is the way in which the Arabs state what is, in principle, a form of vitalism.

The animal soul, *anima sensibilis* or *vitalis*, comprises two classes of powers, the motive and the sensitive. These are elaborately subdivided. The motive powers are those which (*a*) command movement, the *vis appetitiva* or impulse including desire and aversion, or those which (*b*) execute movement. A distinction is made between the faculty of desire and the faculty of aversion, the former being the *vis concupiscibilis*, the latter the *vis irascibilis*. The former of these is described as an expansive power, the latter as contracting, the distinction being apparently transferred from the sphere of physiology to that of psychology, probably under direct influence from the Stoic tradition. Something might be said in favour of a true psychological distinction between the desire to possess and the purpose of overcoming, a point developed from this terminology by later writers. Passing on to the cognitive powers, we find the power of apprehension is divided into the outer and inner senses. The outer senses are the usual five, also counted as eight, not in the Stoic fashion, but by including under touch four distinct species of discrimination, namely for hot and cold, for dry and wet, for hard and soft, for rough and smooth.

This distinction obviously goes back to the doctrine of the four elementary qualities and does not really amount to a recognition of difference between a sense of touch and a temperature sense, though the suggestion of such a distinction is implied in the language. In dealing with the separate senses Ibn Sina follows Aristotle, with such additions as were due to the later medical writers. In particular the problems of vision are discussed at length and with some advance on earlier statements. Ibn Sina was one of the first, if not actually the first, to state that the crystalline lens is not the seat of the visual image but only presents an image visible to an observer: the optic nerve was according to Ibn Sina the organ of vision, for he does not arrive at any statement about the retina.

Ibn Sina deals at length with the inner senses. Under this head come the powers called common sense, *vis formans* or *formativa*, *vis cogitativa*, *vis aestimativa* and *memoria*.

The common sense, which receives and unites all the separate sense impressions, is only formally distinct from the second power, the *vis formans*, or power of retaining the sensible forms. When, for example, we apprehend the movement of a body in space, the external sense gives us a number of sensations; to obtain a notion of this as a whole, or to sum the series of sensations, we require a power which is distinct from that of immediate apprehension, for the result is a compound of present and past data. The characteristic of the *vis formativa*, then, is that it conserves the image; it is a primary retention, akin to memory; it may also be called *phantasia* (imagination), since in it the merely sensible is converted into the imaginable, i.e. into a form that can be re-presented after the presentation is over and ended. The name, *vis formativa*, is intended to mark this essential change of character by which the sensation, a physical event, becomes a treasured form, a psychic possession.

The third inner sense is the *vis cogitativa* (also *imaginativa* or *collectiva*), which is not a power of the intellect but only a power of the *animal* soul (*anima* as distinct from *intellectus*). Such processes as abstraction or association belong to this 'inner sense.'

The fourth is the *vis existimativa* or *aestimativa*, a kind of opinion or judgment which is produced by the *anima* and is more akin to a feeling about things than to an intellectual grasp of them. This is equivalent to what we call instinct in animals; in man it is a 'prejudice' or opinion. The example given is that of a man who, seeing a child, *feels* that he ought to treat it gently; so that this power is a kind of judgment in which the grounds of the judgment or the reasons for it are not consciously elaborated by any intellectual process.

Fifth and last is the memory, the full power of preserving the forms which are acquired in experience.

The powers here described are classed as 'animal powers,' that is to say, they are attributes of the organism composed of body and soul. As they are organic powers they have definite relations to the extended organism, in the sense that the power of sight has a definite relation to one part of the organism, the eye. Though these inner powers have no scientific organs they have specific localities. The outer sense organs are in fact no more than localizations of powers, and there seems to be no reason why one should not localize the inner functions. The brain is the organ for all of them, and the divisions of the brain are specialized areas. So the powers are localized thus: the *vis formativa* has its seat in the anterior cavity; the middle cavity is occupied by the *vis cogitativa* in the fore part and the *existimativa* in the hinder part; the posterior cavity is the seat of memory. This was an old doctrine, but it took a new lease of life from Ibn Sina.

As we noted above, Matter is for Ibn Sina an independent reality. The body, as a material thing, is produced by a mingling of the elements, and each element has its own form; so that the form of the body is a product of the other forms, which are merged in its being. But this form is not the soul. Whatever Aristotle may have meant, Ibn Sina declines to accept the doctrine that the soul is the form of the body; on the contrary, it is a separate independent reality, which is only united to the body accidentally, that is to say, without any relation which affects its essence. All those powers which we have described, both vegetative and animal, are made possible by the union of the soul with the body: but if we go beyond these we come to other activities which belong to the soul itself. These are described in the doctrine of the Intellect, which comprises (*a*) the *intellectus activus*[1] or practical reason of Aristotle, and (*b*) the *intellectus contemplativus*. The former is not treated with any originality: the latter is described genetically and analytically in what may be regarded

[1] In scholastic terminology *operativus*.

as the classic statement of the Arab teaching. By analogy with the general view of the cosmos we get the idea of a pure potentiality, a blank state of being,[1] which precedes all production or activity: opposite to this at the other end of the series of states is the pure actuality, the separated Form or *intellectus agens*. The continual operation of pure Form on the material or potential reason of the individual produces an ascending scale of perfections: the pure potentiality becomes endowed with the primary truths and then becomes *intellectus possibilis*, or nascent intelligence: advancing to further knowledge, the *intellectus* is said to be *in actu*: next it becomes a complete and independent system of thoughts or fully developed intellect (*adeptus acquisitus*): finally a higher stage may be reached by a few, which is the intuitive knowledge of the most supreme intellects, the prophets and the 'holy spirits.'

A little light on the real significance of this description may be obtained by considering the simple example given of the development indicated. A child may be regarded at first as capable of writing, though unable to write: after instruction he will be able to write in the sense of copy-writing; finally he will be able to write from the inner prompting of his own mind. The basis of Ibn Sina's distinction is a passage in Aristotle,[2] but the expansion shows an interest in the fact of development. For the rest, the doctrine of the intellect is Arabian Neoplatonism and has no interest in connection with psychology, though hitherto hardly enough attention has been paid to the subtle changes which the Arabian versions of Greek writers introduced into the later scholasticism and then into Cartesianism. It is of interest from this point of view to notice how in Ibn Sina the germs of sensationalism and of occasionalism are equally preserved. Nothing is required beyond exclusion of the *intellectus agens* to leave a sound doctrine of the senses and the intellect: nothing more is needed than the conversion of the *intellectus agens* into an ever-acting God, a subtle turn of the phrase '*Deus Illuminatio mea*,' and occasionalism emerges.

4. ALHAZEN

The labours of Ibn Sina in compilation and speculation were followed by a relapse into inactivity. There are no more great

---

[1] The *tabula rasa* of Alexander.   [2] *Ethics*, ii. 4.

systems to be studied, but there remains one name of real importance, the astronomer and optician Alhazen. Those who have
studied and described the works of this isolated genius have
unanimously agreed to rank him (by analogy) with Helmholtz.
There is little or no relation between the ideas or the methods of
Alhazen and those of Helmholtz, though some curious anticipations of later views have been found in the Arab's theories. The
analogy is most striking when applied to the two writers as phases
in the history of thought. In the earlier period we have the Neoplatonic background, and sharply defined against it the man of
practical schemes and acute observations, who is, however, no
mere empiric. In the later period the modern Neoplatonism of the
Hegelians floats cloudlike behind the figure of the scientist who
combined with the most rigorous investigations of natural processes no slight inclination to see in his work a significance that
must ultimately transcend the sciences.

Alhazen, whose full name was Al-Hasan ben Al-Hosain ben
Al-Haitam, was born at Basra in A.D. 965. The first stage of the
process which transferred to the Arabs so much of the Greek
literature was then ended: a more independent development
succeeded it, and brought an extension of interest into the mathematical and physical sciences. Alhazen had an inclination for the
sciences which seems to have been 'debauched with philosophy.'
He maintained in theory that the flooding of the Nile could be
regulated, was deported to achieve it, realized his own incapacity,
and lived in concealment from the wrath of the Khalif Al-Hakim
until 1021. This enforced retirement was occupied by copying
and writing books, more than one hundred treatises on mathematics and astronomy being ascribed to Alhazen. Among these
there is no work on psychology, and the Arab would hardly have
considered his ideas as a contribution to that subject, but he is in
fact a link in the chain which runs from Aristotle and Ptolemy
through Witelo and Roger Bacon (p. 300) down to Helmholtz and
his successors. As such a link history is honoured in remembering
him.

The only work of Alhazen which concerns us is the one entitled
Al Manazir, in the Latin version *De Aspectibus*, which became
known as the *Perspectiva* or *Optica*. This was a work on the
physical doctrine of light which continued the works of Ptolemy
and Damianus. Omitting those details which concern only the

history of physical optics, we may remark that Alhazen starts with the general principle that the eye receives light from objects, the older doctrine that the eye sends out rays having been already destroyed by Ptolemy's school (*c*. A.D. 150). In common with other thinkers of this age, Alhazen accepts without criticism Galen's description of the eye. This was in many respects defective, but Alhazen is only concerned with the organ of vision as a system of lenses and with the consequent problems of refraction. With this scientific interest is united the general Neoplatonic tendency to regard light as something unique; from Proclus onward there was a continuous tradition about the nature of light which made it the basis of intellectual as well as sensitive knowledge. It was therefore no personal idiosyncrasy that led Alhazen from the physical treatment of light to the problems of perception: they were not for him two wholly distinct subjects, but rather one group of subjects whose natural connection was found in what we might call the psycho-physical character of the eye. With this explanation of what might otherwise appear to be a miraculous birth of psychophysics we may proceed to summarize the views of Alhazen on perception by the eye.

It is necessary to recall the general conditions of vision as they are stated in the works which depend upon Galen's teaching. According to this the optic 'nerve' is a channel through which the particular spirits (*spiritus visibilis*) run from the brain to the eye and back again. The images or forms (visible species) which produce vision are conceived as propagated from the object to the eye, taken up in the stream of spirits, and so conveyed inward to the cerebral place of forms (Aristotle) and true centre of vision. This doctrine was open to misconception and usually became unintelligible through the influence of atomistic (Lucretian) views, which made the 'forms' into material things. The genuine doctrine was not this materialism but a more strictly Aristotelian tradition, which was concerned only with the functions of the eye and its 'pneuma.' Alhazen is quite unintelligible unless we remember that he keeps closely in touch with this Aristotelian line of thought, assisted as it was by the Neoplatonic assertion of the immaterial character of consciousness and the importance of psychic activity. Alhazen, setting himself to extend the description of the eye into a description of its functions, thinks of the visible world not as an infinite mass of material objects, but as a system of activities, and so proceeds to an analysis of visual experiences, with very surprising results.

The method and the genesis of the method as here stated are as interesting as any part of Alhazen's work; the emergence of new varieties of thought by what appears to be almost accidental cross-fertilization of old traditions is here shown in a striking way. In every part of Alhazen's work it is possible to see two persistent factors, the practical scientific investigation of data and the theoretical schematism of the Neoplatonic world-system. The sphere of vision offered many problems, and Alhazen took the question of sight as comprising both the outer seeing of the eye and the inner seeing that is of the mind. Compared with the atomists Alhazen is a mystic; compared with the mystics he is a man of science. In a true Neoplatonic manner the Arab sets himself to explain how vision comprehends the invisible. For if a man sees two things and their relations one to another, he cannot do this with the same kind of vision; there is a sight that belongs to the senses and another seeing that is not of the senses. This is the mystery which Alhazen explains.

We must begin with the physiological aspect. Alhazen seems to have been of the opinion that the 'spirits' concerned in vision were the agents producing sensation. Each eye can have its own sensations of the amount and direction of light, but the cognitive part of visual experience is the work of the spirits lying behind the eyes in the channels where the nerves cross—the chiasma. These more remote spirits (which afterwards were located in the fore part of the brain and so come to be the equivalent of the later cerebral centres) have the power which we might expect to find at such a point of union—the power of judgment or comparison. Any given perception comprises (a) the sensations of the eyes, and (b) the activities added to them by the 'inner sense'; it is therefore analysable into given elements and associated elements. Taking first the process of seeing an object, we find that this is either a point to point relation of the eye and the object or it is a visual perception of an object as a whole. The perception of the whole is achieved by movements, the eye thus exploring the object. Here we have explicit recognition of the difference between visual points and the whole field of vision, the latter being constructed by the series of movements which gives the different elements synthesized in the perception of the whole. Such a process involves the power of memory and (in some sense) the reason. This is not the higher deductive reason, but a lower activity which the Scholastics call *cogitatio* and the Latin versions of Alhazen refer to as contributory reason (*ratio conferens*). The exact nature of this operation is more obvious when we consider other points now to be named.

Aristotle had remarked that in perception some elements may be 'accidental,' that is to say, supplied from another source. We say that we 'see' a friend, when really we see a coloured object and recognize it as our friend. Alhazen elaborated this analysis of perception. In perception there is an element of comparison, either of coexisting sensations when we perceive the relations of data given together (e.g. size) or of present and past sensations. Recognition is only another phase of the same kind of activity, and immediate recognition is an unconscious comparison. The doctrine of unconscious *inference* is largely used by Alhazen in the explanation of all the more complex kinds of perception. Following out Aristotle's dictum that we do not perceive a thing as 'this' but rather as 'such,' Alhazen traces out the influence of accumulated experience on perception. If a person perceives an animal of a familiar type, that is to say, an animal of which he possesses already the 'species' or generic concept, he does not explicitly perceive all its parts: he sees enough to justify a kind of unconscious identification of the object with the form or *schema* already existing in the inner spirits. Any doubts as to the real meaning of Alhazen are removed by the statements which he makes as to the time taken by perceptions. He noted that the process takes time, and that this time is reduced when the individual is familiar with or expects to see a certain kind of object: for then the 'species' is ready to hand.

Time and space are two subjects in which our mathematician took a special interest. As regards the origin of perceptual space, he seems to have no idea of the problems and is contented to regard it as a natural possession of man, as in what is later called the nativistic doctrine. Size, magnitude, and position Alhazen regards as objects of judgment, though usually the judgment is made so rapidly that we are not conscious of the act. That the apparent perception is actually a judgment was shown by reference to illusions; we seem to see the moon moving when in reality the clouds move across it. The time-element required for judgments explains the apparent mixture of colours when a rotating circle of different colours ceases to be perceptible as such and becomes a blurred (mixed) colour. It has also been asserted that Alhazen understood the facts which are formulated in Weber's law, for he said that all sensation was a discomfort, but that it could only be perceived after a certain degree of intensity.

It is not desirable to indulge too freely in the comparison of Alhazen with modern writers. It has been asserted that in the *Optica* Herbart's doctrine of apperception and Helmholtz's views on sense-perception are clearly anticipated. The work is remarkable enough without any such extensions of its meaning; it bespeaks for its author a fine sense of distinctions and a great power of analysis; but it is obviously rooted in the science and philosophy of the Greeks. Its naturalism is that of the Peripatetics from Strato to Galen; its subtlety and refinement are akin to the qualities of Plotinus. The influence of the work began to be a force in history after the success of Witelo's transcript made in the latter part of the thirteenth century, and in some details of secondary importance Alhazen has gained by being credited with the points which were added or corrected by that faithful disciple.

5. AVERROES

With Ibn Sina the Eastern school of Arabian philosophy ended its effective life; a train of epitomists closed the procession. The activity of Arab or Jewish philosophers was always very dependent on patronage, and the next home of culture was provided in the West. The Spanish Arabian school included Ibn Tofail (Abubekr), Ibn Baddja (Avempace), and Ibn Roshd (Averroes). None of these was endowed with any originality, unless Ibn Roshd can claim the distinction. On questions concerning the mind we find ourselves back in the old rut: emanations, spirits celestial and super-celestial, and dialectical difficulties about the Active Intellect form the basis and the superstructure of the discussions. It is enough to have stated the earlier forms of these doctrines; there is no call for repetition, but Ibn Roshd must occupy our attention for a while.

Ibn Roshd was a native of Cordova; he belonged to a family of lawyers and was himself a jurist, in addition to being a doctor and a philosopher; after a prosperous career he fell on evil days when the philosophers were no longer patronized; he died in

1198. The Western line ends with Ibn Roshd, as the Eastern did with Ibn Sina: these two stand out across the centuries like twin mountain peaks, wholly different in character, yet alike in their general outlines and in a certain mistiness at the culmination. Ibn Sina clung to the idea of individual souls, destined to individual immortality. It would be difficult to find in that teaching anything more than a dogma; for the Reason is declared to be the real essence of man, and the Reason is that into which the Active Intellect, immense and eternal, continually flows: so that if Ibn Sina was not, technically, a pantheist, one feels that he might as well have been. Ibn Roshd went the one step further and surrendered the dogmatic point that the individual soul is immortal. His doctrine was known afterwards as Monopsychism, the doctrine that there is ultimately only one Soul, that the individual reason is no more than a temporary manifestation of that generic or universal Soul, in the same sense that Humanity may be said to be manifested in the human individual. This is not so much a religious as a logical doctrine; Ibn Roshd is not concerned to prove that God is in all and all are in God: he has followed out the idea of a universal or generic human Reason, which is not identical with the Active Intellect but is related to it as a Passive or Material Intellect. The basis is a dualism of Matter and Form: the soul of the individual is no more than the particular form which constitutes the particular soul, and as such it perishes with the organism. But the Matter, as eternal potentiality, remains; so does the Active Intellect, as eternal Form. These two continually produce individual souls, and it is on this eternal continuity that Ibn Roshd insists. An analogy may make this point clearer. If we assumed Matter and a Creator, the human race might be regarded as an endless material manifestation of one principle, Humanity. This principle would not be identical with the creator: it would have an intermediate existence made eternal by the persistence of its causality. If Humanity is regarded as essentially spiritual or intellectual, the position of Ibn Roshd is clear. What he calls the Material Reason is not the individual Reason, but a generic or racial Reason to which the individual Reason is related as species.[1] This doctrine is therefore not Pantheism, and its historical

[1] It is interesting to remember that Spencer said: 'It (consciousness) is a specialized and individualized form of that Infinite and Eternal Energy which transcends both our knowledge and our imagination' (*Facts and Comments*, 1902).

importance is due to the fact that its interpretation of universality was bound to affect very considerably any theory of the Soul which was based on the logic of universals. For this reason it is continually discussed by the later scholastics in the West. The idea of consciousness in general was ready to hand in the Neoplatonic tradition. The Aristotelian basis to which scholasticism returned in the thirteenth century was firmer ground, and the rejection of this pantheistic tendency was in accordance with the general character of Christian monotheism. The Platonists of the early Renaissance were not disinclined to revive it, and, in this respect, the course of history affords an interesting parallel to the development from Kant to Hegel, the former being more definitely Aristotelian, the latter an admirer of Neoplatonism. The true development of the idea of 'consciousness in general' is to be seen in the Hegelian conception of Spirit (*Geist*) and in the more scientific form given to that branch of psychology in the nineteenth century.

D. *Subjects of controversy in the schools*

I. THE METHOD OF SCHOLASTICISM

The tenth and eleventh centuries were a period of political unrest and the progress of learning was slow; but the definite beginning of scholastic thought may be assigned to this period and the movement of thought from this point to the days of Thomas Aquinas has a noticeable continuity. To understand the character of this movement we must always keep in mind both the matter and the method of scholasticism. The writers are not engaged in the study of man but in the study of theories; their first object is to defend a thesis or a series of theses; and they enlist under some recognized banner to carry out either attack or defence. The method, then, is the academic method in its perfection; encyclopaedic learning, and astounding subtlety are the marks of the great mediaeval champions: they can quote, defend, pervert and controvert with all the baffling dexterity of intellectual fencing.

The matter and the method are very closely united; for the matter is neither more nor less than the particular theses which are defended, or the particular meaning of the theses, or the definition of the terms of the theses. It will help us very consider-

ably to state at once the principal theses which fall within our
scope, as it will be obvious later that a treatise is really a collection
of theses, and all that we require to know is the author's attitude
towards each thesis. The propositions of the great masters are the
foundations of each system: fortunately there were many masters
and stagnation was not possible; the irrepressible pupil could
always arise with his list of things that both were and were not so
(*sic et non*); and that keen debating, by which the later scholastic
synthesis was reached, can still remind us that facts are not
wholly distinct from interpretations and that our own age may
well be charged with less desire for consistency than those
disputants.

2. THE SPIRIT AND THE BODY

Into the details of this physiological psychology we shall make
no further excursions. In view of the reports to be given of later
writers it will be useful to remember the rather confusing effect
of translating Greek terms from their Latin equivalents into our
modern (philologically very complex) terminology. The term
'spirit' means to the average Anglo-Saxon something opposed to
'matter.' Spiritual is therefore the antithesis of material. But in
the eleventh century '*spiritus*' was equivalent to 'pneuma' and
meant the material basis of life. Hence we find *spiritus vitalis*
($\pi\nu\epsilon\hat{\upsilon}\mu\alpha$ $\zeta\omega\tau\iota\kappa\acute{o}\nu$) for the spirits produced from food (aliment in
general): *spiritus spiritualis* for breath: *spiritus animalis* for the
'*ánima*' or highest vital substance, by which man is made 'animate.'
'Animal spirits' are therefore the specific *human* spirits and the
indispensable basis of sense or thought. The animals, as such,
have vital spirits, but nothing above that, unless the error of the
materialist is overlooked. On these points there was no general
consensus. The conflict of interests naturally affected the following questions most acutely:

(*a*) The purely ecclesiastical influence was exerted against any
recognition of the fact that mental powers depended on the body:
usually, however, the senses were left without defence to the
'physical' theorists.

(*b*) A scientific question was raised in the form reported by
Constantine: 'Some philosophers say the spirits of the brain are
the soul, and the soul is corporeal: others say these spirits are the
instrument of the soul, and the soul is incorporeal.'

(c) A question dependent on this is the legitimate question of a criterion of the higher life: if man is distinct from animals, what is the nature of that distinction? Writers in the twelfth century were quite aware of the nature and the implications of this question. Materialists (and heretics) inclined to be generous to animals: they gave them souls because they obviously had sensations, discrimination and voluntary movement. Against this the opponents urged many familiar arguments which all come back ultimately to a profession of faith: man has something wholly different from the brute nature—a *spiritus rationalis* or *incorporeus*. Here we reach the really 'spiritual' spirit. In spite of the rather obvious contradiction of the terms 'immaterial breath,' these writers return by sheer force of assertion to the confused mixture of Greek and Hebrew thought, out of which came originally the idea of a supernatural immaterial Pneuma. The Neoplatonic streams brought down this last and worst sediment of antiquity, from which the subsequent theories were never to be wholly free.

3. SENSE-PERCEPTION

The problems of sense-perception are treated principally in the form of discussions about the nature of 'species.' In every perception there is some effective relation established between object and subject. Aristotle had said that the senses receive the form of an object without the matter. The Atomists had explained the physical part of this process as the emission of species or images (εἴδωλα, Epicurus: *imagines* or *species*, Lucretius) by objects and the transference of these images from outside into the channels filled with spirits. Thus physical and physiological data were supplied; but the process of transmitting these ideas had robbed them of their meaning, and the earlier mediaeval writers did not grasp either the value or the limitations of these traditions. So long as men were content to regard the soul as a mystery there was no acute problem, but as time progressed the inevitable questions arose. The soul as a power of thought is 'indifferent,' and therefore it is necessary to explain why it has a given activity at a given time; it is also necessary to explain how the material process, whether external motion or movement of spirits, becomes a spiritual process. Between them these questions involve all the problems of modern psychology, problems of body and mind, matter and thought, image and idea. What the mediaeval writers contributed to the problem was, first, a growing comprehension of the fact that nothing could be attained by merely treating the physical and the psychic as two disconnected series of facts: and, secondly, an honest attempt to analyse the process of apprehension by the senses. It seemed to them that the soul must become like that which it perceives: for in knowing it knows itself, and when that knowing is determined as knowledge of this or that, the soul must then be knowing itself as this or that. The first essential, then, is a process of assimilation making the soul like the object. As the object is spatially distinct from the subject, it was natural to assert that logically there must be (*a*) the action of the object, (*b*) the transmission of the action, and (*c*) the 'passive' reception of the activity. These were denoted respectively (*a*) *species impressa*, (*b*) *species in medio*, (*c*) *species expressa*. The act of knowing follows on the formation of the *species expressa*: in other words, the external object causes the soul to produce an internal object, and we are said to apprehend when we know this internal object.

4. REASON AND WILL

On the subject of the inner senses (memory, imagination, judgment) we find a general agreement and acceptance of tradition, with differences to be noted later. The more important topics are Reason and Will. Both for the Arab and the European philosopher of the Middle Ages, Reason was the sphere of expatiation. We might regard mediaeval psychology as a theory of Reason without doing it injustice; it is occupied continually with exploiting and exploding theories of Reason. The cause is obvious. Aristotle had not been explicit about Reason. Augustine had given rein to his imagination, though moderately. Both might be interpreted, commented upon, and developed with no obstruction except that of opposed commentaries. The theological factors assist the tendency to make Reason the mark of man's superiority over animals and, in some sense, superhuman. This tendency, most marked where the writer inclines to pantheism, is finally modified into an acceptable intellectualism. The actual difference between man and the animals is then accepted as sufficient, and the powers of the intellect are regarded as immanent, not transcendent. Though this development obliterates the doctrine that a superhuman light shines in upon the darkness of human reason, the original Aristotelian point is not forgotten. That point, the real storm-centre of all the ages, is that the operations of the senses do not wholly account for or produce the intellectual life. The more ecstatic writers start from that point to construct baseless fabrications; the separated intellect was the beginning of a whole system of substantiated abstractions called celestial spirits; human psychology led on to angelic psychology, from which it was no great step to a psychology of the Divine Mind. The results were not directly edifying or psychological: but people too often forget that the terms in which a problem is solved do not always damage the truth of the solution. Though this literature is full of discussions about angels, pure spirits, pure activities and the like, it is obvious that there is really nothing in what is said that does not in some way reflect an experience. The pure spirits are described as having certain selected faculties, which thus become isolated to the mind of the thinker. It may seem absurd to argue about the ways in which angels can know material objects; but it is a useful way of presenting to one's mind the idea of an intellect that has no body, and, on the hypothesis of the scholastics, man was already half way to that state and might therefore rightly interest himself in thinking about it. In the modern contempt for this kind of speculation there is a peculiar mixture of common sense and inconsistency; a textbook of psychology that ventured on such themes would be scouted, while every hymn-book embalms the angelology of the Persians. Perhaps, after all, the contempt, in practice, is the contempt of those who see too little for those who see too much; at least it is most often the contempt of the half-hearted for those who take life seriously. To destroy these doctrines was to change the whole basis of Western thought: the rejection of the superhuman intellect was the removal of a foundation from a structure that rivalled the tower of Babel; when the analytic method asserted its sway, these transcendental realities were written down as subjective and seemed to disappear; perhaps, as we progress, it will become apparent that the disappearance was not so complete as it promised to be.

The Will is discussed at length by most writers. The point at issue is whether the Will depends on the Intellect for the knowledge of the end of action, or whether it is the Will that actually makes the true apprehension of the end possible. This is a question of great interest arising from the Augustinian formula,

'Believe that you may understand.' Those who said that the intellect took precedence (intellectualists) were right in their point that one must know the end in order to aim at it; but the voluntarists turn the flank of that party by using the term Will in two senses. In one sense it is merely a power of choice (*electio*), which presupposes a knowledge of the alternatives; in the other sense it is the whole trend of character, which itself constitutes the Good for us and so colours even the intellectual outlook. This was a deep and true view, but technically the intellectualists regained their ground by pointing out that the character in that sense was an illumination, and that the illumination converted knowledge into intuition, which being an absolute conviction, amounted to knowledge and will all in one. So that while one party united intellect to will, the other persisted in uniting will to intellect!

5. CONSCIENCE

Conscience was a subject which naturally attracted much attention in an age that was predominantly theological. The reflective consciousness of the Stoics produced the explicit idea of an inner judgment or personal conviction, to which they gave the name συνείδησις, the Ciceronian *conscientia*. In the sphere of worldly knowledge this inner conviction is simply the sense of rightness or wrongness in respect of judgments, and as such it persisted during the Middle Ages under its original Latin name of *conscientia*. But this did not suffice for the needs of the mediaeval theologian, who took more interest in the religious sentiments and concerned himself with sin rather than error. At the hands of various writers—Alexander Neckam, William of Auvergne, Alexander of Hales and others—there grew up a body of doctrine about a faculty called synderesis. The name was variously spelled scinderesis, synteresis and synderesis; there was some uncertainty as to its origin and exact meaning, Albert undertaking to derive it from *syn* and *haeresis*, the opinion that clings to a person or coheres with an infallible universal judgment. In reality it was originally the Greek συντήρησις and its origin, for the mediaevalists, has been traced to Jerome's commentary on the vision of Ezekiel. In that commentary the four animals are equated with the powers of the soul, the first three being the Platonic Reason, Spirit, and Desire; the fourth is alleged to be 'what the Greeks called συντήρησις, a spark of conviction (*conscientiae*) in the breast of Adam which, after his expulsion from Paradise, is not extinguished.' From this beginning the word became a technical term for consciousness of sin, the religious conception of 'conscience,' as distinct from a mere sense of intellectual error.

Though the term 'synderesis' was fully established in the days of Albert and Thomas, and still appears in textbooks of psychology,[1] its exact significance from the psychological point of view was not clearly defined. The ordinary term 'conscience' denoted a mental state which the scholastics divided into two parts: *synderesis* was the intuitive grasp of the highest principles in the sphere of practical reason, *conscientia* was the power of applying those principles to particular cases. But the persistent fusion between Aristotelian and Neoplatonic views prevented the scholastics (with the exception of St. Thomas) from being clear as to whether this faculty of the mind was due to nature or training: in other words, they did not decide whether it was an innate 'light of nature' or an acquired power of judgment. The Aristotelian bent of Albert and Thomas leads them to co-ordinate this moral insight with the intuitive reason that grasps first principles in science. But before and after those writers there was a tendency to treat the moral insight as unique. This was, in fact, the first phase of the long struggle over moral sentiments. Albert speaks at times as though it was a question of will rather than intellect, and that also was a point which was destined to remain in dispute down to, and after, Kant's treatment of the Practical Reason; while Bonaventura expresses the mystical (Platonic) view that there is in every creature a natural love of good and a natural remorse for evildoing: their inability to agree was purely temperamental. This discussion, more than any other, produced many fine distinctions, and particularly assisted the introspective analysis of purpose and of emotions.

6. SELF-KNOWLEDGE

A very important topic is discussed under the rubric, Does the soul know itself? This question may be stated in the form, Is there a fundamental activity of the soul as distinct from the mere sequence of states? The discussion is usually diverted to points that have a religious significance: for if the soul does not know

[1] E.g. Maher, *Psychology*, p. 335.

itself, its existence is merely a knowledge of things and it is itself (as some Indian philosophers had said) no more than a mirror of Nature. If Nature is corruptible and will finally pass away, the reflections must also perish and nothing will be left. The problem is insoluble, but its existence served to draw attention to the necessity of a regulative principle. Stated in a more modern form, this topic was essentially identical with the question whether consciousness and the contents of consciousness are to be regarded as identical. In part this subject looks back to Aristotle and the Arabs (the creative reason); in part it reaches forward to the later doctrine that a series of impressions cannot know itself.

7. UNIVERSALS AND THE SOUL

The controversy over universals, which necessarily occupies so much space in histories of mediaeval philosophy, dealt with a subject that offered scope for psychological treatment; but nothing was further from the minds of the disputants. The problem was not approached from the basis of an investigation into the actual processes of the mind; the Realists and the Nominalists were guided by other considerations. Yet the question was ultimately psychological; if the Realists maintained any form of Platonism, they could not avoid at least describing the relation between the real existent universals and the mind: if the Nominalists reduced universality to a quality of thought, they too were driven to explain how the mind gets the universal out of the particular and what is the exact nature of this work of the mind.

The problem of the Universals was both deep and wide; it ramified through every part of knowledge and affected every department of thought. With many of its developments we have no concern, but its relation to psychology is a vital point for the history of that subject, and we must halt for a time to review its different phases.

In the first place, what of the soul? That is usually taken to be an entity, an independent self-subsistent thing. But the question then arises, Is it a name for a group of functions or something over and above those functions, a substance that has or supports those activities? The Nominalist tends toward the position that the term 'soul' is a name for the totality of functions: it is not a *mere* name, a sound signifying nothing: but, on the other hand, it is not the name of something that remains, alone and solitary, when all the attributes are stripped off. The Realist takes the other road; there is a world of Ideas with which the soul has communion by right of its own nature; stripped of the senses and disconnected from the body, it may confront the Ideas or enter the presence of God. A deep chasm separated these two points of view. It was destined to widen as time went on; for the Nominalist became more and more occupied with analysis and the senses, while the Realist developed an introspective psychology; the Nominalists foreshadowed the coming of empirical psychology, while the Realists have their successors in the later mystics and in some forms of Rationalism.

The definition of Reason is the true centre of the controversy. Reason is a term that covers a multitude of notions, and in sorting these out the Realist and the Nominalist find themselves working in the same field. Given the Realistic position as to the soul, Reason has for one of its meanings the activity which the soul puts forth from itself, an intuition into truth or an inner development of innate notions. This definition omits the consideration of truth derived from without through the senses, and some room has to be given, however grudgingly, to those empirical truths. The Nominalistic basis, on the contrary, developed the idea that the senses are the source of knowledge and so tended to make Reason the highest activity of the sensuous intellect. While the Realists were drifting helplessly on to the rocks that make shipwreck of science, the Nominalists were equally liable to come to grief over the possibility of supersensible reality. The spirit of the age dictated the form of the question; the crucial test was the nature of God and our knowledge of God. But we need not confine ourselves to that aspect of the question; the problem is as clear, and more free from controversial points, if we take the laws of nature as the focus of inquiry. For the Realist the universality of those laws was manifest, and Reason was a faculty of universals; for the Nominalist the similarity of particular cases has to serve as a substitute for true universality, and he has to admit that he cannot go beyond that. In a word, the distinction which was afterwards expressed as one between intuitive Reason and calculative reasoning was already latent in the controversy between Realists and Nominalists. The progress of the question was dependent on many factors which only gradually came into action as other branches of study began to develop.

Lastly, we must indicate here another fundamental point. The distinction of soul and body which is implicit in the Realist line of thought eliminates the feelings; in opposition to this, Nominalism combines with its higher valuation of the senses a greater willingness to regard the feelings positively and not negatively. Owing to the erratic development of Mysticism, which at one time poses as rationalism and at another takes refuge in emotionalism, this distinction is obscured. We shall see at a later stage how far the psychological problems were affected by these different tendencies.

E. From Alcuin to Aquinas

1. ALCUIN AND ERIUGENA

While the East was developing the religion and philosophy of Islam, the West had been returning to the primitive levels of the Teuton. The advance of the barbarians had for a time checked the growth of that culture which emanated from the Roman Empire, while it could put in its place nothing but superstition and the simple grandeur of its myths. Then came the age of Charlemagne, the godlike hero who drove back the infidel, and with his restoration of peace and order we find the cause of learning once more in the ascendant.

The scholars of the ninth century are a peculiarly interesting group. During the struggles of the sixth, seventh and eighth centuries Wisdom seems to have fled to the uttermost parts of the earth. In the West this was Ireland, and it is from Ireland that the wise men reappear to go eastward and shine in the kingdom of the Franks. With Ireland must be associated England and Scotland. From these three emerges a line of eminent men which is really distinct in its character: it appears before the Arabic influence begins to affect the thought of the West and has a pronounced tendency toward (a) assertion of the supremacy of the will and (b) investigation of the empirical bases of speculation. At first there is too much dependence on traditional forms, and in consequence the points of interest are not sharply distinguished, but before long these begin to appear, and it is possible to show that there is a fundamental difference between the Realist and the Nominalist, the mystic and the empiricist. Then it also becomes apparent that the strongest nominalistic influence comes from

men like John of Salisbury and Duns Scotus, to which rationalistic mysticism is a complete antithesis.

Alcuin (A.D. 735–804), famous as the moving spirit of the
Carolingian revival, was by nature and circumstances chiefly an
organizer of studies. Among the subjects recognized in the curriculum of the period no room was found for the study of man
except in so far as this was involved in ethics and theology. An
original mind could have put a very large amount of psychology
into these two subjects, but Alcuin, in his treatise *De Animae
Ratione*, merely reproduced the Augustinian theory in outline.
With Alcuin, as with his pupil Rhabanus Maurus (A.D. 776–856),
the soul is the essence of the life of man, but not the basis of the
animal life. Thus the education of the West began again, under
the auspices of Christian Platonism, with a strong bias toward
supernaturalism and a predisposition toward the neglect of the
body and of nature. Against these disadvantages may be set the
facts that spiritualistic psychology asserted the unity of the soul,
that it avoided speaking of 'parts' of the soul, and was a good
basis for the introspective work carried on by the later Augustinian school of mystics.

The greatest speculative mind of the ninth century was John
Scotus Eriugena, another of those who were drawn from the
western islands to the mainland of Europe. His birth, parentage,
character and career are all alike involved in obscurity; but the
little that is known about him reveals a man well fitted for the
times. There is a strong likeness between this man and that
other wandering spirit of the next renascence, Giordano Bruno.
Eriugena was not, strictly speaking, an ecclesiastic, though the
distinction between the philosophers and the divines cannot have
been great at this time. Eriugena seems more like a rhapsodist who
has specialized in philosophic traditions: he comes as the man of
wisdom, to supplement the man of destiny, a point neatly expressed
in the statement that Eriugena was the Charlemagne of philosophy.
In his method and in his matter Eriugena carries us back to the
days of primitive myth: in him is born again the tendency to
pure romance which was the beginning of speculative thought.
But this rebirth is no longer a purely spontaneous beginning: it
has its background and its inherited dispositions: while it draws
inspiration from the most primitive sources of thought and
feeling, it veils its impulses in the stiff garb of traditional phrases.

A wise man must justify his existence by being useful. This primitive notion had not yet disappeared from Western Europe, and the metaphysician had not yet become merely a thinker. If the goal of life is the return to God, there must be a way by which men return: the practical use of the wise man is to show that way. He does not do this by example only, for it would be absurd to suppose that the way is the same for all: he does it rather by theory, the theory of the nature of man and of the kind of action by which the human may become divine. Here then the myth conceals a science of life as practice: the theology is the shell that contains the religion and the ethics, while the ethics is the approach to psychology.

When we come finally to the practical part of this doctrine, there is not much to grasp. Eriugena does not conceal the sources of his formulae: he is rather proud of his learning, and has for his authorities all the writers from Augustine onwards, chiefly the pseudo-Dionysius. But in spite of his learning Eriugena has a distinctive line of thought which marks him off from those whom he quotes. His thought struggles between two ways of looking at life, neither of which he will wholly abandon. Of these one is the empirical, obviously suggested by the Aristotelian element in Eriugena's education: the other is the Neoplatonic theory of logical inclusion, which, by putting the particular in the universal, made the unwary think that it was possible to get the particular out of the universal before it had been put there. So Eriugena becomes, as the result of his Neoplatonism, a realist and declares for the supremacy of reason. At the same time he keeps his belief in the individual, and is compelled to give a place to the will which is not beneath that of reason. These two are therefore co-ordinate, but in a sense it is the will that has the superiority, for the reason only lights the way, while the will is the agent, the power. No critical questions are introduced here: Eriugena has explained the relation of the deliberative and executive powers in the individual, and also preserved his sense of the fitness of things by giving the Supreme Ruler an arbitrary power of decision, the will of God above and the will in man below. This was the way in which the theory reflected its sources and its circumstances. It would be no gain to dwell on the more formal elements, and it is only necessary to record that Eriugena restated them: there is, he says, a *sensus exterior* belonging to the body and not of much account: there is the *sensus interior*, by which we have knowledge of the images of sense and memory: there is discursive thought, intellect proper, and finally the highest stage, the *visio intellectualis*. It is interesting to note that Eriugena calls this the real experience, thus giving strong expression to the fact that experience is essentially the innermost core of the spiritual life, and so anticipating the Victorines, while he has a latent idea that the difference between this gnostic intuition and what the ordinary person calls reason lies in the fact that the former is individual and the latter is social.

2. JOHN OF SALISBURY AND WILLIAM OF CONCHES

In the twelfth century the school of Chartres, founded by Fulbert, was the stronghold of Realism. While that fact is important for historians of philosophy, for the present purpose it is even more important to remember that the great men of this school were Platonists. They form a group sometimes called the Christian Platonists of the twelfth century. Bernard of Chartres (d. 1130) was succeeded by Theoderic, who had among his disciples John of Salisbury. At this period in the history of Western thought philosophical ideas were not precise; almost the only mark of a Platonist by which he could be distinguished was belief in an active principle in matter. This explains what seems to many students a paradox, namely the tendency of the Platonists toward a new appreciation of the world and its phenomena. Platonism, and afterwards the Neoplatonic teaching, had more than once been almost identical with mystic asceticism. Here, in the twelfth century, it appears as the parent and protector of the sciences. The movement can be studied in the work of William of Conches (1080–1154), who began by transgressing the limits of orthodoxy and, being reprimanded, turned his attention to the sciences. This is itself a curious point. From the Platonic basis it was possible for an ingenious mind to build up either a doctrine of the World-Soul or a system of anthropology. The former naturally led to collisions with theism and accusations of pantheism; the latter was a region to which apparently little attention was paid, as the Church had no quarrel with the sciences. From what is know directly and indirectly about the works of William, it is evident that he was a man of great ability and energy. Taken all together, his writings form an encyclopaedia not unlike the work of Rhaban Maur, nor very much in advance of it. The subject was the universe: cosmology, or the structure of the earth and the heavens, was the foundation: a doctrine of elements (earth, air, fire and water) and of qualities (hot, cold, wet, dry) was compiled from the available literary sources; Plato and Lucretius dwelt together in these hospitable pages, and their author subscribed to a doctrine of atoms which was robbed of its natural 'materialism' by being imperfectly understood. By this ascent through nature William arrives at the nature of man, which he describes with great minuteness in an orderly genetic fashion, beginning with the embryo, its development, its animation, its evolution into an independent organism, its relation to its environment after birth, its growth to the adult form, with the consequent narration of the anatomy, physiology, and pneumatology of the normal human being. The last topic, pneumatology, is the traditional doctrine of spirits, including those which subserve the operations of sense and thought. The material for the work is drawn mainly from Constantinus Africanus and exhibits no novel features so far. As a contribution to the literature of the period the work is important on account of its form and limits. It is presented as an account of human nature and human life which ascends from matter to mind, and is naturalistic if not materialistic. The highest human function, thought, is here closely connected with the spirits of the brain; the soul of man is 'a spirit which, united with the body, gives man aptness to discriminate and understand.' At the same time William does not deny that the soul is substantial, independent and separable from the body; he merely implies that such topics are not part of that natural history to which he limits his attention. As mental operations he names *ingenium, opinio, ratio, intelligentia, memoria*. The list is instructive for two reasons: it includes intelligence as simply the developed form of thought and therefore ultimately derived from sensation: it introduces as a datum the natural power of perception called *ingenium*. Presumably this term is equivalent to a modern conception of 'awareness' as the real beginning of mental development. For *ingenium* is defined as *'vis animae naturalis ad aliquid cito percipiendum.'* It is introduced as the specific mark of the rational creature, and seems by definition to contradict the whole tradition of a passive sense-receptivity.

But on these subjects William of Conches had but little to say, and we must remain uncertain how much insight into the nature of the mind he really possessed.

Other writers of the twelfth century were occupied with theories that showed an increasing opposition to realism in logic and a growing interest in the physical aspects of human life. Adelard of Bath (c. 1116) follows Plato and Augustine in his psychology, making the soul 'entirely independent of the body' and intellectual knowledge wholly innate. He travelled in Greece, Spain, Asia Minor and Egypt, and was instrumental in extending the knowledge of Galen as reflected in Constantinus Africanus. Abelard (1079-1142) was chiefly important for his critical attitude and his influence in bringing to notice secular topics. 'He fixed the attention of his contemporaries on the soul, its power of abstraction and its function in the genesis of knowledge,'[1] but beyond this he made no contributions to psychology.

The tract De Intellectibus has been ascribed to Abelard, but is now regarded as due to some other writer of this period. It has some importance as indicative of changes then taking place. The main topic is the distinction of conception from sense, reason, imagination and other faculties. The essay seems to be largely based on Aristotle, perhaps on the sixth book of the Ethics, with Boëthius as mediating authority. Emphasis is laid on sensation; all knowledge is said to depend on the senses: imagination mediates between sense and intellect, being a confused perception of the soul—a remark that seems to anticipate the later doctrine of confused or indistinct ideas. On the whole, the points made are logical rather than psychological. In some respects material may have been drawn from Aristotle's Analytics, which were then newly acquired.

While the author of the De Intellectibus opposes sense to judgment, John of Salisbury (d. 1180) inclines to treat sensation as a primitive power of judgment. John was a man of wide experience and keenly critical in his attitude toward the school logic. In his opposition to the formalism of current teaching he represents the first vague movement toward the outlook of the Renaissance. Seeing the barrenness of a mere dialectic, he emphasized the need of studying the genesis of knowledge, which means in practice substituting for logical formulae a consideration of actual

[1] De Wulf, History of Mediaeval Philosophy, E. Tr. p. 193.

methods of thinking. The soul is defined, in the Platonic manner, as simple and immortal; but all knowledge is said to originate in the senses, for sensation is the means by which we come into relation with the world of things. There is a world of immaterial realities which are known by the intellect, and absolute truth is attained by knowing the 'eternal reasons' (*rationes aeternae*), but the chain of faculties rises from the senses with no intrusion from without. The relation of the intellectual powers to the physiological basis is also considered, so that we may recognize in John of Salisbury a definitely naturalistic tendency, antagonistic to the Arabian influences.

3. HUGH OF ST. VICTOR

The scholastic lines of thought were not the only ones developed or suggested in the twelfth century. Two others deserve notice, namely the atomistic doctrines and the purely mystical.

(1) We have already noticed that certain of the scholastics were prepared to adopt atomistic theories in the sphere of cosmology; but that did not prevent them from advancing other views of the soul. The atomism of the Cathari and Albigenses was more complete; they followed the Epicurean School in believing that the soul perishes with the body. In so doing they relied upon the analogy between human and animal souls; as the soul was asserted to be in all cases immaterial, it followed that, in the case of animals, an immaterial principle can perish; and what ground is then left for making an exception of the human soul? This is one of the few suggestions of a comparative method in psychology to be found at this time; it would have been more successful perhaps if it had been applied to a more suitable topic than immortality.

(2) The mysticism of the twelfth century was given its classic exposition in the Abbey of St. Victor. Abelard's unsparing dialectic had driven William of Champeaux to the shelter of this institution in 1108, and from that time onward it became the centre of a movement which combined practical austerity with a theoretical and literary opposition to all rationalistic tendencies. The greatest thinker of the school was Hugh of St. Victor, originally a Saxon noble who belonged to a German monastery. He came to France in 1115, at the age of twenty, and in 1133 was made director of studies at St. Victor: he remained there till his death in 1141,

and was succeeded by Richard, under whom the school maintained its character and high repute till 1173. Mediaeval and
modern writers are unanimous in giving Hugh the credit of
making the school famous. Great in learning and in character, he
was not devoid of originality, and his influence was a constant
factor in all the later scholastic philosophy. It may not be wholly
fanciful to see in Hugh's temperament the signs of a distinctively
Teutonic influence; in any case we have here to deal with that
line of thought which runs from the school of St. Victor down to
Meister Eckhart and the German theologians.

Mediaeval psychology is so inextricably mixed with other
subjects that it is easy to miss the developments which emerge
from time to time as the writers shift the centre of interest. Yet
the germs of many sciences are to be found in the works of this
era, and the Victorines may be described as authors of a psychology of the religious or contemplative life, intended to be a supplement to the physiological and analytical psychologies which
represented the Arabian or Aristotelian influences. It is true that
their basis was Augustine and that they were themselves sufficiently trained in the teachings of the schools to be aware of their
affinities, but it is also true that they expressed in their own time
a distinctive view of the inner life, and by so doing made to contemporary thought a unique contribution.

Before stating the more introspective part of Hugh's teaching
we may notice that his position is primarily animistic. In man
there are three 'forces,' the natural, the vital, and the animal.
Natural force has its place in the liver and controls the blood and
the humours of the body. Vital force is located in the heart; on it
depend heat and respiration. Animal force is in the brain: that
part which serves for sense in the anterior regions: that which
controls motion in the posterior: and that which operates in
thought in the middle region. Hugh traces various stages in
psychical life, according as it appears in plants, animals, and
men. The soul is described rather than defined; in itself it is
spirit, but in relation to the body it is soul, and in that relation
becomes the possibility of vegetative and sensitive functions. The
soul is known through the functions which manifest its presence
—that is, through the motions of the body. But these (objective)
motions do not prove the reality of the soul: we must begin with
self-knowledge, and our knowledge of the souls of others must be

constituted in the main by belief. Hugh emphasizes the knowledge of the self as the one certain datum and as the basis of our knowledge of God, thus mediating the transition from Augustine to Descartes (*'Cogito, ergo sum'*).

While we may assert that the soul *is*, it is necessary to explain more fully the exact nature of its being. All that changes has some share in being, for the very continuity of change implies being continuously in changes. In other words, change requires for its basis a permanent reality, which (after Augustine) is declared to be God. God alone is the one self-contained Being: the soul is not such a being for it has a definite beginning, is allied to the changing body, and in its activities exhibits changes. But these changes, from ignorance to knowledge, from pain to pleasure, are changes which it knows: and since it knows them it must be a permanent substratum of all changes. Thus self-consciousness is the evidence for the permanent nature of the soul, and that justifies us in calling it a substance. That the soul is a substance cannot be proved by argument: the ground for that assertion is immediate self-knowledge.

The soul, then, knows itself to be an independent substance distinct from the body. As such it is spirit: all souls are spiritual, but all spirits are not souls; for spirit is the generic term for the incorporeal, while soul is the special term for a spirit united to a body. As there are pure spirits, so there are spirits that seem to be identical with bodies. The spirits of animals are not distinguishable from their material substratum; they are merely souls, principles of life, and cannot be truly called spirits: while the souls of men are at once spirits and souls, because they may be separated from the body. This amounts practically to denying that animals really have souls in the ordinary sense, for they lack reason, which is the distinguishing mark of the human soul.

The self-consciousness which proves the being and the spirituality of the soul also proves its simplicity. On this intuitive basis Hugh builds his definition of the soul as substantive, spiritual, simple, and immortal. He rejects the doctrine of a spiritual matter, maintains that the soul is indivisible in every part, and in general restates the principles of the Augustinian doctrine. In all these revivals of the Christian Neoplatonism founded by Augustine the salient feature is the assertion of personality as the central psychological fact.

The pure spiritism of this tradition makes all the more important the question of a relation between soul and body. How can the immaterial non-spatial soul have any relation to the extended material body? This problem was, as usual, given an extensive significance; it included the relation of God to the Universe, and the union of the divine and human natures in God. We pass over those aspects and confine ourselves to the nature of man, a mystery which Hugh thought greater even than that of the Incarnation. Hugh argues the point dialectically: every union of different things implies some degree of similarity or affinity: this is supplied, in the case of soul and body, by the harmony of the body: only when that harmony is realized can the soul be united to the body, and the harmony is then the cause of the union. The explanation was neither original nor satisfactory; it was an echo of Pythagorean doctrine transmitted through Boëthius; it savoured of the old doctrine that like knows like; and it developed automatically into a profitless disquisition on the 'number' of the body. The only element of value was the idea that the life of the soul (not the spirit, but the soul) is dependent on the perfection of the organism; pain and death are derangements of the inner harmony which destroy the soul by dissolving the union of spirit and body. We can only say of this theory that it is no worse than the physical theories of intermediation: and that the problem is not as yet much nearer a solution. Hugh really believes in a mysterious unification which depends upon the simplicity of the soul; that simplicity overflows, as it were, into the body and produces a unity of the body as well as a unity of body with soul. This union constitutes the 'person' as distinct from either body or soul taken abstractly. Hugh lays emphasis on this idea of the person; but he found no support for his line of thought.

We need not expect from the mystics any serious contribution to the physiology or the psychology of the senses. In these subjects Hugh is content to follow others: the tradition was well defined, and there seemed no need to do more than give the senses a definite place in the general scheme as a means by which the soul is roused to know itself and God. The case is similar with the question of desires: ethical distinctions take the place of psychological analysis and the doctrine of the Fall of Man colours the whole treatment.

The reason and the will are of more than vital interest to Hugh,

yet here too the work is more interesting as theology or as literature than as psychology. In the famous passage of the 'three eyes'
we reach the central conception of the mystical school. The soul,
says Hugh, stands midway between the world outside itself and
God within itself. It has an eye by which it sees the outer world,
the eye of the flesh; it has also an eye by which it sees itself, the
eye of reason; it has also an eye by which it sees God and the
things that are in God, the eye of contemplation. In the first
state of bliss all things were clearly seen, but sin entered in and
the eye of contemplation was destroyed, the eye of reason was
dimmed, and only the carnal eye remained clear. For that reason
men now see the things of this world more clearly than they see
the soul or God.

Hugh's description of what is included in the process called
reasoning has distinct historical interest because he makes no use
of the 'active intellect' as we find it among the Arabs and later
scholastics. His exposition follows more closely that of Aristotle;
the incentive to reason is furnished by the senses which supply
the data; the forms are received by the soul and the process of
reasoning consists in reaching at the meaning which the material
thing only symbolizes. Hugh's example explains this. The world
of things is a book which the intellect reads: the data of the senses
are like the written signs which the mind in a certain way receives;
but the written word is not the real material of thought, for by
means of those symbols the intellect reaches the meaning, a
spiritual reality which it can take up into itself. The simile was
destined to be a standard explanation of the difference between
the material object of knowledge and the immaterial content of
thought.

Reason as a faculty of knowing is only one aspect of the inner
life. If we turn from the outer to the inner we find that the reason
has certain qualities which make it significant in a wholly different
manner. The knowledge which we have through the senses is an
extension of the self; reason overcomes this tendency to diffusion
by restoring unity: where the senses are extensive the reason is
intensive. This intensiveness is the real content of the idea of
self-consciousness; the unity of the personal life, not the reduction
of all consciousness to a simple point, is what Hugh strives to
explain; the intensive character of reason is really a quality, not
another kind of quantity comparable to the plurality of sense.

The goal of reason is to know the self, and therein to know God. The three kinds of activity typified by the 'three eyes' are related one to another as stages in the progress to perfect knowledge; the understanding applies itself to the sensuous data, collects itself into a knowledge of its own life, and passes then beyond itself to the knowledge of God. Reason is therefore transcendent in two directions; it transcends itself when it goes out to objects no less than when it goes out toward God. In both cases the transcendence of the act is accompanied by assimilation, so that the soul progresses from state to state, not passing beyond itself actually, but yet always going beyond its present limits to a greater perfection. This temperate mysticism compares favourably with the more elaborate doctrines of 'intelligences'; it shows a clear appreciation of the relation between transcendence, as a passage from one state to another, and immanence as the abiding quality of the conscious life; we transcend our limitations most when we are most truly at one with ourselves. The distinction of transcendence and immanence rests upon the distinction of object and state. If we think of objects (things), ourselves and God, we naturally speak of the first and third as being outside us. But all objects as known are assimilated, and the knowledge is not the thing, but the inner state which takes on a quality corresponding to the object. The difference, then, between knowledge of things and knowledge of God is a difference in the quality of the inner states, due to the different conditions which produce them; the objects in the world are the conditions required for the production of sense-knowledge, and they are responsible for the resulting inner state; God is the required condition for knowledge of God, and His perfection is the ground of that perfection which belongs to such knowledge. In describing the states Hugh uses the terms *cogitatio*, *meditatio*, and *contemplatio*. As pure states these are not entirely dependent on the character of the objects; it is possible to contemplate the sensuous objects, and that form of contemplation is *speculatio*; but as a rule *contemplatio* is understood to be the activity of the soul in comprehending the supersensuous.

It is important to grasp the immanence ascribed to thought in this doctrine, because mysticism rarely achieves so critical a result. It is more usual to make the goal of mysticism an illumination from without: Hugh abides by the doctrine that the evolution of the intellect explains all its states. It is also more usual to express the goal of mysticism as a feeling which transcends intellect. That is a later form of mysticism: the mysticism of Hugh belongs to that phase of its development which is bound up with the belief in intellect as the supreme form of the conscious life. As a consequence of this, belief and will are made subordinate to intellect. Belief or faith is more than opinion, but it is less than knowledge; it is concerned with things hoped for and not seen, but it vanishes with attainment and intellectual vision: '*nam si vides, non est fides.*' The will is fundamentally a principle of movement; as such it requires an end given by reason; nothing is willed unless it is first known. Even in animals the idea, as sensuous picture of the object, is the root of impulse and the guide of appetite.

This position, though clearly stated, avoids none of the cardinal difficulties which it involves. The theological and ethical interests, so prominent in all the theories that hung upon the Augustinian and Pelagian doctrines, required some decision upon the question of free will. Hugh's position involves the old difficulty of rational determination: the reason shows the will what it should choose, and therefore choice is ultimately dependent on the light of reason. The Socratic position that error arises from ignorance is changed by Hugh into the doctrine that error arises from sin: but that amounts ultimately to natural depravity and explains nothing, while it leaves us with the persistent fact that depravity means inability to see rightly the truth that reason would otherwise grasp.

4. ALEXANDER OF HALES

One of the great masters of the thirteenth century was the Englishman, Alexander, called after his birthplace Alexander of Hales (now Hailes, Gloucestershire). He lived till 1245, a Franciscan teacher, honoured long after for his extensive learning. His work, *Universae Theologiae Summa*, has the encyclopaedic character common to all writings of this class; it comprises the Creator and His works, including in due course man, body and soul. His work has some importance historically as the chief point at which the Christian tradition is modified by Arab influences.

Alexander bases his doctrine on the idea of a substantial incorporeal soul, supporting the view of Augustine against the Aristotelian idea of 'Form.' The soul as substance is distinct from the substance of the body; the two coexist with apparent unity, though the soul is specifically that which moves the body (Plato).[1] At this period two extreme doctrines were under discussion, the materialism of the (heretical) atomists (David of Dinant and others) and the pantheistic spiritualism of Avicebron. Alexander rejects the idea that the soul arises from primitive matter, agrees with the Arabian doctrine of spirit, but refuses to identify that spiritual ground of all existence with God. In this way Alexander evolved the idea of a spiritual matter (*materia intellectualis*). While the argument is curious, the result is good; the soul is thus made an independent reality, neither confounded with body nor regarded as superhuman; in other words, beyond its being 'poured into' the body ('*anima creando infunditur*') there is nothing unique in the soul except its immediate characteristics. Matter is distinguished by its extension: the spiritual has no such mark. In this position lies the beginning of the later scholastic development, its maintenance of spirituality along with independent existence.

Following the Aristotelian scheme, Alexander proceeds from substance to properties. The soul is simple and indivisible. The vegetative and sensuous powers do not precede the rational soul, as some argue from the study of embryos ('*quod obicitur de embrione*'), but the soul itself prepares the corporeal powers and completes them; hence if those instruments are again destroyed, the soul still keeps its powers of sensation and imagination (namely, after death). The relation of these powers to the soul— that is to say, the relation of the plurality of functions to the unity of substance—was a standing topic and comes in due order into Alexander's scheme of exposition. The problem was confused at this stage by the fact that differences were deduced both from the nature of the acts and from the organs. So long as the rational, sensitive, and vegetative 'parts' of the soul were localized in the head, the heart, and the lower organs respectively (after Plato), there was sufficient reason for the distinctions. But Aristotle distinguished functions rather than localities; and such differences as might be said to exist in thinking and willing could not be brought under the other principle of local distinction. Avicenna and the author of the *De Motu Cordis* led Alexander to emphasize

---

[1] Expressed by Alexander thus: '*In homine est principium movendi secundum voluntatem non dependens a motu coeli*' (Endres, 205).

the physiological side of the question, the problem of vitality and vital operations. But he cannot admit that the soul is related to psychic functions as vitality is to vital functions; this (nominalistic) view was not in favour at this date, and Alexander maintains confusedly that the soul is distinct from its powers.

From this point Alexander goes on to discuss the senses and then the reason. The majority of this part is a discussion of earlier doctrines, guided by a desire to unify Augustinian and Peripatetic theories. The distinctively theological bias of Alexander's work is shown in three main points, the idea of *sensualitas*, the form in which freedom of the will is stated, and the emphasis on synderesis. The first is a term for all the lower activities, both sense and desire; the term *sensualitas* is meant to indicate that these all belong to the body as infected by original sin. Free will is for Alexander a faculty distinct from will and intellect; it is an absolute power of determination. Synderesis is a term that begins from Alexander to take a place of importance in mediaeval systems; its meaning has been stated above (p. 262).

The historical significance of Alexander's formulation of doctrine is due to his place in the development of scholastic thought. Equipped with considerable knowledge of the ancients and the later Arabians, he presents a union of doctrines whose incompatibility he does not seem to recognize. Where practical and religious interests guide his thought he is authoritative; for the rest, his compilation is crude and serves primarily as a starting-point for later dissensions.

5. ALBERT AND AQUINAS

The great names of Albertus Magnus and Thomas Aquinas bring us to the climax of the thirteenth century. These two created what we may call the scholastic synthesis. The time had come when it was possible, and very necessary, to create an authoritative body of doctrine. The process was mainly one of selection and combination; the greatness of these men was shown in their grasp of the possible solutions of the established problems and their power of systematic presentation. In the particular sphere of psychology they cannot occupy any very conspicuous place for this very reason; we have already stated the doctrines as they arose, and a complete description of these systems would involve wearisome repetition. Moreover, the unity of these systems is mainly due to the recovery of Aristotelian theories, now being rapidly acquired from Greek and Arab sources; so that the dominant feature, in psychology, is the Peripatetic character of the conclusions.

Albert led the way with a massive collection of doctrines that covered all the ground but fell short of the Thomistic system in respect of consistency. The comprehensive monograph of Schneider amply demonstrates his assertion that Albert really failed to produce any definite system; his views are both Peripatetic and Neoplatonic in the old confusing way, and even on the same topic he frequently arrives at contradictory conclusions. A brief epitome will show how matters stood.

The soul is defined as both form and substance of the body. The idea of Form is drawn from Aristotle, but the mediaevalists believed that a form is dependent on its substance and is annihilated when the substance is resolved into its elements; in other words, that a form is an attribute. Consequently, to save the soul from such dependence, the scholastic doctrine makes it a substance that gives form. As such the soul is, for immediate observation, the organic principle of life which cannot be divided from the organism; but it is also at the same time separable as a substance, and Aristotle gives place to Plato when we pass from the organism to the soul in and for itself. Meanwhile this much is gained: the soul and body, in other words the organism may be taken as the object of independent inquiry. In this way philosophy and religion acquire independent spheres or subject-matters; and this is important, because the sphere of philosophy is thus segregated and comes, in practice, to be a true science distinguishable from theology.

The soul is united to body, not to matter. It follows that a process of formation goes on prior to the union of the soul with the body. This process is the work of the *vis formativa*, a natural power which controls the evolution of the material body up to the point at which the soul is united to it. Here, therefore, there is a duality; the soul is a rational principle coexisting with the vital principle; they limit each other in so far as the soul does not cause the evolution of the bodily form, and the *vis formativa* does not evolve into a rational principle. Vital functions and intellectual functions are therefore coexistent but not unified; the animal organism is the instrument which the soul uses; it is the medium by which the soul completes its activities, as the musician completes his activities by means of the musical instrument.

Some interest attaches to this position on account of its partial simplification of earlier views. Albert retains two terms, body (or *forma corporeitatis*) and soul; but he has no intermediaries between these. He also rejects plurality of souls and reduces all the 'parts' of the soul to aspects of its activity. The soul has degrees, namely vegetative, sensitive, and intellectual. This repeats the familiar classification of Aristotle, with some elaborations derived from Arab writings. The vegetative soul is the form of the physiological life; it includes as its faculties the nutritive, augmentative, and generative powers. The nutritive power acts by means of natural heat (*calor naturalis*), which includes *calor digestivus*, *calor coelestis* and *calor animalis*. The first of these is the heat in the organism; the second is the heat contained in the things assimilated; while the third is in the soul, being vital heat. The augmentative power is the power of growth. The generative power is put last as being the final cause of the others; the end of nature is to preserve and multiply its types.

Upon the sensitive degree of the soul we hear nothing that is new. The outer senses are the five special senses and the common sense. It was not usual to reckon the common sense among the outer senses; but Albert does so because he regards it as their complement. The object of the senses acts upon the subject so as to produce an image (*forma sensibilis*); this is completed by an act of the soul which grasps the content of the presentation. While the *forma* is the image of the object, this mental grasp of the thing is an *intentio*. Albert here unites the language of Aristotle with the meaning of Augustine; in Aristotle the sense is passive, while in Augustine it is an activity of the soul; Albert has grasped the point that an event in the organism, such as the acquisition of sense-images, must be made the object of an activity, if sensation is to result. Thus, a noise produces an organic change which is the sensible form; if this is followed by a conscious grasp of the image, it becomes a sound.

The analysis here reproduced had been made before Albert's time and had given rise to a characteristic chain of ideas. Having introduced the image as sensible form, some thought it necessary to introduce another factor to unite the image and the subjective action, the idea. The more metaphysical theorists made light the intermediate factor, believing that the soul was enveloped in a body of light, and that this light mediated between the physical and the psychic events. That view Albert rejects as nonsense. A second class of theorists ascribed perception to another agency in the soul itself, multiplying powers needlessly. Albert believes that the facts are adequately explained by the action of the object on the subject, without further interposition. This is one of the instances in which he simplifies current theories.

The common sense, described after the manner of Aristotle, is concerned with the common sensibles; it also discriminates, and is the agency by which we know that we have sensations (consciousness of self). The vexed question of the relation between special and common sensibles is treated with some originality. The point in discussion was the union of the common elements with the special data; that is to say, the way in which space, time, figure, motion, and rest are actually given in relation with a sensation of colour, sound, taste, smell, or touch. Albert believes in a kind of reciprocal action and consequent union. The special object is perceived first by the special sense and then by the common sense; the common sensible is first perceived by the common sense and then by the special sense. For example, a coloured object is so perceived that the colour is first the object of the sense of sight; then the common sense perceives the colour to be extended: thus the final object is both a colour extended and an extension coloured, which ultimately comes to the same thing as a synthesis of matter and form in perception. On the other topics (discrimination, consciousness) nothing new is suggested.

Imagination in the narrow sense is the storehouse of forms (*thesaurus formarum*) and is also called *vis formalis*. The term Fancy (Phantasia) is used as the equivalent of *imaginatio*, and also in a wider sense to include reception of forms (*imaginatio*), production of forms (Fancy) and valuation of forms (*vis aestimativa*), or instinctive valuation of particulars as objects of desire or aversion.

Memory is not the storehouse of forms but of intentions. Forms, as we saw above, are images received from objects; intentions are activities directed to those forms. If, as Albert says, memory is the storehouse of intentions, it follows that memory is the preservation in consciousness of previous activities of conscious life. This is the Augustinian view. Albert actually accepts both the Aristotelian definition, that memory is an act of sensuous imagination accompanied by a sense of time, and the Augustinian idea that it is the equivalent of continuous consciousness. From both of these he distinguishes Reminiscence as voluntary recall involving the intellect. While memory is the reproduction of a particular sensuous fact, qualified by the sense of time, reminiscence involves the active reproduction of another idea related to given idea; this is taken to involve a common concept, related to the separate ideas as genus to its species. Since the generic concept is peculiar to man and involves intellect, reminiscence is an intellectual process and is not reached by animals.

The intellectual powers are divided primarily with reference to the difference of their objects. That which deals with probable truth is opinion; this is inserted as an intermediate power, in the manner of Plato and Aristotle.

The Reason (*Intellectus*) is the faculty that grasps the supersensuous. Here the important question in the thirteenth century was that of the *intellectus possibilis* and *intellectus agens*. Against Averroism Albert maintains that the *intellectus agens* is not a principle of knowledge outside and above the individual; he goes far enough to make all knowledge an immanent activity. But he will go no further. The soul cannot attain the highest truths without a separate, non-sensuous faculty which actualizes the passive intellect, as light makes actual the colours potentially contained in things. Albert thus retains a dualism in the sphere of the intellect. The process is conceived as follows: the data of the senses are illuminated by the active intellect, which thus reveals the universal element latent in them; the potential intellect, by abstracting the revealed forms, gradually becomes actual —in other words, the actual body of our knowledge is a growing system which is accompanied, psychologically, by a growing clearness in our ideas. This experience of the inner clearness and joy of intellectual satisfaction is the one sure feature in this maze of explanation.

For the rest, Albert maintains the traditional distinction between Reason and Understanding (*Intellectus* and *Ratio*) which had come down from Plato through Aristotle. He also recognizes the active elements in the life of the soul, the *vis concupiscibilis* (ἐπιθυμία) and the *vis irascibilis* (θυμός). In this direction nothing of importance was achieved: the treatment of desire and will remained merely subordinate to that of the intellect, even though Augustine's influence tended to correct the balance of interest.

The account given above of Albert the Great can be taken as applying in the main to Thomas Aquinas (1225–1274). The relative merits of these two writers have been variously estimated, but no one will disagree with the general statement that Albert excelled in scientific matters, while Thomas surpassed him in subtlety and systematization. So far as psychology is concerned, we cannot find much ground for the superiority usually attributed to Thomas: the ideas of the master overshadow the technical subtleties of the pupil. Their agreement extends so far that we may here confine ourselves to two principal objects: the first will be a general statement of the scholastic doctrine, the second, an indication of the last touches given to it by Thomas and of their significance.

The most obvious feature of the whole movement called scholasticism is the steady restoration of Aristotle's doctrine. After the earlier Platonism, Arabian teachings begin to occupy the scholastics. The task of assimilating Arabian psychology proves to be ultimately the task of annihilating the Arabian doctrine of the intellect. This step is definitely progressive because it ends with a clear assertion of the immanence of all psychic powers in the individual. Intellect is defined by Thomas as the faculty of intellectual comprehension; the importance of the definition is in the implied rejection of a universal, superhuman intelligence in which all human beings partake. From the given definition it follows that intellect is individual; each person's intellect is no more than the individual's actual intelligence.

After this cosmic dualism is cleared away there remains the dualism within the individual. The Aristotelian treatment of the soul is not satisfactory to the Christian philosopher. For him the soul must be both separable from the body and immortal. The proof of these points is not a part of psychology; the assertion of them affects a psychological theory in the consequent difficulty of uniting that kind of soul to a body. The difficulty is obscured by speaking of the soul as the form of the body, with the added qualification that the form is, in this case, substantial. That is the point at which the theologian forsakes Aristotle.

In reality the point is not of much importance. So long as the theology is kept out of the psychology, there is no reason why the analysis of consciousness should be vitiated by such irrelevant considerations. But the method of psychology is not conceived by Thomas with clearness; the true analytic method is mixed with the synthetic method of Plato, and, in spite of all assurances that the real unity of man is what experience reveals, we ultimately come to the question, How is the unity possible? For the powers of the senses and of imagination are organic, but the intellectual powers are not organic; there is therefore a dualism to be overcome, and some explanation must be given of the way in which the sense-experience is taken up into the higher work of intellect. Before attacking that point some preparatory remarks may be helpful.

Scholastic psychology, as we see it in the works of Thomas Aquinas, is rightly called spiritualistic. The nature of the soul is described in harmony with revelation; from this is deduced the nature of consciousness. The example set by Augustine was followed, and the testimony of consciousness to its own nature was accepted as indisputable. The knowledge of self is therefore primarily intuitive; the soul knows itself to that extent, but no further. The essence of the soul is not movement but knowledge; it cannot produce knowledge except in the way of reaction to a stimulus. The object known acts upon the sense and produces an organic change; upon this there follows consciousness of that change; the activities of the different sense-organs are united in the central 'common sense,' where there is also recognition of knowledge as distinctively one's own knowledge. In spite of the antiquated formulae in which the writer expresses these ideas, it is clear that the description makes room for a physiological process, a psychological event, and a distinct process of a higher order; these are, in fact, the nerve-excitation, the sense-perception and consequent apperception. The common sense also achieves a synthesis of all the elements.

In the days of Thomas Aquinas it was already obvious that the weak point in the constructive psychology of the age was the relation between the senses and the other functions of the soul. Thomas made a bold attack on the problem, but only succeeded in giving a description of possible stages in the transition from 'outer' to 'inner.' The material change (physical and physiological action of the object) is followed by a spiritual change (*immutatio spiritualis*) which is called the *species sensibilis*. This is an inner change co-ordinated with the sense-impression and constituting the significance for consciousness of what is (externally considered) an impression. This was no more than a reproduction of Aristotle's formulae about impression (τύπωσις) and qualitative change (ἀλλοίωσις), and may be regarded as originally an unobjectionable way of describing the genesis of some contents of the mind. But the distinction thus made between *species impressa* (stimuli) and *species expressa* (reaction and consequent apprehension) was destined to harden into a system of different entities and give rise to endless disputes which presupposed that the dual function here described was an actual meeting and fusion of 'images.'

The scholastics refuse to identify mind and matter. St. Thomas rejects all forms of materialism, including the mediating views of the soul as arising from the mixture or harmony of elements in the body (Empedocles, Galen). He argues that the intellect is not a form of sensation. The rational principle is therefore in no sense part of the physical organism, though soul and body when united form the actual human organism. On this basis we can expect no development of the physiological view of the senses; that was a task for which Thomas was not equipped by nature or training. On the other hand, having emphasized the difference between mind and matter, he treats the processes of sensation, imagination, and thought with considerable acuteness. In the main Aristotle is reproduced; the outer senses are described; then the inner senses, namely the common sense,[1] memory, instinctive valuation (*vis aestimativa*) and imagination. At this point there is a change in the nature of mental processes; the transition from images to concepts is a transition from the sphere of sense to the sphere of intellect. The dualism of the system obtrudes itself at this point. There can be no sensation without an object; also, there can be no thought without a content; but how the sensuous forms become contents of thought we are nowhere told. Scholasticism condemns by anticipation the doctrine of empiricism, asserting that sense never becomes intellect; it looks forward to the doctrine of Kant in its twofold assertion that sensation without intellect is never universal, and intellect is an activity wholly

---

[1] Thomas here diverges from Albert by transferring the *sensus communis* from the outer to the inner senses.

distinct from sensation. St. Thomas is sustained, in the last resort, by his faith; the problem is to be regarded as a mystery, and the power of God as Creator of all things can be the only explanation of the ultimate unity. This belief accounts for several bold assertions. Soul is said to be united immediately to body; there are no intermediaries, such as the *spiritus physicus*. The intellect is declared to have the power of reaching, through a process of abstraction, the essence of objects, which it then universalizes; a view which clearly implies that intellect and intelligible essences are created for each other by God.

A complete account of Thomas's views could only be given at the cost of repeating most of what has been already ascribed to Albert. The reader is asked to remember what has gone before and to reflect for a moment on what is to be developed later. We have here already the cleft between mind and matter which Descartes will be found developing later; we have, too, the Cartesian principle of union through God; and, at the same time, there is more than one suggestion of that later Aristotelianism which Kant so ingeniously elaborated.

Chapter Nine

THE CHALLENGE TO AUTHORITY

A. Introductory

During the first three-quarters of the thirteenth century scholarship was estimated more highly than originality. The work of interpreting Aristotle absorbed the energies of the great writers, and for a time little or no attention was paid to nature. Here was a flaw which gave an opportunity for both criticism and reconstruction. The times were not favourable to either procedure, but efforts were made in both directions. The problems of mind and of matter could be regarded as problems of nature, and an opposition to traditionalism naturally presents itself as an appeal to two great sources of knowledge, experience and experiment. From this point of view mysticism and natural science may be regarded as aspects of one tendency, for mysticism is based on the idea of experience, and science on the idea of experiment. Mysticism is represented in various degrees by Bonaventura, Gerson, and Eckhart; Roger Bacon and Witelo are most prominent in the sphere of science: while Duns Scotus, Ockham, and others represent the development of thought in more strictly theological circles.

Naturalism and mysticism are, in many respects, poles apart. Macchiavelli and Montaigne had little in common with Eckhardt. But in one basic respect they are connected—they both exemplify challenges to authority. Much of this challenge in the Renaissance period took the form of replacing a Christianized Aristotle by a rather self-conscious Platonism or of a sedulous cultivation of the pagan spirit of antiquity. Even Macchiavelli had an almost adolescent fixation on the Roman Republic and Montaigne often bores us with his classican erudition. But this return to antiquity was only one facet of the revolt. Men began also to look more carefully at nature. Leonardo really looked at the human forms which he depicted; their theological significance was of minor importance to him. Similarly Macchiavelli noted quite dispassionately what actually happened in the politics of fifteenth–sixteenth-century Italy. Religion could be regarded by him as a useful form of social cement. This attitude to nature was made possible partly by the declining importance of the Church as a political and moral force due to the moral corruption of the Church itself as well as to the rise of national sovereigns supported by wealthy traders and bankers, partly to the great widening of men's outlooks occasioned by the discovery of America, the improvement of communications and the invention of printing, and partly to the beginnings of physical science. Leonardo contributed to the sciences of optics and acoustics—the sciences concerned with looking and listening. This concentration on what is actually there and how we actually see it is significant. It explains, to a certain extent, the connection between naturalism and mysticism, the connection between the stress on outward seeing by a natural scientist like Roger Bacon and inward seeing by a mystic like Eckhart. They said in effect: 'Why spend years trying to reinterpret Aristotle when nature lies before us waiting to be explored by hand, ear, and eye? Why search for the wisdom of the past when the inner eye can reveal God at work in the castle of the soul? We can find out these things for ourselves; the key to the natural and supernatural world does not lie in the past. It is ready to hand. . . .'

In the seventeenth century, when these trends of thought found more coherent expression, there was little in common between the interests and stations of Francis Bacon and George Fox. Yet we find Bacon making explicit the method of careful observation as the key to the secrets of nature whilst George Fox proclaimed an experimental way of living guided by the inner light as the key to salvation. This stress on experiment and on experience were two different aspects of the revolt against authority, of the rise of individualism. The individualistic movement which culminated in Protestantism and in physical science had its roots in the thirteenth century; it was much more than an ideological reflection of the rise of commercialism. In its essentials it dated back to Socrates, Protagoras, and the early Ionian scientists.

The function of mysticism in the mediaeval period can only be understood by reference to the dominant intellectualism. The prevalence of Aristotelianism tended to exclude from academic expositions any real analysis of the affective states. In relation to the dogmatic theology of the later Middle Ages, mysticism appears as a more or less irregular offshoot; it allies itself to systematic thought, but always with an inclination to emphasize aspects of life which the systematic thinkers treated lightly. In the thirteenth century there was already a line of demarcation between learning and piety; and the pietists or mystics were strong enough to express their views adequately. In this class of work we find some valuable attempts at an introspective study of the soul and the first beginnings of a deeper psychology of emotions, principally religious emotions. At first this is hopelessly confused in method. The writers begin without properly understanding that in discussing such a topic as the love of God they must consider the emotional state and not its object. The theological bent of the writer often obscures the real value of his introspective analysis because his language makes no proper distinction between the psychological element of feeling and such other questions as the duty of cultivating the feeling. Owing to this want of clearness a large part of the work done is irrelevant to psychology and can only be treated by drastic expurgation.

B. Ethico-religious

I. BONAVENTURA AND ECKHART

In 1253 John of Rochelle resigned his chair in the University of Paris. He had been a pupil of Alexander of Hales and acquired from his master a taste for science which was shown, in his treatise *De Anima*, by the unusual amount of attention paid to physiology. No successor could be found to carry on his work until finally John Fidanza was elected, henceforth to be known as Bonaventura. He continued to teach for many years, became General of his order, and died in the same year as Thomas Aquinas (1274). Bonaventura was a Franciscan, and therefore belonged to a society whose traditions were primarily those of prayer and preaching. He was known as the Doctor Devotus, later as Doctor Seraphicus, and his spirit was before all things devout.

It is not so much the philosophical doctrine as the spirit of the age that we look for in the work of Bonaventura. The influence of the schools can easily be detected. Bonaventura was fully equipped with the learning of his day; but there is clearly another factor at work in the shaping of his interests. St. Francis of Assisi died when Bonaventura was five years old (1226). That was the period which produced the *Roman de la Rose*; before the close of the century both Germany and England had developed the use of the vernacular tongue; Dante belonged to its later years; in art, literature, and science there was new life in abundance. It seems almost a law of nature that under such circumstances there should be a tendency among reflective minds to distrust schemes and formulae: the stir and change of the world's activities enter into the scholar's conception of man's nature.

In detail Bonaventura clung to the traditions, but even so there was a choice of opposites. The Victorines had already laid the basis of a doctrine widely different from the Dominican systems. Bonaventura has not much to add to the work of Hugh of St. Victor, and may be regarded as a faithful follower of that Augustinian trend. Here we meet again the *Itinerarium mentis ad Deum* with its various stages and divisions. Here, too, we find the view that theology is practical rather than theoretical, to which the necessary complement is the high valuation of the will. Bonaventura begins in a temperate way the movement toward voluntarism.

Bonaventura's work remained a persistent factor in the thought of the thirteenth and fourteenth centuries. In the main it was no more than a revised Augustinism which gradually tended to reproduce the main points of the Neoplatonic teaching. A century later than Bonaventura, Gerson (1363-1429) vigorously supported the mystical doctrines of this school and gave new strength to the old Neoplatonic view of the inner light. In the meantime the German school of theologians had begun from Eckhart with a strong religious movement that was destined to affect the current of speculative thought in many different ways. Historical research has shown the importance of this somewhat crude expression of feeling not only in the religious life of Germany but also in that philosophic development which begins more formally from Leibniz. Eckhart's mysticism had less of the scholastic affinities that bound Bonaventura to his contemporaries. Though less refined and accurate, it was far more forcible in its expression of the idea of personality as constituted by will and feeling, while its language was free from traditional associations.

The inheritance of thought is inevitably also an inheritance of words. It would be difficult to estimate the amount of influence which is exerted by a well-defined system of terms; but there can be no doubt that Eckhart gained considerable freedom by using the German language. His thought still ran in the well-worn channels of tradition: the Victorines influenced his outlook; his idea of an ultimate unity of thought and will in a supreme state of love was neither wholly new nor wholly unique at the time. Yet to Eckhart belongs the credit of giving the traditions a new value. The word *Gemuth* may be said to mean what Plato meant by θυμός; it is hardly distinguishable from the Neoplatonic κεντρόν, the inmost point of self-conscious unity; it absorbs the function of the spark, *scintilla mentis*, which had become the key-word of mysticism. Yet it eludes exact equation with any of these terms and creates its own atmosphere, remaining as obvious and yet as indefinable as the term 'personality.'

We may agree, then, with Siebeck, that Eckhart marks a distinct movement from the scholastic doctrine of faculties toward a more adequate view of feeling. It would be hazardous to ascribe to Eckhart any definite conception of that doctrine of feeling which is associated with the names of Tetens and Kant. It is true that he uses very freely the analogies of sense and dwells on the affinity between religious exaltation and sensuous enjoyment. But such phrases as the Biblical exhortation to 'taste and see that the Lord is good' were enough to account for this, and what is specifically lacking in Eckhart is any adequate treatment of such psychological truths as might be deduced from these spontaneous utterances. The dominant tendency towards uncritical emotionalism which was the popular side of Eckhart's teaching becomes more marked in his successors, Tauler and Suso, and in his contemporary, Richard Rolle of Hampole.

2. DUNS SCOTUS AND WILLIAM OF OCKHAM

The opposition to intellectualism which distinguished Bonaventura and Eckhart appears also in the work of Duns Scotus and William of Ockham. Both of these great schoolmen were British by birth, though, in accordance with the habit of the times, their education was Catholic. New currents of thought were beginning to run in the English Universities. Roger Bacon was drawing attention to the study of nature and the natural sciences, completing in this way the work of men like Grosseteste: Oxford was opposed to the Thomistic doctrine, and its attitude helped to inspire Duns Scotus with a spirit of critical antagonism toward the great Dominican. The centre of academic thought was still in theology, but many divergent interests began at this time to enlarge the views of its exponents. Scotus reached Paris in 1304. Eleven years before (1293) Henry of Ghent had died after seventeen years of vigorous and original work. The influence of this teacher as a link between the days of Thomas Aquinas and of Duns Scotus ought not to be overlooked. In the main a follower of Augustine, Henry tended to emphasize the importance of the will and may be counted among the voluntarists. Henry also raised some acute questions about *species*, realizing that knowledge of God and the self could not be mediated by representative images. The doctrine of *species* had degenerated into a theory of images imported from without into the sensorium. In opposing this error Henry was only reinstating the original doctrine, according to which the *species* is not a passively received image of the object but a determination of the sensuous activity. Here we find already begun that struggle over the theory of perception which lasted through the seventeenth and eighteenth centuries. Though Henry made some advance in developing the activism of the Augustinians, he was unable to explain the higher mental activities without a superfluous doctrine of illumination.

The Scotist position is the most complete form of the voluntaristic doctrine. Duns Scotus struck at the root of the whole matter by declaring that the end of all existence is not the speculative knowledge of God, but the personal satisfaction which constitutes unity with God. Faith, then, is not an intellectual but a moral state; it is the possession of a desire which, consciously or unconsciously, moves men toward a natural good. This desire is the moving force at the level of sensation; as will it reappears to be the motive force in the sphere of reason. As desire grows into will, so all experience grows from part to whole. But if there is any real progress in this movement, the end differs from the beginning; the whole is subsequent to, not co-existent with, the parts. If the soul is known immediately, it is known in and by itself, *totaliter*. This Duns Scotus denies; we know ourselves mediately —the soul is not the only cause of knowledge: experience is made by us; for this making objects are needed; the soul co-operates with the objective existence in building up experience.

Here the idea of growth and development is vigorously put forward. The consequences are also seen in part. The process of constructing experience begins from the 'clean slate,' and is explained in the terms of Aristotle with the addition of that voluntaristic element in Stoicism, the doctrine of assent.[1] At first man has only a confused knowledge of the self: we cannot tell at any one time what will emerge from the depths of consciousness: belief does not require that we should know, but only that we act. Yet this empirical view does not serve Scotus to the end; some things the soul attains which are not given by objects, certain immediate truths which are presented to us by this theory without

[1] See *H. P.* i. p. 171.

explanation. The result is again a compromise between pure empiricism and a doctrine of the active intellect.

The treatment of the will as basis of right action is more satisfactory. Scotus makes a genuine attempt to explain the actual relation between knowledge and purpose. The cognitive part comes first; we have the idea before we consciously use it as means to an end. But there are two kinds of thinking (*cogitatio*); first thoughts are merely events, the appearance in the soul of ideas, among which one is clearer than the others. This is the material upon which the will acts; its function is to retain the indistinct thoughts, directing itself to them and controlling their relations to the central power of thought.

At this point Scotus seems to have attained a rather striking view of the problems which now occupy psychologists in the sphere of attention and apperception. He is so far from regarding knowledge as the determining cause of will that he speaks of an *intellectio a voluntate imperata*, not, of course, the *prima cogitatio*, but that which Scotus calls *secunda*. Beneath these thoughts which the will makes clear there may be many indistinct or incompletely actualized thoughts: the will turns to these and exerts itself to raise one of them to clearness. Conversely, with the cessation of the act of will, the idea tends to lapse from distinctness.

While this is a logical and perhaps inevitable outcome of a consistent voluntarism, it has some claim to be considered original. The method of exposition adopted by Scotus makes the point still more interesting for the historian, since it appears to anticipate in principle the later ideas of a fringe of consciousness. Scotus remarks that in the field of vision there is one point of distinct vision and many indistinct elements: he adds that if this is possible in sensation it is much more possible in the sphere of intellect. Making allowance for some obscurity, we can hardly refuse to admit that Scotus here intends to make the content of the mind equivalent to a confused impression produced by the object and a clear perception determined by the active exercise of attention.

William of Ockham (1300–1347) was a force in his day, but his influence on psychology was indirect. His nominalistic position (perhaps more correctly described as conceptualism) was essentially a plea for simplification. Ockham represents the final outcome of the movement that began with John of Salisbury, a sane and broad conception of the mind free from cloudy metaphysics. Ockham's life was spent in an age of ferment. The great objective universals, Church and State, were dissolving into a multitude of particular existences, and Ockham as a political theorist entered into the spirit of an age that was beginning to feel the concrete value of particularism and individualism. Ockham's ideas were embodied in his logical writings; he seems to have taken little interest in the psychology which might have supported his logic, and contented himself with rejecting *species* and asserting that the source of all universals was to be found in the mind's power of abstraction.

3. BURIDAN

Siebeck has rescued from obscurity a pupil of Ockham—John Buridan, who became rector of the University of Paris in 1328. Buridan is best known for his discussion of freedom, a new but inadequate analysis of the conflict of emotions. Here we are more concerned with a wider question, that which Siebeck calls the 'psychic mechanics' of Buridan.

In full conformity with the spirit of Ockham, Buridan emphasized the essential unity of the mental functions and the superfluous character of the earlier lists of faculties. Previously the 'parts' of the soul were quoted as comprising the five senses, the common sense, and then the *virtus phantastica*, *cogitativa*, and *memorativa*. Buridan reduces the first two to one, the cognitive power; with this he retains memory, which may be sensuous as well as intellectual, for he grants this power to animals. But intellectual memory is not distinct from cognition, for it is simply a form of knowing which involves a time-element. Thus memory is made one with the *vis cognoscitiva*, which includes also the imagination. Retention and recollection are declared to be identical in nature : there is not one faculty for preserving ideas and another for reproducing them, but power to recall ideas is dependent on the act of thinking, which is, as it were, added on to the acquisition of ideas by the individual and makes connections that facilitate recall.

Siebeck[1] further shows how Buridan discussed the question

[1] As I have not been able to see Buridan's work, I have relied for these details on Siebeck, *Beiträge zur Entstehungsgeschichte der neueren Psychologie*, Giessen, 1891.

of the 'span of consciousness.' We may perceive distinct things with distinct senses, but are the objects all equally clear? Every percept has a plurality of parts, but we do not actually perceive all the parts: we perceive them as a totality (as a writer would now say, a schematic whole). When the object is small we perceive the whole rather than the parts; but if it is large we perceive the parts better. What we perceive is in fact regulated by the Will, that is to say Attention—a repetition probably of the point made by Duns Scotus (cp. p. 295). In consequence, there is a rising and falling of ideas as they become relatively clear or obscure, a process which Siebeck regards as similar to the Herbartian dynamics of the mind.

Buridan further notes that there is an element of relativity in perception: grey near black appears brighter, while next to white it appears darker: in fact, there is no absolute value in colour· ('*certus gradus coloris*'). In this sphere there is a distinct sugges-tion of later ideas when Buridan says that a small change is not immediately noticed: but he attempts no measure of the incre-ments required and may be simply repeating ideas found in Alhazen (cp. p. 254). In his discussion of pleasure and pain Buridan employs his idea of mechanical interaction and points out that the increase of a feeling involves a decrease in the inten-sity of other feelings. The soul strives to maintain the pleasant and reject the unpleasant; its forces are therefore divided when both are present, a state of mixed feeling which Buridan admits.

There is an old story that Buridan said an ass standing between two equally attractive bundles of hay would be unable to move toward either and would starve where it stood. This is now regarded as apocryphal, but it is like other stories in being good enough to be true: it serves to show how clearly the mechanical principles must have appeared to be the essence of Buridan's teaching.

4. ST. THERESA

The renewed interest in man and in nature led to a fresh comprehension of many older doctrines. To this the mystics made a considerable contribution. As the best example is the work of St. Theresa, and this has been excellently treated by Ribot in his study of Attention, exposition and valuation can be achieved most adequately by quoting the passage from Ribot.

'In order to trace this ascending progression toward absolute unity of consciousness, of which even the most concentrated attention is but a very faint outline, we need not have recourse to probable hypotheses, nor need we proceed theoretically and *a priori*. I find in the Castillo Interior of St. Theresa a description, step by step, of this progressive concentration of consciousness, which, starting from the ordinary state of diffusion, assumes the form of attention, passes beyond the latter, and by degrees, in a few rare cases, attains to perfect unity of intuition. The illustration in question is exceptional and single, but in the present matter one good observation is better than a hundred second-rate ones. The observation deserves, moreover, our fullest confidence. It is a confession made at the behest of the spiritual power, the work of a very delicate mind, and a very able observer that well knew how to wield language to express the finest shades of thought. Furthermore, I must request the reader not to allow himself to be led astray by the mystic phraseology in which the observation is couched, and not to forget that here a Spanish woman of the sixteenth century analyses her mind in the language and ideas of her time; we shall be able, however, to translate the same into the language of contemporaneous psychology. This task I shall now attempt, endeavouring at the same time to point out the ever-increasing concentration and incessant narrowing of consciousness that we have noted, as they are described from her own personal experience.

'There exists, says she, a castle built of a solitary diamond of matchless beauty and incomparable purity; to enter and to dwell in that castle is the supreme aim of the mystic. This castle is within us, within our soul; we have not to step out of ourselves to penetrate its recesses; though, nevertheless, the road thereto is long and difficult. To reach it we have to pass through seven stations: we enter the castle through the seven degrees of "prayer." In the preparatory stage we are still immersed in bewildering varieties of impressions and images—occupied with "the life of the world"; or, as I should prefer to translate it, consciousness still follows its usual and normal course.

'The first objective point, or stage, is reached through "oral prayer." Which, interpreted, means that praying aloud—articulate speech, in other words—produces the first degree of concentration, leading the dispersed consciousness into a single confined channel.

'The second stage is that of "mental prayer," which means that the inwardness of thought increases; internal language is substituted for external language. The work of concentration becomes easier: consciousness, to prevent aberration, no longer requires the material support of articulate or audible words; consciousness is now satisfied with a series of uncertain images unfolding before it.

'The "prayer of recollection" (*oraison de recueillement*) marks the third stage. What this means, I must confess, slightly puzzles me. In this state I can only perceive a still higher form of the second period, separated from it by a very subtle shade, and appreciable only to the mystic consciousness.

'Up to this point there has been activity, movement and effort. All our faculties are still in play; now, however, it becomes necessary "no longer to think much, but to love much." In other words, consciousness is about to pass from the discursive form to the intuitive form, from plurality to unity; it tends no longer toward being a radiation around a fixed point, but a single state of enormous intensity. And this transition is not the effect of a capricious, arbitrary will, nor of the mere movement of thought left to itself; it needs the impulsion of a powerful love, the "touch of divine grace," that is, the unconscious co-operation of the whole being.

'The "prayer of quietude" brings us to the fourth station; there "the soul no longer produces, but receives"; this is a state of high contemplation, not exclusively known to religious mystics alone. It is truth appearing suddenly in its totality, imposing itself as such, without the long, slow process of logical demonstration.

'The fifth station, or "prayer of union," is the beginning of ecstasy; but it is unstable. It is "the meeting with the divine betrothed," but without lasting possession. "The flowers have but half-opened their calyxes, they have only shed their first perfumes." The fixity of consciousness is not as yet complete, it is still liable to oscillations and deviations; as yet it is unable to maintain itself in this extraordinary, unnatural state.

'Finally it attains to ecstasy in the sixth degree, through "the prayer of rapture." "The body grows cold; speech and respiration are suspended, the eyes close; the slightest motion may cause the greatest efforts. . . . The senses and faculties remain without.

... Although usually one does not lose all feeling (consciousness), still *it has happened to me to be entirely deprived of it*; this has seldom come to pass, and has lasted but for a short time. Most frequently, feeling is preserved, but one experiences an indefinable sort of agitation, and although one ceases to act outwardly, one does not fail to hear. It is like some confused sound, coming from afar. Still, *even this manner of hearing ceases when the entrancement is at its highest point.*"

'What, then, is the seventh and last station that is reached by "the flight of the spirit"? What is there beyond ecstasy? Union with God. This is accomplished "suddenly and violently . . . but with such force that we should strive in vain to resist the impetuous onset." God has now descended into the substance of the soul, and becomes one with it. This distinction of the two degrees of ecstasy is not, in my opinion, without reason. At its highest degree, the very abolition of consciousness is attained by its excess of unity. This interpretation will appear well grounded upon reference to the two passages above italicized, viz. "It has happened to me to be entirely deprived of feeling," and "this manner of hearing ceases when the entrancement is at its highest point." We might cite other passages to this effect from the same author. It is remarkable that in one of her "great raptures" the Divinity appeared to her entirely without form, as a perfectly empty abstraction. Such, at least, appears to be the gist of her own words: "And so I say that the Divinity is like a transparent diamond, supremely limpid, and much larger than the world." In this I can discern nothing else than a simple rhetorical comparison, a literary metaphor. It is, indeed, the expression of complete unity of intuition.'

C. *Speculative*

I. ROGER BACON AND WITELO

The years that divided Alcuin from Thomas Aquinas lie across the page of European history like sunlight between shadows. So far were these ages from being 'dark' that they seem rather to have been the glorious age that divided two eras of darkness, one in the sixth and seventh centuries, the other in the fourteenth and fifteenth. Before Europe plunged into that second epoch of anarchy and confusion, the thirteenth century blazed out in a last triumph of achievements. From the beginning of those five centuries circumstances gave a unique character to the progress made, and history has tended to accentuate that character by speaking of orthodoxy and heresy, theology and ecclesiasticism as though they were synonyms for mediaeval life. The Church was indeed predominant, but its rule was catholic and it protected all manner of men against its one enemy, the World. Not theology alone but all branches of learning were its concern, and not least the scientific branch. Yet the decline of this catholic spirit was rapid: the Inquisition was foreshadowed in the thirteenth century when Roger Bacon, the incarnation of the highest development of his century, spent his last years in prison.

Roger Bacon was not the beginning of the scientific movement: he could better be described as its last representative. Born in the first quarter of the thirteenth century (c. 1215), Bacon went from Oxford to Paris about 1240; his principal works were written about 1266, and from 1278 till his death in 1292 (?) he was shut off from the world in his prison. The effective part of Bacon's life belongs therefore to the years between 1235 and 1265. The development of European literature had begun to include a scientific line of thought with Adelard of Bath (p. 271), who translated Euclid into Latin, and the school of translators established by Raymond, Archbishop of Toledo, contributed some valuable material. Among the contemporaries of Roger Bacon, Albertus Magnus was honoured as a master of the sciences, William of Moerbeke encouraged scientific research without much actual knowledge, and Grosseteste was eulogized by Bacon himself in the expressive phrase 'he knew the sciences.' Nor should John Peckham be forgotten, a pupil of Bonaventura, a teacher at Paris and Oxford, and at his death in 1279 Archbishop of Canterbury: among his works were treatises *De Perspectiva* and a *Tractatus Spherae*.

A general history of the sciences would have to go further afield in this wonderful century and record many important discoveries. For the psychologist there is not much of primary importance. When attention was directed to experience rather than experiment there was at least the possibility of subtle introspective work; when experiment was emphasized the situation was more novel, ideas were less mature, and the very notion of applying experiment to the mental processes was not so much as entertained. The most important of the results are achieved with no consciousness of their ultimate significance, and foundations are laid upon which no one thinks it necessary to build. In a sense it is true to say with Windelband that 'the fruitful development of empiricism during this period was only in the line of psychology,' but to maintain that truth it is necessary to take empiricism as covering such widely different attitudes as those of Henry of Ghent (p. 283) and Roger Bacon. Some distinction is here required, and it will be convenient to consider as separate questions the special scientific movement and the general influence of Bacon's experimentalism.

Among the special sciences only one was at this time closely related to psychology, namely optics; and in this we have to deal only with the transmission of earlier achievements. The recognized authority on optics at this time was Alhazen (p. 252), whose work comprehended both physical and psychological material. In the thirteenth century the contents of Alhazen's work were given a new lease of life by being incorporated almost bodily in the *Perspectiva* of Witelo. The relations of the learned men of this period are well illustrated by Witelo's history. He came from the east of Europe, probably Silesia, and found his way to the more enlightened regions of Italy, in particular to Padua, where in 1260 the University was reorganized; later he journeyed to Viterbo and came in touch with the culture of the West, for there William of Moerbeke was producing a translation of Proclus; to William he dedicated in 1270 his *Perspectiva*. This work differs in some details from that of Alhazen, but is so far a reproduction of its teaching on all psychological points that no analysis of it need be given here.[1]

Bacon's work *De Multiplicatione Specierum* shows an intimate knowledge of Alhazen. Dr. Bridges says, 'Whether Bacon and Vitello (Witelo) ever came into contact there is no evidence to show.' Bacon probably knew enough Arabic not to be dependent on Witelo or the anonymous translation he used, and of Moerbeke Bacon had a very low opinion. In any case the two contemporaries, Witelo and Bacon, supply an element which is not usually recognized in surveys of the thirteenth century, and

[1] The idea that Witelo knew Arabic and made a translation is untenable according to Baeumker. Klemm errs in repeating that story. Witelo used a Latin version by an unknown hand, probably one of the Toledo translators, but perhaps not Gerard of Cremona, as Bridges stated.

was almost lost in the succeeding centuries. For while others were engaged on the nature of the faculties, these men of science had diverged into another path and were expounding with some clearness the principles of an associationist doctrine and a view of the mental processes which can be regarded as empirical in method and conclusions. The ineffectiveness of this movement justifies the belief that at the time it was no more than an incidental phase of a wider interest.

In that wider interest is to be found the ultimate significance of this scientific movement. Alhazen had employed direct observation; Witelo's Neoplatonism was tempered with mathematics; Bacon surpassed them both in his grasp of the idea of experiment as an independent approach to truth. Though still inclined to the outworn doctrine of the *intellectus agens* and a firm believer in astrology, Bacon had grasped some principles that might have carried him a long way if he had not been so sternly checked. The dynamic view of nature was one of those principles. Another was the belief that matter is not the inert recipient of forms, nor form the universal agency which develops the potency of matter. Bacon regards these terms as names given to the aspects of things: the things themselves live and move in a world untouched by dialectic and unreached by the mere play of the intellect. What applies to nature applies to man. Soul is nothing without body, body is nothing without soul. The individual is the real starting-point. To this conclusion the mystics came by one road, and along another road the scientific minds reached the same goal. On both fell for a time darkness and obscurity, till new circumstances once more favoured the onward movement of thought.

2. THE MYSTERIES OF NATURE

The first sign of a change from the disputes of the schools to the study of nature could be detected in the works of Albertus Magnus. By the end of the thirteenth century Albert was renowned for independent research and for a knowledge of things natural as well as supernatural that was one of the wonders of the age. From Albert the whole range of the sciences received a new impetus: the thirteenth century saw the production of a book *De Natura Rerum* by Thomas von Cantimpré, and the fourteenth century was illuminated by a comprehensive encyclopaedia of natural history in Conrad von Megenburg's *Book of Nature*

(1349). This wider study of nature took effect on the study of man almost at once. In 1501 Magnus Hundt, Professor in Leipsic, wrote a book on the *Nature of Man*, and made use for the first time of the term 'Anthropologia.' In these works we see the process by which the naturalistic treatment of man developed its later forms. It is impossible to read Hundt's book without feeling that it belongs to a new period. Its material is antiquated and its illustrations provoke laughter: yet it is inspired throughout by a genuine interest in the natural life of man. The whole economy of man is set forth in order—food, blood, humours, anatomy, and characteristics. The soul is treated briefly and in epitome only: the centre of interest seems to have shifted from soul to body and in place of a psychology we have the rudiments of descriptive zoology.

Throughout the sixteenth century there was a steady growth of interest in this study of man as a part of nature: theological modes of thought were thus, to some extent, counterbalanced, and greater weight was given to scientific pursuits. But the progress of science was hampered by tradition, quite apart from the sphere of religious prejudices. No one seemed able to approach the kingdom of nature without some prejudice derived from Pliny or some erratic legend from the *Physiologus*. In their eager zest for novelties the new writers were willing to credit any reports that endorsed old fables: sirens, mermaids, headless men and men with tails were faithfully described and elegantly depicted in volumes that are still the delight of all booklovers. An age of wonders was preparing the way for an age of science: imagination sowed its wild oats before reason could control the literature of natural history. The great work of Gesner[1] has many references to curiosities, but while he merely notes the reports, the later writers tend to discuss the cases as established facts. A profound belief in the infinite possibilities of nature was beginning to supersede the older ideas of passive matter and limited potentialities; it was quite commonly felt that nature might do anything, that it was absurd to deny any assertion merely on the ground that the thing was impossible, and what cannot be denied is always partly believed. The significant result of this was the realization that the dividing line between man and the rest of nature was not drawn

---

[1] Conrad Gesner, *Historia Animalium* (1551-8), one of the foundations of modern zoology. *De Anima Liber* (1563), confined to subject of senses.

so clearly as had been supposed. Awkward questions arose: for it was necessary to decide when a man ceases to be a man—whether six fingers are a disqualification, or inverted feet, or the absence of an eye, or the possession of two heads. On the other hand, are animals ever capable of developing human qualities? What can be said of the monk-fish or the bishop-fish? Matters were becoming complicated, and in the mass of new discoveries the ancient categories seemed inadequate. The problem of the nature of man in this new sense was definitely faced by one author, whose genial treatise will repay a little expenditure of time.

In 1574 Levinus Lemnius wrote a book *De Occultae Naturae Miraculis*. He adopts a very decided attitude on our problem: form, he says, cannot deprive a creature of the right to be called man, provided it is the offspring of human parents: centaurs and such-like are not human, have no rational soul, and no hope of resurrection. The last was the important item. If we read Lemnius a little further we get some more decisions that help us to understand his times. Naturalism is wonderfully developed in this little work: all the stories about monsters are accepted, but the general principle is laid down that natural causes explain them all: mind and body are both subject to changes due to climate and the different regions of the earth: humours, not evil spirits, cause diseases: even the power of speaking in unknown tongues is not due to possession but to latent memories, for if it was a daemon that spoke from within he might as well go on speaking after the possessed was cured of the disease. The spirit of scientific inquiry shows itself in the remarks of Lemnius on conscience. Conscience, he says, is most effective in the morning: the evil vapours are then removed and the pain of conscience (like a headache) accompanies the memory of sin: to confess the sin is to gain relief, for feeling, if pent up, corrupts the humours of the body: David usually repented in the morning, and he has testified to the good results. Conscience is very dependent on one's mode of life and one's complexion or constitution: sailors, innkeepers, tightrope walkers, usurers, bankers, and small shopkeepers usually have little conscience: theirs is a busy life. The sedentary and the melancholy, on the other hand, have too much conscience: they foster imaginary sins and repent unnecessarily. The young sin and are not troubled: the sick and the aged magnify their faults and brood over their deeds.

Lemnius is hardly a classical psychologist, but after the academic disputes of the preceding centuries there is a refreshing clearness and sanity in these observations. For they entirely give up the usual generalizations about the inborn knowledge of the good, and show the variety of human nature and human occupations. The curiosity which sought out strange things was not the only one to be found at this time: there was also genuine observation and a new power of seeing the meaning of ordinary events. The Bible was still quoted fantastically, but to illustrate rather than to prove. Above all, man had become a part of nature in a sense that can be felt rather than explained: and this was the case not only in matters of structure and diet, but in questions of behaviour, and the springs of action. From such naturalism as that of Lemnius we must look to the naturalism of Macchiavelli in order to grasp the whole significance of the new outlook.

3. MACCHIAVELLI AND MONTAIGNE

Beside the lists of faculties and functions through which the psychologist strives to make his subject a science, there is another mode of thought, more concrete and more vital, which has for its medium poetry, romance, history, and politics. All these agree in one point: they take the individual as a unity rather than a plurality, and begin in consequence where analytic psychology ends. The product of this method, whether a poem or a novel or a biography, may be a psychological work; but it eludes the psychologist by ignoring his mode of exposition; it differs from his schemes as a photograph differs from an anatomical chart. For a long time anatomists operated on apes as a substitute for human bodies; they learned much, yet were often misled. In a similar fashion psychologists tended to dissect a mind which was either prehistoric or had never really existed as a human mind: the fifteenth century corrected the errors of both methods.

For the new psychology that now emerges we have to look to new sources. It was created in part by Macchiavelli when he undertook to study life as he found it before his eyes. It is impossible to say exactly when and where this new way of thinking begins, but in Macchiavelli's work there is a definite exposition of the conscious life of man from a point of view which supplements, if it does not wholly supersede, the previous expositions. Dante, Petrarch, Boccaccio, can all be quoted as forerunners of this political theory; they all turned toward the living force of the individual and presented in their different ways a concrete picture of the inner life. They expressed the new idea that human life is a type of force, not a mere relation between form and matter. They tend, therefore, to express what has been aptly called the autonomy of thought. Discovery and invention objectified this independence of individual life: new instruments, new crafts, and new worlds all helped to make men feel that their powers were not limited to the mere repetition of ancient things; if they could create, they might think of themselves as creative. The time had not arrived for a comprehensive grasp of this fact; the point of view had first to be elaborated in the different departments of human activity. In politics this was achieved by Macchiavelli; in the study of life and character by Montaigne; in art and science by Leonardo da Vinci; in the sciences as a whole by Galileo. A full account of these men and their work would cover the whole range of thought in this era; the limits of our subject condemn us to the ungracious task of selecting from the mass of their achievements a few relevant details only.

All the work done at this time has two characteristics; in part it is a direct appeal to experience, in part a revival of ancient ideas. The relation of Macchiavelli to the ancients and to the scholastics can be expressed in a sentence: he turns from Plato to Thucydides. In a sense, Macchiavelli was a moralist: but he substitutes for the usual exposition of what ought to be a statement of what actually constitutes average character and conduct. To this extent Macchiavelli is a sociologist rather than a moralist, and his observations are the germ of later movements toward social psychology. But the essence of a social psychology is the consideration of individuals as social products, and that idea is not to be found in Macchiavelli. For him the individual is the first object to be considered: man and circumstances are the two factors which explain all events and all social conditions. Society here appears only as a repressive agency, from which the genius or the man of power escapes. Later theorists rejected this point of view, but Macchiavelli talked of what he saw: he expressed clearly a part of the truth, though he did not escape the insidious influence of too much study of Livy, with the consequent tendency to think first of isolated historical figures.

Fifty years after Macchiavelli's death Montaigne began to

publish his essays (1580); they became a literary force which has to be reckoned with in the history of psychology in general and in detail.

Regarded as a whole, Montaigne's work is an embodiment of the thought that there are no essences and no universals. An essence is an eternal and unalterable form of Being; but for Montaigne nothing is thus fixed or unchangeable. He turns from the idea of the soul to the idea of experience, not to dissect it and arrange its parts under given heads and categories, but to collect its varieties and show that their complexities refute all systems. It is the variety of human experience that charms Montaigne. He describes the strange mixtures found in great men: the fierce brutality and sudden tenderness of an Alexander, the tenacity and ambition of Julius Caesar alternating with petty vanities and absurd anxieties—and so rejoices in Nature's love of contradictions. When he describes freaks and strange abnormal births, Montaigne does not regard them as exceptions to the laws of Nature: he prefers to draw attention to the infinite resources of God, Who gives us the usual and the unusual alike. What are the normal and the regular, he seems to say, more than privileged cases? And this privilege is not of nature; it is a creation of our minds, the offspring of presumption. Against human presumption Montaigne rails continually; here, if anywhere, he breaks his own rule and proclaims a universal disposition, an essential vice. Through presumption men are led to say what is or is not part of the essence of God; through presumption they make laws for nature and marvel at the way nature ignores those laws; through presumption they define the soul, explain the self, say which impulses are good and which are bad. All these things Montaigne abjures. He cites all the different views of the soul ever recorded and deduces from their contradictions the hopelessness of the task. We do not know the soul, he declares; he adds that there is nothing astonishing in that, seeing that we do not know anything else 'in its essence.' In saying what things really are, people usually imply that which ought to be: there may be no earthly example of the definitions they construct, but this fact affects them not at all: what cannot be found on earth may be imagined in heaven.

It would be unjust to expect from Montaigne more than a mood and some illustrations. The illustrations are in fact multiplied to weariness: the infinite variety degenerates into chaos and palls. In refusing to aim at any system Montaigne becomes superficial; he goes far enough to see that distinction is not separation but fails to discover any way of expressing the unity which is implied in denying the separation of objects. We can excuse him for talking loosely of the senses and postponing the problems of memory while he tells another story; but we look for a real development of the 'passions' and resent the dilettantism that cannot be troubled to solve the problems it raises. Such is the case, and as such it must be accepted. The real outcome is a new feeling about the varieties of human experience. For Montaigne does not only ignore the headings and divisions of the traditional teaching; he leaves us with a subtle but undeniable feeling that they were pedantically foolish.

A few prominent points stand out as isolated contributions to the knowledge of man. Being sceptical of all dogmas, Montaigne is inclined to question the rigid division between men and animals: he repeats the arguments of Plutarch and of Porphyry for the rational character of animal behaviour. He is equally open-minded about the nature of theological speculations, quoting St. Augustine's words to support the view that in expressing the attributes of God man only expresses his own qualities. Here and elsewhere Montaigne clearly anticipates the main point of Kant's attack on rational psychology: the limitations of knowledge are a favourite theme of the sceptical essayists, and Montaigne recognizes very adequately the psychological character of many religious beliefs. He does not wish to deny them, but to measure them; they are forms of experience, and, as such, real. Conscience, too, is real; it is the product of custom, varying with times and places, as may be seen by comparing different countries and ages. Socrates had a 'divine sign': there is nothing unusual in the fact that sudden promptings are often good, for in some minds they are prepared by previous discipline and unnoticed meditations.

So Montaigne continues, ever changing from one topic to another, always inclined to simple and natural explanations, denying nothing except 'presumptions,' and unceasingly reducing everything to the plane of experience. It might be said of Montaigne that it was his function to bring psychology down to earth. That which was regarded as above the mind he reduced to processes or contents of the mind. He studied behaviour and was mainly objective in method. He studied himself, but in this, too, he was objective; his introspection was conducted as though with the help of a looking-glass; he tells us that he has no violent passions, that his memory for names is weak, that in recalling names he often sees only the first letter—constructing in this way an inventory of the characteristics which he observes and which he assumes anyone else might observe in him. In all this there is no trace of purpose; he does not undertake to mend his faults, he merely states what they are, that you may know one more variety of nature: he never becomes a mystic, his introspection is not of that kind: he tells you the disposition of his mind as he tells you his height or his complexion. On such deep questions as the freedom of the will he does not care to say more than is implied by a discussion of the extent to which the body actually obeys the will. The Stoic ideal, as an ideal, seems to him admirable: but personally he does not feel adapted for it!

While this indirect destruction of philosophies is the significant outcome of Montaigne's work, one other element has particular interest for the historian. In the *Essais* (ii. 14) Montaigne touches on the 'pleasant imagination' of a mind exactly balanced between two equal desires: he quotes the problem of choosing between two quantities of money absolutely alike, and says that the Stoics explained this choice between indistinguishables as merely accidental.[1] Montaigne objects that two *experiences* are never quite alike; in the sight or the touch of an object there is some slight difference which attracts, 'though this may often occur imperceptibly.' So in another place (i. 20) he tells us that the will does not control the different parts of the body; they have their own affections which do not wait on our permission: the motions of the face betray our thoughts; the heart, the lungs, the pulse ignore the central authority; an agreeable object spreads in us the fever of desire imperceptibly: there is in it no consciousness of will or of thought. This theory of subconscious factors is no chance element in Montaigne. He uses it to demolish the presumption that man knows himself and rules himself; he uses it to explain the Socratic 'daemon': he took it undoubtedly from Augustine, who had already used it to show that the body is partly independent of thought and will. The idea is of interest because it forms the link between Augustine's definition of sensation (*quae non latet*) and

[1] Cp. p. 297. Buridan's problem.

Leibniz's definition of apperception. It has been maintained that Leibniz was directly inspired by the passage of Montaigne's *Essais* (ii. 14) and that his statements reflect the fact that Montaigne spoke of the 'imperceptible' where Leibniz would say 'inapperceptible.'

4. POMPONAZZI

The various movements already described were paralleled by changes in academic teaching during this century. For two centuries a process had been going on which could only end in a complete revision of the teaching that satisfied the thirteenth century. The sciences of nature as distinct from man could go out more easily from the enchanted circle of authority: they were of the earth and might be allowed to return to it. But what was to be the result of all this ferment upon the belief in the soul and its immortality? This became the test question. 'Tell us about the soul!' shouted the pupils in the classrooms of North Italy; they were not to be put off with excuses nor satisfied with old formulae. The teachers as well as the pupils were in a state of turmoil over the new doctrines: for most of the chairs in philosophy were held by men trained in medicine: the leaven of new ideas and new methods was at work in their brains.

The honour of taking the most decisive step belongs to Pietro Pomponazzi. Born in 1462, trained in the school of philosophy and medicine at Padua, he became in 1492 the most prominent teacher in that University. The school of Padua was at this time pre-eminent in the world of letters. Its influence was not confined to one town, but extended over the whole of North Italy, for its teachers were transferred to other centres, such as Ferrara or Bologna, and through its brilliance Italy became the leader of the New Learning. The chief interests at the close of the fifteenth century were literary or philosophical. Science had hardly begun to assert its pre-eminence: since the attempts of Roger Bacon very little had been done, and the influx of new material after the downfall of Constantinople tended to make the men of learning anxious to settle accounts between the old interpretations and the new evidence. We arrive here at the last stage of the process which began with Alexander of Hales, and here, too, we reach the last formal dispute over the meaning of the Arab and the Greek doctrines. Pomponazzi's work was the pivot on which the whole system of academic psychology turned to face in the new direction. In the detail of his work there is little to interest a modern reader: his problems are those of the later Middle Ages, and his conclusions are merely decisions of the points at issue in the schools. The immortality of the soul and the true nature of reason are his principal themes: he had the courage to strike at the most vital parts of the enemy, though it must be admitted that this sort of thing was at the time quite in the fashion and does not imply any very startling display of boldness. In character the work done by Pomponazzi is controversial rather than constructive: we look in vain for any system, but if one turns from the earlier *Summa* to Pomponazzi there is a distinct sense of relief: so much is left out, and the blanks are so eloquent. Take, for example, the great questions of the earlier treatises. Is the soul immortal? Reason, says Pomponazzi, cannot prove it. Is the soul separable from the body? Experience never shows us that separate existence. What is the life of the soul apart from the body? There is no material for an answer. These and other similar topics Pomponazzi teaches us to treat with the eloquence of silence.

In the time of Pomponazzi the literature of philosophy was divided between the scholastic system of Thomas Aquinas and the teaching of Averroes. The difference between the two masters came to a head in the question of the pure intellect. At one time Averroism was favoured by the authorities, who supposed that it taught the essential affinity of the human with the divine soul, but when they perceived that the Arabian teaching was really pantheistic, they formally condemned it. At this juncture the influence of the classical scholars brought the work of Alexander Aphrodisias into prominence, and the point then at issue was the correctness of that commentator's version of Aristotle. In this confusion of opinions Pomponazzi undertook to explain the real meaning of Aristotle. The result was original in one sense, for Pomponazzi undoubtedly restated the teaching of the *De Anima* in a forceful and adequate way. The difference which still remained between the original Aristotle and the new version need not detain us: for the purposes of history it is more important to consider what notions Pomponazzi brought into vogue and how far they represent any material gain for the theory of mental processes.

In his treatment of sensation Pomponazzi succeeds in removing part of the errors that had crept into the doctrine of species. The point here was simply the question whether the sensible object should be spoken of as something passively received and afterwards apprehended, or whether the sensation and the sensible species should be identified. The latter alternative, which Pomponazzi supports in agreement with the trend of nominalistic psychology, amounts to a clearer appreciation of the distinction between physical things or organic processes and the psychic results. In adopting this position Pomponazzi at least came nearer to the original meaning of Aristotle, namely, that the object of sense is actualized along with the sensation, and is to be described, when regarded as purely objective, as potentially sensible. Instead, then, of supposing that the object produces a species or copy of itself and that this species is the real cause of sensation, Pomponazzi goes back to the view that sense is an activity not caused by but conditioned by the presence of objects. This implies not only a direct relation between mind and its objects, but also a close union between mind and body. For the whole doctrine of species had been required in order to bring together mind and matter, the spiritual as something superior and the material as inferior. Pomponazzi adopts a subtle and at the same time a very sound view of the relation between mind and body. For all the functions of sense body is required: there is therefore a close union, but not such an absorption of mind in body as to justify materialism. Some functions of the mind, Pomponazzi thinks, do not require physical organs, and it would therefore be wrong to speak of the soul as material. On the other hand, even these higher functions, abstract thought and the work of the intellect, do not carry us beyond the proper sphere of human experience: they imply no superhuman power operating from without, but are simply those operations of the intellect by which we see clearly that there is activity as well as passivity, and that consciousness is a real datum.

It was natural that Pomponazzi should find himself in difficulties over the question of substance. It was almost impossible at that time to declare anything to be an independent existent without committing oneself to the idea of substance. Yet Pomponazzi is inclined to regard substance as an inference, and not as the separate object of an intuition. It is not so much an object of the common sense as something given in the separate senses and then eliminated as common to them. In the general description of the senses Pomponazzi adds nothing to Aristotle, but he makes a criticism of the Arabian scheme of faculties which has some importance. The point which Pomponazzi is most anxious to maintain is that the soul is both mortal and immortal: mortal because it requires for all its functions the immediate or mediate basis of experience (immediate in sense, mediate in *cogitatio*), immortal because it is not the product but the presupposition of all experience. Pomponazzi interprets the famous saying of Aristotle, that reason comes from without, to mean that it is not conceivable as the product of the organism or as the result of sense-experience. This was probably what Aristotle did mean: in any case Pomponazzi did well to insist that reason was immanent in man as a function, and that consciousness has an independent existence as known, though it is always 'immersed in matter.'

To the objector who would maintain that there was no possible union between a spiritual and a material nature Pomponazzi had a ready answer. The list of powers which was usually accepted included the *vis cogitativa*. This had been inserted between the imagination and intellect as a kind of intellectual process distinguished from the intellect itself by the inferiority of its occupations. It was easy to point out that the admission of this power really undermined all objection to a union between intellect and matter: in spite of its difference of degree the *vis cogitativa* was essentially intellectual. The other argument was no less valid, though not so keen a dialectical weapon. If, says Pomponazzi, soul and body are divided, no power can reunite them. 'Soul and body would have no greater unity than the oxen and the plough.'

The simplification of the doctrines of sense and of intellect is the most distinctive part of Pomponazzi's work. Many other points were treated with freshness and vigour, but they were not new. What Pomponazzi has to say on attention, e.g., is merely the Stoic doctrine of the tension of spirits: the peculiar grading of animals which recognizes higher and lower levels of the animal consciousness is also Stoic. These and similar points which have been noticed as original points in Pomponazzi by his admirers are now, with more adequate knowledge of the Arabian systems, seen to be no more than a proof that Pomponazzi was essentially a scholar, and wrote with a genuine respect for experience, but not with any store of new details drawn from observation.

D. Medical

1. VESALIUS AND HARVEY

The general tendency which has been described above required for its advancement a radical change in the scientific description of the human body. In this department of knowledge the work of Mondino had remained since the fourteenth century a solitary monument. At the beginning of the sixteenth century the dissection of human bodies was more freely permitted and some progress was accordingly made. In 1510 Sylvius discovered the 'Fossa Sylvii,' and in 1518 Berengar von Carpi gave the first description of the conjunctiva, but the originality to which these discoveries testify was united with a persistent belief in the infallibility of Galen and no radical change was made until Vesalius appeared. The great work of Vesalius, *De Humani Corporis Fabrica*, was produced in 1543: it came after the days of Sylvius and after the discovery by Servetus of the lesser circulation of the blood: the pupils of Vesalius were able to find errors and omissions in his work, so that it is obvious that, without detracting from the courage or the acuteness of Vesalius, we may recognize that the time was ripe for new developments. The progress was rapid; artists were engaged to prepare anatomical charts that exhibited the organs with commendable exactness: the nerves were at last separated from the tendons and ligaments and traced along their various courses: the fiction of the bone in the heart, so long handed on from generation to generation, was destroyed by the simple process of observation: the walls of the chambers of the heart were declared, against the received authorities, not to be porous. As this last discovery proved that the blood did not travel through the walls, it was necessary to look for some other explanation of its movements. Servetus solved part of the problem: Fabricius came wonderfully near solving the other part, but it was the pupil of Fabricius, Harvey, who proposed the idea of circulation and demonstrated its superiority over the earlier ideas of ebb and flow. The numerous problems which had been slowly making the old ideas untenable were now solved by a new formula.

Great discoveries are often accepted slowly, but their greatness is shown by the way in which they penetrate every department of knowledge. Harvey's discovery made his contemporaries ask themselves how much of the current teaching on any subject would stand such shocks as this. In particular the doctrine of Galen had been the mainstay of the ancient idea of the airs in the body, concocted in the heart and distributed over the body by the arteries. The new doctrine of the body and of the circulation left no room for these fancies, but time was needed before each separate consequence of the new theory could be realized and valued. In spite of all that was implied in the new doctrine we find the old doctrine of spirits continuing to flourish. This was more a matter of neurology, but here too there seems to have been great progress and yet little radical improvement. The crucial point in the teaching of Galen was the question of the difference between the motor and sensory nerves. Galen explained the difference of function as equivalent to difference of structure, the nerves of motion being hard and those of sensation soft. No progress was made beyond this point until Rondeletius (*c.* 1550) declared that all nerves are isolated from one another, that they proceed uninterruptedly from the brain to the extremity, and consequently that all cases of paralysis are to be explained by obstruction of the nerve and not by condition of the spinal marrow. The statements made by Rondeletius were experimentally demonstrated by Laurentius, without further progress being made. Then Varolius showed that the spinal cord was not a simple prolongation of the cerebellum, but composed of four distinct parts, two originating in the cerebrum and two in the cerebellum. Finally, Laurentius and others noticed that the spinal nerves have double roots and that the nerves develop into knots or ganglia after leaving the cord. Yet the distinction of the sensory and motor nerves as nerves that arise from different roots was not made for another century and not fully accepted till fifty years later.

2. VILLANOVA AND PARACELSUS

The revolt against authority in the sphere of medicine led in many cases to the revival of contrary opinions that had no great merit to recommend them. The return to nature introduced the minds of men to a world beyond their grasp: the emancipated thinkers plunged into premature attempts to comprehend man and the universe in one formula. The result was a chaos of ideas drawn from all sources and a fantastic semblance of system. Some of the authors of these systems were primarily concerned with occult medicine, others with the pure speculative interest in the interpretation of the harmony of the universe. The theory and system of occult medicine rested on the assumption of the *spiritus*, the vital spirits in man. Roger Bacon stated the principles of this occult therapy in a way that showed clearly how it arose from the belief that a magnetic fluid resides in the body and that sympathy is a real bond of unity between different bodies. Arnauld de Villanova, who lived during the last half of the thirteenth century and was among other things a doctor, gave much attention to this theory of spirits. To understand the importance of this movement it is necessary to remember that it was opposed to the current belief that the treatment of the sick should be regulated by the times and seasons. Incredible as it seems, there is little doubt that the professional doctor did not require to see his patient or diagnose his condition: the prescription was regulated by the date of the month and other attendant but irrelevant circumstances. To the modern reader the occult therapist seems fantastic: we miss the point that he was returning to the actual observation of conditions, and that if he spoke of spirits that did not exist he none the less was in immediate touch with the object of his study. Arnauld undoubtedly represents a movement in medical science akin to that started by Roger Bacon in physical science, but in theory he does not go beyond the common idea of a relation between macrocosm and microcosm such as had been taught by Hippocrates: the real development of the doctrine of spirits was postponed till the sixteenth century.

The most bizarre and exotic figure of the sixteenth century was Paracelsus. No less than his famous contemporaries he took the entire universe as the particular subject of his researches. He touched upon all things, adorned most of them with new titles and obscured as much as he revealed. It is not the achievement but the spirit of the man that commends him to history: the noisy, quarrelsome, opinionated, cheese-fed countryman thundered out his views on God, the Universe, and Man in a way that could not be ignored. His views can only be judged relatively; we must see them on the background of scholasticism to appreciate their value. There is hardly a trace of the usual arrangement of things or the usual divisions. The universe as a whole is divided into the Creator and the created: the created world includes the celestial and the terrestrial spheres, so that men have three kinds of knowledge, corresponding to these three objects. These kinds are knowledge from the flesh (senses), knowledge from the stars (science) and knowledge from God (spiritual). The terminology is in the best style of obscurantism, but the explanations are reassuring. Knowledge of God rests on purity of heart: the condition required here is the moral disposition, that Faith which Augustine before, and Luther in this generation, made the basis of the religious life. Knowledge of nature rests on the combination of theory and practice: experience is the only source of knowledge about the things of the world, but Paracelsus does not mean by experience the mere accession of sensations. For him experience is the life of thought, not altogether a common thing, because there is something about the man of genius that makes him distinct from the common herd: everyone can look at things, but only the elect can see the hidden reality of them: in brief, genius is not to be explained merely by training and circumstances. Paracelsus himself must have felt that there was something to justify this opinion in his own career, the career of a man born to make much out of every chance occasion, to see where others saw nothing, above all to produce continually ideas and theories that seemed to have no connection with the times and places of his life.

The doctrine by which Paracelsus is best known is that of the *Archaeus*, or occult vital force. The soul, according to Paracelsus, is the breath of God in man, as stated by Moses, Plato, the Stoics, the Cabbalah, and other authorities! With this the practical science of man has nothing to do. Over against it is set the system of natural powers, as distinct from the supernatural power of the soul. Here the divergence from the teaching of the schools consists in the fact that the material part of man is given a real independent existence: it is not matter as dead and formless, but matter as the womb of all things created. This is the characteristic note of this naturalism, the common distinction which all the expositions share. The system of the *Archaei* was a crude and fantastic way of expounding this notion, which we shall find repeated in other forms in the later history of vitalism.

3. CARDANUS, TELESIUS, CAMPANELLA, AND
   SCALIGER

To talk of the system of Paracelsus is to argue oneself deficient in the sense of humour. He neither planned nor chanced to produce a system. Others, however, did come nearer to that achievement, either by design or by accident. Of these Cardanus, Telesius, and Campanella are three well-known examples, very typical of the large designs and incomplete structures that belong to this period. The works of Cardanus include all possible subjects, natural and supernatural. Much he writes is flagrant nonsense which the author does not seem to believe himself: he wavers particularly between his emotional belief in all manner of spirits and his professional medical opinion that the recorded ghosts or incubi are to be explained by pathology. We should be disposed to pass over Cardanus as somewhat too erratic to be trusted if it were not that he had a genius for detail, made a reputation that still endures in the history of mathematics, and was a distinct force in the seventeenth century. Cardanus has nothing to tell us about psychology in the ordinary sense: his outlook is purely objective, and what he has to say about the light of God in the mind is an echo of earlier writings. It is on such a subject as language that Cardanus is able to distinguish himself. Having travelled all over Europe and in Scotland, he was in a position to realize the different varieties of intonation and detect in them the signs of the gradual development of human speech. Languages, he tells us, differ through climate and through habit: the use of language is to express the movements of the soul according to the distinct genius of each nation. This was no more than a hint toward a science of language, but it was a hint not entirely lost. Cardanus was also the author of the rather peculiar division of human faculties into the three classes memory, reason, and imagination which was adopted by Francis Bacon as the basis of his classification of the sciences. This classification is probably meant to distinguish between experience, the process of reason which completes experience, and the productive imagination: we shall have occasion to notice again the tendency to use memory as equivalent to sense-presentations consciously perceived.

Cardanus, Telesius, and Campanella present a distinct cycle of thought passing through a very typical form of evolution. Cardanus is predominantly objective and gives no account of the processes of the mind when it thinks. Telesius shares with the others the general naturalism of the Italian schools, a naturalism which had its home in Italy but was shared by all the wandering scholars and magicians of the age. But the striving after system is

more apparent in Telesius, and with it there is a greater consciousness of the need for a theory of mental action and of knowledge. Man, we are told, is distinct from the animals because of a
certain *substantia immissa*: in animals there is only the seminal
spirit, and this is clearly required also in man, as is evident from
his corporeal structure and physical needs. Thus in man there are
two kinds of spirits, two distinct agencies, not merely a soul
united with matter, but material spirits and something of a higher
nature. The latter can be ignored while we consider the corporeal
life of man, and so drops out of all serious consideration. This
was the standard method of avoiding the theological part of the
doctrine of man. Once fairly rid of the supernatural, Telesius
begins to develop a very independent theory of the functions of
the organism. In animals, nerves have channels: these must be
full of something: it is invisible and therefore must be spirit.
Spirit also resides in the blood, for when blood is fresh spilt it
smokes or steams. Given this basis, a kind of ambiguous materialism, Telesius is able to persuade us that the basis of experience is
motion: the soul is set in motion by things, being subject to
expansion and contraction, as the Stoics had said. As we proceed,
the dependence of this theory on Stoicism becomes more and
more apparent. The beginning of motion is in the nerves—that is
to say, the animal spirits in those tubes are set in motion by the
action of the object: as the object is material, this soul (at least)
must be material, since it is capable of being moved by material
things. But Telesius is aware of the distinction between sensation
as a physical process and sensation as a psychic event. He is also
dimly aware that the idea of the senses as passive had concealed
some confusion between these two things. The Stoic idea of
activity is therefore carefully preserved: the real sensation is not
the movement as it affects the organ of sense but the actual effect
on the spirits which go out as it were to meet the incoming shock.
The spirit is thus made the real subject of the sensation: the soul
is not confined to any one part, and therefore perception takes
place instantaneously—a point doubtless subscribed to the theory
by one of the Neoplatonic lecturers in the school of Padua.

As sensation is here made an elementary function of the animal
spirit, and as the other spirit does not seem to be wanted for the
ordinary operations of the mind, there was no reason why Telesius
should not proceed to describe the operations of the mind as

higher forms of sensation. This he actually proceeds to do. Modifying Aristotle by a mixture of later activism, he proceeds to make a continuous series of mental operations, from sensation up to the co-existence of many images in the mind, which is equal to the understanding. The critical part of this doctrine is the memory. Telesius assumes that every sensation, being an activity of the spirits, is also a tendency, more or less active, toward the repetition of the same movement. Consequently a second perception is distinct from a first by reason of this difference in the nature of the movements: a perception is a sensation completed by the activity of the mind, which contributes elements not actually contained in the presentation: a memory is a sense-presentation persisting in the spirits: a recollection is a sense-movement initiated from within: the storing of images combined with the power of discrimination and of comparison constitute the elements of reason. Thus the analysis of the understanding is reduced to three terms, *memorari*, *reminisci*, and *commemorare*. The terms are significant, and show by themselves the underlying idea, namely that neither sense nor reason falls outside the natural activity of the individual. By thus interpreting sensation as an activity of the organism not separated by nature from the reason: by practically ignoring the pure reason and throwing emphasis on the complex activity of comparison and discrimination: finally, by presenting the whole as a natural process tending toward a perceptible good, the preservation of self, Telesius has anticipated the principal parts of the anthropological teaching of Bacon and Hobbes.

Telesius has been likened to Condillac. There is at least a general resemblance in the two theorists, both in regard to their good and bad points. Just as Condillac was considered to have made too little out of the subjective activity, so Campanella seems to have found this particular defect in Telesius, whom for the rest he is content to follow. With him the cycle is complete. Science has developed the conscious expression of a theory of mind, the theory has been developed in the interests of that objective life from which it sprang, and there has resulted a sense of its limitations and the desire for some more complete expression of the nature of man. If we fail to find this among the philosophers of nature, we are not likely to discover it among the disputants of the schools. Yet they contributed their share to the general progress, and it is time to see the results of these manifold activities as they are mirrored in the purely philosophic literature of the age.

The *De Subtilitate* of Cardanus was the stimulus which provoled Scaliger to write his *Exotericarum exercitationum liber XV de Subtilitate ad Hier. Cardanum*, a book printed in 1557 and afterwards frequently reprinted. Julius Caesar Scaliger (the elder) was one of the great intellects of the age: in addition to philological works he wrote translations and commentaries: he had a partiality for Hippocrates, Theophrastus on plants and Aristotle on animals. We may assume that much of the ancient and some of the more recent views on life and nature were known to Scaliger, though he appears to have been a violent, boastful, and unreliable writer. The attack on Cardanus was primarily an exhibition of bitterness, but it had, and it retained, a certain importance, due in part to its author's learning and in part to a genuine power of analysis. Scaliger has been quoted as the first exponent of the muscular sense, on account of his statement that in walking a man can know the position of the foot without a 'sensible species' to represent that position, and that weight is not, strictly speaking, perceived by touch. He says: '*Appensum filo plumbum grave sentitur: manus tamen filum, non plumbum tanget.*' A clear distinction between active and passive touch seems to be indicated here. Also Scaliger doubted whether one single 'species' was sent from the brain to effect a movement; he suggested a continuous chain of such species, and this has been regarded as a description of 'innervation.' Habit was described by Scaliger as the quality of movements and as residing in the moving parts themselves; habits are produced by actions, consist in organic adaptation, and are closely akin to instincts. The inherence of the habit in the muscles is illustrated by the example of the bullock, which thrusts with the head before the horns are developed.[1] While these views clearly mark an increase of scientific interest in such inquiries it is difficult to assess the value of the statements. Cardanus appears to have recognized a difference between passive and active touch, so that Scaliger's views may. be only an extension of that topic. The recognition of a sixth sense peculiar to the sexual organs was certainly due to Cardanus, but it was probably derived by him from Stoic traditions.

[1] After Galen, *De Usu Partium*, i. 3.

E. Educational

1. VIVES

Juan Lius Vives was an itinerant Spaniard, a native of Valencia, who spent part of his time in England (1523–1528), lectured at Oxford, was patronized by Wolsey and Sir Thomas More, had a quick and comprehensive mind, and from much travelling acquired a large outlook combined with a genuine knowledge of humanity and a very defective sense of system. Neither psychology nor scholarship was his strong point; he made his mark principally as a reformer of educational ideals by showing his generation the sense in which life is more than letters. What Vives wrote is a curious mixture of ancient thoughts and new ideas. He adopts the old lines of construction; Galen supplies the physiological part and Aristotle's analyses fill out the programme. But there is a conspicuous irregularity about the whole matter: Aristotle is suddenly dropped in favour of a moderate Augustinism: elaborate Arabian subdivisions of faculties are enunciated, and then a sudden effort at simplification comes as a surprise; flashes of insight keep the reader in a state of expectation and uncertainty.

Vives begins with the division of things into organic and inorganic. The organic world includes (*a*) plants, (*b*) plant-animals, (*c*) birds and quadrupeds, (*d*) the superior animals. Plants have a nutritive power (*facultas altrix*). We expect to find next a class that has sensitive powers, but Vives chooses to distinguish those that have only the outer senses (plant-animals) from those that have both outer and inner senses (birds and quadrupeds): the *vita rationalis* is the distinctive mark of mankind. The nutritive faculty is elaborately divided into the attractive, retentive, digestive, purgative, expulsive, distributive, and incorporative powers! The sensitive powers are treated as usual, with two noticeable differences. Aristotle's 'medium' is treated as though it was an atmosphere through which material 'species' were transmitted; its function is to spiritualize the sense object so that less of the crude object reaches the sense organs. In brief, Aristotle and atomism are uncritically combined. His was an example often followed in the next two centuries.

On the senses of sight and hearing Vives is weak. On the sense of touch he makes the interesting comment that the experience of heavy and light is distinct from that of soft and hard, and that the former are related to the whole body. This has been declared to be an early exposition of the 'muscular sense' (cp. p. 322), but it is difficult to say quite what was meant. It may have been simply an original observation of fact, for Vives was the kind of man to notice things that happened to himself or his friends, and his points are often illustrated by anecdotes that testify to a growing appreciation of first-hand data. Thus he tells us:—'When I was a boy at Valencia I was ill of a fever: while my taste was deranged, I ate cherries: for many years afterwards, whenever I tasted fruit, I not only recalled the fever but also seemed to experience it again.' This narrative has a modern tone, and the same may be said of the remark that man expresses by laughter what animals express by other movements, for example, the dog by wagging its tail. Here was a promising start for a comparative study of the emotions. A somewhat cruder note is struck when Vives betrays the physiological analogy underlying his conception of mental functions. In the nutrition of the body, he says, we find first reception, then retention, and finally elaboration of the material. In cognition there are similar steps: first comes imagination or the reception of the mental food (images): then memory (retention): then there is phantasy, combining and fusing: finally judgment (vis aestimatrix). How long, we may ask, were psychologists (perhaps unknowingly) satisfying the love of system by this kind of parallelism? How far · does the metaphor still rule us and make us think too grossly of mental digestion and spiritual rumination? Perhaps the metaphor really died with those 'spirits' which went up from stomach to brain, and yet it may survive in other forms. Vives at any rate has confessed his method and betrayed his thoughts.

The greatest part of the work of Vives is occupied with topics now to be mentioned. He undertakes to discuss the nature of the soul; he rejects the idea that it is a, harmony, and declines to believe that it is produced in and through the formation of the body, because in that case the souls which were alike would be in bodies that were alike: but (in fact) the elephant, though most like human beings in mind, is most unlike them in body. In brief, we cannot know either the nature or the origin of the soul, but only its outward expressions. For this flash of insight Vives has been called the father of empirical psychology: he was, however, a neglectful parent, for he spent the balance of his time on metaphysical productions, trying to prove that mind and body are related as light and air. Here we have again Augustinian ideas emerging, and the whole classification of faculties is finally taken from Augustine—namely, intellect, will, and memory.

Here we may find another point of considerable interest. The intellect as such (*mens particularis*), which is the person's own mentality, and not any superpersonal intellect, is described as beginning with the *intellectus simplex*, the elementary grasp of the meaning of a presentation. This germ of thought then grows and expands into a system of thought by the action of various mental operations named *consideratio, recordatio, collatio, discursus, judicium, voluntas, contemplatio*. This catalogue is formidable, but it deserves attention: for Vives had an exceptional feeling of the vitality of mind: he seems to feel its life and growth as though it were a visible thing of flesh and blood. Every term in this catalogue marks a real advance, and the goal is complete development, for contemplation is here used as equivalent to fruition, the restful enjoyment of attained knowledge. The scheme itself might not suggest this sense of vitality, but the details make it impressive. An affection or concomitant feeling, says Vives, increases the strength of memory: that is to say, the idea abides because we have not merely *had* it but also *lived* it. Interest and attention are emphasized, for they are the living aspects of the procession of ideas. Association is discussed, not as mere association of ideas, but rather as a statement of the way in which experiences cling together; the law of association is here formulated for the first time in its most general terms, and, since animals are also guided by it, association is more closely related to feeling than to reason. Beneath the life of thought there is the unnoticed flow of experiences: impressions are received when there is no conscious attention, and the fact is only realized some time after. Sometimes we know an event took place, but afterwards fail to recall it: there was at the time no attention, and so reflection (*consideratio*) fails to bring back the lost detail.

Finally Vives supports both nominalism and voluntarism. The picture we have in the mind is made up of attributes only: the understanding puts them together to make the compound object. Voluntarism comes out in the assertion that knowledge only serves to find an object for effort (conation). In connection with the tendency toward nominalism an important point arises. Is the *simplex intelligentia*, which Vives opposes to the *composita*, a doctrine of 'simple ideas'? If it were so, the fact would be of some historical interest. What Vives actually says is that the copula belongs to the faculty of judgment; it is an addition to the given data. That is only intelligible on the assumption that the elementary presentations are regarded by Vives as units of thought: form and colour, for example, being separate data which the inner sense first unites in the judgment that 'this form is coloured.' That was undoubtedly the natural way to work out a nominalistic psychology; it seems to be the right interpretation of what Vives says and most probably marks a stage in the progress of thought toward Locke's teaching.

It would be easy to point out confusions in this work of Vives, but there is more profit to be got from a frank recognition that his genius, though erratic, abounded in suggestive thoughts. He is in that respect a typical figure of this age of unrest, still labouring under dead formulae, and yet often conscious of quickening impulses. The last and in some ways the most significant part of the work is on the 'passions.' This is so far a practical discussion, with ethical and educational bearings, that we may postpone its consideration until that aspect of the century can be reviewed as a whole (pp. 328, *sqq*).

With Vives psychology received a new impulse mainly because his first interest was education: he approached psychology 'from the point of view of effectiveness in instruction,' and 'his study of psychology was rather the product and accompaniment of his educational activity than its originating impulse.' This explains very largely the fresh elements in the psychology of Vives: the high *a priori* road is abandoned and the variety of the soul's manifestations begin to take rank above the formal deduction of its powers. Unfortunately Vives was too busy to do more than show how the direct study of the mind might be furthered by a careful analysis of the process of learning.

Proof of a widespread interest in the psychological basis upon which educational theories should be built is to be found in various treatises of the century. For the most part they follow the vague efforts of Erasmus to define character and aptitude, the *natura specialis* of the individual. Sturm in Germany, Elyot and Wotton in England, gave teachers an impulse toward the study of character and temperament, but the only definite attack upon the problem was made by Juan Huarte, author of the *Examen de Ingenios para las Ciencas* (1575), translated into English as 'Examination of Men's Wits.' Huarte belonged to Spain, the land of Vives, and his work may be described as a further development of the teaching of Vives with a more emphatic bias toward problems of education. A fanciful correlation of faculties with subjects mars the value of Huarte's work, but we may agree that 'what most interests us is the fact of direct concern for psychological analysis as a specific aid to the right adjustment of instruction.'

The general significance of this movement may be summed up briefly. The progress of learning, the revival of classical knowledge, and the growth of a new individualism had as one of their results a fresh interest in the methods of imparting knowledge and building up character. Since the great educators of this age always aimed to master the secrets of character and character-building, they were naturally led further and further into the problems of connate tendencies, instincts, varieties of memory and degrees of intellectual capacity. Uniformity ceased to be of interest; the *natura specialis* became the object of study; the variety of nature is most apparent in children and young people, so that a theory of the mind which begins from differences and from the point of view of growth or development is a natural outcome. Individuals living in communities tend to appear uniform in character; to the superficial or untrained observer they seem to be all of one pattern. This tendency persists, for example, in Erasmus, whose *natura specialis* clearly implies as its background a *natura universalis*. Here the logical universal conflicts with the scientific; the abstract idea of man is retained along with the new concrete idea of individuals. This is a mark of transition. When the sixteenth century closes we find ourselves appreciably further away from the mediaeval thought and nearer Locke or Rousseau. This is due to the fact that for the educator interest centres upon the understanding rather than 'pure reason,' and when the understanding of the child has been described as something 'made,' it is easy to go one step further and look on the human understanding, the adult mind, as also for the most part a manufactured article. The work of Locke is here foreshadowed; it only remains to note that the emotions still escaped attention, awaiting their resurrection in the work of Rousseau.

The mixture of theory and practice which characterizes all

educational reforms, makes that profession a natural bridge from the abstract to the concrete. A similar quality belongs to the sphere of conduct, and in the psychology of conduct the men of the sixteenth century found a need for fresh and concrete modes of treatment. The first step in this direction was to emphasize natural qualities, taking a cue from the physiological basis of temperaments. Telesius, who made virtues and vices into innate tendencies, and Vives, who used the distinction of warm and cold blood to explain the difference between courage and caution, are examples of the naturalistic tendency. A more subtle point was made by Scaliger when he asserted that brave men feel the force of an insult in those muscles which serve for striking, while the less pugnacious type are affected in the organs of speech. This we may especially commend to those modern writers who reduce all consciousness to terms of motor-innervation! Another writer, Neuhus, boldly makes purity of heart equivalent to purity of blood: thick and impure blood is the cause of irreverence, irreligion, and shamelessness. As usual, the innovators went to extremes in emphasizing this physiological view of morals.

The avowed object of these theorists was to treat the emotions with no reference to moral values; they aimed at a theory of the passions which would make these phenomena purely a matter of 'physics,' meaning by that term what we should now call natural science. The movement was supported by a general revival of interest in the details of character and its expression. From temperaments, as treated by Galen, the interest spread to Physiognomics, exhibited partly in translations from Aristotle, partly in more original views which had been fostered by Leònardo da Vinci's study of expressions from the artist's standpoint. Physiognomics was divided into a general and a special science. While some concerned themselves with national or individual characters, others studied the face, the hands, the feet, the different periods of life or the different sexes. The literature of the subject became large and full of detail. In spite of the lack of any unifying principles, the whole movement was a decided contribution to what would now be called Individual Psychology.

A full account of all the contributions made under these different heads would take a disproportionate amount of space. It must suffice to note them as signs of the times, and pass on to the treatises which deal with the emotions. Melanchthon led the way toward a physiological method in dealing with these states of the soul, defining joy and sorrow in terms of expansion and contraction, which ultimately comes down to movements of the heart and blood. But the classic exposition was given by Vives, whose work may be more fully considered because it is the best example of the work done at this time.

Vives rejects the Stoic views and openly declares that the whole course of life is regulated by feelings; feelings can obscure perceptions and are not subordinate to intellect, but frequently hinder or destroy the intellectual activities. Emotions are rooted in dispositions, so that a dominant tendency will colour all a man's thoughts, either continuously or periodically. These dispositions can be changed physically by diet, mentally by training; for an opinion often lies at the root of an emotion, and change of opinion changes the emotional attitude. This point leads on to the favourite topic of Rhetoric as the art of exciting or allaying the emotions of men, a phase of Aristotelian teaching which was revived at this time. The individualistic tendency shows itself in the lengthy treatment of self-approbation, the egoistic sentiment which directly or indirectly pervades all the actions of some men, even though the victim of the tendency does not recognize its presence. The addition of a little pessimism to this doctrine would have given it the quality of the maxims produced by the French in the eighteenth century.

On the basis of these general statements Vives builds a descriptive psychology of the emotions. The physiological treatment of the emotions fell short of completeness through failure in studying the phenomena inductively. Vives made a beginning of such a study, and his work on the 'passions' marks a new era in the history of that troublesome subject, not by virtue of a new classification, but rather on account of the careful way in which the phenomena are described.

The fundamental passion is Love; men love that which they consider good, for the good has a certain natural agreement with the individual's nature, and as such is both attractive and satisfying. The human being loves itself most of all, and next those whose interests or activities harmonize with its welfare. The benevolent love those whose welfare they promote, but the recipient of kindness has a less degree of love because his gratitude is mixed with shame. Love is strengthened by sympathy, as the

mother loves most the child whom others dislike: it is increased in
reconciliations, for the temporary intermission and restraint serve
to increase its power; but many checks or disappointments can
convert it into hate. Desire, hope, and joy are also concerned with
the good according as it is wanted, expected, or confidently
believed to be attainable. Evil arouses anger, which is most
intense when feelings are thwarted: sensible pain, such as a blow
struck in anger, arouses less violent resentment than that which
follows an insult. In the matter of anger men differ greatly, some
being quick to feel it and quick to cease from it, others being
moved more slowly but nursing their wrath for long. The sense
of injury involves some desire for revenge, but this is sometimes
satisfied by obtaining the means to inflict harm without actually
employing them. A less violent state of feeling than hate is that
called resentment (*offensio*). This is a tendency to be sensitive
about past, present, or future acts regarded as possibly injurious.
It is properly a disposition; often mere novelty excites it; the man
who stays too much at home finds the world barbarous and
stupid. The feeling of hate arises from persistent anger or from
grudging: we hate most strongly when there is a basis of love,
that is to say when the object is one that excites the deepest
interest. Pity, as it increases love, tends to diminish hate.

Vives discusses also fear, respect, modesty, grief, longing, pity,
envy (a contraction of the mind which is all the worse because it
is concealed, while other feelings are shared), jealousy (a form of
fear, anticipating that a good will accrue to one whom we hate),
and indignation, the only affection which rests on the idea of
merit and implies moral valuations. The description of these
different moods and emotions is fresh and varied, but its exact
quality, depending on the finer points of detail, is not reproducible
in an epitome. The work was carried a stage further by Laelius
Peregrinus who published in 1598 a little book that may best be
regarded as an essay in the empirical psychology of the feelings
and an appendix to the essay of Vives. The point common to both
and characteristic of this new tendency is the acceptance of the
two movements, attraction and repulsion, as the basis for grouping
inner movements of the feelings. This method now superseded
the division into concupiscible and irascible passions, which had
so long dominated the mediaeval traditions.

In this, as in many other points, we find the conclusion and summary of the work represented by Bacon. In the *Advancement of Learning* (Bk. vii, chap. iii) Bacon wrote what was at once an epitome of the progress made and a clear direction of the course to be pursued afterwards. He adopts the practical tone and writes of the 'cultivation' or 'cure,' i.e. 'care' of the mind. As a programme of practical or applied psychology the chapter deserves careful attention: its historical importance is shown by the fact that the French Encyclopaedists openly adopted the Baconian scheme of sciences, and modern psychologists have often noted that their work actually fulfils the demands of Bacon's programme.

'The first article,' says Bacon, 'of the culture of the mind will regard the different natures or dispositions of men.' These he finds have already been studied by the astrologers, who professed to say that 'some are by nature formed for contemplation, others for politics, others for war.' This primitive type of vocational psychology did not commend itself to Bacon, but he rightly recognized that it was trying to do what otherwise remained wholly neglected. Next to the astrologers the poets were to be ranked as exponents of a concrete individual psychology, in which they were surpassed by the 'more prudent historians.' The defects of this work were obvious to Bacon, but he thought it might be taken as a beginning for more systematic inquiry, 'so that an artificial (i.e. scientific) and accurate dissection may be made of men's minds and natures, and the secret disposition of each man laid open, that from a knowledge of the whole, the precepts concerning the cures of the mind may be more rightly formed. And not only the characters of dispositions impressed by nature should be received into this treatise, but these also which are otherwise imposed upon the mind by the sex, age, country, state of health, make of body, etc. And again, those which proceed from fortune, as in princes, nobles, common people, the rich, the poor, magistrates, the ignorant, the happy, the miserable, etc.'

The magnificent sweep of this outlook may be left to the reader's approbation without comment. What Bacon could have done to supply the detail in each or all of these departments we shall never know. Apparently the idea was not unique: as the previous pages have shown, there was a strong though diffuse current of thought setting in this direction, and many minor works floated for a while on that river of time which Bacon accused of bringing down only 'what is light and tumid.' Among these may be mentioned the work of De la Chambre, of Cordemoy, of Neuhus and of Clarmont. In the history of literature and of science these works have been eclipsed by the greater achievements of Descartes, on the one hand, and of the French moralists on the other.

PART

III

Chapter Ten

THE GATEWAY OF METHOD

A. Introductory

The revolt against scholasticism culminated in the seventeenth century. The achievements of the physical scientists had by now become as much a challenge to the old ways of thought as the national Churches had become to the old methods of ecclesiastical organization. The Aristotelian contemporaries of Galileo refused to look through his telescope to test their theories about the moon and the planets; they were not impressed when the 100 lb. and 1 lb. cannon-balls, dropped from the tower of Pisa, arrived at their feet at approximately the same time, thus refuting their theory of natural fall. But anyone who used his eyes could see now that the Aristotelians were wrong in many of their dogmas. No longer did the new physical sciences commit a 'rape of the senses.' The Inquisition was the only effective answer to Galileo's demonstrations.

The startling development of astronomy, mechanics, and optics was accompanied by systematic substitutes for the old Aristotelian explanations. Francis Bacon and René Descartes, in their *Novum Organum* and *Regulae*, expressed the new spirit of confidence in the ability of living men to discover the secrets of nature for themselves; they also provided the tools of discovery—their books. In an age of new men and new social and economic opportunities belief in the power of the book took the place of reverence for tradition. Just as Macchiavelli had written his *Prince* for those who wished to start afresh or overthrow an established tradition of government, so Bacon and Descartes proclaimed that the way out of the hallowed wasteland of forms and species lay through the gateway of method. Their books provided the signposts. It is important to realize that they both shared the view that method was the key to knowledge although they disagreed about what the required method was. Descartes, with his eye on the success of the new physical sciences, saw in mathematics the key to knowledge. He thought that the physical scientist, like the geometer, should isolate by intuition certain 'simple natures' or essences; a clear and distinct perception of these would provide a certain foundation from which nature's secrets could be rationally deduced and demonstrated. Bacon distrusted the axiomatic approach and saw in the careful observation of nature, the collection of data, and the cautious generalization made by a judicious man like himself the only safe way of arriving at knowledge. Both Bacon's and Descartes' methods are examples of what may be called dogmatic methodism—the view that success in science is the result of following a definite method. It is a particular example of the belief in the magic of technique which succeeded the trust in traditional ways of thought and action. This basic similarity between the rationalists and so-called empiricists of the seventeenth century is seldom noticed.

The rise of the physical sciences and the dogmatic methodism which accompanied it both exerted a great influence on the development of psychology. Descartes' reflexology modelled on mechanics, Locke's inventory of the human mind, and Hume's self-conscious attempt to model psychology on Newtonian physics are the first examples of this dual influence. The later history of psychology, as will be seen, is riddled with attempts to apply recipes like those of measurement, operational techniques, or starting from 'pure data' in the laboratory, just as it is studded with ideas and theoretical concepts drawn from other sciences like chemistry (e.g. Watt), physiology (e.g. Beneke), biology (e.g. Ward) and dynamics (e.g. Lewin). Of course the influence of dogmatic methodism and of physical science are connected; for, if it is assumed that there is a recipe for success in science, it will be natural to apply in a young science the techniques and concepts which have proved useful in a more established one. The infiltration of other sciences into psychology is healthy in so far as it shows that the separation between the sciences is quite arbitrary but dangerous in so far as it derives from dogmatic methodism.

In spite of the misguided trust in technique exemplified by the guide-books of Bacon and Descartes, they were both enormously influential and important figures in the development of science. At the time when they wrote the triumphs of quantitative techniques needed noising abroad as an answer to the qualitative procedure of the scholastics. Similarly the importance of sense observation in science needed to be stressed as a corrective to the one-sided rationalistic exaltation of mathematical deduction. The fact that both rationalists and observationalists overstated their cases and presented them in rather misleading ways is of minor importance compared with the services which they rendered in freeing inquiry from the shackles of scholasticism.

Before considering the details of the psychologies which sprang up in the wake of the new physical sciences and the dogmatic methodism which accompanied them, it will be as well to examine in more detail firstly what the relevance of these new sciences was to psychology and secondly what the details were of the recipes provided by rationalists and observationalists for the guidance of psychologists.

B. The influence of other sciences

I. GENERAL

The principal sciences of the Middle Ages were astronomy and optics, both of them having special features to recommend them. Astronomy was more or less concerned with the heavens, and was therefore the science of the ultimate immovable reality, a most dignified affair even though in form it was created by Ptolemy. Next to this celestial science came the study of light, which fascinated the minds of men in each successive generation and slowly passed from the region of imaginative metaphysics of light to the mathematical study of refraction and reflection. In the progress of astronomy at the hands of Copernicus and Galileo we see the real decline of the mediaeval system of thought, the disappearance of that world in which it had lived and grown old Similarly in the progress of optics the writers are consciously attacking one of the fundamental doctrines of their age. We may accept today a new discovery about the properties of light or a new type of lens with scarcely a sensation of any kind: in the seventeenth century such an event was closely connected with the question of the reality of the world in which men lived and the problem of happiness in this life and the life to come. For since the first consideration of man was to justify the ways of God and show that the facts did not wholly disprove the existence of Providence, every new statement of things observed had to be securely fastened into a general scheme by specific (and irrelevant) comments on the relation of the particular item to the wisdom of the Creator.

Apart then from the general question of scientific advance, these two sciences have a particular relation to the development of thought. They represent the crucial point at which science and belief came into contact, and the second of them, optics, is concerned with that which was from the earliest times regarded as a privileged sense, superior to all the other senses of man.

2. ASTRONOMY AND MATHEMATICS

The astronomy of the Middle Ages had been revolutionized by Copernicus and Kepler. Copernicus' heliocentric hypothesis was revolutionary not just because he postulated the sun as the centre of the solar system, but also because his view intimated that it was a matter of convention whether the sun or earth was regarded as being the centre point. This shocked the orthodox because of the theological importance of terrestrial man as the centre of creation. His theory was accepted by his followers not because of its empirical verification, which had to await the invention of the telescope, but because the facts of astronomy were thrown into a simpler and more harmonious mathematical order with the sun as centre. The Platonic-Pythagorean picture of the universe as a harmonious mathematical structure had survived as well as the Aristotelian conception of nature as a hierarchical structure of different and irreducible qualitative species. This surviving tradition lent a degree of metaphysical respectability to the theory—especially when it became known that some of the ancients—e.g. Aristarchus—had put forward a heliocentric theory. Copernicus and Kepler were steeped in mathematical mysticism; even Galileo, like Plato, regarded God as a great geometer. Kepler, it is true, combined his Pythagorean picture with an insistence on appeal to observation which he had learnt from Tycho Brahe. But his mathematical bias led him to equate the real qualities of the world with those that were mathematically tractable. By thinking mathematically the physical scientist was penetrating to the ground-plan of the astronomical universe.

Galileo brought this mathematical unveiling down to earth. His terrestrial mechanics revealed terrestrial phenomena as amenable to the same treatment. In opposition to the Aristotelians he held that mathematics was the instrument of discovery, logic only of criticism. He is justly famous for evolving what is now called the Galilean method of explanation. This involves isolating a typical phenomenon and, after only a few critical experiments, deducing by mathematical manipulation a vast number of conclusions that go beyond those already revealed by experience or experiment. For instance, once we have ascertained that the path of projectiles is a parabola, we can demonstrate, without recourse to further experiment, that their maximum range is 45 degrees. This concentration on 'pure cases' with systematic variations in a few different experiments was a departure from the Aristotelian insistence on collecting a great number of cases and making inductions on the basis of simple enumeration. Galileo allowed a place for both sense-observation and mathematical reasoning in his description of his method. If anything he placed more importance on the latter than on the former. The senses present us with a problem. We take a typical phenomenon and by thinking about it resolve it into sections. We isolate those simple elements of it like its extension, figure, and motion, in terms of which it can be translated into mathematical form. We quantify the variables involved and deduce mathematically conclusions which will be true of this and any similar instance. For the sake of conviction and in order to make sure of our prognosis we then confirm the adduced conclusions by experimental observation. The senses may often be raped without aids like the telescope; for mathematical reasoning reveals the real world behind the sensible phenomena. The Aristotelian qualitative differences are not irreducible; they are expressions of the underlying, immutable, mathematically amenable reality—matter in motion.

Galileo is properly to be regarded as the first to practise consciously what is now called the hypothetico-deductive method of inquiry. The scientist formulates tentative hypotheses to explain puzzling phenomena; he works out deductively the consequences of these hypotheses and compares them with actual observations. If the observations fail to confirm the hypotheses he reformulates them and tries again. And so science goes on. The hypothetico-deductive method seemed like magic in his hands because he was able to combine mathematical reasoning, which gives exactness, with experimental observation. He had no fear of using hypotheses which often seemed highly speculative; for he had a technique for testing them.

Galileo, however, was renowned more for his experiments than for his descriptions of what he did. This was a pity. The methodologists who exerted most influence each stressed elements in Galileo's technique to the exclusion of the other elements. Descartes concentrated on mathematical deduction and the isolation of elements that were mathematically manageable. We cannot understand his rules for inquiry without bearing in mind this background of astronomy and mathematics; for it was Descartes who tried to make explicit the methodological assumptions of those physical scientists who, openly or secretly, regarded mathematics rather than Aristotelian logic as the guide to nature's underlying ground-plan. Unfortunately his account was very unbalanced because he placed so little emphasis on observation as a necessary accompaniment to mathematical deduction. This defect in Descartes was more than amply compensated for by Locke and Hume who, following Bacon and sharing his inadequate understanding of the importance of mathematical deduction in physical science, founded the observationalist tradition in scientific method and in psychology.

3. OPTICS

Aristotle's views on light and colour suffered from two principal defects. He knew too little about the structure of the eye and too little about the problems of refraction and of focal points. The period with which we are now dealing was the time when these defects either had been or were in process of being rectified. Kepler's knowledge of the purely optical parts of the process of vision, the action of light in passing through lenses and the relation of the convexity or concavity of those lenses to the point at which the rays come to a focus, enabled him to attack Aristotle's theory of a transparent medium. According to Aristotle an object ceased to be visible when it was in contact with the eye because the medium was then excluded: according to Kepler the medium was entirely unnecessary because in any case the rays of light would not converge as required for vision under such circumstances. The extreme case of actual contact was not important, but the general explanation of near and far-sightedness was involved and Kepler had the advantage of explaining vision as a special instance of the general laws of optics. Then, again, the defective condition of science previous to this period had made it possible to regard the image visible in the eye as the actual object of vision for the person possessing the eye, because the rays were regarded as staying in and not passing through the lenses. Kepler, distinguishing between the reflection from the eye and the actual transmission of light through the lenses, rejected the common view that the crystalline lens was the place in which the rays came to a focus and so arrived at the new doctrine that the retina was the seat of visual stimulation, or, as he puts it, the place where the converging rays meet the spirits from the brain.

This discovery met with a somewhat unexpected obstacle in the discovery of the 'blind spot' which was detected by Mariotte (1668) and seemed to refute the whole theory by being at once the point of entry for the optical nerve into the retina and itself devoid of sensibility to light. Mariotte was induced by this discovery to assert that the choroid and not the retina was the part of the eye which directly subserved vision, but Haller and Bernoulli explained away the apparent objections to the retina. The position of Kepler was thus ultimately established.

Optics and dioptrics form an important part of all the greater philosophical treatises after Kepler's time. Descartes wrote at length on the subject, and Hobbes spent many years on its problems. Both of these writers grasped the importance of the subject for a general theory of sensation. They acquitted themselves as philosophers with credit, but this credit was due rather to their reform of philosophy than their contributions to science. Nothing of real importance was done till Newton produced his physical analysis of the spectrum. This gave a new turn to the question of colours. Hitherto the basis for a discussion of colour had been either visual experience or the mixing of pigments. Newton's method was different from both and in itself was simply an objective physical analysis. But Newton still persisted in treating black as one of the colours, though this was consistent only with the psychological point of view. The whole question of colour as a part of physiological psychology was thus left in confusion, waiting for the union of physical, physiological, and psychological data.

In addition to the question of the nature and action of light and to that of colour the consideration of vision leads to the question of the perception of space. As it became clear that in vision there was no picture sent from the object to the mind, and, further, that in any case the picture would not arrive in the mind with the place of its origin marked upon it, the philosophers were harassed by the difficulty of explaining the fact that visual images are taken to indicate external position. Descartes, being at once philosopher and physicist, could not avoid the problem, but he offered no real solution. As regards the physical part of the process he maintained that vision was wholly a matter of motion, light was a movement, the movement came from the object to the outer organ, the eye, and passed thence to the inner organ, the part of the brain in which the nerves of the eye terminated. Descartes did not commit the error of supposing that the inner organ had for its object the outer organ; he regarded the outer organ as no more than a medium for the transmission of the motion, so that the resulting motion which arises in the brain comes directly from the object. Between the eye and the object the line of light stretches like a rod, being a continuous line of matter in motion: the brain is directly affected at the part at which this line terminates inward and we know every change in the position of objects by the corresponding change in the affection of the brain. By this means we localize in space the different objects we perceive, and if we ask further how we know the space in which we so localize things we are told that this is done by a kind of innate geometry. Here we pass from the empirical side of Descartes' system to the *a priori* idealistic side: the idea of space is joined to the perception by the co-operation of God. For the world of our experience is not really known directly through the senses: we have no ultimate ground for saying that the object causes the idea: we can only suppose that God would not make our lives an eternal hallucination. The results of this teaching will be seen in the work of Malebranche: its significance cannot be grasped without further details of the relation between mind and body.

4. MECHANICS AND CHEMISTRY

For those who accepted it Harvey's discovery of the circulation of the blood involved a profound change in the conception of the relations between soul and body. The idea that the soul was at once the basis of life and of thought now began to give place to a more distinct conception of the difference between the physical processes and the psychic activities. The progress of physiology made it increasingly possible to think of the movements of the body as capable of explanation without reference to that soul which had so long been defined as the principle of movement. This new direction of thought shows itself more or less distinctly in all the writers who discuss from their various points of view the nature of the soul.

In the seventeenth century two distinct influences were at work. One of these came from the progress of mechanical science and was adopted, by those who accepted Harvey's conclusions, as the natural corollary of this discovery: they argued that the circulation of the blood was a mechanical process and that the rest of the processes in the body might be reduced to mechanical operations. The other influence came from chemistry and was reinforced by the observation of processes not regarded as mechanical, the chief instance being that of fermentation. In their relation to physiology these influences appear as deciding the difference between the mechanical and chemical schools. We may begin with the latter as representing the older tradition though in a new form.

The beginning of the chemical school is to be found in Paracelsus. In the seventeenth century his doctrine was advanced by Johann Baptist van Helmont, a man whose work was a strange mixture of religious beliefs, mystical expansiveness and keen insight into facts. His principal work, the *Ortus Medicinae*, was published in 1628: he died in 1644, more than a century after the death of Paracelsus and sixteen years before the death of Descartes. He was by nature a mixture of the different temperaments of Paracelsus, whom he consciously followed, and of Descartes, whom he unconsciously resembled. The central point of his teaching, for our present purpose, is the treatment of the relations between mind and body. Everything, he declares, has a living spirit, which he variously describes as *flamma*, *aura*, or *spiritus vitalis*. This is present in metals as a principle of cohesion, in plants as a composite humour, and in animals and man as a substantial vital principle. In this part of his teaching Helmont follows the 'cosmic philosophy' of Paracelsus and recalls the Stoic theory of Pneuma as it appears in Philo and the Neoplatonists. The theosophy of the seventeenth century was closely allied to the Stoic-Philonic tradition, and to that same source we may ascribe the distinction made by Helmont between men and animals: the vital spirit is common to both, but man is only like the animals: in essence he is the image of God. Helmont declares that man cannot be defined as a rational animal: on the contrary he is a spiritual being clothed in a body. Man is thus above the animals; but Helmont declares, against the Pantheists, that man is not essentially one with God. The body is mortal, but the mind is immortal.

Some minor points made by Helmont are of interest. The true knowledge of God is to see things intellectually (*intellectualiter videre*). The soul cannot know itself through reason merely or through images, but only through the recognition that the truth of being (*veritas essentiae*) and truth of understanding (*veritas intellectus*) are united in all real knowledge. The first of these statements is a good formula for religious experience, while the second expresses the significance of intuitive apprehension: the union of the two anticipates all that Descartes meant by his *cogito ergo sum*.

We pass on to Helmont's physiological teaching. This is a form of chemical physiology. The two principal terms which he introduces are *Gas* and *Blas*, the former being carbon dioxide, the latter a vital force akin to the *archaeus* of Paracelsus. In animal organisms the Blas utilizes the ferments, which appealed to Helmont as occult processes of change and a kind of universal life in matter. These ideas were employed by Helmont to explain the process of digestion in which he recognizes six stages. With these we are not concerned until we come to the fifth, in which the blood of the arteries is changed into the vital spirit of the *archaeus*, and the sixth in which this *archaeus* enables each part of the body to assimilate its nourishment. The vital and the animal spirit Helmont declares to be identical. Thus with Helmont the 'nutritive soul' is really a vital principle whose workings are at least analogous to ordinary fermentation.

So far Helmont was a man of science. His more speculative mood is expressed when he deals with the sensitive soul. This is the property of man; strictly speaking, plants and animals have no soul; in man it is the ruling principle, controlling the *archaeus* and all the lesser agencies; it acts through the brain and nerves, but its own real seat is in the pylorus, in the orifice of the stomach.

This last idea, as old as Homer and not unknown to the ancient Hebrews, is supported by sundry arguments which need not detain us. It is enough to point out in conclusion that Helmont has greatly helped to give the physiological processes an independent status, that he has elaborately explained the origin and use of 'spirits,' and has kept the sensitive soul apart from these in a place of its own: while the immortal mind is a pure adjunct wholly unexplained.

Six years after the *Ortus Medicinae* Glisson produced his theory of 'irritability' (1654). It passed unnoticed and we leave it till we come to Haller in the next century. The dominant line of theory goes from Helmont to Willis, whose *Cerebri Anatome* (1664) comes after the death of Descartes. Descartes himself contributed nothing to physiology; he was embedded in the stratum of theories which we are now considering. Willis, though a famous and thriving doctor, was not a genius; his work was a skilful combination of ideas, some of which were his own, some were picked up through intercourse with the greater men of that galaxy which was the first nucleus of the Royal Society. Our interest in Willis is confined to his explanation of sensation and movement and to his significance as a classic representative of his age. Willis upholds the animal spirits in a way that does not differ essentially from the ordinary tradition. While Descartes looked upon the spirits as purely physical, Willis prefers to call them by the older and more ambiguous name of corporeal soul. He divides this soul into two parts, one in the blood and the other in the brain and nervous system. The former is described as a flame: in other words vital processes are a form of combustion. Here Willis scores a point against Descartes' idea that there is an 'innate heat' in the heart; Willis more correctly maintains that the heart gets its heat from the blood. Willis had some peculiar ideas about the corporeal soul which he assigned to the brain. He believed it to be a light and even maintained that it was visible; some warm-blooded animals 'emit a visible flame or fire at night only.' An 'ingenious man' told him that 'after an extra good bout of wine he could see to read print clearly on a very dark night.' This curious symptom may have been one of the facts which turned Willis to the general subject of sensations, in which he showed a very creditable interest, and he is still handed down to fame as its investigator in the term *Hyperacusis Willisii*. As a neurologist Willis achieved much, and his classification of the cerebral nerves was a work of permanent value; it remained supreme till the close of the eighteenth century. Willis regarded the nerves as solid fibres, not tubes: they are 'like cords lightly strung, extended from the brain and its appendages' to all parts of the body. The same nerves function in sensation and motion; in sensation a movement is transmitted from the extremity to the brain; in voluntary movement the brain originates 'an impression or impetus' from within outwards. As the animal spirits are not in the nerves (as tubes), they are to be considered as passing along them on their surfaces. In this 'Willis may be regarded as dimly striving to explain nervous phenomena on the hypothesis of a specific nervous fluid.' This was a change in the physiological theory of sensation, but it produced no fundamental change in the concept either of sensation or volition.

The localization of functions in the brain is thus stated:—'It seems allowable to conceive of the middle regions of the brain constituting an inner chamber of this (corporeal) soul fitted with dioptric mirrors, as with windows. The pictures or images of all sensible things admitted into these secret places by means of the ducts of the nerves, as by means of tubes or narrow openings, first pass through the corpora striata, and then are represented on the corpus callosum as on a whitened wall. And so the things which give rise to sensation induce perception and a certain imagination.' By 'a second undulation' these images get to the cortex of the brain and give rise to memory, being stored in the folds of the cortex. The image now vanishes; so that the undulation of the cortex is the physiological counterpart of memory.

According as the image is suggestive of good or evil, impulse arises and so the spirits 'being excited, look back upon the object' and bestir themselves to remove or retain it.[1]

Willis proposed to explain all the life of animals through this physiological mechanism: the *anima brutorum* is with him quite distinct from the *anima rationalis* of man. He acknowledges that he had not explained how this corporeal soul 'perceives that it feels and in accordance with that perception is driven into various passions and actions.' It is to his credit that he saw the difficulty of passing from motions mechanically connected to motions selected and directed. In man, he says, 'we can readily understand that the rational soul looks upon the images and impressions presented to the rational soul as to a mirror and according to the

---

[1] Quotations from Foster, *Lectures on the History of Physiology*, pp. 270–7.

conceptions and emotions thus derived exercises the acts of reason, judgment and will.' Others, however, did not so readily understand that, and the doctrine which Willis expounded was easily developed into a pure materialism. Some eminent men of science (Mayow,[1] Stensen, Lower) did not approve of the vital flame or the 'lucid soul.' The animal spirits, however, in some form or other, remained a cardinal point of physiology and physiological psychology. Boerhaave (d. 1738) at Leyden discussed the theory and from Boerhaave it went into the mind of La Mettrie to assist his materialism.[2] Toward this Willis made a substantial contribution by his attitude on the question of reflex action. He defined a reflex action as a motion that depends on a preceding sense-stimulus and returns directly to its source, not attaining to any higher levels. He thought that the seat of imagination might be reached by the nerve currents without any change in the reflex character of the resulting movement. Also, in addition to the acquired memory in the cerebrum he recognized a natural memory in the cerebellum, this giving his adherence to an organic memory distinct from intellectual memory (*Cer. An.* 211). On some points Willis was in error: he held that the ventricles of the brain secrete humours, though this was already disproved by Schneider; he continued the doctrine of spirits, though others (Fernel, Plater) had already questioned it, and the work of Mayow[1] was destined to dissipate the whole subject by giving a more adequate account of the chemistry of physiological processes. Yet at the time Willis was a power second to none, and it was largely his influence that kept interest focussed on the decaying problem of the seat of the soul.

Vieussens (1641–1716) devoted considerable attention to the relation between physiological structure and psychological activity. He showed the influence of both Willis and Descartes, for he localized the *sensorium commune* in the corpora striata and the *imaginatio* in the centrum ovale. These parts being closely connected, Vieussens thought he could explain the relation between sensation and thought. In any sensation there are movements propagated to the corpora striata where the sensation as psychic event takes place. The same movement extends to the centrum

---

[1] Mayow's nitro-aerian spirits were the first step in the discovery of oxygen. F. Bayle (1622–1709) employed a method of hardening the brain which subserved neurology, as the later methods subserve nineteenth-century progress.

[2] See p. 522.

ovale where the 'first imagination' occurs; in other words, the sensation may be said to be presented in the centrum and every sensation is inevitably united with this kind of *presentation*. This scheme of motions is then used to explain *representation*, where the movements within the centrum ovale explain what might be called centrally excited experiences. These constitute a class of experiences which are essentially representative but have a degree of sensation, due to the fact that the motion extends outward along the course of the original sensation. In this case the objects seem to be actually presented, but with less clearness and intensity than when they cause a sensation.

Claude Perrault (1613–1688) was the most important opponent of the Cartesian mechanistic theories. He was a predecessor of Stahl and, according to Haller, a source from whom Stahl borrowed. His chief work, *Essais de Physique*, was published in 1680 and contained a considerable amount of work on sense-perceptions. Perrault did not accept the pineal gland as in any sense a privileged 'seat of the soul'; the soul according to him is connected directly with the whole body and controls all activities, both of movement and sensation. Since thought or consciousness is the essence of the soul, Perrault draws the conclusion that it must have knowledge of all its operations; the body is not an unknown appendage of the soul but its persistent object. This view requires for its support the assumption of two kinds of knowledge, the clear knowledge of thought and the obscure knowledge of organic sensation. Perrault explains the genesis of this difference; we pay little attention to what goes on inside, and consequently those operations pass from the sphere of attention to that of habit. All the organic functions are thus the work of a spiritual principle, but have lapsed from the highest apperceptive degree of attention; the heart, now apparently quite mechanical in its action, was once directly controlled by will; and all other movements are, as Hartley said later, secondarily automatic. It is obvious that Perrault approaches from the side of medicine that view of life which Leibniz developed from the basis of metaphysics.

In the year in which Descartes died (1660) George Ernest Stahl was born at Anspach. He lived till 1734, so that he belongs primarily to the close of the seventeenth century though his life and work extended well into the eighteenth. Early in the seventeenth century medical science had taken different paths according as it moved in the iatromechanical school of Borelli or the iatrochemical school of François de la Boë (Franciscus Sylvius, distinct from Jacobus Sylvius). Borelli was an admirer of Galileo, and travelled to Florence to see that hero of science. He published mathematical and astronomical works, but the desire of his heart was to write a treatise on animal motion. He achieved this; though the work *De Motu Animalium* was not published till 1680, after his death. It was preceded in 1664 and in 1667 by the tracts of Nicolas Stensen, a Dane, also known as Steno in Latin. Stensen and Borelli between them refute the idea that spirits or corporeai airs can bring about muscular movement. Borelli approaches very closely to the idea of irritability as resident in the muscles; but that was only fully realized later (by Haller) and the significance of this mechanic of the body lies in its point of view, its method, and its complete antagonism to the doctrine that movement depends entirely on the current of animal spirits (as in Descartes).

Sylvius is of no interest to us except for the fact that his school produced the doctrine of Stahl. The real beginning is in Van Helmont; Sylvius developed Helmont's chemical theories in a less mystical way; Stahl had more of the imaginative power of Helmont. Stahl maintained that chemical processes in the living body are quite different from the analogous processes (ferments) in things. The reason given for this was that in animal organisms the sensitive soul pervades every part and presides over every operation. Thus the Cartesian idea of the body as a machine is openly opposed; Descartes and Borelli might have been reconciled, but there was no possible reconciliation of Cartesianism and Stahl's doctrine. There is no need to discuss the details of Stahl's physiological chemistry: it is enough to say that he rejected all Helmont's intermediary forces and held to the simple position that spirit and matter are united by motion, that the processes of the animated organism are not all explicable by chemistry, and that the sensitive soul must be brought in to make our theory of life complete. This theory, the new animism, has a long history and will be met again later.

An important result of Stahl's general theory was the closer connection it established between psychology and medicine, and the consequent tendency to pay greater attention to psychic factors in explaining abnormal conditions of the individual. Stahl maintains that the soul builds the body; diseases are processes by which the soul strives to remove what hinders its operations. Diseases of the soul are abnormal conditions which arise when the normal activities are hindered by obstructing factors, described as due either to the nerves or the feelings. Thus Stahl begins to lay proper emphasis on those mental derangements which arise from the passions, distinguishing between the effects due to physical disposition and those which arise from the operations of the soul, as (for example) the working of the imagination. Stahl supports his position by many acute observations: the sight of food makes the mouth water; a mere association of ideas can change liking into disgust and produce actual vomiting; the mere thought of a medicine sets up contractions in the stomach. These facts prove the direct action of the immaterial vital principle on the material organism. To this action Stahl set no limits, making digestion and circulation dependent on the purposive action of the soul. Such extreme views were not capable of actual proof, and they brought discredit on the more acceptable parts of the theory, counteracting the effects of Stahl's refutation of the Cartesian mechanical standpoint. But for this the animistic view might have had more success, since its rejection of animal spirits, its opposition to all intermediation between soul and body, and its recognition of a simple action of mind on body by the production of motions in the organism, were all valuable contributions to a sounder psycho-physical position.

C. *The observationalist[1] method of induction*

The movement represented in Italy by Galileo's *Il Saggiatore* (1623) was paralleled in England by Bacon's *De Dignitate et Augmentis Scientiarum*. First published in 1605, but reproduced with this title in 1623, Bacon's work was more ambitious but less penetrating than that of Galileo. As a reformer of method he opposed the debased Aristotelianism of his age and expounded the new inductive methods. A complex character, a man not wholly devoted to science but interested also in affairs of state, with a keen eye for human motives and a desire for literary fame, Bacon united in a curious fashion the qualities of the essayist and the system-maker, of Montaigne and Telesius. With some new

[1] For the label 'observationalist' I am indebted to Professor K. R. Popper, whose views on scientific method I have largely adopted. (Editor.)

ideas he combined a great deal of credulity and a habit of accepting traditions uncritically. He enters into the history of psychology as the author of a classification of the sciences in which he assigns a place to the science of the soul: the effects of this scheme of work can be traced in more than one of Bacon's successors.

The whole doctrine of man is here divided into '*Philosophia Humanitatis et Civilis,*' the study of man as such and the study of man as citizen. The former of these is subdivided into doctrine of the body and doctrine of the soul. Prior to this Bacon thinks there should be a general science of man: a laborious collection of evidence about individuals should result in a concept of man formed in a purely empirical fashion and designed to show the actual nature and limits of human capacity. This part of the scheme reflects the influence of that movement toward scientific anthropology which had already begun. After these should come the study of the union of soul and body, including the study of expression (physiognomics) and the interpretation of dreams. The general object of these two branches of study is to determine in what way and to what extent the humours and temperament of the body affect the soul: also, how the soul affects the body. In the subdivisions of the scheme the first is concerned with the body: the headings there given are taken from the encyclopaedic treatises of the times and call for no comment. The second is the doctrine of the soul. One part of this is to be devoted to the spirit in the theological sense, the breath of God. This *anima rationalis* is derived from inspiration and by inspiration it must be treated: it is consigned to theology. The sensitive soul is a created thing and can be treated as one among other natural objects: that is to say, it may be treated physically as an object of natural science. Bacon made room in his scheme for the study of divination and fascination or the action of imagination upon bodies: but as he did not do more than create a scheme it is not necessary to say more about the dubious items.

More than anyone else at this period, Bacon excelled in making plans which were not carried out. When we turn from the scheme to actual achievements there is little to say. Bacon's writings show the strong impression made on him by Telesius. He regards the souls of animals as altogether material, a mixture of fire and air, situated in the head, running through the nerves and fed from the spirituous element of arterial blood. In animals this is the chief soul: in man it is the organic instrument of the rational soul. In the sphere of the senses Bacon did a little experimental work on the nature of sound, but did not advance from physical to psychological problems. He divided the faculties of the mind in a way already suggested by Campanella into three classes, memory, imagination, and reason. To these he ascribed respectively the 'disciplines' of history, poetry, and philosophy. More interesting than this dubious classification is the famous division of the idola. Bacon shows a distinct tendency toward a broad treatment of the mind. To him we owe the often quoted remark that the human understanding is not a dry light but is suffused and coloured by will. Among the idola he reckons natural prejudices, *idola tribus*, which are connate tendencies that affect the individual's thoughts. This is in direct contrast with the idea of human intellect as the repository of eternal truths, a universal essence alike in all. Followed to its end the thought would lead to a voluntaristic doctrine and produce a fruitful study of the actual varieties of the human mind.

Bacon did not follow out this or any other of his suggestive propositions, but the ideas which he expressed ruled the progress of inductive or experimental psychology all through its development. It is to the nineteenth century that we must look to see the full outcome of this comprehensive outline. The distinction of objective and subjective psychology, the study of the expression of emotions, the inquiry into human faculty based on statistics— all these are direct fulfilments of the plan for a comprehensive study of the human mind which Bacon partly originated and partly codified as it came to him from the Italian school of the sixteenth century.

In the history of science Bacon's major claim to fame rests on his *Novum Organum*, his substitute for Aristotelian logic as the tool of discovery. Like Galileo he objected to syllogistic reasoning as a way of understanding nature; it forced assent only, not things. But he differed from Galileo in his distrust of mathematics and abstract axioms. One typical instance of a phenomenon he regarded as useless to the scientist; rather he must collect countless instances under different conditions. All the realms of nature must be scoured by teams of sedulous research workers. Well-attested facts must be recorded in a central clearing house without any 'anticipations of nature' or provisional hypotheses. Rather these facts must await the judgment of the man who can give an 'interpretation of nature.' Method is the key. Method will guard us against our inveterate tendency to generalize too soon, to 'anticipate' nature. Nature is a book written in a finite alphabet. If countless words or instances are collected the key or letters of the alphabet will emerge, the forms in the facts will be discovered. The method of discovering these forms or generating natures was to compile tables of instances— tables of presence, absence, and degrees. In all examples of heat, for instance, it will be found that motion is co-present, co-absent, and co-variant with heat. The induction then follows that motion is the form or generating nature of heat.

This account of the inductive method was developed in much more detail and in a far less crude and metaphysical manner by J. S. Mill in the nineteenth century. The tradition of scientific method in England between Locke, Bacon's successor in the seventeenth century, and Mill was almost unbroken. British psychology grew up with this tradition. As will be seen by studying the work of Locke, Hume, Hartley, Hamilton, and many others—especially Bain—the view was tacitly accepted that scientists must start from facts or observations, preferably measurements; these are to be collected carefully and cautious generalizations made which do not go beyond the collected data. These generalizations, or empirical laws, are then to be related in a similar cautious manner under theories or higher level generalizations. In psychology the result was sensationism and associationism. By careful mental observations the well-attested facts or mental contents were collected together and sorted out under a variety of classificatory schemes. The generalizations were concerned with the laws of association or the various ways in which these mental contents were assumed to be connected. There were practically no variants on these pictures of and generalizations about the mind until the beginning of the twentieth century in British psychology. This was the extent of Bacon's influence.

No one, with any sense of historical perspective, could question the importance of this general outline of inquiry at the time when it was written. Bacon called upon inquirers to look at nature if they would learn her secrets. This may seem rather obvious advice to us now; but it was not then so obvious or so free from personal danger. Unfortunately the judicious Lord Chancellor, in his cautious distaste for hasty generalizations, overlooked the importance, indeed the indispensability, of hypotheses in science. Instead of saying that hypotheses, however arrived at, must be *tested* by observation, he maintained that we must *start from* observations in order to arrive at 'interpretations' rather than 'anticipations' of nature. He overlooked or knew nothing about the practice of Kepler and Galileo who certainly 'anticipated' nature in their search for a rational order. Not only was Bacon quite wrong in thinking that an orderly arrangement of data by itself will make the right 'interpretation' obvious, there being no method or recipe for inventing hypotheses to co-ordinate observations; he also failed to see that a hypothesis is indispensable to the collection of data since the selection of certain data out of a welter of sensory experience demands some way of determining relevance. Scientific data are always relative to the inquirer's existing knowledge, his interests, the problems which he wants to solve, and the type of solution that he expects. In fact an experiment in science implies the deliberate observation of expected results, not gaping open-mouthed at nature. Countless people must have noticed queer-looking objects in clay cliffs; they only became 'data' to a Darwin collecting fossils to test his evolutionary hypothesis.

Bacon's neglect of the use of hypotheses in science was paralleled by his disregard of deduction of which mathematical deduction is the most precise form. Here again he ignored or was ignorant of the technique by means of which Galileo achieved such startling results. In science there is often a long deductive journey between the hypothesis put forward and the observations of nature which will confirm or falsify it.

It is worth recording that sensationism and associationism, which were the main characteristics of British psychology up to the early twentieth century, were the by-products of dogmatic methodism in general as well as of the attempt to follow Bacon's advice for inquiry. The stress on starting from well-attested data issued in the search for simple incorrigible sensory elements which could form a reliable starting point for building up knowledge. We can readily see that Locke's simple ideas which come in through the windows of sense serve a similar function to Descartes' simple natures. Both provide some foundation of certainty for the erection of the edifice of knowledge. Locke's blank sheet of a mind had to be passive because otherwise we might make mistakes about the simple sensory elements which provide a sure foundation for knowledge; Hume's impressions and ideas, bound together by the principles of association like Newtonian mass-points bound together by gravitational attraction, were the creation of his belief that we could be certain, at least, about isolated impressions of sense. The picture of the mind in these cases was dictated mainly by preoccupation with recipes for obtaining certain or highly probable knowledge. Psychology was epistemology in disguise. This is regrettably true of a great deal of psychology right up to the middle of the nineteenth century. This connection between psychology and epistemology, which dates right back to Protagoras, explains why so much has to be said about the history of epistemology in a book on the history of psychology.

Bacon, therefore, was a mixed blessing to science in general and psychology in particular. Without him the view might never have arisen that scientific laws emerge after methodical collection of well-attested data—a view that Galileo and the prominent scientists never held—and psychology might have been spared its storehouse and cinematograph pictures of the mind popularized by Locke and Hume. On the other hand, perhaps, the observational basis of science had to be stressed in an extreme way in order for headway to be made against the rising tide of rationalism. Attention was focussed on sensory observation. This may well have mattered more to science in general than the caricature of its method and more to psychology in particular than the caricature of its mind.

D. *The rationalist method of deduction*

As the sixteenth century drew to a close the changes already made in the existing system of knowledge were summed up by a decisive revolution. René Descartes was born in 1596. He was educated in the Jesuit College of La Flêche, but his early training in that institution did not prevent him from acquiring the sceptical mood which the prevailing disagreement among theorists had made almost a fashion. In the history of psychology Descartes inaugurates a new era, not merely because he restated many old views and united in a novel manner the results reached by philosophers and physiologists, but first and foremost because he was gifted with the power of actually experiencing the new freedom of thought. When others were acquiring traditional formulae Descartes was living again through those primitive efforts of the mind by which sciences were first created. Apart altogether from considerations of doctrine and the inquiries which can so easily show where this or that opinion had a prototype, the work of Descartes must be counted truly original for wholly different reasons. Nothing that may be said, and must be said, to show how thoroughly Descartes was steeped in the thought of his contemporaries and the tradition of mediaevalism, should be allowed to obscure the fact of supreme importance. The fact was the recognition that the very existence of truth depends on the effort to make ideas clear; the thinker must experience the connection and unity which he asserts; the spirit which upheld the motto *credo quia absurdum* must be for ever abandoned. As the embodiment of this new gospel of intellectual sincerity Descartes' *Meditations* may be classed with Augustine's *Confessions*. A general resemblance between these two has been often noticed, but attention has been misdirected to similarities of expression. More important than such literary coincidences is the profound fact that Augustine brought to an end the effective philosophy of the ancient world by retiring into the sanctuary of the heart. Descartes inaugurated the effective reunion of the inner and outer worlds, the world of introspection and the world of scientific prediction, by going forth from the inmost chambers of the intellect to the boundaries of its new domains.

The methods of the physical scientists like Kepler and Galileo were much better understood by Descartes than by Bacon. In his famous vision Descartes saw that mathematics was the sole key needed to unlock the secrets of nature. Soon afterwards he invented analytical geometry. He postulated an exact one to one correspondence between the realms of number and of geometry, the nature of extension being such that its relations must always be expressible in algebraic form. Conversely, algebraic or numerical truths could always be fully represented spatially. He concluded that the whole realm of physics would be reducible to geometric qualities alone. If all other qualities like sound and colour and smell could be shown to be appearances of extended and figured magnitudes in motion, mathematics would indeed reveal nature's ground-plan. In the context of the astronomy and mechanics of his day we can understand Descartes' boast that, given matter and motion, he could make a world. We can also understand his reluctance to meet Hobbes who inexorably concluded that mental characteristics also were causally dependent upon motions of the corporeal organs.

Descartes' famous method and his rules for inquiry are best seen as his attempt to make explicit the procedures of mathematical reasoning. Like Plato Descartes thought that knowledge must be certain if it is really to be called knowledge. He tried to show how certainty could be attained. In the main his account was similar to Galileo's without Galileo's insistence on the importance of experimental checks. The senses present us with problems. We have to think about the characteristics of the phenomena presented and isolate the difficulties under examination. Isolation enables us eventually to discriminate the several constituent natures of a complex object; knowledge begins when we have a clear and distinct 'intuition' of the simple natures like figure, motion, and extension which are incapable of further analysis. By combining simple natures, intuitively revealed, we are able to make complex deductions in the same sort of way that Pythagoras' theorem can be deduced from a few simple axions which contain simple notions like 'straight,' 'equal,' and 'greater than.'

Descartes thought that all men were alike in their capacity to perceive rational connections; differences were due either to prejudice, or to defects of will, or to failure to observe the right method. If the data were arranged in an orderly way, if nothing was accepted as true which was not clearly and distinctly perceived, if the difficulties under discussion were properly isolated, and if frequent reviews of the steps in reasoning were made, we simply could not go wrong. Knowledge awaited anyone who was prepared to follow the correct method.

Rationalism, as a theory of inquiry, was strong where observationalism was weak. Descartes, like Galileo, stressed the importance of deduction in science. He saw that to explain a phenomenon is to deduce its occurrence from some more general and often highly abstract assumption. He was misled, however, by his paradigm of Euclidean geometry into thinking that the adequacy of the explanation is guaranteed by the self-evidence or clarity and distinctness of the postulates from which a phenomenon could be deduced. The real characteristics of the optically revealed world were lighted upon when, as it were, there were flashes of light within the mind. Metaphors taken from optics seemed to percolate into Descartes' theory of knowledge. In science basic postulates need not, as we have discovered, be illuminated by the glow of self-evidence. The history of science is littered with abandoned postulates which, at one time, were thought to be self-evident. Conversely even Newton was hesitant about adopting his basic postulates because they did not seem to be self-evident. They soon became so to later generations, self-evidence being mainly a matter of habituation. The acid test of postulates in science, as Galileo suggested, is whether consequences deduced from them agree with observations. A scientist does not worry about certainty and regards all his postulates as tentative. He is prepared to discard any which are empirically falsified. Descartes, being preoccupied like Plato with certainty and taking mathematics as his model, where sense-perception is of minor importance, made a rigid separation between sense and reason and almost completely neglected the importance of sensory observations in testing hypotheses. The senses can only decide between two postulates which are intuitively equivalent. The hypothetico-deductive method of Galileo, in Descartes' hands, retained its deductive but lost its hypothetical character.

It is almost superfluous to add that Descartes' dogmatic methodism is a superstition. His claim that all men can win their way to knowledge provided that they follow the right method will not bear examination. There are no rules for achieving adequate explanations. Discoveries are not made by men with the book of the words in their hands. Newton had a hunch that the motion of the planets in relation to each other could be explained by deducing them from the same laws which explained the motion of freely falling bodies on earth. The story of the apple may be apocryphal but it represents nicely the idiosyncratic way in which hypotheses may originate. There are no stereotyped rules for arriving at hypotheses; there are only certain general counsels of prudence for testing them and for publishing them in such a way that others can check up on them. The new man cannot be successful in science by referring to a guide; he must steep himself in a tradition and acquire all sorts of skills which no textbook can teach him. In science all men are not on a level; neither can they become so, as Descartes thought, by careful conning of a technique.

Descartes' psychology was a consequence of his methodology. As he has been called by some 'the father of modern psychology' it will be useful, before embarking on the details of his system, to select the main lines of his influence in advance.

Descartes is most famous for his dualism of mind and body, which follows from his method of deduction. Explanation, for Descartes, involved deduction from simple natures clearly and distinctly perceived. Between physical natures like figure and extension on the one hand and mental natures like thinking on the other hand there seemed to be no qualitative similarity. It therefore seemed out of the question that physical events could be deduced from any postulates describing mental events and *vice versa*. The body, which was physical, was therefore explained on mechanistic lines. It was a machine like an animal body. Like the rest of the physical world it could be treated by the quantitative techniques of the physical scientist. The workings of the mind, on the other hand, could not be treated by quantitative techniques; they could only be understood by introspection. When Spinoza later suggested that the mental could be subjected to quantitative treatment so that emotions could be studied like lines, planes, and bodies, he was only developing Descartes by suggesting that the separate science of mind could also make use of mechanical categories of explanation. This was a theological heresy that even Spinoza was reluctant to publish in his lifetime. It is true that Descartes did not hold consistently to his dualism of mind and body. The machine of the body, he taught, was regulated in voluntary movements by the mind which switched over the animal spirits at the pineal gland rather like a signalman regulating an automatic railway. This primitive picture of the control of nerve impulses was glaringly inconsistent with the Cartesian method of explanation, as Spinoza later pointed out. And it was the two world picture with its derivative dual modes of inquiry which was foisted on psychology by Descartes. We thus find growing up a mechanistic biology and physiology alongside of a separate science of mind using only the method of introspection. Watson and Pavlov on the one hand and Titchener and Wundt on the other were the final flowers of Cartesian dualism. They were his descendants in more than their concentration on what they deemed mind rather than body or what they deemed body rather than mind. In their use of ultimate units like reflexes or sensory atoms as explanatory principles they were following up, also, the Cartesian search for simple natures from which the motions of the body or the workings of the mind could be rationally deduced.

Descartes, as is well known, in his search for certainty, hit upon the proposition '*Cogito, ergo sum*' whose precise meaning has been a standing bone of contention to generations of philosophers. Whatever Descartes in fact meant by it the assumption steadily developed that we have prior knowledge of the mental—of our own mind-pictures, as it were, which come between the mind and external nature. If we will but look into ourselves, so taught Locke, Berkeley, and Hume, we can settle psychological disputes because nothing can be more certain than our own awareness of our mental pictures. Hume championed psychology as the basic science. The categories of the other sciences like causality, continuity, and so on, were genetically explained in psychological terms; but the categories of psychology itself, oddly enough, seemed in need of no further explanation. This shows Descartes' influence even on one whose fame rests mainly on the death-blows which he dealt to Cartesian methods of explanation. But how many psychologists, even now, are free from the assumption that most beliefs, except their own psychological ones, have a psychological explanation which somehow is relevant to their validity? Psychologists have, in the main, outgrown the view that psychological disputes can be decisively settled by comparing introspective notes; but the Cartesian doctrine of the logical priority of the science of mind dies very hard—even harder, perhaps, than the Cartesian view that there can be a separate science of mind.

The final general trend of Descartes' influence can be summed up in the label 'intellectualism.' Psychology, because of its close link with epistemology, had a strong cognitive and intellectualistic bias. This was strengthened and perpetuated by Descartes. The investigation of conative factors was more or less neglected, with the exception of Spinoza, by most psychologists right up to the end of the nineteenth century when the advent of biology began to change the direction of interest. It is significant that Descartes' main interest in conative factors was epistemological; he had recourse to them in order to explain how people make mistakes.

Dualism, atomism, 'psychologism,' introspectionism, intellectualism, mechanistic physiology—these are the main heritages of Descartes. These trends are as much the consequences of his methodology as of the details of his psychological system. Indeed, he was the father of modern psychology if 'modern' denotes up to the start of the twentieth century. There are many who would maintain, when they consider his heritage, that his revolt against Aristotelianism did more harm than good to the development of psychology.

Chapter Eleven

THE RATIONALIST TRADITION

A. Descartes

I. PHYSIOLOGY

In physiology Descartes had the advantage of coming after Vesalius and being acquainted with the discovery of Harvey. He studied anatomy and made dissections for himself, but where he differed from the physiologists he was usually wrong; his strength lay in his readiness to adopt the results reached by others. In the sphere of physiology everything seemed to point to self-explanatory processes. The circulation of the blood was a mechanical process requiring for its explanation only the matter and the motion of the heart. Descartes showed his natural inclination by trying to make this motion dependent on the heat in the heart, a divergence from facts which revealed how much Descartes could sacrifice strict scientific procedure to imaginary systematization. Digestion, too, was now explained by the chemical properties of secretions; science no longer favoured any special faculty of digestion. Over and above these genuine contributions to the view of man as a machine, there was the fact that mechanical models were among the wonders of the age. Descartes was greatly impressed by the clock-work structures which were to be seen at Nurnberg and elsewhere. The gardens of the aristocracy were adorned with fountains so constructed that the water running in the tubes would move mannikins, play instruments, or even produce sounds like words uttered by lay-figures. Descartes saw an analogy between these water-pipes and the 'tubes' in which he thought the spirits moved; the absence of voluntary action was evident in the case of the statues, and this was paralleled by the fact that movements of the body are also frequently executed without conscious intentions. Thus Descartes arrived at the *undulatio reflexa*, the action unaccompanied by will, for which he has been described as author of the theory of 'reflex action.' We may give Descartes credit for recognizing that all movements are not supervised by a will-to-move, and possibly for some knowledge of the fact that movements are performed by decapitated animals. But it is very necessary to remember that the *undulatio reflexa* of Descartes was essentially a mere rebound of particles, a mere ingoing and outcoming of an actual stream of subtle matter. In the language of the nineteenth century 'reflex action' means a co-ordination of centres with a considerable degree of integration —all of which was not considered until the latter part of the eighteenth century. Much of the confusion which seems prevalent in accounts of the reflex-action theory is due to not recognizing the difference between Cartesian theories and later physiological observations. Descartes was primarily interested in the analogy between mechanical and physiological action; he saw only the points of resemblance between reflection of light, reflux of water, and reflex action. The modern neurologist would see chiefly the absence of resemblance.

2. THE BODY AS A MACHINE

Though Descartes did not produce a formal system like those of the scholastics, he intended to include in his work all the standard topics. He would have treated the cosmos as a whole if his work had been completed, beginning from stones and metals, and ending in man and God. The familiar lines of the ordinary system are only obscured by the absence of the familiar terms and rubrics. It is from the general consideration of the cosmos that we come to man, and the objective science of man or anthropology is the background of psychology. The body is part of the world of matter, it is a certain portion of matter peculiar to a man. As matter it may be dealt with scientifically, which, for Descartes, means mechanically. The soul does not move the body, nor is it the principle of life; death is not due to the absence of the soul from the body, but when the bodily functions cease the soul withdraws. Thus, in opposition to earlier views, Descartes removes from the concept of the soul every part of the concept of physical life. Physical life is essentially movement, which depends on the muscles, and these in turn depend on the nerves. The corporeal principle of movement is a kind of fire, a natural heat which resides in the heart. This internal heat causes the blood to circulate; it also produces by rarefaction a kind of quintessence of the blood, the subtle airs called animal spirits. 'These animal spirits consist of the finest particles contained in the blood, which are filtered from the arteries through minute pores into the central cavity or ventriclè of the brain. From this ventricle they pass into the nerves, and, by flowing down the motor nerves and from them into the muscles, they cause the latter to become distended laterally, and therefore to shorten and so bring about the movements of the parts of the body. According to Descartes' scheme of the nervous system, the motor nerves open from the ventricle of the brain by valved mouths; the sensory nerves also have their central terminations in the ventricle, each being connected with the valve of the motor nerves; when, then, any impression is made on a sense-organ, the sensory nerve affected plays the part of a bell-wire, it pulls open the valve to which it is attached and so allows the animal spirits to flow down the corresponding motor nerve and to bring about the appropriate reflex movement.' Though it has now only historical interest, this scheme has been stated in the words of Professor McDougall (*Body and Mind*, p. 51) at some length because it was destined to form the basis of nearly all the physiological psychology which the seventeenth and eighteenth centuries produced. It affords a proper understanding of the way in which Descartes understood the relation of the soul to the body, for if the soul is in some sense present to this machinery at the critical point of transmission from sensory to motor channels there is ground for asserting that the soul may direct the movement of the animal spirits and make possible the required development from action to conduct when our philosopher is called upon to explain his ethics.

In accordance with the original Aristotelian scheme Descartes recognizes two levels of conscious activity: the soul thinks, remembers, and wills by itself, while its union with the body makes possible the sensuous operations of the common sense, imagination, and instinct. As the principal 'seat of the soul' Descartes selected the pineal gland. This selection was peculiarly unfortunate from a physiological standpoint, and we can hardly doubt that the quality which recommended it to Descartes was the uniqueness of this gland, and that in this uniqueness Descartes found the physical counterpart of conscious unity. In mitigation of this disparaging explanation there is the possibility that Descartes was merely following a fashion; apparently as early as 1641 a certain Jean Cousin discussed in a 'thesis' the question,

An κωνάριον *sensus communis sedes?* A thesis is usually a symptom of some popularity attaching to its subject.

3. THE SENSES

The senses were divided by Descartes into two classes, the outer and the inner. The outer senses are the usual five senses, touch, taste, smell, hearing, and vision. On these Descartes has nothing essentially new to say, with the possible exception of vision, which is treated primarily from the point of view of dioptrics. The essential features are the same in all the modes of sensation, for they all express a relation of the three factors, sensitive soul (*anima sentiens*), external object, and intervening nerves. The objects are, for Descartes, constituted by the union of extension with motion, so that the relation of each object to the body is a relation of co-extension and motion. The motion is transmitted from the outer to the inner extremity of the nerve, and from the inner movement we derive all the effects called sensations. The transition here made from quantity of movement to quality of effect, was not made by Descartes in ignorance of the difficulties. To remove the obstacles no means were available except that form of procrastination which works by intermediaries; the movement of the nerves was said to produce upon the pineal gland an impression, such as a seal might make on wax, and by this impression the soul was stimulated to produce an idea. At the last critical point, then, Descartes falls back on traditional metaphors. He thinks, indeed, that motion in the physical world is identical with activity in the spiritual, and therefore the transition from the last motion to the adjacent (?) activity is not really a leap, or at any rate the *saltus* is (in the scientific sense) 'negligible.' The new scheme, if inadequate at this point, had the merit of simplifying matters by dropping the old view that a picture *like* the object was deposited in the brain. For 'likeness' must be substituted a very attenuated conception of 'correspondence.' As all motions, in terms of situation and velocity, are pure quantities, Descartes saw that the qualitative differences of sensations were not properly explained by his principles. For this there was no cure except to begin again from the other end and throw the burden on the 'nature of the soul.'

All the senses are forms of touch, as Aristotle had said: but they have distinctive characteristics. Touch itself usually seems easy to explain and many are deceived by the apparent ease. Vision, on the contrary, seems extraordinarily difficult: the object is more or less distant, the organ exceptionally refined, the results exquisite and mysterious. The difficulty of passing from motion to sensation is here most distinctly comprehended, and consequently the powers of the theorist are here most severely taxed. The primary objects of vision are light and colour; as secondary objects Descartes enumerated position, distance, size, and form. Sight is dependent upon three things—object, inner organ (nerve and brain), and outer organ (transparent parts of the eye, etc.). Assisted by the advances made during the century, Descartes was able to give a rational account of the physical and physiological conditions of vision. Light is a motion transmitted from a luminous body in straight lines through the air or other transparent bodies to the eye (*Dioptr.*, i. 6). As light is purely motion, not (as the corpuscular theory maintained) minute particles of matter in motion, Descartes thought that the transmission of light was instantaneous: the thrill or vibration of the luminiferous substance occurs simultaneously at all points, as the jerk given to a taut line takes effect simultaneously at both ends. This and the corresponding view that the movement of the nerves is propagated instantaneously were alike erroneous, but the error did not affect the most valuable part of the conclusion, namely that vision depends on the communication of a motion originating outside the eye to the optic nerve and its inner terminus. For this the formula is: *Actionis vis ex objectis visus emanans ad oculos nostros diffunditur* (*Dioptr.*, i. 5). The result of the physical and physiological processes is an image of the object, but the image is not itself the vision nor is it even what is seen. The *actionis vis ex objectis* requires as its complement another *vis* which is the innate power of the eye and goes forth from it to the objects: *quae oculis innata ad illa pergit* (*Dioptr.*, i. 5). Here Descartes is once more face to face with the central problem and compelled to justify his claim to superiority over the mediaeval doctors. In one respect that superiority is manifest: there is more economy of thought in Descartes' exposition of sense-processes, and therefore a superiority of method. A passage like the following is decisive: *licet autem haec pictura, sic transmissa in cerebrum, semper aliquid similitudinis ex objectis, a quibus venit, retineat, non tamen ob id credendum est, ut supra monuimus* (*Dioptr.*, c. iv), *hanc similitudi-*

nem esse, quae facit, ut illa sentiamus, quasi denuo alii quidam oculi in cerebro nostro forent, quibus illam contemplari possemus. We need not stop to inquire who held this 'representative image' theory: it is enough that its nature is here fully exposed and adequately refuted. As a consequence all problems of light, colour, and visual space are made subjective, since they are effects which can only be produced in the sensitive soul. Perception of distance was explained by Descartes as dependent on *mutuam quandam conspirationem oculorum (Dioptr.*, vi. 11, 13); the inversion of the retinal image was negligible, for the image was not the object of vision; thus in some degree Descartes comprehended the significance of accommodation of the eye and the symbolic character which sensations have in their relation to the total experience of the individual.

The Cartesian dualism penetrates to the uttermost limit of things. In sensation there is the dualism of *motus* and *idea*, the content and the form *(Dioptr.* c. vi. a 2). This idea is the *idea materialis* of later writers, described *(De Hom.*, a 70) as a figure traced by the spirits on the surface of the pineal gland. When the soul is united with this machine (that is, when it is attentive) it produces a spiritual idea corresponding to the material idea, and this is the function called imagination. There are then three degrees of organic activity: there is outer perception, there is the inner perception of material ideas, and finally the inner perception of pure ideas. This scheme does not realize the expectations aroused by the vigour with which Descartes began; there is an obvious lapse into formalism. Similarly, the *sensus interni* are grouped and arranged in an artificial manner. A distinction is first made between natural appetites and 'passions.' The former comprehend all affections of those nerves which extend to the stomach, *oesophagus*, and adjacent parts: these are principally hunger and thirst, though Descartes includes in the same category feelings of pain, irritation, and general 'tone,' since these too are perceived by the soul as being inside rather than outside. This is the link which connects these appetites with the passions. To the latter Descartes gave much attention, and we must return to the subject later. Before leaving the classification of the organic activities, which so far has included outer sense, imagination, and inner sense, some account should be given of the activities which belong to the soul itself. If we think only of the soul, the outer and inner senses are to be called 'passions,' since in them the action of the soul is always aroused and determined by objects. Then the activities of the soul are forms of ideation, and we find in this class the familiar doctrines of active imagination, memory, and recollection, and finally the highest operations of reason. On these topics Descartes offered no views that were superior to those of Aristotle or Augustine.

4. THE MIND

One cardinal feature in the work of Descartes is the definition of the mind as essentially a thinking thing, *res cogitans*. Upon this basis, remembering that the mind is a substance, we expect to hear what it is that the mind thinks. This question Descartes undertakes to answer by a method which is partly introspective, partly dogmatic and scholastic. He asserts, dogmatically, that the mind can function without the aid of the brain. 'I have often shown,' he says, 'that the mind can work independently of the brain; for clearly there can be no use of the brain for pure intelligence, but only for imagination and sensation' (*Med.*, ii. Resp. quint. ad obj. 3). This is a clear statement that the mind has activities that are nothing but its own motions, the *actus purus* of earlier writers. The operations of the mind when it thinks are ideas; so the pure activities will be ideas that have no dependence upon the world of objects either for their origin or for their truth. These are the so-called innate ideas. As these ideas do not originate from causes external to us, they arise in the form of memories, and experience is only the occasion for our consciousness of their existence. This view of the innate is as old as Plato, and Descartes seems to have adopted this theory at first without much serious reflection. But objections and criticisms quickly caused him to shift his ground. He declared that he meant by innate ideas no more than an indefinite potentiality of thought: the ideas exist only potentially and become actual in the process of experience. But this later position is equally full of difficulties for Descartes. It is excluded from the beginning by his idea of substance: the mind is not merely the sum of possible ideas; it is a thing, and that fact haunts Descartes to the end. After having once said it, Descartes strove earnestly to unsay it in every way except by open recantation. The goal at which he was aiming was the complete separation of all mental processes from physical processes. He felt, as Plato and Aristotle had felt, that the physical events preceding consciousness of an object never actually explain the consciousness; whether we think of universal ideas or particular ideas, the idea as such is a fact of consciousness and nothing if not that. So in spite of many partial contradictions and many changes of front, it seems correct to say that Descartes' 'innate ideas' amount ultimately to no more than this assertion of independent reality, crossed and confused by the use of the scholastic formulae of substance. This view is strongly supported by the attempt at a catalogue of innate ideas which Descartes was led to make.

Believing in the self-evidence of consciousness and inclined to be introspective, Descartes naturally finds such notions as those of God and the self most distinctly innate. They seem to be in the mind; they are not adventitious, as is the idea of an object like the sun; they are not made up out of separable elements as are the ideas of centaurs and hippogriffs. A feeling of certainty and inevitableness belongs to them, and Descartes by a 'spontaneous impulse,' writes them down as ultimate, underivable, and eternally true. On further reflection he finds many other ideas that can claim to be innate for the same reasons. The axioms of mathematics have a longstanding claim to be called innate; the ideas of figures, such as the circle, are ideas that have no real external counterpart, for the *absolute* circle is not given us in experience; space, time, motion, and all the primary qualities depend more on mind than on outer perception; in fact ultimately *everything* depends on mind in so far as it is an idea and not a thing.

The general statement of the nature of innate ideas, as made by Descartes, leads to the specific question of the relation between ideas and images. The current theory of perception postulated three terms, an object, an image of the object, and an idea or mental grasp of the image. This scheme implies a universe of objects reproduced in a universe of thought; Descartes rejects that scheme and is then driven back on the problem of the ideas as effects of some agency. If the idea is not an effect of the object it must be an effect of the subject, a product of subjective activity. In the second case, the producer is at the same time the product, and the idea is no more than a state of consciousness (*modus cogitandi*). But the actual distinction of image and idea is still untouched; it will be necessary either to deny the distinction or reinterpret the subjective activity. Descartes chooses the latter course. Ideas are classed by him as (*a*) innate, (*b*) adventitious i.e. dependent on external conditions, and (*c*) made by the mind (factitious, complex ideas of imaginary objects). As ideas these are all mental; as images they are presented with the concurrent help of the body. The distinction between the image and the idea depends therefore on the part played by the body. The image has the peculiarity of being apparently corporeal; if that means that it is a physical event, we are no farther advanced, for the image remains on the other side of the gulf between matter and mind; similarly, if an image is truly mental, why is it distinct from the idea? Descartes sees vaguely that a pure introspective analysis of mind cannot find any distinction between image and idea. The later scholastic position, that an idea may be real without having a corresponding reality to depend upon, has developed in Descartes to a grasp of the fact that all inner states are on the same level psychologically. But the problems which belong to the theory of knowledge corrupt this insight. Descartes persists in thinking that the idea of a centaur would be changed if some real centaur came into existence; he also thought (after Anselm and before Kant) that the idea of God was (as mere idea) dependent on the existence of God. Overlooking this confusion we may credit Descartes with a grasp of the fact that ideas cannot be both inside and outside the mind; consciousness is pure immediacy. To be 'in the mind' is nothing else than to be a phase or aspect of mental life. Next to the mind comes the brain, and the image, if it is more than the idea, is a brain process. In this way Descartes works out a dualism different from that of external object and internal image. The object and the image are for him alike corporeal; the idea and the concept are mental. To the passage quoted above in which Descartes says the brain is needed only for imagination or sentiency, we may add another explicit statement: 'no corporeal species is received in the mind; pure thinking is performed without any corporeal species; imagination, however, which can only arise in the case of corporeal things, needs species, which is a truly corporeal thing; to this the mind applies itself, though the species is not received into the mind.' The language is scholastic, but the point is new, namely that brain processes are no more than conditions of mental processes. Whether Descartes was right in saying that there are any mental processes not dependent on brain-process and whether he rightly understood the relation of image and idea, remains to be seen.

Descartes did not say all this in one place or at one time, but a comparison of his various statements shows that he vacillated between two distinct positions. At one time he thought of the innate ideas as a 'very few' divinely implanted possessions of the thinking substance. At another time he clung to the unassailable position that thought is thought, a bare affirmation that served to mark him off from any encroachments of materialism. As a development of this affirmation he was prepared to say that he never meant by 'innate ideas'[1] anything more than the potentiality of thought and that the modes of thought included all the contents of consciousness, sensations, perceptions, judgments, and intuitions. As this was the point which Descartes reached in the later writings we must accept it as his real teaching. It is clear that he denied any materialistic tendency in his teaching; it is also clear that his objections to materialism were rooted in his nature, for he was a rationalist at heart, a scholastic by early training, and tempered his pursuit of physiology with a liberal amount of mysticism and theology. The occasional use of such terms as *notiones communes* suggests the Stoic element in Descartes' education; we know how popular those doctrines were at the time, and it is probable that they greatly influenced Descartes; but the form in which Descartes states his views seems to show that they were not consciously adopted from any school.

5. THE PASSIONS

The two factors, mind and body, have now been treated as distinct. It remains to see what Descartes said about the organism as a living unity of opposites. This part of his teaching is comprised under the term Passions of the Soul; it is the psychophysical part of the whole system.

The term passion denotes a change or affection in a thing which does not arise from the thing itself. In the case of the soul it will include all the phases of conscious life which are dependent on the action of agencies external to the soul. Thus the sensations are passions; the lower form of memory, the mere retentiveness, is a passion; Descartes goes so far as to say that *all* forms of

---

[1] Descartes speaks of *ideae* as *innatae, ingenitae, insitae*. Also simply as ideas which are in our mind or which we have.

knowledge are passions. By thus including under the 'passions' perceptions, feelings, emotions, and the processes of induction and reasoning, Descartes shows that he intends really to oppose the will to the intellect. The soul is active only in volition, which includes attention, recollection, and phantasia (cp. p. 365); in cognition it is passive. Descartes retains the belief that truth belongs to those ideas that correctly represent their sources, the objects. If the will intrudes, it can only assent to the necessary connection of ideas; otherwise it perverts the truth into error.

The doctrine of the passions depends upon the idea of spirits. All passions originate in the sensations. When Descartes defines the term further he distinguishes the emotions from sensations and from volitions. Sensations are passions which we refer to external objects, e.g. smells, sounds, colours. Volitions are emotions which arise from and are caused by the soul itself. So Descartes finally means by passions those inner states which are states of consciousness, but at the same time have their real cause in the agitation of the spirits. They are both inner states, with no external counterpart, and intermediate states, neither wholly physical nor wholly psychic. They are determined from without and from within. The exciting cause, e.g. of hate, moves the animal spirits, but the nature of the individual's character modifies the nature of the passion through the brain. The brain being the chief seat of the soul, the two activities meet at that point. In this way the will or activity of the soul has the power of modifying the passions and changing their psychic values. Every passion has an inner and an outer phase. The natural disposition is the inner phase; the object which stimulates to action in accordance with this disposition is the other phase. Education produces character or fixed dispositions, so that the doctrine of the passions leads into the doctrine of conduct or ethics. The training of the will and the control of the passions thus form the psychological part of Descartes' ethical reflections.

To complete the psycho-physical part of the doctrine it is necessary to note that Descartes makes the brain the seat of the passions. This is directly opposed to the view that they should be localized in the heart. The heart is usually affected and all passions are accompanied by a feeling in the heart and in the blood. This is a secondary effect due to the close connection of the animal spirits with the blood; it is a subordinate physical quality of the passions. If the passions were purely an affair of the heart and the blood they would not be subject to control through the will. That they are capable of such control and that the mind has the power of changing their nature is a cardinal point steadily developed by later Cartesians. Descartes himself roundly declares that conduct is ruled by thought; good judgment suffices to produce good action. The Socratic phrase is repeated, *omnis peccans est ignorans (Ep.*, i. 110), and no sign is given by Descartes to show that he wished to modify the strict interpretation of this. Socrates may have meant by 'knowledge' a complete state of conviction; but Descartes does not show any inclination to adopt what would be a correct but tautologous formula for action.

Two points deserve notice. First, that ideas and feelings tend to be associated. In the *Passions* (ii. 107) Descartes says, 'when we have once joined some corporeal action with a thought the one never presents itself afterwards without the other also presenting itself.' This implies both the recall of feelings and the general principle of association. The education of character is achieved by causing a union between feelings and ideas, so that they are ever afterwards united. Secondly, Descartes gives attention to the purely physical side of emotions and explains them as primarily intended to secure suitable responses to given conditions. The sight of an animal is a perception to which is added immediately the emotion of fear with consequent tendency to flight or to self-defence. This process does not involve the intellect; the passions do not proceed from reason or will; the full perception of our own mental state is rather the effect than the cause of the bodily adjustments. This looks like an anticipation of the James-Lange theory; it has the same tendency to put the physiological process before the developed emotion; but in origin and nature it is probably a way of saying that Providence gives us instinctive emotions. Descartes believed in pre-natal emotions as well as innate ideas, deriving them probably from reminiscences of the Stoic doctrines.

6. DESCARTES COMPARED WITH ARISTOTLE

The reader has probably concluded, long before this, that there is no unity in the doctrines of Descartes. The fact is obvious. The only task that remains is to distinguish and identify the various lines of thought that here converge.

At one extreme we have a purely rationalistic element. The essence of mind is thought, and the fact that some ideas are declared innate makes the doctrines of Descartes a spiritualistic psychology. Here we have a continuation of pure scholasticism. At the other extreme we have a naturalistic element. Apart from the innate ideas, the content of consciousness is furnished from the body through the passions; this is an empirical element, though not in Descartes a materialistic tendency. The sharp definition of the extremes leads to a continual insertion of inter-mediary factors. Between soul and body come the spirits which are undeniably Stoic in origin and mark the persistence of the theories handed down from Galen. The Stoic doctrine was known to Descartes, for he mentions Zeno and Seneca; but even without this direct evidence it is obvious that the ethical part of the writings of Descartes is thoroughly Stoic and shows the influence of contemporary revivals of Stoicism. The monism of the early Stoics is not acceptable to Descartes; he is more closely allied to the later Platonizing Stoics, both in his ethical views and in his treatment of the soul as distinct from the body. Cicero probably exerted some influence on his mind, and his phrases occasionally recall the language of Epictetus. The dualism which he maintains is primarily scholastic and so, indirectly, Aris-totelian. It is not correct to say that Descartes 'had defined mind, in opposition to Aristotle, as exclusively thinking substance.'[1] Aristotle never supposed that mind as such was anything more than a principle of thought. In fact, Descartes and Aristotle are remarkably alike. They both start from a basis of natural philo-sophy; they both regard sensation as a matter for empirical treatment and value sensations and emotions as primarily the data of the natural life. Descartes agrees with Aristotle in dividing the psychic activities into two classes. One class includes sensa-tion, retention, and the processes of discursive thought. The other includes the activities of the soul which seem to be pecu-liarly its own, those which Aristotle assigned to reason ($\nu o \hat{v} s$). Descartes' definition of soul corresponds to Aristotle's idea of the reason; both come in from without, furnish the ultimate principles of thought, and may be considered apart from the composite human nature. The mind is for Descartes what the reason was for Aristotle. The two part company most clearly on the question

[1] Wundt, *Human and Animal Psychology*, E. Tr., p. 3 (1896).

of the *soul*, not the mind. What Aristotle would have described in terms of a principle of life, Descartes attempts to describe mechanically. It is very doubtful whether Descartes had the advantage in that point. He disentangled himself from the meshes of contemporary Aristotelianism; he broke away from the mere repetition of words without meaning; but in all that he was acquiring for himself a grasp of the truth which had been lost with the decay of Greek civilization. As time progresses it becomes more certain that Aristotle's concept of the organism must be preferred to the Cartesian machine and operator.

7. ANIMALS AS MACHINES

There is a curious passage in the history of Descartes' mind which deserves to be studied for the light it throws on the development of thought at this critical point. The passage in question relates to the notion that animals are machines, a very natural and sensible idea if rightly understood; since Huxley has taken it under his protection we need not labour the point but give a brief account of Descartes' own views and then indicate the real importance which belongs to the topic.

It had been customary from the time of Aristotle to distinguish three uses of the word soul and three grades of being, namely plants, animals, men. Since Descartes proposed to confine the term soul to reason, the question whether animals have souls can only be taken to mean: Have animals a rational soul? As Descartes had also declared the human body to be a machine, and everyone agreed that man was a rational animal, the most elementary logic could show that an animal was wholly what man was in part, to wit a body, and therefore a machine. So far the point is clear, but Descartes was not quite sure what his own statements meant. At first he was content to treat animals as machines: he was at that time fresh from the pursuit of physiology and also very much inclined to regard machinery as the true type of self-explanatory causation. In his eagerness to be rid of all occult causes he was ready to disregard some obvious facts. At this period he could see no distinction between a sound organism and a perfect clock. But as time went on these impulses grew weaker. The force of analogy began to assert itself. He hinted at the possibility of a different principle, the instinct. While he began by speaking of animals as mere machines, he ended with the much more moderate statement that it was not possible to prove they could think. In the interval between his earliest and his latest views he grants that these organisms may give sensations and a kind of consciousness which does not amount to thought. In general his position is that reason in the proper sense is peculiar to the human mind. In human life there are many actions that do not come into consciousness; they are reflex activities which the organism carries out without the intervention of mind. These are operations of our animal nature, our bodies as machines. The human and the animal world overlap at this point. Instead of saying with the Scholastics, that the vegetative and sensitive souls are merged in the rational soul as the higher form, Descartes regards the human body as an animal organism united with a rational soul. Animals can then be regarded as bodies only, and this is the point which Descartes never wholly abandons. If he goes so far as to suppose that some obscure sensations accompany its operations, it is because his idea of body develops into the idea of an organism which acts as if it had psychic qualities.

Fundamentally, then, we may regard this much disputed proposition, animals are automatic, i.e. self-contained, machines as merely a forcible way of eliminating animism from physiology. But apart from the mere statement of the view, there is the question of its historical place and significance. It is not a question of animal psychology at all, for it is concerned neither with animals nor with psychology, except in that wide sense in which the human being can be called simply an animal. Even the disciples of Descartes saw that the consequences were important, and there can be no doubt that Henry More hit the mark when he said that the whole idea arose from the prejudice against giving animals a claim to immortality. There can be no doubt, too, that this was not all. Descartes disliked the sentimental attitude toward animals: he rightly thought the popular ideas about their powers were gross exaggerations: he lived in close enough contact with the beliefs about human souls taking up their abode in animal bodies to feel the immense advantage of a more scientific view of the matter. Yet even here he blundered, for his sharp distinction between soul and body made it more than ever possible to regard the body as a place occupied by a soul, and so reduced the possible objections against its dwelling in all and every kind of body. Descartes, in fact, lost his way, believing as he did that moral qualities belonged only to men and that no one could prove animals to be reflective moral beings. Proofs might indeed be wanting, but statements were abundant. Apart from Pliny, who counted religion among the moral virtues of elephants and endorsed the ancient idea that those animals lifted up their trunks in prayer, Lactantius had been generous enough to ascribe morality, without religion, to animals. Omitting Porphyry, whose influence had waned many centuries before, and the queer stories which supplied the place of earnest inquiry for the whole period of the Middle Ages, we find Rorarius (1554) maintaining that animals have reason and make a better use of it than man. In the same year Gomez Pereira, in a book called *Antoniana Margarita*, had upheld a similar position, the source of which can easily be traced to the Stoic idea of instinct, that natural faculty in all created things which operates undisturbed when the reason does not intefere with its promptings. Thus for a century before Descartes there had been a distinct tendency to dispute the primacy of man in the moral sphere. It was argued that if man was made in the likeness of God, but had defaced that likeness by his arbitrary choice of evil and his fall from grace, the animals (having no such freedom of will) preserved what Cicero had called their uncorrupted nature; they are either created evil or not evil at all.

The tide of opinion was turning against man. The reason for this is to be sought in the whole change which came over the dream of human perfectibility. The end and aim of knowledge had for long been put in the world above; its significance had not been of this world. Hobbes, the contemporary of Descartes, following in the steps of Macchiavelli and of Bacon, states abruptly the opposite point of view: for these men knowledge was power, the peculiar power of the human being by which he could devise more cunningly than other animals, by which he could secure advantages for himself and satisfy desire. The intellect that invented gunpowder was not amenable to the old definitions: it was a new variety, and these writers believed in adapting their definitions to the facts. The curious inquirer could find in Hobbes the curt remark that speech enables a man to utter what he does not think, that it leads him to deceive, and so 'by discourse man is not made better, but more powerful.' He might go further back still and produce from Paracelsus some bold statements that could only have escaped notice through being regarded as utter insanity. The discovery of America gave trouble, and some dispute arose as to the origin of the American Indians. The authorities boldly ruled in 1512 that they were descended from Adam and Eve. In 1520 Paracelsus declared that there had been another Adam, as if there could have been two first men! He delivered himself further as follows: 'It cannot be proved that the men who inhabit the hidden countries are descended from Adam: but it is credible that they were born there after the deluge: and perhaps they have no souls. In speech they are like parrots and have no souls unless God be pleased to join them in the bonds of matrimony with those who have souls.' We are left in no doubt about the intention of Paracelsus to write a new account of the origin of man, for he says explicitly that Moses wrote theologically and according to the faith, but was not acquainted with natural science. Further in 1616 Vanini suggested that man was originally a quadruped: Vanini was burned. In 1665 Peyrere talked about Pre-Adamites[1] and in the same year a work was published anonymously in English, which seems to be the beginning of the history of the word Anthropologie in the English language. In this book Anthropology is divided into Psychology and Anatomy, and the writer announces that 'of the former we shall in a distracted rehearsal deliver our collections.' In 1677 Matthew Hale discussed the primitive origin of man, and from that time onwards a series of works on comparative anatomy, on pygmies, and on other allied topics prepared the way for the appearance in 1735 of Linne's *Systema Naturae*, where we find man treated zoologically.

These few dates and titles show how the teaching of Descartes about animals comes midway in the development of a large theme. The focus of interest was man and the question at issue was not so much the scientific analysis of animal behaviour as the adjustment of man, now declared to be in part a machine, in his relation to animals. The issue of the discussion was finally that which Descartes vaguely indicated, namely that as body man belongs to the animal kingdom, as mind he belongs to another realm. While Descartes confused the subject by treating this other realm as sometimes merely psychological, sometimes ambiguously spiritual,

---

[1] Isaac de La Peyrere (1594–1676) Prae Adamitae, sive exercitatio super versibus 12, 13, 14 capitis V. Ep. D. Pauli ad Romanos.

the sequel shows that it was possible to advance from his position to a general theory of man divided into physiology and psychology.

Whatever may be said of previous suggestions it was the work of Descartes to give wider significance to the question of automatism. His followers and defenders saw this aspect of the problem, and the consequent ventilation of his views brought to light many interesting points. Ignatius Gaston Pardies (*Discours de la Connaissance des Bêtes*, 1672) and a certain A. Dilly, author of a work on the soul of animals, published at Amsterdam 1691, were the chief writers concerned. Dilly argues that the growth of the embryo precedes consciousness, that movements easily become automatic, that somnambulists act unconsciously, that speech and the playing of instruments are systems of movements which depend solely on the nature and disposition of the organs. Pardies argued that it was simpler to explain the lamb's fear of the wolf through some automatic principle than to suppose the animal first learned to think the wolf could harm it. The theologians were attacked in flank by the assertion that it was more creditable to the Divine Wisdom to create an organism that automatically preserved itself than to complicate matters by adding consciousness. Regius declared that the education of animals was achieved by repetition of acts which produced new dispositions of the brain substance and so caused a regular flow of spirits to certain muscles. The same writer fell back on the early physiology of the emotions and explained the love of the animals by the temperature of the blood; the presence of the agreeable object causes physiological changes affecting the heart, while danger produces movement through affecting the spleen and the gall. Pardies further quoted the irrational fears of human beings, as, for example, the effect of a mouse on the feelings of a woman. In short, the whole movement, though curious in its focus and interests, produced a considerable amount of able writing which is closely akin in its results to the good and bad points of the later attempts to show how far consciousness is an epiphenomenon. Pardies clearly was not far from the views on emotions afterwards made popular by the James-Lange theory.

B. Gassendi, Hobbes, and the reaction

I. GASSENDI

In his views of man, and especially in that part which concerns the soul, Descartes belongs to the last phase of the mediaeval tradition. He belongs to it by reason of his preoccupation with questions that should have been excluded and also by reason of his reliance on ancient theories, particularly Stoicism. Emancipation from the tendency to regard man as a fragment of a divine substance enclosed in another substance not divine was hardly likely to come from the Stoic mode of thinking. Those who had other ideas on the subject were inclined to favour Democritus in their physics and Epicurus in their philosophy of mind and conduct. To this class belonged Gassendi and Hobbes, two great contemporaries of Descartes, who form an interesting complement to his influence in the seventeenth and eighteenth centuries.

Gassendi belongs to the old school of writers, the producers of comprehensive encyclopaedias. His life was comparatively uneventful, the peaceful life of the studious priest who was known and respected as a mathematician, a scholar, and a philosopher. His work was a careful and very sane compilation of teachings guaranteed by the quotation of numerous authorities and marked only by one striking peculiarity, the respect paid to Epicurus. Since the ninth century Epicurus had gone out of favour, incurring more and more of the odour of unsanctity. To revive his teaching was therefore a bold step, but it was taken by Gassendi very cautiously. In his psychology there is very little to show Gassendi's divergence from the more popular and respectable Stoicism, or from the improved Aristotelianism of his generation. Yet there are marks that differentiate this system. Gassendi tries to reduce all phenomena to matter and motion, excepting only the immortal soul in its separation from the body. Sensation he regards as primarily a mode of motion, possibly identical with the movements observed in plants and certainly found in animals. From the senses all knowledge is derived, though a higher faculty is required to elaborate from that basis the abstract and general ideas. From the senses Gassendi goes on to the imagination in the usual course: he marks his dissent from Platonism by making memory equivalent to the formation of folds in the brain substance, so that the retention of ideas is equivalent to the permanence of these fields. Gassendi took a keen interest in what was taught at that time about the organism, and he inclines to revive from Aristotle a biological interpretation of mental operations. This turn of affairs has a subtle significance.

The evolution of Aristotelianism had two aspects. So long as Aristotle was confused with Neoplatonism the emphasis fell on the master's doctrine of intellect. When a better knowledge of Aristotle coincided with a better knowledge of facts, it was possible to keep in touch with the scholastic tradition by quoting Aristotle, and also absorb the new naturalism by drawing those quotations from the neglected parts of Aristotle. Sufficient notice has not been taken by historians of the fact that the Stoics were eastern in temperament though Platonic in doctrine, while Epicurus was more purely Hellenic and more allied to Aristotle. The genuine Epicureanism which Gassendi had at his command serves him as a guide to those aspects of Aristotle which were not usually emphasized. His psychology therefore differs only in this matter of emphasis and is not really at variance with the Aristotelian scheme as worked out under the main headings of sense, imagination, and reason. The real significance of this Epicureanism reveals itself in the sphere of morals and of the passions, where the Aristotelian eudemonism comes to the front in its Epicurean form. This is the point common to Gassendi and Hobbes, and to it we shall return after estimating the position of Hobbes.

2. HOBBES

Thomas Hobbes has been proclaimed the father of empirical psychology, but that honour has since been transferred from him to Vives, from Vives to John of Salisbury, and bids fair to get back in time to Aristotle. Yet there is a reason why it should have been given to Hobbes sooner or later, though that reason is not the one usually alleged. The facts which seemed to justify the claim were the treatment of motion by Hobbes.

This was worked out in the greatest detail in his work De Corpore (1655) which was his definitive work on the philosophy of nature. He had intended it to be the first of a trilogy—On Body, On Man, on Citizen; but the upheavals of the Civil War wrenched out of him his civil philosophy in De Cive and Leviathan before the details of his natural philosophy had been completed. The De Homine, the second work in the trilogy, was to follow later in 1658.

Though Hobbes is often claimed as one of the founders of analytic philosophy, he was also one of the most imaginative system builders in the history of thought. Those for whom the main task of philosophy is to prevent other people from talking nonsense quote with relish Hobbes' celebrated remark: 'For words are wise men's counters, they do but reckon by them; but they are the money of fools . . .' But they seldom pause to consider what Hobbes envisaged that wise men should do when they reckon with words, when they build scientific systems.

'When we calculate the magnitude and motions of heaven or earth,' said Hobbes, 'we do not ascend into heaven that we may divide it into parts, or measure the motions thereof, but we do it sitting still in our closets or in the dark.' This striking quotation from De Corpore presents vividly the problems around which his philosophy of nature and mind revolved and intimates the kind of method by which he thought a solution should be sought. The problem that haunted Hobbes was simply man's ability to sit in his closet and picture the world outside, to roam over continents in his imagination as Drake and Magellan had roamed over uncharted seas. 'Of all the phenomena or appearances which are near to us, the most admirable,' he says, 'is apparition itself, τὸ φαίνεσθαι; namely, that some natural bodies have in themselves the pattern almost of all things, and others of none at all.' It is recorded in his prose autobiography how he found himself in the study of some learned men who were discussing the cause of sensation. One of them asked derisively what sensation was anyway, and Hobbes was astonished to find that no one of them could say. From this time onwards Hobbes could not rest until he had answered both these questions for himself. What was this mysterious power in man by means of which he could register what was going on in the world around him and store up his impressions for use on future occasions? Why did men, unlike other natural bodies, have in themselves the pattern almost of all things? We must first consider the *method* by which Hobbes hoped to solve these problems before we turn to the actual solutions which he suggested.

From the point of view of method the picture of Hobbes sitting still in his closet calculating the magnitude and motions of the heavens is like a cartoonist's insight into the essential. Hobbes flourished at a time when observation and experiment were fashionable amongst English intellectuals. The Royal Society, with its strong Baconian emphasis on observation and the method of induction, was to burst forth in 1662 from the chrysalis of the 'invisible college.' Yet Hobbes, for all his continental reputation, was never asked to join. It is true that he attacked the universities as hotbeds of Puritanism and Catholicism and that the Royal Society had a strong Puritan bias; it is also regrettably true that his attempts to square the circle in Chapter 20 of De Corpore were mercilessly exposed by Wallis, one of the leaders of 'the invisible college.' But his alienation from these brilliant and pious men was even more deep-seated; it sprang from his contempt for the inductive method and his unswerving allegiance to what was thought to be the rival method of deduction. It was this method which he thought that wise men should employ when they used words to reckon by. In his view the followers of Bacon spent too much time on new-fangled devices and experiments and too little on deducing consequences from the fundamental theory of motion pioneered by Galileo and his disciple, William Harvey. They preferred their eyes, ears, and finger-tips to their brains. Philosophy, he thought, could only be advanced by those who were prepared to sit quietly in their closets and use their brains instead of scouring the earth and gaping at the face of nature.

The genesis of Hobbes' devotion to the method of deduction is well known. Up to the age of 40 he had made no contribution to philosophy. His sole academic achievement had been a translation of Thucydides—a timely warning to his countrymen of the dangers of democracy. But on his second journey to the Continent he came across, quite by chance, a copy of Euclid's *Elements* in a gentleman's library. 'By God,' said he, 'this is impossible,' as he traced the demonstration back to the simple axioms from which it started. 'This made him in love with Geometry'—to quote Aubrey. He became completely enamoured of a method by means of which important and seemingly indubitable conclusions could be drawn from premises that no one could help accepting. He need no longer proffer judicious warnings to his country-men; he could promulgate necessary truths. 'The skill of making and maintaining commonwealths, consisteth in certain rules, as doth arith-metic and geometry; not, as tennis-play, on practice only.' So, too, in natural philosophy. To understand nature we must start from certain primitive notions which are clearly defined like body, accident, motion, space, time, cause, and so on. A combination of these primitive notions will eventually generate a deductive system in which the ground-plan of nature is set out . . . 'therefore, they that study natural philosophy, study in vain, except they begin at geometry. . . .'

Having mastered the magical method of geometry Hobbes was now ripe for the imaginative idea by means of which he thought he could explain sensation. In 1636 Hobbes made a pilgrimage to Italy to visit Galileo. In his verse autobiography he relates how, on this his third visit to the Continent, he was obsessed by the omnipresence of motion. Nor was this surprising to one who could grasp the implications of the heliocentric theory of the heavens put forward by Copernicus and Galileo's crude formulation of the law of inertia. Was not the earth itself rotating on its axis and revolving round the sun? In the old Aristotelian world-view rest had been regarded as the natural state of bodies. We must begin from the evidence of our senses which tells us that things only moved when motion was imparted to them by a mover. But Galileo, through his training in geometrical thinking, was able to conjecture that *motion* was the natural state of bodies. They continued in motion to infinity unless they were impeded. Thus Hobbes' obsession with the omnipresence of motion was his mental acclimatization to the revolutionary theories of Galileo. What excited Hobbes was the possibility of deducing new consequences from the law of inertia to spheres in which it had not yet been applied. Harvey had tackled the circulation of the blood. Could not Hobbes apply this new theory of motion to psychology and politics? And thus his imaginative idea was born: 'For seeing life is but motion of limbs. . . . For what is the heart but a spring; and the nerves but so many strings; and the joints but so many wheels, giving motion to the whole body, such as was intended by the artificer?' Life is a race with no other goal but being foremost. There can be 'no contentment but in proceeding.' Liberty is 'an absence of the lets and hindrances of motion.' Individual differences in wits are due to differences in quickness or 'swift succession of one thought to another.' Desires and aversions are motions towards and motions away from objects. And so on. Everything was an appearance of bodies varying in size from the astronomical to the atomic, moving at varying rates. Even thinking itself was but motions in some internal substance in the head. The appearances were scientifically uninteresting. What mattered was the mechanical ground-plan revealed to the geometer.

Thus Hobbes' solution to the problem posed by the learned doctors about the cause of sense consisted in looking at a familiar process in the unfamiliar way which he had learnt from Galileo. To quote his prose biography: '. . . it occurred to him that if bodies and all their parts were to be at rest, or were always to be moved by the same motion, our discrimination of all things would be removed, and (consequently) all sensation with it; and therefore the cause of all things must be sought in the variety of motion. Then he was led to geometry to learn the varieties and modes of motion. . . .' Apparition, which he found so wonderful, was to be viewed as a kind of meeting-place of motions. Our sense-organs were agitated by external motions without which there could be no sensation. To give the entire cause of sensation would require an analysis of all motions in bodies external to us which were passed on by direct contact or via some medium. The answer to the learned doctors must consist in deductions from a general mechanical theory. These Hobbes proceeded to provide.

The selectivity of perception was explained by suggesting that while the organ retains motion from one object, it cannot react to another; similarly in attention the motion from the root of the nerves persists 'contumaciously,' and makes the sense-organ impervious to the register-ing of other motions. The explanation of imagination was a straight deduction from the law of inertia:

'When a body is once in motion, it moveth, unless something else hinder it, eternally; and whatsoever hindreth it, cannot in an instant, but in time, and by degree, quite extinguish it; and as we see in the water, though the wind cease, the waves give not over rolling for a long time after; so also it happeneth in that motion, which is made in the internal parts of man, then, when he sees, dreams, etc. . . . Imagina-tion therefore is nothing but decaying sense.'

The decay, of course, is not a decay in motion. For that would be contrary to the law of inertia. Rather it comes about because the sense-organs are moved by other objects. This explains the vividness of dreams. For in sleep there are no competing motions from the external world. When sense-impressions are constantly crowding in on us, the imagination of the past is obscured and 'made weak as the voice of a man in the noise of the day.' Thus the longer the time that elapses after sensing an object, the weaker our imagination.

There is something almost incredibly hard-headed and naïve about Hobbes' gross materialism. To say that sensation and the conceptual processes are nothing but motions is rather like saying that kissing is simply a mutual movement of the lips or that work is moving lumps of matter about. Hobbes, too, was aided in this rather monstrous piece of metaphysics by using terms like 'agitation,' 'celerity,' 'disturbance,' and 'tranquility' to describe mental processes; for these terms have meaning as descriptions both of physical and psychological happenings. Hobbes could thus talk like a physiologist and preserve the common touch of everyday psychological description. He did not, however, seem to be sufficiently aware of the sort of gap that he was bridging. For the distinction between sense and imagination is not simply that imagination is decaying sense any more than the distinction between imagination and memory is that the latter involves only the addition of a sense of pastness. For these activities have different names because they imply different logical criteria. Psychologically speaking, perceiving may be the same as imagining in a given case. When we say, in spite of this, that we did not imagine something, we are making a logical point, not a psychological one. To perceive is to see something that is really there; to remember is to be right about the past. There is no place in a purely mechanical theory for criteria such as these.

In the theory of action Hobbes' great historical importance was to generalize the concept of 'efficient cause' of the natural philosophers and to apply it to man as well as to nature. 'A final cause,' he said, 'has no place but in such things as have sense and will: and this also I shall prove hereafter to be an efficient cause.' How then did he introduce efficient causes, in the form of antecedent motions, into the sphere of human action?

The transition from nature to man was effected by the introduction of the concept of conatus or 'endeavour.' He defined endeavour as 'motion made in less space and time than can be given; that is motion made through the length of a point and in an instant or part of time.' In brief, it was used to designate *infinitely small* motions. Hobbes took over this technical term from the physical scientists and generalized its application to bridge the gap between physics, physiology, and psychology. By means of it he was able to postulate minute unobservable motions in the medium between the object of sense and the brain, and he used it also to explain how movements coming from outside bodies were passed on through the body so that they eventually led to the gross movements observable in desire and aversion. He was thus able to suggest an explanation of all human actions in terms of efficient causes. External objects worked on the organs of sense and produced not only images but also minute internal motions which proceeded to the heart and thus made some alteration or diversion of vital motions, or the motions of the blood. When these incoming motions helped vital motion it appeared to us as pleasure and the body was guided to preserve the motion by staying in the presence of the stimulating object; and conversely with pain. Appetite and aversion were the first endeavours of animal motion. Thus the postulation of these minute motions made it plausible to suggest that human action as well as the movement of projectiles could be mechanically explained in terms of efficient causes or antecedent motions. For, after all, men do move towards and away from objects and each other. And, of course, he was right in saying that human actions have efficient causes—external stimuli, movements of the sense-organs, internal motions, and so on. But this does not mean that a list of any such movements could ever be sufficient to explain actions. For actions are distinguished by the goals towards which movements are directed; the goal makes the movements part of an action of a certain sort. And since we cannot specify which movements must be involved in attaining the goal, so also we cannot specify precisely which antecedent movements are sufficient to initiate behaviour.

This kind of logical difficulty was even more glaring in Hobbes' theory of the passions. For most of our terms at this level of description are either like 'ambition' in assigning a certain kind of objective to an action or like 'honesty' in classifying an action as being the application of a certain rule or convention. It is most unplausible to suggest, as Hobbes did, either that such terms imply anything specific about the efficient causes which initiate behaviour of this kind, or that such behaviour could be deduced from a theory concerned only with colourless movements. For a gross muddle of explanatory models is involved. Terms like 'ambition' and 'honesty' derive their meaning from a model of behaviour peculiar to goal-directed and rule-following activities, which is of quite different logical type from that of mechanics. In this explanatory model an agent is assumed to have an objective (like being a professor, in the case of 'ambition'), and to have information about means which will lead to this objective in a manner which is both efficient and in accordance with certain conventions of appropriateness (as in the example of 'honesty'). This model forms a kind of explanatory ceiling in understanding human behaviour just as the mechanical model of bodies pushing other bodies formed an explanatory ceiling in the seventeenth-century understanding of nature. Now physiological descriptions can state necessary conditions for behaviour conforming to this model; for it is a truism to say that we cannot plan means to ends unless we have a brain. Similarly, physiology can state conditions under which this type of behaviour breaks down. A man with a brain injury may well be insensitive to social pressures. Obviously physiological theories are extremely relevant to explanations of action at the molar level of behaviour. But this does not mean that there is a deductive relation between them—that behaviour can be deduced from the physiological description alone.[1]

Hobbes saw that it was man's capacity for using symbols in deductive reasoning and in descriptive languages which distinguishes him from animals, together with the theoretical curiosity that goes along with it. But he even suggested a mechanical explanation of language in his crude causal theory of signs. This was a grotesque failure because he never properly distinguished logical questions of the reference of signs from causal questions of their origin. Similarly, he gave a mechanical explanation of choice. Will, he held, simply is the last desire in deliberating which emerges after an oscillation of impulses. Here again, in his writings on free-will, he never properly distinguished questions about the justification of actions (their reasons) from questions about their causes. A person who deliberates rationally about means to an end will be influenced by logically relevant considerations. For him there is a difference between good and bad reasons for a course of action. Now any mechanical theory, even if it has recourse to minute motions, must face the glaring inappropriateness of giving causal explanations of such transitions which involve insight and the grasp of relevance.

As a matter of fact Hobbes' theory of the passions and his emphasis on the role of speech in human affairs had very little connection with his mechanical theory, except the kind of language in which his epigrammatic pronouncements were couched. It is to be understood much more in terms of his political preoccupations and the influence on him of Bacon and his early classical studies. Thus in his political theory, the basic movements of approach and avoidance appear as the desire for power and the fear of death. But a traditional classification of the passions is stuck on very loosely to a mechanical foundation. And Hobbes never properly resolved the contradiction between such a foundation and his stress on the arbitrariness and conventionality of speech and social institutions.

It has been said that Bacon exercised no influence on Hobbes. The remark is probably true in the sense meant. The historian of philosophy looks for influence in similarity of views and phrases: it is true that Bacon was noisily inductive and Hobbes equally noisily opposed to experience, that Bacon ignored mathematics and Hobbes made himself ridiculous by his pretensions to refute the Oxford professor and to square the circle. But these are superficial points. The real affinity between Bacon and Hobbes was in their common contempt for the schools and, still more, their common love for influence and power. Born in 1588, Hobbes was at Oxford from 1602–3 till 1608, and emerged with little appreciable gain. His knowledge of science and of the anti-scholastic movement was gained in subsequent travels. He then

[1] See pp. 760–1 infra.

came under the notice of Francis Bacon and acted as translator of
his works. More important than this for the development of his
mind were the translations he made from the Greek, namely the
history of Thucydides and the *Rhetoric* of Aristotle. Hobbes was
affected by Thucydides in the way in which Macchiavelli had
been affected a century before. The strong realism, the moving
picture of strong personalities, the frank exposition of natural
passions, all these appealed directly to the active nature of the
man. The *Rhetoric* of Aristotle served as a useful commentary on
the art of managing those passions. In the second book of the
Rhetoric we are told how the arts of language may be employed to
gain one's ends. The war of words is the highest form of that war
of all against all which Hobbes saw around him: it is the strife
that goes on when physical force gives way to the conflict of wits.
Words make for knowledge, knowledge is power, and the most
fundamental passion of man is the desire for power. We need not
wonder then that Hobbes found most interest in the passions of
men, their feelings of liking and disliking, or that he regarded
these passions from the point of view of their management and
employment. In this way Hobbes comes very near to a purely
social psychology, concerning himself most with individuals in
their mutual relations. Technically there is no such social psychology to be found in Hobbes, if the term social indicates the study
of the individual as produced in and through society. But in
another sense the great value of what Hobbes has to say lies in the
fact that he thinks more of individuals than of the parts of individuals. This is the force that emanates from Hobbes continuously,
the force of the man who has said in clear language just the things
we know about one another. But Hobbes quickly goes on to
political matters: all that he gives us is a sketch of the kind of
mental operations we may expect to find in the ordinary individual.
The phrases are new because previous writers had not taken them
from this source: in reality they are transcribed from that second
book of the *Rhetoric* of Aristotle.

The fundamental difference between Plato or the Stoics and
Aristotle or the Epicureans lies in the estimate of the passions.
For the genuine Stoic a passion is always a derangement of
reason, not an access of power but a loss. For the Stoic pleasure
is a passion as well as pain: they are disturbances of reason.
Gassendi and Hobbes choose the other line of thought. They

regard pleasure as something positive, something which is the object of desire, and good because it is desired. The psychology which leads up to this ethical valuation is therefore the reverse of the traditional. It recognizes desire as both natural and good. It refuses to distinguish between the higher and lower types of desire, but regards all desire as fundamentally the striving of the organism after its satisfaction. The desires may be rational or irrational, but they cannot be distinguished as natural and moral because in the first instance all desires are natural, and, in the second, the good which makes morality is itself no more than the object either of collective or of particular desire. This then is the new point of view, a fresh conception of the natural man, a dynamic standpoint that sees in every person an eternal striving which creates the ends it strives to attain. The whole matter is summed up in the famous sentence:—'So that in the first place I put for a general inclination of all mankind, a perpetual and restless desire of power after power, that ceaseth only in death.'

3. MORE AND CUDWORTH

The work of Hobbes was received with indignation. The quality of his method was not called into account, but the nature of its effects was quickly appreciated. The chief opponents, Henry More and Ralph Cudworth, were united upon one point: they affirmed the reality of that higher Reason which had been quietly ignored by Hobbes. This revived Platonism was not destined to formulate its psychology in any effective manner, but Cudworth at least deserves credit for a sincere defence of the active and constructive powers of the mind. If quotations are a proof of erudition, Cudworth was a very learned man. Unfortunately his whole work is controversial, and the few points he makes are hidden in a mass of citations and abusive epithets. The contemporary method of disqualifying the opponent was to prove his atheistical propensities.

One of the best statements of Cudworth's doctrine is given in the *Eternal and Immutable Morality* (Bk. iv. ch. 6). He asserts, first, that the soul is not a '*meer rasa Tabula*, a naked and Passive Thing, which has no innate Furniture or Activity of its own.' He proceeds to show that some ideas require a 'more inward and vital Principle,' a natural determination to do some things and avoid others. The main thesis is 'that knowledge and intellection cannot possibly spring from sense, nor the Radiation or Impresses of Matter and Body upon that which knows, but from an active Power of the mind as a thing antecedent to Matter.' He adds that 'sense itself is not a mere Passion or Reception of corporeal impresses without, but that it is an active energy and vigour.' Cudworth approved the Cartesian doctrine because it sets matter so definitely apart from mind; it is acceptable to him just because it seemed to assist the refutation of materialism. If matter, then, is not a source of mental activities, it follows that the mind must have its own activities, if we are to explain consciousness at all. But at that point Cudworth fails. He quotes Plato to prove the essential superiority of the soul, but goes no further. The promise of a psychological analysis which would elaborate and make intelligible the doctrine of the 'vital principle' is never fulfilled. It was not Cudworth but Leibniz who ultimately succeeded in showing that the formulae of pure sensationalism were inadequate.

C. The Occasionalists

The truest line of development from Descartes is that which follows out the spiritualistic phase of his teaching. This was done most distinctively by the Occasionalists.

I. GEULINCX

Arnold Geulincx (1625–1669) emphasizes those points in the Cartesian doctrine which lead to the conclusion that consciousness is never dependent for its changes on the outer world. The mind is active in thought, and every change of consciousness is a phase of that activity. But consciousness testifies to the fact that some of its changes do not depend on an antecedent act of will. It is inferred that all such changes are due to some other will, which can only be the will of God. To this purely dialectical treatment of the question Geulincx adds the plain fact that effects are produced in the soul *through* the body: the physical organism is the means which God uses to produce in our minds the states which are not voluntary.

Descartes had struggled to attain clear concepts. His successors fell into the error of substituting separate realities for distinct concepts. Occasionalism created its own problem out of Cartesianism; for Descartes would not have seen the matter in that light. Geulincx contributed nothing to the history of psychology except the decisive statement that there is no intermediate state between clear thought and purely physical processes; he ignored the possibility of mental processes which are not consciously presented to itself by the mind.

2. MALEBRANCHE

The mystical or Augustinian factor in the Cartesian psychology found an able exponent in Malebranche. In this case we find a recurrence of the influences which affected Descartes in his early days. For Nicholas Malebranche was a recluse by nature and a priest by education. What La Flèche did for Descartes the College de la Marche and the Sorbonne did for Malebranche. After these years of learning there came no such years of wandering as had moulded Descartes. The theological student became a priest of the Oratory of Jesus, a spiritual organization which enabled men to devote themselves to meditation and preaching without actually taking the vows of the Catholic Priesthood. Malebranche was therefore at once a mystic and a Christian, without being a strict adherent of the Catholic system. His initiation into Cartesianism was a kind of conversion; he chanced to pick up at a bookstall Descartes' *Treatise on Man*. His nature reacted to the influence almost violently; he fell in love with it; a new light irradiated his mind. Malebranche clearly belonged by nature to those who are capable of sudden and dominating illuminations.

Geulincx had left the body in the position of an instrument which the superior Will uses to affect the mind. Malebranche took the next step and abolished the intermediary. We know all things by the direct action of God on the mind; and this knowing is rightly called a vision, for it is as insight that Malebranche grasps the essence of knowledge. All knowing is a kind of intuition; but it is not wholly dependent on our will to know; there must be a power not ourselves that causes some of these inner activities; and this can only be the power of God.

The theological influence is manifest. But Malebranche was not in sympathy with those reactionary theologians who opposed the new philosophy; his adherence to Augustine made him favourable to the new doctrines and his real power of introspection enriched his thought. He took firm hold of the Cartesian principle that all consciousness is an affair of the mind, an inner state. But he does not maintain that there is a direct primary intuition of the self. He opposes to current Cartesianism the (scholastic) view that we know the body better than the soul. As the eye does not see itself, but things, so the soul does not know itself, but the body. The growth of knowledge is, therefore, a continuous self-revelation dependent on experience as a process and on God as the condition of that process. The language and the thought are both strongly reminiscent of Christian Platonism and akin to Augustine's Neoplatonism. The result is little more than an intense appreciation of the mystery of knowledge. The origin of ideas from sensations is rejected, the doctrine of innate ideas is also rejected: we are left only with a potentiality of knowledge actualized by the only real Cause, the Divine Power.

Though we might expect from Malebranche nothing but metaphysics, an examination of his works reveals many acute observations of detail. The Augustinian point of view always favoured introspection and was capable of yielding valuable results on that method. Anxious to prove that what men usually call a sensible object is really a determination of our inner powers, Malebranche arrives at the doctrine that an object is equivalent to a complex of ideas. From this follow two conclusions. The elementary processes of the mind are not isolated sense data, but compound perceptions analysable into associated groups of ideas. With these perceptions there enters a principle of relativity; the size of an object, for example, is perceived relatively to a standard given by the size of the person perceiving it. The knowledge given by the senses serves only for the preservation of life; it is essentially a process of adjustment to ·the surroundings, and is not to be regarded as absolute in character. In place of the direct transference of an image from the object to the mind, we must suppose that sense-experience is an activity and that a perception always involves a number of associated elements over and above that element which is the occasion of the activity. This principle Malebranche applies at some length to the perceptions of distance and magnitude; the moon, for example, appears larger on the horizon that at the zenith because in the former position it is compared with other objects in the field of vision. A similar relativity enters into the perception of distance and motion, including under motion the passing of time. Time is measured by its content, which is experience; pleasant time is short, painful periods are long.

The experience which Malebranche supposes to be the ordinary unit of unreflective thought is called by him *sensation composée*. In this sensation he frankly includes an act of judgment, but distinguishes this 'natural judgment' from the *explicit* act of 'free judgment.' The natural judgment (*sensation composée*) is really a union of associated elements. We call it the 'object' because we fail to discuss its elements, and then commit the error of attributing the sensation to the object. To detect and dissipate these errors is the object of Malebranche's work on the mind. His main interest leads Malebranche to deal with the reality of mental phenomena. He points out that there is no direct knowledge of the sense organs; a person who is seeing a patch of colour before his eyes is not conscious of the process which goes on in the retina. It is therefore wrong to suppose that the psychological image as such testifies to its own origin. In fact the same result can be obtained either by stimulating the outer or the inner end of the nerve; in modern terms, peripherally excited and centrally excited images are equally 'real' in so far as they are experiences. Malebranche thinks that the 'little threads' or nerve-endings in the brain may be agitated by the animal spirits, and that is his way of describing a central excitement. He notes that after gazing at a bright light we see a patch of yellow light in the middle of an object to which we transfer our gaze; this is due to the fact that the original excitement subsides gradually. The soul does not perceive the retinal changes; it merely experiences a series of colours, at first white and yellow, changing to orange, red, and blue. Malebranche is fond of little experiments, and what he says about changes in experience is usually elaborated with sufficient detail to show that real observation underlies his analysis.

Under the title of Sensation, Malebranche treats the first level of experience. The results are worth noting. The crude notion of 'objects' is destroyed; the experiences are accurately described; a pure psycho-physical parallelism is introduced by showing that the physical changes accompany the experiences, but are not either the cause or the object of the mental changes; a synthetic principle is shown to operate in sensation because each sensation, though apparently simple, can be analysed into parts naturally compounded and in some cases contains as one of its factors an unconscious judgment.

The second book of the *Recherche de la Vérité* is devoted to the subject of imagination. The first part deals with the subject analytically, discussing the nature and origin of images, or, as Malebranche puts it, the physical causes. The seat of the soul is a problem to which Malebranche attaches no importance; it is sufficient for his purpose to correlate the mind with the organism as a whole. To such factors as digestion, climate, and the action of the nerves in regulating the circulation of the animal spirits Malebranche gives careful attention. With the corporeal and the mental life thus closely correlated Malebranche attacks the problem of connection between the images and then discusses memory. The parts of the fifth chapter (*Recherche*, Bk. II. Pt. i. ch. 5) dealing with these points have been universally recognized as a remarkable treatment of the subject.

Whenever the soul has fresh ideas new traces are formed in the brain; conversely, when new traces are formed new ideas occur. Between these two series, the corporeal and the mental, there is no causal relation; their relations depend on the act of God; the union of the ideas with the traces depends on identity of time, on the will of man, and on the will of God. First as to time. If the idea of God has been presented to my mind at the time when the brain has been struck by the sight of the letters J A H, I shall hereafter think the idea of God at the sight of those letters or, conversely, the thought of God will be accompanied by a confused sense of those letters or of the sound of that word. The will of man operates by using this fact to connect ideas with traces and so make certain signs fit to act as means of communication. Lastly, the will of God makes some traces to be natural signs of objects, so that the traces are not indifferent, but serve only to arouse particular ideas. The trace left, e.g., by a tree will accompany the idea of a tree and no other idea.

Similar to the connection between the trace and the idea is the connection of the traces themselves. Identity in time is the reason why traces are connected one with another: in other words, all association is by contiguity. Some associations are variable, others invariable. This is due to the fact that conservation of life is the final cause of all activity. Hence the trace of an object about to fall and crush a person is indissolubly connected with the trace corresponding to the idea of death; the result is the desire to flee. Similarity is not recognized by Malebranche as a distinct kind of association. The only principle which he employs is that of identity in time, so that association by similarity is really a case of identity, the later experience reviving the earlier by means of those elements which are identical in the two complex groups of traces. This view agrees with Hamilton's Law of Redintegration and with many later expositions of the process of reproduction.

Memory is explained by Malebranche as a habit of the organism (*Recherche*, Bk. II. Pt. i. ch. 5). This follows from what has been said about association, and it explains all the marvels of memory detailed by St. Augustine in the tenth book of the *Confessions*. For an Augustinian this view of memory is hardly orthodox; but Malebranche refuses to dilate on the subject further. Habit is the facility with which the spirits move in certain parts of the body; memory is the facility with which the spirits move through the paths they have made in the brain—that and nothing more. It is astonishing that Malebranche abandons so completely the favourite stronghold of the spiritualists, and his action is an eloquent testimony to the influence already exerted over psychology by physics and physiology. Yet it would be rash to regard this teaching as wholly empirical; whatever Malebranche says must be understood as implying the mystery of the soul united with, but never truly of one nature with, the body it accompanies.

The second part of the book on Imagination contains an interesting contribution to individual psychology. The differences between men and women, the characteristics of different ages, the tendency to lose flexibility and become old in error as well as wisdom—these and other topics occupy our author's mind. He remarks that a prepossession can colour all one's judgments: the ravages of a new disease, for example, impress a man; they make deep traces in his brain; wherever he looks he begins to see signs of that disease: a student who had written several volumes about the cross, saw a cross everywhere; in short, the prejudices of which Bacon spoke penetrate every man's judgments. Commentators are singled out for special mention as bigoted and preoccupied persons.

From individuals or groups Malebranche goes on to a kind of social psychology which seems inspired by Bacon's 'idols of the tribe.' The subject is announced as being the 'contagious imparting of strong imaginations.' These are apt to develop selfishness and destroy civil society, but God has given them natural bonds of unity which consist in certain dispositions of the brain inducing them to imitate their fellows, to form similar judgments, and feel like passions. This imitative tendency operates partly in the mind, partly in the body. By the mind we feel the inclination to acquire the esteem of others, and this inclination secretly induces us to affect the speech, the gait, and the style of our superiors. Hence fashions in dress and speech, and the tendency to extravagances in social habits. By the body is understood the brain, and the influence which produces imitation of the second kind is the dominating power of the strong imagination over the weak. Strong imagination in some cases consists in being entirely occupied with some special idea, a condition of the brain which amounts to madness; in others it consists in power of grasping and expressing ideas, a power which makes its owner able to exert great influence: to be filled with an idea is to have the power of inspiring others, and to feel deeply is to be fitted for arousing deep feelings in others. After two chapters of examples Malebranche devotes a third to the analysis of Montaigne's character and influence, an original piece of writing which by itself would give its author a unique position in the history of the century.

The preceding remarks have been based mainly on the first two books of the *Recherche de la Vérité*. The third book deals mainly with the pure reason, and affords no new material. The fourth book contains a notable contribution to psychology in the treatment of natural altruistic inclinations. Malebranche recognizes a direct feeling of joy or pain aroused by the joy or suffering of others. This has a purely instinctive basis (iv. 13), as we see from the fact that pain causes a cry produced involuntarily by the 'machine,' and that this cry is felt by all human beings with the same emotional quality. This is a clear statement of the doctrine of sympathy and may be compared with the 'primitive passive sympathy,' of modern psychology. Further on in the same book a theory of play is based on the doctrine of final causes: the young are given by God a delight in those movements which keep the channels of the animal spirits open and so facilitate all later activities.

But while such points as these may still be found to sustain the work, on the whole the later books are less psychological than the earlier: the religious, speculative, and ethical interests predominate while the original acuteness and discrimination seem to fail. In judging Malebranche's work this fact should be borne in mind. As a whole the *Recherche* is not a work that is consciously psychological; the striking points made by the writer are of undoubted value, but they are set forth as incidents in a general account of experience which is dogmatic and unsatisfactory. Malebranche hardly attempts to connect the higher with the lower mental processes, and so fails ultimately to explain either group.

D. *Spinoza*

1. ORGANIC UNITY

The real achievements of men like Descartes and Malebranche can be valued without any direct reference to the conflict between philosophy and religion. But when we review the general trend of a school or a sequence of writers, there comes to light a certain similarity or divergence among them which seems to be proof of other invisible forces attracting or repelling the minds of these men. This sense of conflict between observation and belief comes sharply into consciousness when we turn from the Christian to the Jew. Indifferent as psychologists may well be to such distinctions, it was not possible at this time for truth to emerge without traces of the particular source from which it came. Through the Middle Ages and through the Renaissance the Jews had maintained a literary tradition which, if we are not too careful to separate Arab and Jew, might well be described as in no way inferior to the work done by the Christians. In all the topics that began or ended in questions of science both Christian and Jew went back to the classical work, the earlier or the later Greek products. But while the opposition of soul and body was the distinctive mark of the orthodox Christian writings from the beginning down to Descartes, the Jews were not committed to the same point of view: the inferiority of the senses which Philo had taught was an intellectual rather than a moral defect, and was to be overcome by effort rather than by an act of divine redemption. On the other hand, progress in the spheres of science and of education had tended to make the Christian writers more inclined to emphasize as means of grace the human agencies, especially self-control with its assistant factors, knowledge of the body and (psychophysical) habituation. This was the essential point of contact between Descartes and Spinoza. Though a native of Amsterdam and intellectually a child of the new school, Baruch de Spinoza (1632–1677) was by descent a Spanish Jew, and his attitude toward the philosophy which he found in vogue was permanently affected by the bias of his temperament. This is seen at once in his divergence from the Cartesian doctrine of mind and body: the dualism is rejected and a fundamental unity postulated. As a result of this we find no attempt to give any distinctive place either to memory or to will: the sequence of ideas, regulated by association and the order of experiences, suffices to explain memory: the will is not a power that overrides natural causation, but the form which desire takes when it is united with ideas, in other words when it occurs in the more complex types of consciousness. In Spinoza, even more than in the preceding writers, we find the view that philosophy is a way of life. As such its centre is the doctrine of conduct, and under the term 'ethics' Spinoza includes the whole doctrine of man, his relation to the universe, his nature as a created being, and his possibilities. The conceptions of organism and conduct dominate Spinoza's philosophy, and, as the agent is an individual and a unity, it is logical for Spinoza to treat soul and body as a unity, a single being of which these are distinguishable aspects. By so doing Spinoza lays the foundations of a theoretical parallelism and maintains that every bodily event coexists with and is co-ordinate with a mental event. This is not to be regarded as identical with a modern psychophysical parallelism: on the contrary, it is simply a metaphysical doctrine of identity applied to the sphere of conduct in which the ordinary consciousness sees a dualism of desire and will, flesh and spirit. For psychology this metaphysical basis is only important when it leads to new views on the actual course of experience, and this it does mainly in one point: as compared with Descartes, Spinoza inclines to be purely psychological and to trace connections between mental states without the help of that physiology which seemed to Descartes indispensable. For the rest, there is in Spinoza another vein of thought too often overlooked. As he moves away from the Cartesian dualism and toward the concrete unity of the agent there is more and more evidence that Machiavelli and Hobbes are influences to be reckoned with, and the reflective reader will continually catch echoes from those writers as he follows Spinoza's treatment of the fundamental *conatus*, or notes how rigidly he excludes the moral values when he deals with the strength of motives. Inspired very largely by his predecessors, the Aristotelian Jews of the twelfth century, Spinoza is able to look through Hobbes to Aristotle and so to amend the mechanical tendencies of his age by taking what in modern times might be called a biological direction: for in the end it is clear that the organic structure and the development of character as an organic whole is the focus of Spinoza's work. With these general ideas in mind we may proceed to consider in more detail the doctrine of the passions as expounded by Descartes and Spinoza.

2. THE PASSIONS: SPINOZA'S DEVELOPMENT OF DESCARTES

In spite of the many ways in which it is both inaccurate and inadequate, Descartes' treatise on the emotions must be reckoned one of the landmarks in the history of psychology. The views expressed in *Les Passions de l'Âme* are curiously complex, and the novelty of the treatise consists largely in the compromises it offers. Descartes' own interest was occupied with the mechanical aspect, and when he was called upon to give advice about conduct, he naturally thought first of the physical and physiological factors in behaviour. In this way Descartes was led to a position strikingly akin to some modern views; as Ribot has said, Descartes' method is 'that of physiological psychology and not that of spiritualistic psychology, which quite improperly lays claim to him' (*Psychology of Attention*, Eng. trans., 30). We may add that lack of historical knowledge is the cause of this and other obvious errors committed by writers who never look beyond the stock metaphysics of 'the ancients.' But in fact Descartes was not very anxious to alarm the powerful interests which still guarded the inner sanctuary of feeling; he probably felt that the time for open speaking had not yet come, and in any case the occasion for which Descartes began his treatise did not call for unmitigated candour.

The polite society of the seventeenth century, when it aspired to advanced thinking, was predominantly influenced by Stoicism. The intellectual ladies of the period read Seneca, and it was one of these, the Princess Elizabeth, who induced Descartes to write those letters on human happiness which formed the germ of the later treatise on the Passions. Thus, somewhat to its detriment, the treatise was from the beginning under the shadow of ethical aims, and Descartes never fully succeeded in making his mechanics of the passions independent of that Stoic teleology which made palatable his earlier letters. Moreover, there is a genuine lack of clearness upon points which had been continuously discussed by writers from Plato to the Renaissance.

We cannot acquit Descartes of being uncertain whether things are sought because they are good or only because they excite motion in the organism; we cannot acquit him of failing to notice how the phenomena of the passions actually present themselves and preferring to give a deductive account of what should occur when a typical individual is acted upon by what ought to be good or bad for his nature. Beyond a doubt Descartes still thought of things as naturally good or bad, pleasant or unpleasant, in the fallacious manner of Platonism.

There is no need to dwell on defects natural to such a writer at such a time; the good points are more novel and more interesting. The passions are 'perturbations of the mind' in some sense, but new meaning is now given to that phrase. In the wider sense of the term, all disturbances of the reason are 'passions,' and sensations may be put under that heading: in the narrower sense passions are emotions, and it is with the emotions that we shall now be occupied.

In spite of the original separation of mind from body, Descartes frankly admits an interaction in the cases of the emotions and of the will. He aimed to distinguish concepts rather than to separate things; it is the concept of thought which excludes every element in the concept of the body: if Descartes took the passions as a fact, he did not abandon or confuse that principle. It remained open to him to treat the phenomena descriptively; and if some phenomena required both concepts for their explanation, Descartes had no reason to shrink from employing them. He defined the passions as 'perceptions or feelings or emotions of the soul which appertain to it peculiarly and are caused, sustained, and strengthened by the activity of the animal spirits.'

They are, therefore, psychophysical events, and the definition is so far from being revolutionary that it may be regarded as giving, in concise terms, what had been implied in every ancient or mediaeval view, namely that emotions belong neither to pure reason nor to mere matter. But the older doctrines were content to be negative and emphasize the antithesis between feeling and pure reason; the new doctrine was marked by new principles of classification and description.

As regards classification, the two main heads of *concupiscibile* and *irascibile* are now rejected as inadequate; a wider basis is sought in the conception of emotion as a function of the organism varying with the different relations between object and subject. Yet it is obvious that Descartes was still controlled by the idea of distinct faculties, was still sharply opposing emotion and will, and thought that a small number of fixed types would be adequate for a complete classification of all possible emotions. As regards description, the emphasis falls on the activity of the animal spirits, but leaves uncertain the exact part played in each emotional state by the intellectual apprehension of a situation and its meaning. In principle, at least, the problems of James's theory of the emotions are apparent here. The exact manner in which mental and corporeal factors are united in an emotion seems to have been conceived by Descartes as different in different emotions; also, there is some discrepancy in the statements themselves. In general, on the basis of the physiology already described (p. 360), we may say that an idea which includes movements of the body directly affects the animal spirits so as to produce the implied movements: thus the idea of danger includes the idea of defence, and the appearance of a dangerous object will arouse through the soul movements which avert its action. Descartes is well aware that one of the links in this chain of causation is a judgment of value; he accepts the fact that an emotion is caused by the relation of some external datum to the person, and that this relation only exists in and through the person's valuation of the object. To sustain his mechanical explanation Descartes is compelled to make this appreciation a brain-process capable of moving the animal spirits in an unique manner and so changing the character of the blood. In modern terminology, this might be considered as equivalent to explaining emotions by vasomotor disturbances and changes in the secretions. Descartes was inclined to accept such formulae but he was not ready to reduce emotions to nothing but physiological processes. The emotions are instru-

ments which subserve purpose; they tend to the good of the
creature, because when the will is weak they provide bodily
dispositions which make easy the actions that ought to be performed; they belong, in short, to a divinely ordered cosmos and
are so far a part of the intelligible world that Descartes thinks
they must be akin to intelligence, and some emotions are regarded
as caused by the soul in which they occur, so that the physical
changes are mere concomitants. Descartes, no less than the
Stoics, felt the necessity of making room for 'passions that the
wise man may have,' and he followed the Stoic example in making
some emotions qualitatively different from others. These were
points in which Descartes failed to be consistent or wholly free
from the traditional prejudices.

The 'simple and primitive passions' are six in number—
Admiration (Wonder), Love, Hate, Desire, Joy, and Sadness.
Admiration is 'a sudden surprise of the soul, which causes it to
consider with attention those objects that to it appear unfrequent
and extraordinary. Thus, in the first place, it is caused by the
impression in our brain representing the object as rare, and,
consequently, as worthy of exceptional consideration; and in the
second place by the movement of our thoughts, which by virtue
of that impression are disposed to tend with great force toward
the locality of the brain in which the impression rests, in order to
strengthen and preserve it there; as they are also disposed, through
that impression, to pass from thence into the muscles that serve
to maintain the sensory organs in the same position in which they
are, in order that, if originally formed by the organs of sense, the
impression may be further prolonged by their support.'[1] On this
Ribot remarks that 'all the elements which we have endeavoured
to point out in the mechanism of spontaneous attention are
therein clearly enumerated; namely—the augmentation of nervous
influx in consequence of the impression; its partial conduction
toward the muscles; the action of these muscles in order to
"support" and "to strengthen." ' These are points likely to be
emphasized in a modern psychologist's view of Descartes. Apart
from the accuracy of the description, Wonder is for Descartes
the counterpart of novelty in the impressions: it alone of the
emotions has an object which is not primarily either beneficial or
harmful: it is, as it were, the emotion which pertains to pure

---

[1] Text as translated in Ribot, *Psychology of Attention*, 30 (*Les Passions*, ii. 70).

intellectual activity, being for Plato the beginning of philosophy. As Wonder is thus unique, all passions are reducible to the two heads, Wonder and Desire. Love and Hate are forms of desire; and, as the desirable may be an object of intellect, there is a distinction between purely intellectual love and that love which depends on the 'heat of the heart,' which has no object, and consists entirely in a 'pathological' condition or pure *passio*. Here we seem to have the distinction upon which Kant afterwards relied in order to set the emotion which Duty inspires outside the sphere of lower impulses. Descartes rightly notices that popular terms are psychologically incorrect; gratitude is a feeling, but ingratitude is simply a name for a class of actions and is not another specific emotion; desire is positive or negative, not being the opposite of aversion but rather a state which may operate in the way of attraction (desire to have) or repulsion (desire to be rid of): whether we pursue or avoid, we express equally in different ways the fundamental desire for the better, that is the desire to preserve and increase vitality. In showing how the popular terms confused difference of effects with difference of emotions Descartes illuminated an important part of the subject. He found no intrinsic difficulty in the fact that the organic effects differed because he had already explained that the emotion was a state of the animal spirits and the blood, while the effects were secondary products due to further (kinaesthetic) action on the nerves and muscles.

The scheme of classification ultimately reveals itself as somewhat abstract but undeniably simple. If we assume the prior importance of the soul as *res cogitans*, we may give to the intellect its special emotional state, Wonder; if we proceed to consider as the fundamental type of action the effort after self-preservation, Love and Hate will be attitudes of self-maintenance in relation to present good or evil, Desire a corresponding attitude in relation to future good or evil: finally success or failure in the struggle for more and better life will be felt as joy or sorrow. Other subsidiary emotions are described by Descartes, often with acuteness, but never without irrelevant suggestions of the purposes which these states subserve. Already the lines are laid down upon which Spinoza was to build a still more elaborate system of self-preservation.

For Spinoza mind and body are aspects of a fundamental unity. The nature of the body is the cause of passions or affections; the nature of the mind is the cause of the ideas of these bodily affections; and as these two, the physical and psychic, events occur together, the emotions are states at once of mind and body. In this sense, and not in the Cartesian sense of interaction, the emotions or affections are for Spinoza psychophysical. As the basis is a unity with two aspects, Spinoza begins with a tendency which belongs to that unity, namely the effort of self-preservation, the fundamental will to live or *conatus quo unaquaeque res in suo esse perseverare conatur* (*E.*, iii. 8). When this effort is referred to the mind alone it is called Will. Will is the name for the *conatus* when accompanied by consciousness of its activity. When we regard it as arising out of the whole nature of man, mind and body, it is called 'appetite.' Appetite can therefore be called the essence of man, *ipsa hominis essentia*. If we add to this that appetite may be either unconscious or conscious, we get the further distinction between appetite and desire (*cupiditas*), desire being appetite consciously apprehended as such (iii. 9).

From this point Spinoza proceeds to systematize the emotions by a rigid logical deduction. The primary emotions are three in number: *Laetitia* (joy), *tristitia* (grief), and *cupiditas* (desire). These are not strictly co-ordinate, but related rather as substance and accidents. Desire is the determination to action which arises directly from the tendency to self-preservation. Joy and grief are attributes of this fundamental state, arising from consciousness of success or failure in the effort. As the effort to attain fuller life is itself the very process of being (*ipsa hominis essentia*), joy and grief are the conscious equivalents of increased and decreased vitality (iii. 11). The actual pleasure or pain (*titillatio, dolor*) are parts of those emotions, being strictly the corporeal parts of the whole consciousness of increased or decreased vitality. Apparently Spinoza intended these to be purely corporeal, on the level of appetite, that is to say, not accompanied by consciousness. It is not clear whether by that he meant these to be wholly apart from consciousness or only a kind of implicit consciousness.

The point must be settled, if at all, by reference to the general theory of 'adequate ideas.' The emotions, strictly speaking, involve an idea of the object; love, for example, is a mode of consciousness (*cogitandi*) as including an idea of the object loved.

Thus appetite and desire differ as blind impulse from conscious pursuit. Similarly a mere feeling is blind, and in that sense unconscious (devoid of any 'idea'); an emotion is a higher state involving more mentality. But emotions are inferior to intellectual operations, because at this level the ideas are 'inadequate,' confused by the intrusion of factors due to the body (iii. 3). To this distinction another is added, namely between those affections of which we are ourselves the cause and those which are due to external causes. Thus there are the following degrees of consciousness— (a) cognition of the first order, including (1) individual perceptions, (2) signs and images: (b) general ideas, *notiones communes*. These are produced as 'blurred images' by the failure of imagination. Finally there is *intuitus*.

Ideas or states of consciousness are thus divided into (a) adequate, and (b) inadequate. The former involve action, the latter are passive states (sensation, imagination, emotion). The 'idea' (or degree of consciousness) constitutes the basis of classification for the emotions: so that our affections will be divided also as (a) active, and (b) passive. First comes the analysis of passive states.

The passions are in variety infinite; but a principle of classification can be found from the fact that the passion is qualified by the idea. The accompanying idea can be either of an external object, or an internal cause, or of an object wanted. The primary affections can be treated on this basis as follows:—

Joy: with the idea of external cause is Love.
Grief: with the idea of external cause is Hate.

From these two follow certain derivatives: (1) Sympathy and antipathy are affections of joy and grief due to latent causes. A person acquires a dislike for an object A because it suggests B, another object already disliked. We might call this the transference of emotion by association of ideas. (2) The converse position is illustrated in the case of approval (favour) and indignation. If a person A, toward whom I have no feelings, confers a benefit on B whom I love, A becomes the object of a feeling for B. Similarly, if A harms B, I am indignant with him. A more subtle point is added to this. The emotion is sometimes caused by an action benefiting or harming a thing in which I am interested, e.g. my house or my garden: but it may also arise when the object is like me, e.g. when it is another person. Here no direct previous interest is assumed, but the idea of another person is so far akin to my idea of myself that a similar emotion is produced (iii. 27). This is the principle called by Spinoza *imitatio affectuum*, according to which similarity of ideas is the cause of similarity of emotions. If the basis is grief, this becomes commiseration,[1] and there should be a term to express the corresponding emotion when the basis is joy: this term is sought in vain (iii. 22, Pt. 2). (In German *Mitfreude* expresses the idea, and *congratulation* in English is sometimes a strict antithesis to *condolence*.)

Pity (*misericordia*) has its basis in love (of the object in distress), but is actually a state of grief; it differs from commiseration only in being more general and more akin to a habit or disposition: it is, in fact, 'tender heartedness' and properly denotes a readiness to appreciate the moods of others. Its opposite is Envy, or the tendency to refer all events to oneself; the envious person rejoices in the sorrows and grieves at the good fortune of others. This very subtle analysis is dominated by Spinoza's conception of the *conatus*. It is our striving to get ahead of others that makes us feel the reverse of their feelings: their loss is our gain and their gain our loss: the real basis here is a kind of universal hate. The *conatus* expresses itself in relation to other persons as competition: we strive to prevent others from possessing such things as can only be possessed by one: from this competitive attitude (*aemulatio*) arises envy. Children show this tendency: they do as others do from the mere desire not to be left out; they cry when others cry, from sheer desire not to let others cry all by themselves; the surest way to make a child want something is to pretend you want it yourself (iii. 32). As Spinoza points out, envy or grudging operates only in a limited sphere; the farmer envies the other farmer's crop, not the politician's fame; in short, we envy when we feel that we might have obtained some good if it were not already another's.

These more permanent states of mind are contrasted with the 'fluctuations of the mind,' or mixed emotions, when we love and hate the same object at the same time (iii. 17). Of these mixed states jealousy is a typical example.

Spinoza makes extensive use of the idea of association and of

---

[1] This is usually called sympathy; the distinct and more accurate use of that term by Spinoza should be noted.

reproduction. Propensity and aversion are due to such factors; they are forms of joy and grief related to objects associated with ideas of good and bad. The house in which our happiest days were passed is not in itself good: it is a cause of joy *per accidens*. Here Spinoza deals with wonder or astonishment; he does not follow Descartes, but makes it a state of mind accompanied by any other emotion. Thus we may feel astonished at the character of a person; if this is associated with the idea of harm it becomes dread (horror); if fear is the associated element, consternation is produced; if the virtues of the person are recalled, there is veneration. The opposites of all these emotions are grounded in contempt; as we admire abnormal wisdom, so we feel contempt for extreme stupidity; if we condemn what we hate, there is a sentiment of mockery (*irrisio*), as the downfall of an opponent causes merriment in our hearts.

Hope and fear are classic examples of mixed states (cp. p. 433); they pass into carelessness or despair when the element of doubt is eliminated.

In the category of affections accompanied by the idea of something internal as cause, Spinoza puts self-love or 'acquiescence in oneself,' and its opposite, humility: also repentance, which is not a virtue, but a twofold evil, for it involves a previous evil desire and a consequent state of grief. Where self-esteem is based on ignorance there arises pride, 'a kind of delirium,' and abjectness: both are due to incorrect judgment of one's own worth. When this judgment is mediated by a reference to others we have pride and shame, 'joy and sorrow accompanied by the idea of some action on our part which we represent as praised or blamed by others.' Shame in this sense should be distinguished from shame as a virtue, whose opposite is shamelessness.

From cupidity arise several states. Desire when accompanied by a sense of obstruction becomes longing: this is practically a form of Grief, but depends upon desire finally. Love gives rise to gratitude, the desire to make due return of affection. Benevolence is desire arising out of commiseration. In these cases desire and love are united. When desire and hate are joined they cause Anger and vengefulness. If the hatred is not reciprocal, but the person is well disposed, cruelty arises from hatred. The opposite of cruelty is the state of clemency, which is not a passion but a control exercised by reason. Other passions, such as voluptuous-

ness, avarice, etc., arise from Desire, distinguished by their
objects only.

3. THE INFLUENCE OF REASON

We now pass from the passive to the active states.

Reason constitutes character by restraining passions; but the
restraint is only achieved through other passions. The Cartesian
maxim is opposed by Spinoza when he says '*Affectus nec coerceri
nec tolli posse, nisi per affectuum contrarium et fortiorem affectu
coercendo*' (iv. 7). The general name for strength of character is
Fortitudo, including *Animositas* (strength of mind) and *Generositas*
(nobleness). These are desires which tend only to the useful. By
these we set the greater good of the future before that of the
present, and in general subordinate impulses to calculations.
Sobriety, chastity, and such virtues are due to this control of
'presented' by 'represented' ideas, as Spencer afterwards expressed
it. *Generositas* is the social virtue corresponding to the individual
virtue of *animositas*; it is the rational striving after the improvement of others and their attachment to oneself. Nothing is so
useful to a man as his fellow-men; the goal of conduct is a life of
reason, which requires reason in others for its peaceful development. We can learn to know our own passions, and in that knowledge they will cease to be passions. This is the state of virtue,
the attainment of the true end of desire, and the highest (because
most fully conscious) level of self-preservation. By this road
Spinoza returns to the ancient doctrine of Theoria, the *vita con-
templativa* in which all principles of action are harmonized.

The dualism which Descartes maintained left him with a
faculty called Will, essentially the faculty which operated in free
choice of actions and in restraint of desire. This, as a psychological factor, had no real place in Descartes' scheme: it was an
ethical residuum. Spinoza makes Will fundamental in so far as it
is *conatus*. Ethically considered, what we desire is what we call
good; and so far the basis is voluntaristic, with an obvious recollection of Hobbes. But the good, if it is not merely a name for
things, but the name for things as valued, is constituted by knowledge, and therefore our will for the good is not an independent
faculty, but simply enlightened effort. Among Spinoza's predecessors Maimonides emphasized knowledge; Chasdai Crescas

counted love the supreme state: Spinoza's *amor intellectualis* reconciles the opposition. This is not a faculty, but an acquired state which emerges as the product of mental development. It might be made a theme for an essay on Spinoza's attitude to religion, but that is not relevant to our subject. The final *intuitus* is a timeless state, in the language of metaphysics: psychologically it is a completely adequate idea. The meaning of this will be clear if we recall Spinoza's view of the relation between intellect and imagination. Time enters into imagination: it has, so to speak, a perspective and is liable to produce illusions analogous to optical illusions. We may know an action tends to evil: but if the evil is far off, if there is a long interval of time placed between us and it, it may be presented as imaginary evil and not as positively bad. That is a true and valuable indication of the effect which time has on practical estimates: it may serve to show how far Spinoza was from meaning by his *intuitus* any emotional or ecstatic condition. In the end there is no faculty of Will, no *Voluntas* over and above the separate *volitiones*; only the concrete Self remains, fully developed, expressing itself in actions which are voluntary because they are fully conscious.

E. *Leibniz and Wolff*

1. LEIBNIZ'S BACKGROUND AND IMPORTANCE

The work of Leibniz was so brilliant and so full of inspiration that it has often seemed to be the spontaneous birth of German philosophy. 'We speak with pride,' says Dessoir, 'of a German psychology: in the time of Leibniz there was for the first time an imperishable German culture.' In a sense this is true, but the statements of Erdmann are more true. 'German rationalism,' he says, 'owes much to Leibniz, but he is not its only parent; few of its representatives are to be regarded as merely continuing to work out what he had suggested. The great majority of them drew their inspiration from Englishmen and Frenchmen, almost as much as from Leibniz and Wolff.' The movement was, in fact, cosmopolitan from the beginning; Leibniz himself was cosmopolitan in life, character, and thought, and if as a matter of convenience we speak of a 'German philosophy' in the eighteenth century, it is because the locality is more distinctive than the thought. What is true of the general philosophical systems is still more true of the psychological works. They succeed one another in a chain of expositions which show the continual assimilation of imported theories and a gradual movement from the over-developed supernaturalism of the seventeenth century to the hard naturalism of the late eighteenth century. Through this development in all its phases runs one consistent thread of connection. Leibniz emphasized the spontaneity of the soul; for him the work of the mind was something more than a mere arranging, sorting, and associating of the given; it was essentially productive, creative, and freely active. From this point two questions arise. Apart from rhapsodies, to which Leibniz inspired more than one writer, the strenuous thinkers wrestle with the definition of this activity and the obvious necessity of admitting that however much the activity is and remains an 'inner' activity, there is an 'outer' activity also to be considered, both as actual agency and as the source of raw material for all manner of apperceptions or synthetic activities. This complex of problems is frequently presented as a mere antithesis of Locke and Leibniz. That formula does justice to neither of these names, as the sequel will show, and therefore it is better to begin by avoiding the errors which might arise from the use of those names; though nothing is gained by obscuring the fact that as the struggle develops English empiricism becomes the archetype of one doctrine and the monadology forms the germ of the other.

Gottfried Wilhelm Leibniz was born in 1646 at Leipzig. The Thirty Years War was still raging; it terminated in 1648, and Germany was then at the lowest ebb of its prosperity and culture. The active life of Leibniz fell in an age of reviving aspirations; in 1700 the Berlin Academy began its existence and marked the formation of a definite centre of learning in Germany and the determination to rival the French Academy. Though German in its locality, the Academy was cosmopolitan in respect of its members, and the predominant influence was French. Paris was the real focus of Europe at this period, and it is not surprising that Leibniz should have chosen to live there during some of the best years of his life, though the beginning and the end were spent in Teutonic provinces. Descartes died in 1650, but his influence was still powerful; Arnauld, Hobbes, Spinoza, and John Locke were contemporaries of Leibniz. Malebranche died one year before Leibniz: Newton lived for eleven years after him. In

England the Royal Society was founded when Leibniz was beginning his college courses; five years later (1665), the *Journal des Savants* began to appear; in England, France, Holland, and Denmark science was enjoying an age of prosperity and progress.

To reach this world of science and speculation Leibniz had to go beyond the borders of Germany. Within its limits war and theology were most in evidence. The national characteristic which Leibniz never stripped off was that desire for peace which comes from long wars and that turning of the mind toward its own inner welfare which was the core of mysticism. Boehme died in 1624, but the genuine spirit of mysticism lived on in Spener till 1705, and with this temperate mysticism, the religion of the Pietists, Leibniz was well acquainted. His buoyant vitality did not yield to the more negative aspects of mysticism; against pantheism and absorption he maintains pluralism and individuality. The inwardness and the impenetrableness of every life are the two foundations on which Leibniz built.

The complexity of the training, the life and the character of Leibniz is an important fact for the understanding of the eighteenth century in Germany. The strong background of scholasticism, the early influence of Pietism, the brief period of German academic training, the long years of change and travel, the continuous union of study with business—all these factors made Leibniz an epitome of human experiences and a point of attachment for the theologian, the metaphysician, and the social reformer alike. Unsystematic and often incomplete, his theories are full of tempting possibilities and overflow with the redundancy of the Italian Renaissance, to which he was in many ways closely allied. In psychology as in the other departments of knowledge it is to the general attitude that most attention must be paid if Leibniz is to be justly estimated; next to that come the isolated lines on which that attitude found expression. Among these the most important is the Law of Continuity.

2. CONTINUITY, ACTIVITY, AND REPRESENTATION

Originally developed in the science of mathematics and in the study of quantity, this was transferred to the study of life. Its application to the problems of life and mind led to the idea of a continuous uninterrupted scale of Being, which at once involves the doctrine that these are degrees of mind. These degrees do not exist only in the sense that animals and men differ in the degree of intellect each possesses; there are infinite degrees of psychic reality. Again, if we pass beyond the apparent separateness of each living unity, we find a deeper principle of continuity: every thing not only exists but it coexists, and its relations to other things are at once outer and inner. Confining ourselves to the application of this metaphysic to psychology, we find it leads to the assertion that every unit, which the materialist would call an atom, is a centre of force, a living reality. Instead of an atomistic doctrine Leibniz propounds a theory that is only to be called individualistic. The idea of the soul gradually wins its way to the heart of the whole system; psychology becomes the clue to the universe, the microcosm reveals the secret of the macrocosm.

In this way Leibniz ultimately builds up a philosophy that is ruled by the idea of conscious forces ceaselessly active. From Aristotle he takes the idea of potency; from Plato he gets the idea of an indivisible spiritual essence. The two are combined in the new idea of the monad, which is a pure energy known and interpreted through our own self-consciousness.

The doctrine is novel because it is neither realism nor idealism, neither materialism nor spiritualism. Its affinities can only be indicated by calling it naturalism spiritualized. The ultimate elements are endowed with life and motion, and that involves some degree or potency of consciousness. The unconscious, what we call dead matter, is therefore only relatively unconscious; it has the least possible degree of consciousness. Organisms are composed of monads with varying degrees of consciousness; the nature of the monads determines the position of the organism in the scale of life. The rational human being takes the highest place (omitting the nature of God) and includes an infinite series of lower monads. This fact is the explanation of the degrees of consciousness in the experience of the individual. Clear consciousness is distinguished from more obscure states by the degree of intensity. The law of continuity is invoked to prove that a perception rises by degrees to the stage of actual realization. The lower degrees are *petites perceptions*; the actualization of these in consciousness is called apperception. This doctrine is the focus of all that Leibniz has to say about consciousness. Its significance requires more detailed consideration.

According to Leibniz every monad is impenetrable. It follows that nothing enters into or goes out of this metaphysical reality. Applying this principle to the problems of sensation (for the psychology of Leibniz is throughout applied metaphysic), we arrive at the conclusion that there can be nothing but changes in the states of the monads; passivity and receptivity are thus eliminated, and in their place nothing is left but the power of representing, the fact of presentation. This is most clearly stated in the *Principes de la Nature et de la Grace*, §§ 1–4. 'The perception is the inner state of the monad, representing the things outside' (§ 4): 'the perceptions are representations of the composite in the simple' (§ 2). Each monad, we are repeatedly told, is a mirror of the universe. The metaphor is significant. From the earliest times sight was the sense which prompted the most important explanations of knowledge, and in the later periods from Alhazen to Berkeley it is the theory of vision which most effects the general theory of perception and reality. Leibniz, a mathematician and acquainted with optics, finds in the same sphere an expression of his intuitions. As a mirror receives rays of light and redirects them, as the image in the mirror is not an image which the mirror itself absorbs or assimilates, so the mind represents all things not by *receiving* them but purely by being in a *relation* to them. There can be little doubt that Leibniz intended to overthrow the doctrine of outer as opposed to inner senses; or that his famous declaration, 'the intellect is innate to itself,' was formulated to avoid the difficulties which arose from insisting that anything is carried over from object to subject when sensations occur. The 'pre-established harmony' was in reality a name for nothing, a mere symbol of the inexplicable. The net result is the clear recognition that the elementary activities of the mind are conceivable only as its activities; that analysis only reaches down to those elementary activities; finally that no juggling with sensations can make them into 'outer' existences.

Returning to the principle of continuity, we may consider the relation between the confused and the clear perceptions. There are four terms denoting two main divisions and two minor divisions. The condition of mere relatedness is called 'obscure,' and would be represented in the state of mind which did not even distinguish itself from its object. Opposed to this is the 'clear' condition where such a distinction is achieved either distinctly or indistinctly. The two other stages are the lower and higher degrees of awareness, for the perception may be 'clear' but not distinct, or both clear and distinct. This scale is in effect a true genetic analysis, akin in spirit and method to the *itinerarium mentis* of the mystics; it is the journey of the soul to perfection. It is essentially an explanation of the intellectual life *a priori*, i.e. from the basis of its reasons and in reference to its form. It is not, properly speaking, a criticism of Locke; it is merely another and a different theory. It suffers obviously both from lack of means to supply the contents of experience and lack of knowledge about experience. The well-known examples of the murmur of the ocean which must contain the separate sound of each wave, and of the colours, e.g. green, which is a mixture of blue and yellow, are primarily examples of the errors into which great men can fall. For the assumption that the experience is composite because the ground or reason (not cause) for it is composite, must be regarded as unjustifiable. Leibniz (and Kant after him) was misled by the analogy of the miscroscope into thinking that an object could remain the same and yet progressively develop before the mind. The microscope reveals the infinite plurality in unity, the endless parts implicit in a whole; therefore (it was argued) intensive magnitude is equivalent to implicit distinctions, and attention or introspection makes those distinctions explicit. The fallacy here was the assumption that what is implicit in things must also be implicit in the consciousness of the things. Many things may be contained in (implicit in) a box, but the eye which sees the box does not see its contents; nor does the mind which thinks of yellow necessarily think of the green and blue 'implicit' in it. This error in the use of the term implicit deserves careful notice. It not only serves to explain many later attempts to get out of concepts what was never in them, but it also led onward to a renewed belief in experiments on the mixing and fusing of mental elements.

Unity and activity are the two fundamental terms of the monadology, and their importance overshadows all distinctions of faculties. The only kind of distinction which Leibniz does trouble himself to make is that which concerns the difference between having a state and moving into a state, the rest and the motion of the soul. What has been said about perceptions is a description of any simple act of 'mirroring.' If this were all, we should have to admit that the state of perception was really a passive state and utterly dependent on the objects; for a picture in a mirror only changes in conformity with the motion of the reflected objects. But having explained that the content of the mind, its sum total of knowledge, is equivalent to the relations which it bears to its total environment (the cosmos), Leibniz proceeds to add a most significant factor. As merely knowing we reflect the known, but as living souls we are thereby affected, have feelings, struggle to maintain or reject, and so exhibit a 'tendency to pass from one presentation to another.' This is what is called will, and Leibniz proceeds to treat it in the manner of Aristotle and the Peripatetics of the Middle Ages. Will is described as fundamentally a striving after the Good. The Greeks had already distinguished three kinds of good things, those that are good in themselves, those that are good in themselves and for some ulterior end (as exercise which promotes health), and those that are good only as means (e.g. medicine). On this basis, with a reference also to Aristotle's treatment of deliberation, Leibniz distinguishes the primitive will for the good (*volonté antecedente primitive*), the secondary will for the evil which is combined with a good (*volonté moyenne*), and the will as act of choice which results from deliberation (*volonté finale*). The exposition of this doctrine in the *Theodicée* (§ 119) shows both the depth and the confusion of its principles. The confusion is due to the idea of an ultimate good, the optimistic bias characteristic of Leibniz; through this the conation of Hobbes and Spinoza is made into a transcendental will which may be legitimate in a *Theodicée* but is not psychology. The depth is attained by realizing that the will emerges from the sphere of *petites perceptions*, from the unnoticed and perhaps 'unconscious' factors which in their totality make up the dark ground of the life of desires. This was the point which made Leibniz the beginner of a new voluntarism. A brief anticipation of some later theories will show the meaning of this rather obscure point.

The rationalism of Leibniz is obvious; he follows the Cartesian path and makes the ideal of life a state of clearness in which the truth is seen and acted upon. But from that highest point of perfection hangs a long chain of other states, more or less unclear, but not less filled with activity. It was possible therefore to develop from Leibniz a doctrine of feeling of which the keynote was the power of unclear elements to produce unique states of mind. Art in general, and music in particular, was taken to be a sphere in which clearness was not even an ideal; its aim was purely stimulation of the total life of the soul by exciting and blending the subrational elements, the blind forces of the *petites perceptions*. Thus in one direction Leibniz promoted the movement which ends in giving a distinct position and value to the feelings, while at the same time it remained possible for Herbart to quote Leibniz as his forerunner in the theory that the Will springs out of the relations between presentations.

3. WOLFF'S SYSTEMATIZATION OF LEIBNIZ

A student of Leibniz who had never seen the criticism of Locke in the *Nouveaux Essais* would be impressed chiefly with the emphasis laid on the activity and the self-sufficiency of the soul. There would seem to be an affinity between the independence of the monad and the pure intuition of the Cartesian maxim, 'Cogito, ergo sum.' In order to develop the monadism of Leibniz into a complete philosophy it would be necessary to explain the nature of the monad in a way which would conform with the usual divisions of philosophy and, consequently, to evolve from Leibniz a formal psychology. This could most easily be done by interpreting the inner activity of the monad as pure self-consciousness. Granted the standing problem of interaction, that is to say the persistent tendency to regard consciousness as having no relations with the world of things which would explain the presence in it of ideas referred to that world, it was also natural to present this psychology as primarily the account which the soul gives of itself as the product of its reflections. Wolff, endowed with a genius for order and system, very conscious too of the ineffectual character of the Leibnizian exposition, performed the ungrateful task of constructing from the fragments of the master's teaching a standard body of doctrine. For his basis he takes the *vis representativa*, the power of the mind to think its own thoughts. This, in some form or other, becomes the peculiar mark of German psychology, which remains afterwards the type of all psychology founded on the idea of activity. The importance of the point justifies a further expansion of its bearing on psychology.

The English psychologists in the main set out from the idea of the contents of the mind and explain the unity of consciousness by the natural affinities between these contents which are at various times described as associated, chemically united, or physiologically assimilated. All these are metaphors which ultimately explain nothing, but the point maintained without fail is the necessity of going from the plurality to the unity. Leibniz definitely set the unity first, and consequently left to others the task of showing how the plurality was possible. The honours were well divided, for if the former method never seems to attain any real unity, the latter never seems to show cause for any of the ordinary mental conditions which the common man takes to be the effect of sense-impressions. While Locke's terms might give offence by suggesting that the outer sense was separate from the inner power of reflection, Leibniz caused an equal amount of heartsearching through his union of outer and inner sense in one graduated scale of consciousness. What was 'outer' for Locke was 'inner' for Leibniz, and if the former could not get the sense material over into the mind, neither could the latter get it up into the higher plane. In the sequel we shall see how this question is settled: for the present it is enough to remark that the *vis representativa* has to do duty for both the subjective and the objective element in an act of consciousness.

The *vis representativa* is the real beginning of Wolff's psychology. This monumental work is still accorded honourable mention in the histories of philosophy, but it is presented as a deplorable instance of misapplied talent. A certain degree of injustice can be detected by anyone who values systematic thinking more than the invention of systems. The fervid genius of Leibniz achieved great things in many departments of knowledge: Wolff was essentially an instructor and more inclined to judge the final outcome of the whole theory than to defend paradoxes. From the first he was no very strict disciple of Leibniz. He dismissed the monads, substituting for them the atoms of the natural philosophers. He also paid little attention to the pre-established harmony, thinking that the parallelism of physical and psychical states was all that could be established. The science of the mind, at any rate, has no real dependence on these prefatory rhapsodies, and Wolff deserves some credit for having declared the study of the mental powers to be the foundation of all philosophy. This, too, had been said by Leibniz, but it is repeated by Wolff in a more pertinent form. Leibniz was interested in what for the sake of distinction may be called pneumatology. Wolff realizes that this is not a real substitute for the current systems of psychology, any more than a mystical confession is a substitute for a catechism. His task as a teacher was the creation of a new catechism, and as such the outcome must be estimated. He begins with a distinction between rational and empirical psychology which is a distinction of methods. Rational psychology is the deductive part of the science in which the necessary elements can be proved apart from observation. For example, since the material is wholly distinct from the immaterial, the necessary conclusion is drawn that the changes which we observe in consciousness arise from the activity of the soul which always tends to pass from one presentation or state to another. The states of consciousness are therefore changes, each of which has its sufficient reason in a preceding state. This is formal enough, but it amounts to no more than an explicit statement of what was involved in the doctrine of Descartes and Leibniz: it leads to the adoption of a pure parallelism. The psychophysical parallelism taught by Wolff is elaborated with the help of the traditional Aristotelian scale of functions. The physical part of an experience consists in the operation of the organism and the production of an idea in the brain, a material idea. The psychic part begins with the activity of the latent power of the soul, which is the actual sensation and the lowest degree of mental life. The powers of the mind are divided into lower and higher, the division coming as in Aristotle at the point of transition from involuntary to voluntary operations, that is to say in the distinction between retention and recollection, or between receptive and creative imagination.

At this point the significant feature of the Leibnizian influence begins to lend another character to the system of Wolff. Emphasis is laid on the spontaneity of psychic action: the products of this activity are not mere reproductions of the ideas united in the lower powers, but new creations: the poet and the painter have the power of creating new forms, and the work of genius is the full expression of this unique capacity. Here Wolff makes prominent the Platonic factor in the work of Leibniz and, somewhat unintentionally, mediates between the Platonism of the Renaissance and the Neoplatonism of Schelling or the aesthetic mood of Schiller. For the rest, only two points call for mention. The moderate attitude of Wolff allows him to recognize the value of physiology for the understanding of the human being, and his recognition of this part of the science of man prepares the way for the later views of the organism which ultimately took the place of the metaphysical 'harmony.' In opposition to this is the refusal to treat the passions as other than cognitive states: in the recognition of perfection lies the essence of pleasure, and this coincides with the attainment of the good which every creature strives to realize in its conscious life.

In conclusion the main points of Wolff's teaching may be stated briefly. He accepts the *apperceptio* of Leibniz. He builds up his system entirely from the elementary psychic facts called ideas or presentations. He defines sensation as *representatio compositi in simplici*, the representation of the complex physical object in the simple nature of the soul (e.g. the sensation of colour). He develops the law of mental reproduction as a law of redintegration; for when a present perception forms part of a past perception, the whole past perception tends to reinstate itself. To every process of the mind corresponds a modification of the body, an *idea materialis*. As there are no gaps in nature, so in the mind there is no gap between the lowest and the highest operations.

Wolff as a psychologist was at the same time retrograde and progressive. His peculiar inability to grasp the spirit of the monadology accounted for his tendency to see in it only a variation of the Cartesian themes and to begin his own work from the dogmatic '*Cogito, ergo sum*.' For him, too, psychology is a subdivision of metaphysics and not to be regarded as a natural science of the mind. Against this backsliding must be reckoned some important virtues. Wolff named and defined empirical psychology, though he made no significant contribution to it: he mediated between Cartesian spiritualism and the monadology by recognizing physiology as a complement to introspection and advocating a psychophysical parallelism which was sufficiently advanced to be dubbed materialism by his enemies. The extinction of Occasionalism was the most happy result of this sensible point of view. In all his work Wolff failed to be truly creative, but he classified, ordered, and defined almost the whole body of existing philosophical sciences. No more systems were needed, and, as usual, the next movement consists chiefly of emendations along with the elaboration of departmental subjects.

Chapter Twelve

THE OBSERVATIONALIST TRADITION

A. British empiricists and associationists

1. LOCKE

At the close of the seventeenth century speculative thought seemed likely to fall back into the chaos from which Descartes strove to rescue it. The various parts of the Cartesian doctrine were developed, refuted or travestied by innumerable writers. Hobbes had been weighed by theology and found wanting: public opinion was quietly conscious that the revival of mysticism and Neoplatonism which assisted the defeat of Hobbes, could not be dominant for long. What had been temporarily lost was the idea of method: it was this that Locke restored. As the question of method is the clue to Locke's teaching, and the relation of Locke's idea of method to his training in medicine has not been adequately emphasized in the past, we may preface our account of Locke's view by quoting the advice to Molyneux in which the position is fully stated:—'I perfectly agree with you concerning general theories, the curse of the time and destructive not less of life than of science—they are for the most part but a sort of waking dream, with which when men have warmed their heads, they pass into unquestionable truths. This is beginning at the wrong end, men laying the foundation in their own fancies, and then suiting the phenomena of diseases and the cure of them, to those fancies. I wonder, after the pattern Dr. Sydenham has set of a better way, men should return again to this romance way of physics. What we know of the works of nature, especially in the constitution of health and the operations of our own bodies, is only by the sensible effects, but not by any certainty we can have of the tools she uses or the ways she works by.' The recollection of this passage will make clear the real meaning of what Locke says about the human mind.

John Locke was born in 1632. He was nearly sixty when he finished the famous *Essay* (1690), so that we may rightly see in it the distilled essence of a lifelong meditation. It was not only written toward the end of his life, but also brooded over long before, as we learn from the commonplace books. The purpose and the plan of the work occurred to its author as early as 1670, and these ideas had their root in still earlier meditations and experiences. Locke was not an academic person; he loved freedom and disliked the fetters of tradition and a curriculum. His education was complex. At Oxford he learned the current Aristotelianism, afterwards to be derided by him; there, too, he acquired the principles of medicine and practised fitfully and informally all his life. On the Continent he learned something of Descartes, Gassendi, and the Montpellier school of philosophical physicians. His life was of a kind to prevent absorption in abstract theories or the rigidity of conservatism. It is remarkable that in the end Locke's great work reflects so little of his life and so much of his character. Locke's medical training might have led him toward current materialism, but he consciously declines to deal with the physical aspect of mind, and nothing remains of his medical science except the practical bent of his thought. A different man would have allied himself to one or other of the Cartesian developments; Locke is not strictly Cartesian, nor a follower of Hobbes, nor a disciple of any definable sect. He wrote as he lived, with an independent outlook on facts and theories.

Out of the fullness of his own heart Locke undertakes the cure of intellects. He did not write about the soul or compose a formal psychology; he wrote an essay, and his subject was the understanding, its nature and its limitations. Locke's psychology has to be extracted from his works and torn from its context, with some loss of significance. Only the method really belongs to his work as a whole; the rest is tentative and incidental. But the method is psychological; it may be described as 'psychogenetic,' for it traces the formation of the understanding from its beginning to its full development. Yet this is not a 'genetic' method in the true sense. Locke does not describe a process that takes place in time; he has no idea of evolution; in the spirit of his age, he creates a starting point by a principle of analysis and proceeds to explain complexity. His medical science was too crude to suggest the idea of embryonic thought or lead him to treat the mind as an organism.

The beginning is made with a clean sheet. The mind is declared to be at first a *tabula rasa*. The doctrine of innate ideas is refuted on the ground that no such ideas are found in the mind of children or savages. Locke refers only to the writings of Lord Herbert; he probably meant to include the Platonic theories revived by the Cambridge Platonists, but he had personal relations with the Cudworths that may have prevented him from being too definite. In any case his object was to deal only with experience, and by experience he meant a process that falls strictly within the limits of life and death.

The first book of Locke's *Essay* is not really a part of his psychological work; it is a chapter on anthropology, greatly influenced by contemporary accounts of uncivilized races. It had an interest of its own in showing how travel was widening the thoughts of men about the races of mankind, but otherwise it is of secondary importance. As Lord Shaftesbury said, 'innate is a word Mr. Locke poorly plays on.' But Locke's beginning had one significant feature—it excluded the possibility of regarding consciousness as wider than the immediate field of thought. In other words, the possibility of developing the Cartesian doctrine by means of *latent* ideas was decisively excluded.

Locke avoids, when possible, the traditional forms of expression. He makes his own terminology. For him the word 'idea' means 'the object of the mind when it thinks'; sensation denotes the effect which constitutes experience of an object as its cause, and reflection denotes a reaction of the mind upon the original experience. Looked at in another way, sensation may be ascribed to the outer sense and reflection to the inner sense. The influence of Descartes is shown in this treatment of reflection; in making it an original power of the mind, and not subsequent to sensation, Locke has committed himself to the support of such an inner power as would properly belong to a 'thinking thing.' Not observing that and avoiding any definite statements about mind or matter, Locke presents reflection as a function owned by nothing. The attempt to start from a pure experience, which is Locke's real aim, is thus corrupted at the root.

The analysis of experience begins, then, with some tacit assumptions. As it proceeds these assumptions clamour for more explicit recognition. Sensation, we find, is capable of giving only certain kinds of knowledge. Some of the ultimate contents of consciousness are due to demonstration, others are intuitive. The outer sense is the means by which we are brought into relation with things; the inner sense gives us knowledge of ourselves. What is the nature of this process? Is there a relation of causality between the object and the mind? If so, Locke ignores the very problem which Descartes found most intractable; and the inner sense becomes more unintelligible than ever. These are the points thought out by Berkeley and Hume. Their attitude will be seen later.

In the course of his construction of experience Locke introduces other factors. His common sense revolts from the idle talk of faculties. To say that the act of willing is due to a faculty of willing amounts to mere tautology. But Locke's rejection of faculties is followed by the adoption of powers which have no advantage over faculties except in being less definitely real, in the scholastic sense. Locke wishes to shift the point of view from agencies to activities; he thinks more of the classification of phenomena than of the distinctive sources to which previous writers had assigned the different types of experience. The aim was good; the method preserved the Cartesian tendency to make consciousness the sole basis; but the execution of the design was inadequate. This (as Herbart pointed out[1]) was especially the case in the passages referring to Memory and to the span of consciousness. In both these places Locke betrays his tendency to pass uncritically from ideas to some agency which manipulates the ideas, or from the content of consciousness to something over and above that content.

So far, then, we find that Locke begins with a classification of the contents of consciousness according as they are given, by the senses, or produced, by the activity of the mind. We can proceed to see how he describes each of the recognized types of activity.

Sensation implies no activity; it is a process which brings over to the mind that which determines its activity. In Locke's words: 'when I say the senses convey into the mind, I mean, they from external objects convey into the mind what produces there true perceptions' (E., ii. 1, 3). This is not very satisfactory as an explanation, but the purpose of the words is clear. Locke really thinks the sensation consists in a motion of the animal spirits (E., ii. 8, 4), but he desires (after Descartes) to distinguish between the physical fact and its psychic result. His interest ends when he has declared that sensation presents objects 'whether we will or not,' and he compares the mind to a mirror that cannot 'refuse, alter or obliterate the images or ideas, which the objects set before it do therein produce' (*E.*, ii. 1, 25). Bodies produce ideas in us by 'impulse,' a motion being transmitted by 'our nerves or animal spirits' to the brain. This applies both to primary qualities, i.e. bulk, figure, texture, and motion of parts, and to secondary qualities. The phenomenal or subjective character of perceptions is proved, psychologically, by the experience of heat in one hand and cold in the other, when both are held in the same water. This is only to be explained on the assumption that heat and cold are 'nothing but the increase or diminution of the motion of the minute parts of our bodies.' This establishes the required distinction, between the objective nature of the cause and the subjective character of the effects in consciousness.

While sensation is the name for a physical process, perception is 'the first faculty of the mind exercised about our ideas.' It is also 'the first and simplest idea we have from reflection' (*E.*, ii. 9, 1). While we have no innate ideas we may acquire pre-natal ideas through experiences in the womb. The newly born child shows an intense desire for experiences, particularly for that of light. Perception is a power that belongs to animals (in a lower degree) and to man. Plants act mechanically, as in the case of the 'sensitive plant,' but animals have sensation: a point on which Locke differs from Descartes. Perception also involves some degree of judgment. In the case of a man born blind, the mere sight of an object like a globe would not produce more than the idea of 'a flat circle variously shadowed.' This shows that the ordinary adult perception is a complex activity involving judgment. So that our actual perceptions are coloured by other experiences and affected by habits of mind. Locke here shows what we shall have occasion to notice again, namely a clear idea of the unity of consciousness: a single aspect of the mind is regarded by him as implying its whole nature.

From perception Locke proceeds to consider retention, memory, and recollection. He connects the affections with retention, remarking that those ideas are most lasting which are originally accompanied with pleasure or pain (*E.*, ii. 10, 3). He also remarks that the permanence of memories may depend on the constitution of our bodies and the make of our animal spirits. In memory or 'secondary perception' the mind is usually passive; in saying that it *may* be active Locke shows that he regards the passive state as more normal.

Memory or retention makes the mind capable of comparing, and so attaining 'that large tribe of ideas comprehended under relation.' Naming and abstraction follow from that. Abstraction is one of the ways in which the mind manipulates the simple ideas; the others are combining ideas to make complex ideas (beauty, gratitude, a man, an army, the universe), and relating ideas. In this way the increasing complexity of the mind and its contents is explained.

The later editions of the *Essay* were enriched with new material. The chapter on The Association of Ideas was part of the later additions; the discussion of desire and will was another. The nature of the chapter on Association seems to have escaped notice. It makes no reference to the 'Laws of Association,' shows no sign of acquaintance with Aristotle or Hobbes, and does not even begin with its apparent subject. It is upon the unreasonableness of men that Locke seizes; it is the cure of minds that seems to him most important. The real topic, then, is the way our ideas cling together; in other words, the nature of our complex minds. Some ideas have a natural connection with others: so much Locke assumes as self-evident. But the actual union of ideas, which at any given time constitutes our thought, is not such a 'natural' affair: the motions of the mind are like those of the body in being variable in relation to the general condition. But an absolutely normal person is an ideal, scarcely ever realized; most people are not quite sound in body or mind, there is no one who has not some degree of madness (*E.*, ii. 33). The changing course of thought is not guided by reason, though there are always reasons for a change. Custom produces habit, and there are habits of thinking, of determining in the will and of motion in the animal spirits. How far habit is a physical effect, Locke will not say. It seems as though all habits are 'but trains of motion in the animal spirits, which, once set going, continue in the steps they have been used to, which, by often treading, are worn into a smooth path, and the motion in it becomes easy, and as it were natural.' But whether the series of ideas depends upon the physical series Locke will not decide. The whole question of association is a question of the constitution of the mind; accidents of time and place do not wholly regulate it: feelings enter in and the whole composition of our thought may be affected by some innate or acquired antipathy. Locke sees the significance of this for the educators; he thinks they look after health of the body and forget the mind. That was where the observer and the medical adviser showed his bent. But we should like to hear something more about antipathies that are not acquired but natural. This seems to indicate a depth of introspection not reached before; perhaps the addition of this chapter was a mark of progress in Locke's thoughts. However that may be, the disorders of the mind come in for elaborate treatment. The cementing of ideas by brooding over wrongs; the dislike of that which has caused pain; the slow work of time in changing the mental outlook when reasoning quite fails; curious oddities and eccentricities that have secret causes in associations; all these are noted with astonishing freshness and skill. The whole chapter reflects the united qualities of the physician, the liberal thinker, and the keen observer of men.

2. BERKELEY

Locke, Berkeley, and Hume form a chronological sequence conveniently named the English Empirical Philosophy. Under the convenience of this title lurks a temptation; those who yield to it regard Berkeley as essentially at one with Locke and Hume, ascribing variations to theological interests. For the history of metaphysics or philosophy in general such a superficial reckoning may be adequate. Doubtless in the main points Berkeley did mean what Locke had meant; they both aspired to philosophize in a manner worthy of gentlemen and Christians. But in the finer details there is a significant diversity. George Berkeley, sometime Bishop of Cloyne, was born in 1684 and died in 1753. In 1687 Newton published his *Principia*; in 1690 Locke published the *Essay*; in 1696 deism was revealed in Toland's *Christianity not Mysterious*. Berkeley began his academic life in 1700, when he entered Trinity College, Dublin, and these were the forces which then controlled the thoughts of all by attracting or repelling. The young philosopher was acquainted with the 'new way of ideas'; he did not suffer from any obstructing prejudices, and he did not lapse uncritically into an idle fondness for novelty. As a result Berkeley's work combines great originality with strong conservatism. His first work, the *New Theory of Vision*, shows the brilliant cleverness of the young man; his last, *Siris*, shows matured wisdom. While the *New Theory* only touches one subject directly, it indirectly affects all Berkeley's views. Its main positions are restated in the works that deal with knowledge and with theological doctrines. Its empirical character is reflected in everything which Berkeley says about knowledge. But as time progressed its author gradually ceased to be limited by its terms; the extent to which a study of sensation, however acute, falls short of the full study of man, gradually became obvious to Berkeley. Though a scholar in the truest sense, Berkeley was no recluse. He knew the society of his day, was acquainted with such eminent men as Addison and Swift, travelled on the Continent, and saw in England the extremes of prosperous corruption and impoverished virtue. The well-known effort to establish a centre of plain living and high thinking in Bermuda, which brought Berkeley to America but ended in nothing, remains to prove that Berkeley's spirit of adventure was not limited to the world of thought. When justice has been done to the significance of the *New Theory of Vision* it will be necessary to render justice also to the adventurous spirit which rises in the *Siris* to other levels and looks upon new fields of speculation hardly yet fully explored.

The *Essay* toward a new Theory of Vision, first published in 1709, must be reckoned the most significant contribution to psychology produced in the eighteenth century. It merits this title on two distinct grounds: for it was not only an original treatment of the topic, but also a classic example of method. In point of method the *Essay* has been rightly described as the first instance of clear isolation and purely relevant discussion of a psychological topic, and this penetration to the strictly relevant detail is in fact the secret of Berkeley's success. In order to show exactly what constituted the merits of this new theory it will be necessary to cast a look backward.

Before the eighteenth century dawned the worst errors in the conception of vision had been corrected. The form of the eye, the function of its constituent parts, and the nature of light had been brought into the sphere of scientific knowledge. The attempts made to solve the problems concerning perception of distance and size were unfortunately vitiated by a special kind of error, the tendency to suppose that perceptions were made up of conceptual elements. The interest in optics and dioptrics produced elaborate treatises on the geometrical aspects of the subject, and men's minds were full of lines and angles. They slipped from that into the habit of speaking as though the angles at which the rays of light converge were the real data for judgment of distance. Though more refined in its details, this was not different in nature from the old notion that the image in the pupil is the primary object in visual perception. To explain the *perception* of distance by a 'natural geometry' of this kind was no less absurd than to explain the pain of a wound as dependent on knowing the scientific name for the nerve affected. In brief, the prevailing emphasis on knowledge, on the cognitive powers, was a source of errors from which only genius could shake itself free.

So long as the eye-states or the brain-states were taken as the equivalents of experience it was difficult to shake off this 'natural geometry.' Consequently the idealists were in the best position to make innovations, and in this respect due regard must be paid to Malebranche. The treatment of distance and magnitude by Malebranche (*vide* p. 389) was strikingly original. In its main principles it clearly anticipates Berkeley's doctrine, and the fact that the typical problems (such as that of the apparent size of the moon) are common to both these writers, increases the similarity of the two discussions. It is difficult to estimate the amount and value of Malebranche's influence on Berkeley. The *Recherche* was well known in England; Locke undertook to refute Malebranche and Berkeley makes reference to him by name. On the other side of the account must be reckoned the extent to which both writers deal with material that was common property, and, most important of all, the extent to which Malebranche overlooked what Berkeley regarded as fundamental, the part played by touch.

Scientific opinion was unanimous on some preliminary points. It was agreed that as a rod extending from the eye to an object would only be visible at the end near the eye, distance in the sense of depth of space could not be an object of pure vision. There was also a general acceptance of the facts known as aerial and linear perspective, that is the estimation of distance as accounting for the indistinctness or smallness of objects known by near experience to be distinct and large. The problem of perspective, which had been of primary interest to the great painters, really involved the central idea which was now emerging, the idea of arbitrary intelligible signs of which distance was an interpretation. This was the real extent of Malebranche's work. As a metaphysician Malebranche divorced the mental processes from the physical and regarded the former as a system of relations which are true of but not akin to the objective system; our ideas of the world contain its meaning as the words of a book contain the thoughts and feelings of its author. This idealistic position is adopted by Berkeley, but the psychological groundwork is different. Though experience plays a large part in Malebranche's work, even to the extent of admitting direct experiment, it is not sense-experience as such. For Malebranche the perception of distance or size is a synthesis of judgments which are not made explicitly (as inferences) but implicitly and inevitably; hence these judgments are called *sensations composées*.

The difference between Malebranche and Berkeley is great, though the superficial likeness of the two expositions often leads to hasty assertions of identity. The nature of the difference becomes more intelligible if we remember that Berkeley makes a reference to Locke's *Essay* (ii. 9, 8) where the basis is not a synthesis of judgments but a co-existence of the data from different senses in one judgment. That is the English empirical basis from which Berkeley starts and by which he separated himself from the whole atmosphere of Malebranche's work. If we remember this connection with Locke and also that with 'the learned and worthy Mr. Molyneux,' a tutor in the University of Dublin when Berkeley entered there, the differences between Malebranche and Berkeley will not be hard to understand. One instance will make it clear. Malebranche said the moon looks larger at the horizon than at the zenith because there are intermediate objects which affect the 'composite sensation'; if we shut out those objects the size of the moon appears to be increased. This conclusion Berkeley explicitly denies and adopts the explanation of difference through density of the atmosphere, which was the theory supported by Regis against Malebranche.

Berkeley's own theory depends on the assumption that extension and magnitude are primarily objects of the sense of touch. Hence distance and visible magnitude have a constant relation to touch; for the child begins by handling objects as it looks at them, and so learns by imperceptible degrees what the visual image means in terms either of touch (movement over the surface) or motion (movement from far to near). This is an empirical derivation of the perception of size and distance, due allowance being made for development. It implies a theory of space and of things as occupants of space which seems to be unhesitatingly adopted; no analysis is made of space apart from the questions of more or less extension and the 'outness' of objects.

Historians have noticed casually how much affinity there is between Berkeley's idealism and the teaching of Plotinus. Vision is at all times a subject which leads the mind from consideration of the senses to reflection on the inner light. Judging from changes of expression and from the way in which passages were changed in successive editions, Berkeley was never ignorant of the general problems which are bound up with a theory of vision. This is shown by the vigour of his onslaught when he attacks abstract ideas. Taking the word 'idea' with all its burden of acquired meaning, he demands a visualization of every mental content. Consequently he becomes nominalistic; for every image implies an object which can produce an impression, but no such object or image is given to correspond with the general and universal terms. Logically Berkeley could reach the same conclusion; for since objects are defined by him as collections of ideas, there could be no sense in abstracting an idea from an object which is itself essentially an idea (*esse is percipi*). So far the traditional view of the idea (*species impressa*) dominated Berkeley's arguments. But another traditional view claimed his attention and grew in importance as the theological outcome of his nominalism became evident. If we only know objects through 'ideas imprinted on the senses,' there can be no knowledge of the self or soul; for it is absurd to suppose that the soul impresses itself. In this indirect manner and in direct descent from the mediaeval problem expressed in the question 'Does the soul know itself?' Berkeley came to the point of seeing that his premises were inadequate. He admits that we have a notion, not an idea, of ourselves (*Princ.*, § 89), and this is the beginning of a significant change in the whole outlook. In the second edition of the *Principles* a reference to relations was introduced; it was now admitted that the idea of a relation was not to be confused with a relation between ideas (as impression); moreover, time and, in the *Siris*, number were now seen to be something not impressed on the mind as a sense-datum but constituted by an operation of the mind in a different sense, a specific act. Finally, then, the original objection to 'abstract ideas' must be revised. Number and personality are two notions which refuse to fit the original scheme; assisted by Plato's *Theaetetus*, Berkeley virtually abandons the empirical position. We may regret the lack of any proper development of the new point of view, but its inauguration is important and deserves more notice than it has received. At a later date we shall find a similar demand for a new psychology being made in the interest of serial order, form, and relations. At a period so uncongenial it was not probable that such a demand would meet with response, however clearly it might be formulated.

On the whole Berkeley felt no need for a physiological supplement to his psychology. He would settle the whole matter so far as psychophysiology is concerned by announcing that the brain is an idea (*Princ.*, § 146), a method that has found favour with later idealistic writers. But this attitude also seems to have proved unsatisfying to the more mature Berkeley. He wrote on Passive Obedience, and had occasion to speak of 'natural antipathies implanted in the soul' and of custom as a second nature. He declared that all rational beings are by nature social, and warned men against following emotions arising from the blood and humours. In brief, when conduct was the subject of his reflections, Berkeley was compelled to consider human nature more concretely than he had been at first inclined to do. He could still write wittily about a new kind of snuff which might be administered to a person and enable the soul to attach itself to some other pineal gland! To the Cartesian dualism Berkeley could never descend. But the 'spirits' of Willis exercised a subtle attraction. They too were not unlike light! And so, in the end, Berkeley's psychology has the appearance of a reformed doctrine. Ideas have ceased to be the alpha and omega; form and relation have become factors in knowledge and an index of mental 'acts' which are not Locke's 'operations,' of 'notions' which are not 'ideas'; finally the limitation of thought to God and the soul has been overcome far enough to admit recognition of secondary (scientific) causes and allow our author to remark 'that there is really such a thing as vital flame, actually kindled, nourished and extinguished, like common flame, and by the same means, is an opinion of some moderns, particularly of Dr. Willis in his tract *De Sanguinis Accensione*: that it requires constant eventilation, through the trachea and pores of the body for the discharge of a fuliginous and excrementitious vapour; and that this vital flame, being extremely subtle, might not be seen any more than shining flies or *ignes fatui* by daylight. This is Dr. Willis's notion: and perhaps there may be some truth in this, if it be so understood as that light or fire might indeed constitute the animal spirit or immediate vehicle of the soul!' (*Siris*, 205).

3. HUME

The 'new way of ideas,' as understood by Locke, was a description of the human mind more or less governed by the two categories of content and form. It is often said of Locke that he refuted in the fourth book of the *Essay* what he asserted in the second. That point of view is not maintained here. On the contrary, it is asserted that Locke in his second book was concerned primarily with the contents of the mind; he rejected innate ideas as specific innate contents (without thereby denying mental activity as such), because certain persons (not Descartes) were at that time asserting them. In other words, the only source of those ideas which can be referred to external objects must be actually existing objects. In the fourth book we come to the question of ideas that are *real*, but not referred to *things*: the reality of these ideas consists in being what they are, not in being attached to externally existing objects. The critical difficulty which remains when we have accepted this double point of view is to determine the boundaries of the 'kinds of knowledge.' Berkeley's development shows that he became more and more impressed with the importance of the second topic, the form of thought and its constructive aspect. This movement consequently tended to reduce the importance of objects as external agents capable of supplying content to the mind, making them indistinguishable from contents and therefore only psychic events.

This epistemological development had the effect of sharpening Locke's distinctions and giving them the appearance of depending on metaphysical assumptions, primarily that of the difference between soul and body. The result is seen in Hume.

The secret of Hume's success in refining ideas and failure in explaining facts lies in his positivism. Taking that term as a substitute for 'scepticism,' and ridding ourselves of the sentiments which seem eternally bound up with the opprobrious epithet 'sceptical,' we may proceed to estimate Hume's contribution to psychology. A change of terms ushers in the new scheme. For sensation and reflection we are now to read impression and idea. This is intended to eliminate any lingering notion of two sources or two kinds of mental operations. If Locke's 'sensation' pointed to a *res extensa* and his 'reflection' to a *res cogitans*, our new terms will shut out all such implicit references and leave only psychic events differing in the mode of appearance. Impressions are more vivid; ideas are less vivid. Such is the formula by which Hume notifies us that if we enter into our own minds we shall find neither matter nor self, but simply events. Here then we have, at the best, a pure psychology or an analysis of the mind undertaken in the spirit of positivism with no pre-suppositions: it remains to be seen whether pre-suppositions can be thus eliminated or whether the process does not amount to casting out some pre-suppositions in order to substitute others.

The crucial questions for this type of positivism are those of order and system. Hume was from the first aware of his enemy. If an idea is only *weaker* than an impression, we cannot immediately infer that it is therefore older, or secondary, or in any other way equivalent to a 'decaying sense.'[1] To assume that every experience runs its course from a primary impression to a later evanescent stage called an idea is to introduce again the rejected fictions of an object which impresses and a subject which is impressed; this must be avoided, and Hume even goes so far as to suggest that in some cases the idea might come first. He asks whether, given a series of colours, we might not supply a colour which was not actually given, that is to say attain an idea prior to any corresponding impression (*Treatise* i. section 1). What Hume meant by the problem is difficult to see, but the significance of the question lies undoubtedly in the fact that Hume did not intend to regard 'impressions' and 'ideas' as mere names for sense and 'decaying sense.' Yet it is equally difficult to see what meaning can be given to the terms if we are not prepared to treat the force of ideas as in some way having an inverse ratio to their distance from the time of the impression. For introspection does not actually show that every idea is less vivid than every impression;

---

[1] As used by Hobbes, *Lev.* i. ch. 2.

if we admit exceptions it will be necessary to inquire into attention and other selective activities, so that finally Hume's limits will be painfully obvious.

There can be little doubt that the concept of force obtruded itself into Hume's views about impressions. Physical science was still the ideal of philosophers, and Newton was as Locke said, 'never-enough-to-be-admired.' Suspicion deepens into certainty when we come to Hume's doctrine of association. The way was prepared by a perfunctory treatment of memory, which is made equivalent to order and position, and a discussion of relations. The subject of relations is also inadequately treated by Hume, for though he noted a distinction between ideas of relation and relation of ideas, he nowhere explains the significance of either phrase. In the end he is content to state the principles of association as explaining the relations of the ideas one to another and to curtail even this exposition in the later *Inquiry*. The famous passage in the *Treatise* runs thus (i. 1, 3): 'Here is a kind of attraction which in the mental world will be found to have as extraordinary effects as in the natural, and to show itself in as many and various forms.' Our philosopher here speaks the language of physics: he claims to be the Newton of psychology.

Hume's doctrine of Association was at one time thought to be a plagiarism. It was asserted by Coleridge, as an original discovery, that Hume took it from the commentary of Thomas Aquinas on Aristotle's *De Anima*. Evidence was produced that Hume possessed and read a work by Thomas Aquinas, but the proof of plagiarism was weak. Croom-Robertson remarks that Locke overlooked the general psychological importance of association, and Hume took up this point, 'forgetting or ignorant of Aristotle.' In any case, the types of association named by Hume are different from those of Aristotle; Aristotle named similarity, contrast, and contiguity, while Hume's list includes resemblance, contiguity, cause, and effect. Of these the last is the most significant. Locke appears to have regarded association as operative in producing trains of ideas when the synthetic power of the mind was not being exercised. Hume was convinced that the self and its synthetic power were names for nothing but actual connections between ideas: he differs from his predecessors in so far as he does not make association equivalent to some forms of synthesis but a substitute for synthetic activity. Locke was considering why the contents of the mind were sometimes arranged in a kind of unregulated order: Hume, intending to drop all reference to the mind except as a name for the contents themselves, quite logically proceeded to treat the order and connection of the contents as the whole sum and substance of what others regarded as activity of the mind. This and not the mere catalogue of principles was what gave to Hume's doctrine of association its peculiar significance.

In spite of a lucidity in expression which defies competition, Hume was in many respects very obscure. The Enlightenment to which he belonged was always liable to the vice of superficiality. Many points raised in the *Treatise* are hard to understand: the *Inquiry* affords no help, for Hume then omits them entirely. We may grant that Hume's aim was to eliminate all irrelevant factors and treat the nature of man directly, without pre-suppositions and in a positive manner. But the fact still remains that the work done by 'the soul' cannot be wholly ignored: if there is no 'self' to operate, there are still the undeniable operations: and so far as his psychology is concerned Hume is compelled to refund all the requirements by exploiting Belief and Habit. In view of the difference between the *Treatise* and the *Inquiry*, it is justifiable to suppose that Hume lost what faith he originally had in formal principles of psychology. Observation of men and manners led him to think that emphasis should be laid on actions, that introspection was of little value, and therefore an objective description of conduct was alone valuable. It is a mistake to regard Hume as one who aimed to explain mental operations. He regarded the craving for explanation as a mere straining after the impossible. His terms, belief or custom or cause, are descriptive titles for modes of behaviour, tentative formulae which enable us to find our way at any time or place through the bewildering chaos of events. No metaphysical disputes about the soul really touched Hume: he acts the part of the scientific inquirer for whom the 'ultimate reality' is too high so that he cannot attain to it. The outcome of this attitude was, in one direction, a mere neglect of fundamental questions; in another direction it was the revelation of new possibilities in comparative study of men and of animals, but more particularly in the consequent naturalism which gave significance to the emotions and the will. Dispensing with an 'ultimate' here as elsewhere, Hume eliminates from the concept of the Will all suggestion of substantive reality or power: as positivist he accepts nothing but the inner and outer events ('the motion of our body follows upon the command of our will') and the word Will should accordingly be employed only as a name for that class of events in which there occurs an observed sequence consisting of the strongest motive as inner event and change of place as outer event.

Hume takes up the study of the Passions upon the plan used in the treatise on the Understanding. The life of the mind comprehends two classes of 'impressions,' the original and secondary (*Treatise* II. i. 1). In other words, those inner events which have no psychic antecedents are original; the rest are derivative; the former can only be described, the latter admit of some explanation or resolution. In the sphere of the Understanding, the impression is the actual given sensation; to this corresponds the 'original' state of pleasure or pain. In the complex state of mind called a 'passion,' the sensation of pleasure (or pain) would be accompanied by a feeling of hope, fear, or some similar affection, so that the *primary* feeling takes up secondary states, and the scientific treatment of the affections will be the 'experimental' method of discovering the types of feeling, their causes, and their connection with ideas.

Pleasure and pain are the two fundamental facts from which we must begin. Certain states of the organism (heat, cold) are felt as comfortable or uncomfortable, and are in consequence called good or bad. There are also tendencies of the mind which give rise to feelings of pleasure and pain according as they are assisted or obstructed by objects and circumstances; e.g. the distress of an enemy (the term implying previous hatred) is pleasant, as satisfying the tendency toward revenge. Thus the affections can be classed as direct or indirect.

The direct affections include desire and aversion, joy and grief, hope and fear. The states are classed in pairs because the basis is dual, namely good and evil. The distinction between the three pairs is dependent upon additional factors: desire is concerned with good as present; joy, with good as assured in the future; hope, with good as probable though remote. Hope and fear differ somewhat from the other states of feeling through their tendency to mingle. Plato and Aristotle noted this tendency to a mixed state. Descartes restated this and explained it as due to oscillations of the mind in the estimation of probabilities (*Passions*, 165, 6). Spinoza followed the same line (iii, 12), making hope an 'inconstant joy.' Hume does not differ essentially from this position, though he states the mental condition as a mixture of joy and sorrow, rather than hope and fear. Hume also goes further than his predecessors in thinking that similar feelings always have a tendency to produce their opposites: for the feelings correspond with ideas in the mind, and the ideas move by association; as, for example, the idea of impending evil leads to the idea of escape which (so long as it is entertained) arouses the feeling of hope in place of the original fear. This theory of connection is more fully worked out in the discussion of indirect affections.

Direct affections imply nothing more than a cause; indirect affections involve an object as well as a cause. The object may be oneself, or something other than oneself. The types are Pride and Humility, in the case of self-regarding affections, Love and Hate in the case of other-regarding affections. For example, wealth belonging to oneself is the *cause* of joy which has for its *object* one's own increased importance; hence Pride. Pain (as cause) referred to a person (as object) produces the passion of Hate.

It is necessary to notice here that the person is not the cause of the passion; the cause is the inner state which is by us associated with the idea of some person or thing, here denoted as object. This is important, because Hume is anxious to avoid the idea of natural objects of love and hate; he does not believe that there are such natural objects of passions, but that any object, combined with an affection, becomes the object of an indirect affection. Here we see Hume's real drift. The guiding principle of his discussion is the destruction of *a priori* theories which really begin with the idea of objects that *ought* to be loved or hated. This ethical point of view Hume intends to exclude from his scientific 'anatomy of the feelings.'

Love and Hate are not (like pride and humility) mere states; they include an impulse to action. Yet, natural as it would seem, Hume does not deduce benevolence and malevolence from Love and Hate. He classes them as direct, instinctive, and such as cannot be further analysed or explained (*Tr.*, ii. 3, 9). Aristotle declared that Love was a tendency to wish good for another; but Descartes declared this was not the essence of love, declining to consider its nature as identical with its *effects*.

Hume's general principle is clear. He proposes to resolve complex passions into simpler states of feeling associated with ideas. His attempt to do this is technically vitiated by a fault of exposition. The association, as understood by him, could only be the association of the idea of an object with the idea of the feeling. We require to know whether the revival of an idea of feeling is always equivalent to a revived feeling. We also require to know whether the 'association' operates by similarity, contiguity, or causality. Each of these principles offers peculiar difficulties, and it is clear that Hume has followed his own theory too hastily. Nothing but elaborate inductive research could give a satisfactory answer; Hume's idea of 'experiment' exhausts itself in the creation of imaginary cases resolved in a way that illustrates the principles cleverly, but not perhaps rightly.

The finest product of this scheme was the doctrine of Sympathy. Here, contrary to his usual tendency, Hume becomes positively rhetorical. The fact of sympathy is fully recognized, and its importance for the psychology of 'political animals' is clearly seen, but the explanation of this unselfish selfishness is altogether too complex. The idea of another person's feeling is said to be associated with the idea of oneself, and so the required liveliness is imparted to the otherwise neutral conception of another's joy or sorrow. It is enough to remark that Hume himself finally saw that this was mere subservience to the rules of a system, and, seeing it, he abandoned the false method. It is extremely probable that true sympathy is dependent upon the possibility of reviving the memory of a corresponding experience; the ordinary formula is 'I feel for you in your distress, I have known what it is to suffer.' But this is not at all what Hume meant by his analytic explanation of sympathy; it is, perhaps, what he meant when he abandoned that explanation.

The development of the law of comparison produced a more important result. As the idea of association grew more definite, the associated elements became less rigid and atomic. This process was considerably furthered by taking into account the affective side of consciousness. For it was then obvious that the general temper of the mind greatly altered the objects usually called the 'same.' If A is larger than B, B larger than C, the mind accommodated to A would feel C to be much smaller than if it was previously accommodated to B. The idea is not, for experience, a changeless quantity; it is relative, inasmuch as it is presented always in contrast to a preceding state. If this is true in the case of a pleasure contrasted with a pain, it is also true for the sense of space: the small room is oppressively small to the nobleman accustomed to spacious halls; to the cottager it is the ideal of comfort. In short, Hume sees in a new light the fact that all ideation is, in part, feeling; and the continuous change of contents is for the mind a continuous comparison making each state relative to its antecedents.

4. HARTLEY

To this period belong the life and works of David Hartley. Born in 1705, Hartley was trained for the clerical profession, to which his father belonged; but finally he abandoned his calling and became an industrious physician. The complexity of his training was reproduced in his interests; his mind was both exact and speculative, his minute observations were joined with cosmic theories; natural science, mathematics, optics, poetry, physiology, and theology—all in turn attracted his curiosity and absorbed his energy. The work by which Hartley is best known, *Observations on Man, His Frame, His Duty and His Expectations*, was slowly evolved during sixteen years of patient toil (1730–1746). An outline of the theory was first published as an appendix to a medical tract under the title *De Sensu, Motu, et Idearum Generatione*. The larger work was published in 1749, and seems to have attracted little or no attention. In 1775 Priestley edited a new edition, omitting the theory of vibrations and most of the theological discussions. A translation appeared in Germany in 1778[1] and from this a complete edition was issued in English by the author's son in 1801. The real influence of Hartley was thus postponed until the nineteenth century, and the great exponent of his views on the human mind was James Mill.

Hartley's work comprises three parts which are really unconnected. The first contains the physical doctrine of the vibrations; the second is concerned with the operations of the mind; the third treats of the Christian religion. The want of real connection is obvious from the fact that Priestley saw fit to publish the middle part without the other two; and the author himself frankly says,

---

[1] Prepared by Rev. Dr. H. A. Pistorius (Ruegen), with notes and essays, 1791 and 1801.

'the doctrine of Association may be laid down as a certain foundation and a clue to direct our future Inquiries, whatever becomes
of that of Vibrations.'[1] On the other hand the author spares no
pains to show the value of his hypothesis as an explanation of all
the workings both of body and of mind. In this lies the whole
value of his work. The possibilities of a physiological psychology
were at the time wholly unsuspected. Hartley takes his place in
history as the originator of this branch of science. The particular
form of his hypothesis may no longer claim any serious attention,
but the hypothesis itself is of primary importance. That hypothesis is, in brief, that mind and body always co-operate and there
is a physical equivalent for the mental, a mental equivalent for
the physical, operation in every case. The development of this
hypothesis occupies all those parts of his work which concern
our subject.

Hartley leaves us in no doubt as to the origin of his ideas or
the writers with whom he has the closest connections. Newton's
remarks at the end of his *Optics* influence the whole theory of
vibrations. The preface states 'About eighteen years ago I was
informed that the Rev. Mr. Gray, then living, asserted the possibility of deducing all our intellectual pleasures and pains from
Association. This put me upon considering the power of Association.' The 'general plan' is declared to agree with that of Descartes and Leibniz; the point of agreement is the common freedom from 'that great difficulty of supposing, according to the
scholastic system, that the Soul, an immaterial Substance, exerts
and receives a real physical influence upon and from the Body.'
Here there is a clear statement that the basis of the whole work is
not materialism but parallelism, the hypothesis being 'that there
is a change made in the medullary substance, proportional and
correspondent to every change in the sensations.'

The views of Hartley upon sensation as a physical process were
taken direct from Newton's *Principia*. In brief, the object of
sensation produces the idea of sensation by making an impression
on the organism and creating a disturbance of the nerves; these
disturbances are called vibrations and said to be 'motions backward and forward of the small particles, of the same kind as the
oscillation of the pendulum and the trembling of particles of
sounding bodies.' The nerves are regarded by Hartley as 'solid

[1] Pt. I. Sect. i, Prop. ii.

capillamenta according to Newton' rather than 'small tubuli according to Boerhaave'; the theory of vibrations requires the substance of the nerves, spinal marrow, and brain to be uniform, continuous, and devoid of any opacity that might obstruct the ether. For in reality the doctrine of vibrations is a doctrine of ether; the small particles of bodies emit an attenuated Air or Aether, which is a thin elastic fluid; this has a 'repulsive force in respect of the bodies which emit it,' and its particles repel each other. The real transmission of movement is therefore along the surface of the nerves and the nerve acts as a conductor for the transmission of this movement. The use of the lightning conductor would be a good analogy.

It is important to notice that the vibrations are propagated along the nerves, for the nerves themselves only account for the place and direction of the vibrations which are like the 'free propagation of sounds along the surface of water.' The brain is not a gland filled with a secretion, but an expansion of the medullary substance, a mass of fibrils which can be made to vibrate in different directions 'according to the different directions of the nerves by which the vibrations enter.' The nerves and the brain are thus described as instruments which subserve the action of the ether; they have no activity of their own except in so far as they react to the 'repulsive force' of the ether. As we noted above, only place and direction are said to depend on the nerves; the degree and kind of motion, the remaining two 'sorts of difference,' are ascribed solely to the vibrations which depend upon the ether.

The theory of Hartley is not so clear as it would seem to be from the account usually given of it. The term 'vibrations' covers three distinct things, the action of ether, the action of nerves, and the interaction of both these actions. But in the end (Prop. 5) we are told that matter is not endued with the power of sensation; there may even be 'an infinitesimal elementary body' between the soul and the 'gross body,' in which case all this machinery would explain nothing. The hypothesis of vibrations would then be true 'in a very useful practical sense,' yet not so 'in an ultimate and precise one.' This shows that Hartley's references to Leibniz and Malebranche are significant; he was at heart an occasionalist, and occasionalism was a very appropriate theory for one who combined physiology with theology. The fault to be found with this type of physiological psychology is in its speculative character; but Hartley may still claim the credit of being the first to take serious account of the fact that mental and bodily processes are conjoined in the operations of the senses.

The general result of the doctrine of vibrations can now be summed up in a formula. The impression of the object gives rise to vibrations which travel along the nerves to the brain, meet and interact in the brain, and then descend from the brain to the muscles. The chain of causation need not be broken at any point, and the explanation of consciousness either drops out altogether or we are to assume that vibrations are equivalent to consciousness of vibrations. This point was not clearly seen by Hartley; it was the natural ground for accusations of materialism and shows how far Hartley was from understanding the full significance of his own teaching. The activity of mind, here tacitly omitted, was to find its way back into psychology slowly and with difficulty. Meanwhile the supernaturalists were to be chastened with a naturalism which they could not accept and could not refute. The power of this naturalism belonged to its method rather than its matter. If we ignore altogether the hypothesis of vibrations, the scientific method of Hartley would remain undisputed. To apply the method of analysis and synthesis was his professed object; to find a way of reducing all phenomena to a single law after the manner of Newton was his ideal. These principles were maintained, even though at the last it is evident that the dualism of mind and body has not been overcome. Vibrations, Hartley admits, may have no significance in the sphere of mental operations; but the law of Association seems to bridge the chasm. In every creature there is from the first a natural disposition, and there are consequently natural vibrations existing in the body before birth. 'As soon as the child is born, external objects act upon it violently and excite vibrations in the medullary substance'; these are called preternatural. The impression made by the object is, therefore, never 'pure.' The natural vibration (N) has to be overcome by the preternatural vibration (A); there is a tendency for N to establish itself again, but the reflected action of A finally produces a result a. This explains the increased facility which is produced by repetition and habit; for a supplants N permanently, and we have in place of the first nature a second nature. The process, says Hartley, is made more rapid by the fact that 'the several regions of the brain have such a texture as disposes them to those specific vibrations which are to be impressed by the proper objects.'

If we now imagine a number of vibrations A, B, C, D to be excited at one time, the natural vibrations in each part will be partly overcome; so that if A occurs again, B and C and D have a latent readiness to occur. In time this will become a necessary sequence, so that the occurrence of any one of the vibrations will cause the occurrence of all the others. This is the fundamental principle of Association. It is not an association of ideas but of sensations, and of sensations only as being identical with vibrations. It is not the psychological but the physiological law of association that Hartley seeks to establish; the association of ideas follows as a corollary. For the vibration A is the physical concomitant of the sensation A; and the residual vibration which is left when the object ceases to act on the sense-organ (the so-called little vibration or vibratiuncle) is the concomitant of ideation. So we come to the final formula of association: 'If any sensation A, idea B, or muscular motion C be associated for a sufficient number of times with any other sensation D, idea E, or muscular motion F, it will at last excite D, the simple idea belonging to the sensation D, the very idea E, or the very muscular motion F.' As Hartley points out, the only thing association cannot do is to give the sensation D; it is held to be an adequate account of all else.

In thus establishing a connection between sensation, ideation, and motion Hartley gives to association a meaning quite distinct from that given it by Locke or Hume. A closer analogy would be found in Hobbes and, through Hobbes, in Aristotle. For this is not merely a way of saying that we have trains or sequences of ideas; it is rather an attempt to exhibit man as a microcosm, a world ruled by law and by the laws of the universe outside him. Hume could say that association was a kind of attraction and, in a certain sense, all the writers since Newton's time felt a vague impulse toward doing for the world of mind what Newton had done for external nature. But Hartley differs from all these; from Locke in being more systematic and precise about associations; from Hume in emphasizing physiology. In Hartley we see a man whose mind naturally took up and maintained the point of view of the organism as a whole.

The whole work of Hartley is summed up in the two words Vibrations and Association. The former term represents the

elements; the latter, their relations. There are simple and complex sensations; simple and complex ideas; automatic and voluntary or semi-voluntary movements. The character of all associations depends on the previous coincidence of vibrations; some are
received synchronously, others successively: these are the two
types of association. Hartley discusses the senses individually and
shows the operation of both principles in each case: he analyses
the desires of the sexes toward each other in a chapter of some
value, and describes in detail the character of involuntary or
automatic actions, with the steps by which they become, in some
cases, voluntary. The section closes with a significant criticism of
the Stahlians and the remark that 'what is mechanical *may*
both be understood and remedied.'

The third chapter of the first part opens with a section 'Of
words and the ideas associated with them.' In Prop. 79 the following statement is made: 'Words may be considered in four
lights. First, as impressions made upon the ear. Secondly, as the
action of the organs of speech. Thirdly, as impressions made
upon the eye by characters. Fourthly, as the actions of the hand
in writing.' Hartley proceeds to say that 'we learn the use of
them in the order here set down,' so that he intends this to be
both a genetic and an analytic account of speech. As an analysis
it is remarkable and clearly prepares the way for the later work on
speech, i.e. the study of aphasia and its cognates. This is not only
true in the general sense but can be stated explicitly. For Charcot
says (*Leçons du Mardi*, I. 362) that the root of aphasia is in
Hartley, whom he studied thoroughly: he expressly says Hartley
'*a parfaitement reconnu la véritable constitution de ce qu'on appelle
le mot*'; and then proceeds to show the relation between the
analysis quoted above from Hartley and the theory of four elements represented by four images which he himself elaborated.

The protest which Hartley made against animism in the sphere
of medicine accurately foreshadows the general tone of his work
on the 'Phenomena of ideas, or of understanding, affection,
memory and imagination.' All these come under the principle of
association, and this way of analysing them offers nothing of
particular interest. The nature of assent and dissent is a subject
about which a reader would naturally feel curious; but the mysteries of these operations are quickly dispelled. 'The cause that a
person affirms the truth of the proposition, twice two is four, is

the entire coincidence of the visible or tangible idea of twice two with that of four, as impressed upon the mind by various objects.' The rest is in a similar vein.

A section devoted to the intellectual faculties of brutes (Prop. 93) shows a distinct leaning toward a comparative method. Hartley accepts the Cartesian view that all the movements of animals are 'conducted by mere mechanism,' but he would admit that they are not 'destitute of perception.' Instinct is explained as due to natural vibrations, so that animal intelligence and that of undeveloped human beings are closely allied. Animals 'much resemble persons of narrow capacities and acquisitions who yet excel greatly in some particular art or science,' for such persons show great ingenuity in the things to which they are accustomed, but if much put out of their way they are 'quite lost and confounded.' While this does not explain much, it is a theory surprisingly free from narrow prejudices.

The intellectual pleasures and pains are divided into six classes, namely of imagination, ambition, self-interest, sympathy, theopathy, and the moral sense. Vibrations, Hartley remarks, 'seem of little importance in this part of the work.' Everything is in fact explained by association. The most striking feature of this section is the careful observation of facts which it displays, and especially the observation of children. Two passages may be selected as typical of this very commendable treatise on the affections.

The first (ii. 475) is concerned with the 'Affections by which we grieve for the misery of others.' In the case of children the following analysis is given: 'When their Parents, Attendants, etc., are sick or afflicted, it is usual to raise in their Minds the nascent Ideas of Pains and Miseries, by such Words and Signs as are suited to their Capacities; they also find themselves laid under many Restraints on this Account; and when these and such-like Circumstances have raised the Desires and Endeavours to remove the Causes of these their own internal uneasy Feelings or, which is the same thing, of these Miseries of others (in all which they are much influenced, as in other like cases, by the great Disposition to imitate, before spoken of); and a Variety of internal Feelings and Desires of this Kind are so blended and associated together, as that no Part can be distinguished separately from the rest; the Child may properly be said to have compassion.'

The second (ii. 488) belongs to the discussion of 'Theopathy,' and explains the genesis in the individual of an idea of God: 'Amongst Jews and Christians, children begin probably with a definite visible Idea of God; but that by degrees this is quite obliterated without anything of a stable precise Nature succeeding in its room; and that, by farther Degrees, a great Variety of strong secondary Ideas, i.e. mental Affections (attended indeed by visible Ideas, to which proper Words are affixed, as of Angels, the general Judgment, etc.) recur in their Turns when they think upon God, i.e. when this Word or any of its Equivalents, or any equivalent Phrase or Symbol, strike the Mind strongly, so that it dwells upon them for a sufficient Time, and is affected by them in a sufficient Degree.'

These examples of the analytic method in two critical spheres, namely the genesis of altruistic feeling and the construction of the idea of God or religious feeling, will suffice to show this author's skill; it may also suggest his limitations, but Hartley is always worth reading even when he is obviously subordinating his observation to his preconceptions.

[Hartley's work was strongly supported by Joseph Priestley (1733-1804). Priestley deserves mention as author of a *History of Optics*, and also a *History of the Philosophical Doctrine concerning the Origin of the Soul*, a treatise added to his *Disquisitions relating to Matter and Spirit* (Ed. ii. 1777). An energetic and rather voluminous writer, Priestley made no distinctive contribution to psychology, but was effective in promoting the kind of materialism which characterized the second half of the eighteenth century. Unlike the physiological materialism of 1860, this position was based on the Newtonian physics: though the prevalent interest in theology made materialism a term of reproach, this doctrine was little more than a demand for the scientific treatment of human nature. Priestley's historical work is of little value now, but the mere fact of its being achieved at that time in a creditable manner is important. Priestley was a severe critic of Reid and the minor Scottish writers; to some extent his criticisms were unfair, particularly when he fails to see how the problems of knowledge differ from psychological problems as understood by a supporter of vibrations. Priestley thought fit, in republishing Hartley's work, to omit the doctrine of vibrations; this was not good judgment since it tended to leave the associationism unsupported by that general conception of a scientific method which the vibrations implied.]

5. REID AND STEWART

Thomas Reid (1710-1796) may be accounted the real founder of the Scottish school of philosophy. This school claims attention from the historian on account of its duration and its influence; for psychology it did but little, since it took from the first an unfortunate direction. The student of Reid's works might well be inspired with the highest expectations; for the opening promises him a complete renovation of the philosophical sciences by means of a thorough psychological analysis. The result is disappointing. The physiological groundwork is first rejected, especially Hartley's doctrine: and we are told that the relation of a sensation to its external cause must be 'resolved into the will of God or into some cause altogether unknown.' Doubtless Hartley was wrong, but this is a counsel of despair. Reid is also much too fond of saying that he will countenance nothing that degrades the dignity of man, an attitude of mind that savours too little of science and bespeaks a prejudice in favour of sentimentalism. These were both deep-rooted tendencies of the age, and Reid often speaks as if the shadow of the mediaeval theology was still upon him. While the rejection of physiology might have made Reid a good psychologist, this does not seem to have been the case. As a philosopher he took upon himself the task of answering Hume; the disastrous outcome of 'idealism' was to be counteracted by a new realism. So far as the psychological part of this was concerned, all Reid's successors seem to agree in finding faults. Reid was continually at war with a doctrine about ideas which he ascribed to Descartes, but wrongly. He insisted, against this doctrine, on the immediacy of consciousness, and was uniformly understood to mean by consciousness a special faculty. He spoke vaguely of 'common sense,' and made it impossible for anyone to say exactly what that was. Whichever way we turn we seem to meet in Reid doubtful assignations of doctrines to others and unstable doctrines of his own invention.

The real basis of all this confusion seems to have been in the misunderstanding of Aristotle. Dugald Stewart corrects Reid, Brown corrects Stewart, and Hamilton corrects everybody. There is no sound historical learning until we come to Hamilton, and anyone who will read Hamilton's notes to Reid's works cannot fail to be struck with the fact that the whole line of Scottish writers moves from Reid onward by progressive discoveries of an unknown past. Stewart and Brown are particularly prolific in novel suggestions, adorned with footnotes which express their astonishment at the way in which earlier writers had anticipated their most original efforts. To a large extent this is explained by the history of Scottish education. In the history of psychology it was a transition period, consisting at first of a reaction against 'sensualism' and later (in Brown) of direct reproduction from the ideologists who were opposing Condillac.

The Scottish school was primarily a school of philosophy. Its problem was the general theory of perception, and Reid's merits are to be estimated finally according as he is or is not considered to have answered Hume. This subject belongs to general philosophy or to the sphere of epistemology, not to psychology. In the sphere of psychology Reid contents himself with merely stating the elementary and complex operations of the mind, refusing to accept any explanation of what he regards as primary facts, e.g. consciousness (as a faculty) and belief. In this way a large part of mental life is made immediate or innate; that is to say, the importance of the senses is reduced and Locke's 'sensualism' revised. The association of ideas, both name and thing, is rejected in favour of an 'inductive principle.' Reid was both original and right in thinking that 'ideas' are not associated, but his own exposition of 'experience' is equivalent to the process called by others association; if, as is probable, Reid meant to assert the activity of the mind in 'experience,' as opposed to 'association,' his distinction may be reckoned valuable. That this was the case might be argued from the fact that Reid shifted the emphasis from interrelation of ideas to judgment, from mechanical union to something like a creative synthesis.

Dugald Stewart was a man of rhetoric and poetical illustrations. Diffuse in style and unfortunate in his inventions, he is an attractive writer and gives his subject, The Philosophy of the Human Mind, new life and warmth. The spread of general culture was one of the objects at which the Scottish professors aimed; their classrooms were filled with eager listeners, lawyers and men of business, whose presence induced the lecturer to adopt methods foreign to the routine of class work. For the most part Stewart follows Reid, but he differs in many details. The doctrine of association is expounded at great length, though Stewart thinks there are no particular principles of association; anything may recall anything else. Wit, fancy, and invention are three of the spheres in which association is particularly noticeable; and it is worthy of remark that Stewart speaks of habit as controlling association, not the reverse. Another type of association which is quoted is that of space with time; 'we speak of long and short time.' Apparently any customary connection of ideas can be called an association. Association is said to presuppose 'a faculty of retaining the knowledge which we require': it also implies a power of recognizing the thoughts that recur, and this is not a part of the 'association' as usually defined. From this kind of over-subtlety Stewart goes on to discuss the value of a commonplace book and the kinds of memory which excite admiration in society!

In the works of later psychologists Stewart is credited with two distinctive points. In his discussion of attention (chap. ii) he notes the fact that there are gaps in ordinary experience; attention is required as the condition of retention, but 'when we are deeply engaged in conversation or occupied with any speculation that is interesting to the mind, the surrounding objects either do not produce in us the perceptions they are fitted to excite, or these perceptions are instantly forgotten.' It follows 'that a person may be conscious of a perception without being able afterwards to recollect it.' Consciousness and attention together make recollection possible. Consciousness without attention is something different. But Stewart does not actually call these unremembered perceptions 'subconscious.' He regards them as forgotten links which join one idea to another without being remembered; they enable us to make sudden transitions, but 'it requires a considerable degree of reflection to enable the person himself by whom the transition was made to ascertain what were the intermediate ideas.' Stewart speaks in apparent ignorance of any theory of subconsciousness, and does not oppose his view to that theory. There is also some obscurity in his own view, for, if reflection can recall the missing links, there must be some degree of retentiveness in consciousness alone; whereas Stewart ascribes retentiveness to the power of attention. On attention itself he remarks, characteristically enough, that 'every person must be satisfied of its reality from his own consciousness.'

The other point is a criticism of Reid's statement that 'imagination is attended with no belief at all.' This Stewart presumes to call in question, and maintains that an imagination may be accompanied by belief and that 'when imagination is very lively we are apt to ascribe to its objects a real existence.' We then 'feel and act in the same manner as we should do if we believed that the objects of our attention were real.' This is very true. It is also another remarkable sign of general superficiality; for this admission demands a complete revision of Reid's psychology and a new statement of the difference between idealism and realism: but no such revision is attempted.

6. BROWN AND HAMILTON

J. S. Mill, in the introduction to James Mill's *Analysis*, remarked that Brown was not a true successor of Hartley; his work must be regarded as an original effort in a similar direction. This judgment was only partially true. Brown was not a follower of Hartley unable to grasp the principles of his own school. On the contrary, he was an intelligent opponent of Hartley's teaching, a follower of Dugald Stewart, and at the same time anxious to utilize the good parts of Associationism. Brown gives the reader a feeling of insecurity; he is patently over-developed and alive to more possibilities than he can hold in his grasp. Erasmus Darwin attracted him in one direction; the French Ideology drew him the opposite way; he found a temporary resting-place between these extremes and died before his powers were ripe (1820). The key-word of Brown's psychology is 'suggestion.' Rejecting Hume and Hartley, Brown begins with the idea of consciousness as expounded in Reid and Stewart. To this dogmatic basis is added a doctrine of association, not as a principle of cohesion among ideas but as a mode of activity. Suggestion is said to be either simple or relative. Simple suggestion operates in the production of complete ideas, as e.g. in the thought of a friend when the sound of his voice is heard and suggestion adds the elements of his appearance. Relative suggestion is different from this; it explains the power of the mind to supply non-sensuous data, e.g. the right-angled triangle suggests the proportion between the square of the hypotenuse and the squares of the other sides. By this distinction Brown tries to achieve two things. The general principle of association seems to him valid, in so far as it expresses the tendency of some ideas to recall others. But Associationism as a doctrine seemed to err in reducing judgment to the level of sensation and ignoring any synthetic power over and above the separate ideas. Pure Associationism survives in Brown's 'simple suggestion.' The addition of the other 'faculty' of relative suggestion places Brown outside the limits of Associationism.

Sir William Hamilton was one of the candidates for the chair of Moral Philosophy in Edinburgh when Brown died. He was not elected, and only succeeded, sixteen years later (1836), in obtaining the chair of Logic and Metaphysics at that university. This chair he held till his death in 1856. Hamilton's whole life was devoted to the acquisition of knowledge. Medicine, law, classics, and philosophy were the subjects to which he gave most attention, and his writings show an extraordinary erudition in all these branches of learning. At sixteen Hamilton was attending lectures in Moral Philosophy at Glasgow, learning the ideas of Condillac and de Tracy. From Glasgow he went to Edinburgh, from Edinburgh to Oxford, and apparently survived all these experiences with no definite acquisition of dogmas. Hamilton was destined to develop through his own exertions; literary research was with him a passion; from 1829 to 1836 the *Edinburgh Review* furnished a means of expression, and from 1836 the duty of lecturing assisted to concentrate his powers.

Hamilton was a philosopher rather than a psychologist, and we may be excused from discussing his work in more than one aspect. It was as a literary phenomenon that Hamilton really made his mark; his learning was encyclopaedic, and he alone at that time could round off a subject by adequate reference to ancient, mediaeval, and modern continental writers.

Hamilton brought into Scotch philosophy a new conception of Greek and a still newer conception of German ideas. With Hamilton, Kant begins to affect British philosophy, and this influence reinforces the tendency to move from analysis to synthesis. From this point onward it becomes impossible to stay at the level of Hartley's work; for better or for worse the significance of activity, of the Ego, of the noumenal has to be reckoned with. The stronghold of Associationism was attacked by Hamilton when he proposed to explain the recall of ideas by a 'total redintegration.' In place of the link between ideas hitherto regarded as essential to all reproduction, Hamilton proposes to view each idea as a phase (not a part) of mental activity, and explains the view by the term 'redintegration.' Since for Hamilton physiological explanations of memory were merely nonsense and the whole subject was part of the 'metaphysics' of the soul, not much can be expected from this development. Hamilton saw no difficulty in memory; his difficulty was to explain forgetting, and that difficulty he never overcame.

During his lifetime Hamilton exercised an autocratic sway over the British philosophers. The erudition of his works gave them a position of authority almost sacrosanct in character. Yet the work was singularly sterile. A curious entanglement in the philosophy of the unconditioned prevented Hamilton from progressing toward that union of physical and metaphysical ideas for which he was so well equipped. Instead of that progress Hamilton rejected the help of physiology and relied upon the dubious factor of 'mental latency.' This was not a 'subconscious' factor but a real unconscious consciousness, which was neither good psychology nor sound metaphysics. It appears to have been a confused mixture of Hartley's 'minimal vibrations' and Leibniz's *petites perceptions*. In this and many other points Hamilton fused and confused radically different lines of thought; he also created a terminology that would have made Hume regret his nationality still more!

The influence of Hamilton is seen most clearly in the work of Mansel. Hardly anyone in the twentieth century would quote Mansel as a psychologist. The times have changed and the change has been faithfully recorded in that monument of British learning, the *Encyclopaedia Britannica*. For the eighth edition Henry Longueville Mansel, B.D., was assigned the task of writing the article on Metaphysics, and the article reprinted as a book arrived at its fourth edition in 1883. Mansel was a great scholar, acquainted with all the important writers from Aristotle to Hegel. His defects were not personal; they were the excellences of his generation. The article is mentioned here to give a measure for comparison. Its inclusion of Psychology along with Ontology in the general sphere of Metaphysics; its superficial treatment of the senses; its insistence on intuitions, especially moral intuitions; its declaration that the body with its organs, however necessary to certain modes of consciousness, 'is not, in any sense of the term, myself' —these and many other similar turns of expression stamp the article with the characters of the old school. As an accurate statement of theories then in vogue it merits all respect. If anyone will take the trouble to read Mansel's article and then turn to the article 'Psychology' in the eleventh edition of the *Encyclopaedia*, significantly separated from Metaphysics and given an independent status, he will discover why Mansel's work is no longer quoted as standard psychology.

7. JAMES MILL

The idealistic trend faintly perceptible in Thomas Brown and more obvious in Hamilton was a divergence from the path marked out by Hume and Hartley. With the philosophical problem we are not here concerned, and it is therefore not necessary to decide how far Hamilton's theory of perception was a form of idealism or a species of natural realism. The point relevant to psychology is the question whether the synthetic activity of the Ego or the associative power of ideas (as elements of consciousness) is to be emphasized. The latter was the original attitude of Hartley, and to it James Mill remained true. Born in 1773, Mill absorbed in his youth the ideas of Hume and Hartley, became acquainted with the teaching of Reid and Brown, but remained unaffected by German thought till his death (1836). He entitled his work *Analysis of the Phenomena of the Human Mind* (1829), and to that title the whole work faithfully corresponded.

James Mill is the supreme exponent of Associationism. Unlike its founder, Hartley, he was not a physician but a historian, a politician and something of a doctrinaire. His work is a reflex of his character. Mill dispenses with all that he considers irrelevant; he opens abruptly, proceeds curtly and shrinks from excessive illustration. The heading of the first chapter is a quotation from Locke—'I shall not at present meddle with the physical consideration of the mind.' Physiology is left unmentioned, and the subject begins with the elements that are 'most simple,' namely, the feelings we have through the external senses.

The senses enumerated are first the usual five senses, then the muscular sensibilities and those which have their place in the alimentary canal. The order of the senses is regarded by Mill as unimportant; the account given of each sense is perfunctory, but special mention may be made of the fact that Mill includes 'sensations of disorganization,' from external and internal causes. The muscular sense 'has been miserably overlooked,' except by Hartley, Darwin (Erasmus), and Brown; it is specially important because without it we could not have the idea of resistance.

From sensations Mill passes to ideas, which he regards as the remainder left when the object causing a sensation is removed. 'We have two classes of feelings; one which exists when the object of sense is present, another which exists after the object of sense has ceased to be present.' Ideas are explicitly said to be *feelings*; thus Mill goes from sensation to what he calls 'ideation' with no suggestion of any activity. This is the characteristic of a pure Associationism, and Mill is the last writer who follows its course without trepidation. Among other difficulties this method involves ignoring such residues of sensation as after-images; there is no real distinction made between after-images and ideas. Again, the presence of different sensations is made to account for discrimination; the difference is made to account for discrimination, whereas it must to some degree depend upon discrimination.

From ideas we pass to sequences of ideas, and the first question is whether ideas 'occur casually and irregularly, or according to a certain order.' The latter is obviously the case, and the two kinds of order named are the 'synchronous' and the 'successive.' This is quite inadequate, but it satisfies Mill; he thinks the sequence of ideas reproduces the sequence of sensations; if we add vividness and frequency to explain the strength of association, the whole theory may be considered complete.

The principle thus established is next used to explain several other phenomena. Facility, e.g. in addition, is a case of rapid association due to practice. Complex ideas are cases of coalescence, the separate ideas having been so often conjoined that they run into one another. 'It is to this great law of association that we trace the formation of our ideas of what we call external objects.' Further, 'some ideas are by frequency and strength of association so closely combined that they cannot be separated,' e.g. colour and extension, solidity and figure. The 'acquired perceptions of sight' are quoted as another example; colour alone is given by the eye, extension and distance are derived from sensations in the muscles and associated with the sensations of colour.

Some associations are to be called 'indissolvable'—though, of course, Mill means by the phrase that some ideas are inseparably associated; and, conversely, some ideas cannot be united. This psychological incapacity would be very interesting if it were proved to exist; it was a myth of Thomas Brown, who was too apt to confuse logic and psychology. Mill makes better use of Stewart, from whom we may assume he derived the idea of unremembered suggestions (chap. iii); a further point made is the interaction through association of organic and mental states. 'Anxiety in most people disorders the digestion. It is no wonder that the internal feelings which accompany indigestion should excite the ideas which prevail in a state of anxiety.' This is of interest, and in part at least it is true. But as the editor (J. S. Mill) remarks, on this theory only those would suffer from depression who had *previously* had indigestion. In mitigation of this criticism we might say that Mill was not thinking so much of actual depression as of the particular ideas in the mind of the depressed person. Mill thinks there is an association between feeling in general and certain specific ideas; this is a valuable point, though very obscure and treated too briefly. It would be interesting to know whether individuals ever had ideas or groups of ideas that regularly predominated during states of physical weakness or of localized pain such as headache. Our author has not attempted to satisfy curiosity on this point.

Mill's account of the Laws of Association is vitiated by one great defect. He speaks of ideas without noticing that they are capable of being elements in many different sequences; the reader is left with the impression that every idea belongs to a definite place in a definite series. This was a natural mistake for a rigid Associationist to commit, but it was not excusable after the way in which Brown had resolved associations into a general possibility of suggestion.

Under the heading of 'Naming,' Mill pushes his psychology a step further. We have heard about sensations, ideas, complex ideas, and trains of ideas. A name is not an object that acts on the speaker's mind; it is a device by which the speaker acts on another mind. The desire of communication may be satisfied by pointing or by picture-language; but the end is most easily achieved by having a single mark for a group of sensations and associating the idea of that mark with the idea of the group of sensations (i.e. the complex idea of the thing). The method of the Associationists thus seems to stand the test of the transition from things to language.

In addition to names for things (clusters of sensations) we may have names for clusters of copies of sensations; these are the names of imaginary objects or 'all that class of ideas which Mr. Locke has called mixed modes.' These may be called Mental Ideas, as distinct from copies of external objects called Sensible Ideas. Mental Ideas are 'arbitrary,' such as ideas of 'a mountain of gold, of comfort, of meanness.' By thus quoting his examples, Mill passes imperceptibly from imaginary groups of sensible ideas to abstract ideas and, finally, to class ideas. By this disputable process Mill keeps the reader in one plane; language is a system of marks for groups of sensations or copies of sensations;

general names are therefore marks of this kind. Before dealing with that subject some other points require elucidation.

A source of some contents of the mind might be looked for in consciousness. To obstruct this line of thought Mill declares (against Reid) that consciousness is nothing distinct from feelings or ideas. 'To say I am conscious of a feeling is merely to say I feel it.' In other words, behind the given state there is no consciousness to which the state belongs; the state is the consciousness, and therefore it is the Ego. This is Mill's last word to intuitionism and to those idealists who make the ideas belong to a Self that transcends them; it is Hume's position restated. Consciousness is a 'generical name'; so is 'conception'; a group of ideas called 'horse' is the same as the concept of horse, and consciousness is the generic name for the whole sum of concepts. Consistently with this position, Mill makes Reflection a class name; it is 'the notice which the mind takes of its operations,' and as having an idea, being conscious of an idea, and noticing an idea are all names for the same thing, reflection is another word for consciousness. Thus, after the intuitionists, the apperceptionists are disposed of; and Mill ignores all the arguments for unnoticed affections, even those commented on by Hartley.

When Mill comes to the question of classification, his psychology reveals its true polemical character. Plato, Aristotle, Mr. Harris, and Cudworth are included in one sweeping condemnation. There is no 'idea' above and beyond things; there are no 'real kinds'; abstraction is not a process of getting to the essence by omitting the unessential; men have been 'led to class solely for the purpose of economizing in the use of names.' This is the reason why we make one name serve for many individuals; the general name is a mark of innumerable individuals. It is obvious that Mill's theory is beginning to get out of its depth at this point. The situation is worse in the succeeding chapters on Memory and Belief, for the author is in sore need of some degree of activity in order to explain these data, and activity he nowhere admits.

Mill sees no alternative between calling Memory a 'faculty' and reducing it to a complex of ideas. He commits himself to the latter proceeding, and does it as follows. He states first that we could not exist if we had only sensations, or ideas unconnected with sensations, or such series of ideas as constitute imagination.

For then each separate state would be our whole being, and we could not have knowledge. So far Mill agrees with Plato and all other supporters of continuity. We must be able to unite the present with the past. How is this achieved? When I have the idea of an action, I recognize it as an action formerly done by me, I recall by association its accompaniments, I anticipate similar results: this is what is called 'experience.' Nothing is remembered except through its idea; we have therefore to find the difference between ideas that are memories and ideas that are not. Association is essential to memory; it is the sole means of purposive recollection; but these facts relate to the means of remembering, not to the nature of memory. This the author explains as equivalent to the idea of an object, together with the idea of my own former experience. This last point is capable of further analysis. A memory consists of 'the idea of my present self, the remembering self; and the idea of my past self, the remembered self.' In other words, an object A is associated with a past state B, which is linked by a series of intervening states to my present state B^2. This reminds one of Goldsmith's Traveller, who 'dragged a lengthening chain.' It assumes that we get back to an earlier state through 'running over the intervening states of consciousness, called up by association.' But these states are not states of myself unless the identity of the self during the time-interval is admitted. Also, as J. S. Mill notes, nothing is here said about belief, which seems to accompany an idea called a memory. James Mill rightly says, 'It is not easy to treat of memory, belief and judgment separately': but here, as before, he neglects order in his treatment and so makes the whole procedure obscure. Belief in a sensation, says Mill, is another name for having the sensation; that is, belief in a present state is simply a present state. Belief in the past is memory, as analysed above. Belief in the future is the association of an idea with other ideas as its consequences; given an antecedent, we anticipate the (future) results, and so have a belief in a projected idea. Belief in that which is not perceived (e.g. the back of a picture) is a case of association; the same explanation applies to the general belief in *external* objects when we have only the *internal* sign (sensation). The other factor, Identity, is ultimately reduced to Memory. 'The life of one man is one series' of ideas. 'When I say, then, that a man is the same, I merely express my belief in one of these series.' In the case of other men we have observation and memory: in the case of ourselves we have consciousness and memory. This settles the whole matter, if we add, as the author does, that 'the memory of a state of consciousness and the memory of something observed are two distinct things.'

Mill shirks no difficulties; he faces every test of his theory gallantly. He dislikes all mystery, and his sentiment in this respect is thoroughly healthy. He lacks nothing so far as concerns acuteness and, if he does not refute, he very nearly succeeds in silencing, his opponents. The possibility of analysing the self down to the ground in this way is the point of dispute among psychologists; Mill's commentators could not uphold the master, and their remarks show how uncompromising Mill remained to the end. It will be enough to remark at present that the treatment of memory, belief, and identity involves a circle; that Mill fails to show how one series can be one when the point in dispute is whether the parts make the series, or the recognition of the series fixes the parts; that finally this applies particularly to the case of personal identity where we require to determine psychologically whether a past event does or does not belong to the particular series called my 'self.' Mill does nothing ultimately to prevent my 'self' being purely objective to me; my identity is for me what it is for anyone else, so far as Mill goes. But this cannot be accepted without demur. The situation is much the same when Mill comes to the questions of attention and will. He creates a circular definition first; sensations are either indifferent or interesting; we only attend to the latter; therefore to attend and to have an interesting sensation are one and the same thing. Similarly we only will to do what we want to do: we only want to do what is associated with pleasure and with the actions which formerly produced pleasure. In both cases the operation of the simple factors gives the whole explanation. But it is open to the opponent to ask whether a sensation is interesting to the senses, or to the person; whether the quality of being interesting belongs to sensations thus considered; and, if not, whether the explanation explains anything.

Into Mill's other discussions, of logical processes and of moral sentiments, we shall not penetrate at present. They are for him more important than the analysis; the real aim of this empirical groundwork was to eliminate 'entities.' This was done very thoroughly; whether too thoroughly remains to be seen.

8. BAIN AND J. S. MILL

During the first half of the nineteenth century the focus of interest was in Germany. In England there was no great convulsion that formed a landmark in the advance. The English temper had been consistently practical, and could become experimental without pain. The change that came over Germany was mediated by the adoption of English methods and theories, Herbart and Beneke both proclaiming from their respective housetops their indebtedness to Great Britain. The French philosophy had long been in close touch with the British, and might have exhibited the same evenness of development if there had not occurred a temporary aberration, partly political, in the direction of an official idealism. Leaving France for later consideration, we shall now trace the development of English thought and show how it began a new movement, which was in part due to the scientific progress made in Germany, and reached a second distinct stage through the further introduction of German ideas.

James Mill's *Analysis* was a work that belonged distinctly to the old school. It summed up the work of the British psychologists of the eighteenth century, but its last editors (J. S. Mill, Bain, and others) took care to signify their disagreement not only with particular details, but with the whole treatment of the mind. Their fundamental protest against the imputation of 'passivity' is only saved from being a rejection of James Mill's whole work by being diplomatically adapted to the neutral and colourless parts of the work. The new note in the school was activity, combined with an extension of the physiological groundwork that is strikingly in contrast with Mill's perfunctory notes on the sense-organs. This novelty was a reflection on the German physiology, especially Muller's, and we have now to see how this movement was received in England.

From 1860 to 1900 the course of British psychology was determined by three distinct agencies. First comes the new psychology of Alexander Bain; then the evolutionary standpoint was developed in Darwin and Spencer, making it necessary for Bain to revise his doctrines; finally, the position taken by James Ward in his article contributed to the *Encyclopaedia Britannica* and in other published essays led to a second crisis. Bain's last defence of the doctrine that had grown old with him is to be read in the numbers of *Mind* for the years 1886–1887. Bain was a strong debater: he knew all the advantages and most of the limitations of his subject; if we cannot feel to the end that the doctrine is sound, we feel at least that a great cause has been greatly maintained.

It was in 1886 that Bain reviewed in *Mind* the article by Ward: in the next number he wrote a general defence of Associationism. With that he nailed his flag to the mast; he may or may not have realized that the ship was sinking. To understand this climax it is necessary to go back to the year 1836. In that year Bain entered Marischal College in the University of Aberdeen. He was then eighteen years of age, a child of poverty, delicate in health, wonderfully zealous in the acquisition of knowledge. Mathematics, chemistry, natural philosophy, moral philosophy—all these entered into his scheme of studies. Science and philosophy were for Bain inseparable: the philosophy (chiefly Reid) had no inherent quarrel with the science, being itself a 'mental science,' which asked only for peace and the right of self-preservation. Restraint and caution could be acquired in abundance from the philosophical regimen of 1840; some other nourishment was needed to satisfy youth and stimulate progress; it was provided in due course by the physiological work of the Berlin school. Before 1855 Bain had shaped his philosophy of the mind. Empiricism was the fundamental characteristic; induction was the logical principle; the study of the body was to precede that of the mind, and the accumulation of physiological data was to be the beginning of wisdom.

Thus in Bain we see the last pure example of the spirit that had animated the earlier British writers, equally laudable and equally infelicitous. Locke and Hume suffered from excessive respect for Newton and gravitation; Hartley seemed to think that the secret of the Universe could be solved in terms of sound; James Mill coquetted with chemistry; Bain, more fortunate in his choice, united the 'mental philosophy' to the natural philosophy of the body. Whether or not this choice was simply a piece of good fortune we need not inquire: it is enough to know that Bain looked to sciences that were not 'mental' for guidance in those that were, that he took physiology as his ally, and so entered the field with a physiological psychology that was well abreast of new movements, and could hold its own for half a century. If it now seems antiquated we must remember two significant facts. First, that when Bain took up the study of psychology nobody had realized what could be achieved by taking the whole organism as a basis; second, that Bain helped a whole generation of writers to think out the philosophy of the organism and see not only what they could do with it, but also what it could do for them. The elaborate physiology of Bain's works was absent from James Mill's *Analysis*; in Ward's scheme it has again shrunk to minor importance.

There is a well-known passage in which Bain says that mind and body are one, a double-faced unity: 'We are to deal with this, in the language of the Athanasian Creed, not confounding the persons nor dividing the substance.' 'The momentary glimpse of Aristotle,' he says in conclusion, 'is at last converted into a clear and steady vision.' We might not unfairly describe Bain as a true Aristotelian, not only because he did more than anyone else at that time to secure a just recognition of Aristotle's psychology, but also because of his own grasp of the ideas of organism and activity. Yet at the last this judgment would require modification; for the Scotch philosopher thought about matter and mind in the spirit of Descartes rather than of Aristotle.

The nature of Bain's chief works makes a satisfactory reproduction of their teachings almost impossible. The central points are few, simple, and not original: but the real worth of the expositions, as landmarks in the history of psychological literature, consists in their massiveness and their untiring elucidation of general principles by quotation and by observable instances. This was at the time a very necessary procedure; but the inevitable result was the production of the feeling which was tersely expressed by Hoffding when he said that Bain wrote psychology in the spirit and manner of a botanist. This is true in so far as Bain purposely adopted the method of natural science as he understood it. He dispensed entirely with any preliminary assumption either of a soul or a sensorium, or unifying agency; he preferred to deal solely in nerve-currents, 'it seems as if we might say, no currents, no mind' (*Senses and Intellect*, 1868, p. 53); the repetition of those currents and their association, in all degrees of complexity, are for Bain the real explanation of mental processes. For taking the nerves and the brain as an organic unity, Bain evolves from them the elementary states of mind—viz. instinctive muscular movements and the processes of the special senses. Motion, sensation, and instinct together form the basis of the developed life of conscious beings, for consciousness is a unity in which may be distinguished as typical forms, feeling, willing, and thinking. The first phase of cognition is the act of discriminating, with which stand closely connected the consciousness of agreement and the power of retention. The two latter are forms of association, and in explaining them Bain restates with remarkable fullness and completeness the whole doctrine of Associationism.

While in general this is the familiar method of the British school already made classic by James Mill, the part assigned to movement is a distinctive feature of Bain's exposition. Movement and perception are throughout closely allied, and from this basis it is possible to develop a sound doctrine of feeling and will. Though apparently arriving at this position easily by employing the contemporary progress in physiology (which had already done much to elucidate reflex action and other primary forms of spontaneous movement), Bain actually transgressed his own limits as he advanced. The spontaneity which ultimately looms in the background is not wholly explained by the physiological surplus of energy which Bain uses as its equivalent. To his contemporaries this spontaneity appeared no less than a surreptitious appropriation of that activity which was looked upon as the particular property of transcendentalism. To a later generation Bain seemed to stand midway between a mechanical or physiological theory of the mind and such venturesome speculations of those of Maine de Biran or Schopenhauer. He had, in fact, opened the way to that new type of thinking which makes activity its supreme category, and explains all thought and feeling by making the one an instrument of purpose, and the other a consciousness of complemented or obstructed instincts. We can make no attempt here to reproduce Bain's elaborate exposition of detail. It will be necessary to confine our remarks to the general significance of his attitude. This can best be done by showing how Bain was regarded by three great contemporaries—J. S. Mill, Spencer, and Martineau.

The remark made by J. S. Mill at the beginning of his essay on 'Bain's Psychology' is too well known to be omitted here. 'The sceptre of Psychology,' he said, 'has decidedly returned to this island.' For two generations the study of the mind had been either neglected or carried on perversely; Bain restored it to its ancient honour. Mr. Mill was prepared to take Mr. Spencer seriously, but 'though possessing great analytic power he is a less sober thinker than Mr. Bain.' Mr. Spencer, on the other hand, did not feel this lack of sobriety to be any drawback; he was impressed by Mr. Bain's excess of sobriety, and also by Mr. Mill's habit of understanding things without the help of evolution. According to Spencer the work of Mr. Alexander Bain 'is not in itself a system of mental philosophy, properly so called, but a classified collection of materials for such a system.' It was, in fact, what it professed to be, 'a natural history of the mind,' and Mr. Bain is not unlike the naturalist who 'collects and dissects and describes species'; his work is of great value, 'estimated as a means to higher results.' 'To those who hereafter give to this branch of psychology a thoroughly scientific organization, Mr. Bain's book will be indispensable.'

It is impossible to ignore the tone of patronage in this estimate; for Spencer Bain is purely a factor in a greater transition to a new era, a humble and unconscious co-operator in greater movements of thought. In this there is very much truth; it is now a commonplace to say that J. S. Mill never properly appreciated the significance of Darwin and the year 1859, so that we can today see how accurately Mill understood Bain's relation to the past, while Spencer was better able to estimate the future significance of the early works. Neither writer at the time could foresee the course of the next forty years, and for that reason what they thought in 1863 has only a partial relation to either Bain or his works as known in 1903. Without being final verdicts, these estimates have thir own intrinsic value as historical landmarks; and with that excuse another figure will here be introduced.

While Mill was writing in the *Edinburgh Quarterly*, the *National Review* depended for its philosophy largely on the Rev. James Martineau. Unlike either Mill or Spencer, Martineau was regarded as a champion of religion, particularly of those parts which are called 'the essentials'; he was indeed suspected of having renounced all the other parts. However that may be, this trio makes an interesting group of witnesses. In 1860 Martineau wrote an article on 'Cerebral Psychology: Bain.' It breathes a spirit of tolerant compassion, highly characteristic of the constituency represented by Martineau. He was, of course, 'very much in sympathy' with the work as science; in some respects, indeed, Mr. Bain's position deserves nothing but admiration; yet one must protest. The physiologist, treading hard on the heels of the mental philosopher, already claims almost the whole field; psychology is fast sinking to the level of the sciences; there is a 'captivating simplicity' in this idea of a rising pyramid of sciences, whose apex would be the highest animal, Man: 'It seems to promise that we shall surmount all our ignorance, and find Thought and Love, as well as Force and Matter, beneath our feet.' That is, however, a crisis not really to be dreaded; to those who say that natural science can be prolonged until the same line of method runs through mental and moral science, Martineau has one final answer: 'We utterly disbelieve it, and venture to affirm that no refinement of growth in the other sciences has any tendency to blossom in knowledge of the mind.'

This oracle speaks more darkly than the others; its inspiration is larger, and not easily compressed into definitions; it announces, for example, that 'mental science is self-knowledge,' with no apparent sense of the degree to which this illumination fails even to make the darkness visible. In this Martineau was truly representative of a certain type of culture, not unknown at any time. He was a champion of a peculiar form of idealism, derived originally from German sources; he spoke authoritatively out of the depths of his own sincerity, bearing his part in the cloud of witnesses to truths no longer of any interest, and quite unconscious of the way in which he performed synchronously the function both of witness and of cloud. Whatever may be said against Bain's psychology, it cannot be accused of failing to survive Martineau's. Yet for all that the balances are struck very evenly. J. S. Mill felt that what he called the *a priori* and *a posteriori* schools of thought were well matched; perhaps both were as much wrong as right. Martineau knew his strength; when he struck he wounded. He praises Bain's physiology and thinks it would make an interesting treatise by itself; in the psychology it is largely irrelevant; the apparent advance on the earlier writers, Hartley and James Mill, is illusory, consisting of nothing but a new way of talking about 'activity,' which ultimately is only the muscular sense of Dr. Thomas Brown: the basis of the whole work is an 'idealism,' which makes everything subjective and then undertakes, 'given the rudiments of any brute, to construct the perfection of any angel'—by Associationism. Two points made by Martineau are of importance. The first is the declaration that Dissociation precedes Association; the second is the generalization of this principle in the assertion that consciousness is the given unity which the psychologist analyses: the Associationist is too fond of compounding fictitious elements.

This essay is of distinct interest as showing how a futile antipathy to 'cerebral psychology' and a still more futile belief in 'mental science' could be united with criticisms in the main justified. If we now return to Mill's estimate of Bain we shall see first how a trained Associationist valued the work of Bain, we can rely on getting a clear statement of the important points, and reconsider the grievances of the *a priori* philosophers.

The aim of the Associationist cannot be objectionable to anyone, says Mill. The desire to analyse and resolve the higher into the lower is universal: it is open to the *a priori* philosopher to show when it cannot be done. Incidentally, Mill here gives the opponent the inferior ground by asking him to prove a negative; it is, in fact, the ground which the transcendentalist usually clamours for, so he cannot rightly protest. 'The first question in analytical psychology,' Mill continues, 'ought to be how much of the furniture of the mind will experience and association account for?' The residuum is to be left for further consideration. After some general remarks on the excellence of Associationism, Mill commends the physiology of Bain, and comes to 'the first capital improvement' made by Bain. 'Those who have studied the writings of the Association Psychologists must often have been unfavourably impressed by the almost total absence, in their analytical expositions, of the recognition of any active element, or spontaneity, in the mind itself.' This is what Bain has remedied; he has supplied the activity: he has done for Hartley's system what Laromiguière did for Condillac's. 'He holds that the brain does not act solely in obedience to impulses, but is also a self-acting instrument; that the nervous influence which, being conveyed through the motory nerves, excites the muscles into action, is generated automatically in the brain itself.' There is, therefore, according to Bain, an inner activity, producing spontaneous activities, from which the mental powers select those which are to be repeated or prolonged; this is the ultimate basis of voluntary action.

Thus far Mill. On this important point Martineau has very different ideas. He remarks that the sensational psychologists have struggled long with the problem 'of extracting from a primitive passivity the various forms of energy.' Physiology has at last decided the point; Sir Charles Bell has separated the nerves of sensation from the nerves of action; so Mr. Bain follows the same course and divides the functions of action and sensation. This is technically a great improvement; Bain creates 'a fund of spontaneity to set off against the stores of sensation, and make acquaintance with them.' This looks like a dualism, but it is not. 'Though Mr. Bain grants us a spontaneity, he plants it where we have nothing to do with it, any more than if our limbs were spasmodically stirred by a galvanic touch. In his zeal to cancel Hartley's prefix of a sensational stimulus, he forgets to leave any attendant consciousness at the fountain head at all, and makes the movement come, *psychologically*, out of nothing.'

Martineau is not always clear in his thought, but he seems to have the criticism of the *a priori* school focussed on the right point. One of the questions most in need of elucidation in 1860 was that of action; Bain seems to have thought that a physiological formula was enough, and his admirers were evidently confused between the functions of the brain and the spontaneity of the mind. Bain, in short, was temporarily overweighted by the current physiological doctrines.

Returning to Mill we hear further that Bain lays great stress on the muscular sense, but goes too far in making it the principal source of the acquired perception of sight. Association by contiguity has been so well developed (by James Mill) that nothing more is to be said; but Bain rightly insists on association by resemblance as even more important, while he adds 'Compound Association' as a third law, 'where several threads or a plurality of links or bonds of connection concur in reviving some previous thought or mental state.' Here Bain succeeds in explaining 'the singling out of one of many trains'; he explains also 'obstructive association.'

From the 'senses and the intellect,' Mill goes on to consider 'the emotions and the will.' Here he agrees with the critics that Bain is not very successful; 'the attempts of the Association psychologists to resolve the emotions by association has been, on the whole, the least successful part of their efforts.' Mill rightly says that the failure is due to the fact that instead of explaining an emotion, this school is satisfied to show how an emotion becomes associated with an idea. He comments on Fear, and declares 'the proper office of the law of association in connection with it is to account for the transfer of the passion to objects which do not naturally excite it.' The emotion itself, he thinks, can only be explained by physiologists; a much more doubtful proposition. Bain's treatment of the Will is praised in a way that was at the time justified; for Mill is more interested in the general questions of freedom and determinism than in the more minute analysis of volitions. Lastly, we may mention that Mill frankly admits the feebleness of his father's explanation of Belief as due to 'indissoluble associations'; he applauds Bain's declaration that the difficulties are due to regarding Belief 'too exclusively as an intellectual phenomenon and disregarding the existence in it of an active element.' Bain himself, however, drifted somewhat helplessly toward a doctrine of innate credulity, the mental counterpart of his innate spontaneity: 'The inborn energy of the brain gives faith, and experience scepticism.' Belief is, in fact, a primitive manifestation derived from the natural activity of the system. Mill very naturally 'desiderates a more complete analysis.' The more hostile Martineau saw his opportunity in Bain's second volume, and quoted with asperity the passage referring to the 'eminently glandular' nature of 'the tender affections'! British psychology stood now more definitely than ever at the point where objective and subjective psychology part company.

Bain lived till 1903 and was active almost to the last. In 1876 he founded the periodical *Mind* for the express purpose of encouraging the study of psychology. Assisted by George Croom-Robertson, the first editor, Bain made his periodical a real force. during the last twenty-five years of his life. Its pages were open to all schools of thought, and contain, in addition to contributions from British writers, many articles by continental psychologists. The progress and results of experimental psychology were frequently reported at a time when that kind of work was not regarded with much enthusiasm. Bain himself was always ready to profit by new movements, though not quick to change the ideas acquired in his younger days. His second work, *The Emotions and the Will*, was published in 1859, four years after the book on *The Senses and the Intellect*, and the critics noted that it reflected its author's readiness to go further than before in the way of emphasizing activity and development. For Bain psychology was a living practical interest. His *Logic*, his *English Grammar*, his ethics, and his metaphysics were suffused with the colour of his psychology. Though he did not declare psychology to be the one foundation of philosophy, in practice he gave it that position. His idea of its value for education was expressed in a separate work, and his brief but clear statement of the relation between body and mind enjoyed a long enduring reputation. Lastly, we may mention Bain's contributions to the history of psychology. The sketch appended to the 'Body and Mind' shows sound knowledge, though its scope is inadequate; the account of Aristotle's psychology, which is an appendix to *The Senses and the Intellect*, was actually the work of George Grote, and belongs to Bain only indirectly. In the literary history of psychology Bain deserves a place of honour. But he lived through an age of ferment, and was moulded by forces that he comprehended only in part. He will reappear in our history after the movements of the last quarter of the century have changed the scene.

B. Continental empiricism and reactions against it

I. THE FRENCH ENLIGHTENMENT

The eighteenth century was a period of revolution for France both in thought and in politics. With that great climax which is known as the French Revolution we are not here concerned, except to remark that it was a climax and that the steps by which it was reached were neither few nor rapid. The mind prepares what the hand executes, and a just estimate of the century which had its crisis in the events of 1789 must be constructed in part out of an inquiry into the transformations of French thought. The immediate source of the new currents was England, but there were also deeper reasons for the spiritual change which ultimately showed itself in the welcome given to English influences. In the seventeenth century France was aristocratic, self-contained, profoundly ignorant of English thought, and no less profoundly convinced that a country which murdered its king could produce nothing but poisonous literature. In the eighteenth century there was a change. A more liberal spirit began to prevail, travel increased, refugees from England after 1688 settled in France, and after the revocation of the Edict of Nantes whole colonies of French settlers were to be found in England. Thus the channel which separates France from England was bridged by persecution.

Gradually, with the lapse of time, the notion that England was a land of ruthless anarchists became extinct. It was succeeded by an almost equal extreme of enthusiastic imitation. To this above all others Voltaire contributed. Leaving France (1726) in a mood of bitter resentment, this brilliant but acrid person was fascinated by the unaccustomed tone of the new society, especially when its irreligious, frivolous, and free-thinking aspects were most in evidence. In 1729 Voltaire returned to France equipped for that prodigious activity by which he was to teach Frenchmen the incomparable glory of Newton, Locke, Bolingbroke, and others, creating by his efforts that enlightenment which France was destined to experience. In less than fifty years the Paris which Voltaire educated was to gaze in unaccountable rapture on the corpulent and speechless figure of David Hume! Voltaire was the great interpreter; he was ably seconded by the translators who gave to France versions of Richardson, Swift, Pope, and others. The literary activity came first: it was quickly followed by a more complete assimilation of ideas as principles of construction, with the result that new works were produced on the English patterns. In these one feature becomes of great importance. It was the middle-class character of English thought and writing, the attention paid to middle-class families and their daily round of actions, the genial and domestic positivism of the people who had tea and the *Spectator* unwearyingly at the same hour every day—in short it was the natural realism of English writing which seemed to the French a new revelation of the common thoughts and emotions of common people. With a burst of enthusiasm France embraced the idea that apart from monarchs and metaphysics there are ordinary mortals and a science of man.

To the new doctrines Voltaire contributed nothing but an introduction in such works as the *Lettres sur les Anglais* (1733), and apart from the usual accumulation of popular writings there are no writings which deserve detailed mention in a history of psychology except those of Diderot and Condillac. Diderot's work was slight but interesting and influential. He seems to have grasped the inner meaning of the English empiricism and to have been one of the first to interpret its spirit. In his *Lettre sur les Aveugles* (1749) we have an excellent example of that reflective empiricism which sprang from the union of English common sense with French acumen. Diderot's subject was not that of Descartes or of Berkeley: neither vision nor space is treated by him as the topic of chief interest: it is the *man* who is blind, and the *life* of such a man, that are the objects of his interest. The essay has been rightly admired as an informal but none the less valuable contribution to individual psychology. To Diderot the blind man presents himself as a negative instance, to quote the language of that very Bacon whom the encyclopaedists so much admired. As a negative instance, a kind of natural experiment in the art of living without one sense, the blind man furnishes a distinct source of knowledge about the mind. We may ask him what he means by beautiful, by a mirror, by size, distance, or figure. Unlike Descartes or Berkeley, Diderot concerns himself very little with what a blind man experiences on recovering sight: he speaks chiefly about the life that would be lived in darkness. He notes how really hard it is to comprehend this: the judge condemned the blind prisoner to a dark cell and received the reply, 'I have been in that for twenty-five years': we think the sun sets on the blind, and forget that it never rises. Perhaps, says Diderot, the metaphysics and morals of the blind are really different from the normal: the clothing required for decency can hardly be essential to people who see nothing, and the 'light of truth' can hardly be a significant metaphor for those who give to light no such preponderant value.

We will not continue these samples of the method. The letter *Sur les Sourds et Muets* has the same outlook and aim. Many shrewd remarks about language and meaning are mixed with general speculation on the character of a life thus limited. A further flight of imagination leads to the question whether there is not a sense in which all people are deaf and dumb, unable to comprehend what others mean or to express their own meaning in terms of another's experience. Both essays are remarkably suggestive and almost reach the level of a definite attempt to construct an individual psychology, all the more notable because the eighteenth century tended so strongly to enthrone the typical normal man and draw all its pictures on one pattern. By treating the senses in this separate fashion and creating the idea of persons who possess one or more senses only, Diderot came very close to that analytic method which we see more fully developed in Condillac.

Étienne Bonnot, Abbé de Condillac, was a contemporary of La Mettrie and the encyclopaedists, but he stood aloof from them in his work and differed from them in his views. He was born in 1715 and died in 1780. He had great contemporaries, such men as Buffon, Voltaire, Rousseau, Diderot, Helvetius, and d'Holbach. His hard and continuous labour earned him a solid reputation in his own time and extensive influence among later writers. His life was not eventful; the most important task which he essayed, beyond his philosophical studies, was the education of a young prince. This duty he took very seriously, and it seems to have been an opportunity to employ his powers of observation. He was regarded as an authority on the methods of education, and wrote his *Logique* (1779) in answer to an appeal from the educational authorities of Lithuania. In the psychological writings of Condillac we may trace the effects of his interest in the development of the mind, however little the mind of his pupil could have followed the course he describes.

Locke was the author who most directly affected Condillac. In Locke he found an attempt to trace the growth of the mind from its simplest states to its full complexity. He fell at once into Locke's error, the belief that development could be regarded as increased complexity. This point of view was much in vogue, and Condillac was even accused of stealing his method from others, particularly from Buffon, who had hit upon the idea of describing the first man awaking, with all his powers but no experiences, to discover the world around him. The accusation was groundless: the idea was in the air, but Condillac merely followed that quest for a pure experience which had been pursued by everyone since Descartes.

Condillac thought that Locke was wrong in beginning with sensation and reflection.[1] He proposed, instead, to simplify matters still further by beginning from sensation. This was purely a device of method. Psychology for Condillac is a branch of metaphysics, so far limited as to be the science not of the soul

---

[1] Before the *Traité des Sensations*, 1754, Condillac merely restated the position of Locke on this point.

but of the mind. A belief in the substantial reality of the soul and in its activity is pre-supposed; materialism is explicitly rejected; and the action of matter upon mind is accounted for on the principles of occasionalism. Condillac does not begin with the senses: he begins with sensations, taking his stand upon the inner fact with little reference to anything else. Though he recognizes the physiological aspect of mental phenomena, his work in that direction is of no importance: his occasionalism absolved him from its problems but did not save him from being criticized by Bonnet and Cabanis for this deficiency. The advent of anatomy and cerebral physiology really divides Condillac from his successors.

The form in which Condillac states his theory is picturesque. He creates the fiction of a statue[1] and endows it with one fundamental faculty. This faculty is a sense, and smell is chosen before the other possible senses, because it has the least amount of complexity. This sense furnishes the simplest imaginable sensations. The statue is not to be regarded as passive, for a sensation is a mode of consciousness and implies an activity of the soul. It is, however, relatively passive, for it does not at this stage exercise any of those powers which are afterwards brought into play. If we accept this beginning, the rest follows easily. The sensation first received occupies the whole power of the mind, so that its mere persistence constitutes attention. If a second sensation arrives, it bears a certain relation to the former, the perception of this relation constituting comparison. If instead of being together in the mind, the second seems to throw the former sensation back, we have what is called memory. These modes of consciousness are therefore primitive activities which may be described as nothing more than transformed sensations.

The point upon which disciples and critics naturally seized was the transition from sensation to attention. Those who preferred to follow Condillac gave up this point in the master's teaching. Whether definable or not, the position taken by Condillac seems to be due to his exclusion of will from the first sketch of the mind. He did not mean to exclude activity, but he implies that the mind may be so occupied with a single presentation as to

---

[1] A heated controversy arose over the origin of this fiction: it was claimed by Buffon and several contemporaries, but was assigned by the learned to Descartes, Arnobius, Cicero, and even Herodotus!

be absorbed in it alone. He postulates a sort of fundamental interest, and he means by attention a kind of fascination, an activity which is not volitional but composed of automatic retention and interest. This would really approximate to the *idée fixe* of later writers.

To continue the scheme: after the modes of consciousness described, the stage of ideas is reached. Here there are three distinguishable operations of the understanding: when different things, qualities or parts of a whole are considered and judged, there is reflection; when attention is directed to a memory or unites two ideas in a way not given by sensation, we call the process imagination; the union of judgments, finally, is reason.

The same scheme is carried out in terms of the affections. Here the basis is felt want; want, when there is definite direction toward an object, is desire; desires become passions; assurance that the object is obtainable constitutes hope; and when nothing obstructs the mind in its outgoing toward the object, we say there is volition.

A bare epitome of Condillac's exposition hardly does him justice. His aims must be clearly grasped if we are to reach a true estimate of his significance. Incidentally, comparisons are of great use for this purpose. Condillac, as we have seen, makes reflection arise out of and, logically, later than sensations. He does not propose to make an absolute division between ideas of reflection and ideas of sensation; the latter term only means that we think of the ideas as due to the objects of sense, while the former implies that we take the idea simply as a phenomenon. Condillac thinks that Locke did not really get away from the obsession of innate ideas; he is himself more thorough and tells us that all general ideas are merely ways of regarding special or particular ideas. When we consider similarities we move toward general ideas: if we consider differences we make species; as both are operations of the mind there is no need to assume that the general ideas point to any distinct class of objects, the real universals for example. Psychology, within its own limits, must side with the nominalists.

Since sensation is the root of all our understanding, there is no absolute need to have more than one type of sensation. This is the point of Condillac's paradoxical method. Each sensation is, in fact, a single irreducible aspect of the understanding. So that if we start from smell, we may go on to attention to smell, comparison of smells, judgment and reasoning about smells; a sense denotes a complete sphere of understanding, just as a science is limited to one class of objects. The fact that we have five senses only means that we have five different ways of knowing our environment; it is a pure error to suppose that mental complexity can only arise from a plurality of sensations. Condillac thought that the concept of sensation had not been fully elaborated by his predecessors; this was the task he set himself, and his principle work was entitled *A Treatise on Sensations*. The strongest point in Condillac's work is this insistence on the fact that the higher functions of attention and judgment are not to be regarded as an independent stratum of mental life; there is complete continuity in the scale of faculties, and one type of sensation is enough to begin and complete the scale. The further analysis of the understanding is carried out by considering, in detail, what each type of sensation actually contributes to our total knowledge of the world. Smell, taste, and hearing are the most simple; touch gives an idea as well as a sensation, because it conveys the notion of the external object; sight is complicated by the fact that judgment enters into its normal activity. In his treatment of vision Condillac followed Berkeley, for, though in the *Essais* he combated Berkeley's views, he afterwards repented and joined Voltaire in supporting the New Theory. The rest we may leave without further comment.

Condillac is the last writer to follow out the idea of a pure experience on the lines of descriptive analysis. Locke had inaugurated that development, and in his lack of clearness avoided the errors of extreme definition. In spite of his trenchant criticisms, we feel that Condillac had less insight into the complexity of mental life than Locke; psychology, in pursuing the analysis of the understanding, seems to have lost touch with the fullness of life. What was lacking in this respect was provided richly by the genius of Leibniz. At the time when he wrote, Condillac did good service by furthering a general tendency toward direct treatment of the facts of consciousness. His contemporaries felt the inspiration of his work; they rejoiced in a philosophy that freed them from the shackles of metaphysics. Men of science read Condillac; the ideologists proclaimed him the sole French thinker of the eighteenth century. He himself had no doubt about the inferiority of his predecessors. Descartes, he said, had never discovered the real source of our ideas; of Malebranche he said, with becoming smartness, that not knowing the source of our ideas he referred them to God. In acknowledging, as he often does, that we cannot attain these transcendental verities or know anything about God, eternity, substances or even ourselves, Condillac shows a healthy sense of limitations. Yet he failed to see how transcendental his own method was. By starting with his 'statue,' he put himself outside the limits of humanity quite as much as if he had begun with angelic existences. His concept of the solitary individual is as unscientific as any hypothesis can be; it is a new way of deducing entities from nonentity. The merits of the proceeding depend largely on its failure. In spite of himself Condillac uses the term 'we' as if he had begun from a fully developed conscious person. It is on record that at the end of his life Condillac said he had neglected too much the idea of personality, the true subject of the whole analysis. This was the point at which his inadequacy was to be most keenly felt; the next development of French thought, the spiritualism of Maine de Biran, was created by a sense of this defect. Yet Condillac's influence remained paramount; his affinity with English empiricism gave him a place of honour when, after Maine de Biran, Taine urged the return to analysis and joined his praise of Condillac to his admiration for John Stuart Mill. It is supposed that Condillac largely influenced Rousseau and inspired him with ideas on education. Though he began with a misleading hypothesis, developed his subject arbitrarily, and dealt only with one aspect of psychology under circumstances which did not favour a sound treatment, Condillac was a force to be reckoned with for half a century.

In spite of its subtlety and acuteness, Condillac's treatment of the human understanding was not calculated to prove satisfying. It was coloured with a peculiar artificiality; it was redolent of good society, and its very precision seemed to prove it inadequate to nature. Condillac began from a statue, and he ended with what was to the last a lay figure. Upon this weakness the friends and disciples of Condillac were not slow to seize: foremost among them was Cabanis, who was well fitted to supply the defects which were obvious in Condillac, and are perhaps inevitable in any mere analysis of the understanding by the understanding.

Pierre Jean George Cabanis was born in 1757, the son of a

practical man, who in addition to his occupation as a lawyer had been successful in reclaiming barren land and had helped the reforms of Turgot. The son did not appear at first to possess the industrious temperament of the father: he neglected his studies and was in consequence deported to Paris by the indignant parent and left to shift for himself. This rather peculiar treatment explains the extraordinary variety and range of Cabanis's reading. We find in the end that he had an excellent knowledge of Hippocrates and Plato, enough knowledge of Aristotle to correct the general impression that he had declared all knowledge to come from the sense, some acquaintance with Cicero, Tacitus, Plutarch, and Augustine. Among the moderns he was particularly conversant with Montaigne, Charron, Locke, and (of course) Descartes. He had a taste for poetry, and translated at different times such widely different subjects as Homer's Iliad, Goethe's *Stella*, and Gray's *Elegy*. The years spent in acquiring this varied stock of knowledge were not wasted, but they might have proved a dangerous beginning if the young man had not rather suddenly adopted the medical profession, and from 1778 devoted himself to a more disciplined course of life. He applied himself strenuously to the study of medicine, retaining a peculiar affection for the ancients, Hippocrates and Galen, but drawing from them inspiration for the reform of medicine in his own time. We find him afterwards an authority on systems of education, reviving the comprehensive ideas of Plato and moderating them into practical prescriptions for the French Government in its many endeavours to establish a national system of education. We find him also acting as professor of medicine, more inclined to discourse upon its history than demonstrate the practice, yet in his turn dealing with the nature of diseases from what was then a new point of view, and, above all, insisting on the relations of mind and body in every stage and crisis of life. From first to last this was the dominant interest in the life of Cabanis, and it is to this that we shall shortly turn our attention. For Cabanis has been deservedly called the founder of the modern physiological psychology, and his method, by extending the scope of Condillac's work, laid the foundations for the development of the complex French psychology of the nineteenth century.

Condillac was by no means an isolated figure in the French society of the period immediately preceding the Revolution.

When Cabanis arrived in Paris in 1778 he was able through the influence of Turgot to ally himself with one of the most brilliant literary circles ever formed. Around the gracious figure of Madame Helvetius moved such great luminaries as d'Holbach, d'Alembert, and Diderot. Voltaire was affable to the young man, Franklin was his dear friend, and Condorcet was a relation by marriage. Among the great men known as the Encyclopaedists Cabanis was a youth of promise: among the Ideologists he was a mature thinker and a leader in politics and science. A pupil of Locke and Condillac in his own studies, he was the master of the generation that included Maine de Biran, De Tracy and the other eclectics. Admired in his youth, valued in his maturity and honoured at his death, Cabanis became in a few short years the symbol of degenerate materialism, a name to be uttered only with apologies, the type of all those who had trodden the godless ways of science. Among those who directly influenced him must be named Dubreuil, a doctor who laid much stress on the psychic factors in disease, Mesmer and, at a later date, Pinel. These names suggest the source from which Cabanis drew at least part of the inspiration to treat the human being psychologically as well as physiologically. Bichat, Pinel, and Cabanis stand together as the three great exponents of philosophy and medicine during the last decade of the eighteenth century.

Cabanis began his psychophysiological writings in 1795 with an essay on a theme of melancholy interest at that time, the question whether the victims of the guillotine suffer any pains after decapitation. For Cabanis this was not a matter to be treated in any other way than that of scientific deduction, and his view of the question showed that he had already evolved one of the most significant of his ideas on the relation of mental to corporeal life. As it was expressed more fully later, this was the idea that consciousness belongs to a central Ego, *le moi centrale*, and that this central Ego is an epitome of all the separate centres which the nervous system creates. The apparent signs of life which might be exhibited by the decapitated body are then explained as activities of neural ganglia which are relatively independent of the brain or central Ego.

From this basis Cabanis builds up the whole structure of his teaching about the conscious life of man. We notice at once that he is not primarily concerned with Condillac's subject, but Condillac was the most prominent psychologist of the day and

Cabanis feels that he must define his attitude toward that standard. He does so in clear and precise terms. The chief fault to be
found in Condillac is that he will not admit the existence of
instincts in the proper sense: he insists that an instinct is a rapid
inference. For Cabanis an instinct is thoroughly organic, wholly
independent of the central consciousness and therefore wholly
independent of the rational activities. Cabanis identifies the
central Ego with the brain. He does not mean that the brain is
the principal seat and organ of the soul, for he does not propose
to assume the existence of an agency behind the visible agent: by
the brain he means the supreme nervous mechanism which is
indispensable for the operations called conscious. It was from this
point of view that he made his famous statement: 'To form a
correct idea of the operations whose result is thought, it is necessary to regard the brain as a special organ whose particular function it is to produce thought just as the stomach and the intestines
have the special function of carrying on the work of digestion, the
liver that of filtering the bile, etc.' Unscrupulous and perhaps
unintelligent persons quoted this afterwards as the crowning
proof of the materialism of Cabanis: clearly it is a sufficiently
sound analogy which does no more than lay down the fundamental
principle of cerebral physiology in its relation to psychology. The
spiritualists who misused the passage were quite right in regarding it as the antithesis of the declaration made by Descartes that
some operations of the mind, in fact all the important ones, are
carried on without the help of the brain. A very few years after
the death of Cabanis men were again discussing the futile question
whether ecstasy was a non-corporeal state and whether the
'higher' operations of the mind were conducted without the
brain's assistance.

To return to the question of instinct. The fundamental point
against Condillac is that the psychology of the statue excludes all
co-operation in the organism, all sympathetic relations within the
organism, all that unity of operation which Cabanis says that
Hippocrates so rightly insisted upon. Cabanis means to say that a
sense studied in isolation is not a sense at all: the operation of
explaining the mind by adding sense to sense can only be correctly carried out if we begin with the senses as they appear in the
actual organisms of human beings. If the theorist retorts that he
is dealing with sensation in general, he is met with the reply that

that is his particular besetting sin. There is no such thing as sensation in general: a statue might attain such pure sensations, but in the actual living being the sensation is a particular activity which must be regarded as a function dependent on the whole structure and nature of the organism in question.

At this point we reach the line that divides Cabanis from Condillac. Formally expressed, it amounts to a difference on the question of activity. But it is necessary to avoid carefully the error of rushing into voluntarism without further discrimination. One way of criticizing Condillac was to assert that he overlooked the spontaneity of the spirit. This is exactly what Cabanis did not do. He says nothing of the spirit or of will in that sense, regarding them as abstractions no better than Condillac's sensation. He remains true to the method of Condillac, the ideal of analysis, but instead of taking as his basis the understanding he begins with the individual as a living totality of organs and functions. Any given mental event is then a function of this organism and not merely an activity of mind. Cabanis then goes right back to the beginning. Before the first sight or sound reaches the nervous mechanism there is a long period of embryonic development which, though we cannot say much about it, must certainly have some cumulative effects, and these enter as qualifying conditions into the first sensibility of the outer world. Sensation in Condillac's way of using it, is therefore very far from being the real basis of life. The fact is, as Cabanis points out, that we pay far too much attention to the outer sensations. The most important thing for the adult is the acquisition of knowledge, and this fact gives a spurious importance to the avenues by which that knowledge enters. But the science of the mind must not be distorted by that kind of consideration: it must think of the person in the way in which the person rarely thinks of himself. The ordinary individual overlooks just those points which science has to investigate, whether by objective study or by introspection. The persistent background of all isolated activities is the object of Cabanis's researches. Beginning from the embryonic stage of life, he proceeds to indicate the significance of each decisive crisis in the development of the organism. The earlier stages are marked by a lack of stability in mental actions. This stage terminates at puberty, when new developments of the organism produce the most decisive changes of mood and mental outlook. 'The adolescent, haunted by a vague restlessness, ceaselessly plunged in objectless reveries, moved even to tears by the slightest impressions, begins to find pictures in his imagination and inclinations in his heart that surpass his knowledge. While the hearth of the passions is kindled in his breast, his soul, allying itself to all that surrounds it, rushes on to unknown ends—the stature, the features, the manner, the looks, the sound of the voice, all take on a new character.' Similar parallels can be drawn at every new stage of development, and Cabanis rightly suggests that for the full understanding of the human being it is necessary to study all these phases of life—childhood, adolescence, maturity, and old age: and in addition to these normal states the effects of accidents, of mutilations, of intoxication and all the forms of disease should be studied. He included also crime, significantly defined as another species of mental derangement.

Cabanis does not give many details or examples of the cases he had observed: he was more concerned with the reform of method, than with the actual carrying out of researches. The few quoted by him show a keen power of observation, and have in some cases become classic instances. For the later development of the science of man, Cabanis is the most important writer of this period. The proof of this is contained in the mere statement of the subjects to which he gave a new impetus. By his insistence on the axiom that the study of the mind must be closely united with the study of the organism, he gives the psychophysiological point of view a practical basis. His own way of stating this was by saying that there is an inner man as well as the outer man, and this inner man is not a nebulous spirit but the brain and the nervous system. In addition to the outer senses there are also inner senses, not such as reflection and memory, but the senses which represent in our total consciousness the conditions of the inner organs, the viscera, muscles, and membranes. Into every definite act of the mind these enter, not necessarily in such a way as to make us conscious of the part they play, but so as to determine the total state of mind. The question which Condillac has not answered is the preliminary question, What is sensation? The answer which Cabanis proposes is that sensation is a relation between the organism and the object resulting in a conscious condition which arises mainly from the whole trend of the individual's life. It was easy to support this notion of sensation by referring to hallucinations in which the subjective tendency overpowers the normal force of the objective stimulus, and so shows more clearly the degree to which normal perceptions are not passive states of reception but activities. In justice to Cabanis it must be added that he was clear in his mind on the distinction between irritability, sensibility, and perception. He maintains firmly that it is possible to have sensations without sensibility, i.e. without conscious presentation. He thinks that sensation and presentation have been wrongly identified, for nature has provided by means of lower nerve-centres for operations distinct from mere irritability that do not amount to consciously recognized sensations. To the axiom that all knowledge comes by way of sensation Cabanis added the statement that all sensation is not necessarily (clear) knowledge. This rejection of the narrower standpoint of the Enlightenment created a new epoch. From Cabanis arise the various departmental studies by which the concept of psychology was to be continuously enlarged, including the study of abnormal psychology, of national or ethnological psychology, of genetic psychology, and of social psychology. The last was in Cabanis no more than an indirect deduction from the idea of a true education, which Cabanis described (after Rousseau) as the correct development of the natural powers, and then proceeded to treat as a process involving primarily the relations of individuals in society. He saw indefinitely that here was a store of influences distinct from the objects about which children were instructed in schools and involving in their operation all the physiological and emotional life which men agree to consign to the heart rather than the head.

2. BONNET

Charles Bonnet of Geneva (1720–1790) was at first interested in natural science and is still remembered for his *Traité d'Insectologie* (1745), a work which ranks with that of Trembley as a contribution to the study of micro-organisms. This application to work involving the continual use of the microscope ended in weakness of the eyes, and Bonnet applied himself to elaborating physiological, psychological, and metaphysical works of a more general character. In 1755 he published (anonymously) the *Essai de Psychologie*: in 1760 appeared the *Essai Analytique sur les Facultés de l'Âme*, with a supplement (1762) entitled *Considera-*

tions sur les Corps Organisés: after these works more general speculations contributed to spread Bonnet's fame, notably *Contemplation de la Nature* (1764) and *Palingénésie Philosophique* (1769).

Bonnet's psychology is contained principally in the *Essai Analytique sur les Facultés de l'Âme*. This work, published six years after Condillac's *Traité*, is in many respects similar to the earlier work. Bonnet is quite conscious of this and refers explicitly to the points of agreement and difference, with explicit assertion that there was no dependence (*Ess. An.*, 14). There is no reason to doubt the truth of this statement; Bonnet comes forward as one who agrees in the main with Condillac, but proposes to correct the errors of his predecessor (*Ess. An.*, 156). The corrections are of two kinds. In some cases they consist in giving supplementary physiological explanations; in others they arise from disagreement on the question of mental activity.

As regards the starting-point and form of development, there is an extraordinary similarity. Bonnet uses the idea of the statue, begins from the isolated sense of smell, and exhibits the development of the content of the mind as a progressive complexity. At this point Bonnet begins his deeper view; he not only says, with Condillac, that the sensation causes a change in the soul, but adds an explanation of the process. Infinitely small particles set up a motion of the nerves, and the 'neural fluid' (*fluide nerveux*) transmits the motion to the brain; the consequent agitation of the appropriate 'fibres' produces the agitation of the soul.

This addition of physiology to psychology is typical of Bonnet's methods. He insists, in every case, on the insertion of some process of the 'fibres' between the external stimulus and the subjective experience. When we come to 'attention' we find Bonnet objecting to Condillac's views. As the object ceases to act on the organism, the movement of the 'fibres' decreases; there arises in consequence a consciousness of change from better to worse, a desire to sustain the better condition, and therefrom attention. (*Ess. An.*, 47: '*J'entends ici par l'attention cette reaction de l'âme sur les fibres que l'objet a mises en mouvement, par laquelle l'âme tend à conserver, à fortifier ou à prolonger ce mouvement.*') Here Bonnet seems to take an independent position, and explains attention as a specific activity of the soul. But the activity is no more than an inclination to the greater pleasure, a mechanical process, no way superior to Condillac's idea of an 'interest' in pleasure or pain. In the earlier work Bonnet had been more in favour of defining attention as a self-determining activity of the soul; perhaps his reading of Condillac made him change his attitude. The mechanical view, up to a certain point, was more in harmony with his ideas about animals.

Memory is explained by Bonnet with special elaboration of the physiological counterpart. The action of an object changes the original order of the particles composing the 'fibres'; the new order constitutes a tendency to act a second time in the same way; this physical disposition or habit is the explanation of memory. Imagination, comparison, and judgment are explained on the same principles: understanding is simply a higher degree of sensibility (*sensibilité plus relevée* (*Ess. An.*, 261)). The association of ideas is explained through the movement of 'fibres,' so that it can be produced by any cause which results in the movement of different fibres at one time. This is noteworthy, because it involves giving up all explanations based on the original order and connection of impressions; it implies rather a law of (physical) totality, since the only reason for the association is that the fibres have 'something in common.'

Reminiscence requires some explanation which will make clear the *qualitative* distinction between that which is given for the first time and that which is repeated. For reminiscence is essentially having a presentation which is recognized as not being given for the first time. Bonnet solves this problem by saying that a motion of the fibres is different when repeated from what it is when first given; hence the two movements do not fuse, and this difference, when noticed, constitutes the mark of remembrance. The difference in question consists in the greater facility of the second movement, and therefore amounts to saying that memory is a habit of the 'fibres.' Similar empirical principles explain all the higher functions. Personality, the last and highest, is of two kinds; the inferior kind is equivalent to the recognition of the changes that take place in consciousness, a recognition ascribed by Bonnet to animals; this is 'personality improperly so called,' while personality in the proper sense is reflection upon the processes constituting the inferior degree of personality.[1]

[1] Probably allied with the idea of different levels, perceptive and apperceptive, as taught by Leibniz.

In estimating the work of Bonnet two points deserve particular attention. In his own mind Bonnet seems to have considered that he was defending the reality and activity of the soul. In fact, he made the brain and the physiological factors bear the whole burden of the work. Though he declined to be called a materialist, his interest in the animal organism gave his work a materialistic appearance. His empiricism is as thoroughgoing as Condillac's, but his outlook and method give him a different historical standing. He indicates the way of development for a new type of psychology, a distinctive physiological psychology. A passage in the *Analyse abrégée*, § xix, is often quoted as stating the doctrine of specific energies, and in another place Bonnet says, '*chaque sens renferme donc probablement des fibres spécifiquement differentes.*' This seems to have been a speculative thought and in part a deduction from the hypothesis that all external differences are represented by differences in the physiological organ of thought. He declares 'The Intelligence which could have read in the brain of Homer would have seen the Iliad represented by the varied play of a million fibres!'

3. TETENS

Johann Nicolas Tetens (1736–1807) was in 1760 a teacher of physics and metaphysics at Rostock, in North Germany, and later at Bützow, when the University was moved to that place. In 1776 he became Professor of Philosophy and Mathematics at Kiel. In 1789 he was given a position in the administrative offices at Copenhagen: he did not return to academic work, but rose to higher posts on account of his ability as financier and advocate of insurance. A contemporary of Bonnet and a keen student of his work, Tetens was not himself a physiologist: nor was he a mere philosopher. His chief work, *Philosophische Versuche ueber die menschliche Natur und ihre Entwickelung* (1777) showed a new and important combination of speculative power with keen observation. While Tetens had a firm belief in the value of what was at that time called the empirical method, he saw very clearly the fallacy of reducing psychology to terms of mechanics or physiology: he maintained firmly the doctrine that the true method for psychologists is the psychological method.

The nature of this method is left in no obscurity. Experience is the basis; the modifications of the soul are to be accepted as they become known through inner experience; they are to be repeatedly observed, with variations of circumstances; their origin and the action of the forces which produce them are to be noted; the observations are to be compared and resolved, so that the simple capacities, with their operations and interrelations, may be sought out; and these are the essential parts of a psychological analysis that rests on experience. This statement, reproduced almost verbally from the introduction to the *Versuche*, deserves to rank as the first clear statement of a purely psychological method; it has the comprehensive outlook of a Baconian programme with all the advantages of direct relevancy; it accepts the whole spirit of science without confusing the notions of inner and outer reality.

The work of Tetens bears continual and direct relation to that of Bonnet; as Bonnet comments on and corrects Condillac, so Tetens treats Bonnet. In one respect these two exponents of science were united; they both declared that science is concerned only with phenomena. They both believed in an ultimate ground of unity called the soul, but they also believed that science reached no further than its appearances. Both reject materialism; both speak of soul and body as distinct data, though (unlike Bonnet) Tetens would accept a reduction of body to psychic elements in the manner of Leibniz. In any case, the hypothesis of interaction is accepted as the most probable; others are admitted to be possible, but this works best. It was in the valuation of the physical processes that Tetens parted from Bonnet; 'My way,' he says, 'is the way of observation, while that of Bonnet was the way of hypothesis.' In other words, while we can observe both our own experiences and the operations of the organism, the explanation of psychic events from the physical side is too insecure; the brain *might* explain the mind, if only we knew more about it, and if what we said about it were not so largely a repetition of psychological data in another terminology.

The study of the brain has advanced since the days of Tetens, but his main contention is still sound; feelings and thoughts are not really explained by calling them 'movements of fibres'; we should in most cases never discover the function of these 'fibres' if we had not begun from a given experience to find its possible physical correlate. While the help of physiology was neither rejected nor underrated by Tetens, it was regarded by him as limited and usually overestimated.

The attitude of the psychologist toward the data of physiology greatly affects his views on the subconscious. With the English school, Condillac and Bonnet opposed the notion; either there is consciousness or there is an inadequate physical agitation. Leibniz was in favour of subconscious operations of the soul. This fact doubtless influenced Tetens; it was made more influential by his independent recognition of the obscurity underlying the idea of reaction. Physiologists incline to think that if the soul reacts to brain processes, it may derive its knowledge from or through those brain processes. But Tetens has two points to make in this connection. Reaction is only possible where there is power of action, so that the brain does not create, but only conditions, the soul's activity; it is still possible to ask whether this does not admit some activity of the soul over and above these reactions. Secondly, the essential element of feeling may be dependent on brain-effects, but there might also be modifications of the soul due to its own activity which did not achieve any brain-movement, and so failed to be reflected back into the soul. In this way Tetens keeps a place for the unconscious life of the soul, but he realizes more than his predecessors that we only know phenomena, and he is clear that the unconscious is properly a deduction from the idea of method, a metaphysical standpoint rather than a datum.

Tetens does not show any interest in the physiology of the senses; he abandons the objective method for introspection. Under sensations he groups the inner sensations of hunger, thirst, increased and decreased vitality, and in general all that was included in the *sensus interni* of Descartes. The subjective marks of sensation are—(*a*) reference to an object as present, which distinguishes it from a presentation or idea; (*b*) capacity to vary in intensity, extensity, and duration; (*c*) an element of passivity. Sense is described as 'relative,' because it is not derived merely from the nature of the soul, but is conditioned by the state of the organs and by their relation to the objects. Finally it is reaction and therefore in some sense action, but consciousness itself testifies that the action is necessitated, and so far is passive. Driven at this point to say something about the physical conditions of sensation, Tetens agrees in the main with Bonnet; but he regards the whole question as irrelevant to psychology, belonging rather to a different sphere of science and not likely to give any deeper insight into the peculiar problems of the inner life.

The feelings are in part to be identified with sensations, namely as events in the organism. But the sensations have a quality of appropriateness (or its opposite) which constitutes their being felt. The feelings are therefore distinct from other phenomena in being presentations which are not conditioned by external objects (as sensations are) but by inner modifications. The nature of feelings is therefore best described by saying that they are distinguishable phenomena of consciousness which appear as the 'feeling-side' of sensation. Tetens raises the fundamental question —Is the feeling only a phase of sensation, or is it a distinct experience capable of being later in time than the sensation.[1] Tetens decides that feeling is not capable of independent existence; it is by nature a parasite. But if he does not assert its separateness, he does maintain its distinctive character.

In addition to this question of the independence of feelings, there are other points to be settled. We may ask whether all conscious processes are accompanied by feeling, whether feelings are transferred, and whether they can be reproduced. On this first point Tetens decides (against Hartley and others) that feelings may be associated; that is to say, that a feeling may recall or reproduce another feeling without involving any other association (of ideas) to make its presence possible. But Tetens does not stop at this point; he goes further from Hartley and nearer to Bonnet in declaring that the soul has powers of spontaneous action, that the feelings accompanying the presentations of the inner sense are not merely reproduced, and that these feelings are more closely bound up with the accompanying ideas than would be the case in a mere association. Feelings, then, are not confined to the sphere of sensations; all consciousness has an element of feeling. Transference (or transferred association) is admitted. Also feelings may be reproduced, i.e. the idea of a feeling is itself accompanied by feeling; but the idea of a feeling tends to be weaker, though some ideas tend to change into original images, as presentations may become hallucinations.

Sensation has a double function: it establishes a relation between the object and the mind, and produces in consequence a modification of the soul, the Leibnizian 'presentation.' These are

---

[1] Cp. Höffding *Outlines of Psychology*, ch. vi. § 2: 'I took a couple of steps backward and came in contact with a hot stove, which I had not imagined so close: I then felt quite distinctly the sensation of touch before the feeling of pain.'

described as after-effects, echoes, or traces of the original impression. These terms are not to be taken as indicating any actual portraiture of things in the mind; presentations of 'ideas' are not copies but elementary experiences, phases of the soul's life and activity. Tetens here shows the influence of Berkeley and of Hume; we only know our own inner states, so that our immediate world is a world of experiences; but some of these experiences (namely those which we recognize as sensuous) appear as impressions and as relative to external agencies. Reid's doctrine is expressly rejected; that the presentation (or idea) refers to something beyond itself is a fact which only reflection makes clear, though, as a fact, it is implied from the beginning in the confused state of unreflective thought. In this way Tetens mediates between Locke and Leibniz.

The idea is for Tetens closely allied to the after-image. This remarkable opinion arose quite naturally from consideration of the nature of reaction. A sense-impression excites an inner activity which, so long as it remains a continuation of that excitement, is to be described as an 'after-image' or residual sensation. As the original impression becomes more remote the image becomes an abiding presentation or mental content which operates in perception. Finally it recedes still further into the soul and only comes back in the reproductive activities. Somewhere in this series of transmutations we pass over from image to idea, from *idea materialis* to *idea intellectualis*. Tetens recognizes both; in fever and delirium there is evidence that brain-changes cause reproduction of ideas; but in normal thinking the reproduction is an activity of the soul, not primarily of the brain. Perception, reproduction, and imagination are all distinct, but not as 'faculties': they are modes of the fundamental power of presenting ideas (having presentations).

Memory is a power of reproduction which belongs both to the soul and to the physical organism or brain. Four hypotheses are possible: (*a*) The traces of former experiences might be in the brain alone. This was Bonnet's position, but it offers nothing more than a translation of psychic experiences into unproved physical hypotheses. Loss of memory, e.g., may be due to destruction of fibres, but it might equally well be due to purely psychic failure; restoration of memory after an illness is not really explained by the renewed vigour of the fibres, for not only the fibres but also the particular 'traces' must be restored; to assume this is to assume everything. (*b*) The traces might belong to soul and brain alike. (*c*) They might be merely modifications of the soul. (*d*) Some might belong to the brain, others to the soul.

This last hypothesis Tetens would accept. At the same time he regards this question of the 'seat of memory' as illegitimate; the processes are phenomena, the memory as such is not a phenomenon, and since scientific analysis is limited to phenomena, no demonstrable answer to such a question is to be expected. We can only take the least impossible hypothesis. So with association; the fact of association is obvious, but its basis lies outside experience. Association by similarity and by contiguity in time are the two types named; beyond that statement Tetens has only criticisms to offer. He feels that the theory has been overworked; the only real fact is that any idea may recall any other, and some are recalled more easily than others. Behind this general antagonism to the questions of association lies the belief in the soul's activity; it was as a passive linking of ideas that Tetens received the 'associationist' view; he argues that imagination overrides its laws, that a series of ideas can be revived in a reversed order, i.e. in the order in which it was *not* given; also that links in a chain of ideas may be dropped out, without destroying the possibility of reproduction. All these are just observations, but they do not actually achieve much more than a reformation in the idea of 'association.' Tetens affirms the need of action; but after all, associationism was chiefly concerned with the nature, not the fact, of that activity. From his own position Tetens could be more venturous in treating the creative imagination; the material for this is drawn from earlier experiences, but the form of the result is wholly derived from the psychic activity. This conception of a matter and a form, corresponding to data and products of the inner activity, was a large factor in the work of Tetens. It came ultimately to be the core of his doctrine; associationism, he felt, left the data to arrange themselves and their relations; his view, on the contrary, made the data only a part of the content of consciousness and associationism only a partial explanation of the whole mass of psychic processes. Here we find the most significant part of Teten's work—the doctrine of creative imagination (*Dichtkraft*), a point not fully developed, but a real independent attitude capable of evolution. More will be heard of it when we come to Kant.

Form and matter, activity and passivity, come to be the leading terms of this doctrine. Sensation and feeling are (relatively) passive; after-images and ideas are activities, judgment and reasoning still more so. The simplest element of thought is the discrimination of one percept from another, not a comparison of them but a pure recognition of differences as actually presented. Out of this recognition of difference (or mere plurality) arises reflection; the earlier product is the raw stuff of this later and higher process. This 'matter' of thought is not a feeling or a sensation; there is no way from sensation to thought such as was meant by Condillac's definition of *sensation transformée*. Tetens' affiliation to the school of Leibniz is shown by his preference for the term apperception. What he wishes particularly to avoid is the notion that thought arises out of the mere coexistence of data; he refuses to admit that the feeling which arises out of a similarity or difference in objects is the same thing as the recognition of that similarity or difference. Yet Tetens is too keen a thinker to assert that the recognition of relations is an act which creates them; and a very awkward dilemma results. Either the mind creates the distinctions or the distinctions are first made and then recognized; in other words, either the images are apperceived and so made distinct or by becoming distinct they reach the stage of apperception. In attempting to get away from the Leibniz-Wolff position that images are obscure and only ideas are clear, Tetens has brought upon himself the whole problem of attention and activity. On this he has nothing new to say, and contents himself with protesting against the idea that attention is an act of will directed upon a given (passive) content; a view discovered by Germans in Abraham Tucker.

Next to apprehension comes the act of relating. Relations exist between objects, as was generally recognized; for Tetens they exist also between impressions—a point not unlike Hume's doctrine but distinguished from it by the emphasis which Tetens always lays on activity. Hume spoke of the relations we feel, Tetens of those we create. The list of the relations, taken from Leibniz (*Nouveaux Essais*), comprised (*a*) relations of comparison (Identity, Diversity), (*b*) relations of coexistence (Inherence, Time, Space), to which is added causality or dependence. These are the modes of thought; all thinking is judgment, and therefore these are forms of judgment, the categories. Tetens has obviously left the list incomplete, or rather he leaves a gap between these categories of relation and the categories of substance, unity, and reality which seem to transcend the system of relations. There is also some uncertainty whether the relations are established and then made explicit for thought by reflection, or depend entirely on thought. It seems as though Tetens was willing to admit a felt relation in such cases as musical harmony, but in the sphere of thought had not made clear to himself the difference between the relations of ideas one to another and the ideas of relation. Similarly Tetens shares with his contemporaries the tendency to confuse logical relation with psychological connection.

Thinking and Willing are two cognate activities; the former reproduces previous modifications, the latter produces new ones. We do not directly feel the activity of Will; what is given to consciousness is the residual effect. The act of will presupposes the idea of the completed action; we can only will movements by fixing an idea of such a movement as it was previously observed in our own involuntary action. The basis for developed action is therefore the preceding instinctive operation. Will therefore belongs to the higher plane of reflective action; Leibniz had not observed this when he reduced action to the mere idea of the object of volition; for on that basis instinctive action could not be explained. In every action mind and body co-operate; the idea is united with the feeling, the feeling is a conation that has immediate relation to the actual motor processes in nerve and muscle; movement is not a mere act of will, nor is it a mechanical process in which conscious activity has no share.[1]

4. MAINE DE BIRAN AND COURNOT

Though the French philosophers of this period were never very effective, Taine's view of the matter was not the last word.

[1] The account here given of Teten's *Versuche* may appear, to those who have been trained in modern psychology, lacking in systematic arrangement. It is necessary, therefore, to explain that Tetens comprehends the physiological parts of the subject under his conception of '*Entwickelung*,' and to them he devotes most of the second volume. He relies largely on Unzer, and clearly regards the subject as a matter of correlation: the whole question of physical development runs parallel with that of mental development, from birth to death: embryology, physiology, evolution, and epigenesis are here discussed as relevant topics, but always with the proviso that it is a matter of analogy (the relations within the material series being equivalent to the relations within the other series). The details of this lengthy discussion involve continual references to Bonnet, Haller, F. A. Wolf, and other scientific writers of the period. It is not possible at this point to do more than record that fact.

Progress was continually being made, and the evolution was both simple and normal. Condillac did not properly estimate the activity of the mind. Laromiguière (among others) emphasized attention and declared that there were internal as well as external senses: the statue could never have acquired such powers as are implied in the perception of beauty, moral truth, and so forth. The next step to be taken was the full elaboration of a theory of activity with a consequent apotheosis of Will. By the end of 1822 Maine de Biran had accomplished this, and was by virtue of his achievement the acknowledged leader of the reaction towards, spiritualistic psychology. To Taine this was darkness and anathema; yet even he wavers in his attack and makes some admissions which show him to be uncertain whether the spiritualists had not somewhere in their teachings a vein of truth.

This, in fact, they had, quite apart from their metaphysical flights or their tendency to obscurantism. It was an old truth, but France was still without share of it. Leibniz revived it from Plato, and from Leibniz onward it remained a possession of Germany; it was the insight into the fact that relations imply activity. Locke had not committed himself to the kind of language Condillac used; he had not excluded activity, though he had paid more attention to its effects than to its nature. Empiricism, which began by requiring a careful history of the actual life of thought or consciousness, had allowed itself to drift into a false position of appearing to deny the life it analysed. Hence the need of reaction and at the same time the barrenness of the reaction; when the life was reasserted there was nothing more to be made of it psychologically than had been made by Locke or Leibniz. In this connection Biran's development is instructive and typical: it shows a very common misunderstanding of the relation between the form and the content of a science.

Biran began in the spirit of Condillac and the atmosphere of Cabanis. His first work, *Sur l'Influence de l'Habitude à la Faculté de Penser* (1802) may be said to show signs of opposition to Condillac, but its suggestion of a theory of activity was no more than Condillac himself might have developed. Few, if any, of the great thinkers have denied activity; many of the greatest have felt that it was a metaphysical subject, to be approached gradually through the study of its manifestations, the recognizable activities. Biran was inclined to commit the error of youth and begin with the largest ideas. He quickly overcame that and definitely proposed to himself the task of uniting ideology and physiology. This was a very legitimate course to adopt; ideology seemed in need of physiology to give it body and weight; Cabanis was showing the way to a psychological standpoint; the future seemed to lie in the hands of those who could think in terms of both matter and mind. But Biran was not to be appeased by the offerings of the physiologists; he grew dissatisfied with the language of the 'fibrepsychologists' and more anxious to achieve what he called the 'decomposition of thought.' At the stage of his development in which he produced the *Essai sur les Fondements de la Psychologie* (1813–1822), he had passed from sensationalism as he understood it, acquired from Leibniz a belief in activity as explaining those contents of the mind which are not sensations or compounded out of sensations, and made some acquaintance with the developments in Germany down to Kant. The work has been variously estimated; in most cases without any attention being given to its title. The author writes entirely under the limits of the title; his work is not concerned with psychology but with its fundamental presuppositions; it is meant to be a critical introduction to all future psychologies. The criticism is often acute; the constructive parts ultimately collapsed.

Undertaking the 'decomposition of thought' in 1805, Biran announced his opposition to the method of the analytical school. The term decomposition is meant to imply that thought will be treated as a whole admitting distinctions, not as something which is put together by adding parts. As a result of thus opposing the traditional method of beginning from sensations, Biran denies that attention is sensation, or that memory is the persistence of images, or that will is matured desire. Biran has now read the literature of his subject and can criticize Hobbes, Bonnet, and Gall: these writers ignore the very object of psychology, the immediate consciousness itself. Elsewhere he traces this development as the outcome of Francis Bacon's teaching, and says that Bacon has only led his successors *dénaturer psychologie*. The point is well expressed: the science of the mind had actually tended to become the application of the mind to some other science, especially physics or physiology. Biran clearly announces the value and the need of an independent psychology, a pure science of the facts of consciousness.

The ancient theory of the soul was no longer regarded as the object of any science. Biran did not make the mistake of opposing to the empiricist any effete doctrine of substance. He read Locke carefully and discovered how that writer distinguished between soul and self; he knew Descartes' position well enough to realize the fundamental importance of immediate consciousness; finally, he was equipped by Leibniz with the idea of activity. The last point is for Biran cardinal; he links the three positions together and offers as the postulate of his psychology an active Ego defined in terms of actual consciousness.

To make it valid this fundamental proposition has to be worked out in all its implications. The praise which Biran gave to J.-J. Rousseau and Pestalozzi shows his leaning toward a treatment of the mind which will be concrete, practical, and mindful of the affective side. The main lines of development are as usual; attention is emphasized and discrimination made to depend on it; consciousness has four levels—the affective, the sensitive, the perceptive, and the reflective. These differ in the degrees of effort which they exhibit, the first being the life common to man and animals, obscure and devoid of self-recognition; the Ego awakes and surveying its states is said to be sensitive; this mere awareness when concentrated upon a single object becomes perception; the last supreme effort is that of reflection when, no longer dependent on external stimulation, the self dwells within itself and contemplates its own pure reality.

From this point Biran's ideas cease to interest the psychologist. For the historian they have some significance as indicating the continual reversion which generation after generation makes to some well-defined type. For Biran the type was the Alexandrian Platonism. He objects to the view of the atomists that nothing acts on itself; he thinks the soul does act on itself, and that act is reflection; he thinks mathematics and metaphysics are very much alike, for in both the thinker depends upon reflection, which is not to be confused with abstraction; he tells us that 'a philosopher of the Alexandrian school' defined memory not as 'keeper of images' but as a faculty which can produce from concepts a proposition. What the use of this definition may be we are not told; it is admitted to be arbitrary and inaccurate, but it does emphasize activity! Into this idea of activity everything finally enters; out of it nothing returns. The spiritualism which could be developed from Cartesianism through Malebranche, began to come under the sway of theology. The origin of language was again referred by de Bonald to a special revelation; Augustine's phrase, *Deum et animam scire cupio*, was reflected in the titles of works, *De la Connaissance de Soi-même*. The revival of religious enthusiasm checked the spread of scientific inquiry, and Biran, always susceptible to influences, went on from introspective psychology to mysticism. In the Middle Ages the mystical tendencies had helped to create psychology. In the nineteenth century they were no longer helpful and served only to confound the issues.

Biran died in 1824. His voluntarism had run to seed, but not without bearing fruit. The introspective point of view was reaffirmed, but not rightly used. An analysis of will was demanded to supplement Condillac's work on the senses and the intellect; but none was supplied. Cousin treated philosophy diplomatically and aimed at conciliating the theological party. Gratry (1852) attracted some attention by his theory that the infinitesimal calculus was a bridge from the finiteness of man to the infinity of God, and made his psychological analysis a faithful copy of the doctrine of the Trinity.

Jouffroy (died 1842) represented the mediating position which was limited to the declaration that psychology is the science of the self and of self-knowledge. Under his influence Garnier produced a *Traité des Facultés de l'Âme*, which reached a second edition in 1865 and was henceforth regarded as the catechism of this school and its most complete condemnation.

The course of thought during this period was the chief reason why Biran's work fell into disrepute. As Cabanis had been pushed aside because of his 'materialism,' so Biran was shunned because of his 'spiritualism.' In Renan, Littré, and Taine aspects of Positivism were developed and accepted as a relief from obscurantism. Biran suffered unfairly, though his last writings were not calculated to inspire confidence in his psychology. His central doctrine of will was valuable; details of his work deserved to be remembered; he has been described as 'perhaps the earliest accurate introspective observer of dreaming,' on account of his statement that active action is suspended in the dream-state; he also noted that sensation and perception vary inversely, though Hamilton did not admit that Biran anticipated his discovery of this phenomenon. In details of this kind Biran retained a scientific interest, which was derived from the earlier period and gradually ceased to be effective.

Antoine Cournot (1801–1877) was the author of two works which deal with the scope and method of psychology (*Essai sur les Fondements de nos Connaissances*, 1851; *Materialisme, Vitalisme, Rationalisme*, 1875). Cournot regarded vitalism as the true basis of philosophic construction. He was consequently opposed to mechanism and to spiritualism, finding in the sphere of life the manifestation of an unique principle and the demand for a specific method. As life is manifested in a continuous scale of forms, there is no gulf between physiology and psychology: in general agreement with Bichat, Cournot would treat psychology as a natural science and make it a phase of biology. The mark of living organisms is spontaneity, and the spontaneity of mental action is not different in kind from the general spontaneity called life. The vital and the psychic syntheses therefore represent an activity which is neither mechanical nor derivative: in this sense 'innate ideas' may be affirmed as the basis of all individual characters, whether types of body or types of mind. Cournot defends the conception of animal psychology, emphasizing the power of unconscious tendencies and natural instincts, with a process of development through sensibility to a higher consciousness which approximates to a sense of personality. Similarly in man there is a continuous development from the lowest degree, irritability, to the highest level of intellect. Human psychology must be a science of a species or genus, and so must be finally a psychology of human society. In all this Cournot certainly anticipates the later work of men like Bergson and Wundt.

The nature of a transitional era is well illustrated by the work of Cournot. He grasps the significance of scientific method in psychology; he is obviously in sympathy with the standpoint of Cabanis and Bichat, without being persuaded to reduce mental to physical processes. On the other hand, the conception of a 'rational psychology' retains what Biran and others had laboured to establish in the name of spiritualism. For the continuity of life, which is Cournot's fundamental hypothesis, allows him to proceed from sensation to intellect without either degrading the former or exalting the latter: the soul as substance is never invoked to support either higher or lower faculties, but sense and intellect alike are functions and as such simply forms of vital activity.

5. FROM TAINE TO BINET

The history of psychological theories in France entered upon a new phase in 1870. Whatever else may be thought of the work done by Taine, no one would deny his right to be considered the leader of the empirical school and the exponent of concrete practical methods of study. The movement was a reaction for which considerable preparation had been made in several directions. In 1870 France began to realize the full significance of the fact that Cousin was dead. That great philosophical dictator left no successor: there could be no second Cousin with the same power of historical compilation, the same zeal to make the mental sciences part of the national life, the same anxiety to be at once both great and conspicuous. Even before his death rebellious spirits had murmured this was no more than a sophist, a *philosophe-orateur*, and foremost among these was the young and journalistic Taine. Born in 1828, Taine was brought up in the Eclectic school, but at the age of twenty-three abandoned it to take up an attitude of hostility which was fostered chiefly by the study of the sciences, especially anatomy, mathematics, and physics. The result was the usual tendency of the young to feel that the philosophers were not moving as quickly as they should, and in 1856 Taine helped them to move on by the publication of the series of essays entitled *Les Philosophes Classiques du XIXᵉ Siècle en France*. With inimitable literary skill Taine sketched the history of philosophy in France during the preceding quarter of a century, and the book, destined to run through seven editions, was from the first a force to be respected. Such books cannot afford space to be complete and their writers cannot spoil the chances of victory by fine considerations of justice. Taine was not just, but he achieved his purpose, which was the condemnation of the whole trend of French philosophy since the days of Condillac.

We might say that at this time Taine's motto was 'Back to Condillac.' The philosophers had lost the respect and confidence of the men of science, and Taine, with one foot in philosophy and one in science, felt aggrieved at the way in which the national philosophy was falling behind the progress of research. This state of mind implies of course a contempt of metaphysics, and Taine's real mission did not amount to a constructive philosophy but a very limited attack on the points which were of interest to him, the problems of physiology and psychology. We shall enter upon no disputes at present about the value of this kind of outlook, but take a retrospective glance at the developments which culminated in this revolt of the empiricists.

The general idea entertained about the method of Condillac was that it kept to the sure ground of experience and could be trusted. This was fostered by the fact that the spirit of enquiry which was active at the time, co-existing with the supremacy of Condillac, though not otherwise related to him or his method, produced a vigorous movement in the sciences both of body and of mind. Under the somewhat vague term of Ideologist the historian groups men like Cabanis, Broussais, and Bichat, a group of speculative physicians; Destutt de Tracy, Laromiguière, Cardaillac, and other philosophical writers; while the period was made famous by the names of Lamarck, Biot, Flourens, and others whose fame spread over Europe and made Paris the centre of European learning. This pre-eminence passed by degrees from France to Germany, and in 1870 the French were conscious that they had lost to some extent their prestige, and those who looked at things from the point of view of the politician were anxious to find the reason for this apparent degeneration. Taine laid the blame on the spiritualistic school of Maine de Biran, and his sentiments are echoed in all the writings of the empirical school.

The ideologists were concerned with many things beside psychology, but they made one contribution to the progress of that science by their consistent efforts to explain the nature of mental activity. The mere analysis which Condillac made so clear and attractive was superseded by this demand for some deeper penetration into the mystery of the living mind, just as the physiologists were influenced in the direction of vitalism by their dissatisfaction with a mere description of the mechanism of the body. The vitalists were going back to Stahl: the psychologists were really moving across from the territory of Locke to that of Leibniz. The movement was weak and stopped short of the goal. De Tracy and Laromiguière went no further than the assertion of a specific activity which was the active element in the perception of resistance and the contribution which the individual makes to the act by which external reality is perceived. From this point, which belongs to ideology rather than psychology, the school diverged into speculative philosophy tempered by interest in language and signs. The quantity of the work done was not great, but it has a distinctive quality, and the analysis of resistance, with the consequent development of the sense of effort as a fundamental part of experience which could not be given from outside, was an important contribution to psychology. There can be no doubt that the friendly visits of the Scotch philosophers to Paris during this period were accountable for the originality of those who tried to improve on Reid by this same process of emphasizing activity.

Together with this speculative element the Ideologists retained the practical and empirical mood of the age. They were at peace with the men of the world and those who came into contact with the daily needs of men. The politician, the men of culture, the healers of the body were kindly disposed toward these thinkers, and De Tracy has the reputation of being the only philosopher who has invented a new dance. But a very different type of man was coming to the front under the guidance and encouragement of Cabanis. Maine de Biran, though he was a soldier by profession, at times a man of affairs on a small scale, and a figure in the cultured circles of Paris, was at heart a recluse. He withdrew more and more from the outer world to the inner, and traversed the whole road from the empiricism of Condillac, through the physiological psychology of Cabanis and the semi-spiritual psychology of the Ideologists, to a definitely metaphysical view of the soul and a mystical pietism. The power of Maine de Biran's work was shown by the following which he had in the period immediately succeeding his death; it has been shown again less directly by the fact that while Taine and Ribot are regarded as the leaders of the empirical school, Bergson is the advocate of what would have been called in 1870 'Biranism.' The empiricists speak as if French psychology plunged into a deep and dark tunnel just before it arrived at Biran's spiritualism, emerging into the light of day once more at the era of Taine. In any case there is here a clear distinction of aims and methods, and we may proceed to enquire separately into the development of these antithetic standpoints.

The reader of Taine's book, *On the Intelligence*, is conscious at the sight of the first page of some disturbing elements; he has been accustomed to hear about the sense organs, sensations, higher powers, and so on in regular order; but this book seems to be curiously inverted and in addition to its disregard for standard divisions and headings it offers curious paradoxes culminating in the assertion that sensations are true hallucinations. All this requires some explanation which, fortunately, can easily be obtained. Taine is a peculiar combination of psychiatry and positivism. From the school of Condillac and Cabanis there had emerged Pinel, the man who first began to impress people with the fact that mental diseases were simply one kind of disease, not a wholly supernatural event but a form of human suffering to be treated as such. Pinel (1801) had a worthy successor in Esquirol, whose writings from 1817 onwards are regarded as the real foundation of the mental pathology and psychiatry of the nineteenth century. When the subject was properly established and the pathology in question was seen to be really a question of the mind and not to be satisfactorily treated by scourging, purgation, or a sudden application of cold water, there was the usual zeal to collect examples, and the work of the scientific enquirer became the object of public curiosity. The abnormal became a popular topic before 1860, and it was the fashion to look on psychology as a storehouse of curious narratives: the ancient ally of metaphysics was reduced to supplying copy for sensational romances.

It was a just dispensation. While the psychologist in earlier days had been content with an abstract science, the writers of romance had kept alive the observation and description of human behaviour. Now, from that intermediary sphere of hospitals and asylums, from the places where society collects and segregates the products it cannot assimilate, there comes that application of method which alone could make the raw material of novelist into a scientific product. The gulf between sanity and insanity rapidly narrowed and the systematic study of mental pathology led to the idea of a distinction between normal and abnormal mental structures which was totally different from the current conception of madness or of idiocy. From the new point of view not only did sanity and insanity merge their borders in the life of ordinary individuals, but the science of the normal mind, the ordinary psychology, was compelled to recognize as part of its domain what previously had been either excluded or unknown. To Esquirol was due the distinction of illusion from hallucination, together with a more careful elaboration of the significance of organic development as Cabanis had suggested it should be treated. After Esquirol, Michea (1837), Baillarger (1842), and Brierre de Boismont (1845) continued the work of collecting material, studying and describing individual cases. At last a new and fruitful method of studying the operations of the mind seemed to have been discovered. The impact of the new influence on general psychology was expressed, with the exaggeration natural to the circumstances, in Taine's phrase, perception is *hallucination vraie*.

While it was natural that psychology should be most affected by the sciences which either bordered upon or actually shared its territory, there was a more general principle underlying the whole movement which may be regarded as the philosophical basis of the new empiricism. This was the positivism of Auguste Comte. In 1830 the *Philosophie Positive* announced that the world had passed through the age of religion and the age of metaphysics: it had now reached the age of science. The time was ripe for some such declaration and the Positive Philosophy counted among its admirers or adherents such widely different personalities as J. S. Mill, G. H. Lewes, Spencer, and Taine. It was not necessary for the Comtist to accept Comte's doctrines as such: it was enough to sympathize with the general idea, and this was all that the disciples as a whole professed to do. That idea was positivism, not necessarily empiricism but the broad conception of fact as the basis of theory. That this should at once lead to a theory about facts and much discussion as to what were and were not facts, was only the nature of things reasserting itself against formulae; without following the ramifications of Positivism we may note its relation to psychology. Comte himself disregarded the psychology which is based on introspection, a point on which Mill did not follow him. On the other hand Comte's objective mood was a strong stimulus to the study of social relations and social interaction. The two points taken together sum up the significance of Positivism or more strictly Comtism, for the science of mind; as Lewes formulated the psychology of positivism it was a combination of biology, mental physiology, and sociology.

The discussion of Positivism leads at once from France to England, and then back again to France. The English writings were closely watched in Paris, where later the personality of J. S. Mill was known and honoured. Taine incorporated long passages from Mill in his own work, and between 1870 and 1875 great activity was shown in the translation of Bain and Spencer, Taine using his influence to recommend these works to the public. It has been said that France owes to Taine the importation of Stuart Mill and to Ribot the importation of Spencer. Be that as it may, in 1870 France possessed an independent school of thought based on empirical principles in Taine and Ribot, while the school of Biran still diffused through its classroom an odour of metaphysics and Germany.

It is more important to understand Taine as a person than to criticize Taine as a psychologist. There is no need to give any detailed description of his work, *On the Intelligence*. It was essentially a manifesto in which Taine did not so much write psychology as show how he would like to see it written. The contents, drawn from works of physiology, reports of asylums and Mill's Logic have no inner unity and are decidedly entertaining. If they aspired to the dignity of a system there would still remain the fact that Taine never added the other promised volume on the emotions and the will, nor is it easy to see what he would have done with them if he had followed the indications of his treatment of intellect. In a similar suggestive but incomplete way Taine created a type of applied psychology in his *History of English Literature*, of which the monographs on La Fontaine and Livy were preliminary studies. Believing in the concrete rather than the abstract, Taine thought of this Folk-Psychology as the real sphere of applied psychology and deserves the credit of introducing to France this product of German thought. Popularity was Taine's nemesis; the public found his work original and entertaining, but failed to see in it any revolution which would usher in a new era of literary criticism based on psycho-physiological principles.

Much as he disliked the Metaphysical school, Taine never really worked out his own salvation; his empirics were closely akin to 'Metempirics,' and he aimed, more or less consciously, to exhibit the unity of mind as the plurality and then synthesize the plurality. A beginning was made from signs, presumably because they are indisputable realities; thence the author descends to images, to sensations, and to the elements of sensations. The last term denoted homogeneous, imperceptible elements corresponding to neural reflexes, a speculative basis which perhaps anticipated the neurograms of later writers. The return from these depths is made by a synthetic reconstruction of experience, decidedly not the most original part of the book.

Taine was the forerunner and herald of the era that began actually with Ribot. Born in 1839, Théodule Ribot began his professional career as a lecturer at the Sorbonne. In 1873 he published his book on *L'Hérédité Psychologique*, which Taine among others hailed as significant of new and better things. Ribot was in fact applying and extending the general spirit of English thought, and when the opportunity came he was naturally considered the right man to establish in France a school of experimental psychology. The opportunity did not come; it was made. In 1888 the chair of Law of Nature and Law of Nations fell vacant at the Collège de France. M. Renan thought the time had come to recognize psychology as an independent subject, and proposed to convert this chair into a professorship of Experimental and Comparative Psychology. After some delay due to opposition the change was effected, M. Ribot was installed, and psychologists everywhere applauded this sign of progress. From then onwards M. Ribot continuèd his extensive labours. He had given to his countrymen an historical account of English and German psychology in 1879; he had founded the *Revue Philosophique* in 1876 (the year in which Bain started *Mind*), and begun already that long series of monographs by which his name has become familiar to students all the world over.

Physiology and pathology were the moving forces in France during the decade 1880 to 1890. Ribot did not estimate these forces very accurately; he allowed himself to be carried too far by the stream and gave too much importance to the idea that consciousness is an 'epiphenomenon.' This excess was modified in time and from 1888, the date of his work on *Attention*, Ribot became more truly psychological in his methods and outlook. The original animosity against metaphysicians, expressed almost violently in the early historical work, ceased to occupy the foreground, though the main principles remained unchanged.

In 1889 M. Liard, the Minister of Education who ratified the appointment of Ribot, established a laboratory for psychological work at the Sorbonne. To this was appointed as director Henri Beaunis, author in 1889 of a work on *Les Sensations internes*. Beaunis was a physiologist first and foremost; his work was well fitted to rejoice and reassure all who longed to speed the parting metaphysics. But it was no longer a question of putting one doctrine in the place of another. The area was widening more and more; the different sciences began once more to diverge rather than encroach. In the sphere of mental pathology a new era dates from Pierre Janet's work; the physiological standpoint was at the same time more clearly defined by Richet, Grasset, and others. A pure objective psychology was the programme of another group including Marillier, Paulhan, Godferneaux, and Ruyssen. Introspection was accepted as a fundamental part of psychological method by a third group, including Egger, Marion, Derepas, Dugas, and Malapert. Tarde and Le Bon followed psychology along the line of its connection with sociology. In 1896 Recejac made an important contribution to the psychology of religion, while Delacroix in 1908 undertook a study of the history and psychology of mysticism.

Individuals may arrive at a monism which they find satisfactory, but the reduction of all the data to one category is rarely accepted by a whole nation or even a group of thinkers. In France at the close of the nineteenth century there survived in new forms the antagonism with which the century began: the empirical tendency was opposed by the idealistic critics. The spirit of Maine de Biran lived again in Alfred Fouillée (1838–1912), and was expressed in two of his works, the *Evolutionnisme des Idées-forces* (1890) and the *Psychologie des Idées-forces* (1893). Fouillée begins with a general opposition to Spencer: he would abandon all attempts to build a psychology out of 're-presentations'; in places of these *idées-reflets* we must put *idées-forces*. This programme emphasizes all that is dynamic: the affective states are put first, and appetite (*conatus*) is the fundamental explanatory term. As a philosopher Fouillée puts the unity of life first, and by making life essentially activity, gravitated towards a voluntarism not unlike that of Schopenhauer. The intellect is not to be ignored; on the contrary, thinking is of prime importance as the last term in evolution, and this voluntarism is called by its author intellectualist. None the less as a whole Fouillée's work was distinguished by the emphasis on activity, and was thus correctly accepted as an attempt to evade scientific determinism by employing biological rather than mechanical categories.

A similar object is the main feature of Henri Bergson's psychology. Here, too, evolutionism is reinterpreted, and the argument is a counterstroke to the evolutionism then dominant. Bergson's first work, *Essai sur les Donées Immédiates de la Conscience* (Eng. trans. *Time and Free Will*) appeared in 1889. *Matière et Mémoire* followed in 1896. While later works, notably *l'Evolution Créatrice*, have given a more extensive statement of Bergson's philosophy, the main points of the psychology were stated in the first two. One of these was the decided opposition to mental measurements, criticized by Bergson in a vigorous polemic which has become almost classic. The other was the doctrine which turns on the distinction of two memories. The object of this distinction is to separate the habit of the organism from the pure act of memory. From Maine de Biran down to Bergson French thought is continuously exercised on this topic. To emphasize habit is to reduce mental activity to cerebral physiology, as associationism had shown sufficiently. The new philosophy of M. Bergson is primarily a restoration of metaphysics, and is not so much a psychology as an influence reacting upon psychology. Some writers have welcomed it as a force likely to elevate psychology above the level of empiricism; others see in it only a useless regression from the light of facts and experiments to the darkness of unanalysable intuitions.

Such was the character and the distribution of the work done in France during the last decade of the nineteenth century. The group which still remains to be considered under the general title of experimental psychology can best be accounted for by tracing the work of Binet.

Alfred Binet was born in 1875 and died in 1911. When Taine wrote his earlier works Binet was still a boy; as a student he heard Charcot lecturing at La Salpêtrière; he graduated when the English psychologists still formed the ideals of the French school and J. S. Mill especially was the dictator of scientific method. It is a curious fact that Binet never learned German and to a large extent seems to have been indifferent to the progress of psychology in Germany. His earliest works reflected the prevailing interests, e.g. the well-known study of *Animal Magnetism* (1886) (in collaboration with Féré) and of the *Psychic Life of Micro-organisms* (1887). A new direction of thought was foreshadowed in the *Psychologie de Raisonnement* (1886) and in 1892 the work on *Alterations of Personality* showed that its author was moving away from Associationism to a different conception of the psychic life. After collaborating for some time with Beaunis, Binet became assistant director and finally director of the laboratory of the Sorbonne (1894). In 1895 the *Année Psychologique* began its career as the organ of Binet's school, and much of his work appeared in this periodical.[1]

Binet's work belongs historically to the age which followed the first epoch of experimentalism in France. The preliminary adjustments to the new outlook were achieved, and Binet really entered into an inheritance prepared by others. His reputation rests on the further progress made under his guidance. In Germany experimental work had tended to remain an appendage to physiology, an affair of nerves and reactions. Binet has the credit of moving on to comparatively new ground and attacking the intellectual life as a whole by experimental methods. The transitions which mark the different stages of Binet's career have an obvious logical sequence. Interested from the first in psychological phenomena as they are to be found in natural daily life, Binet carries the methodical principles of the laboratory into the street and the school. He constructs a bridge from the place of instruments and isolated problems over to the complex world of characters. His range was thus extended from his earliest studies on micro-organisms to the beginning in 1895 of Individual Psychology, which was then a new department. A more determined movement towards the understanding of minds as unities was then set on foot. The results were intended to be practically useful and were quickly developed in the sphere of pedagogy and legal testimony. The latter application resulted from a long study of memory and suggestibility (*La Suggestibilité*, 1900) which showed how the form of a question tends to determine the psychological reaction expressed in the answer; children particularly were found to fabricate answers, not by deliberate falsehood, but by the construction of 'memories' and ideas which were due to the pressure put upon them by the fact of being questioned. The study of fatigue made by Binet and his pupil, Victor Henri, was an exhaustive research that has become classic (*La Fatigue intellectuelle*, 1898). This was intended to inaugurate a new experimental pedagogy, and the work was assiduously developed by

[1] For details and extensive list of writings, see articles in *Année Psychologique*, 1912.

studies carried out in schools. In 1905, with the assistance of MM. Belot and Vaney, a laboratory for the study of pedagogical problems was founded. From the normal cases it was a short step to the abnormal. In 1904 a commission was appointed to examine the status of the mentally defective in schools. The work was hampered by a general uncertainty as to the definition of the abnormal and the point at which a line could be drawn between the normal, the subnormal, and the abnormal. Binet grasped the full extent of the problem and, having already made a comprehensive study of the different phases of intelligence, was able to construct a scheme of questions which could be used to test any given individual's powers. This scheme, known as the Binet–Simon scale because Simon collaborated in its production, must be regarded as a great achievement. The task was peculiarly difficult. It could only be accomplished by those who had behind their results an enormous mass of detailed research showing the order of development of the human facilities and the normal levels of intelligence at different ages. This 'metric scale of intelligence' has been criticized often and certainly fails to be an exact measure. But none the less it works; it has been found of great use for its original purpose and more generally for the purposes of psychological clinics; and those who build better are ready to acknowledge it as the foundation on which they build.

6. WUNDT

The declaration that psychology must be based directly on experience is not original with Wundt. Locke, Condillac, and Herbart had adopted the same attitude, not to mention Reid or Maine de Biran. The mere collocation of these names shows how indeterminate the concept of experience had been, and how great was the need of a fresh outlook. To this Wundt attained by first abolishing the tacit presuppositions of the earlier methods. He does not undertake to examine inner experience or outer experience as such; experience is merely the given events and the sequence of events. As given, the events are neither corporeal nor spiritual. There is no *a priori* way of deciding whether they are by origin physiological or independent of physiological conditions. It is therefore the duty of the psychologist to employ all the available means by which they can be studied. The scope and method of psychology opens out from this methodological indifference; for in some cases pure analysis will be used, in others physiological conditions will be studied, in others there will be no way of approach except through the study of various forms of expression such as language, myth, art, and religion. This complex system is the true 'method of psychology.'

The conscious employment of all these means for the solution of the psychological problem makes the greatness of Wundt's work. One other aspect of the scheme calls for special notice—the idea of experiment. In reference to this, Wundt made, in 1892, the following important statement: 'We must remember that in every department of investigation the experimental method takes on a special character, according to the nature of the facts investigated. In psychology we find that only those mental phenomena which are directly accessible to physical influences can be made the subject matter of experiment.' Elsewhere he refers to experiment as the means by which we may so control our mental processes 'that the disturbing influence which the condition of observation tends to exercise upon them is counteracted.' By earlier psychologists the word experimental had been used to mean the method of observation; the inductive was opposed to the deductive process. Here we have a characteristic advance. While the previous schools were content to begin the science of thought with the observation of the senses, this experimental method enlarges enormously the subject of sensations, placing them, as it were, under the microscope instead of taking them in the gross. Of this method more later.

Next to the question of method or outlook, comes that of elements. A brief statement of Wundt's views on this subject will preface the way for the later topics. Psychology begins after reflection has become possible; it is by reflection that we get data. When we recall the impression that any particular experience has left on the mind, we distinguish in it three distinct elements—the image or idea; the reaction or feeling; and a third part called effort, impulse, or volition. These three form a unity, but they can be distinguished, and each can be studied separately.

The term 'idea' is here used to comprehend sense-perception, memory, and images of fancy. The characteristic of the idea is that it is present to the mind in the form of knowledge; it is a specific way of knowing. Whether it is an actual image of a presented object, or the image of an object presented in the past, or an illusion, is not at first to be considered; the psychologist must begin with the datum, the image, and not confuse this with the *significance* of the image.

Psychologists of the earlier schools were usually in too great a hurry to reach the object of the idea, to settle whether it was or was not representative of reality. Wundt proceeds from the idea to its elements, the sensations; thence to the elements in the sensations, namely, strength or intensity, and quality. For its production the sensation is dependent upon a stimulus, which may be external (e.g. sound waves producing sound) or internal (processes in the sense-organs and the brain). Since the sensation, as the final result, may vary through conditions of the organism, it is necessary to treat it as dependent on internal as well as external stimuli.

The intensity of a sensation is never separable from some quality, but it is possible to change the intensity alone or the quality alone. We may strike a note on a musical instrument loudly or softly, changing the intensity; or we may strike two notes, changing the quality of the sound. Hence these elements of the sensation can be treated as distinct.

The intensity of sensations becomes a subject for scientific investigation when it is possible to find an exact measurement of different intensities. This was the object of the investigations which led to the Weber-Fechner Law, and Wundt's discussion of the subject is a valuable contribution towards its definition and use. As the method of the physicist is used in dealing with quantity, so in the case of quality it is possible to employ the method of the chemist. 'So that, in splitting up our sensations into quantitative and qualitative units, we are analysing these mental states in a way which recalls the two chief directions of analysis of the material world without us' (*H. A. P.*, 66, Eng. trans.). On these principles Wundt then deals with sight and hearing.

This account of sensation, though no more than a brief indication of the salient features, must serve to illustrate Wundt's method. The place of this subject in the whole scheme of his work may be indicated by saying that sensations are the psychological phenomena associated with the afferent nerves. The next topic is the operation of efferent nerves and their function in the sphere of movement. This is introduced as a question about the immediate consequence of a sensation. The answer is that every sensation, if unhindered, is followed by a muscular movement, called reflex. We have, therefore, as simple elements, first the sensation, then the reflex movement. These reflex movements are in a sense purposive; they subserve an end, and that end is another sensation. For example, a sensation on one part of the skin produces a reflex motion of a limb to that part, and so gives a sense of contact at the same point. The whole process is determined by the structure of the organism, and results in an experience of the position of a given sensitive area. To this must be added the fact that sensations at different points of the whole area of the skin are themselves intrinsically different. This qualitative difference in the sensations constitutes their character as 'local signs,' so that after experience of their position we recognize the place of a sensation as though that place was an original quality of the sensation. This is applicable to the retina as well as the skin, for the muscular motion that follows a sensation of light is a reflex action that tends to bring the stimulus directly upon the most sensitive part, causing in the process a series of sensations noticeably different. These reflex processes are accompanied by sensations in the muscles used. The result is an association of the muscle-sensation with the recognized local sign of the impression. Our adjustments to any given situation are therefore analysable into a sensation, the recognition of its situation, the reproduced idea of the muscle-sensation, and a consequent movement. In this way purposive motion arises out of reflex motion (which is originally in itself purposive, though not intentional), and the psychological explanation of the highest kind of movement of adaptation is achieved.

This part of the general theory has further important consequences. The idea of psycho-physical parallelism is now accepted, and it is assumed that processes can be treated in terms both of physiology and of psychology. A general principle of connection has also been introduced under the name of 'association,' which is here not association of ideas, but a natural coherence of elements such as a sensation and a movement. Given these factors, it is now possible to see how there emerges from the chaos of sensations and reflex motions the ordered experience. The reflex motions become more easy in some directions than in others;

paths of preference are established, practice and habit assist, and the individual acquires a whole system of experience before reflection detects its presence or its complexity. Then the ideas are described wrongly as innate, a remark that applies especially to the idea of space. Wundt is opposed to any view of that subject which does not treat the idea as a complex result. A very skilful exposition of the errors in measurement which are observable in simple experiments, a discussion of the part played by touch and sight respectively, and an application of the Weber-Fechner law to 'just perceptible differences' in measurement by sight, lead up to the final statement that our idea of space is to be explained by the theory of complex local signs. The distinctive features of this theory, as stated by Wundt, are: (a) the view that sight is not educated by touch necessarily, but that (b) the sense of sight is itself a kind of touch, since the skin and the retina are equally areas of sensation with local variation. Earlier theories had been troubled (a) by the factor of distance in vision, (b) by the inversion of the retinal image. Wundt shows how the first difficulty arises from starting with irrelevant notions; it is not the *object*, but the *sensation*, from which the psychologist must start, and the sensation is never 'distant.' The second problem is settled by an adequate knowledge of the ocular movements.

From sensations we may pass to feelings. Here again we find errors have arisen from failing to begin with 'pure experience.' It is usual to speak of sensations as 'objective,' feelings as 'subjective.' But this distinction implies the construction of object and subject; it implies that we are thinking of an object and its relation to us, not simply of the feeling as event. If we confine ourselves to the feeling as event, we find the whole class of affections includes both sense-feelings and the more remote idea-feelings. Hunger is not merely a sensation; it is a felt sensation. 'The ultimate fact is that we sense and feel,' so that the common distinction is really logical (derived from the idea of object and subject), and not psychological. In psychology it is necessary to view ideas as produced from sensations, and to regard feelings as inseparably united with sensations, sensational complexes, and ideational complexes.

A feeling is a simple and undecomposable mental state; it is indefinable, and consequently appears obscure if we take an intellectualistic view of it—'that is, explain feeling by reflecting upon the ideas among which it arises.' From Descartes onward this error of method dominated most of the attempts to deal with feelings (*H. A. P.*, p. 218). The principle of description used by Wundt is based on the difference between sense-feelings and idea-feelings. The skin, the muscles, the internal organs all give rise to distinguishable feelings; the sense-organs unite feeling with cognitive values, and therefore tend to produce an apparent distinction between sensation and feeling. But in reality there is always some degree of feeling in a sensation, and this becomes noticeable in high degrees of intensity (e.g. when a light is dazzling). Similarly, we have continuous feeling of our inner organs, normally repressed, but capable of becoming objects of attention when intensified. In addition to the separate feelings there is a total feeling which is *not* merely an aggregate of feelings; it is not decomposable, but has a qualitative unity which 'corresponds to the ideational unity of consciousness.' The best examples are the oscillatory and discordant feelings: 'affective discordancy is directly derived from affective oscillation,' as, e.g., in tickling, among sense-feelings, and in doubt among intellectual feelings.

As feeling is intimately associated with sensation and ideation, so also is will essential to feeling and feeling to will. Since volition does not always result, feelings may lapse into states apparently devoid of volition. We may, therefore, speak of the degrees of feeling as comprising feeling proper, or an affective mood, impulse, desire, or inhibited impulse. The foundation, then, is feeling, and every feeling is definable as a simple or elementary volitional tendency. We are not called upon to educe the will from some foreign source, nor can we add it on as a 'faculty' to the other processes that enter into consciousness. One or other of these methods is usually adopted: we are either asked to start with involuntary reflex motions, and then observe how the mind notices them and appropriates them, or we are told that will is wholly distinguishable from all other processes. These are roughly the theories dictated respectively by the prejudices of materialists and spiritualists; they reflect the antithesis of science and religion. Wundt, to be consistent, must eliminate these prejudices, exhibit the unadulterated facts, and remain true to the idea of process as opposed to faculty. The result is a complete inversion of popular (and some scientific) accounts of will. Volition, we are told, is fundamental; desire does not precede will necessarily, it is repressed volition; choice is not the essence of will, for choice is itself a selection between volitional tendencies; will is not a conscious use of reflex actions converted into volitions by the addition of conscious choice, for the reflex actions are themselves simply primary volitions. In brief, whichever way we turn we are met by the fact that volition has no antecedent; it is original. Every sensation and every idea has its own affective tone, and so far is an elementary volition. The total state is distinct from the sum of these parts, and it is this total state which is at once the unity of self and the basis of external volition—the action which we usually identify with 'an act of will.'

The analytic movement of this doctrine is now complete. The result is obvious. What is to be said about consciousness is now said; for it is the name of a totality whose parts have all been discussed. The apparent separateness of the parts is only a necessary illusion of method. Psychology is like physiology in this respect: it distinguishes and names parts without continually recalling the organism to our minds, but implies throughout that there is an organism. After the analytic movement comes the synthetic view; for the phenomena which result from the combination of all these parts have to be considered, and this phase of the subject falls outside of the consideration of the parts themselves.

Consciousness is a name for the total state involving sensations, ideas, feelings, and volitions. It is a unity, and at the same time a plurality. As a plurality it suggests the question, How many ideas can be in consciousness at once? The answer is dependent on the question of degrees of consciousness, and really means, How many distinguishable elements can be clearly held by the mind? In addition to these there may be an infinity of indistinct elements. This leads to the separation of perception from apperception, the doctrine of Leibniz which Wundt adopts, with emphatic exclusion of any metaphysical implications. 'The perceived ideas are those which lie in the field of consciousness, while the apperceived are situated at its fixation-point.' Apperception, introspection, attention are all names of complex processes involving ideas, the outstanding character of some ideas, and the feelings associated with fixation, such as strain of the muscles of the forehead in thinking or tension in the ear in remembrance of sounds. None of these terms can be legitimately used for operations brought to bear on consciousness: introspection of experiences is itself simply a way of experiencing; attention to an idea is a way of ideation; all attempts to explain these terms as implying that the 'self' turns round upon and regards mental processes objectively are condemned beforehand by the assertion that the processes in their totality are what we designate by the term 'Self.'

We have arrived, then, at this position. The object of study for the psychologist is a complex system of processes. As processes, none of them is ever repeated or preserved. We cannot think of consciousness as storing up ideas, nor of ideas as emerging on the theatre of action from some obscurity 'behind the scenes'; ideas are not entities, but events. Yet there is a distinction between the total state at any given time and the presentation of the moment. Attention may be determined 'by more remote conscious tendencies which have arisen from previous experience and are not directly related to the particular impressions of the moment.' It is this that produces the impression of activity; for though all processes as such are activities, there is a special idea of activity associated with the relation between established dispositions and the chance stimulus. We may distinguish, then, a passive and an active form of apprehension, corresponding to the fundamental forms of creative activity, impulse and choice. As voluntary action arises out of the total state thus produced, we are now told that 'apperception is the one original act of will: it can exist without the consequences which follow upon other acts of will, whereas these always presuppose as their condition some internal act.'

As we remarked above, Wundt's career as a writer began in the region of 1860. The date is significant, because it shows how naturally Wundt assimilated the spirit of the speculative and constructive thinkers who adorned the first half of the nineteenth century. Wundt is not only a psychologist, but also a logician, a metaphysician, in the widest sense of the term a philosopher. A complete estimate of Wundt's psychology must therefore take some account of the ideas which belong primarily to the wider sphere of philosophy, but none the less suffuse the pages of psychology. At the cost of a little repetition we must summarize a few of the relevant points.

The ultimate elements of the psychic life are sensations and feelings. But experience gives us only complex states; the elements

are, therefore, no more than resultants of a logical analysis. The
science of psychic phenomena really begins with abstracted
factors, hypothetical ultimates. Though in English we use for
Empfindungen the old term 'sensations,' this fact must not be
allowed to obscure our recognition of the difference between
Wundt's doctrine and the doctrine of Locke about 'simple sensations.' Similarly, as Locke's 'elements' were concrete experiences
capable of union or separation, Wundt's elements are far more
metaphysical, and call for a deeper analysis of unity. For Wundt
an experience is always more than a sum of parts: it is something
new, something created, and depends upon an activity called
'creative synthesis.' Looked at from this angle, an individual's
psychic life is not made up of events describable as the meetings
or partings of ideas (or even sense-data), but is a perpetual creation. It is in the light of this conception that we see the real
meaning of Wundt's term 'will.' The will is that fundamental
activity which sustains experience in the making.

At this point, also, we touch the core of Wundt's distinction
between the psychical and the physical processes. Physical processes, the content of the physical sciences, are known mediately
and treated in abstraction from the observing subject; psychical
processes are known immediately, for in them the subject becomes
actual and in knowing them knows itself. This difference is
further developed into a difference between quantitative and
qualitative causality. The product of the factors in the physical
world is equivalent to the sum of the factors, and can be again
resolved into those factors. In the psychical world the result
differs qualitatively from its (antecedent) factors; therefore here,
and here only, we find a truly progressive movement. Since
creative synthesis is characteristic of all psychic activity, the
result is both effect and end: the antecedent, conversely, is cause
and reason. When this principle is applied to the whole evolution
of humanity, it serves a double purpose and constitutes the
principle of psychogenesis. History, then, is to be closely connected with psychology; for the record of progress is a record of
the stages through which psychic activity has continually summed
up its own content and generated qualitatively new products. The
cosmic application of this principle of psychogenesis shows how
the lowest (reflex) activities subserve the production of higher
personal activities, and these again produce the superpersonal

system, the activities of the organic community. The climax, later in time and in logical expansion, of this scheme is the exposition of the 'folk-soul,' a task which Wundt undertook in his *Völkerpsychologie*.

Length of life and indefatigable industry added to great abilities have given Wundt an almost unrivalled pre-eminence among psychologists for half a century. On a broad foundation of physiology, experimental psychology, logic, and metaphysics, Wundt has raised a monument of literary production surpassed by few, if any, individual efforts. Criticism cannot detract from the abiding merit of this great achievement; not criticism but the passage of time reduces to their imperishable elements the vast bulk of these labours. A detailed statement of the fate that has befallen each part of Wundt's system cannot be attempted here. Some parts, especially the voluntarism, and the doctrine of creative synthesis, have leavened psychology in every part of the world. On the side of direct stimulation for work, the laboratories for experimental research testify to Wundt's influence. Neurology, psychology, and the social sciences often echo the words of the master. But with all due allowance for solid results, it must be admitted that the glamour of Wundt's psychology is no longer enthralling. Apart from technical points, the great question which forces itself upon psychologists is that of outlook and method. From some quarters there have come authoritative assertions that Wundt's psychology never actually reached the living reality. Can psychology really progress if it is a compound of innumerable disconnected data derived from carefully arranged experiments and supplementary metaphysical assumptions? Is the immediate total experience ever reached by these roads? The so-called Würzburg school have had their quarrel with Wundt, and may be regarded as the most damaging secession which the Leipzig school has suffered. In America the influence of James and the Pragmatists has tended to reduce the estimation of pure experimental psychology: the varieties of experience, religious or otherwise, cannot be sought *only* in the laboratories. In short, the new psychology of 1880 is now a little old, a little disillusioned, a little wiser and sadder. But no generous student of history would care to emphasize this change of mood as a disparagement of the life-work of Wundt. Progress is itself a kind of critic; but it does not despise the things it must discard.

7. MACH AND AVENARIUS

In addition to the systems of psychology which were built on the scientific work of the century, important revisions of method were also advocated under the influence and protection of the same movement. The works of Ernst Mach and Richard Avenarius are the chief examples of this new doctrine of method.

Mach entered the field as a champion of physics and a declared enemy of metaphysics. His polemic was directed against every doctrine and every method which did not begin and end with elements and analysis. This was an extreme view that could not benefit psychology in more than a limited part of its area. The general doctrines of 'economy of thought' and of the identity of physical and psychic elements have importance for philosophy as a whole, and may be regarded as part of a logic of the sciences: they could be applied to any science, and do not belong peculiarly to psychology. But in his *Analysis of the Sensations* Mach uses these principles to show how they can be applied to the subject of psychology. The work has had great and well-deserved influence. It is a model of acute discrimination, and as an exposition of method may be ranked as a masterpiece. But a doctrine of method does not by itself make a science, and the success which attended the analysis of sensations could not be repeated elsewhere at will. The deduction of a complete psychology from these premises was therefore an error: the criticisms which Mach passed upon the scientific principles of his day helped to produce a new outlook in the sphere of physics and physiology, but the constructive part of his work ended in a complication of elements (sensations) which could not in any degree of complexity produce the required result. For psychology it would appear that Wundt's conception of synthesis and of a fundamental difference between psychology and physics was better and truer than Mach's scheme of analysis.

The real centre of Mach's theory is the idea of evolution as affecting the origin and value of concepts. He approaches this evolution through the history of ideas, and thereby differs from Avenarius, who looks primarily to the evolution of the organism as an individual instrument. The *Kritik der Reinen Erfahrung* is not a treatise on psychology; it is primarily a study of scientific thought; but the strong leaning to biology which Avenarius shows makes his work of interest to psychologists. The idea of 'pure experience' involves a wide programme of reform. The soul, as a principle of explanation, is to be discarded: the processes of knowledge must be described without reference to a soul, and this is ultimately achieved by a new psychology. The spirit and the letter of this new scheme are both biological. The organism is subject to changes which disturb its equilibrium. In accordance with the general principles of life, there follows an attempt to regain the lost stability, and the whole movement from the first stability to the second is called by Avenarius a 'vital series.' The terminology and the symbolism which Avenarius employed were chosen to assist his main purpose, namely, exclusion of all metaphysical implications. A 'vital series' is, in plain language, a sequence of changes in the psychophysical organism: it begins with a disturbance and ends with the natural subsiding of that disturbance. It may be described in terms of body or of mind indifferently: as, for example, we may follow an individual's experience from the first shock of astonishment to the last degree of contemptuous familiarity, and describe it in terms of nerves or feelings. With this beginning it is easy to see that there is a progressive element in experience. The course of a vital series can be repeated, and is traversed with less total disturbance of the equilibrium at each repetition. Biologically, this is equivalent to the formation of habits, habit being the usual name for sequences in organic life which, by reason of established connections, are automatic and economical. If this scheme is accepted as a profitable method, it is clearly possible to extend its operation over the whole field of human development, thus attaining, in terms of a simple unit-process, a complete system of evolution. Our interests do not carry us into that subject. But Mach and Avenarius were both forces tending toward the advance of a more strictly scientific psychology. While men of less intelligence were still hankering after a psychology which would cover both romantic animism and psycho-physical analysis, these two thinkers enphasized the necessity of making science more scientific: they measured accurately the difference between an anthropomorphic doctrine of the soul and a truly objective treatment of psychic phenomena. Every sign pointed at the time to the desirability of seeking for fixed (conceptual) elements, and treating complex states or events in terms of these elements. As a method, this must necessarily make psychology less and less like the popular conception of a 'soul-doctrine.' As we see it in the work of Münsterberg, this doctrine of method demands and welcomes an open rupture between the concepts of psychology and the 'values' of life.

8. EBBINGHAUS AND KÜLPE

Among those who build neither on physiology nor biology, but rely on the experimental treatment of psychological data, the pre-eminence belongs to Ebbinghaus and Külpe.

Hermann Ebbinghaus (1850–1908), Professor in Halle and, later, Breslau, made his reputation by the publication in 1885 of his researches on memory (*Ueber das Gedachtniss*). In these researches he provided a model for this class of work. He believed that the two essential factors were repetition and time, the former tending to create and the latter to destroy the impressions. The *meaning* of what was to be remembered was eliminated, so as to remove that complicating factor: nonsense syllables were employed to secure this condition. The particular law which Ebbinghaus formulated as a result of this research is far less important than the discovery which emerged in the course of it. The experiments showed that if a series A B C D E were learned and forgotten, and then in a second experiment a series A C E was learned, there was an increased facility which implied some association between A, C, and E. As this must be due to the previous exercise, it was shown that A and C were to some extent associated, apart from the mediating B. Ebbinghaus also demonstrated that a series when learned backwards (X to A) takes less time if it is previously learned forwards (A to X). This, again, throws interesting light on the form and character of the association processes.

Ebbinghaus gathered together and systematized his psychology in the unfinished *Grundzüge der Psychologie* (one vol., ed. ii., 1905; vol. ii., completed by E. Durr, 1913). This was quickly recognized as an up-to-date book. It impresses the reader as essentially up to date. The standard questions are all carefully oriented and fully treated; neurology and the allied topics are given adequate space; sensations occupy the place of honour; the ideas and the feelings are grouped next as 'simple forms of psychic activity' or 'elements.' This arrangement is not an artifice; it is a theory in action. Ebbinghaus recognizes physiology as indispensable background; sensation, ideation, and feeling are the elementary data; then the remainder is a question of the operations of the soul, its life as equivalent to the processes into which those elements enter. In the first part Ebbinghaus tells us what the soul *is*, and maintains that there is no unknown residuum over and above the elements described; in the second we learn what the soul *does*. This, again, is no chance collection of statements; its basis is a definite theory which has considerable interest as one more mediation between extremes. Ebbinghaus adopts psychophysical parallelism, and follows the psycho-physical line of development in the part that concerns elements. But he does not believe any purely descriptive psychology can be adequate; we must explain, and we can explain only if we follow a genetic and comparative method. The fourth book, on the laws of psychic life, therefore takes a turn toward the biological standpoint, and the central idea becomes that of self-maintaining action. In this case the term 'biological' denotes method only: there is no attempt to import any matter that belongs to the biological sciences; the matter remains to the end strictly psychological. The forms of psychic life are considered according as we regard (1) the coexistence of simple factors, or (2) their sequence, or (3) the total product of the processes as building up new forms of action, or (4) the connection of these processes with physical activities. The chief forms in these divisions are (1) attention, (2) association, (3) habit, attitude, fatigue, and (4) movement.

This description must suffice to show the chief lines on which Ebbinghaus works. Without attempting a complete survey, we may add one or two significant points which seem to us both distinctive and important.

Having accepted psycho-physical parallelism, Ebbinghaus frankly admits that it presents difficulties. Of these the one most commonly urged is the fact that very small differences in objective stimulation must be credited with great differences in result. For example: a man receives a telegram, 'Your son is elected.' He is filled with joy, and proceeds to act accordingly: but another telegram arrives, 'Your son is rejected,' and the man is accordingly depressed; his actions are totally different. Can we suppose that so small a difference in the letters which act as visual stimuli really accounts for all the subsequent differences? Must we not assume that the interpretation, the psychic factor, is the cause of the physical outcome? Ebbinghaus replies that the difficulty is due to supposing that the neuro-cerebral processes are simple counter-parts of the stimuli, that each letter or word excites one cell or group of cells. But this is not the only possible way of stating the case. A word is not an isolated entity: it has its associations, which, physically expressed, are irradiations from one cerebral centre to others along brain-paths. This is a modification of the view that there is a point-to-point relation between the objective stimulus and the neuro-cerebral centres, and it becomes an essential feature in the exposition of every type of action. It appears, for example, in the treatment of ideas, where emphasis is thrown on the arrangement or order of excitation to explain how things which are objectively similar (words like *Rebe* and *Eber*) can produce dissimilar results. Again, an application of this view is seen in the treatment of attention and memory. Attention implies concentration, which is in physiological terms contraction, or the tendency of neural excitations to converge on a limited area; while memory requires that the excitation should radiate outwards and produce excitation of centres other than that first stimulated.

Other points of interest are the fact that Ebbinghaus, with Lipps, accepts the Unconscious as explanatory principle, that Wundt's doctrine of feelings is rejected, and that association is held adequate to explain all phenomena without 'apperception.' The 'association of ideas' is for Ebbinghaus something quite distinct from the eighteenth-century associationism: rejecting the latter, he accepts the term 'association' as a name for a general mode of activity which is not a relation between 'ideas' at all, but a phase of the organic unity of the soul (psycho-physical system). The will is not either an element or a separate type of action: it is a complex of sensation, association, and movement.

Oswald Külpe, Professor in Würzburg, produced his chief work, *Grundriss der Psychologie*, in 1893. It was translated into English (1901) by Professor Titchener, and is sufficiently well known not to require description in detail. The work is pre-dominantly experimental, and its value consists mainly in the thoroughness with which the methods and results of the 'new psychology' (in this case very closely allied to Wundt's) are stated. In respect of theory, Külpe is, in this work, inclined to agree with Wundt on the cardinal doctrines of feeling, attention, and apperception, though in the question of will he sides with those who reduce it to a complex of sensations and ideas marked specifically by an 'idea of the result.' He defines psychology as 'a science of the facts of experience in their dependency upon experiencing individuals.' He admits that individual differences always meet us; but no science is deterred by that fact from formulating general statements and laws. Physiology is described as inadequate to provide an explanation of psychic processes, and is therefore to be used cautiously: experiment, observation, and introspection are of more use than physiological hypotheses. The emphasis falls mainly on analysis throughout the work.

Though a disciple and follower of Wundt, Külpe has shown himself decidedly inclined to break away from the limits which cramp the work of the master. Though neither a revolution nor a reaction, the movement which began under Külpe's influence, and is now known as the doctrine of the Würzburg school, can only be regarded as a declaration of freedom inspired by dissatisfaction. For the historian this crisis, however mild, is more interesting than many textbooks, and it is excusable to ignore the details of Külpe's *Grundriss* while we lay emphasis on the new spirit which he breathed into the bones of German psychology. As the result of this development was a new conception of method which affects the whole field of modern psychology, the subject will be met again in the later part of our history.

C. *The Beginning of Social and Animal Psychology*

I. SOCIAL PSYCHOLOGY

The general interest in the nature of man, which was a prominent feature of the eighteenth century, became specialized in several directions. Religion and morals constituted one of these directions. From this another gradually diverged, namely that which led to the consideration of man as a social creature. Shaftesbury gave the first suggestion; Adam Smith expanded it and Hume supplied a distinctively political treatment of the subject.

Adam Smith's doctrine of 'sympathy' was a part of his theory of moral sentiments (1759). It was designed to show that men are united by a direct feeling for one another. The proof of this was made to rest on community of feeling apart from calculated self-interest, and Smith made some valuable suggestions afterwards developed into definite theories. But Smith's 'sympathy' was a curious mixture of imitation (as understood by Plato) and practical judgments. Confusion on this vital point reduced the value of Smith's exposition, for it was not possible to pass from imitation (e.g. the automatic reproduction of an actor's movements) to that exercise of judgment which marks the action of a man claiming justice for a friend in distress. Smith expressed most adequately the dissatisfaction aroused by the followers of Hobbes, but he made no substantial contribution to the psychology of conduct beyond indicating that the moral sentiments should be explained by means of the actual development of a social nature.

The confusion between motor impulses and rational direction of action was a defect that remained incurable in Smith's writings. The doctrine of sympathy lapsed, but the Utilitarians, having turned their faces to the world, began to see in it new matter for thought. Hume discovered that good and bad were employed to denote relative rather than absolute qualities. This relativity explained the idea we have of types; the virtue of one man is measured in relation to the vice of another and is different in degree rather than kind; man himself appears eminent because he is compared with animals inferior in his peculiar advantages. Similarly we must judge types of character as differences in the degrees to which the principal elements are developed. The priest and the soldier are instances of qualities developed under different influences and in different proportions: the mixture makes the man. Nations can be treated in the same way; they are specialized types of man produced largely by 'contagion.' Man is by nature very imitative, and union in one political body gives endless opportunity for the acquisition of resemblance. Hume in his *Essays* is prepared to assert that all national characters depend on 'morals,' i.e. on intellectual factors;[1] we can 'discover everywhere signs of a sympathy or contagion of manners, none of the influence of air or climate.' This thesis Hume defends at length, making only slight abatement of its dogmatic generalization. The correctness of his examples need not be discussed; it is enough to show

[1] Following the French use of *morale* as distinct from *physique*.

in what way Hume treated the idea of national characteristics and to record in its proper place this early attempt to give a psychological explanation of their uniformity.

There is a psychology which has for its object the social nature of man and another which treats individuals as they are met in the life of a society. This second type, a system of reflections on human beings, was essentially French by nature and origin. It had taken form at an earlier stage in La Rochefoucauld and La Bruyère; it was formed again and very differently by Vauvenargues. Born in 1715, physically wrecked by hardships during the campaigns of 1742–43, overtaken by death in 1747, Vauvenargues left a mark on the literature of character by his *Discours, Caractères and Reflexions*. As Pascal marks the extreme development of the pessimistic valuation of human powers and La Rochefoucauld the corresponding cynical estimate of human duplicity, so Vauvenargues is the typical advocate of the more balanced optimism which came as a reaction against both. The natural goodness of man is once more asserted; the affections are taken as the real basis of character; naturalism is defended against supernaturalism by the argument that all volition is a function of passions and ideas which co-operate to produce human action. Vauvenargues deals primarily with types of conduct and draws concrete pictures of those types. The theoretical part of his work is vague; the descriptive is more precise and realistic. He complains that teachers aim to dull the vivacity of children when the impulsiveness and energy of their characters should be heightened and directed rather than repressed. In such points as these Vauvenargues reflects the tendency of his age, while he anticipates the attitude of the Encyclopaedists and of Rousseau.

From 1750 onwards a form of positivism developed continuously in France. The theory of morals moved steadily away from the spiritualistic basis of the theologians and preachers; exhortation gave place to a positive mood, associated with a keen sense for the relativity of moral valuations and a tendency toward the explanation of conduct through circumstances and places. The old antithesis of soul and body was exciting opposition from two classes of men, the anthropologists and the men of the world. This movement, too often branded as materialism and consequently misjudged, was represented by La Mettrie,[1] who drew

[1] *L'Homme Machine*, Leyden, 1748.

his inspiration partly from medical studies under Boerhaave, partly from direct observation of his own experiences during a fever. These influences were accentuated by a sense of opposition against the current idea of man; they were consequently allowed to produce exaggerations which must, however, be measured in relation to the contemporary state of opinion. La Mettrie's position was that of the psychic anthropologist; in other words he was seeking for an explanation of life in terms of both body and soul. The result was undoubtedly crude, but it was movement in the right direction. Beneath the bald statements that the senses are the source of all knowledge and that man is a machine only superior in degree to the animals which Descartes called machines, we must look at the deeper meaning. For here we find the most outspoken rejection of that doctrine which regarded man as wholly unique, a fallen angel, a corrupted image of God. The philosophers ignored La Mettrie because he had no philosophy; the theologians perversely judged him as a corrupt moralist; historians stigmatize him as a materialist. While none of these judgments is wholly wrong they are all in part irrelevant. It is as a naturalist that La Mettrie should be classed, and his work should be ranked with the work of men like Huxley or Spencer, who in their day suffered similar treatment. Nothing was more conspicuously absent when La Mettrie wrote than the idea of man as a creature whose life is conditioned by physical states. That idea was to grow and La Mettrie should have the honour of being one of the first to stimulate that growth.

La Mettrie was probably responsible for the general tendency exhibited by Helvetius. In 1758 appeared the essays entitled *De l'Esprit*, an untranslatable phrase which is reduced to insignificance by being made equivalent to 'on the Mind.' Helvetius was not proposing to write a treatise on the soul; nor was he concerned to produce a new analysis of the understanding. The subject of the work is man as a social unit, and the *esprit* is the 'genius' of such a man, in the old sense of genius as it survives in 'genial.' The range of the essays would be very curious if we were to regard them as parts of a textbook of psychology or of an essay on the understanding. Man is taken to be an intellectual, moral, and political creature; in other words, he is an animal capable of intelligent action, fit for the society which evolves manners, and developed enough to have laws. The germ of the work is the intention to produce a general guide to clear ideas for those who no longer believed in the 'soul' of the metaphysicians nor cared for the narrow cynicism of La Rochefoucauld. The first essay (in four chapters) deals with the 'mind considered in itself,' and is a perfunctory statement of the general empirical doctrine that sensibility and memory explain the contents of the mind; error is due to passions or to ignorance of the facts which would be required to form a complete judgment. The second essay, entitled *Of the Mind relatively to Society*, is the real beginning. The exposition is diffuse, adorned with quotations, references, and examples. The most fundamental point is the assertion that interest is the constructive force in psychology and in conduct. This is considered in relation to individuals, small societies, nations, different ages and countries, and finally the whole world. Interest operates as a principle of selection; we value the actions of others in relation to the ends which have interest for us, and in fact we only understand others from the point of view of those interests. This is not difficult to prove in the sphere of morals; one nation praises what another blames; the courtier values attainments which to the scholar seem insignificant; the fanatic is enraged at the low standards of the average good man. All standards are therefore relative, a conclusion to which men naturally inclined when the study of anthropology was beginning to supply data for a sociology distinct from theological ethics.

The third essay deals with the relative importance of nature and education. Man is by nature normally well endowed to achieve a high level of mental power; but the achievement is conditioned by the opposed forces of inertia and passions. Progress depends on attention and involves activity; inertia would prevent this but for the fact that men acquire dominant passions or interests which heighten activity and fix attention. Passions therefore have their use; the affective part of the man is the living force within him which leads to high endeavours under the guide of reason and social approbation. The fourth essay expands this topic further in a series of discussions on faculties, such as imagination, sentiment, wit, and taste. It concludes with a brief treatment of education.

The significance of the whole work lies in its character as an epitome of current tendencies. These were, chiefly, the tendency to make social pressure and social relations the reason for the various characteristics of men and nations; the tendency to lay slight emphasis on the intellect and pay more attention to the passions (envy, pride, avarice, ambition) which depend upon the social form of life; lastly, the tendency to see in the adult a complex product of education, defined as an art dependent upon the 'knowledge of the means proper to form strong and robust bodies and wise and virtuous minds.' The first and last word to be said on Helvetius is that he developed the positivism of La Mettrie in the direction of social anthropology.

The original impulse toward a comparative study of men and manners was given to France by Montesquieu (died 1755). Voltaire and Montesquieu returned from England in the same year (1729), inspired with a new outlook on the world, the outlook of Locke's school. But Montesquieu was no psychologist, and his attempt to make climate and soil explain mental characteristics was the irritant that produced innumerable denials of any such complete relation between the physical and the moral. Hume and Helvetius are equally emphatic in their assertions that no such simple explanation can be recognized as adequate. Voltaire propagated the doctrines of Locke but made no contributions to psychology; the Encyclopaedists as a whole were drawn away from the scientific basis to the sphere of controversy and belong to a general history of religious and moral writings. The speculative writings of the Encyclopaedists proved a hindrance rather than a help; the formulation of a definite 'atheistical' or 'materialistic' position brought discredit on the genuine naturalism which was its original source. The great need of the time was for substantial scientific investigation, without which Locke's work must needs have failed to bear fruit. The new light in which the English empirical school had worked was now waning; the reconstruction for which it was adequate had been accomplished; and not until it was definitely superseded by a yet greater brilliance could there be another and a deeper insight into nature. Before noting the movements of scientific thought at the end of the eighteenth century some notice must be taken of the work done in comparative psychology, for as yet this sphere of inquiry was entirely under the influence of that empirical doctrine which had removed many defects but was itself in need of renovation.

2. ANIMAL PSYCHOLOGY

During the second half of the eighteenth century the Protestant attitude toward authority and the critical spirit of the Enlightenment combined to produce the idea of a natural religion. Religion based upon reason was opposed to religion based upon revelation; man was supposed to attain the truths of religion by his own powers and not by the special gift of God; the human being was specifically the religious animal. Thus the old question about animals in general was again raised. The position was very complex. Descartes had said that animals were machines; the extreme rationalizing party argued that men were animals and therefore also machines; the extreme religious party drew a hard and fast line between men and animals, stifling inquiry; the moderate religious party was inclined to argue the question and show from the facts that animals were neither machines nor reasoning creatures. As the last party appealed to observation, both they and their opponents diligently collected evidence and so incidentally laid the foundations of comparative psychology in its first form as a comparison of men and other animals.

The standard teaching on the nature of animals was the simple assertion that they possessed blind instincts, but the limits of these powers were only vaguely determined. Writers like Montaigne, who affected contempt for human presumption, were pleased to revive extravagant stories of animal intelligence. The work of Rorarius came into esteem and was printed as a rationalist manifesto. In 1713 Thomasius Jenkin repeated the examples used by Plutarch and Rorarius in what he called a *Philosophical Defence of the Souls of Animals*. Leibniz was driven by force of metaphysics to admit only a difference of degree between men and animals, not being able to deny immortality to brutes. This position was converted into a definite platform by the Leipzig Society of the Friends of Animal Souls in 1742. La Mettrie (1748) represented a more experimental tendency, basing his view of the affinity between men and animals on the structural similarity of man and the apes, following thus the comparative anatomy of Willis (*De cerebro et de anima brutorum*). Condillac also contributed a discussion of the subject which had a decidedly scientific turn. His *Traité des Animaux* (1754) was partly an attack on Buffon, whose mechanistic views he criticized severely, and partly an exposition of his own doctrine of sensations applied to the animal world. This second part contained many acute observations on the development of faculties in animals, the chief point being to prove that they advance under the influence of their needs and their environment just as men do, but actually never arrive at the level of arts, sciences, morality, and religion.

Condillac was not a naturalist and his views had no root in observation. Charles George Leroy, who repeated and extended the work of Condillac by his *Lettres philosophiques sur l'Intelligence et la perfectibilité des Animaux* (1764), had all the qualities which Condillac possessed. Born in 1723, Leroy went to the school where Diderot had been educated, learned his philosophy from Condillac, maintained a friendship with the learned men of the time and was attached as keeper of woods and forests to the court of Louis XV. A courtier in some degree, a man of good understanding and a practical woodsman, Leroy was a useful man to employ in the writing of an article on 'Instinct,' or on the habits of animals. Darwin reckoned him a good observer, and more than one observation recorded by him has become classic. But the knowledge of detail did not prevent Leroy from being silly in some of his work, especially in his proof that animals count up to six!

The Encyclopaedists had a natural bias against the traditional (ecclesiastical) doctrine of instinct. In 1754 Hermann Samuel Reimarus had produced a work dealing in part with the question of animal intelligence: a more definite discussion of the same topic followed in 1760 and became a popular work republished in 1762 and 1773. Reimarus was creating a stir in Germany by his opposition to the idea of revelation; he was a centre of theological disputes, an 'advanced thinker' in those days. A man of wide reading with a taste for cosmology, Reimarus is decidedly scholastic in form and method. He had some idea of biological and psychological principles, but spent too much energy in the formal demonstration of the difference between plants, animals, and men. At the end we find that animals are credited with instinct but not reason, as Thomas Aquinas said. Reimarus opposes the 'automatism' of Descartes and the 'mechanism' of Buffon, believing that animals are created with natural impulses and 'powers,' but not with substantial souls such as men possess. The value of the work done by Reimarus lay chiefly in its careful elaboration of the zoology of the period. Leuwenhoek, Roesel and others had studied the structure of animals, and the wonders of insect life were new to the public. Sensation, attention, recognition, and involuntary connection of memory-images could be shown to be phenomena of animal life. But comparison and reflective thought, the formation of concepts, Reimarus denies to animals. These are the higher capacities which distinguish man. Apparent cases of inferences drawn by animals are adequately explained by association and the instinctive expectation of similar results from similar situations, such as the familiar action of the dog running away at the mere sight of the uplifted stick. The 'arts' of animals—the weaving of the spider, the cell-building of the bee, and other similar operations—Reimarus ascribes to innate impulses determined by specific structures. The establishment of this point is one of the objects of the whole undertaking, for Reimarus is particularly anxious to show that determinism is characteristic of all infra-human activities.

The German Enlightenment was religious in tone, and Reimarus carried that tone into his discussion of animals. The French enlightenment was of a different kind, and Leroy, influenced by the Encyclopaedists, attacks Reimarus as much as Cartesian automatism. For Leroy the question of a spiritual essence has no interest; he works on the assumption that man is a superior animal and that the superiority is explained by greater development of powers common to man and the other animals. While Reimarus is critical and conservative, Leroy is uncritical and rash. Many of the points discussed are common to both writers, but Leroy is distinguished by his consistent development of Condillac's sensationalism. He distinguishes between the state of nature and the state of culture, arguing that the difference produces corresponding differences of intelligence. Parallel with this can be set the differences between primitive and civilized men. Animals have sense-faculties, but their individual needs create specific interests, and so the senses develop differently in different species. To sensation is added memory and 'ideas acquired by reflection'; animals compare and judge, as for example when a fox prepares to leap over a wall, it judges the possibility of doing so safely. A young animal makes mistakes that an old one avoids: this proves some development in the capacity of judging. The practical man, the hunter and trapper, knows this fact from his experience. Leroy proceeds to assert that animals know the time of day, count, converse, have social and ethical sentiments—in fact, all complex forms of sense and feeling, but not pure abstract thinking. Particular attention is paid to the development of feelings among animals. The fundamental tendency to self-preservation is accompanied by feelings of insecurity which lead to formation of societies; that these societies are formed and maintained by self-interest, was, for the circle in which Leroy moved, an obvious and commendable fact. Mandeville and his *Fable of the Bees* were not forgotten. Animals do not act unselfishly; on the other hand they are free from brooding hate, and only quarrel in the seasons of sexual excitement and competition. The sexual relations are curiously described, with a touch of gallantry. The parents love the offspring, sympathy abounds, the mates are chosen and the union is a genuine marriage with mutual respect! The age was fond of exalting the 'natural' relations and accusing its own artificiality; it is easy to see how recklessly all the 'natural affections' are here transferred to animals. We begin to lose confidence in this writer of letters on animals. Yet apart from the exaggerations, many good things are said. In regard to the will, Leroy says it begins in self-preservation; it develops through curiosity into a will to know; finally it reaches the level of 'free will.' These animals seem to be precociously human, but Leroy makes an important reservation. In essence animals and men are not distinct; but animal life is simple and its needs, being few and easily satisfied, do not drive individuals to perfect their powers. There is no real social life, no articulated speech, no higher refinement, because no forces carry the animals to such complicated levels of existence. Needs produce activities, and without needs activities lapse. So Leroy came at least within sight of a theory of development based on use and disuse; he expressly says that the organism transmits acquired aptitudes, and he quotes examples of the way in which unused faculties lapse. Here we reach the main point against Reimarus. Instincts are not special and providential gifts; they are habits acquired under the pressure of needs and converted by use into dispositions or connate tendencies.

In spite of exaggerations Leroy made excellent use of his knowledge. The work of Reimarus 'smells of the lamp'; that of Leroy is a curious mixture of natural history and artificial philosophy. The vitality of Leroy's *Lettres* is well shown by the way in which his name recurs in the writings of Lubbock, Romanes, Darwin, and Ribot. In passing from Reimarus to Leroy we pass from the old to the new, from the spirit of the eighteenth to that of the nineteenth century.

PART

IV

PART

IV

Chapter Thirteen

PSYCHOLOGY BECOMES
SELF-CONSCIOUS

A. *Introductory*

In German psychology in the nineteenth century two main trends were discernible which are of methodological interest. Psychologists were very preoccupied with the self or soul as a possible object of study; they were also very concerned about themselves and the status and terms of reference of their developing inquiries.

Both these trends were traceable back to Kant. Kant himself made few contributions to psychology, but he initiated the climate of opinion of the nineteenth century by his attempt to make explicit the methods and presuppositions of science—especially Newtonian physics—and by his distinction between the phenomenal and the noumenal self. To take the last point first: Kant maintained that we have two selves—the phenomenal self whose structure and content could be analysed by epistemologists and whose outward manifestations could be studied in the discipline which he called anthropology, and the noumenal self which was a presupposition of experience but about which nothing could be known save in moral experience. This distinction led to endless disputations about whether such a noumenal self exists and whether it is a possible object of study. Herbart clung tenaciously to the idea of the self and sought to show that although it can never be an object of psychological study, nevertheless it must be retained as a metaphysical construct necessary as a presupposition for psychology. Beneke denied the necessity for this metaphysical starting point, claiming that the 'prime faculties' of man provide a solid enough basis. Fechner's fascination with the soul, not just of man but of the world as well, was the imaginative idea that permeated his empirical work. Lotze reintroduced the soul not simply as a metaphysical postulate but as an object of psychological study.

Kant's second contribution to the German tradition of psychology was his contention that science is characterized by mathematical as well as by empirical description. His celebrated fusion of the empirical standpoint of Hume with the rationalist standpoint of Wolff involved the aphorism that an empirical inquiry is as scientific as it contains mathematics. This was an extrapolation of Newtonian practice, and as a methodological prescription it had a profound effect on successive psychologists. It introduced the craze for measurement in psychology and reinforced the yearning for scientific respectability amongst psychologists which had started with Hume's *Treatise*. Thus Herbart made a point of claiming that psychology was a science and that it could employ the mathematical method. He tried to compile a kind of statics and dynamics of the soul. A mere description of internal phenomena was not enough for him; he tried to formulate mathematically precise laws of consciousness, although he accepted Kant's view that it was impossible to experiment on the mind. Fechner followed Herbart and, of course, is famous for his employment of mathematical techniques in psycho-physics. He established new methods of measurement and ushered in quantitative experimental psychology. The use of mathematics was to him, a trained physicist, the obvious way of giving precise expression to his panpsychism. Weber's law seemed to him to be an exact expression of the identity between body and mind. His number mysticism led also to the foundation of experimental aesthetics. The work of Fechner is an object lesson in the inseparability of science from metaphysics. Beneke shared Herbart's passion for making psychology scientific, but he preferred physiology to mathematics as a paradigm of scientific inquiry. Lotze returned to the Kantian position that there can be no exact science of our inner life. Although interested in details of physiology he ranked scientific description of fact as inferior to metaphysical intuition of essence.

Many would regard the legacy of Kant as a disaster for psychology. It perpetuated the rigid distinction between the outer and the inner with its accompanying assumptions both that there is a radical difference between what we know of our own minds and what others know of them and that overt behaviour alone can be scientifically described. The nemesis of this dichotomy was behaviourism on the one hand and introspectionism on the other. It also led people to believe that they were not doing science unless they were using mathematics. We have, therefore, the tendency developing for psychologists to explore all methods of obtaining quantifiable 'data' often without any fruitful assumptions to test. The combination of observationalism with the Kantian prejudice about mathematics encouraged the view that science progresses by the accumulation of measurements, the noticing of correlations or laws between the sets of measurements, and the final relating of laws under theories. Psychologists, increasingly self-conscious about the status of their studies, thought that respectable scientific theories would emerge if only enough mathematics were used in making the initial observations.

The main function of measurement in science is surely to facilitate the testing of hypotheses by expressing them more exactly.[1] Quantitative techniques enable scientists to answer precisely questions unearthed by cruder qualitative methods. But there is little point in going round measuring unless the object of devising such measuring techniques is the testing of interesting hypotheses. Measurement by

[1] Of course mathematics can be used most profitably also for the building of theories. But psychologists in the main have only used mathematics for making statements about observed phenomena. See Appendix A of J. F. Brown's *Psychology and the Social Order* for detailed treatment of this topic.

itself does not produce scientific hypotheses any more than do laboratories or grants for research. In the physical sciences a tremendous amount of preliminary qualitative analysis not only preceded the use of quantitative techniques, but also provided assumptions about the physical world which were incorporated in measuring devices. The lever law, for instance, which gives the relationship between weight and distance, enabled instruments to be built which permitted the fundamental measurement of weight in terms of distance. The clock is a similar device based on the velocity law. The qualitative experiences of daily life provided the necessary basis for the quantitative attack by Galileo on a variety of problems in the seventeenth century. But psychologists attempted to measure without sufficient qualitative knowledge of functional relationships which would both enable them to follow up relationships worth exploring and provide the necessary basis for measuring devices. Though Fechnerian psycho-metrics and the measurement of intelligence which started with Binet have developed enormously, neither type of measurement has made much contribution to the systematization of psychological theory. Fechner himself was passionately interested in measurement because, as a physicist, he wanted a precise confirmation of a highly imaginative metaphysical speculation. Far greater contributions were made to the advance of psychological theory by people like Freud and McDougall who did not bother themselves with premature attempts to measure than by those who were obsessed with the necessity of obtaining quantifiable data. The advance of science depends upon the development of imaginative assumptions as well as upon exact techniques for testing them. To invest in the latter without the development of the former is like buying a combine harvester for use at the North Pole.

B. Kant's critique of speculation

I. THE ATTACK ON RATIONAL PSYCHOLOGY

The work of Kant belongs, in respect of time, to the last quarter of the eighteenth century; in significance and effect it belongs to the nineteenth century and the twentieth. The different writings mark the various crises of Kant's life and, for the historian of ideas, his biography is identical with the record of his literary productions. These fall into three groups, conveniently classified as the pre-critical, the early critical and the later fully critical group. The pre-critical period is dominated by the rationalism of Wolff; the second period is marked by greater attention to the analytic work of the English Empirical School; the third period shows a synthesis of the doctrines of Locke and Leibniz, which then passes into the definite philosophy of Kant. When we come by this way to Kant's final position we inevitably pass out of the sphere of psychology into that of epistemology and it becomes necessary to consider, as a separate topic, the effect which Kant's philosophy has upon the concept of psychology as a science. To avoid confusion these subjects will be treated separately; after the statement of Kant's psychological doctrines we may return to consider the relation of Kant's conception of knowledge to the departmental science of psychology.

The most important feature of the Wolffian psychology, as a whole, is its doctrine that all psychic phenomena are degrees of reason. This doctrine, called dogmatic intellectualism, leads to the assertion that sensations are confused ideas; between sensation and understanding (or reason) there is only a difference of degree, and the whole scale of mental activities can be regarded as consisting of degrees of reason. In a word, sensation is to be regarded as confused or obscure understanding; reason is distinct or clear understanding. The language and the thought of this dogmatic intellectualism are reproduced by Kant in his earliest work: he thinks of the soul as a mirror of the universe, includes in its content the latent or unconscious perceptions, and regards the emergence of ideas out of sensations as a progress from confusion to clearness. Platonism, mediated by Leibniz and Wolff, is therefore the first tendency of his thought.

Though Kant rarely refers to the works of others, he was continually engaged in the study both of ancient and modern writers; when he does mention a name it signifies that he has found a distinctive contribution to his own progress. After the first preoccupation with Leibniz and Wolff, it is in Hume, Hutcheson, and Locke that his interest finds satisfaction. The famous reference to Hume indicates that the reaction began from the study of that philosopher's trenchant criticisms. But this was no more than a beginning, for Kant was at once driven back toward the position of Locke, and it is from Locke that he really makes a fresh departure. In 1762 Kant expresses the opinion that an animal may have clear and distinct ideas without necessarily attaining to reason; there is a fundamental difference between distinguishing things from one another and knowing the distinction between things. If this difference is established, it follows that we can detect qualitative differences in the contents of our mind, and we are compelled to separate the natural or physical process which results in a distinct image from the other logical activity which leads to the inner recognition of the distinction itself. Here we see the steps by which Kant returns to a position that involves the separation of sensation from reflection; we expect an immediate recrudescence of Locke's thought and terminology. Kant moved slowly. There was no impetuous rush into premature attempts at a system of thought. The situation was surveyed from various points of view, and the next most significant step was taken in his consideration of Swedenborg's works. The *Dreams of a Ghostseer* is an essay on limitations. If there are spiritual beings, beyond the range of common experience, there can be no reason for refusing to accept the statements of privileged persons about the actions and the mode of life of those beings. But then, where shall we stop? Kant saw that this was a test case: his mind begins from that point to dwell consistently on the question, Where shall we stop? The result was the critical philosophy—an elaborate statement of where one ought to stop. For Kant does not content himself with the question of the supernatural; he sees that it is not essentially different from the question of the super-rational, and if we include both these in the vague term super-sensuous, it will be necessary to examine the whole question of the relation between sense, reason, and reality.

The first result was a change in the idea of sensation, quickly followed by a modification of the opposition between sense and reason. The intellect is now regarded as the faculty which makes explicit that which forms the content of our sensuous life. Sense and reason are therefore mutually limited; there cannot be objects for sense which are never given in experience, nor objects of the understanding which have no relation to the senses. This correlation gives Kant a critical attitude, which we see applied by him to the idea of the soul. This is a typical example of the way in which an idea may be converted into a thing. Rational psychology was founded on the idea of the soul as an entity; in other words, as a possible object of a sensuous experience. Kant rejects this, and by so doing frees himself from the whole Platonic tradition. Descartes had never seriously challenged the idea of the soul; nor had Locke. Changes of method had never reached the point at which the question of any possible relation between a soul and a world of objects would be debated. Kant saw that it was not possible to speak of a soul which entered into relation with a system of pre-existing things. That consciousness which Descartes put in the forefront of his speculations is not for Kant a function of the soul; on the contrary, the new attitude is clearly defined by the assertion that the soul, in this sense, is in the consciousness, it is an idea. Hume had perhaps taught Kant that reflection is never actually a withdrawing of the soul into itself, nor is it a power by which the soul observes itself. As Hume confessed that when he entered into himself he found only the existing idea and not a permanent total self, so Kant admits the conclusion that experience is made up of experiences, that the idea of the soul is equivalent either to the substratum or to the totality of experience, and that it can for that very reason never be given in any single experience.

2. KANT'S 'ANTHROPOLOGY'

Here, then, is the real beginning of 'psychology without a soul.' In distinction from many who have used that phrase, Kant did not propose to deny the reality of the soul in the same way in which it had been asserted; his treatment of Rational Psychology is not dogmatic but critical. The first result was a clearer conception of the limits of psychology; in place of the previous inaccurate use of terms we are given clear distinctions. The science of the soul is called Pneumatology: the study of man as part of nature is called Anthropology; under Anthropology in general comes the specific department called Psychology. Since the critical philosophy teaches us that we only know phenomena, psychology as a science will be concerned with the phenomena or outward manifestations of the ultimate self. Psychology, as distinct from theory of knowledge, must accordingly be sought in Kant's work on anthropology (*Anthropologie in pragmatischen Hinsicht*, 1798). The title itself proclaims that psychology is now to be regarded as an empirical or pragmatic discipline only: since its particular sphere is that of inner phenomena, it may be called a natural history or description of the inner sense.

The scheme of the *Anthropologie* is adapted to the threefold division worked out in the *Critique of Judgment*, namely, knowing, feeling, and willing. These terms denote the least possible number of classes to which the phenomena can be reduced. If we speak of these as faculties, it is necessary to remember that they are such only as being unitary groups, not because each term stands for a distinct agency. In the sphere of knowing Kant distinguishes sense and understanding, the passive and the active aspects of that process. Kant diverges here into a defence of the senses which serves to warn us against under-valuing their importance or regarding them as an inferior degree of reason (§§ 8–10): they are like the people in a state who are under the ruler in the sense that they place themselves at his disposal, but not in any other sense 'inferior'—a reminiscence from Plato. The sphere of sense includes imagination, or the power of envisaging sensuous images; and intuition, or direct presentation. The senses are also to be distinguished as outer and inner. The outer sense includes the affections due to those stimuli which affect the organs of sense and also those which arise from states of the body, the 'vital sensations' of heat and cold. The addition of the latter draws our attention to the fact that Kant is carefully avoiding any expressions that would imply the action of outer objects on the soul. The older view, which always speaks as though things lying beyond the surface of the body produced effects inside that surface, is assumed to be made impossible by the work of the critical philosophy. We must no longer use the terms outer and inner as though they meant outside and inside the skin. The new point of view deals only with the distinct character of the different contents of consciousness; everything is really 'inner' in one sense, but there remains a pragmatic difference, a distinction in the significance of those contents according as they imply objective or subjective reference.

That which is technically called the inner sense is limited to the perception of time. While the outer sense has many immanent differences (sight, hearing, touch, taste, smell) and involves the form of space, the inner sense·is the mere consciousness of a time-order. As actually known the inner and outer sense always coalesce, so that time and space are the forms of all sense-experience; but Kant certainly regards the inner sense as in some way more fundamental. Incidentally it may be noted that neither space nor time is regarded as a product of experience; logically they are presuppositions and psychologically they are incapable of genetic explanation. This view of space is known as the nativistic doctrine and is open to dispute; the question as to time is not regarded as equally disputable.

Imagination is either productive or reproductive. In either case

it consists in the power of presenting objects for intuition when
they are not actually given, an activity without a stimulus. This
activity may either anticipate experience or follow it. In the
former case, which is that of productive imagination, the pure
intuitions of space and time are brought into play and enter into
the experience as it were from our side, i.e. as purely subjective
elements. This, needless to say, is an obscure point in the Kantian
exposition. In the latter case imagination has the complete experience for its material: its work is seen in the power of the artist to
form a mental picture of the object which he intends to create; it
operates also in the association of one idea with another upon
which depend memory and prevision; finally it is the condition of
those forms of association which lead to abstraction, classification, and analogical reasoning.

The second book of the *Anthropologie* discusses the feelings.
These are regarded as distinct; they are not merely abnormal
conditions of the intellect or in any other way to be reckoned as
part of the life of the intellect. None the less, they inhibit the
intellectual powers, and so far Kant can agree with the Stoics in
regarding them as undesirable. The principle of 'apathy' is
expressly cited with approval. But while pain and pleasure are
thus regarded as obstructing pure reason, the understanding
can unite the idea of them to the ideas of good and evil, and so
produce a quickening of the will. But, though useful, these
feelings remain distinctively pathological and distinct from the
feelings called aesthetic. Kant seems to have been uncertain
whether these two kinds, the pathological and the aesthetic, were
really species of one genus, but in the *Anthropologie* they appear
as such.

The closing sections on will, character, disposition, and temperament have no claim to be regarded as novel or important. In
fact, the degree to which Kant was steeped in the thought of the
eighteenth century is nowhere more obvious than here. This can
be said with no disparagement. The statement implies that Kant
took more interest than is usually recognized in the daily routine
of individual thoughts and feelings; that he was not ignorant of
the spreading interest in man as a social animal; and that these
lectures, delivered for so many years, may really have contained
what Kant himself regarded as the indispensable groundwork of
a constructive philosophy.

Kant's psychology, when thus picked out and presented separately, is seen at once to be decidedly meagre. But what it lacks in quantity is compensated by abundant suggestiveness and an almost unlimited power of generating problems. The meagreness is due largely to the fact that Kant takes psychology to be of little value; it is for him wholly empirical, and consists of an elementary doctrine of faculties amplified by the inclusion of such descriptive matter as might have been culled from novels or improving stories. Kant, who would quote no one as the source of his critical doctrine, frequently refers us to Fielding for his psychology! This is significant for two reasons: it shows how Kant limited his psychology to pragmatic anthropology, and it also incidently heralds the coming of a new psychology which shall be a science of behaviour. For Kant is a mediator: he considers that the pure intellect of the rationalists and the pure matter of their opponents are equally ridiculous; sensationalism is right, provided that it is the right kind of sensationalism—provided, that is to say, that it is critical.

The stimulation which Kant has supplied perennially for a century to innumerable writers must be held accountable for many discussions of his 'psychology.' We halt instinctively at the 'Kantian era'; we feel that a man who said so much ought to have said something on this great subject. Yet the fact remains that in reality he said nothing, and we reluctantly pass on. But if we now pass on we must change our direction. Again and again men have arisen who were not, properly speaking, psychologists, but were none the less factors in the history of psychology. Theologians, mathematicians, and doctors have all in their turn impinged upon the moving body of psychology and redirected its course. With Kant it was not discovery but criticism that gave a new direction, and in view of much that has been said it is necessary to define at this point the exact estimate of Kant which will be carried over into the last part of this history.

3. KANT'S IMPORTANCE

When it was stated above that Kant had nothing to say on psychology, the term was used with strict reference to the last years of the eighteenth century. At that time there existed two distinct points of view, one a formal treatment of the soul, the other a disorderly curiosity engaged in collecting the materials for an uncreated science. Kant's critical work was destructive of the former because it made impossible the deduction of the facts of consciousness from an arbitrary definition of the soul. The latter Kant supported by his *Anthropologie*, for he was not devoid of sympathy with inductive methods, and preserved to his death a keen interest in phenomena which readers who never look beyond the *Critiques* do not appreciate. But this anthropology Kant declared could never be a science. The reason for that statement was Kant's conviction that mathematics was the one and only type of true science. Granted that position, Kant's judgment remains true. It is frequently stated that Kant condemned psychology because it could not be made a science, and that Herbart did what Kant declared impossible, while Fechner's use of mathematics destroyed the last remnant of Kant's objections. The statement has no relevance. On the contrary Kant has been justified by the increasing recognition that mental phenomena are, as he said, in 'the flux of time,' and therefore inherently incapable of being brought under the laws of a timeless (mathematical) order of reality.

Kant's constructive works, including a *Rational Psychology*, were never written, and we are left with nothing but the preparatory criticism. The measure of his success and failure seems most adequately indicated by stating that his recognition of the variety of human experience was never brought under any such regulative principles as might be furnished by evolutionary and biological standpoints. Between the mathematics of the seventeenth century and the biology of the nineteenth there was an interregnum. Kant as a philosopher supplied new matter for thought by the invention of epistemology, but in many fundamental points he seems to be looking vainly for what had not yet appeared. Between the dogmas he could not support, and the deeper appreciation of phenomena which he could not reach, Kant remained motionless. Yet the negative attitude had its positive effect. Later generations looked back to Kant as a deliverer and acknowledged in him the beginning of two great ideas. Of these the emphasis on the practical reason and on belief may be regarded as the reaction of pietism against intellectualism, while the assertion of a synthetic activity as the central feature of consciousness was the preservation of what was best in Leibniz. The significance of these two points must be fully grasped.

4. PRACTICAL AND THEORETICAL REASON

(a) *The Practical Reason.*—In the *Anthropologie* and elsewhere Kant dealt with the objective aspect of conduct, the social order, law, and custom. As objects of various sciences these are phenomena; one phase of society succeeds another and the student arranges their sequence in the hope of extracting a law of their coming and going. If such a law could be formulated life could be reduced to a mathematical formula. But the actions which make history, though they can be taken in abstraction, are not abstract; they have their source in the living reality of the individuals. Kant therefore excluded the sphere of rational action from the domain of science as he understood it, that is to say from the domain of necessity. The metaphysics of freedom do not concern us here; the point of interest is that by this declaration Kant gave new life to the belief in personality, in that totality of the individual self which is called character and consequently for psychology recreated the standpoint of voluntarism which was in danger of succumbing to the mechanical type of analysis. In theory as well as in the significant use of the term *Gemüth*, Kant here revived the outlook and temper of the mystics (e.g. Eckhart).

For those who had grown up in the atmosphere of dogmatic religious teaching Kant's writings were novel and inspiring; the psychological treatment of religion in modern times goes back to Kant through Schleiermacher. But on the lower plane of morals there is less to applaud; in separating ethics from psychology Kant committed the error of exploiting 'pure' forms where no such purity exists. It may be very true that emotions are 'pathological,' but the point at issue is whether conduct is ever exhibited by an agent devoid of such emotions. This we must deny and face the paradox of Kant's work, which is the fact that he humanized religion and hypostasized ethics.

(b) *Theoretical Reason.*—A similar defect mars Kant's treatment of the theoretical reason. The root of evil in both cases is the tendency to treat the capacities of men as though there was some disembodied 'consciousness in general' about which the philosopher could make statements eternally and immutably true. The defect is less apparent here because Kant breaks new ground by attacking the problem of knowledge separately. This is what is meant when Kant is said to have invented epistemology. As a study of the structure of thought this science brought to light many valuable points, first and foremost being the idea that knowledge is not the product of ideas that arise out of experience and then systematize themselves in accordance with sundry affinities called 'laws of association.' On the contrary, Kant rightly declared that the mind must be regarded as a structure regulated by principles which are ultimately its own activities. Before Kant's time the psychologist was not unlike a physiologist who tried to explain digestion, without any reference to the organism, as a process by which various foods introduced into the stomach analysed themselves and distributed themselves conscientiously to their appropriate places in the organism. It was Kant who first saw clearly that such a procedure was wrong and that we must start from the mind to explain the ideas, not from ideas to explain the mind. Psychologists have, in most cases, recognized this merit in Kant, and all the modern work founded on the conception of the unity of consciousness is indebted to Kant. But for the rest Kant belongs to the logicians rather than the psychologists, and his theory is more important for discussions of validity than for the study of the mental structure.

The most difficult question to be answered is whether the Kantian *Critiques* are really based on psychology or on some other principles of analysis. The problem will be met again when we discuss the position adopted by Fries. Here we shall deal with a few isolated points. Kant asserts that sensation is a passive receptivity; this is modified later by the introduction of formative principles (time and space) and of imagination as a power which selects and groups the data. The actual contents of the mind are therefore really very complex products, and as no actual experience can ever give us the unformed data, as in fact the passively received matter has no existence apart from some formative activity, it is difficult to see what significance can be attached to Kant's conception of sensation. A modern critic would also point out that in fact sensations are modified by their relations; after great heat a moderate warmth seems chilly, and so through all the senses; there is a kind of self-arrangement which is not the work of the mind, and however far we penetrate there is never a mere chaotic multiplicity of states.

This serves to show that Kant had his limitations. He was

unable to see that his outlook was limited to the operations of reason; he still thought of the 'higher powers' as the sole organizers of conscious life. He attempted to modify the rationalism of this view by creating inferior powers called categories which were to be regarded as the indispensable preliminary activities of consciousness. These categories were not logical formulae; they were functions in and through which the structure of thought must be developed. But can such categories be found? If they make experience possible, is not the question of their nature a psychological queston which must be answered before we pass from the statement 'these are the valid forms' to the more ambitious declaration 'these are the necessary and only forms' of all thinking? It is true that Kant did not use the term *a priori* with any reference to time, nor did he imply a psychological priority, but the point in dispute is whether Kant's avoidance of the psychological was not his chief mistake and the cause of his failure to recognize adequately that a real development is not the same as a formal synthesis.

This problem is too large for our scope and must be left without further argument. Something will be added as our history proceeds. The idea that Kant's true basis was psychology will be found elaborated by Fries: the Kantian tendency to make Reason a thing apart will be seen abounding in the Hegelian movement: the emphasis on Will and the moral life will be reaffirmed by Schopenhauer. From all these something may be learned, and in some sense all nineteenth-century philosophy is a commentary on Kant. But even this galaxy of writers does not exhaust the sources; the real significance of Kant's attitude is not felt until we reach the modern attempts to get away from piecemeal experiences and secondhand physiology into the region of that indivisible consciousness which they all presuppose. But Kant, one imagines, would have smiled discouragingly at the idea of an experimental method for the investigation of thought and will: the times have changed.

C. Herbart's mathematical psychology

I. THE SOUL AND PHENOMENA

The tendency of the post-Kantian psychologists to begin by transcending the Kantian limitations is shown once more in

Herbart. Just as Fries adopted the general Kantian position with the intention of making the connection between the Self and its phenomena more explicit, so Herbart believes that it is possible to make metaphysics the basis of psychology. The influence of Kant is seen in Herbart's view that experience is the source of true knowledge, but experience is taken in a sense wide enough to include certain implied conditions. Of these the chief are persistence and unity; experience implies a unifying agency and indestructible elements. In this way Herbart becomes dogmatic in his teaching about the permanent which underlies phenomena and about the ultimate nature of the elements in consciousness. This position was unfortunate. Herbart agrees with Fries in tending toward anthropology; his interest develops along the lines of psychology, and the metaphysical presuppositions ultimately become superfluous.

Analysis, the method of science, requires plurality. The unity must therefore be equal to synthesis, not a 'pure unity,' but that complex unity which coexists with a plurality of parts, an organic unity. The analytic method is accepted by Herbart. This method gives us first the elementary psychic activities; then there is that complex unity of activities which we call 'self'; finally there is the bearer of the activities, the Soul as the underlying 'Real.'

A great many errors might be expected to enter in with this notion of the soul. But Herbart actually avoids them all. While insisting that metaphysically we must retain the soul in order to explain the possibility of unity and the origin of the first activity, Herbart explicitly affirms that 'the simple nature of the soul is wholly unknown, it is an object neither of speculative nor of empirical psychology.' Since the Ego is known as a system of activities, psychology does not require to go beyond these activities. As a science it knows nothing but phenomena.

Though it is not easy to put oneself into the position which Herbart takes, it is ultimately worth the trouble. For Herbart's general knowledge of philosophy enabled him to grasp the whole significance of psychology as a natural science and as a philosophy of mind. The tradition which he inherited spoke of psychic phenomena as phenomena or manifestations of the soul. But why should there be phenomena? If the soul thinks of its own nature (as the Comtians said), why should it ever do more than think itself? Why should it not either be a subject thinking a subject, or simply lapse into nonentity? To this question there is really no answer; the problem is attacked in the wrong way and the way of science is blocked. This result condemns the method; it is part of the work of science to find methods that will give results. If a beginning is made from the phenomena it is possible (Herbart thinks) to prove both the fact and the nature of the soul; this is the true metaphysic of psychology. To begin from the soul is a false metaphysical process.

Though Herbart does not fully accept Kant's attitude toward psychology, he cannot be accused of backsliding. Kant had intended to remove the 'soul' from the sphere of phenomena; but the gap between the phenomena and the unknown basis of the phenomena was filled in with faculties. Herbart pushed this process one step further; the faculties give place to a multitude of independent 'ideas' or activities. In short, the soul is reaffirmed as an actual datum, its whole content is made equivalent to the sum of persisting ideas, and these ideas are treated as the primary irreducible elements of psychic life. It is not difficult to understand how such a theory should give occasion for offence and receive very different interpretations. Lotze's direct criticism is deserving of all respect; but it seems to be based on some error. Lotze says, 'According to this psychology, if the soul was ever active at all, it never was active but once. It asserted itself against the stimuli which came from without, by producing the simple sensations; but from that point it became passive, and allows its internal states to dominate its whole life without interference.' Here Lotze speaks as a supporter of another kind of psychology; he misses in Herbart 'the eye which perceives the relations obtaining between the single ideas.' Herbart is not proposing to treat psychology in that way. Taking the natural sciences as his guide, he aims to reduce consciousness to simple elements and their combinations; it is of the statics and dynamics of the mind that he speaks, and ultimately comes to the idea of a mathematical psychology, which can dispense with the idea of the soul. On the other hand, it is clear that Herbart did not consider that he was dropping that idea. On the contrary, his whole theory of psychology depends on the doctrine that every single element is an activity of the soul. This is especially obvious in his view of ideas or presentations which are not transmitted from outside into the mind, but are reactions of the original underived agent. Lotze seems to miss this vital point in not seeing that Herbart's 'soul' is never the place in which events happen, but the actual agent partially manifested in each distinguishable activity. If this were not so, the idea that there is a constant tendency towards equilibrium could never have been elaborated by Herbart as it was.

The result is actually that psychology becomes empirical. The extent of this empiricism must be considered with some care, for at the time when Herbart wrote, 'empirical' might mean either that the psychic events were alone to be considered (as in English Associationism) or that psychology could be treated as a natural science. Herbart's position is midway between both these views. The postulate of the soul makes this psychology an applied metaphysic; and Herbart explicitly denies that it is possible to treat psychology experimentally. On the other hand, he thinks that psychology can be made an exact science, and to show this he invented his own peculiar mathematical formulae. No attempt will be made to follow that line of development; it was unique, and found no subsequent supporters. For it was not in principle the same as the later mathematical expression of ratios and differences which is exemplified in the Weber-Fechner law, though undoubtedly much encouragement for that later method was derived from this striving after exactness and scientific expression.

Phenomena are in perpetual flux; in other words, the most obvious thing about consciousness is its perpetual tendency to change: even though we try to retain one presentation, it slowly dwindles in our grasp. This general fact gives Herbart his starting-point. By an idea we mean the outstanding point, the summit or peak, on the surface of an ever-heaving consciousness. If we imagine a light shining on a sea of rising and falling waves, the analogy may assist us to grasp Herbart's conception of 'arches' and 'summits.' Every single idea travels, as it were, on the path of a semi-circle, from a point below the level of consciousness upward to its zenith; it then goes down again and gives place to another. This process continually goes on; it is the business of psychology to find its laws.

Returning to the question stated above, we look first for the starting-point of the whole process. The only active quality ascribed to the soul is the tendency to preserve itself. The separate activities are special cases of this general tendency to self-preservation. Our experience is constituted by an objective disturbance and a subjective reaction. The position is therefore realistic in so far as a real objective element is assumed, but idealistic in making the whole content of the resulting state of mind consist in a particular kind of inner activity. Herbart has taken from the English psychologists the doctrine that there are no innate ideas; from the same source he derives the idea that the variety of the inner states is directly due to the variety of external conditions; but he diverges from them in making the unity of the soul his ultimate basis and so avoiding the necessity of finding some bond for (atomic) ideas.

2. SELF-PRESERVATION AND THE PRINCIPLES OF MENTAL ACTION

Having attained both unity and plurality (two essential categories for all thinkers at that time), Herbart proceeds to develop the laws of mental action. A certain amount of energy is expended in every act of self-preservation. It is this energy that carries the presentation up to the summit; that is to say, makes it a conscious presentation. If a second disturbance follows, the total amount of energy is divided; what the second gains the first loses, and therefore as the second rises into consciousness the first dies away. This principle, applied to the whole diversity of mind, explains its perpetual movement and its perpetual self-preservation. No presentation ever disappears completely; it only becomes infinitesimal in respect of its energy, which is equivalent to becoming a negligible factor until some access of energy raises it again into consciousness.

We must deal leniently with this doctrine. Its value is great, if we regard it as an attempt to give an intelligible description of facts. In detail it has many defects. Herbart constructed mathematical formulae to explain the rising and falling of presentations. He seems to have thought in these terms, or in terms of architecture (arch, summit) where others would more easily think in different forms. But all are metaphors alike, whether they are terms of mathematics or of 'waves' or 'streams.' In spite of a vigorous beginning, the formulae soon dropped behind the requirements, and this phase of almost Pythagorean number-worship was in the end neither a help nor a hindrance. The most interesting point to notice is that the number-theory is here used to reduce differences of quality to quantitative measurements. The reason why one presentation is ousted by another is their incompatibility, their difference in meaning. But while every idea must have both content and activity, there is no sure basis for the conversion of degrees of difference into degrees of activity. The peculiarity of Herbart's doctrine consists in this very conversion; the logical opposition, as between affirmatives and negatives, is fused with the inner activity of preservation and put forward as an actual struggle. It may be true that we experience a strain in thinking that an object is both long and short; but the strain is not a measure of the energy of 'long' and 'short' as ideas. In the sphere of sensation this or a similar law might hold good; in the sphere of ideas as such, without reference to emotional accompaniments, it is a rash assumption. For Herbart it is fundamental, as his terms continually show. In fact, every mental operation is described as twofold; every presentation is both a presented content and a presentative activity. When the contents conflict, the activities are opposed; this is the assumed relation and the point by which the whole system stands or falls. Presentations are classified as similar, disparate, and contrary. Contrary presentations are (as activities) in conflict; they hinder one another, and one is said to be 'arrested' by another. Similar presentations fuse, and so reinforce one another. Disparate presentations (e.g. those of sight and touch) unite but do not fuse; they are said to be 'complicated,' and, as activities, they are co-operative.

The whole state of the mind is determined at any given time by the degrees of activity belonging to each element or presentation. Thus the elements a, b, c, d, . . . , according to their respective qualities, will be either clear or obscure, and they will stand to one another in different relations which can be measured as degrees of distance from the point at which they become relatively negligible. This point of least activity is called the threshold of consciousness. Below the threshold the contents exist with no measurable activity; they are not annihilated and they continue to affect the whole consciousness; they are not unconscious, but subconscious. Here a further distinction is introduced. When the contents of the mind attain equilibrium there is a static condition which would, presumably, continue if no fresh disturbances occurred. But the objects of the outer world continually enter in;

they continually disturb the equilibrium which tends to establish itself in consciousness; there is therefore a threshold for static conditions and another for dynamic conditions. If a presentation has been through the process of conflict and succumbed, it is below the static threshold and as good as dead; if, on the other hand, its energy is unexhausted and its obscurity is due to not having asserted itself, it is describable as below the threshold in a different sense: it is below the dynamical threshold. This distinction of statical and dynamical thresholds amounts, therefore, really, to a difference of point of view; the descending presentations are exhausted, the ascending presentations have the strength of their youth unimpaired.

From simple presentations we pass on to fused and complicated presentations. The principles are identical; the only difference is that, in experience, we must deal with masses of ideas, and consequently consider not merely the relation between a and b, but also between a and b and c, or a plus n and x. Collective presentations and total states now enter as factors, and the problem resolves itself into the relation of the Ego, as the totality of acquired mental contents, to each new element introduced. This relation is one of reception or opposition. The entrance of a new element constitutes a perception. If it is rejected it falls away; if it is received it is taken up into the existing totality and is said to be apperceived.

The term apperception is the mark by which Herbart is known to most readers of psychological works. It is also the most obvious sign of the general influence which Leibniz exerted over Herbart. It denotes two processes, distinguished according as the apperceived element is derived from without or from within. The process has the same character in both cases; a new element, relatively unstable, is taken up into an existing mass of presentations and thus incorporated in the permanent body of presentations. When the new element comes from without, the process begins with a sense affection which is at first only an event *in* consciousness; apperception makes it a *part of* consciousness, because the sense-affection rouses into activity the pre-existing Ego as a complex of presentations with which the new element must fuse, or else perish.

Under some circumstances the process begins with the upward movement of what is normally weaker and therefore repressed;

then an analogous reaction takes place on the part of the complex which is normally stronger, and a struggle ensues, ending in a new equilibrium. In sum, this is a doctrine of association, but the mere association of ideas as understood in the English school is qualified by the assertion of spontaneous ideas which represent an activity not recognized in the ordinary formula of Associationism.

It is obvious that in this description the term consciousness is used in two senses. In the wider sense it includes all psychic events; in the narrower application it denotes only what is actually known to be in consciousness. This dual use of the term is not an accident; it is an integral part of Herbart's system. Not every psychic event is noticed at the time of its occurrence; experience shows that some events remain latent until they get an opportunity of emerging into full consciousness. Also, there are at one time more factors in consciousness than can be comprehended in the scope of observation. From this follow several deductions. First, that some components of consciousness exist as a vague margin, like objects beyond the range of a light. Second, that apperceptive consciousness is equivalent to attention. Third, that the real meaning of 'inner sense' is explained by the fact that apperception is to perception as perception is to its external condition; for the perception is external to the apperceiving mass, and the inner sense is thus provided with an object for its activity.

Other points follow logically from this position. We observe that people have interests; the musician notices discords, the scholar notices a false quantity, the nurse hears the sound in the sick room when others do not perceive it. In short, all perception owes its power to a relation between its quality and the quality of the individual's dominant complex of presentations. Attention, then, is reducible to the activity of the apperceiving masses; that is what is meant by the inner activity of the mind when it attends. Attention is here analysed into (a) the activity of existing mental states and (b) the fact that apperception increases and develops the content of the presentation thus reinforced. It is a characteristic of Herbart's whole method that the activity of the mind should be resolved into the complex interaction of the elements. This principle is applied to the problem of feeling, of desire and of volition. Pleasure and pain are concomitants of the struggle between presentations; when the combination of forces through which a presentation becomes established is in excess of the requirements, there is a feeling of pleasure: tension between presentations is a source of pain. In view of the earlier theories, which made feelings into confused intellection, it is necessary to notice that Herbart makes the clearness of the presentation quite independent of feelings. This is especially the case when the source of unpleasant feeling is below the threshold; when, for example, we clearly perceive a fact, but have a sense of dissatisfaction about it.

Desire and volition, not being distinct 'faculties,' are resolvable into the activities of presentations. When a presentation, though opposed, gradually attains predominance, with accompanying feelings, it constitutes the state of desire. If action is possible, desire becomes volition. Since the course of life tends to create permanent complexes of presentations which usually overcome all others, there is a tendency to establish desires which are similarly permanent; these we call 'character.' This is the climax of Herbart's system.

In view of the numerous criticisms passed upon Herbart's doctrine of feeling, the interpretation implied in these statements may be in need of further explanation. According to Herbart, feelings are capable of being treated as one aspect of presentations. This is usually regarded as one more example of the doctrines which make feeling dependent on knowing. It is true that Herbart regards feeling as arising in the sphere of ideas. But he is not actually taking sides in the time-honoured controversy on the primacy of intellect over will, or will over intellect. He aims at a deeper unity. The idea is an activity; the soul is a unity that cannot be divided against itself, and resists the tendency to be divided between conflicting presentations. Feeling is the concomitant of this activity, inseparable from it. Here Herbart reminds us strongly of Aristotle's formula, that pleasure accompanies unimpeded activity. The emphasis on the ideas of organism and of habit recalls the same original, for Herbart does little more than develop the Socratic idea that true knowledge implies feeling, and feeling directly affects knowledge. This may not be applicable to all cases, but the principle is maintained by Herbart in reference to the education of the mind. In this connection it is true that the ultimate object is to produce a union of knowing and feeling. Habit means psychologically a union of ideas which no longer involves conflict and effort; Herbart's object is to explain how this state may be produced. He speaks elsewhere of feelings which arise outside the circle of ideas; here he is concerned with what we might call mental feelings. The truth of his doctrine might be illustrated largely from the pathology of the mind; here it is enough to point out that the kind of knowing out of which feeling is said to arise is not a mediaeval 'cognition,' but that which Herbart has already translated from passivity to activity. Whatever may be said ultimately of this view, it is not correct to speak as if Herbart was attaching the feelings to some passive form of receptive knowing. Most criticisms seem to labour under this misreading of the text. Yet on this point rests Herbart's claim to have provided a psychology specially applicable to education. It was the interest in mental growth and in the union of right thinking with right feeling that led Herbart to understand how closely the qualities of character depend on the complete fusion of knowing and feeling in one indivisible state of mind, evolving into the kind of clearness which is only attainable through self-expressing actions.

Kant had declared that there was a process of apperception in which the consciousness of self was united with consciousness of the given object. This point was taken up by Herbart as a problem; the method hitherto followed must be finally justified by its applicability to the problem of self-hood.

The essential feature of mental growth and expansion is described by Herbart in terms of apperception. Though the soul is a metaphysical postulate, it is not a psychological datum; all that we have given is the sum of presentations existing at any time; this is what we call 'self,' and it is this that we denote by the 'I' in 'I think' or 'I will.' If we say 'the snow is white,' our statement is to be interpreted, psychologically, as meaning that the snow-complex includes the white-perception as an element; this is a typical *objective* judgment. But the statement 'I think' looks different; it seems to be subjective and to imply a wholly different operation. If so, our psychology must split into two; the operations of the mind must be different in judgments of sensation from what they are in judgments of reflection; outer and inner sense must be opposed as well as distinct; and, ultimately, the 'I think' will take on a peculiar character, recede into the inner sanctuary of the soul, and be a fruitful germ of mysticism. To overcome this tendency is really the object of all the anti-Hegelian 'scientific' psychologists.

Since apperception is a process in which a relatively stable mass takes up and absorbs a less stable presentation, it will be obvious that the scale of apperceptive levels is without limit. This logical consequence Herbart accepts. Just as the snow-complex assimilates the white-presentation, so the ego-complex itself may assimilate a presentation; this is, in fact, only the general mode of psychological procedure converted into an apparent judgment about the self. But there must be a knower as well as a known; I cannot put my whole self outside myself and then take it back; the ultimate apperceptive mass must contain all the factors, subjective and objective, that appear in the psychological ground of judgment. If the term 'I,' used in a series of judgments, such as I think, I will, I feel, I speak, has any distinctive significance, it must stand for an apperceptive mass which is capable of assimilating these differences; it must therefore be the most permanent and the most general system of presentations.

This solution satisfies the requirements. The 'I' of our consciousness is explained, but not explained away; it is made intelligible within the limits of scientific psychology. Other advantages are also attained. The Ego is not allowed to lapse into metaphysics and become transcendental; it moves, it grows, and it changes; yet it tends to persist, to be relatively permanent, and to harden into a resisting force, just as character does. It does not convert itself suddenly into a substance, yet its inmost nature escapes us just because the attempt to grasp it is a process in which it operates, and by its operation moves on to a higher degree of Being. Herbart never forgot that a science does not limit its subject by defining it. The subject of psychology seemed to him to be unlimited; he anticipated that the greater part of it would remain for ever unknown; but he found in this no reason to despair of the science, for all sciences are in the same position. As the natural sciences are not adequate to the subtlety of nature, so the science of mind cannot make an immediate advance to the absolute limit of knowledge. The horizon continually recedes as the explorer advances; that is the mystery and the charm of progress, not its condemnation.

3. CLASSIFICATION OF MENTAL ACTIVITIES

So far we have been considering mainly what Herbart calls 'fundamental principles.' We now pass to empirical psychology, the second part of Herbart's *Lehrbuch*. As we require an analysis of the mind, it becomes necessary to find some principles of classification. The doctrine of faculties has hitherto furnished a kind of classification, and the subject can be formulated by discussing the value and the defects of that proceeding. A very fundamental defect is the tendency to observe only 'the social, the educated man, who stands on the summit of the whole past history of mankind.' Psychology has tended to neglect all but this ideal type, the rational man; it has dealt with *a* type, not *all* types: its method has been unscientific because it reaches only limited statements which it exalts into universal facts. If we take into consideration children, savages, idiots, and abnormal conditions of the average mind, the universality becomes very doubtful. 'There are no universal facts,' says Herbart; 'purely psychological facts lie in the region of transitory conditions of individuals.' The cut-and-dried system of faculties is therefore condemned by the very nature of the facts which it pretends to systematize. What can be done with such materials?

In the first place, observation gives us extreme points, such as animals and men. Psychologically these are desirable as extremes of sense and reason; the animals have the lower faculties, man has the higher. But the gradations are infinite; every activity passes gradually into another; so that the sense of animals is to some degree rational, while the reason of man is always largely sensuous. We can classify mental activities according to their quality as presentations, feelings, and desires. The degrees of higher and lower will be found in all these; the common distinction of sense and reason must be taken to indicate a confusion of two things, namely, the degree of development and the character of the activities. Herbart proposes to unite these classifications, which then give the following general scheme:—

	Presentation.	*Feeling.*	*Desire.*
Higher	understanding	artistic	rational will
	judgment	moral	passions
Lower	imagination	pleasure	instincts
	memory	pain	appetites

This picture of the mind is so far new that it may be said to abandon entirely what is usually called the doctrine of faculties. Its historical affinities are interesting. By looking toward all conscious beings and not thinking only of the rational educated man, Herbart puts hinself in the position taken by Aristotle. His idea of extreme and mean states is an obvious recollection of Aristotle. His general scheme, with its parallelism of theoretical and practical activities, shows the same source. For immediate inspiration Herbart did not require to go further back than Leibniz, to whom he owes, among other points, the ideas of continuity and activity. Finally, in rejecting the idea of pure reason and refusing to break the ascent from sense to reason, Herbart intends to show his opposition to Kant and his preference for the anthropological standpoint of the Greeks. Herbart shares with Plato and Aristotle the belief that there is no ultimate explanation of the soul's nature or being; he feels, as they did, that the infinite diversity of life mocks our little systems of classification, while the hope of progress drives us on to divide and unite eternally. The extraordinary range and power of Herbart's mind will be increasingly obvious as we describe his teaching. At this stage we can only indicate the way in which he goes back behind all the formalism of the preceding century to the fresher spirit that knew no scholasticism and no doctrine of faculties.

Before Herbart's time psychologists had combined the idea of a scale of activities with the idea of faculties; this fact is noted by Herbart and criticized. The systems to which he refers are— (a) those which take one basis, sensation, and present every activity as a transformation of sensation; (b) those which treat sense and reason as coexisting parallel lines. The objection to the first is that it can give no account of the way in which the higher activities conflict with the lower; in other words, it never explains the struggle between reason and sensuous impulse. This is a fact, and Herbart declines to follow a method that must ultimately exclude the phenomena of the moral life. The objection to the second is that it involves a faculty of Reason, for which there is no evidence. In this discussion Herbart adjusts his relations to empiricism and transcendentalism, thinking of Condillac and Kant especially. The ethical remarks appear at first irrelevant. 'The greatest evil,' says Herbart, 'is quite as little purely sensuous as sensuousness is pure evil.' Here, however, we have an important point. The manipulation of psychological schemes is rarely free from prejudiced suggestion. Herbart detects the motive which, from Plato onwards, led to the description of sensuous impulses as 'lower.' It is not only psychology that must be made scientific; ethics must progress to meet it. So long as rational conduct and moral conduct are identified, neither can be properly understood; in brief, Kant's idea of the practical reason will lead us astray if we steer from the first toward a will devoid of sensuousness. Herbart is ever on the watch for those cross-purposes which make false beginnings; with the science of the psychologist he combines the art of estimating psychologically the motives that have produced other systems.

At this point Herbart inserts another criticism which may be noted since it makes clearer the progress of his thought. Unreflecting thought speaks of the self or Ego as taking its material and then giving to that material its unity. Kant restated this common belief as a cardinal doctrine, declaring that 'all combination is a spontaneous act of the power of representation.' Herbart declares that 'everything like this Kantian assertion must disappear completely from the dogmas of psychology.' As we learned above, Herbart makes the elements do their own work; the Ego is for him the relatively permanent apperceptive mass of ideas; this notion of a 'act' is offensive to him just because he thinks of unification as a perpetual process, going on even below the level of consciousness, and declares the Ego to be a product rather than a producer of unity. If we do not imagine that we can analyse a given static Ego, but in place of that consider only the empirical data, we must arrive at the conclusion that there are no strict lines of division between men and animals or between higher and lower faculties.

If we are clear on two points, namely, that all things continually change and that classifications are only instruments of science, there is no particular reason for dropping the usual terminology. Herbart actually adopts the familiar scheme, and discusses presentation, outer sense, inner sense, reproduction, feeling, desire, and will. Omitting the commonly accepted ideas about these, we may notice the special points which distinguish Herbart's treatment.

(a) It should be noted that Herbart regards sensation as the material of experience; it is an organic process which passes into perception when the mind discriminates. The mere sensation is not analysable because it is either a mere bodily change or rises into the state of consciousness called presentation. All that we can do with sensations is to group them in classes.

(b) The inner sense is not indicated by any perceptible organ; it is assumed in order to explain our apprehension of our own condition.

(c) The most significant feature of the inner sense is the production of series, such as space, time, number, degree (intensive magnitude). These forms of perception are not innate or a priori; they are ways in which the mind relates one to another the individual perceptions. The difficulties presented by space are summarily treated by Herbart: as we can observe our own inner activities, we can abstract from those activities and think the relations without reference to the objects originally given in the relations. This is the origin of geometrical space, arithmetical numerations and all similar constructions.

The idea of series is important. Empiricism treats sensations as occurring in time and as sequent, thus creating an insoluble problem. For if one sensation gives place to another, how will the mind ever reach the point of having a plurality of sensations to compare or unify? T. H. Green asks, in reference to Hume, how can a series sum itself? In Green's sense of the terms, it cannot. But Herbart understood what was wrong with the empirical expressions and began with the kind of series that does sum itself. In the first place, Herbart does not talk about sensations, but about presentations. These are activities which overlap; as the first a is followed by b, it diminishes gradually; similarly b diminishes as c supervenes. The series, therefore, sums itself as it is created, for the last state C is equivalent to a plus b plus c, each element existing in its own relative degree of strength. Other series may be formed, such as l plus m plus n, p plus q plus r, and these other series may cross the original series if any one element is common to two or more, as e.g. f plus b plus g. Again, the relative strength of the different elements in a series varies from time to time, and some elements may drop below the threshold of consciousness. In such a case the series is shortened. These points taken together furnish a satisfactory explanation of (a) the formation of series; (b) the possibility of arriving at the idea of series as such; (c) reproduction, or the revival of past ideas from present states of consciousness; (d) processes of memory where the whole series of actual presentations is abbreviated and only certain elements of the series are retained.

The idea of series is used to explain the facts which gave rise to the doctrine of 'association.' Herbart sets himself to explain not only the reproduction of a sequence of ideas, but also the order of that reproduction. If we have first the idea A, this becomes a when displaced by B; the real union is therefore between a and B. The next state of consciousness comprises a_2 plus b plus C, and so on. Then, since a and not A is the real associate of B, if we start again from A, there will be no revival of B until A has become a. The order of reproduction is thus established by means of the ideas themselves and their qualitative relations. As this is a simple law of connection deduced from the unity of the soul, it makes the so-called Laws of Association superfluous; Herbart discards those laws in favour of a general interconnection existing continually in the whole mass of presentations and operating as we have indicated.

Feelings, that is to say all forms of pleasure and pain, can be classified as—(a) those which arise from the nature of what is felt, e.g. aching teeth; (b) those that depend on mental conditions; (c) mixed feelings. Here the second class is of interest, because it indicates the difference between desire and feeling. Desire does not necessarily arise out of feeling, for some feelings are caused by unsatisfied desires. Herbart detected a difference between feelings of pain, such as toothache, and feelings of tension or anxiety: he rightly noted that the feeling of ineffective effort (as in trying to untie a knot) may amount to positive discomfort; he failed to make any further analysis of such conditions. The acceptance of mixed feelings is a reminiscence of Locke.

Passions are 'rooted desires,' while emotions are 'transitory variations from the state of equanimity.' Emotions are often described as stronger feelings, but this is an error. The strongest feelings are often equable, as e.g. love of one's country. Emotions tend to make one's feelings dull; an emotional nature tends to insipidity. Herbart here anticipates the distinction now expressed by the use of the two terms sentiment and emotion; sentiment being the tendency toward emotions of a certain kind, emotion itself the active outbreak occasioned by some particular existing cause. It is also worthy of notice that the physiological theory is not rightly regarded as opposed to Herbart. Ribot has pointed out that Herbart (*Lehrbuch*, 58 (100)) speaks of laughter as an 'affection' which has a physical reverberation and reacts through the body on the mind. Further, this is asserted of all *Affecten*—emotions.

Desire is a tendency to action, either to attain the desirable or avoid the undesirable; or simply as a general tendency to action determined by the existing mental condition. Herbart here reproduces the Aristotelian scheme of relations between desire, deliberation, and will. This leads to the conclusion that reason is 'neither commanding nor law-giving,' and, as Aristotle and Hume had declared, 'the reason doth not move to action.'

Herbart regarded his scheme of mental processes as the right basis of ethics; he thought it was also eminently fitted to furnish a science of politics and a theory of 'the destiny of man.' In this respect Herbert was reviving the broad outlook of the Greeks and to a large extent consciously adopting and revising their doctrines. In the case of ethics he shows a persistent opposition to the ideas of freedom, and the supremacy of reason, which Kant had taught, or led others to teach. Those ideas are treated by Herbert as contrary to the actual processes of the psychical mechanism and irreconcilable with the idea of continuity. Freedom, in the sense of spontaneous activity, is always realized; but the progressive complication of ideas does not admit any sudden and disconnected assertion of one's 'self.' This follows quite logically from Herbart's identification of the Ego with the dominant mass of presentations. The theory of apperception involves the following consequences:—deliberation of the interaction of ideas or masses of ideas; will is the final stage of deliberation; every volition reflects the relation of the forces in the mind at the time of choice; character is the equivalent of persistence on the part of any complex of presentations, being therefore a habit of mind; an act of will as an event becomes an element in psychic development, since it can be presented, and no presentations are wholly lost. Herbart lays stress on the point that we have a memory of will; he desires to get away from the concept of will as a mysterious expression of a self lurking somewhere behind the normal processes of mind, ready to strike a sudden blow without any 'phenomenal causality.' In all this he is, of course, opposing the Kantian development of 'transcendental will'; he has a rooted objection to the transcendental. His emendations of the current psychology of conduct show the influence of Locke and Hume.

4. BEYOND PSYCHOLOGY

'Psychology,' says Herbart, 'will remain one-sided so long as it considers man as standing alone.' From this we might well expect an elaborate social psychology. But Herbart's development in this direction seems to have been warped. He objected to Plato's parallel between the individual organism and the State; in its place he proposed another which differs only because the psychological basis is different. In place of the Platonic conception of three main 'parts' of the soul and of the State, we have a multiplicity of individuals (presentations) struggling together, the formation of parties in the State (presentation-masses), and the determination of the character of a community through the character of the successful and dominant class. All this throws more light on Herbart's powers of imagination than on social psychology. At the same time there is truth in the idea that the individual has a tendency to shape his own character by thinking over and adopting the tone of the society in which he lives. This was the good point in Plato's view of 'assimilation,' and the doctrine of the *Republic*, that the temper of the community is at once the product and the maker of the individual's temper, was the point that Herbart retained as an element common to his own and to Plato's exuberant imaginations.

Lastly, Herbart did not flinch from a psychological description of the 'destiny of man.' Here again Platonism is very much in the ascendant; yet there is some foundation also, in the general system, for these last thoughts. It is a cardinal point in Herbart's system that no activity of the soul is ever lost again. Eternal life is therefore a possible idea; it is 'an infinitely gentle fluctuation of concepts.' No proof of this is given; the note is dogmatic: 'since the soul is immortal, the career of the individual man cannot be confined to the earthly life.' Since the condition of permanence is equilibrium, eternal life is a perpetual calm. 'The concepts of the child that has died young would very soon approach their general equilibrium, and so also the thoughts of the man of peaceful conscience, who is simple in his actions and desires, and not destined to any great change. On the contrary, no restless far-reaching mind, fettered by the world and suddenly torn therefrom, can attain the stillness of eternity otherwise than by a passage through violent transformations which, owing to entirely changed conditions, may be still more stormy and painful than those by which the passionate man is so often tormented in this world.'

The value of this passage as a theory of the state after death need not be judged; it is quoted here for the light it throws on Herbart's own mind. For him experience was the only ground of explanation. But he would never admit that everything can be explained. Mathematics he took as the type and symbol of exactness; but he knew that it was essentially no more than a principle of method. Metaphysics he regarded as indispensable, because, sooner or later, the limit of the demonstrable is reached and the mind strains after some hypothesis whose guarantee is the system which it makes possible. This width of comprehension and depth of insight make Herbart one of the truly great thinkers known to history.

Herbart's work exercised a persistent influence on many subsequent treatments of psychology. The immediate circle of the Herbartians included principally M. W. Drobisch, Theodore Waitz, W. F. Volkmann. Drobisch emphasized the need for an empirical psychology and retained the mathematical form of exposition. Waitz inclined to make psychology into a natural science, following Drobisch in this respect, but ignoring the mathematical vein. Volkmann's *Lehrbuch der Psychologie* is a monumental work covering the whole field of general psychology, and comprising historical sketches that show a wide and deep knowledge of the history of psychological theory. These works, however, offer no essentially new point of view. The next important move which takes us from the original Herbartian theory to a new phase was made by Lotze. Parallel with Herbart's work and in some respects closely akin to it was the reform of faculty-psychology made by Beneke.

D. *Beneke's restatement of 'faculty' psychology*

1. BENEKE AND HERBART COMPARED

Friedrich Eduard Beneke was a contemporary of Herbart. Writing in 1824 to Herbart, Beneke said, 'independently of one another we have both arrived at the conviction that if psychology is to solve the problems which have been raised, it must undergo a thorough reform.' This statement was not accepted by the disciples of Herbart; they would not admit that Beneke had followed an independent course, declaring that in all essential points Beneke stole his thunder from Herbart. To the whole sum of charges Beneke made, in his *Neue Psychologie*, a spirited reply which is worth considering in detail.

The facts of the case are simple. As Beneke said, Herbart and he both saw the need of reforming psychology. They both meant that psychology must be made scientific; both, without knowing it, thought that the term 'scientific' could only mean 'like one of the other sciences.' Herbart inclined to take mathematics as the ideal type and model his psychology on that science. Beneke leaned more toward physiology, talked platonically about the 'nurture of the soul' and drifted from that into biological terms when he had to consider functions. Both tacitly accept the old assumption that psychology can only be a science if it can be reduced to the form of some *other* science. But of the two Beneke seems to have chosen the better way of being wrong, and his defence of his doctrine against the Herbartians is a singularly interesting piece of polemical writing.

The defence begins with facts and dates; no man is wholly original, and he himself owes his mental furniture to all the books, teachers, and acquaintances from whom he has derived knowledge or inspiration. He names Schleiermacher, Jakobi, Rousseau, Tetens, Garve, and Aristotle; all these he had mentioned in earlier works as recognized sources of his own ideas; to them may be added the English school, Kant, Fries, and Plattner. Only after his acquaintance with these and when his mind was formed did Beneke read Herbart's *Introduction to Philosophy*. From that time he read and appreciated Herbart, but these facts seem (to Beneke) to disprove even the possibility of plagiarism.

Mere biographical details are of no interest apart from what they prove. The charge of plagiarism can be met another way, by showing that in reality Beneke has not followed Herbart. Taking up the individual points Beneke explains where he differs from Herbart. First, he differs in respect of the basis of psychology; he has not used nor wished to use Herbart's metaphysical basis nor his mathematical procedure. Secondly, he will not allow that any part of philosophy comes before psychology, for psychology is the fundamental discipline; this position he claims to have maintained not only as a theory but in practice, for he has based metaphysics, logic, the philosophy of religion and ethics upon psychology, making philosophy an organic whole in a way that was not possible for Herbart. Thirdly, Herbart is an idealist in psychology; he himself is a true realist because he maintains that in sensuous perception something is given us directly by things. Fourthly, the active element in consciousness is with Herbart derivative; Beneke makes it primary. Fifthly, persistence is asserted by Herbart for all ideas, but with the added qualification that the obstructed ideas survive below the threshold of consciousness; Beneke means by persistence an actual survival in consciousness. Sixthly, if the idea of association is found in Herbart, it is found also in Aristotle and the Stoics; Herbart has no monopoly of it. Lastly, Herbart has planned a reform of psychology, but not actually achieved it; he himself has planned differently and succeeded because of the difference. These, then, are the points which Beneke cites as distinctive of his work. We may now proceed to consider his teachings.

2. THE 'PRIME FACULTIES' AND THEIR DEVELOPMENT

The accepted starting-point for all philosophical disciplines was, in Beneke's time, experience. The word was common to all, but the understanding of it was various. For Beneke it means the course of conscious life, taken primarily at the level of maturity. If we take the ordinary man or the typical mind as the central point, we have also as points of reference the mind of the child, which is less mature, and pathological cases which are divergent from the normal. Contrast and comparison will enable us to analyse the mind, and a regressive method will furnish its history.

Men are infinitely various; the mature mind has a character which makes it unique. To explain this without unwarranted assumptions we must assume that the mental life is a system of activities and that the mode of action is from the first determined by the nature of the individual. The content of the mind is therefore due to the interaction of native disposition and circumstances. The native disposition is identical with the 'prime faculties' (*Urvermögen*), which are distinctive forms of sensation and movement. These 'faculties' are not separable from impulse and striving, so that mental life begins with a tendency to realize native powers and proceeds by assimilation.

Here we may pause to take stock of the results. The starting-point has been defined, and, while the soul is in no sense a mere receptacle for impressions or a *tabula rasa*, the requisite presuppositions are reduced to a minimum, including only sensibility, movement, and objects. The presupposition of objects is intended to mark Beneke's disapproval of Fichte's method, which he elsewhere declared to be the influence that had made Herbart go too far. The disciples of Herbart claimed that their position was established by 'experience.' Beneke denied this on the ground that the Herbartians could never really get back to experience at all; there was no road from their base to their goal. In this Beneke was right; it is always possible to go too far in the search for ultimates, and Herbart, by starting from metaphysics, showed that he had not fully appreciated the Kantian teaching or adequately learned where to stop. Beneke reforms psychology without transforming it; he explains phenomena without going beyond them or deriving their being from the earlier stage of their not-being.

This last point of method is the guiding principle of his explanation of the unconscious. The unconscious is not an underworld from which the conscious states arise by a miracle of resurrection. All mental states persist, as it were, in the same plane. But they disappear from direct consciousness in various ways. They may enter into more developed states in which complexity is represented by a change of quality; or they may persist beyond the horizon of actual thought. While many writers speak as though there was a scale of degrees of consciousness and it was possible to go below the zero point to the subconscious, Beneke regards this as an error. For the subconscious is then only a name for the vanishing-point and all below it, a Not-Being out of which none but the Hegelians could evolve the Being of real consciousness.

What, then, is the process of development which explains the passage from the simplest to the most fully developed states of mind? In the beginning there are 'prime faculties' which by nature determine the character of stimuli. The child turns to the light or takes pleasure in some colour; it retains an impression which is never wholly lost, for, if the same impression is received again later, it is not like the first. It is both another and a second impression; second, because the first survives into it. In course of time this procedure results in a definite consciousness of the impression, a true experience; the subsequent development is a multiplication and complication of these experiences. In and among these experiences as events there is a continuous unity which reveals itself in the consciousness of relations and the reactions of the mind as a whole, at each stage, upon the newly acquired elements. Throughout this process, which is described as a process in time involving real increments and not mere 'self-development' in the Fichtean sense, the outer experience and the unconscious area are continually sending in their contributions. These two constitute the 'beyond' from which the conscious life perpetually derives its matter. As Beneke speaks of 'faculties' as original data, so he speaks of new 'faculties' as continually arising. This language seems to have given unnecessary offence. By 'faculty' in its first use Beneke means no more than the unique character of the human mind, beyond which it is profitless to seek for a starting-point; analysis cannot go on to infinity, and the facts indicate that there is something distinctive about mind, else education would be vain. The child, says Beneke, differs from the animal, it has greater possibilities, and those possibilities are its 'faculties.' Similarly, as development goes on, the basis from which the person reacts must change; in other words, new faculties arise. If we are not obsessed with the idea that the word 'faculty' must indicate bad psychology, it will be obvious that Beneke's use of it does not prevent him from reforming the wrong idea previously associated with it. His statements then appear to require neither correction nor comment.

In the *Lehrbuch der Psychologie*, Beneke describes four fundamental processes. Of these the first two, namely, the initial process of sensation and perception, and the production of new 'faculties,' have been stated in the last section. The third is the process of reproduction as determined by the formation of 'traces' (*Spuren*). The fourth is the law of attraction or association. These will now be stated more fully.

The doctrine of 'traces' is one of the outstanding features of Beneke's psychology. On closer inspection there seems to be little novelty in any part of it except the name. After dealing with stimuli and the primary power of reaction, Beneke proceeds to show how the activity of the mind develops. As he is opposed to innate powers, he must substitute for this hypothetical store of resources a gradual acquisition of power due to assimilation. This is done by the supposition that every activity of the soul once aroused never wholly disappears again; it remains as a 'trace,' and it shows itself in the tendency of the mind to acquire specific modes of actions or 'dispositions.' These acquired dispositions take the place of the 'innate' ideas and are intended to explain the presence in the mature mind of what, in the language of physiology, might be called specific energies. Through these traces the mind acquires greater independence in relation to effects produced from without. Hence there arise new kinds of activity, such as the striving after what is not presented (desire) or the effort to remember; in general 'the trace is that which lies between the production of an activity of soul (sense-impression) and its reproduction' (*Lehrbuch*, 29).

Of the traces as such we are not conscious. They do not enter into consciousness, but they enter into the conditions under which we become consciously active. There is a natural temptation to think of them as structural changes in the brain and nerves, but Beneke refuses to admit that psychology derives any help from physiology. The body grows by assimilation; so does the mind. But introspection shows that the mind reproduces what it acquired before; it is not like a tree that puts out new leaves, for it puts out on occasion the old leaves again.

The independence now acquired by the mind is shown in another way. There is a persistent tendency toward equilibrium, which is attained by transferring elements. At a lower level we are to suppose that the stimulus absorbs the available activity of the soul. But as development proceeds and complexity increases, this is not the case; a certain excess of activity is produced and becomes mobile. For example, love and joy heighten the mental activity; as Beneke would say, these elements (or forces) are transferred to the side of the perception, and its activity is made more intense by this reinforcement. Conversely, hatred and sorrow abstract our powers from the object with which they are associated and reduce the activity by which they are presented. Here, indeed, Beneke seems to have fallen a victim to his own use of terms. Translated into the ordinary phraseology, this is clearly only a way of stating the facts of interest and attention, made difficult by the supposition of a plurality of invisible elements.

Here, as in many other points, Beneke is too anxious to achieve some striking expression which will show his opposition to Herbart. In Herbart's system the ideas are made to conflict and mutually repress each other; logically this should lead to mutual annihilation, though that is in accord with the letter rather than the spirit of Herbart's teaching. Beneke substitutes for that conflict of ideas his own theory of movable elements, to explain by external reinforcements the relative strength of different elements at different times. As a theory of attention this has some merit, and may be regarded as leading on to the position afterwards developed by Ward and Lipps.

The historical importance of Beneke's work is to be found in its opposition to all forms of transcendentalism. If this is forgotten his writings lose much of their interest. There is no longer much tendency to speak of faculties, intuitions or reason in such language as offended Beneke; we feel now that 'psychology as a natural science' is no longer a startling title for a treatise. The changes that have ended in the present situation were beginning in Germany when Beneke wrote his 'Textbook.' The remembrance of this fact reconciles us to his repeated refutation of innate ideas, the inner sense, pure reason; his own explanations of the psychic life are a continuous polemic against those terms and theories. As Beneke knew, the ground had been well prepared. For a counterblast against 'pure reason,' he could look to Hobbes; for the idea of 'reflection' he went to Locke; the whole history of eighteenth-century thought furnished materials for a new construction, and when we come to that construction it often sounds like an echo of English Empiricism. Beneke had no desire to conceal the fact that he meant to use the English psychology to refute German idealism; the outcome of this effort was a psychology obviously compounded of English analysis and German synthesis, a compound that was in its day the quintessence of sober speculation.

Beneke, as we have seen, began with simple elements, not simple ideas but (after the German manner) original forces. The soul, he said, has powers; in fact, it is no more than a totality of powers. If we ask what these powers are, the answer is given in a list of activities; we know the activities, and there could not be an activity without a pre-existing power. After this nothing remains but to describe the behaviour of these powers and write a life of the average soul. Sensations are described and we learn their nature and relative importance; then comes Reproduction, and we are told that 'memory' is not a faculty, it is simply a power of reproducing ideas dependent upon the fact that 'traces' were left behind after the original experience. Beneke seems quite satisfied with showing how wrong it is to say that we came into the world bringing our memories with us; psychologically, at any rate, one cannot begin life with a past. Beneke's own explanation is robustly empirical: it is the doctrine of the Association school with proposed amendments. The objection, says Beneke (*Lehrbuch*, 86) to the usual theories of Reproduction is that they are much too general in their statements; their laws are such that no explanation is given of the actual results, as, for example, when we are told that a revival is due to association by similarity, as if one idea were never 'like' more than *one* other idea. Something better than this must be attempted.

When an experience lapses from consciousness it loses something; to bring it back again that loss must be supplied. This is the fundamental explanation of all reproduction, but it would not seem to explain much unless further developed; it seems indeed to have been underrated, being at least a thoughtful attempt to solve the most difficult problem in psychology, and for that reason an elaboration of Beneke's statements may be admissible.

In the case of sensation the best result is attained when the stimulus is exactly adequate to the capacity. This adequacy is not equivalent to a fixed quantity; it is relative to the actual capacity at the time. If a person has been long in the dark, a small amount of light may be dazzling, if a sound is expected for a long time it may be heard, though a much louder sound would usually go unnoticed. These observations, interpreted psychologically and not physiologically, suggest the convergence of forces upon the given stimulus, causing it, in consequence, to come over from the not-conscious to the conscious area of the soul. An objective stimulus and a portion of the not-yet-conscious psychic material are regarded as being in the same position; they are both, for the time being, part of the not-self. The objective stimulus excites latent powers when it produces a psychic result; something goes out to it and qualifies it for conscious actualization. Similarly, when an idea is out of consciousness, it may be reinforced from the existing field of consciousness, and so brought over into that field. Analogies in this kind of subject are necessarily misleading; but, as Beneke says elsewhere, we are compelled to use doubtful parallels to make these matters intelligible at all. Here we might use the example of a system of lights dependent on one main source of strength, gas or electricity; as one is turned down the others grow brighter. The changes of consciousness are a fact which we cannot hope to explain fully; the only question is what explanation is to be preferred. Beneke's view is that the elements are qualified by relations such that one rather than another is affected by every change. If an accident in the street makes me forget that I have urgent business on hand, when the excitement is over the forces of the mind will again converge upon the supposed thought and raise it to consciousness.

The advantages of this theory are twofold. The fault of the ordinary associationism lies in joining together particular ideas; Beneke's theory admits the reproduction of all ideas at all times through any adequate transference of forces. The fault of Herbart's method lay in making the elements too individual and resolving the mind into a collection of ideal forces. Beneke's view treats the single presentation as a function of the total psychic activity. The difference between Herbart and Beneke is probably not so great as Beneke liked to think; yet something is here gained by treating the soul as a moving system of forces rather than a place in which separate forces struggle together.

Reproduction is the central theme of Beneke's psychology. If that has been satisfactorily explained, memory and recollection are successfully withdrawn from the list of ultimate faculties. Intellect and reasoning can be explained on the same lines by showing that groups and series of ideas tend to come into existence and fuse into concepts. Judgments are not operations of a super-sensuous 'Reason,' but express the psychological relation between an individual object of thought and the series or group in which it is placed. Such a judgment as 'I am here' implies no intuition into a metaphysical Self. Its psychological ground is a group of ideas fused into the concept 'Self' and made to converge upon one intensified element. As the intensified element is variable, the whole group tends to become independent of these special convergences; thus the *abstract* conception arises, not being abstracted in reality, but rather differentiated through continually having its identity repeated with partial variations.

These cases, of the Self and of abstraction, show what Beneke means by saying that his psychology is the basis for metaphysics and logic. He was still more concerned to make it serve as a basis for religion, ethics, and education. To explain how this was done we must briefly consider his treatment of desire and will. The activity of the soul is made the starting-point; the soul is essentially active, for it is force rather than substance. The effort comes before the presentation (*Lehrbuch*, 167), for the soul strives from the first to realize its own primitive powers. A sense-impression, as it ceases to employ a primary force, sets it free. Collateral with those liberated forces there is normally uneasiness, due to the existence of unrealized and therefore unsatisfied powers. The former are strivings *after something*, wants associated with definite satisfactions; the latter are blind strivings which (being un-attached and by definition mobile forces) automatically converge on the strongest of the allied psychical forms. A striving or conation is therefore either a specific want or a vague unrest. The latter state leads to actions that are suggested either by others, in the case of children and empty-minded persons, or by an idea which is naturally strong. The former case is that of imitative action; the latter is illustrated by the process of waking from sleep, when there is first a general activity and then consciousness of the last occupation or of some important business.

According to Beneke the fundamental activity passes into conscious effort when the stimulus is no longer adequate. If an experience is pleasant, when it begins to cease as a full stimulus it gives up part of its energy, and this part is converted into remembrance of the pleasure or into desire. There is no absolute division between these two, and in general Beneke recognizes no opposition between knowing and striving such as the earlier writers made between passive and active powers. All striving, therefore, is presentative in some degree, if the mind is mature; the laws of the presentational consciousness can be directly applied to this sphere, and the principles of aggregation, complication, and dispositions reappear as explanations of moods, inclinations, and passions.

The passage from conation to action affords some difficulty. In the sphere of action there is a difference between involuntary and voluntary movements; involuntary movements are due to a capacity for action and an adequate stimulus from outside;

voluntary actions, if they are not to be consigned to some mysterious 'Will-Force,' should be analysable into similar factors. Beneke rises to the occasion. The idea of an end as desirable is equivalent to a certain degree of effort; so far, then, the available force is exhausted, and there is no reason why the desire for an object should not be satisfied by the idea of the object. But other 'primary faculties' are present, and if these are free they transfer themselves to the idea of the end, swell the stream of forces and produce, over and above the ideas, the appropriate actions. This exposition is offered as satisfactorily explaining the origin of desires, the fact that desires and tendencies often remain latent for long periods of time, and that at different times different inclinations break out into action. The theory claims the merit of treating all these phenomena as events reducible to common principles of natural forces without the special intervention of new faculties.

We cannot follow Beneke into all the details of his work. The reader will now be prepared to hear that productive imagination and thought are equivalent to new combination rather than creation of elements; that will is a desire combined with a presentational group or series; and that the whole range of conscious activity, up to the achievements of genius, can be analysed as complex forms of conation and representation. A third main class of phenomena now calls for consideration; in addition to knowing and willing there is also feeling. Feeling is immediate consciousness; it is either consciousness of a state of the inner conditions, or it is due to a relation between those conditions and the idea of some other possible condition. Feelings are a distinct class of phenomena, but not a distinct class of activity; they are a kind of direct valuation of activities. As we have seen above in the case of pleasure, the memory of pleasure, desire for pleasure and feeling of pleasure are really variations of the same act. The classification of the feelings can therefore be based on the four fundamental processes. (1) Feelings may be due to objective causes (the stimuli) as in the case of feelings of contrast, change, etc. If the previous subjective state is a factor here, we get feelings of novelty, astonishment, etc. (2) A second class of feelings has for its ground the 'primary faculties' and their relations to the stimuli. Feelings of liveliness and excitement are of this kind, and the whole range of aesthetic feelings; for we *feel* the beauty of an object in proportion as we are conscious of inner states which we project into that object. As a deduction from this, it follows that different people are capable of different feelings in relation to the same object; and development changes our aesthetic values; the child finds in her doll her own moods; the adult has other interests which give a new character to all joys and sorrows. (3) The fusion and congruence of ideas is the ground for another type of feeling. We have a feeling of clearness when there is uniformity of action among presentations and 'traces'; if the number of elements is inadequate we feel obscurity, and if elements of different kinds are mixed the result is a feeling of confusion. A feeling of worth, combined with a feeling of agreement between individuals in respect of values, constitute the moral feelings. This disposes of the 'innate faculties' by which the 'moral' had been kept separate from the natural. It is hardly necessary for Beneke to tell us that he is opposing Kant. (4) The union of unlike elements also gives rise to many feelings, e.g. the feeling of inclination toward another person, arising from unanimity in opinions and purposes. These are the four roots of all feelings; the growth and development of the feelings follows the course of psychic growth in general, that is to say there are traces left by feelings, aggregations of like feelings, dispositions and all the other processes which end in the fixed character.

E. Schopenhauer and von Hartmann

1. THE SOURCES OF 'WILL' PSYCHOLOGY

On the philosophical side there were many sources from which might be drawn inspiration for a fresh exaltation of the Will. Leibniz obviously could be drawn upon for the conception of impulses preceding and determining clear consciousness. Reid was actually taken by some to have taught a form of intuitionism which could be called psychological vitalism; and Hume's reduction of mental life to a sequence of beliefs implied the priority of active belief over intellectual calculation. On the scientific side the vitalism of the school of Montpellier (Bordeu, Grimaud, Barthez) was opposed to both mechanism and Stahlian animism; life, they declared, was not inexplicable either as mechanical or intellectual (i.e. consciously teleological). For this school life and instinct were closely connected; both were forms of spontaneity, aspects of the mystery of life; and instinct played in natural history the part which was assigned in physiology to the vital principle. Schelling made this spontaneous life-principle cosmic, a development greatly assisted by the discovery of electrical phenomena and the misunderstanding of 'animal magnetism.' The romantic tendency of the period was a source of strength for all theories of this kind. Genius was felt to be something over and above mere individual activity, something expressive of the cosmic in man. Against the romantic tendency to drag in a cosmic spirit two other factors were operative. One of these was the recognition of centres of consciousness lower than the brain, an idea already met in Cabanis and more fully evolved by Bichat. The other was the evolutionism of Lamarck, which gave a racial history to individual characteristics and made the development of the organism dependent on psychic impulses. Combining these various but convergent thoughts, it is easy to see that it was possible to regard the thoughts of the individual as a narrow sphere of intellect resting on a broad basis of unconscious growth and construction. If to this is added the interest in Eastern philosophy which began from 1800 and for a time made the Vedanta quite the latest thing in philosophies, we have the sum total of the external factors which controlled the work of Schopenhauer. The internal factors of upbringing and disposition cannot be ignored in the case of one who thought philosophy was a function of temperament, but they are to be found in the accounts of Schopenhauer's life.

2. SCHOPENHAUER'S REINSTATEMENT OF THE WILL

We should not require to' discuss Schopenhauer if we had nothing to mention except his speculative metaphysics. Of that part of his work little need be said; the Kantian concept of the self as the source and bearer of phenomena is converted into will; the indefinable is thus defined, but as this is not volition, being the presupposition of all volition, it is soon declared to be Will-in-itself, and so passes out of the reach of psychology. Though the system constructed by Schopenhauer thus tapers away into impossible concepts, its point of view brought into relief some fruitful ideas. The philosophic mind tends frequently to value the processes of thought overmuch; it puts its view of knowledge in the place of actual activities and regards rational conduct as necessarily a product of reason. But the character of an action is not necessarily the same as its cause; instinct, for example, may lead to action that is rational in its methods and results, though not in origin. The relation between intelligence and intelligible conduct is not a known quantity, but a problem.

If Schopenhauer was hasty in asserting that Will was the right name for the ground and root of all things, he was freed by his own act from the overestimation of intellect. The phenomena of animal behaviour suggest (to any but a Cartesian) that there may be forms of action that achieve rational results without conscious processes of reason; below the animals there seem to be various degrees of life in which activity is less and less associated with intellectual processes, until at last the line is crossed and we come to the inorganic and to simple motion. This inverted evolutionism moves from intelligence to force. By calling force 'blind will' it obscures its illogical transition, but cannot wholly veil the movement. We cannot get back again from force to will, nor from the blind cosmic will to the individual act of choice. Yet, for all that, there may be some profit in the point of view; and it may be admitted that Schopenhauer has given a new impetus to the search for the relation between the span of conscious purposes and the obscure factors that dictate our choice. A summary of the strong points in the position will show how far this attitude is worth considering.

The doctrine that we only know phenomena is not rejected by Schopenhauer. Normally we have before us in thought only a part of the total possible contents of the mind. Knowledge is thus a limited part, a section of the whole being that lives and acts. The whole self, if it has an active unity, is identical with the whole sum of forces that drive us on from moment to moment. In other words, there is an impulse that escapes our notice, continually emerging into consciousness, but as a whole remaining below and beyond the span of intellectual comprehension. As some had declared the 'Thing-in-itself' to be the organism, Schopenhauer declares it to be the vitality resident in the organism. His view is thus biological, where it is not merely metaphysical; when he proclaims his own originality he is justified if we think only of modern tendencies, but in everything but its language and its excesses this view is a restatement of Aristotle's doctrine of the fundamental conation, persisting through all the scale of organic life, variously combined with and modified by corresponding degrees of conscious realization.

Metaphysics apart, we owe to Schopenhauer an important element in modern thought, the restoration of the will. The recognition of the will has steadily grown since he wrote his most famous work; the view flourishes now in the various theories of the will to power and the will to believe. But we must pass from this subject because Schopenhauer never descended from his loftier speculations to consider the will in a scientific psychological manner. Instead of that, he made speculative excursions into topics closely allied to his main theme and furnished new suggestions for the psychology of ethics and aesthetics.

The historian of philosophy finds Schopenhauer's system dull; it is infected with Eastern nihilism, and may be criticized as based upon a confusion between will and intellect. The psychologists, such as Ribot, find in Schopenhauer neither system nor dullness; they forgive him his metaphysics and dwell admiringly on his insight into nature and his subtle analyses. The whole trend of Schopenhauer's interest is toward the most fundamental impulses of the animal nature. With none of the cynicism of the eighteenth century he takes up the theme of love in the frank spirit of the unsophisticated Greek. Plato, in the *Symposium*, had sketched a theory of sexual attraction and hinted that it owed its strength physically to the nature of human beings, metaphysically to the purpose achieved through its agency. Aristotle ranked the sexual impulses with the desire for food and drink, a triad of innate forces which permeate the whole structure of the rational being. Those who still think of intellectualism as the real psychological doctrine of the greatest Greek thinkers might reflect for a time on the place they gave to the passions when they spoke of the earthly life and not of the last things. This lost stream of naturalism, after centuries of subterraneous persistence, wells up again in that essay which Schopenhauer called his 'pearl.'

At this point we emerge from the metaphysics to the full light of experience. When he is of most value, Schopenhauer stands exactly where Kant stood; his statements refer to 'phenomena,' and his position is 'anthropological'; he does nothing to solve his original problem, because his ultimate 'Will' is a blind spot; he derives nothing from his metaphysics except a guiding principle that might have been reached from observation, and his views on the departmental topics of ethics and aesthetics can be accepted for their real worth, with no reference to a cosmic Will.

3. VON HARTMANN AND THE UNCONSCIOUS

The name of Eduard von Hartmann (1842–1906) is usually linked with that of Schopenhauer, though Hartmann regarded himself as having neither master nor disciples. The only work by Hartmann which is directly and exclusively concerned with psychology is *Die Moderne Psychologie* (1901), a review and criticism of the chief psychological writings of the nineteenth century. This is a work full of erudition and very instructive. It is like most of Hartmann's writings in being frankly personal, and undisguisedly written to show how much psychology has lost by not using the author's doctrine of the Unconscious. For Hartmann the Unconscious is the fundamental active principle in the universe. It is not identified, as by Schopenhauer, with the nature of will, but is a synthesis of will and intellect, a creative force in which resides the principles of construction, and on which, therefore, depends the meaning of all creation. In this way Hartmann makes teleology fundamental, a point which makes easy the statement that instinct is action that embodies a purpose, though without knowledge of the purpose. Into the metaphysics of the Unconscious it is not our present business to inquire, but there are certain respects in which this point of view is vital to psychology, and later developments will be made more intelligible by a statement of the essential details.

Though to some of his contemporaries Hartmann appeared to be wholly original, two-thirds of the doctrine of the Unconscious was already almost a commonplace. Confronted with a bitter opposition, Hartmann was shrewd enough to realize the advantage this gave him. He points out that there are three kinds of 'unconscious' reality. First, there are the physiological processes, which the doctrine of reflex action among others had made important. Then, second, there are the psychic processes which do not come into the focus of consciousness; and these, too, were more than ever recognized. Lastly, in distinction from this second or 'relative unconscious,' there is the absolute unconscious. Hartmann argued very effectively that the first and second were widely acknowledged, that so far many people were actually incomplete followers of his doctrine. He argued also that science favoured the first two meanings of the Unconscious, and that by accepting the third philosophy and science would be forever united. The immediate response was very small, but as time progressed Hartmann was not only read by the general public which supported him at first, but also granted a hearing by more competent audiences. In the present state of affairs no one is anxious either to reassert Hartmann's doctrine or to deny that he powerfully influenced the development of nineteenth-century thought. Whatever Hartmann said always came back to the one and only essential conclusion—the Unconscious must be accepted. And it has been accepted. Some writers almost apologize for using the term 'rational.' The old habit of putting 'clear ideas' in the foreground is almost obsolete. We are told that men live by impulses; that actions express the efforts of a vital energy which moves darkly on the wings of heredity through the generations of men; that we do not act from conscious reasons, but rather construct reasons to explain what has been done in and through us. The soberest psychology of the twentieth century is leavened by these ideas. In the analysis of conduct, normal or abnormal, the idea that consciousness does not really act, but rather serves to recognize and appropriate the actions of an unconscious force, is everywhere to be met. It is true that Aristotle said, 'the understanding moves nothing,' and Hume repeated the idea in the statement that 'the reason doth not move to action,' but it was Hartmann who elevated these phrases to the dignity of a cosmic interpretation, and, by sheer force of wide application and manifold repetition, made them subtly penetrate or openly dominate the minds of men. We cannot deny that Hartmann was right in his antagonism to 'professorlings.' Both Schopenhauer and Hartmann were anathema to the typical lecturer, and both have come to be regarded as in some way expressing a phase of experience which is better known to the heart than to the head. If we feel that the truth has been guessed rather than expounded, if we grope blindly for something tangible to formulate and tabulate, but only end with a conviction that eludes the categories, this is perhaps the natural outcome in a sphere which is implicitly devoid of logic. The same is true of Nietzsche, who also belongs to this group. He, too, has been proclaimed as one of the great psychologists, and much that he has said is a real contribution to the analysis of the human mind. It is at present one of the most significant paradoxes of psychology that every attempt to define it recoils from the impact of some historical antithesis. Descartes and Pascal, Hegel and Herbart, Hartmann and Wundt—what phrase that has any but the vaguest connotation can spread itself over all these claimants?

F. Fechner's experimental pan-psychism

1. FECHNER'S INSPIRATION

The study of Fechner's life is one of the most instructive ways of following the progress of thought in the nineteenth century. Born in 1801, Fechner lived through all the vicissitudes of European science which occupied the middle of the century; he died in 1887, the spectator of a new world of ideas. Leipzig was the city in which Fechner spent his life as a student—that is to say, his whole life after 1817. His career began with poverty and the study of medicine. The latter ended in disgust and such complete academic success that Fechner realized the degenerate state of his chosen profession. Meanwhile poverty led the young student to make translations of French scientific works. In 1820 Fechner's mind was filled with the dreams of the 'Naturphilosophie,' and inspired by its cosmic outlook. In 1824 he had completed his translations of Biot's Lehrbuch der Physik and Thénard's Chemistry, and asked himself whether the 'Naturphilosophie' could have furnished a single one of the facts discovered by the method of the French school. In this, as in many other points, Fechner's experience was the experience of Germany in miniature; the land of Schelling and Hegel looked to France as the complement and antithesis of its own speculative mood. At this stage Fechner became interested in physics, and wrote some valuable treatises on electricity. The transition from physics to physiology and psychology was made in 1838-1840, when the problems of colour vision were subjected to an experimental treatment.

The work of these years ended in the nervous collapse and almost complete blindness which obstructed or wholly prevented all further undertakings until the end of 1843. When he resumed his duties as Professor, Fechner devoted most of his time to speculative problems. As early as 1836 the life after death had been the subject of a work issued under the pseudonym of 'Dr.

Mises,' but the publication of *Nanna* in 1848 marked the full development of that cosmic philosophy which was always united by Fechner with the minute detail of experimental research. In 1851 appeared another exposition of this cosmic thought, the *Zend-Avesta*; in 1855 the doctrine of atavism was defended against speculative philosophies of nature; lastly, in the year 1860 the *Elemente der Psychophysik* was completed. During the remainder of his life Fechner was engaged chiefly in a study of the principles of aesthetics and in defending the doctrine of the *Psychophysik*.

Looked at from the point of view of contemporary history, Fechner's mind is a result of two very distinct influences—the romantic philosophy of the post-Kantian school and the scientific development of the second quarter of the nineteenth century. Even the psycho-physical standpoint is an outcome of the '*Naturphilosophie*'; it is a concrete instance of that ultimate unity of the sciences which the doctrine of an Absolute postulates. To Fechner, as we know, the idea came as a revelation. Lying in bed on the morning of the twenty-second of October, 1850, he saw the vision of a unified world of thought, spirit, and matter linked together by the mystery of numbers. So it was, perhaps, that Pythagoras saw the quality of sound transformed into a measurement! The distinctive feature of Fechner's insight was its power of sustaining research; it grew by induction, and did not exhaust itself in mere abstractions. But the same expansiveness of mind showed itself in other directions, in *Nanna* and *Zend-Avesta*. Here we see the mystical spirit of the '*Naturphilosophie*' asserting its claims against the analytical tendency of the eighteenth century. Mathematics and mysticism are not so very far apart by nature; Herbart is a good example of the close alliance between metaphysics and numbers. Pythagoras, Plato, and Proclus illustrate in their different ways the deep-rooted sentiment that the secret of the world is to be grasped by the mathematician; in numbers they saw the inner unity of immediate practice and ultimate reality. Hegel became more and more addicted to the study of Proclus, not altogether to his advantage. From Proclus it is a short step to the philosophy of the East, the original home of mystery and numbers. Schelling, Hegel, and Schopenhauer all exhibit tendencies that seem foreign to the course of European thought; they recall the vague spaciousness of the East and its reflection in the semi-Oriental Alexandria. From 1820 to 1830 Hegel delivered his annual lectures on the philosophy of history, and pictured to his audience the life of the East as 'a dream, not of the individual mind, but of Absolute Spirit.' The West was just beginning to discover the East; Hegel could quote from Colebrooke and remind his hearers how new the knowledge of Eastern literature still was. This new influence, one of the acquisitions of the nineteenth century, must henceforth be taken into account. Schopenhauer felt the attraction; Hartmann succumbed to the 'drowsy syrops of the East'; Fechner had his *Zend-Avesta*, followed in later years by the oracles of Zarathustra.

All through the centuries thought had been observed trailing a cloud of speculation; saints and scientists seem to present themselves ultimately with the same golden halo, worn with complacence or irritation according to their respective temperaments. And here, in the middle of the nineteenth century, we find the same problems that troubled Plato still unsolved, and a mind that embraces Platonism and Atomism, repeating again the lost formulae that should exorcize the mystery. It is time to face the matter squarely.

Psychology, of course, has nothing to do with metaphysics; the psychologist asks, 'What are metaphysics?' in the tone of the man who said, 'Who is my neighbour?' When the issue becomes practical, this kind of destructive innuendo fails; the psychology proves to have a private metaphysics at least, or it avenges itself by giving a psychological explanation of all other metaphysics. In this the psychologist shows a true instinct; to offer a psychological explanation of the metaphysical mind is to invite a psychological explanation of the psychologist's mind; but this the psychologist can reserve for himself. Ultimately, without doubt, there must be in some sense a psychological explanation for all systems of speculative thought. Whether that means the consequent rejection of all such systems, as exploded fictions, is quite another question. To give a psychological explanation of a course of thought is not the same thing as proving it a form of madness. Yet there is no doubt that to the average man giving a psychological explanation of a system of ideas means really discounting its value; it is as if you tapped your skull with your forefinger and looked knowingly at the audience. If your action does not imply that the author of the system was mad, it would at least be taken to mean that his ideas were 'peculiar,' very much his own, not universal.

This is the crucial point. It so happened that the epoch into which Fechner was born had seen this very fact dawning upon some minds. All systems of thought, says the Hegelian, are explicable in terms of thought; they are explicable psychologically, if you take the right kind of Psyche, the pure spirit, the absolute. With this declaration the ages of the world run back; the language of Heraclitus was converted into scientific German, and Europe was told most emphatically 'though the Logos is common to all, most men live as though they had a private wisdom of their own.' With Heraclitus must be joined the last exponent of the Greek traditions, Plotinus. If we are to believe that man is the last and highest product of nature, can anything disprove the conclusion that in reflective thought the creative reason knows itself? Can anything counteract the wonderful fascination of this belief when it is seen to abolish the dull stupidity that looks animal-like on things and never sees them to be only the outward show of laws, principles, ideas—a slumbering thought. Is it, after all, a mistake to busy ourselves so much in division and analysis and classification? Do we not fail to enter into the very heritage of all human thought, that higher unity in which the mind is one with itself, that intuitional life of the spirit compared with which the days of our intellectual labours are like the dissociated images of dreams. In India, says Hegel, the absolute spirit dreamed; when it awoke it was in Germany.

The romantic school, then, was more psychological in its own way than its opponents will admit. Like Wisdom of old, it *did* nothing; it only undertook to show the meaning of what was done. Wisdom, said Aristotle, is above practice; the means do not create the end, it is the end that dictates the means; and wisdom is the inner realization of the end or purpose immanent in all action. If so, the formulae are secondary; spiritualism, materialism, monism, atomism, are all names for processes, stages in thought; they serve their purpose not as eternal truths, but as adequate hypotheses. And in psychology the same will be true. The definition of the soul will be a hypothesis that serves to make action more intelligible; if it is limited to that function it may be hampered by its own limitations. Descartes achieved much by limiting his concepts; progress abolished the limitations. In the end it may be true that inorganic, organic, plant, animal, man are all names for limitations; they may stand for divisions as artificial as the counties in a geographical map; nature may ignore them as the earth ignores its political boundaries.

It is, therefore, not irrational to have more than one way of looking at things, to value divisions as working principles, and at the same time to question the value of the divisions. It is not irrational to co-ordinate the psychical and the physical and yet maintain that the psychical is never wholly physical. In biology, cerebral physiology, and psycho-physics this is equally true; they all involve a unification of distinct spheres, and so testify to a unity beyond the distinctions. Fechner saw this in a peculiar way; his mind was occupied with so many diverse spheres of thought that the very diversity annihilated itself; he could belong wholly to none of them. His *Psychophysik* was not the mere invention of a science; it was the attainment of a new plane of thought. As the diversity of nineteenth-century thought came to a point in his work, so from him the new diversity emerged. The centre of controversy shifts to the question, How much of the inner life actually enters into this sphere of measurement and quantity?

2. PSYCHO-PHYSICS

Fechner's *Psychophysik* belongs to the later period of his life. Both in point of time and of logical sequence Fechner seems to have come to the problem of consciousness from a 'physical philosophy' in the old sense—the sense in which Aristotle applied it to the Ionians. The outlines are comprehensive, and the categories include all being. The existence of parts implies a whole; every atom has its place in an organized totality; if it belongs to nothing else, it belongs at least to the cosmos. The atom is the physical unit; by the help of this idea of discontinuity we can construct practical interpretations of nature, such as the law of gravitation. Nature, therefore, is a complex of concepts (for the atom is primarily conceptual) and laws; it is nothing dead and cold, the lifeless matter of the materialists. Nor does Fechner mean that matter is the bearer of an animating principle, that inner life of which the primitive hylozoism had spoken. Abandoning the '*Naturphilosophie*,' Fechner moves toward the earlier Kantian standpoint. Phenomena and the order of phenomena are the real material, the stuff of our thinking; nature is experience looked at from an impersonal point of view, the point we usually call 'objective.' The other point of view is the subjective, that which is peculiarly each individual's possession. There is no need to linger over the detail of this theory in its scientific aspects; it will be enough to remark that Fechner speaks of three forms of nature—the inorganic, the organic, and the cosmorganic; that these are distinctions depending partly on the point of view taken, partly on the degree to which the unity of system is actually realized in nature. The inorganic is usually regarded as the basis from which scientific thought should begin. Fechner adopts the reverse method; the inorganic never produces the organic, whereas the organic is liable to degeneration, and even in the normal state the 'mixed natures' of the animal world contain a large percentage of inorganic material. An organism cannot be said to *contain* life: its own organization is its life; and life is that form of mechanism which stands out distinctly through its own attributes; it is, so to say, nature's mechanism. Organization and the presence of system, along with the equivalent of laws, are therefore the ultimate terms. Organization is presented to us in very different forms and degrees. If man is primarily an organism, a soul in a receptacle, what ground is there for separating organization from 'soul' or life? Fechner abides by his logic; there is none. Plants, animals, man, stars, the universe—all these have organization in their degree and their way; all, have, therefore, their own life and their own 'soul.'

This climax is a severe strain on the trusting disciple who felt secure in the wake of an atomist and a man of science. Fechner's public in 1850 was composed chiefly of the aesthetic type of lady who could see the soul in the flower and derive from the plucking of a blossom all the thrill of a public execution. Yet there was real value in this line of thought. If it overreached itself, it did not sin more than its antithesis, materialism; against the current views, which must put an end to all subjectivity, it restores the value of experience without degrading observation. So far as the study of human life and behaviour is concerned, it has the advantages of the time-honoured Aristotelian doctrine—it stands by the organism against mere materialism and mere spiritualism. In a sense, there was nothing very new in all this. Kant had already destroyed the bald antithesis of mind and matter; Spinoza had adopted a fundamental unity; and Leibniz had spiritualized atomism. But in two ways Fechner made a distinct position for himself. In Spinoza and Leibniz the ontological element persists; Fechner drops the whole subject of the 'thing-in-itself,' and takes the level of experience as itself the real bedrock. In Kant the critical tendency evolved into a dogmatic scepticism, which stated unequivocally what was to be acquired from nature. This was notably the case in reference to the sphere of psychology or pneumatology. Fechner, accustomed to experimentation and the adventures of the laboratory, applied to the world of science that doctrine of belief which Kant reserved for the world of conduct.

The really difficult point about Fechner's method and system is its refinement, or what the ordinary man would call its 'abstractness.' The ordinary man thinks easily of mind and matter; he finds it difficult to regard them as points of view, not as antagonistic substances. If you try to persuade him that it is more 'concrete' to talk of unity, organization, and law than to discuss the mind alone or the body alone, he grows restless, and if you declare the distinctions of science to be 'categories,' he thinks you are destroying its 'reality.' This is the first ground of the objection to the *Psychophysik*: the plain man defies anyone to measure his mind, and in this he is backed up by all the devotees of 'common sense' (used as Reid used it) and their next-of-kin, the intuitionists. This has the misfortune of being irrelevant: one does not really measure anything *absolutely*; the very essence of measurement is comparison, analogy, relativity. When the plain man says it stands to reason that a thought cannot be measured, he means measured 'absolutely.' He is superabundantly right. Yet the same man would say he was strongly excited, violently agitated, or deeply stirred; he would understand quite well the science of the valet who measured his employer's temper by the broken furniture; he would admit, in short, that mental states do have physical equivalents as a matter of mere co-ordination, and that you can 'measure' psychical activity just as much (or just as little) as you 'measure' a child's growth by pencil-marks on a door. The first requisite is to know what you want to do; the next is to discover the means. A more detailed account of the *Psychophysik* will make this part of the subject clearer.

The germ from which the *Psychophysik* ultimately developed is to be found in Weber's experiments upon the senses of touch, sight, and hearing. Fechner began by believing that there *must* be some connection between the physical stimulus and the sensation. He remained for a time unable to formulate this connection, but finally adopted the belief that the relative increase of the bodily activity might be equivalent to the increase of psychical intensity. There the matter might have remained but for a correspondence with Wilhelm Weber, the electrician, which started Fechner on experimentation. The results of these experiments seemed to support the hypothesis, and Fechner then found that his position had already been reached by E. H. Weber, the physiologist. The difference between Weber and Fechner lies in the fact that the former laid no emphasis on the significance of his discoveries for psychology; he reached his results as a physiologist, and looked no farther.

Outer psycho-physics is the name Fechner gave to the science of measuring sensations by the required stimuli. The methods which he formulated are three: first, that of the just observable difference, the discovery of minimal thresholds; second, that of right and wrong cases; third, that of average error. The general formula which serves as theoretical summary of the doctrine is that the sensation is in proportion to the logarithm of the stimulus. For the technical elaboration of this and the mathematical formulae employed, we must refer the reader to the original, or to the many expositions available in textbooks. In general, it is obvious from what has been said that the core of the whole matter is the correlation between outer or physical and inner or psychical expressions of energy. Fechner does not contemplate any transmission of energy from the outer to the inner; the scale of changes in the outer sphere is, and remains, parallel to the scale of changes in the inner sphere. Some of the inner changes are not correlative to outer stimuli, but occur in consciousness as a self-contained and self-preserving system of energies. Attention, for example, seems to be of this kind, or the action of memory, for in the rise and fall of these activities there seems to be implied a system of stimulations analogous to that which had been more successfully studied in the field of sensation. This part of Fechner's work, which seems to be a translation of Herbartian notions into a mystical form of 'wave-theory,' has not retained the attention of psychologists. None the less, the driving force of Fechner's whole life was concentrated on this point; for if the psychic energy is always conserved and yet actually falls below a zero point of actuality, we seem able to follow consciousness itself into an underworld, a world under the threshold of our realized being, a world which must then be no other than the abiding-place of a general consciousness of which life is but a ripple on the surface. The attraction of this speculative outcome is never wholly exhausted. The term 'threshold' is partly a scientific term for the limit of perception, partly a name for the borderline between light and dark, here and hereafter, individual and universal consciousness. Fechner united both uses of the term; later psychology has divided them. The experimentalist keeps the former; the latter we find again, not only in worthless lucubrations, but also in earnest inquiries such as those of Myers and James; though the value of these inquiries is not yet such as to give them a place in the records of psychology.

The law known as the 'Weber-Fechner Law' has been so often described and discussed that we may be excused the task of repeating its definition. Its fundamental point is the fact that a sequence of sensations, regarded as inner events, can often be shown not to follow, point for point, the increase of the stimulus. If we suppose that a light is perceived when it has a value as stimulus equivalent to 10, and that we notice a change in that light when the stimulus is equivalent to 12, it follows that (a) the interval between 10 and 12 has no perceptible counterpart, and (b) that a stimulus equivalent to 20 will have to be raised to 24 in order to cause a perceptible difference. Given the possible truth of this hypothesis as an assumption, the work of the investigator consists in finding out how far it is true for all kinds of sensation, or for all parts of the scale of sensation in any one case, and also in determining what is the *minimum sensible*, the 'threshold' in each case. Volumes have been written on this subject, many of them valuable, and the results seem to be (a) that the law does not apply so widely as at first it seemed to, and (b) that psychologists are not agreed as to whether the proceedings concern them or not. The first question, being a matter of details, we cannot consider further. The second may be illustrated briefly, as it is obviously at bottom a question concerning the nature and scope of psychology.

James, with characteristic completeness, says: 'Fechner's book was the starting-point of a new department of literature, which it would be perhaps impossible to match for the qualities of thoroughness and subtlety, but of which, in the humble opinion of the present writer, the proper psychological outcome is just *nothing*.' In spite of this, the subject is 'a chapter in the history of our science'; moreover, it is a very long chapter in James's *Psychology*. Ultimately James consigns this whole 'department of literature' to physiology. This was one of the outstanding views of the subject, seen more soberly exhibited in J. Ward's article 'An Attempt to interpret Fechner's Law.' In this article (*Mind*, 1876) Ward adopts the view that the law should be given a physiological rather than a psychological interpretation, provided that a physiological explanation of the facts can be given. Such an explanation he finds in Bernstein's researches, which seem to establish the propositions that (1) a stimulus-wave in its passage along a nerve-fibre remains throughout of equal strength, (2) but on reaching the centre is irradiated, and (3) meets with continuous resistance, which (4) is proportionate to the strength of the wave at that point. From this physiological basis it is possible to express the intensity of a sensation in terms of its irradiation or neutral extension. Against Fechner it is urged that he gives no explanation of what he means by intensity. If intensity is equivalent to irradiation, and if the propositions of Bernstein are true, Fechner's formulae would be the indirect measure of sensation and the direct equivalent of physiological processes.

The Herbartians received all psycho-physical doctrines with reserve; they maintained in general that immediate experience can only be known in one way—immediately. To some extent Ward's position in this article is on their side. Another supporter of their position (not to mention such professed Herbartians as Volkmann) was Lotze. The main point of the opposition was the assertion that Fechner did not pay enough regard to the psychical side of the matter. If the variations of the stimulus produce differences of quality as well as quantity in the resultant consciousness, and if in any case the results are conditioned by inner activity (attention), these formulae seem to state a very small part of the whole matter. That they express *something* no one wishes to deny; what is implicitly denied by these criticisms is the assumption that Fechner's works unveiled the mystery of sensation.

Fechner remained to the end of his life ceaselessly active. He made his own reply to the more important criticism in a new statement of his position, entitled *In Sachen der Psychophysik*, 1877. This was not the last word, for it preceded G. E. Müller's *Zur Grundlegung der Psychophysik*, which moved Fechner to write a *Revision* (1882), which was to take the place of the original *Elemente*. In 1887 he added an important statement of his views in the article 'Ueber die Psychischen Massprincipien und das Webersche Gesetz' (*Phil. Stud.*, iv. 1888). The *Revision* was edited in 1889, two years after its author's death, by Wundt. The objections or criticisms which appeared in Fechner's lifetime cover the whole ground, and present all the principal views which have been advocated up to the present. The objections were classified by Fechner, and the list here given will be found more fully described in Ribot, *German Psychology of Today* (E. Tr., 169. Cp. Klemm, E. Tr., 245). They are:

(1) That the laws and formulae of psycho-physics are not supported by facts of experiment.

This contention was made by Hering during the years 1872 to 1875. Later authorities have shown that (*a*) Weber's law cannot be converted into a general law for all sensibility, and (*b*) that it holds only for some senses within definite limits.

(2) The law has only a physiological value. Of this view Bernstein was the main supporter, as quoted above.

(3) That the mathematical expression of the formulae is wrong. This related to the fact that Fechner correlated an imperceptible stimulus with what he called a negative sensation. Though the stimulus is imperceptible, it must be given a quantitative objective value, say 1. Then to the objective 1 corresponds the subjective 0; but the two series of stimulus and sensation should start from an equal position, both being either 0 or 1. This point does not seem to have more than formal value, for (if I understand Fechner rightly) he meant by negative sensation what others mean by latent or unconscious factors (e.g. Herbart or Lipps), which are positive in function, though less than a perceptible totality.

(4) That Fechner ignores the real character of mental processes; they are biological rather than mathematical in their own nature. This objection is far-reaching, and has been often repeated in later writers. It involves (*a*) the view supported by von Kries, that psychic states are intensive, and for such 'magnitudes' there is no known method of measurement, because there is no constant

unit. To make measurement possible the increments of sensation should be equal; 'in a series of sensations e, e_1, e_2, we cannot say that the change from e_1 to e_2 equals the change from e_m to e_n.' This is (b) a special case of the general objection that life processes cannot be reduced to the abstract form which a mathematical treatment requires. Similarly, Boas raised the point that different intensities are equivalent to different qualities, so that a light A cannot be called two or more times greater than another light B, since the sensations a and b differ one from another as much as a light differs from a sound. Whether this objection really makes *all* measurement in psychology impossible is a point that still remains in dispute. It is sufficient for the present to show by these quotations what views were held about Fechner's work in the twenty years that elapsed between the publication of his *Psychophysik* and the last defence which he himself published. As the psycho-physical interpretation, which Fechner gave of Weber's law, was seen to be valueless, a choice remained between the physiological and the psychological interpretations. These were defended by G. E. Müller and Wundt respectively. The subject underwent considerable modification at a later date, and must be deferred until we come to more recent experimental work.

G. Lotze's soul psychology

I. SPECULATIVE PHILOSOPHY

Rudolph Hermann Lotze was born in 1817. In 1834 he entered the University of Leipsic, and studied medicine and philosophy for the next five years, qualifying as *docent* in both faculties in 1839. Lotze thus began his career in the circle of E. H. Weber, from whom he learned those scientific methods which always tempered the speculative quality of his mind. Though his first work was entitled *Metaphysic* (1841), Lotze secured his first literary success in the sphere of the sciences. The air was still full of the problem of vitalism; Müller at Berlin still held to the idea of an 'imponderable substance' which no analysis could reach or resolve. Lotze in 1842 declared himself an opponent of this vitalism; he sided with those who thought that this was a remnant of metaphysics for which science had no place. But even at this stage Lotze's position exhibits his characteristic subtlety and that definite lack of certainty which so often annoyed his friends and exposed him to his enemies. Life, for Lotze, is a system of activities. It may be explained as a mechanism, without even the usual admission that it is 'ultimately' inexplicable. Yet, for all that, materialism is wrong.

In 1844 Lotze became Professor of Philosophy at Göttingen, and from this date begins the series of works which most especially concerns psychology. After writing two books on aesthetics and one on physiology, Lotze produced, in 1852, the work entitled *Die Medicinische Psychologie oder Physiologie der Seele*. The date and the title are both worthy of notice. In the next quarter of a century, many books were to appear on the subject of 'the physiology of the mind'; this was the great prototype. In the sphere of the natural sciences the influence of Hegel was now both dead and buried; only the memory of the '*Naturphilosophie*' remained, a spectre of idealism driving the more timid to take refuge in the obscurity of unilluminated 'facts.' Under such conditions courage was needed to enable anyone who valued his scientific reputation to say anything that sounded speculative: Lotze emerged as one who had shown that courage. With his contemporaries, he rejected Hegel; against his contemporaries he clung to the belief that idealism still remained the true way of thinking. With one hand he deals out the facts of science, with the other he supplies those principles which unite and systematize the facts.

'I called on Lotze,' says Helmholtz, recording a visit to him in Göttingen, 'but found him too hypochondriac and slow, so that I could get very little out of him.' Helmholtz was, perhaps, not quite the kind of man to whom Lotz would talk freely; the philosopher would feel too acutely how inadequately his thoughts could be demonstrated or his theories established by experiments. The unique position of Lotze was made for him by training and by nature; none could accuse him of lacking scientific knowledge, and his word carried weight when the mere philosophers went unheeded. Yet it was primarily as a philosopher that Lotze cared to be heard, and he suffered in consequence from a double responsibility. Though the struggle between science and philosophy, the mechanical and the ideal, was the inner process of Lotze's mind, it did not end either in disruption of thought or in despair. For him they were reconciled in a unity that was not either Hegelian or Kantian, though, like the former, it was idealistic, and, like the latter, it was critical and ethical. In the sphere of psychology, to which we must confine these remarks, this unity was shown in the grasp of facts, the simultaneous retention of the phenomenal and of the real.

The enlightened reader will see that this is the preface to the 'question of the soul' as it appears to Lotze. The mediaevalist raised the question in the form, 'Does the soul know itself or only its acts?' Kant brought psychology under his general ruling that we only know phenomena. Hegel declared for a transcendence of the phenomena. Lotze advocates a new answer which depends on a new statement of the question. If the soul knows itself in its acts, if, in fact, the error has lain in the persistent separation of Being from Doing, there may still be a more adequate grasp of the whole reality in a doctrine that revises the method first, and then translates into its own terms the language of observation. This was Lotze's aim; the study of his psychology must begin with the clear understanding of this point of view.

The distinctive feature of Lotze's psychology is the retention of the concept of 'soul.' The exact interpretation to be given to this term will be more easily seen later; it requires to be mentioned here because it is the beginning as well as the end of the whole theory. The soul is active, but not in such a way as to evolve its own experiences. Its activity is conditioned by the operation of extensive things, so that the order of procedure in time begins from the stimulus and its consequence in sensation. Lotze here parts from the method of Fichte; he does not admit that the soul can generate experiences without the external occasion, though he has to admit that no direct reason for this limitation of action can be demonstrated. In opposition to the other contemporary trend of thought, the materialistic, Lotze sharply divides the physical event from its psychic equivalent; the stimulus is, therefore, reduced to a mere occasion, in explicit agreement with the original doctrine of the Occasionalists.

2. THE DETAILS OF LOTZE'S SYSTEM

While the actual process by which the physical becomes psychical remains a mystery, the stages can be empirically determined. The outer object generates an inner sense-stimulation, which is continued in the nerve as conductor, till it arrives at and is transformed in the central organ; here the soul is affected unconsciously, and the conscious reaction is a higher grade dependent on attention. This analysis is sometimes stated more simply in the three terms, 'stimulus,' 'neurosis,' 'conscious sensation.'

Lotze treats the nervous system as a pure mechanism; its function is to mediate between the object and the central organ; it transmits only motion and not sensation. The idea that each part of the nerve may have its own sensation as the accompaniment of its motion is explicitly rejected; a nerve acts only as being subject to shock and capable of regaining its equilibrium. A certain degree of habit arises from continuous repetition of this action, so that in time the nerves become 'specific' in their action. To this extent they might be said to have 'specific energies,' but the doctrine of specific energies as held by Müller is rejected, and very little importance is attached to this modified form of the doctrine.

In the same way Lotze admits the value of Weber's Law as a statement of objective fact, but declines to give it any real psychic interpretation. The psychic changes are changes of quality; they correspond to the quantitative changes of the stimuli; but since the psychic units are distinct qualitative sensations and form a discontinuous series, the Law gives us no real knowledge of the inner relation between physical and psychical series. To say that a change in the rate of vibrations of the ether corresponds to a change of colour is to state two facts in their relation; it explains nothing.

For Lotze the world of inner experience is wholly distinct from the outer world of physical forces and events. If we now pass on to consider this inner experience, the language of the physical sciences can no longer be employed. Motions can be described as having degrees of strength or as being opposed to one another; but one presentation as such is not 'stronger' than another, nor can such events as perceptions be described as 'opposed' one to another. Here, then, Herbart is definitely rejected. There are differences in the elements of an experience; some are more impressive, more lasting, and more inclined to occupy the field of consciousness. But all these are qualitative differences, to be reduced to a qualitative basis if any explanation can be found. In short, it is in the language of values and not of mass or force that we must express this variety and its relations. With Lotze, as with all the idealist psychologists, memory is the crucial instance; there is no faculty of memory, no cerebral organ, no 'storehouse of ideas': only the living continuity of the soul and its power of reproducing its own previous activities.

It is interesting to observe how accurately, though perhaps unintentionally, Lotze repeats the arguments of Plotinus. But the question has become more complex than it was in the days of Plotinus, and we require to see how far Lotze meets that increased complexity. The subject of memory is no longer to be regarded as something unique; it is one aspect of the general question of mental reproduction, and when memory has been defined, it is necessary to give an account of its processes. There must not be any contradiction between these two parts of the theory if it is to prove satisfactory.

First as to memory. Lotze regards the soul as the receiver of incoming currents and the initiator of outgoing currents. If we admit any distinct kind of action that can be called mental, if there is any difference between man and the machines, it is necessary to allow that there intervenes between the afferent and the efferent neutral currents a third factor. We may say, then, in the first place, that a psychic factor is not to be excluded *a priori*. Having cleared his ground, Lotze proceeds to give his reasons for not treating memory as a mere precipitate of impressions, a storing up of injected copies of things. In opposition to this view, he maintains that memory does not, in fact, keep any such pictures; what it really retains is a kind of scheme, a plan of action, and the term 'memory' really denotes the power of acting again in the way in which one acted before, with a recognition of the fact that the action is qualitatively like a previous action. This might be described as, in essence, the typical form of a spiritualistic interpretation of memory. It seems to involve—at least, in Lotze's way of stating it—the following additional points: The experiences which have once formed part of the life of the soul can never again be wholly lost. The external event, as such, does not necessarily enter into the life of the soul, for it may go unnoticed; but if it is noticed it involves attention, and is in some degree woven into the web of consciousness. Finally, the inner process is different in kind from the receptivity of sense, for there is in memory no shock of stimulation; the memory of a pleasure is not in itself pleasant, it is an activity to which all colouring is incidental. Pure inwardness and the necessity of attention to constitute the remembered process—these are the characteristics of memory that make it at once the product and the proof of independent psychic activity.

So far we have not gone much beyond the doctrine of the ancients, of Plato and of Plotinus. When our philosopher remembers his science, the strain begins to tell. He is compelled to mention the cerebral motions, those weak oscillations which accompany the act of remembering. These would give no trouble by themselves, for it would be easy to say that they represented the use of the body as instrument of the soul. But there are other facts to be faced that come much nearer home. There are hallucinations which can only be explained if more emphasis is thrown on those motor accompaniments that Lotze would fain keep in the background; there are pathological cases which make it difficult to say that memories never perish unless we boldly add that they retire into some inner sanctuary; there is also the damaging admission that people differ in the kind of memory each possesses, for some have memory for places, others for words, all of which suggest a close relation between memory and the sensory basis. It is certain that all these points cannot ultimately dispose of the theory that the soul has an independent reality, and that the memory exists even when it fails to give outward manifestations of its existence. But the question that must continue to haunt the reader is whether any profit really attaches to such a view, whether, after all, the opponent is not right when he says that there is no such thing as memory, there are only memories. To choose between these two views is really to choose between psychology as applied metaphysics and empirical psychology.

After what has been said on memory, the subject of reproduction in general can be dismissed quickly. Psychologists of Lotze's type have no interest in elaborate theories of association. They maintain that all ideas are equally reproducible, and the particular reproduction is dependent on nothing but the general conformation of consciousness. If we state this as the tendency to form mental series, and to repeat a series as a whole whenever a part is made prominent by circumstances or by increased intensity of thought (activity of the soul), we see at once the affinity between this view and that of Herbart, and its relation to associationism. Lotze's position here is that which appears as typically German at this period. It belongs also to that British school which began under German auspices with Sir W. Hamilton, and has continued to speak of redintegration rather than association. As Lotze does not adopt the particular theory by which Herbart accounted for actual reproductions, and does not admit that there is any force in ideas that enable them to struggle with one another, he has to look elsewhere for the factor that determines any one set of ideas to occupy the attention. He finds this in the feeling which accompanies the thought, for feeling is allied with interest, and this brings us back to attention, which gives the required activity. In another sense of the term, feeling is the equivalent of the total mental state, and this general feeling is also used by Lotze to explain the recall of ideas. There can be little doubt that this is an important factor, and that the groups of ideas which so often seem to come into the mind without cause are given their prominence by organic changes which themselves are due to still more remote causes rarely detected. This point Lotze derived from his knowledge of mental diseases, where there is more chance of studying the relation between general conditions and their accompanying ideas; but the principle is equally good in normal states.

Feelings are for Lotze a distinct class of phenomena; they are not to be deduced from sensations or ideas, or any interrelation of these. In his earlier works Lotze was more inclined to emphasize the physiological conditions of feelings; later he united with this a teleological ground of explanation. Feeling in general is the equivalent of harmony or disharmony, between a neutral stimulation and the ordinary function of the nerve. When the harmony is retained—when, that is to say, the stimulus is neither too great nor too small—pleasure results; when the harmony is disturbed, pain is felt. But since the sensation itself is given by a nerve-oscillation, and every sensation is distinct from the feeling which may accompany it, we seem to have used up all the available machinery. The facts of analgia make it impossible to identify the process that underlies sensation with that which underlies feeling; a special centre for feelings is equally impossible. The remaining possibility is that a nerve may have two modes of action—the functional activity which ends in sensation, and a destructive or reconstructive activity known by the soul as feeling.

This explanation, which as a physiological hypothesis cannot be proved and as a psychological doctrine has no direct utility, is for Lotze a product of teleology. From the question of the *nature* of the feelings he turns to the question of their *purpose*. Purpose, in fact, becomes for Lotze a ground of complete scientific explanation, and is regarded by him as an essential principle of method. Psychology is applied metaphysic just for this reason, that the data cannot be comprehended under the mechanical formulae to which the sciences of nature rightly restrict themselves; the life of the spirit is essentially purposive, and only to be interpreted in the light of purpose. A feeling of pleasure or of pain seems a needless addition to the cognitive side of sensation. If we can know by touch that a thing is hot, why should we also feel it to be *too* hot, painfully hot? Here, indeed, is a metaphysical problem. But assume that the pain leads to a consciousness of action, or that the pleasure produces reflection on the psychic condition itself, then feeling is given a place in the system of life. It is the process by which consciousness becomes aware of itself; it is the agency that converts consciousness of objects into consciousness of self.

The opponent could with no great difficulty brand this doctrine as idle speculation, but for one consequence: upon it depends the explanation of impulse, desire, choice, and volition. To describe these as operations of the organism before it acts is not a proceeding that satisfies everyone; it is too much like describing hunger as the condition of the organism before it eats. But if these subjects are seriously attacked, the centre of gravity seems to shift from one part of the exposition to another, from the physiological to the metaphysical, from the empirical to the speculative. This shifting is very apparent in Lotze. From neural processes he passes to activities that have only 'secondary' neural equivalents; from these to activities to which nothing physiological seems to correspond; finally, to new categories such as activity and value, that seem no longer part of the world in which we touch, taste, or smell. This may be a justifiable procedure. The complexity of data may render all other treatments less adequate. The empiricist may acquire his convincing simplicity only by suppressing facts; the idealist may be wrong in neglecting the principles which science overworks; there may be room for a mediator, an idealistic realist—in a word, for such a man as Lotze.

3. PSYCHOLOGY WITHOUT METAPHYSICS?

It is an open question whether a psychologist can be an idealist or a realist. He should perhaps be simply a psychologist. But apart from collectors of detail and writers of monographs, history has failed to produce a psychologist who was not a philosopher of some kind; and it is notorious that a rejection of all metaphysics is the most metaphysical of all positions. The fruits of the sciences may be plucked by every chance comer; yet the tree that bears them must strike its roots deep or quickly wither away. Lotze's psychology has not perished yet. For that reason, if for no other, it deserves a careful valuation, root and branch. The central problem is the question of method. Is psychology a branch of physiology, or a department of metaphysics? To call it a science is ambiguous. If by science we mean a natural science, what is the meaning of nature? Is there one nature for science and another for philosophy? Is metaphysics necessarily the antithesis of science? The answer depends on the most fundamental of all sciences—the science of categories, terms, or classification. A new point of view, as opposed to a discovery of detail, is essentially a reform of the categories.

The term 'metaphysic' merely denotes ontology; it implies, therefore, ontologism, or the manipulation of data under the category of substance. Confining our attention to psychology, this means the explanation of psychic phenomena by the use of the term 'soul' as equivalent to an underlying substance. This was the essence of that rational psychology which Kant criticized. The doctrine of faculties was really a form of this psychology; for one soul it substituted a group of souls, complicating problems without advantage. Under pressure of criticism, the faculty-doctrine was converted in two ways: some said that ideas were the ultimates, treating them ontologically in the end (Herbart); others said that a faculty was the name of a class of phenomena, a form of psychological nominalism. Against this last position it is easy to bring the old argument of realism. If the phenomena are so classified on account of their real nature, the name of the faculty represents a real inner unity which controls the classification and makes it real. If, further, all the phenomena have an inner unity and constitute a genuine class, there may be a significant name for that unity. Taken in this sense, the term 'soul' has significance, and psychology is the science of the soul.

The retention of the term 'soul' is thus primarily a logical necessity; it is at once retained and transformed. In its new meaning it is the symbol of a new point of view. The ontologist regarded the soul as a transcendent reality; here it is immanently real. Kant is justified; we only know phenomena. But the phenomena are not the cast-off clothing of reality; they are its concrete self, its flesh and blood. In psychology we can have no skeletons; there is no anatomy of the soul. If we strain the term physiology so far as to speak of mental physiology, it is because the term has a kind of universality. As we may speak of life without necessarily meaning life of the body, so we may speak of physiology without thereby indicating only the physiology of plants or of animals. The conservation of energy may be a law without any determination of the question whether we know all the forms of energy. The very term phenomena seems, then, to be a term of art, a convenience of thought; and if it has not a correlative 'reality' it is meaningless. Taking the phenomena as aspects of reality, Lotze treats the two terms as equivalent to plurality and unity. Both being implied in the given actuality of life, only one further distinction remains: we *know* the plurality as object, we *are* the unity as subject.

This discussion of the philosophy of psychology is made necessary by the fact that later writers use Lotze's results without repeating the process here briefly indicated. The effect upon all who share Lotze's position is seen in the following points: While ·physiology is not rejected as irrelevant to the life of the soul, it no longer usurps the whole field as it did in the materialism of 1860. The double point of view is translated by such a writer as James into a distinction of knower and known, the 'I' and the 'me.' Further, activity is restored to a central place as something without which it is not possible to present a complete statement of facts. Lastly, by a combination of the idea of process or activity with that of unity (the unity of consciousness), modern psychology revises the doctrine of association, and enters upon the phase which is distinguished by the predominance of 'apperception,' taken not directly from Herbart, but indirectly through Lotze. The value of these and other results due to Lotze's influence must be considered as we reach them in their particular setting; here it is enough to indicate the place and circumstances to which they belong historically.

H. Brentano and Lipps

1. BRENTANO'S NEO-SCHOLASTICISM

Among modern psychologists Brentano holds a curious position. The adjective most commonly applied to his work is 'old-fashioned': embedded in the following narratives of the 'new' psychology we find references to the 'older type' as presented by Brentano, accompanied with cautious indications that in many points the work is important. For the historian this collision of the new and the old is a matter of exceptional interest. Let us recall the fact that Brentano wrote in 1874; that Fechner's *Psychophysik* was then fourteen years old; that Wundt had laid the foundations of his work and begun to acquire ascendancy and vogue, though the laboratory was not yet in operation. We may recall also the fact that Brentano had the bias of a Catholic theology to shape his course—a fact that shows itself indirectly in lengthy citations from Aristotle and vindications of Thomas Aquinas. It is not surprising that the outcome was a work of great literary merit, well-informed and up to date (in 1874), a bone of contention for subsequent writers and a model of keen criticism. Brentano has been called a neo-scholastic, but the emphasis must be laid on the word 'scholastic.' Brentano's modifications of the old in face of the new, and the new in face of the old, are so far fundamental that the work is never in danger of being regarded as a futile resurrection of dogmas.

The *Psychologie von empirischen Standpunkte*, so far as it ever went, comprises two books, the first on psychology as science, the second on the psychic phenomena in general. The first book is concerned entirely with questions of method. Here the chief point is the insistence on experience as immediate, ultimate, and incapable of error. The source of all psychological experience is the inner perception, for without this we can never know what an idea, a judgment, a desire, a feeling, or a volition really is. Inner perception is to be distinguished from inner observation; while we can perceive outer objects and then observe them, we can never 'observe' experiences of the inner perceptions. Most of the errors in psychology, Brentano thinks, have arisen from a confusion between perception and observation (in this sense); from it, too, has arisen the scepticism of those who reject psychology, as, e.g., Comte did. Here, it would seem, Brentano revives the mediaeval problem, Does the soul know itself? He decides that it does. For while it is true that 'we only know phenomena,' in the case of the soul the phenomena are the acts, they are functions without any remainder in the way of material substrate. Consequently, there is no difference between the terms 'soul' and 'psychic phenomena.' Since the soul is its acts, psychology can be defined as science of psychic phenomena or as science of the soul indifferently.

The definition of psychology as 'science of the soul' can be traced back to Aristotle; but the history of thought since Aristotle shows a continual limitation of the term 'soul,' which now means consciousness rather than 'principle of life.' There has also been, at times, a tendency to make the different sciences into opposed spheres of reality, as we see in the opposition of the physical to the psychic. Brentano rejects this opposition. On the one hand, these oppositions too often lead to conflicts—e.g. the attempts of some writers (Maudsley among the chief) to reduce psychology to a form of physiology. On the other hand, if we recognize the unity of the sciences, there is room for all as specialized fields which supplement each other. Brentano's defence of introspection is not the prelude to condemnations of other methods. His final conception of method includes self-observation as based on the recall by memory of experiences; observation of the experiences of others as shown in speech, actions, and all forms of expression; study of animals and of children, of abnormal individuals, and different grades of civilization. He would give a large place to physiology, but not admit that it is the basis of psychology (Horwicz, Maudsley), and to mathematics, but not in the Herbartian way. Measurement and statistics are mathematical processes which assist the psychologist: we can measure extensive quantity, such as time-duration, but intensity cannot be measured. Brentano criticizes the Weber-Fechner doctrine in a way that has been often followed since; the two points are (a) that exact determination of psychic processes by such methods is obstructed by intermediary physiological processes; (b) that intensity is a factor which complicates all psychic processes, through attention especially, and cannot itself be either eliminated or estimated.

The second book, on psychic phenomena, deals with two points mainly—the Unconscious and the problem of classification. Brentano regards all theories of the unconscious as perversions due to influences from physiology. We may say of this that historically the notion of the unconscious did arise from the conception of reflex action and the consequent doctrine of higher and lower levels, but Brentano makes the subject too simple by reducing it to the question whether unconscious consciousness is conceivable. Such a treatment is no longer instructive in view of the later developments of the subject. On the question of classification Brentano makes his most characteristic point. Taking the Kantian division of sensation, feeling, and will, he examines each of these operations, and finds that introspection does not give any pure sensation, but always a mode of reaction to a situation. He rejects the principle that in psychology we can form ultimate classes of those elements which are not further reducible (Kant). On this basis, seeing and hearing would have to be regarded as ultimate classes: in fact, there would be an infinite number of irreducibles. Brentano's own principle of classification is the mode of relation to the immanent object. This gives as classes presentation, judgment, and feeling. As Brentano says, this classification divides Kant's first group (knowing) into two, but unites Kant's second and third (feeling, willing) into one.

To understand how this classification can be justified, it is necessary, first, to understand the general position. Usually, emphasis falls on the object of the psychic process: for example, we say that we see a colour, distinguishing the act of vision from the object. But the 'immanent object' is the content of the act; psychologically the colour and the seeing are one: we have simply 'colour-in-consciousness.' By thus having it in consciousness we recognize it: which means that we affirm it—that is to say, judge it. Usually judgment is described as being 'about something.' We are told that the judgment 'A is B' says something about A. But Brentano means that consciousness of A as A is itself judgment. We need not concern ourselves about objects (the colour seen), but only about the inner fact that a colour-presentation is given. Though we never experience presentation apart from affirmation (judgment), these are distinguishable. What Brentano aims to achieve is twofold. First, he would get away from the whole question of the individual's relation to an (external) object. Secondly, he would revive the scholastic view of *intentio*—that is to say, the act itself apart from its (outer) object but inclusive of its determination (immanent object). The differences between acts can only be established by the appeal to experience. We do (or do not) experience a difference between presentation, judgment, feeling. Those who do will agree with Brentano: in any case there is no other court of appeal. Some light is thrown on this subject by reading Brentano's criticism of Bain. Bain had declared that belief was a primitive attitude of mind, which comes very near to saying that we have sensations and also a belief in the fact that we have them, the belief accompanying but not resulting from the sensation. Brentano calls this 'unfortunate,' because belief implies as its ground a judgment, so that Bain should have gone deeper, and then he would have reached Brentano's position. In his progress away from physiological and experimental psychology, Brentano comes into close contact with the sphere of logic, and his view of judgments has penetrated many systems of logic. This was natural for anyone deeply versed in mediaeval thought, but the experimental psychologist is inclined to regard it as reactionary.

2. LIPPS'S PSYCHOLOGY OF 'FORCE'

Twenty-one years after Wundt's first essays, four years after the laboratory was opened at Leipzig, Theodor Lipps began to publish his works. From that year (1883) to the present time Lipps has remained one of the foremost writers in the philosophical world. His first work, *Grundtatsachen des Seelenlebens*, was a comprehensive survey of the field of psychology, inspired by wide reading of British as well as German authors. Numerous works since then have served to mark the growth of this writer's views, and something not unlike a school of thought has grown up about this central figure. The *Leitfaden der Psychologie*, in its third edition (1909), may be taken to represent the developed form of Lipps's psychology: other works concerned with logic and aesthetics cannot be considered here.

Born in 1851, Lipps belongs to a generation that was influenced but no longer dominated by Herbart. In the perspective of time Kant was seen in his correct relations; Hegel had already been reduced to his right proportions; a sane and critical idealism was the natural tone of the period. Such an idealism, when not primarily concerned to expound its ultimate metaphysic, can appropriate much that belongs to the realist, and, in fact, the system of Lotze had shown that an ideal realism is not an impossible conception. For psychology this might prove the most useful attitude to adopt. In relation to the idea of the subject, it supports the assertion that consciousness is an independent sphere and that psychology is the science of experience as we know it immediately. In relation to the object, it allows its adherents to assert that the object of knowledge is not a mere projected image but an indispensable datum, not a product but a presupposition of experience. This was the view adopted by Lipps, and it may be described as Kantian in spirit, in some aspects Herbartian, and at the same time influenced by the teaching of Wundt. The foundations of this kind of psychology are the two propositions that the inner life of consciousness can only be dealt with immediately, and that activity is the mark of all conscious processes.

The former proposition defines the relation of this psychology to physiology and to physiological psychology. As a principle of explanation physiology is rejected; so far as concerns all attempts to deduce conscious processes from cerebral or neural activity, or to localize mental functions, physiological psychology is a nonentity. Self-observation is the one and only method. This is not to be taken as a rejection of all experiment; on the contrary, both outer and inner experiments, experiments on the correlation of stimulus and sensation as well as on the processes of association, memory, and reaction-time, should be employed. These are subsidiary aids, means of arriving at answers to questions; if we want numerical and statistical results, we may obtain them in this way. But much remains beyond the reach of any laboratory experiment; and even where this method assists us, we can never forget that the data must end in a psychological truth, so that 'one can be an experimental psychologist only so far as one is already a psychologist.'

In this type of psychology all the emphasis falls on the experience as an immediately known activity. Consequently the objective event called sensation is barely within its limits. Sensation as a psycho-physical process only interests the psychologist in respect of its meaning; otherwise it is a mere x. The process and the soul which lives through the processes are equally unknown; with a decided swerve toward Hume, Professor Lipps postulates the reality of the soul and its processes, but takes as the limit of recognizable processes the presentation. The sphere of psychology begins at the point where this recognitive experience emerges. The presentation presupposes a real process on a lower level, which is its determinant; to present is to present something; to be aware is to be aware of something; that something cannot be any external thing or event—it must be the earlier determination of the soul. This determination remains as a 'trace,' the elementary 'memory-trace.' Such 'traces' constitute memory and are implied in 'association.'

The psychic processes can only be explained by assuming that they involve from the first a certain condition of the psychic substratum, the (postulated) soul. Hence the lowest limit is of the nature of a reaction; the reaction leaves a trace; the collective product of traces is the 'habit' of the soul. Here, then, we have innate dispositions, constructive activities, and certain progressive states of soul called 'acquired dispositions.' The terms (*Spur, Anlage*) recall the language of Beneke, but the nature of these fundamental concepts seems strangely like that of the Arabian Aristotelians, who distinguished the primary intelligence from the *intellectus adeptus*!

The exposition of the psychology thus defined begins with 'elements' and elementary laws. Sensations are classified as usual; attention is described as a heightened activity; and here we come to a crucial point—the Laws of Power. Psychic Power is a term here used for psychic life viewed as activity. If, for example, a person directs his attention to a colour, what is the total process? Simply the seeing of the colour. In other words, attention is not an activity capable of being added to or subtracted from the sum of activities upon which psychic power is expended. We must rather think of this power as a permanent force, sometimes distributed, sometimes concentrated. When the force is concentrated we are said to attend; for then the major part of the force is drained off into one channel. As the force ceases to operate in other directions the number of the objects presented is reduced.

Special notice has been drawn to this point for several reasons. In the first place it shows how Lipps throws his psychology into the scheme of a science which deals with force rather than matter. The materialism of 1860 was over and a new era had dawned. The study of energy succeeded the apotheosis of matter, and energy has the advantage of being a neutral category. If the opponent claims that conservation of energy is a law which prevents anyone from saying that brain-movements pass over into thoughts, the psychologist may retort that the law should include psychic energy and conserve that along with the rest. Herbart's position could then be re-edited as a doctrine of forces tending to equilibrium, which is, in the end, exactly what this author does. Consciousness is equivalent to a certain 'height' attained by a process; below that level the process exists as an unconscious sensation or idea. This, we are told, must not be read as though there could be an unconscious consciousness; what is unconscious is the process. The relation between the process and the consciousness is analogous to the relation between heat and light; if the vibrations of the luminiferous ether increase in rapidity, radiant heat passes into light. We cannot say the heat causes the light; nor must we say that the process causes the consciousness. Some would say that the unconscious process is really the psychological brain-state; but that, too, our psychologist rejects because it leads to the unprovable thesis that mental states are caused by brain-states. Finally, the unconscious is declared to be a concept, justified by the help which it gives in explaining the gaps in the causal connection of psychic events. The concept of the unconscious must be regulated by two principles; the term applies only to what has appeared or will appear as conscious, and that which is unconscious acts as a persistent factor in the totality of the psychic life through qualitative differences due to its operation.

Energy is subject to different kinds of condition. Quantitative conditions are one kind, and may be in the form of intensity (the thunderclap), or mass (the mountain range), or significance (portent). These are describable in terms of energy because they condition the 'concurrence' of forces; the psychic activity is prevented from distributing itself and brought to a focus. Another kind of condition is that of the negative and positive 'value-energy,' the pain and pleasure of experiences. Frequency, the basis of familiarity and of habit, is another type. Infrequency or strangeness may attract attention also, these being the positive and negative types of 'dispositional energy.' Fourthly, there is a 'contrast-energy,' a directing of force which depends on the diverting of a concentrated energy from its usual course. The idea underlying this description is that of a unitary force which has both quantitative and qualitative attributes; direction is plainly here only a matter of quality, for a new direction is equivalent to a change of character. The facts observed are not unusual; that 'what is new is also interesting' was discovered long ago. Does the statement really gain anything by this translation into terms of energy?

Granted the general theory of 'psychic force,' attention, memory, association, and dissociation can easily be stated in terms of concurrent and divergent lines of energy. We pass over the detail of that statement in order to explain the higher processes.

Lipps bases his analysis on a distinction between the soul in its relation to things and the consciousness in its relation to the processes involved in that relation. The lower level is constituted by that relation; it is the sphere in which events merely happen; a sensation, e.g., simply occurs. The higher level is that at which the processes which occur on the lower level are the content of consciousness. The two levels are therefore describable as (at least relatively) passive and active, respectively. Sensation is passive; imagination is active. Conation is analogous to sensation, being the point from which activity proper begins. The point common to sensation and conation is their position outside of the organizing activity which is called apperception. Historically, this theory must be regarded as another phase of the 'inner sense' doctrine, a restatement of Leibniz's apperception, Kant's synthesis of the matter of thought with the 'I think,' and Herbart's doctrine of apperception. However little its author might admit it, the guiding principle of this analysis is the idea of incoming and outgoing currents. Both are within the life of the soul, but this assertion does not rob the antithesis of its significance; perception is self-directing, apperception involves gripping the contents and redirecting them by means of the inner mental force. A complex system of distinctions is then required to bring this theory to completion. The individual may be determined to action or determine the self to act; the contents of the mind may acquire relations or relations may be imposed upon them; the receptive attitude may give place to the questioning attitude (the source of judgments), and so on. The subject of apperception is treated elaborately by Lipps, but in principle it amounts to a description of the ways in which the contents of consciousness can be manipulated by reflective thinking. Thus, the contents arrange themselves at the lower level by processes of dissociation and assimilation; at the higher apperceptive level the grouping of the contents is regulated from within, and we get the phenomena of discrimination, serial order, analysis, and abstraction—i.e. the elimination of a factor in a complex whole by purposive selection.

Next to apperception, the most characteristic term in this psychology is *Einfühlung*. Knowledge may be of things (sensation), of the self (apperception), and of other selves. The last source of knowledge is *Einfühlung*, or self-objectification. This doctrine of *Einfühlung* is most useful in the explanation of aesthetic and ethical modes of consciousness, but it plays an important part in the general theory of objective thinking. Every object of thought has qualities which depend on this transfusion of the self into the given. A line, for example, is not only *seen*, but also felt to be straight or curved; the vertical line appeals to us as upstanding, it suggests an act of rising up, it seems to call on us to follow the path it indicates. In this way all that we denote usually as bare qualities of things are really the overflow of our own activities into the outer world, and as we live in them so they become living realities for us.

The doctrine of *Einfühlung* is clearly in its essence a form of animistic thinking. We might regard animism as its unreflective form, and therefore it may be said to derive support from the study of the primitive mind. It serves Lipps as a basis for the explanation of language. The word is not something created by the mind and then associated with the object. On the contrary, the name and the thing are two phases of the original unitary experience; the proposition is the more complex system of words which has reality in so far as the total experience is revived by it; and, finally, the communication of thought is the still more complex condition in which the objectification involves other persons, and a further inclusion of their minds as objects of *Einfühlung*. In this way we arrive at an explanation of those states of consciousness which combine in their unity things, selves, and other selves.

Chapter Fourteen

THE INROADS OF PHYSIOLOGY AND BIOLOGY

A. Introductory

The progress of psychology was deeply affected by that general development of the scientific temper which was so marked a feature of the nineteenth century. More than any other department of inquiry, the sphere of psychology was liable to be invaded by primitive and emotional interests which hampered its progress. Among the effects of the work done during this century must be counted as by no means the least important that moral evolution which, by transforming prejudices, created a new environment for disinterested workers. From this general development of the Western mind we pass on to the specific points in which psychology is related to other sciences. The subject is large, and the space available for it small; there will be much to omit and much to condense; but nothing could justify a failure to point out the subjects which everyone interested in psychology can follow more adequately elsewhere. To simplify this part of the narrative an indication of its purpose and scope will be given.

Without arguing the rights or wrongs of the case, the historian has to accept the fact that a modern psychology frequently, not to say usually, lies between two points: it emerges from anatomy and physiology, and it terminates in a region where those sciences cease to guide. The purpose of this chapter is to indicate the points at which the study of the mind has historically been in contact with sciences of the body or of nature in general. These will be found to be as follows: (a) The study of the brain as the organ of conscious action, which moves from a rough outline of its complexity as equivalent to a system of faculties toward a refined analysis of its structure in relation to more refined conceptions of function, the whole being a history of the problem of localization; (b) the study of the nervous system as a whole; (c) leaving the regions of anatomy and physiology, we then pass to the allied sphere of the experimental study of such functions as touching, seeing, hearing; (d) this involves considering the progress of physics as instrumental in researches upon the senses; and (e) leads to the subject which forms a limit to our scope, the field of mental pathology. It will be obvious that in all these discussions the guiding line is the progressive refinement of method and result. For example, descriptive anatomy begins with the brain surface and terminates in a study of levels and of structure, giving rise to histology; neurology advances from broad distinctions to the difficult problems of the neuron; psycho-pathology emerges as the last phase of a history that begins with chained maniacs and stops (for the present) at the subtleties of hysteria. The history of psychology, which will follow this groundwork, will be essentially the history of a similar refinement, often dependent upon the changes of opinion which science has suggested or made possible

The influence of biology proved to be the most far-reaching of all influences coming into psychology from outside the philosophical, religious, and medical traditions from which psychology, in the main, has developed. But its full influence did not make itself felt till the end of the nineteenth century and beginning of the twentieth century when men who had been trained in Darwinian biology started to study man in the same sort of way as they studied animals and to use the same sort of explanatory hypotheses for human behaviour. There was, however, a transitional period before the rise of various schools of psychology in the twentieth century when the biological outlook exerted a correcting rather than a radical influence on the old traditions of 'ideas' psychology. The systematizers, Ward, Stout, and James, for instance, though strongly influenced by biology, were what we would now call 'philosophical psychologists.' They were interested primarily in traditional topics like the relationship between perception and conception, the self and self-consciousness, the association of ideas, and so on; but what they said on these topics had a different emphasis. Stress on conation, on plasticity and adaptability, and on function was beginning to replace the old interest in cognition, faculties, and structure. But psychology remained predominantly introspective. The mind rather than behaviour remained the centre of interest; the difference was that a more biological account was given of mental processes. We must wait till the early twentieth century until we can see reflected in the various 'schools' of psychology the full realization of the significance for psychology of Darwin's revelation that men are, after all, animals, and that the same sorts of questions can be asked about men as about animals and about animals as about men.

B. *The influence of physiology*

1. EIGHTEENTH-CENTURY PHYSIOLOGY

The latter half of the eighteenth century was full of important events in the history of the sciences. Many of them directly affected the character of contemporary views about life and mind; others, though ineffective at the time, were the first beginnings of the greater achievements of the nineteenth century. A brief account of the work done during the years 1750 to 1800 is a necessary prelude to the study of the most recent phases of psychology.

In the sphere of the special senses Vision continues to be the focus of interest. After the appearance of Berkeley's work a large number of contributions were made to this subject. The progress achieved was due to careful investigation of detail, showing that the science of optics was rapidly becoming more stable and more sure of its own specific problems. The famous Cheselden case (1728) appeared to present a unique opportunity for determining the vexed question of the relation between vision and touch: but, in fact, it remained to the end of the century a doubtful asset, and in his *Aphorismen* (1793) Plattner returned to the position that perception of space is confined to sight, the perceptions of the blind by touch being confined to sequence in time: for the blind, said Plattner, time takes the place of space.

In 1738 the work of R. Smith, *A Complete System of Opticks*, presented a critical survey of this subject, along with an essay on *Distinct and Indistinct Vision*, by Jurin. The latter is noteworthy for its treatment of the phenomena of after-images and contrast. Newton had treated after-images as psychic phenomena, a view which could only be held on the basis of the ancient notion that the eye has an inner light which can 'emanate.' Jurin aimed to give an explanation of these ideas by supposing that the original stimulus persisted and caused a reaction by which the opposite sensation was produced. This view has been regarded as anticipating the general purpose of Hering's work. It was reasserted at the end of the century by Venturi, *Dei Colori Immaginarii* (1801), who 'maintained that the changing tints of after-images excited by the pure colours of the spectrum proved the existence of a multiple function for each nerve-fibre.'[1] In this statement there is the

[1] So stated by Burch, *Proc. Royal Soc.* lxvi. 204 (1900). I have not seen the work of Venturi.

further point that Bonnet had practically enunciated the formula of 'specific energies' (see p. 465), and Venturi is opposing the conception of 'one fibre one function.'

At this date the subject was limited to phenomena of successive contrast. Buffon, and after him Father Scherffer, undertook investigations upon this subject. Scherffer, for example, painted flowers with their complementary colours: the theory here implied was that of four colours. The work of Wünsch (*Ueber die Farben des Lichtes*, 1792) showed that a mixture of three colours could be made equivalent to any colour. The way was thus prepared for Young's theory, since these investigations showed that the number of primary colours was small and that each colour sensation was the function of some nerve-structure specially adapted to it.

Among other topics discussed in this period were the following: the duration of sensations of light, measured (after Newton) by Segner (*De Raritate Luminis*, 1749); measurement of sensibility by Bouguer (*Traité d'Optique sur les Gradations de la Lumière*, 1769); the process of accommodation, which occupies most of the prominent writers (Camper, 1760, Porterfield, 1759, Haller). The work of Priestley on the *History and Present State of Discoveries relating to Vision, Light and Colours* (1772) was the most important addition to the general literature of the subject.

Before the seventeenth century had closed the mechanists and the animists were two clearly distinguished types of theorists in physiology. As against iatrochemists and iatromechanists Stahl may be said to have had some justification: but his theory required modification and his point of view survived in the kindred but different theory of the vitalists. The starting point of this vitalism is to be found in the doctrine of irritability.

In 1672 Francis Glisson, Professor in Cambridge, wrote a work, *De Natura Substantiae Energetica*, in which he ascribed to the muscles a power of responding to stimulation, and described this 'irritability' as a general property of living matter. This was a new idea in so far as it substituted for a specific faculty of motion a more adequate concept of a general property of the tissues. But Glisson obscured his teaching by speaking of this irritability as a perception of irritation, and the point was not developed further. When the fact was again brought to notice a century later by Albrecht Haller, it was supported by more adequate proof and stripped of irrelevant additions. Haller treated the fact of irritability as a physiological datum and dissociated it entirely from sensibility; he was concerned only to demonstrate the properties of living tissues, and he reckoned irritability and sensibility as fundamental characteristics of vitality: he consciously opposed this irritability to the elasticity of inorganic substances.

The significance of Haller's views on irritability was differently understood by different speculative writers. If, as Haller's teaching suggested, all those parts of the body which possessed irritability were endowed with a life of their own (a material life, so to speak), what need had they of a 'soul'? The opportunity was obvious, and it was quickly taken by La Mettrie. Moreover, La Mettrie insisted on dedicating his work, *L'Homme Machine*, to Haller, who was assiduous in repelling this dangerous and self-elected friend. Haller sums up the point thus: 'Since irritability remains after death, since it is found in detached parts of the body which are withdrawn from the empire of the soul, since it is found in all the muscular fibres, since it is not dependent on the nerves which are satellites of the soul, it is clear that it has nothing in common with the soul, that it is absolutely different; in a word, that irritability does not depend on the soul and consequently the soul is in no sense this irritability.' This protest did not save Haller from being associated with the materialistic movement, especially as the rapid progress of research made further inroads on the traditional view of the soul.

Haller was a pupil of the great Leyden school, the school of Boerhaave and Albinus. One of the principal merits of this school was the attention paid to the study of the nerves, and the researches made on this subject prepared the way for successes not actually achieved at the time. Haller still retained the doctrine of animal spirits; he was their last great advocate, but even he considerably reduced their functions. The spirits were, at this time, supposed to be produced in the cortex, but Haller showed that the cortex was not the seat of sensation nor even the sole and only originator of movement: the white matter of the cerebrum and cerebellum was the real basis of both. Haller accordingly rejected all previous attempts to determine the 'seat of the soul,' and thus made room for a new beginning in the doctrine of localization. On the other hand, great importance was attached to the convolutions of the brain. Memory was explained as the persistence of impressions on the brain-substance, and a prodigious amount of area was required to accommodate even the memories of an ordinary individual. The convolutions gave the supporters of this antiquated psychology new hopes that room might still be found!

Under the combined influence of the two dominant ideas, irritability and animism, R. Whytt (1714–1766) and Unzer (1727–1799) laid the foundations of a doctrine of reflex action. Descartes had treated the facts which he observed as cases of mechanical reflection, analogous to the reflection of rays of light. The eighteenth-century physiologists had reached a much more developed stage; they were no longer concerned with mechanical reflection but with vital reaction, and to explain this it was necessary to show a connection between 'feeling' (this term being used to denote an action of the sensory nerves which does not arrive at the level of consciousness) and consequent (unintentional) motion. Observations of decapitated frogs suggested to Whytt and Unzer that the spinal cord was the mediator between 'feeling' and movement in some cases, and this was designated reflex action. A more definite interpretation of the data was given by the Hungarian, Prochaska (1749–1820).

Under the term *vis nervosa* Haller designated the power of the nerves to excite the actions of the muscles. Prochaska adopted the term in a wider sense as a general name for all the phenomena observed in the study of the nervous system. Thus the term really ceased to be the name of a thing at all: it became the symbol of a group or class of observable facts which were to be described without reference to any hypothesis. The description thus begun is now a classical example of scientific work. The *vis nervosa* was declared to be in the nerves, apart from the brain; it could be divided; it acts only in response to stimulus and is presupposed in all irritability. Irritability belongs to muscular tissue, sensibility belongs to the nerves. The nerves are only conductors, for the true centre of sensation is the brain; consciousness may or may not accompany sensation. Prochaska gave a very definite account of the reflex action, describing it purely as the transference of motion from the sensory nerves to the motor nerves, a process which could occur automatically without the intervention of consciousness.

To Haller's definition of the *sensorium commune* as coextensive with the white substance of the brain, Prochaska (and Hartley) added the medulla of the spinal column. Unzer and Prochaska adopted the view that the ganglia are also sensoria, capable of controlling reflex movements without reference to the cerebral centres. Thus the general description of the neural action which accompanies sensation and movement was brought to a high state of completeness. For the activities of thought Prochaska reserved a soul or psychic force distinct from the physiological *vis nervosa*. This distinction did not prevent its author from applying to the higher faculties his ideas of localization. The localization of the sense functions was naturally to be looked for at the point where the nerves concerned had their inner termination: to this Prochaska was tempted to add localization of 'faculties,' such as imagination, perception, and memory, anticipating the methods of Gall.

The sciences of life were now well on the way toward regeneration. After doing good service for many centuries, the nerve-tubes and their 'spirits' gave place to a doctrine of 'fibres,' a change which explains much of the novelty in the psychological theories of Hartley, Bonnet and all the so-called 'fibre-psychologists.' Haller's doctrine of irritability inspired the French school of medicine with new ideas which took form as the Vitalism of the three B's (Bordeu, Barthez, Broussais). This was at first no more than a principle of method expressing the belief that vital phenomena are not reducible to the formulae of inorganic life; unfortunately it grew from a method into a cult and, being adopted by German enthusiasts, passed into an entity called *Lebenskraft*. For half a century it was by turns either the motto of anti-mechanists or a pure nuisance.

Recently attention has been drawn to the works of Swedenborg, which in date precede the last mentioned writers. Swedenborg's *De Cerebro* (1745) has been said to give 'the essential features of the modern doctrine concerning the relative positions of the motor centres in the cortex of the brain': while the theory of 'cerebellula' is asserted to reach the same results as the modern neuron theory. To such merits the historian cannot be indifferent, but Swedenborg's contemporaries appear to have remained in ignorance of these achievements. Prochaska's elaborate historical notes do not mention Swedenborg, and the recognition of his merits has been the outcome of modern research.

Of deep and lasting importance was the work of Bichat, known to science as the founder of modern anatomy. The work of Vicq d'Azyr and of Soemmering was bringing general anatomy to a high state of perfection. Bichat (1801) gave a new turn to the science by investigating more minutely the tissues of the organism in order to discover the actual location of diseases. At the same time, comparative anatomy in the hands of Cuvier and others began to take a definite position among sciences. At an earlier date Trembley (1744) had inaugurated the study of micro-organisms by his observations on fresh-water polyps, and in 1745 Bonnet produced his *Traité d'Insectologie*. Taken together, these achievements increased rapidly and remarkably both the range and depth of the sciences of life. Next came the *Theoria generationis* of C. F. Wolff (1759), which stated a true doctrine of development applicable to plants and animals. Goethe's *Metamorphoses of Plant* (1790), an independent statement of the same principles, secured for Wolff's theory the acceptance which had been obstructed by Haller's rejection of 'epigenesis.' The concept of development now began to be active in many directions; in addition to Wolff and Goethe, Kant, in 1755, supported it by his statement of the nebular hypothesis. Buffon's *Histoire Naturelle* (1749), in spite of errors and omissions, was a force working in the right direction, and its wide sweep of speculation helped to educate his generation in the art of comparative thinking. Kant's *Anthropologie* (1775) showed that the old barriers were breaking down and the evolution of man from animals was no longer regarded as outside the range of sane speculation.[1]

The sciences can never be wholly separated; they continually exhibit a unity of interaction. From pure thought to chemistry is a long journey, but the stages are well marked and nicely graded. The 'spirit' of the ancients was the breath of life; for the physiologist respiration is a function of the organism, and respiration has certain aspects which can only be explained by the chemist with his analysis of combustion. Preliminary work achieved by Black (1760) and by Priestley (discovery of oxygen) culminated finally in Lavoisier's demonstration that men, animals, and plants have a function of respiration which can be expressed in terms of chemical combustion: the original dictum that 'the breath is the soul' was thus at last reduced to its true significance.

While the operations of the organism were thus attacked

[1] Erasmus Darwin's *Zoonomia* (1794) belongs to the class of ineffective suggestions toward an evolutionary system which this age produced.

separately and seemed to be justifying the 'materialists,' the general study of functions supplied another point of view. Life was defined by Bichat as 'the complex of functions which resist death,' and in this modified form vitalism went on its way. Bichat classified the functions as organic and animal; the former constitute a group which is independent of the will, the latter are subject to the will. For the history of speculative thought this division has great importance. If it is accepted, there is obviously a light and a dark side of human nature; there is a realm of activity in which man knows what he does, and at the same time there is another realm in which actions go on autonomously. Man is thus a creature divided against itself; nature in him goes on in its eternal course, necessarily making irruptions into his voluntary life which he barely notices; in a word, the whole system of conscious activities becomes an upper structure built on a dark foundation of natural processes which obey the transcendental 'blind will' of nature. The significance of this physiological scheme for later writers is to be seen alike in Schopenhauer's theories and the whole range of 'theories of emotion.'

2. PROBLEMS OF LOCALIZATION

A general localization of functions in the brain was attempted at a very early date. This was transmitted through the Middle Ages to modern times, losing its influence in the seventeenth century through the predominance of a kindred topic—the seat of the soul. The writers of the eighteenth century remained under the influence of this idea of a 'soul,' and made few attempts to deal with the higher functions of the intellect from the point of view of physiology or anatomy. The subject was therefore almost untouched when Gall and Spurzheim (1805) produced their ambitious attempt to distinguish and locate faculties numbering in all thirty-five. This 'Cranioscopy,' afterwards called 'Phrenology,' was more allied to physiognomy than to anatomy or physiology, and may be classed as a transition from such a doctrine as that of Lavater to the later experimental study of the cerebral structure. The distinction of faculties was crude. The comparison of different cranial formations, from which the localization was deduced, can only be described as still more crude. Neither the method nor the result was received with favour in scientific circles, though some great medical men supported them. In

England and America it was made popular by the work of George Combe (1788–1858), still treasured by hopeful parents, who expect to attain a prophetic knowledge of their children's abilities from an examination of their 'bumps.'

In spite of his unfortunate cranioscopy, Gall was an able anatomist, and credit is due to him for studying the brain and for insisting on the importance of establishing relations between cerebral structures and psychic functions. The great opponent of phrenology, Flourens, is the best witness to cite; he testified to Gall's skill as an anatomist, and declared that the proposition, 'the brain is the exclusive seat of the soul,' was to be found in science before Gall, 'but one can say that since Gall it reigns there.' Gall said of himself: 'I leave unsought the nature of the soul as of the body. . . . I confine myself to phenomena.' Lewes (*History of Philosophy*, ii. 414–54) devotes a long chapter to Gall, and while fully admitting the ultimate failure of his work, declares that his method and outlook were the beginning of a new era. In brief, Gall effectively overcame the lingering tendency to isolate man from nature; 'he concluded that the mind consists of a plurality of functions, a plurality of organs became the necessary corollary of this proposition as soon as the relation between organ and function was steadily conceived.' By way of contrast, Lewes quotes from Sir W. Hamilton the assertion that 'no assistance is afforded to mental philosophy by the examination of the nervous system, and that the doctrine or doctrines which found upon the supposed parallelism of brain and mind are, as far as observation extends, wholly groundless.' This view, by far the more popular at the time, was made more vicious by a readiness to admit that such a parallelism was tenable in reference to the 'lower functions' and in the case of animals. Hamilton's view was not so absurd as Lewes makes out; it was just as natural to reach that extreme from the subjective point of view as it was for Gall to reach the opposite extreme from exclusive attention to the brain. For Gall's method was spoiled by disregard of subjective analysis and a consequent ignorance of the very functions which he ascribed to the brain. Even the study of the organs was left undeveloped, but the current tendency to assign all kinds of physical results to such a faculty as 'imagination,' without further inquiry into anatomical relations and physiological properties, was decisively checked. The opposition developed along the lines of psychology and anatomy. Herbart opposed the phrenologists on the ground of the unity of mind; Flourens, on the ground that the cerebrum itself is a unity. The latter position could be maintained or refuted only by observation and experiment; it became accordingly the centre of a long struggle between the most eminent anatomists.

It was characteristic of the earlier stages of the discussion that a few experiments should be regarded as giving results universally valid. Flourens (1794–1867) made skilful experiments on the brains of pigeons (1822–24), and came to the conclusion that all reflexes were maintained after removal of the cerebrum; that all thought and volition was a function of the brain as a whole; and that there were no distinguishable 'centres.' This was a very natural result to attain, for several reasons. In the first place, it is extremely difficult to say exactly what effect is produced by a surgical operation on so complex a structure as the brain: the excision of a part may not have been complete, or it may have produced collateral effects by causing inflammation or degeneration of other parts; while the necessity of waiting till the wound has healed introduces all the possibilities of redevelopment in the area excised, or of vicarious activity acquired by another part. The possibility of vicarious action, such that any function temporarily lost might reappear if sufficient time was allowed as the acquired function of some other part of the brain, was for a time the strongest point in favour of Flourens, chiefly because it afforded an explanation of the recovery of functions even when that was due to inadequate operations on the alleged centres.

The original craniology of Gall was followed by the modified localization theory of C. G. Carus and Huschke. This, like its predecessor, was based on a faculty-doctrine, though in a refined form. The faculties of ideation, sensation, and volition were taken to be the fundamental psychic divisions; the forepart of the cerebrum was allotted to the first, the middle portions to the second and the cerebellum to the last. Apart from differences of terminology and a more extensive knowledge of the appearance of the brain, this did not differ essentially from the doctrine of Galen and his Arab followers. This doctrine, held up to 1850 by Carus and Huschke, was succeeded by the teaching of Flourens, which held the field up till 1870.

One of the earliest and most famous attempts to assign an area of the brain to a function was made by Bouillaud, a disciple of

Gall. Cases of aphasia (loss of the power of speech) had been described as early as 1742, but the honour of first studying the facts and connecting them with a lesion of the brain belongs to Jean Baptiste Bouillaud, Professor of Clinical Medicine at La Charité, Paris.

In 1825 this professor declared that the frontal lobes were the parts mainly concerned with speech; but, in spite of the 114 cases quoted to support the view, it is generally thought that Bouillaud was misled by his own views on phrenology. In 1833 fourteen cases were recorded by Andral which did not support Bouillaud, and his ideas were temporarily eclipsed until 'in 1836 Dr. Marc Dax called attention to the great frequency of loss of speech in association with right- rather than left-sided paralysis.' As *right-sided* paralysis would indicate lesion of the *left* hemisphere, Bouillaud found a new supporter in Dax. Lastly, in 1861, Broca definitely announced that loss of the motor power of speech was due to lesion 'of the posterior part of the third frontal convolution of the left hemisphere.' This disease he named 'aphemia'; the term 'aphasia' seems to have been introduced by Trousseau. The subject was studied by Hughlings Jackson (1864), Bastian (1898), Karl Wernicke, and others. Broca's aphasia consisted essentially in loss of the power of speech, and was regarded as a loss of motor power. Wernicke distinguished another type distinct from this motor aphasia, namely, sensory aphasia—i.e loss of power to identify the auditory words, the individual being able to talk much and badly. Wernicke localized the area affected in these cases close to that indicated by Broca. Matters were now more complicated. Sensory aphasia is a defect of mental power, and might be regarded as a mental disease coinciding with a defective connection between the cortical and the subcortical motor tracts. This subcortical motor aphasia goes by the name of anarthria, and has been described by Dejerine and Bastian.

An important aspect of this problem is the way in which it led to a fresh conception of the complexity of action. Kussmaul (1876) divided sensory aphasia into verbal deafness and verbal blindness. Charcot enumerated four types, adding to motor aphasia, verbal deafness, and blindness that state called agraphia. This requires that we should think of a word as analysable into four elements—the auditory, the visual, the graphic or schematic, and the articulatory. With this goes the important point that individuals differ in their tendencies to emphasize one or other of these aspects—a principle that has been applied to the sphere of memory, where it is found that some people remember sounds rather than forms (visual impressions), others recall what is seen rather than what is touched. To this we owe the valuable distintion of mental types, as James puts it: 'In some individuals the habitual "thought stuff," if one may so call it, is visual; in others it is auditory, articulatory or motor; in most, perhaps, it is evenly mixed.' The types are denoted as visual, auditory, tactile, and motile (*Principles*, ii. 60).

Though strongly supported, the theory of Broca was not unanimously accepted at any time. Trousseau doubted its absoluteness; Bernheim (1894) maintained that the various centres were fictitious, and the whole matter could be reduced to lack of co-ordination between the higher and lower centres; Charcot and Pitres noted cases of aphasia in which Broca's centre showed no lesion. But the great year of trial for the whole question was 1906, when Marie and Monakow indepedently reached conclusions that vitally affected the whole status of the problem. In the main Pierre Marie's contention amounts to a rejection of that psychophysiological view of language which (after Wernicke) divided the 'inner language' into images which were either verbal, auditory, visual or motor, assigning a different centre to each. He asserts that in all cases there is a general decrease of intellectual power, and not a loss of one function without impairment of the general mental vigour; there may be cases of anarthria, or lack of power to produce the symbols (speech, writing) which express the ideas, but this is not true aphasia; the essence of aphasia is not a specific lesion, as Broca thought, but a general mental defect which cannot be localized as Broca localized it, though the evidence tends to prove that the disturbance is connected with Wernicke's (intellectual) area.

A second era in the study of the brain began from 1870. Electricity had then become available as a means of stimulating definite areas, and in consequence it was possible to experiment on the cortical surface to discover the specific relations between various tracts and the functions which depended upon them. The principal names of this period were Fritsch, and Hitzig, Ferrier, Munk, Horsley, Schaefer, and Beevor.

This was not a return to the phrenological doctrine, because it was no longer an attempt to equate brain areas with faculties; the scientific character of the inquiry was vindicated by restricting the problem to the purely experimental basis, and collecting the reports on various operations which seemed to show that specific areas when electrically irritated produced specific actions; conversely, by the method of agreement and difference, excision of these areas would logically be followed by inability to perform the same functions. Fritsch and Hitzig, anticipated in part by Hughlings Jackson, declared against Flourens that there were motor areas in the cerebrum; but even then the results were not entirely reconcilable, and Goltz returned to the position of Flourens as regards the higher functions, though with many doubts and compromises.

From this point began a triangular contest. Goltz, a pupil of Helmholtz and Professor of Physiology at Halle (1870–72) and Strassburg (1872–1902), maintained that Munk had gone too far in his geography of the brain: he denied the possibility of ever attaining such an accurate plan of circumscribed areas as Munk tried to evolve. This amounted really to the maintenance of different hypotheses: Goltz championed the hypothesis of the unity of the brain; Munk that of its divisibility and plurality. Both were far too scientific to suppose that a hypothesis was more than a working principle; it was in both cases a definition of a general attitude, and the whole controversy shows a most creditable readiness to accept facts, when undeniable, from the opponent. The inconsistencies which resulted were not so much a weakness as a strength, for they arose from the continuous acquisition of fresh data and the consequent desire to attain more adequate hypotheses. The third party to the struggle was the Italian school, chiefly Luciani and Seppili. Their work was guided by the general conception of the brain as a complex of areas which overlap. In this hypothesis localization would be possible, but it could not be so definite as Munk maintained. Every centre or localized function is regarded on this scheme as having greater and less degrees of intermixture, so that the total area upon which a given function is dependent can be regarded as having a focus or centre and a fringe. This hypothesis clearly has the advantage of a mediating theory; it helps to explain many of the complications which arise from operations on the brain, and to give a reason for the agreements as well as the differences between the supporters of the two other hypotheses. Its value is only to be decided finally by the progress of direct investigation.

As it will not be possible to enter into this subject more fully, a brief indication of the main results will be given here. This will serve to show the general relation between physiology and psychology: it will be of use also in the later discussion of the problem of psycho-physiology and psycho-physics.

In 1872 Meynert, a physiologist of the Austrian school, described the structure of the cerebral cortex in a way that is still on the whole correct. The importance of Meynert's researches for the psychologist consists in his areas of 'projection areas' and association-fibres. The attempt to localize functions in the brain by experiments requiring extirpation was far from successful; it was followed and supplemented by a more developed method. The first part of this was the direction of attention to the point at which nerve-fibres enter the cortex of the brain; the second, begun most definitely in 1878 (by Bevan Lewis and Henry Clarke), was the examination of the structure of the brain with a view to distinguishing its strata—that is to say, the differences and relative positions of the tissues of which it is composed.

This tendency was part of a general movement. The earlier descriptive anatomy of the body was succeeded by the development of histology, including this histological analysis of the brain. Parallel with this work there has also been the evolutional study of the brain, a product of the comparatively recent science of embryology. This part of the work done on the brain is associated primarily with the name of Flechsig, who studied the exact stage at which myelinization takes place in the different parts of the cerebrum, and distinguished accordingly 'projection areas,' or sensory centres, from the later 'association centres.' At present a number of different methods are employed to define the nature of 'brain as an organ of mind,' to use Bastian's well-known expression. The study of the brain at different ages shows that the parts develop in a sequence, and this serial development can be equated with the corresponding acquisition or perfection of functions; conversely, loss of function can be equated with the condition of the brain if observed post-mortem; direct experiments on animals furnish collateral evidence in so far as comparative anatomy reaches to the functions of the brain. This last method was overworked in the earlier period, and probably also by

Flechsig. From the very fact that man holds a unique position in the matter of brain development, it follows that the utility of observations made upon animals is limited; and the complex character of brain activities, with the possibilities of educating the centres, has militated against the acceptance of Flechsig's results, which, it is said, he wrongly asserted to be true of the adult brain after observing them only in the immature stages.

3. PROBLEMS OF NEUROLOGY

Considered structurally in relation to the body, the brain is a complex union of nerves. The structure and workings of the brain can therefore be understood only in proportion as the nerves are studied. The most important event in the early history of neurology was the discovery made by Dr., afterwards Sir, Charles Bell that the nervous system is dual in character. The discovery seems to have been made in 1807, published in 1811 in an essay entitled *An Idea of a New Anatomy of the Brain*, communicated to the Royal Society in 1821, and finally stated in a work on the nervous system in 1830. Bell announced that the nerves connected with the spinal centres by anterior roots are employed in conveying motor impulses from the brain outward; from the posterior roots spring the sensory nerves. This was further demonstrated by Magendie in 1822, and established as the distinction between efferent and afferent systems. Bell afterwards showed that the cranial nerves also fall into two distinct classes, so that a dual system was proved to exist in the brain and definite courses for efferent and afferent impulses could reasonably be looked for.

The next most important step was taken by Marshall Hall (1835), following Legallois (1811), and associated with Johannes Müller, who added experimental verification (1835). The possibilities of reflex action had been lying dormant since the time of Descartes, though a few observations on the movements of decapitated creatures are recorded. Legallois (1826) and Flourens (1837) established the existence of a respiration-centre, thus giving a physiological supplement to the work of Lavoisier. The significance of the movement was shown in the work of Marshall Hall ('The Reflex Function of the Medulla Oblongata and Medulla Spinalis,' *Philos. Trans.*, London, 1833), which finally rejected all but the mechanical elements in reflex action and clearly showed that it is distinct from conscious volition. The doctrine of reflexes played a large part in the evolution of opinion from 1840 to 1870. That complete and apparently purposive actions could be carried out by 'spinal' animals (i.e. animals deprived of the higher brain structures) was a fact immediately discussed in all its bearings, both scientific and sentimental. Whether such actions are purely mechanical, or indicate that the lower centres have a consciousness of their own, was to be for many years a question hotly disputed. Just as the ancients had been puzzled by the fact that some animals could be subdivided, and have as many 'souls' as they had parts, so the moderns were for a time astonished at the prospect opened up by this conception of centres which belonged to man and yet did not live in the watchful eye of his Free Will. Meanwhile the more scientific aspects of the question were followed out, and a group of well-known physiologists (Purkinje, Remak, Henle, and Müller) added continuously to the sum total of knowledge about nerves.

During the earlier period attention was directed chiefly to the muscular system, and to those reflex actions which consisted in adjustments to external stimuli. A new turn to the question was provided by Claude Bernard in 1851. This famous teacher of physiology opened the way for many discoveries that have thrown light on the relation between neural activity and such organic processes as nutrition or secretion. In particular, Bernard studied the condition of the blood-vessels when the sympathetic nerve was cut, and his observations coincided both in time and nature with those of C. E. Brown-Séquard and Ludwig. To these three principally we owe the present developments in the sphere of vascular neurology—that is to say, the progress made in the study of the influence exerted by specific nerves (vasodilator, vaso-constrictor) on the blood-vessels, and the consequent changes which may be produced throughout the body by the sympathetic system. This has become an important chapter in the book of knowledge about human life. For the viscera and all the 'inward parts' are directly or indirectly connected with the brain. Not only may the internal states produce changes in the nervous system which affect perception, memory, and thought, but also perceptions, memories, and thought seem able to transmute their values into bodily changes. How these data are useful in psychology will best be seen in considering theories of the emotions.

When the phenomena were regarded as truly reflex, and consequently action arising at one point of the system might produce effects at another, the complexity of the problem was increased. In particular, all the problems of inhibition were brought into greater importance, for the application of a stimulus was found to produce contrary and paradoxical results, from which have been derived theories of 'antagonism' and of inhibition due to 'drainage.' That lower centres should be controlled by higher centres is obviously important for all development of conduct, and the subject of 'central inhibition' was taken up by Setschenow, who thought it was possible to determine an 'inhibitory centre' in the brain. Since that time the tendency has been to study correlation and co-ordination rather than pursue the search for 'centres.' As science advances it becomes more and more necessary to think that the real 'organ of mind' is the body.

The distinction of higher and lower centres, as used above, recalls the fact that in the decade after 1860 Spencer's evolutionary formulae came into fashion. Among those who used it effectively must be named Hughlings Jackson. He recognized in the nervous system three levels of evolution, and assumed that the nerve-centres have the function of 'representing' every part of the body. The levels are characterized by different degrees of specialization, an idea derived from von Baer, and by degrees of complexity, as conceived by Spencer. The lowest level has direct representation of impressions and movements (sensori-motor); after. this (automatic) stage comes a second level, in which the earlier representations are re-represented, subserving increased complexity, specialization, and integration; the highest level is that of the cortex (excluding specifically motor areas), and its function is re-re-representation in the highest synthesis which makes possible thought and volition. The nature of this evolutionary scheme is tersely expressed by saying that it postulates progress from the less to the more organized, from the automatic to the voluntary. It is a scheme intended to have reference to the nervous system only; consciousness, when it occurs, is a parallel phenomenon which merely accompanies neural process.

Another important theme is the development of the neuron theory. A beginning was made by A. V. Waller, a Kentish physician, 1850, with the observation that when a nerve is severed the part furthest from the cell degenerates, while that which is attached

to the cell recovers; from which it followed that the cell supplies
the nourishment and constructive power of the nerve fibre. In
1858 Joseph von Gerlach, of Mayence, began to employ a solution
of carmine for staining sections, and so made distinct the central
nerve-cells lying in the brain substance. The later methods of
Weigert, Golgi, Ehrlich, and Nissl are extensions and variations
of this method. The result is the modern conception of nerves.
In theory this originates from the wider doctrine of cells as it was
taught by Schwann and others, and originally appeared as a description of nerve-cells. The later form of the doctrine is distinguished from the earlier by incorporating and extending the work
of Waller and of Virchow. In place of the term 'nerve-cell,' it is
now customary to use the term 'neuron,' to indicate the complex
unit which consists of the ganglion cell, the axis cylinder, and
the tree-like branching processes (dendrites). In principle, a cell
is an independent unit of life, and it was therefore natural for the
speculative psychologists to think that cells were equivalent to
ideas, and that association between ideas had a physiological
counterpart in the paths by which activity passed from cell to
cell. The 'brain-paths' have had a long and honourable career as
a picturesque 'physiology of the higher processes,' but that career
is drawing to a close. Matters are not quite so simple as that view
suggests, and for the present there is a suspension of judgment
and a desire for more details.

The original doctrine of reflexes, as stated by Marshall Hall,
was the basis of many hopes that all relations of outer and inner
might be solved in some analogous fashion. But Hall was not
right in supposing that he could draw a rigid distinction between
volitional and reflex processes. More recent work (especially that
of Sherrington) has shown that there is an interplay of these
processes, and that the afferent and efferent currents are not
mere 'reflections' (as a ray of light might be reflected from a
mirror), but are connected through a complex mediation which
involves many nervous changes. The original conception of reflex
action has therefore been reconsidered and elaborated by the
introduction of reference to different levels of neural activity and
their integration in the 'reflex arc,' or, more correctly, 'reflex
circuit,' for the sensori-motor processes are really, as processes, a
continuous production of changes. Similarly, the neuron theory
has brought with it a considerable increase in problems awaiting

solution, particularly that of continuity. The natural discontinuity of a cell system is somewhat modified by the presence of those extensions which seem to reach out from cell to cell and establish contact. But the contact cannot be assumed, it must be observed; and it is doubtful whether any such observation has up to the present time been achieved. From the psychological side, interest is attached primarily to the possibility of the intermittent connection. For if the physiological basis is to be taken as equivalent to any kind of psychic process, it should admit of breaking as well as making connections. Some have maintained that contact is established only in and through states of excitement, so that the excitation of a centre would be the occasion for union by contact with other centres—psychologically attention would condition association. Unfortunately, on all these subjects there is no unchallenged view and no final agreement. For the possible variations of opinion the reader is referred to the works of the neurologists, notably Golgi, W. His, van Gehuchten, and Ramon y Cajal. The continuity of the 'sensorium' has been maintained by Held, Apathy, and Bethe; the intercellular bridges by Henson. Nissl thinks the grey matter is a conducting medium, while Cajal was inclined to favour temporary contact by expansion.

Finally, there are the problems which still belong to the sphere of conductivity. 'What is it which is conducted along the nerve?' Any satisfactory answer to this question is extraordinarily difficult. There is no visible motion of the nerve; no pull or push is exerted through it; no 'animal spirits' circulate rapidly through it to constitute the nerve impulse. The solution of these problems, if it were possible, would not come within the scope of our history. It must be enough to point out that this is the logical terminus of the evolution. If we grant any psychological value to localization and to the finer anatomy of the brain, it is at least illogical to neglect the dynamic aspects of these structures. But at present very little can be said on this subject, and the work so far done can scarcely be given any meaning in terms of consciousness. Chemical analysis of the brain yields certain results of a purely chemical kind, of which perhaps the demonstration of the presence of phosphorus in cerebral matter is the most clear and important example. This has also had some popular vogue, but the motto of 1860 (without phosphorus no thought) has long passed into the limbo of untruths. A new interest in the matter of 'conduction' was aroused by the doctrine of 'innervation,' according to which the agent in voluntary acts could experience the expenditure of effort as a positive outflow of spiritual vigour. This was clearly the old animal spirits coming back. The question dropped once more when it was shown that there was no psychological 'innervation,' but that all consciousness of activity was conditioned by the afferent, and not the efferent, currents.

This unfortunate lapse on the part of spiritual psychologists into a mystical doctrine of volitional energy has been partly the reason for the neglect into which the physiological problem fell. There seems to have been continual confusion between the innervation as a fictitious outflow of will power and innervation as a demonstrable physiological fact. Consequently, 'academic physiology had heard the term "nerve-energy," but it did not use it; it left it to the manufacturers of magnetic belts or electric boot-soles.' But the evidence for some kind of specific nerve-energy went on increasing, and led to statements of its possible nature. 'Dr. Hale White was the first English writer formally to enunciate the doctrine of the objective reality of nerve-force, which he did so far back as 1886, when he coined the term 'neuro-rheuma,' or flow in a nerve. Sir Victor Horsley and Dr. Sharkey have concurred in this teaching.' A later and more elaborate theory has been stated by Dr. McDougall, who links up the concepts of neurone and synapse with that of 'neurin.' Here we must leave the subject, for whatever may be said upon it could only be recited here if our annals were designed to reach the most modern times. As this sphere of research is made extremely complex by the fact that electrical phenomena accompany neural conduction, so that possibly a combination of mechanical, physical, and chemical processes must be postulated for every total process, any brief statement of 'facts' would be no more than misleading.

4. PROBLEMS OF SENSE-PERCEPTION

The nineteenth century was destined to witness more than one fundamental change both of thought and of expression. Among the most important changes must be reckoned that which has taken place in the treatment of sensations. The eighteenth century was, for the most part, contented with the division into external and internal senses. This was itself liable to confusion with the cognitive distinction between outer and inner sense. The student of psychology who follows the growth of the subject from Locke to the most recent times will frequently find how utterly these terms cloud the issues. Theoretically, the outer senses give us knowledge of objects or stimuli external to the organism; the inner senses report on events in the organism; while the 'inner sense,' as faculty of knowledge through reflection, is an internal agency for grasping the cognitive 'impressions.' Leaving this last meaning out of account, we may deal with the other two.

Clearly sensations as such are neither outer nor inner; some other considerations must arise to justify these terms, and that is actually the desire for useful classification. For some purposes the source of the stimulus may be a basis of classification; outer is then equivalent to epiperipheral, inner to entoperipheral. But for other purposes a different point of view may be selected, as in the distinction between mechanical and chemical senses; or we may adopt the standpoint of function, and speak of the senses as receptors, using such terms as exteroceptive (stimulated from outside), interoceptive (stimulated by internal organs), and proprioceptive (stimulated from the states of the tissues—e.g. muscular sense). The influence of evolutionary modes of thought, which emphasize order of emergence in organic development, has led to another mode of grouping according as the sensations depend on organs of vitality, mobility, or sensibility.

It was natural that crude experience should give most attention to the ordinary 'five senses'; but from early times additions were made to that list, and we find constant reference to vital and to muscular sensations. In this, as in other cases, the statements recorded are often ambiguous, and we can say without further qualifications that systematic work on these topics first began in the nineteenth century. In part this progress was dependent on advances in physiology. Such works as those of Beaunis (*Les Sensations Internes*, 1889), Horwicz, Schneider, and Funke represent close elaboration of physiological and psychic processes. By this work we may say, in brief, the vague notions of the 'inner sense' were fixed and made verifiable. The results were not significant for cognition, since the data did not belong to that sphere, but they became indispensable factors in theories of action where impulses dependent on total organic states regulated by hunger, thirst, or sexuality are predominant.

Next to the vital sense and the organic sensations in general comes the muscular sense, also included by older writers under the general head of 'inner sense.' The modern use of the term is hardly correct, for psychologically we should say sensation of movement rather than 'muscular sense.' Since the older views of a sense for muscular effort or a sense of innervation have been discarded, the term 'muscular sense' is a mere survival. The modern term *kinaesthesis* may be taken to represent the modern notion, which actually is based on (*a*) clinical and experimental proof that sensations of movement do occur, and (*b*) the discovery of sense-nerves along with motor nerves in the muscular system.

Lastly, as a final expansion and classification of the old 'inner sense' doctrine, we may note the development of knowledge about skin-sensations. Out of the vague conception of 'common feelings' there have emerged specific determinations of sensations for touch, pressure, and temperature. For the theory of touch E. H. Weber's work was fundamental (*Ueber den Tastsinn und das Gemeingefühl: De Subtilitate Tactus*, 1834). Hering's treatise on the *Temperatursinn* (Hermann, iii. 2) forms a landmark in the history of that topic. To the same field belong the often quoted essays of Blix and Goldscheider on cold and warm spots, first studied and described in 1882-85. A new phase of the subject was opened by the work of Dr. Head, who formulated a distinction between protopathic and epicritic sensations (1905-1908).

We shall now return to the earlier period in order to trace the movements which resulted in new views on the nature of sensation, in particular of sight and hearing.

In 1833 Johannes Müller was appointed to a chair of physiology at Berlin. The establishment of this chair marked the recognition of physiology as an independent sphere of science, and from this point begins a long line of important contributions to physiology and to psycho-physiology. Müller was a philosopher, as a thinker a worthy successor of Haller, whose *Elementa* was still the standard textbook, and was only superseded by Müller's *Handbuch*. He was one of those comprehensive workers whose ideas seem to be fully expressed only by a generation of men; biology, physiology, and psychology began afresh from him, and his ideas were developed by such men as Schwann, Virchow, Helmholtz, and Du Bois Reymond. His work marked the beginning of a new era in the history of science in Germany, for it checked that tendency to vague generalization which it was Hegel's misfortune to have stimulated beyond due measure. On the other hand, Müller was indebted to the philosophers for a general attitude toward science which was the opposite of narrow specialization and dogmatism. The great result of the philosophic movement in Germany was the production of a general belief in the unity of nature. This manifested itself in a consistent tendency toward the union of distinct points of view. The best example is that with which we are now most concerned, the union of the inner and outer through the combination of physiology (and later physics) with the earlier notion of psychology. We cannot do better than begin with the subject most prominently connected with Müller's name—the specific energies of the nervous system.

The term 'specific energies' is used to denote the doctrine that a given nerve has one and only one kind of reaction to a stimulus. The optic nerve, for example, may be stimulated by light, by electric shock, or by a blow, but the result will always be of the same qualitative order—a sensation of sight. This doctrine has several interesting aspects. One writer has pointed out that from the earliest antiquity there had always been an assumption of some sympathetic bond between the object and the eye, or between the external process and the inner physiological process. 'The real importance of what is called Müller's Law of Specific Energy is that it contains an explicit denial of any necessary qualitative connection or resemblance between the physical processes of stimulation and the psycho-physiological changes associated therewith in the sense-organ and "consciousness." ' Helmholtz spoke of it as 'the empirical exposition of the theoretical discussion of Kant on the nature of the human mind.' This affinity between Müller and Kant is noticed by Wundt, who adds that the doctrine has a strong likeness to Kant's views on *a priori* forms of sensation. Mueller's opponents declared that this was really a doctrine of innate physical dispositions, and to it they opposed a doctrine of 'indifference.'

Among Müller's many achievements are to be mentioned experiments on the sense of sight and on the action of the vocal cords; his theory of colour contract and of colour sensations produced by pressure; and the researches on the Bell-Magendie doctrine of nerve-roots already mentioned. Each of these studies was destined to expand in the ensuing thirty years, and they will be met again in their later forms. Here we shall follow the development of Müller's views on sensation and allied questions. Müller maintained that the nerves run from the periphery to the brain in such a way that the peripheral order and arrangement is reproduced in the brain; from which it follows that the stimulation of any area of the periphery is copied, or schematically reproduced, in the brain. This bears directly on the vexed question of the perception of space, which Müller thought was given by the nerves of touch, sight, taste, and smell equally; hearing was the only exception. E. H. Weber subjected the problem of touch to experimental analysis, and made this subject peculiarly his own. Müller, in addition to such subjects as instinct, gave special attention to the problem of visual sensation. In accordance with the general idea of 'specific energies,' Müller regarded the phenomena of light, darkness, and colour as dependent on the qualities inherent in the visual substance. This subjective treatment was the counterpart of the objective physical view taken by ·Newton, and was equally inadequate in its isolation. A complete theory of vision could not be deduced from this solitary proposition. Müller naturally adopted Goethe's views on colour, being compelled to stand by the immediate experiences in his analysis. He regarded visual perception of space as primarily dependent on an original consciousness of bodily extension. The subject has at first no perception of objects as external; the outer world is a product of experience. Similarly there is at first only a perception of space as having two dimensions, the equivalent of the retinal image and the stimulated points on the surface of the retina. The perception of depth is an element added by the progress of experience. Müller also was the first to give a satisfactory account of binocular vision, showing that there are points on the retina of each eye which so correspond that an object stimulating two corresponding points is perceived as one. This was established anatomically by tracing the course of the optic nerves and showing how the chiasma or crossing of the nerves provides for the union in a single result of two distinct retinal stimulations.

Müller followed Kant in regarding the idea of space as immediately given; it was developed, but not originally produced, by experience. The actual extension of the retina and the knowledge of its extension were taken by him as one original datum. The Herbartian psychologists did not admit this innate idea of space, but tried to give an account of its genesis. Herbart, and after him especially Waitz, felt the necessity of reducing extension to intension; the given sensations, they held, differ only in intensity, and therefore the only ground for the perception of space is a number of sensations differing in quality. Experience may be said to show that as the eye moves the sensations change in quality, for that which is clearest in one position becomes less clear in another, and a number of clear presentations then coexist with a number of partially clear presentations. These form a qualitative series, and both space and time are psychologically qualitative series. It is possible to reverse the series in some cases, namely those of space, and in this way space is distinguished from time. To Herbart belongs the credit of seeing that objective spatial order must be reached by psychology from a subjective series which is spatial in a different way. But it is necessary to remember that the retina is primarily a part of the whole sensitive surface of the body, and to consider what may be said about the rest of that surface, the skin.

Sight is a special case of touch. While Müller at Berlin was dealing with the problems of sight, his great contemporary at Leipzig, E. H. Weber, was making discoveries about the sense of touch. Müller's pupils include Du Bois Reymond and Helmholtz; Weber was the master of Lotze. Taken together, they form one of the most remarkable groups of scientific workers the world has ever seen. During the years from 1830 to 1860 they contributed epoch-making discoveries to such different sciences as physiology, physics, medicine, and psychology, while the last added a new chapter to the history of philosophy. The physiology of touch, it has been said, began with Weber. The vague idea that we know the spatial extension of our bodies was put to the test of experiment by Weber, with the result that he discovered the need of a certain distance between two points subjected to pressure before the points could be perceived to be two and not one. Further investigation showed that the required distance was different for different parts of the body, and a number of experiments were made by which the fineness of this sensibility was determined for each part.

The physiologists did not agree among themselves as to the explanation of these facts in terms of structure and nerve-endings. That, however, does not concern us. The psychological aspect of

the matter, the perception of space by touch, was passed over by
Weber, who believed that sensations never give immediately an
idea of space; they are only the occasions which bring into action
that innate power by which we perceive things spatially. The
field was left open to the psychologists, and the Herbartians were
ready to supply a theory of tactual space, in principle the same as
that given for visual space. The experiments of the physiologists
and the deductions of the metaphysical psychologists thus
remained disunited, if not discordant.

Herbart and Waitz deduced the spatial order of perceptions
from the unity of the soul and the consequent struggle which it
makes to preserve that unity, ending in series of presentations
more or less repressed. George supplied another element by
laying emphasis on motion, asserting that externality and position
in an external world are due to reflection upon experiences of
change due to movement.

The development of this subject reached a climax in Lotze's
theory of 'local signs.' Lotze followed the Herbartians in one
respect; he stood firmly by the doctrine that sensations differ
qualitatively, and therefore extension as quantitative is translated
into the language of quality when it is perceived. The problem as
viewed by Lotze is purely a problem of order. Space, as some
great receptacle of things, is left entirely out of view. The general
problem of *a* space, and the question whether this is perceived or
not, is simply left untouched. Lotze probably saw that the troubles
into which Kant's followers had fallen were due to beginning at
the wrong end, and discussing space before properly settling
the question of spatial order. It was comparatively easy, after
Herbart's work, to see that experience gives us sufficient basis for
assuming that when we perceive two or more things, the plurality
of the perceptions is equivalent to the perception that the objects
are external to one another. There are, of course, distinctions
which are not separations; we may distinguish the thing and its
value without giving them spatial relations; but when we do
separate we create spatial relations. Lotze is clear that the question
is primarily psychological, and he sets himself to show what
must be given in order to explain spatial order as a fact of experience. In this Lotze frees himself from the limitations of the
physiological treatment of sensations, and avoids falling into the
particular metaphysical quandary of the Herbartians.

Müller, as we have seen, took over Kant's view of space, and did not profess to amend it. Waitz could be refuted in a sentence: If space is generated from the different degrees of strength which the perceptions attain, then two impressions on the same area with different degrees of strength would be perceived as being in different parts of space. Lotze starts from the fact that where there are perceptions of difference there must be differences to be perceived. If each area of the body has such a difference, each sensation will have a quality distinct from the sense of touch as such; there must be a nervous process corresponding to this difference of quality, over and above all the nervous processes corresponding to other characteristics of this experience (degree of pressure, pain, etc.).

Lotze explains his theory by an analogy. If a person transferred the contents of a library from one place to another, he would first label each book; when he put them in their places, he would be guided by the labels, the signs of their spatial order (*Microcosmus*, iii. 2). The point of this analogy is in the fact that the actual space is irrelevant; a book is not in the same *space* when it is in a new library, but it is in the same *place* relatively. The value of Lotze's view depends wholly on this point. He maintains that the essence of spatiality for the mind is the recognition of a certain kind of order which is represented ideally by qualitative differences. This view is a part of Lotze's ideal-realism. It has its difficulties, but it is acknowledged to be the best hypothesis which idealism can produce to explain space in terms of experience. The objections of physiologists, that they cannot find the neural counterpart of these 'local signs,' would not affect Lotze; the relation of the psychological to the physiological data is such that psychology is justified in setting problems for physiology, saying to it that the function is known and the organ must be looked for. There are also other possible objections which can be brought against the theory, but its virtues deserve to be considered first. One point is particularly instructive. Weber, having discovered that two points of pressure are only distinguished as two when the intermediary space is sufficiently great, was then compelled to say that the consciousness of the points was accompanied by a consciousness of the intervening space which was *not* perceived. This unfortunate explanation was the most natural deduction from the doctrine that the perception of space as a whole preceded experience. Lotze could not correct this. For if the points are distinguishable, their local signs differ; if the signs do not differ, they are not distinguished. An observer might see that what the person called one point of touch was really two; but the experience of the observer must not be confused with the experience of the person observed. But in some respects we observe ourselves, and if the whole question of localization is taken up, it will be necessary to consider how far the mature experience is complicated by remembrance of previous experiences in which the sense of sight and of movement may have co-operated. Lotze's theory sets no limits to the education of the senses which may be achieved in this way.

Lotze's theory was restated with greater detail by G. Meissner (*Beiträge zur Physiologie des Sehorgans*, 1854) and survives to the present day. But its rival also flourishes, and the details of the contest form a large part of the theory of spatial perception during the nineteenth century. The broad lines of theory, to which this sketch must be limited, were continually shaped by details of observation and experiment. The period from 1830 to 1870 might well be styled the classic period in the history of optics and the allied subjects. In 1834 W. H. F. Talbot, the inventor of photography, described the effect produced by a rotating disc with black and white sections; he formulated the law still usually called 'Talbot's law.' The credit of the discovery was actually shared by Talbot with the Belgian, J. A. F. Plateau, who is also known as author of the method of differences. In 1838 the researches and inventions of Wheatstone, discoverer of the stereoscope, gave new food for thought, particularly on account of the way in which they showed the disparity of the visual images. From then onwards we meet a number of names famous in the annals of science, as, for example, Brucke, Dove, Donders, Brewster, Listing, Volkmann, Chevreul, Nagel, Panum, Fick, Hering, all of whom made one or more important contributions to the subject of vision. The period came to a climax with Helmholtz, who summed up and co-ordinated the work of his predecessors. In 1868 Helmholtz gave his support to the local sign theory, and designated it the empirical theory of vision. The essential elements of that theory were (*a*) difference between the sensations of various parts of the retina depending on their local difference, and (*b*) a capacity for learning the significance of these differences for purposes of motion and direction of action in the world of spatially related objects. On the other side (nativistic), Hering maintained (1879) that the local sign or space-value is given to consciousness immediately, without the mediation of sensations of movements (Lotze). There the matter remains, so far as concerns the so-called empiricist and nativistic theories. A third type of theory has been called 'genetic,' and may be regarded as a development from the Herbartian doctrine. The difference between the various standpoints is not actually so clear as these nominal oppositions would suggest; and to a large extent the genetic theory is a compromise. On the one hand it rejects the purely nativistic argument; it relies, at the same time, on local signs as ultimate data, and traces the complete formulation of the spatial perceptions to a process of fusion. Wundt has elaborated these ideas, and Lipps supported a similar theory based on fusion without reference to movement. That the whole subject is capable of another treatment seems shown by G. E. Müller's article, 'Ueber die Localization der Visuellen Vorstellungsbilder.' He applies the method of the Würzburg school, and finds localization to be affected by conditions and attitudes of the subject. This suggests that the earlier work was too exclusively physiological. Among recent writers a general dissatisfaction is the most obvious feature: no definite explanation is yet attained. For example, Külpe reserves judgment, after rejecting the existing theories. W. McDougall (*Body and Mind*, p. 307) thinks 'we have not advanced beyond Lotze.' Stumpf and James take space as a primary datum. Ward and Stout employ the term 'extensity' for the particular quality of a group of localized sensations which have implicit space order.

5. VISION AND HEARING

Following the track of history, we have been led on from sight to touch, from touch to the problems of localization and space. Another topic occupies a prominent place in this period—the discussion of the visual sensations. In addition to what is known about the anatomy and histology of the eye, the study of visual sensations may be approached from the side of their stimuli (the Newtonian analysis of light) or their actual nature as experiences. It was the latter question that attracted Goethe's attention, and led him in 1812 to give a description of colour blindness. Goethe's interest in colour was mainly aesthetic; he was concerned with the actual sensations which could be experienced, and desired to find out what general feelings were associated with different colours, an interesting topic that might be profitably pursued. From this point of view, black and white are to be reckoned as 'colours,' a view which came to Goethe directly from Aristotle. Aristotle, Goethe, and Hering constitute one distinct line of investigators concerned with sensations as experienced.

In 1819 Johannes Evangelista Purkinje, a young graduate in medicine from Bohemia, wrote as his inaugural dissertation a work on subjective visual phenomena (*Beiträge zur Kenntniss des sehens in subjectiver Hinsicht*), which attracted Goethe's attention. Later he became Professor of Physiology and Pathology at Breslau, and until his death in 1869 continued to make valuable contributions to many different departments of science. As a physiologist he is remembered as the first to use the term protoplasm, as the discoverer of the ganglionic cells in the brain and those fibres which bear his name; but he is to be mentioned here on account of his work on the subjective visual experiences which are caused by galvanic stimulation and on the relation between brightness of colour and intensity of light. The so-called 'Purkinje phenomenon' is the fact that with decreasing intensity of light the colours with short wave-lengths become relatively more visible. Green and blue survive when red and yellow fade. 'In a summer evening, for example, the green of the marshes may be seen against the blue of the sea long after the golden rod and tansy have lost their colour, and after the old red farmhouse has turned gray.'

Thomas Young was an extraordinary genius, a brilliant linguist, famous in physics as the author of the wave theory of light, an authority on the phenomena of tides, an expert Egyptologist, a decipherer of hieroglyphs—in fact, a prodigy. By profession Young was a doctor, with degrees from Göttingen and Cambridge, and a practice in London. He has been called the 'father of physiological optics,' and it is as the first expounder of what is now called the Young-Helmholtz theory of colour-vision that he claims notice here. The possibility of reducing all colours to three fundamental colours and their mixtures was recognized before Young's time; his particular contribution (1807) was the suggestion of a physiological basis consisting of three sensation processes assigned to three kinds of nerve-fibre independent in their action.

Young's theory remained as he left it until Helmholtz began the researches which finally appeared as the *Physiologische Optik* in 1867. Apart from its achievements in detail, this work of Helmholtz, together with that on hearing, gave a new impulse to all attempts at an interpretation of perceptions through analysis. For Helmholtz was a man of philosophic mind. His father was devoted to the idealism of Fichte; the young Helmholtz saw the futility of that 'nature-philosophy' which ruled the Germany of his youth; he spent his days and nights in the pursuit of knowledge, with a craving for exactness as the only salvation of the spirit; and in time medicine, mathematics, and physics became for him the means by which the inner world of thought might objectify and realize itself. This fact gives Helmholtz a place in the history of speculative thought akin to that of his teacher Müller, and not vitally different from that of the young Lotze. The attitude common to all these is that of the man who has a theory to apply, and is aware that his theory must wait on detailed investigation and inductive reasoning. The theory formulated by Helmholtz was based on the belief that every sensation as it is immediately known signifies but never copies an objective fact. It is the task of science to discover and express in its own language that objectivity to which the subjective experience points. An attempt to deduce the objective reality from the subjective movement of the spirit is, on this view, worse than absurd; in other words, Fichte, Hegel, and the '*Naturphilosophie*' were useless, not by accident, but by their very nature. The '*Weltanschauung*' of Helmholtz has a grandeur of its own; it also proved fruitful in shifting the centre of interest from speculation without facts to speculation allied with experiment. The two great fields in which Helmholtz worked—those of vision and hearing—are good illustrations of his theory; in both there are elements and factors which enter into experience, yet could never be deduced from experience without the aid of science.

In the particular case now under discussion the colours of any ordinary experience are found to be either mixed or pure. The latter, stated by Helmholtz as red, green, and violet or blue, are to be considered as pure sense-processes, requiring therefore separate physiological bases described as nerve-elements capable of one kind of activity only. The production of a colour sensation is, on this theory, to be ascribed to the activity of all or some of these three 'fibres,' each having a distinct kind of process, and responding to distinct kinds of stimuli (the different wave-lengths of the different colours in the spectrum analysis). For purposes of experiment a given stimulus is employed, complex in nature; a given sensation is produced; and it is assumed that the resulting perception of colour is equivalent to the physiological changes produced by the stimulus in the 'substances' of the retina. For example, a wave-length R affects the substance R^1 alone, causes a neural process in the fibres leading to the visual centres, and produces the perception of a red object.

As this is not a psychological analysis, it is not open to criticism on that basis. Just as the painter learns to mix pigments so as to produce certain results, the physical experimenter learns to mix stimuli, and the physiologist adds a complementary theory of the processes that result from those stimuli as suggested by the structure of the visual apparatus. If we ask what connection this has with psychology, we may say that it has none. But it is owing to work of this kind that psychological works have in fact changed their character and their contents. The sensation, which is the real starting-point, is a psychological datum: if we desire to know the relation of that sensation to the external world as it is known to science, this seems to be the way in which the gulf between subject and object can be bridged. This desire is the source from which has come the intermediary science called 'physiological psychology.'

From the Young-Helmholtz theory of three colours, we may now go back to Goethe's four colours, and consider its physiological basis as constructed by Hering. In its original assertion of six colours, this theory contained the old (Aristotelian) confusion of brightness and colour. Hering distinguished the quality of brightness from that of colour, but retained the six elementary forms—namely, (a) white and black (toneless), and (b) blue, yellow, green, red (toned). A toned colour, says Hering, may be regarded as made up of four primary components, two toned and two tone free (black and white). This position is reached by taking the four toned colours as equivalent to two pairs (red-green, yellow-blue), one component of each pair coexisting with black and white. 'In any red-yellow colour—e.g. orange—we have accordingly to distinguish three bright, pure components (red, yellow, white), and one dark (black); but in any green-blue, three dark (green, blue, black) and one bright.' Thus we get a 'four-colour' theory, suggested by a physiological assumption of four substances which separately undergo constructive or destructive processes (anabolic, katabolic) set up by stimuli. The further consideration of this theory belongs to physiology, and is a matter of detail. At present there is no final basis for judging the two theories, and no way of deciding which school will ultimately prove to be right.

The necessity for a theory different from that of Young or Helmholtz arose from the fact that the physical doctrine of light affords no explanation of after-images and simultaneous contrast. This point, which Goethe emphasized, was elaborated in 1865 by Aubert (*Physiologie der Netzhaut*) in a theory based on four fundamental colours. Hering's view is regarded as a development of this teaching. Almost at the same time (1866) Max Schultze declared that the rods of the retina function in perception of light, while the cones give both light and colour perceptions. This was restated by Parinaud (1881; *La Vision*, 1898) and von Kries (1894), apparently in each case as an independent discovery. Since two mechanisms (rods, cones) are here employed, this is known as the 'duplicity-theory,' and now ranks with the others as the third important theory of vision. All the theories have given rise to much dispute and many variations, which cannot be explained here on account of their technical character.

For the details of the various theories of vision the student must consult the standard works on the subject. The sketch offered here is no more than an illustration of the movements which have constituted the more obvious differences between earlier and later treatments of the subject. The main points to be emphasized are the following:

(*a*) The sense-data, the visual experiences, can be observed under experimental conditions. This process helps to determine accurately the factors which at a given time control behaviour.

(*b*) A similar method applied to the behaviour of animals shows how far the retinal stimuli are effective factors in the life of animals.

(*c*) Something may also be done, from the study of literature or by direct experiment, to decide whether there has been an evolution of the colour sense in the history of mankind.

It is obvious that if satisfactory results can be obtained, they will form an important body of knowledge about human and animal behaviour. It may ultimately be possible to construct a formula of evolution from a primitive state of sensibility to the most subtle discriminations of colour. It may be possible to determine whether colour perceptions are functions of the visual apparatus as a whole or are strictly cerebral. It may be possible to understand the psycho-physical processes so adequately that emotional values can be correlated with colour schemes through the general organic processes which accompany the varying stimulations experienced as colours. While these and many other possibilities open out to speculative minds, it is at present necessary to recognize that the speculative element is large, and that existing theories of vision command general assent only on the most fundamental points. In addition to anatomical structure of the eye, as a necessary preliminary, the psychologist is most concerned with the differences between direct and indirect seeing; colour blindness; relation of the colour effect to (1) length of the light-wave, and (2) intensity of the stimulus; combination of stimuli and colour-mixture; effects of spatial proximity as giving contrast-values; and, finally, the time-relations of the stimulations as affecting questions of adaptation and the formation of after-images.

Helmholtz treated the sensations of sound as thoroughly as sensations of sight, and with even more decisive results. He possessed, in addition to his unrivalled knowledge of mathematics and physics, a singular ingenuity in the construction of the instruments which were required to test his hypotheses. This faculty enabled him to foresee where difficulties would arise, and to anticipate the points at which the practical application of the theory would reveal its weakness. The subject of sound was in need of that particular kind of synthetic thinking which Helmholtz was able to give it. After he had once entered the field, he supplemented the shortcomings of innumerable other workers; he supplied mathematical men with finer points of physics, showed the teachers of physics how to develop mathematical methods, visited famous organ-builders and gave them valuable hints—in short, held together in one comprehensive group the different aspects of a subject wide enough to include theories of tuning-forks and Chinese music.

The particular contribution made by Helmholtz to this subject was the description of 'clang colour.' It is a matter of common observation that what is usually called 'the same note' is very different on different instruments. Helmholtz explained this different 'colour' of the fundamental sound as due to the presence of over-tones, showing that the number and intensity of these over-tones was different for different instruments, and that these differences corresponded with the difference of the experience. As mathematical physics progressed in the analysis of the sound or objective stimulus, and as in consequence the difference of one sound from another could be expressed in vibrations and complexes of vibrations, the physiologists were called upon to discover a structure sufficiently complex to take up or respond to the distinguishable tones. The general knowledge of acoustics favoured the hypothesis that the human body contains an instrument sufficiently complex to produce sympathetic vibrations corresponding to definite wave-lengths. The Helmholtz-Hensen theory is the resulting compound explanation of hearing: for Hensen, taking the vibration-theory of Helmholtz, showed that the basilar membrane is structurally adequate to the work required by this hypothesis.

This theory makes large demands on the imagination. It seems to rest primarily on a conception of specific energies, since it requires for each stimulus a special physiological element capable of responding to one, and only one, stimulus. It must therefore suffer from any suspicions that may be roused as to the validity of specific energies. As early as 1879 James (*Psych.*, ii. 169) said that he was disinclined to accept the theory, and in 1886 his position was strengthened by Rutherford's views, communicated in that year to the British Association. Work done later by Rayleigh on sound, and by Ewald and Meyer on hearing, have tended to show that James was right in thinking 'the Helmholtzian theory is probably not the last word in the physiology of hearing.' The new point which most affects the general theory is the fact that (according to Rayleigh) it is no longer correct to regard the periodicity of the sound-waves as ceasing where the nerve process begins; on the contrary, the periodicity is continued from the sound-waves to the nerve-currents. If this theory is finally established, it will bring to an end the doctrine of specific energies. It may also involve, both for seeing and hearing, a new interpretation of the basis of qualities, providing in differences of period a common denominator for interpreting differences of tone and of colour.

The work of Helmholtz has called for special notice, not only as an advance in respect of details, but also as the real basis of experimental psychology. The method used by Helmholtz was not that of the mere specialist: it was distinguished by its synthetic character and its tendency to break down the departmental character of the sciences—a character which is not so much due to the nature of things as to the nature of man. The existence of departments of knowledge is a convenience highly prized by those who find one thing enough for them to do; it is the privilege of superior abilities to override the distinctions. But the ability must be of the right kind. Helmholtz united one subject with another by filling up each one individually until it overflowed into another. This was a way of maintaining the unity of knowledge which was consciously chosen and followed as a reformation of the decaying 'Naturphilosophie.' Experimental psychology came into existence in this way, and in the light of this genesis it must be estimated. Historically, we should perhaps have begun with the famous enunciation by E. H. Weber of a general law governing the relations between stimuli and sensations. This was not done because Weber's statement was a mere by-product of physiology when that science was only emerging from obscurity, and its great exponents were not conscious of any intention to develop a new union of the spiritual and the material. This expansion of the whole subject was the work of Fechner.

6. FEELING AND EMOTION

During the last quarter of the nineteenth-century the more eminent psychologists uniformly complain that the subject of feelings is the most obscure part of the science. For many reasons this subject steadily acquires importance as the century draws to a close and it may usefully be regarded as one of the directing lines in the historical development. For this reason a few pages will be devoted to the attempt made by Horwicz to construct a psychology entirely on the basis of feeling.

In the region of 1850 two antithetic lines of development were still running parallel—the older Hegelian and the newer natural-istic lines. The former waned as the latter waxed, and the single outstanding feature of the next fifty years was the advance of physiological and biological conceptions. The Hegelians, represented by Erdmann and Schaller, were doomed from the first by the fact that they treated the feelings as a phase of the dialectial movement, which was supposed to explain the evolution of the spirit in man. As the physiological basis is not known immediately by consciousness, it was disregarded. The failure of Hegelian psychology was mainly due to this belief that what is not itself a phase of consciousness cannot be used to explain consciousness, a point of method which ultimately rules out physiology, neurology, and natural evolution. The wider basis taken by Lotze in his *Medicinische Psychologie* (1852) furnished the most authoritative and effective foundation for the new developments. In this we find emphasis laid on the action of nerves and muscles, vital activity, and reflex action. Lotze himself was inclined, in his later writings, to say less about those things; but scientific interests made his earlier work more effective among his contemporaries than the later productions. Much to his annoyance, in later years Lotze was often quoted as a supporter of the purely mechanical interpretation of life and mind. In reality both Lotze and George (1854) were attempting to give due weight to both the mechanical or involuntary movements and the consciously-directed system of actions. The feelings were regarded as concomitants of neural action, either in the sense that excessive action is pain, appropriate action pleasure, or in the more general sense that pain is the lowering, pleasure the raising, of vital feeling. If the latter view is restated on the assumption of a natural impulse to live, psychology can be constructed, as by Fortlage (1855), on the basis of impulse alone. Of this particular attempt we may say that it lacked inductive method, and consequently was simply pseudo-scientific.

The Herbartian school more or less strictly followed the master's doctrine that feeling is reducible to relations between ideas. An attempt to make this view acceptable in a new atmosphere is seen in J. W. Nahlowsky's book, *Das Gefühlsleben* (1862; second ed., 1884; third, 1907). The new point in this work was the union of the original doctrine with Lotze's conception of vital activity. The struggle of the presentations which Herbart formulated as a doctrine of conflicting or co-operating energies, added and subtracted mathematically, here loses its abstract nature and becomes a concrete exposition of desires and feelings. But the essence of the Herbartian doctrine is that presentations are original. Consequently, feelings are derivative, and must either depend on ideas or come into a circle of ideas, as it were, surreptitiously. Nahlowsky abandons the theoretical basis so far as to distinguish between lower and higher feelings—that is, between feelings as dependent on sensations (colours, sounds, and the like) and feelings dependent on ideas (aesthetic, moral). The former can only be treated physiologically, and if it is maintained that the physiological process, by increase or decrease of activity, produces *felt* differences, it is no longer possible to avoid the argument that this doctrine requires for its completion a theory of the unconscious.

So at least thought Hartmann, not without a prejudice in favour of that theme. He, more even than the others, consciously aimed to reconcile the philosophers and the physiologists. As idealist, he thinks a feeling can only exist in consciousness; an unfelt feeling is an absurdity. He thinks, too, that all feeling is either pleasure or pain; further, qualitative differences are really differences in the accompanying sensations or ideas. But these sensations and ideas have their degrees: they sink below the threshold of clear envisagement; they persist in some degree, and their existence is revealed by the dim, uncertain character of the total feeling. Passing by the difficulties of the 'primitive atoms' and the synthesis of these 'atomic feelings' into feelings 'above the threshold' (all of which is a medley of Herbart, Haeckel, Schopenhauer, and Darwin), we can do justice to the fact that Hartmann came by this devious route to a very adequate recognition of the complexity of the emotional life. His 'absolute Unconscious' (*vide* p. 578) might not commend entire acceptance, but he had made a new era by not only accepting the physiologists as his allies, but also engulfing them, as it were, in the bottomless depths of his metaphysics.

The last extreme step in this development was taken by Horwicz. Here the situation is inverted, and in place of efforts to adjust the feelings in their relation to the rest of psychology, we find psychology as a whole adjusted to and based on the doctrine of feeling. Adolf Horwicz (1831–94) entitled his work *Psychologische Analysen auf physiologischer Grundlage*. As he himself remarks, the title was like many others, but the book, unlike others with the same title, was true to its name. The work appeared in three parts at intervals (1872, 1875, 1878), and there are signs that the times moved faster than the writer. The first part is a general exposition on the lines of a modern textbook—that is to say, it begins with the physiological propaedeutic, deals with sensation, consciousness, reproduction, association, and analysis of our 'ideas.' Though now obsolete, the physiological part of the work deserves praise. Without being original, it is well selected, and also successfully combined with the psychological parts. Horwicz had learned something from G. H. Lewes in this matter. In the second and third parts we find the author obviously feeling that Wundt's work had already passed the limits of his own ambition, and so continuing to the end with a novelty that had already ceased to be new.

Between the publication of the first part and the issue of the second (*Analyse des Denkens*) Horwicz had time to read his critics and estimate his own success. He finds it necessary to tell the public what points they had missed. These were primarily the relation of sense-feelings to common feeling and the reduction of memory to a gradually complete reaction of feeling. In other words, Horwicz had reduced everything to feelings, and he continues that process in the *Analysis of Thought*. The basis is the neural system and its functions. The ideal for psychology is to reduce all forms of psychic activity to elements which are as well known in their physiological aspects as the sensations. A sensation is a nerve-movement, and the new cerebral physiology indicates that the brain has sufficient complexity to justify the assertion that the higher processes are analysable into complications and irradiations of the primary nerve-cell excitations. Horwicz thought that Darwinism supported his view of feeling as the original form of all consciousness; feeling leads to movement, which, as the reaction of the organism, iş equivalent to primary involuntary attention. Sensation is purely subjective: in itself it conveys no knowledge, for we have to learn that an objective stimulus of a certain kind is its cause. Feeling is always accompanied by impulse to act: sensation is always incipient movement. The coexistence of these gives the higher complex state in which there is tendency to motion and choice of possible movements. Thinking is a process in which we anticipate the results of action, and consequently feel inclined to one course rather than another. Though the 'metaphysicians,' whom Horwicz dislikes, have attached great importance to thinking, it is, on this view, no more than a sequence of ideas controlled by feeling and accompanied by more or less obscure movements. It might be said that 'abstract' or theoretical thinking could not be covered by this description. To meet the objection, Horwicz explains that all search for causes is the satisfaction of feeling. We stumble, and then go back to see what caused the stumbling, so that we may feel more sure about our future course. The most complex science is not different in kind from this simple procedure. It is an elaborate satisfaction of feeling achieved through the driving force of desire (as felt), ultimately the desire to gain pleasure and avoid pain. We are, of course, exhorted to take the terms 'pleasure' and 'pain' in no Cyrenaic sense, but as equivalent to the increase or decrease of vitality.

The last stage of the *Analysen* was a work on the feelings, which seems to have fallen flat and was criticized as neither original nor useful. In fact, Horwicz was more intent on constructing psychology from the basis of feeling than on producing a psychology of feeling. In spite of the many defects in this work, there are elements of distinct historical interest. We may grant that it fails at the crucial point. It does not prove that feelings exist at first apart from all other psychic modes; and it does not satisfactorily generate knowledge out of feeling; while ultimately its physiology lapses into schematism and false analogies. But on the other side must be reckoned the many subtle observations of detail, and the broad fact that Horwicz had a true sense of the course which psychology would follow. He does not pose as a materialist, but he coins the significant phrase, '*Ohne Blut keine Gedanke.*' He uses the concept of feeling to attain a unified view of consciousness, adopting a method which was to be more successfully handled by those who took will for their unifying factor. He faces squarely such problems as that of 'synthesis,' and makes an honest attempt to show how unity of conscious life is conditioned by the neural substrate and its complex network of cells. He makes, in short, the kind of contribution to psychology which was to be expected from a physiologist, and he disappoints our expectations because he is not a physiologist capable of making the required inductive researches.

The period from 1860 to 1880—the era of G. H. Lewes and Spencer in England, of L. Dumont in France, and of Horwicz in Germany—shows the beginning of a desire to explain the 'problems of life and mind' from a new point of view and a new basis.

The inspiration of these writers was drawn from the widest outlook on nature, the first glimpses of a comparative psychology. The next decisive movement was to be produced by a fusion of two methods, one dependent on expression and the other on introspective analysis. The 'expression of the emotions' is a subject which for the British mind is inseparably associated with the name of Darwin. Spencer, Piderit, and Wundt have made contributions to the same subject. The principal interest in these works was centred on the origin of the movements which express emotions, and the possibility of showing that facial or other expressions were the residues of primary actions. So, for example, Darwin explained showing the teeth in rage as the residue of the earlier and more barbarous process of actually biting.

It was theoretically maintained that these manifestations of emotion were only the outer signs, and that, however much these might be repressed, some physical expansion or contraction was a concomitant of every emotional state. The experimental proof of this was given by Mosso and Féré. Angelo Mosso, Professor of Physiology in Turin, wrote a book on fear (*La Paura*, 1889), which quickly became a classic of its kind. Charles Féré, a pupil of Charcot, wrote on *Sensation et Mouvement* in 1887. In the same year Carl Georg Lange produced his famous monograph, *Ueber Gemüthsbewegungen*, which has close affinities with the views that James propounded as early as 1884 in *Mind* and restated in his *Principles* (1890). The development and significance of the points common to those works show the general character of the change which came over the theory of emotions during that period.

The general trend of movement was here, as always, from the more to the less obvious, from the outer to the inner, and in the main centred upon the importance of the vasomotor system. Mosso invented apparatus for measuring the expansion and the contraction of the lungs and the blood-vessels, thus bringing these modes of expression under experimental control. Féré conducted researches chiefly on muscular energy, and believed that the general outcome of his experiments was the proof that appropriate stimuli cause expansive activity, inappropriate stimuli cause contraction.

The general emphasis on these organic phenomena, particularly the variations of blood-pressure, took effect on psychology in the form of a theory that what is called an 'emotion' is in reality a reflection in consciousness of the organic changes taking place. This may be called the 'peripheral' theory. The peripheral theory can be so called because the essential feature is the emphasis laid on the order of events: first comes the objective stimulation of the senses; then the inner organic changes and consequent movements; finally, the consciously recognized state of mind. Briefly and in concrete: we see a bear; we have a sudden redistribution of the blood, the heart beats more strongly, the legs move rapidly in a manner that increases the distance between us and the bear. The observer, or our self when normal, declares we were frightened. A fondness for popular expressions, and a tendency to such epigrams as 'We are sad because we weep,' enabled James to advertise this doctrine, but made the consequent ideas about it obscure.

Lange and Sergi in Europe, James in America, have been the principal exponents of this teaching. It has met with vigorous criticism, chiefly on the point of identity; for James said (at one time) that the muscular and other organic readjustments were the emotion,[1] a pure identity of physiology and psychology which the author did not wholly mean nor finally defend. Though the phrase 'James–Lange Theory of the Emotions' is now widely current, it is not an exact title of anything. Lange (and Sergi) were openly discussing the physiological aspects of behaviour in what people usually call 'emotions.' James was attempting to show how far the cognitive aspect of the total state or condition was qualified by emotional factors. In other words, James meant to say that an 'idea' (e.g. idea of the bear) does not cause emotions as a match might be said to cause a fire; but along with the 'idea' there is a total organic reaction which makes the 'idea' itself a unique personal event, and welds it into that concrete psycho-physical process called experience. In these broad features the theory still survives. It has that kind of vitality which provokes strife and enjoys change. One obvious defect in the whole movement from Lotze onward is the fact that physiological considerations abound, to the exclusion of the equally important data of

[1] *Mind*, Vol. 9, 1884: 'The bodily changes follow directly the perception of the exciting fact and . . . our feeling of the same changes as they occur *is* the emotion.'

chemistry. This last phase of psycho-physiological doctrine we take as the limit of its history, and shall therefore not venture to give any account of its present state beyond indicating that, if the main point of the peripheral theory is as stated above, the further study of bodily changes, which reaches to changes in chemical processes and in secretions, is on the whole inclined to amplify rather than annihilate it.

The whole purport of the peripheral theory is condemned by the supporters of the central theory, namely, Wundt and those who partly or completely follow him. Historically, this view may be regarded as a development of the Kantian; for Kant leads the modern school of thinkers who insist on (a) giving to feeling an independent position, and (b) regarding it as the subjective complement of the objective processes (sensation, ideation). We must remember, of course, that in the strict use of terms these are all subjective processes, and that the distinction is ultimately between more and less subjectivity.

Wundt regards feeling as equally original with sensation. He therefore differs from Herbart, who would derive feelings from relations between ideas, and Horwicz, who would derive sensation from feeling. If we call the former an intellectualistic view we may distinguish Wundt's as a psycho-physical doctrine. As such, it is a species of the general class of theories previously called 'central.'

The reader of these pages has probably felt some uncertainty about the meaning of the terms 'sensation' and 'feeling'; still more about the relation between those psychic states. The uncertainty is natural, because it exists also in the writers who have been discussed, and Wundt has given a clear statement of his position on these points. 'Sensations are present in all immediate experiences, but feelings may disappear in certain special cases, because of their oscillation through an indifference zone. Obviously, then, we can, in the case of sensations, abstract from the accompanying feelings, but we can never abstract from sensations in the case of feelings. In this way two false views may easily arise— either that sensations are the *causes* of feelings, or that feelings are a particular species of sensations.' These two views being rejected, Wundt puts forward his own view that feeling can be most generally described as the reaction of the total consciousness upon the incoming sensations or ideas. This reaction is not purely psychical and, as it were, disembodied process: it involves physiological factors. When we have 'psychical compounds made up of affective elements' (emotions, volitions), the expression clearly shows the presence of such factors, and we may therefore assume that probably some physiological accompaniment exists in the case of simple feelings. Wundt conjectures that 'in the case of feelings and emotions we have chiefly changes in inhibitory innervation, originating in the brain and conducted along the vagus (etc.).' Further, Wundt thinks there is one central region of the brain which serves for the 'connexion of the various sensory centres' and also for 'inhibitory innervations.' For further details the reader must go to Wundt's writings: these extracts are made to explain the terms 'psycho-physical' and 'central.' The standpoint is psycho-physical because it makes feelings independent psychic events and at the same time postulates a physical complement, but does not reduce either of these terms to the other. It is central rather than peripheral because the feeling, being irreducible, cannot be explained as a direct reflection of the incoming current of the sense-nerves through out-going motor channels.

Wundt's further treatment of this subject becomes an elaborate schematism of classification. In this the most obvious feature is the use of certain fresh principles. The writers of the eighteenth century classified the feelings by objective marks, as self-regarding, other-regarding, and so on. The more strictly psychological method then adopted was to reduce all feeling to pleasure and pain, leaving the differences to be defined by reference to sensations or contents (aesthetic, intellectual, religious, political, etc.). Wundt treats the feelings as a 'single manifold, interconnected in all its parts,' and distinguishes certain 'dimensions' (agreeable and disagreeable, exciting and quieting, tension and relief). This treatment has not commanded any general acceptance. For Wundt, emotions are equivalent to a succession of feeling, and are accordingly treated as complex forms of feeling. The names for emotions are consequently names for typical groups of feelings, not for certain invariable and definable psychic states. The physical phenomena have only a symptomatic value, and do not give any reliable knowledge of the emotional experience. James is said to have mistaken symptom for cause, and therewith dismissed. Wundt attempts to characterize the typical forms of emotion (relying on his earlier treatment of feeling), but virtually denies the possibility of making an adequate classification, partly because emotions occur in times and circumstances not suited for the experimental methods, partly because the possible permutations and combinations of the factors (quality, intensity, form of occurrence) have no known limit. In this part of his work Wundt seems to assume that an inductive study based on observations can have no scientific value. One of the points at which later psychologists diverge from Wundt is this very conception, which practically amounts to the dogma that what is not subjected to the conditions of the laboratory is not scientific psychology.

Lehmann's work is an attempt to satisfy the demands of the 'peripheral' and 'central' theories by compromise. On the one side, it gives full weight to the physiological data and the views of Mosso, Féré. Experimental work of great value has been done by Lehmann in the construction of tables showing the physical disturbances that accompany emotional strain. On the other side, attention is given to the psychical variations (especially in the matter of the accompanying images). Lehmann accounts for the origin of emotion on purely physiological grounds: the course of the ideas during emotions involves loss of energy; the feelings are the reflex psychic effects of harmony or disharmony between supply of and demand for energy. This hypothesis seems to be one of those which cannot be proved, and might be disregarded. Lehmann accepts only two qualities in the sphere of feelings, agreeable and disagreeable, thus joining those who reject Wundt's 'dimensions.'

7. ZIEHEN

The physiological bias which characterized Horwicz is seen again in the work of Theodor Ziehen, *Introduction to the Study of Physiological Psychology*. This work is one of the best known textbooks. Ziehen, afterwards Professor in Berlin, wrote it in 1891, when he was at Jena; it has attained to many editions in German and in English. It is marked by directness of expression, firmness of opinion, and a broad-minded disregard for consistency. Ziehen's basis is neurology. His main points are the doctrine of association, the futility of 'apperception' (especially Wundt's), and the supreme value of experimental work. 'Association of ideas,'

says Ziehen, 'is a brief term designating the process of the reproduction of ideas.' The chief law is that 'each idea reproduces as
its successor either an idea that is similar to it in content, or an
idea with which it has often appeared simultaneously.' Here, then,
are two principles—similarity and simultaneity or synchronism.
These may also be termed internal and external types of association. The explanation of the 'process' assumes sensory-cells and
memory-cells. Ziehen admits that this physiological substratum
is 'wholly hypothetical as to particulars,' but claims that it is
'absolutely correct' in its fundamental features.

Wundt's 'apperception' is here called an 'over-soul' and rejected
as superfluous. All unification is traceable (if any) to the brain-
cells in their relative excitability. The reason why a sensation a
becomes associated with a memory image b, rather than any other,
is found in the fact that the corresponding ganglion-cell B, and
the paths of conduction leading to it, have been trained or 'tuned'
by previous excitation, and are proportionately more sensitive to
similar excitation. This, as the author notes, was Bonnet's principle, and Ziehen is, in fact, re-editing the 'fibre-psychology' with
the help of Meynert and other physiologists. Similarly, attention
is analysed into the action of sense-stimuli, which prevail over
the other competing stimuli through resemblance of the new
sensation to the old, and the distinctness of the memory-images
which are recalled or associated with it. Attention is determined
by the 'associative power' of a sensation, which is dependent on
(1) intensity, (2) agreement with the latent mental image, (3)
strength of the accompanying emotional tone, and (4) the chance
grouping of the latent ideas. The belief that we exert a particular
kind of 'activity' in attention is due to the fact that more or less
latent movements accompany our thinking. There is no real
distinction between so-called voluntary and involuntary thought.
'We cannot think as we *will*, but we *must* think as just those
associations which happen to be present prescribe.' With this
dissolution of 'the will,' and a corresponding statement that the
ego is 'a peculiar complex of associated images of memory,' we
reach the logical conclusion of a purely deterministic physiological
psychology.

Though drastic in his analysis and his use of doubtful quantities
like memory-cells, Ziehen does not venture to exclude altogether
psychic factors for which there are no available physiological

bases. The projection of sensations in space and time is one of these. Also there is the question of fine details of action, where the total result of the stimulus seems to contain elements not easily explained without psychic factors. Such points are commonplaces of the criticism directed against completely physiological explanations of behaviour. Ziehen meets them by admitting the gaps in the parallelism, but he seems to override their importance by an optimistic belief that time and patience will provide all that the present, confessedly inadequate, physiology lacks. Clearly the failure is in the physiology, for we have the psychological facts, and nothing would be wanting if we were not bound by preconceived ideas to search for some material substratum. The physiological psychologist has a curious way of declaring that psychology must remain incomplete so long as physiology is inadequate—as if one might say that the water supply is inadequate because there is no vessel to hold it. Ziehen thinks apperception is to be dismissed because there is no centre for it—that is to say, no brainvessel to contain it. Wundt's particular localization may be unfortunate, but the argument that this 'metaphysical' item must be discounted for want of room is itself neither more nor less than an applied metaphysic.

8. MÜNSTERBERG

The antithesis between association and apperception becomes in Ziehen and others so marked that it seems as if psychology must either overcome it or degenerate into faction. The most important effort to achieve reconciliation was made by Münsterberg, and constitutes one of his distinguishing marks. Hugo Münsterberg may be included among German writers because he was at least equally divided between Germany and America. Born in Germany, he became Professor at Harvard; originally a writer in German, he has published works in German and Anglo-Saxon indifferently. Originally known as an associationist in psychology, he later became responsible for a type of activism (*Aktionstheorie*) with idealistic tendencies. In experimental work Münsterberg has taken a continuous interest, and in recent years he has been prominent in the field of applied psychology. To this phase of his work we cannot give any further attention beyond naming the following titles: *Beiträge zur experimentellen Psychologie*, 1889–92; *Psychology and Crime*, 1909; *Psychology and Industrial Efficiency*, 1911; *Harvard Psychological Studies*, 1903–1906. The work of first importance here is the *Grundzüge der Psychologie* (1900), of which the first (and only) part is devoted to discussion of principles. The earlier work, *Die Willenshandlung* (1888), should not be forgotten.

The 'action-theory' has definite historical affinities. Association tends to make mental life depend on sensation and the consequences of sense-stimulation: it is therefore in a way to be called 'peripheral.' Apperception is the name for an activity which is 'central,' and a doctrine of apperception logically involves emphasis on attention and inhibition as activities of the psychic life. This is, broadly, the antithesis shown in modern psychological writings. Münsterberg gives primary importance to the motor activities of the cerebral centres. While the associationist regards the intensity of the sensation as equivalent mainly to the strength of the external stimulus, Münsterberg inverts the position and maintains that the strength of the sensation is equivalent to the centrifugal activity—that is to say, the work done by the cerebral centres.

Every sensation, which means here every content of consciousness, corresponds to the transition from excitation to discharge as occurring in the cerebral cortex. Since it is a fact that there is antagonism between motor centres, and that the action on one inhibits the action of another, this 'act-theory' is held to be a valid explanation of attention and inhibition. For a sensory stimulus is always received under conditions which constitute a predisposition to action; consequently it finds some motor nerves already excited and others already inhibited: the unit of the conscious life is the psycho-physical state which includes sense and motion. This unit is what Münsterberg calls sensation. The task of psychology is to reduce all complex states to these elements; the quality of the sensation is determined by the spatial position of the path of discharge, and the liveliness of the sensation depends on the strength of the discharge. Following this line of thought, we reach conclusions similar to those of Ziehen, namely, that every psychic operation has a physiological counterpart; that the mechanism of the neuro-cerebral system is responsible for all happenings, and the will is simply perception of an effect produced through the body and accompanied by sensations of muscular effort.

Though Münsterberg's hypothesis has had a somewhat solitary

life, it merits attention as an effort to recognize adequately the crisis occasioned by the disagreement of psychologists. To make psychology a science, Münsterberg thinks that some definite causal series must be adhered to. Such a series is not given in the mental life, for it is full of gaps and apparently causeless changes: it may better be found in the sphere of physiology, in the brain processes and their accompaniments; but if we are to avoid irrelevancy and deal with those physiological events which are relevant to psychology, we must be able to name a definite point at which the physiological datum is also a psychological datum. This, we are told, is the sensory-motor process. The suggestion is attractive because such a process unifies passivity and activity, sense-receptivity and ideomotor activity, the whole afferent and efferent currents of life. Such a union could be exemplified in reflex action at the lower level, and if we are prepared to see in all 'higher' processes only the multiplication and complication of one elementary process, then perhaps the sensory-motor units can be so added and multiplied, combined and complicated, that psychology will be an 'exact science.'

At this juncture a new phase develops. This psychology has purposely eliminated what the plain man calls 'himself.' If the plain man has a headache, science is not interested in his naïve assertions about his 'head'; it flatly contradicts his 'experience' and tells him that his headache is 'really' an auto-intoxication located somewhere else. Similarly, when the plain man says his 'will' was active, the scientific psychologist regards this as a statement of symptoms, an indication that the person is actually experiencing changes of muscular tone or sensations of muscular contraction; though the plain man has no more idea of these than he has of the chemical fermentations which constitute the 'objective' phase of his headache. To make psychology a science honoured among sciences, Münsterberg would make it 'objective' in this sense. This purpose, and the need which gave it birth, must be duly recognized; for whether this way of achieving the end is right or wrong, the need is certainly a real product of historical evolution. Throughout his works Münsterberg relies mainly on the muscular sensations as affording the required objectivity; the biological view that touch is the fundamental sense, together with the emphasis on reflex movement which biology favours, doubtless point in this direction. Yet the position is of doubtful value. The pressing question is simply whether this type of psychology does not become scientific in exact proportion as it ceases to be 'psychology.' To assert that point is to reject rather than criticize, for Münsterberg openly proposes to define psychology as 'objective': those who think it must be subjective are irreconcilable opponents.

When we hear that a psychology is 'scientific' we expect its author to insist on the value of experiment and measurements. Münsterberg began by modifying and ended by rejecting psychic measurements. He has also expressed himself very emphatically on the danger of overestimating the value of experiment. Having cast out of psychology all that constitutes the plain man's idea of 'personality,' he makes room for it elsewhere. For psychology the 'heroes' of history are mechanisms whose actions can be regarded as complex processes reducible to stimulations and discharges in the centres of neural excitability. But that is not the whole matter. There is also a subjective point of view. This, however, is another science, the so-called *Geisteswissenschaft*. In this way Münsterberg squares his account with the historical sciences and becomes, outside of psychology, a supporter of idealism and voluntarism. This is not so paradoxical as it is sometimes made to appear. In the development of the doctrines of method, with which Münsterberg is so largely concerned, there has come to view a problem which is not yet clearly formulated, and that problem is this very question of the relation between history and psychology.

C. The influence of biology

I. SPENCER

Herbert Spencer produced his *Principles of Psychology* in 1855, the year in which Bain published his first book. While the majority of the best-known writers of this period were Scotch, Spencer was an Englishman, sharing this peculiarity with Darwin. In his childhood he was encouraged by an intelligent father to take an interest in plants and animals; he avoided the education offered by Universities, but was taught mathematics and mechanics well enough to become an engineer. In 1839 he began to be interested in wider spheres of thought through reading Lyell's *Principles of Geology*. A further period of engineering was terminated in 1846, after which the versatile young man became sub-editor of a paper, the *Economist*. The career of the philosopher began from this point; the publication of *Social Statics* in 1850, and the beginning of an acquaintance with Huxley, Lewes, J. S. Mill, and others were the first beginnings of those philosophical studies and friendships which lasted till 1903. The composition of the *Principles of Psychology* really began in 1853, with the exposition of *The Universal Postulate*, afterwards included in that work; the editions of the whole work appeared in 1855 and 1876.

The year 1860 marked another crisis in the history of European thought. This was the year in which Spencer opened a subscription list for the production of a 'synthetic philosophy.' Five volumes out of the proposed ten were ready before 1874, and this instalment included the *Principles of Biology* and the *Principles of Psychology*; the remaining volumes were to include the *Principles of Sociology*.

Spencer's choice of a title for his work was fortunate; his importance lay primarily in his outlook, and that outlook was above all things 'synthetic.' Before Darwin published his *Origin of Species*, Spencer had taken hold of the idea of development. The idea was by no means new; it could be found fully active in the earliest Greek philosophy; it had taken a mystical form in the school of Plotinus; the Arabians suspected its significance; it had emerged again in full force among the German writers of the first quarter of the nineteenth century, and attained a comprehensive expression with some attempt at detail in the work of Goethe. But it continued to lack both detailed proof and universal application. Spencer undertook the latter; Darwin supplied the former.

For the achievement of his task Spencer required an infinite mass of data. His friends thought that the time for such an undertaking had not arrived; it was, perhaps, already past. The rapid increase of material even then proved too great for the powers of a single individual; the human encyclopaedia is a phenomenon of the Middle Ages, which can be reproduced today only by such 'superorganic' bodies as learned societies or syndicates. In details Spencer is often inaccurate; the conception and the method were his more enduring contributions to the history of thought. The idea of an Absolute came to him from Kant, through Hamilton; his appreciation of the empirical and practical aspect of knowledge must have owed much to his long apprenticeship to engineering, perhaps also to the training which his father gave him, as a child, in the observation of plants and animals. The combination of these two views was the object which Spencer set before himself, the goal to which he moved steadily through long years of financial troubles, physical weakness, and unrecognized labour. He began with *First Principles*, proceeded to trace the origin of forms out of primitive formless matter, and so arrived at the sphere of organic structures and life. The guiding principle of the treatment is the idea of a continual adjustment between the different parts of the universe. This idea, at the point which touches psychology, is expressed in the definition of life as 'the continuous adjustment of internal relations to external relations.' Biology is the science of life in general; the science of conscious life or psychology treats in the same way the processes through which the conscious organism maintains itself in relation to its environment.

In the classification of the sciences psychology appears as a division of biology, coming between and mediating the transition from biology to sociology. This was in itself an important contribution to the idea of the psychological sciences. By relating conscious life so closely to the general idea of the organism, Spencer produced a change in the attitude toward psychology; he made clearer the sense in which psychology is a *natural* science. The movement aroused great opposition from the advocates of the supernatural quality of the soul, but this was a passing phase that belongs only to the history of culture. In its general significance Spencer's point of view has become universal, though objections of another kind, based on a different conception of psychology, will have to be considered later.

Spencer inherited the achievements of the departmental sciences as they were formulated in the second quarter of the century. Among these was the idea of conservation of energy, which Spencer at first adopted unreservedly. At this stage he was a supporter of the 'interaction' hypothesis; it was possible for mechanical movement to be converted into heat, heat into light, and therefore ultimately for the physical to be converted into the psychic process. This position Spencer afterwards deserted, adopting in its place the 'two-aspects' theory. Similarly, his original position required a definite exposition of the way in which the inorganic evolved directly into the organic; this also was not forthcoming. The opponent, therefore, had more than one weak point in the system to attack. But in spite of these failures to carry through the ultimate principles of the system, Spencer's scheme remained valuable and stimulating. It is not as a final metaphysic that Spencer's philosophy is to be judged; its affinity with the evolutionism of Schelling is limited to its cosmic character, but, unlike that Panlogism, the synthetic philosophy is predominantly inductive and still holds its own as a suggestive, if not wholly true, co-ordination of facts.

One of the permanent results of Spencer's work is the growing tendency to separate objective from subjective psychology. Before 1870 physiology and psychology had begun to overlap, and some had maintained that physiology was the real science of mind, while others held that psychology was equally a true science. Psycho-physiology was thus in a very indeterminate position; a science of behaviour was somewhere latent in these complicated ideas of mind and body. Some popular works, still current, belong to this stage of development. W. B. Carpenter, a physiologist and Registrar of the University of London, attached to his *Principles of Human Physiology* (1852) an outline of psychology, which became later a separate and lengthy book called *Principles of Mental Physiology* (1874). Beneath the mass of facts and stories which occupies most of this work there lies a purpose to exhibit the power and reality of the human will, a purpose that was inspired by Martineau. Put forward as 'a contribution to that science of Human Nature which has yet to be built up in a much broader basis than any philosopher has hitherto taken as its foundation,' the work had merits and deserved its popularity.

To this epoch also belonged a group of men who, without definitely working as psychologists, were active agents in the progress of thought. Sir Benjamin Brodie deserves to be remembered; also Sir Henry Holland; and T. Laycock (*Mind and Brain*, 1860). Curious notions were produced as the offspring of a new and premature alliance between the science of mind and the science of body. Such phrases as 'ideagenic tissue' puzzle the reader, and serve to make visible the darkness of this region. Most famous among these products is the word '*cerebration*.' For the benefit of those who still reverence its charm we may quote the remark of Dr. Ireland: 'Cerebration—what a name for thought! When the liver secretes bile, one does not say that it hepatates; or when a man breathes, we do not say that he pulmonates.'

But in spite of crude phrases the efforts of this generation were attended with some success. Laycock grasped the idea that memory might be fundamentally organic, and be analogous to vital processes in plants and animals. The most definite exposition of the general doctrine was produced by Henry Maudsley (*Physiology and Pathology of Mind*, 1867). His works have remained standard contributions to the study of many psychic processes, normal and abnormal, but his adoption of the view that consciousness is a by-product of brain-processes made his work more acceptable to physiologists than psychologists.

It is significant for the understanding of Spencer's psychology that its author began with the 'superorganic,' the society, rather than the individual. In 1854 Spencer's articles in the *Westminster Review* were concerned with 'Manners and Fashion' and 'The Genesis of Science,' in both of which the development of complexity from simplicity is the guiding idea. In the case of the sciences there is an instance of primitive activities becoming gradually specialized and differentiated; in this case we must think of the mental capacities developing along with the sciences, a mutual action and reaction of outer system and inner thought. This idea was reinforced by the embryology of Baer; for Baer's law of development also insisted on the point that development proceeds from the undifferentiated to the differentiated. A common formula was thus found for individual and social 'organisms,' and the way seemed open for a reconstruction of the universe in the light of this formula. The 'Psychology' came next.

Before the *Principles of Psychology* appeared in a second edition (1872) the *Principles of Biology* had been given to the world in 1867. The Psychology presupposes the Biology, for the phenomena of conscious life are a department of life in general. This gives 'mental science' a place in the general catalogue of sciences; henceforth it will be recognized as one of the natural sciences. But this is no more than a device of method; unlike materialism, which thrusts the psychical phenomena into a particular corner of the universe, the evolutionary method of Spencer is indifferent to distinctions of matter and mind; the one dominating question asked about anything is not 'What is it?' but rather 'Where does it come in the scale of things?' As Aristotle located man between the animals and the gods, so Spencer wedges him firmly in between less organized individuals and those other organisms which presuppose the individual as an element. It is in his grasp of these formulae which give the mind a chance to arrange and connect things that Spencer excelled. As a result he was able to throw out the most inspiring ideas for the attainment of knowledge, and a scheme such as he suggested for 'The Comparative Psychology of Man' was more than equal in value to the whole of his own 'special synthesis.'

It is difficult to do justice to Spencer in any one department because his work lay rather in the sphere of co-ordination and correlation than in that of specialized research. Whether anyone can successfully unite sciences without being a master of each and all, is a question which it is convenient to ignore in this connection. The result of the general survey in its bearing on psychology may be briefly indicated.

If we begin from a primitive matter, or a primitive force, of which matter is a phenomenon, and arrange a scale of phenomena which culminates in Man, we may naturally expect to find that the most crucial point is reached when the structure of the nerves has to be explained from the point of view of sensations. Here the formulae must either carry us over by their own acquired impetus, or the synthetic philosophy will succeed in everything but the synthesis. Spencer looked to Germany for help; as Bain quoted Müller, so Spencer quotes Helmholtz. The sensations of tone are built up from units; every sensation in fact is a composite product; the unit is a nervous shock; this is the least common denominator of all sensations, and must therefore be the stuff of which our experience is made by integration and differentiation.

From biology in general we are thus led to neurology and to psychology. Having in this way prepared a place for psychology Spencer does little more than drop into it the traditional Associationism. Psychology proper is somewhere eluded in this procedure; life in general narrows down to conscious life, and then suddenly expands again into complicated integrations of neural and psychic activity. The life of the mind is brought under the general rubric of a correlation between inner and outer activities. The conscious creature reacts to a stimulus, is conscious of the reaction, can have a presentation of the object to which the stimulation is referred, can have later a re-presentation of that primary psychic event, and so on in ever increasing degrees of removal from immediacy. But all this does not ultimately amount to anything, as psychology, except a repetition of Sir William Hamilton's metaphysical psychology. To the absolute division of psychosis from neurosis, Spencer verbally commits himself, hoping to arrive safely at the end of his work by the aid of 'parallelism.'

2. LEWES, MILL, AND DARWIN

The retention of Associationism and the habit of dealing only in large schemes seem to be the reasons why Spencer affected the psychologists so much and the psychology so little. Spencer's ideas and plans were to be carried out by later workers in the fields of anthropology, sociology, and comparative psychology. Meanwhile normal psychology gained almost nothing from Spencer; psycho-physics did not interest him; and where the language of biology seemed to be unsuitable, the ancient rubrics had to be inserted. Yet the Associationists were obviously a disunited party. Stuart Mill was restless on the subject of passivity; he lost no opportunity of saying that his esteemed father had overlooked it, and congratulated Mr. Bain on having noticed it. In 1873 Mill died; he may be said to have looked upon the promised land and died still looking. In his own direct contributions to psychology he attempted no minute analysis or systematic collection of data. His interest was more general, controlled chiefly by the desire to put the study of man and of society on a positive basis. This was a phase of the 'Positivism' which Mill adopted from Comte; but Mill differed from Comte nowhere more than in matters of psychology. Martineau astonished his contemperaries by calling Mill an idealist. The astonishment showed how widespread in 1860 was the belief that no scientific thinking could fail to be 'rationalist,' and no rationalism could fail to be materialistic. Martineau recognized in Mill a different strain, a leaning to what was commonly regarded as the peculiar attribute of orthodox speculation; for Mill insisted on the dignity of man, on the value of introspection, and on the supremacy of character.

All these were signs of the times. A tendency to revive old controversies about 'freedom of the will,' a renewed desire for some doctrine of man that did not cut up the living personality into 'ideas' and then ingeniously reunite the parts with the glue of 'association'—these were the marks by which some new development might have been predicted. Psychology was not the only field of change; in politics individualism was subjected to new and trenchant criticisms; sociology was beginning to restate from a new basis that 'evolution of the spirit' which Hegel taught; British philosophy in the hands of T. H. Green definitely renounced its antecedents and began to ally itself with German modes of thought.

As we have already indicated more than once, the conflict between the leading writers was making evident the need for some clear statement on the scope and method of psychology. Attention was diverted from the construction of systems to this preliminary question, and from the answers offered there emerged a new sense of what was to be attempted. The answers themselves were very different in character and represented the various types of thought then in vogue. George Henry Lewes spoke for physiology and positivism; Mill was in favour of a practical psychology, with modifications due to his belief in personality; T. H. Green was more deeply affected by German idealism, and felt nothing to be so necessary as the complete reform of the concept of consciousness. These three, to whom Huxley might be added, are typical representatives of the secondary forces that made for rightness in this critical time.

To the problem of method George Henry Lewes contributed a whole book, published in 1879, after his death: it sums up the situation before 1879, and expresses a definite standpoint and programme. Lewes begins by noticing what was stated above, that 'physics and chemistry advance with rapid strides to a fuller and more exact appreciation of their respective phenomena. The same may be said of Biology, but cannot be said of Psychology.' The subject of psychology is declared to be the human mind, considered 'as the product of the Human Organism, not only in relation to the cosmos, but also in relation to society.' Emphasizing this relation to society, Lewes defines Psychology as 'the analysis and classification of the sentient functions and faculties, revealed to observation and induction, completed by the reduction of them to their conditions of existence, biological and sociological.'

The conditions of existence are further defined as the structural mechanism and the medium in which it is placed. This is clearly modelled on the biological formulae of Claude Bernard; it means for Lewes the rejection of the idea that mind is an 'entity inhabiting the organism,' and society 'an artificial product.' Lewes regards psychology as a branch of biology, and defines it as the science of the facts of sentience, not of consciousness. By this change of terminology he hopes to avoid any suggestion of a gulf between mind and life; the 'spiritual facts' are a distinct sphere, but not more than that; they are the sphere of sentient functions as distinct, for example, from the 'conditions of their production, which is the sphere of Physiology.' Physiology is in fact dependent on psychology; psychology is dependent on physiology, for sense on its receptive side is an organic function; so that a theory of the soul requires a combination of subjective and objective data.

Lewes believes that every organic state is both physical and psychic. By using the term 'sentience' for consciousness he means to imply that sensibility is a 'vital property of tissue,' which may or may not rise into consciousness. To call psychology the science of consciousness is to limit it; for consciousness is only a part of sentience. The antithesis of mind and body is a mistake which has arisen from regarding the distinction between 'conscious' and 'unconscious,' as equivalent to the distinction between 'mental' and 'physical.' This 'paradox of Descartes' must be rejected; we have no 'grounds for degrading any action of a sentient mechanism from the psychical to the physical sphere solely because it might pass unconsciously.' The mechanical process may be conscious, and the conscious process is always mechanical; the processes may be classified, but not under the rubrics of Body and Mind. Lewes therefore refuses to accept the view that a decapitated frog responds to a stimulus unconsciously: he believes that the nervous centres of the spinal cord are fully sentient, and that reflex action is accompanied by sentience. This affects his interpretation of mechanism. He will not speak of sentience as directing mechanism; he refuses to separate the two, and therefore takes 'mechanical' to mean according to law; there is psychic mechanism as well as physical mechanism, or rather there are distinguishable factors in what is actually a psycho-physical mechanism.

Biology is placed by Lewes between Cosmology and Sociology; psychology is a department of biology. This classification is dictated by the emphasis which Lewes lays on the relation of mind to society, and of society to the mind. In brief, he thinks of psychology as studying sentient processes in the organism and intelligence, which is sentience developed through social relationships. As a discipline psychology is the basis of education and government, a view which he shares with Spencer and Mill; language, science, art arise from this social medium, constituting the data of collective psychology; history takes its place among the sources of psychological data, for some experiences are 'only possible to the collective life.' The method of psychology includes, (a) the subjective analysis and introspective method, (b) the objective analysis, the observation of data furnished by history, the study of animals (only intelligible 'by a light reflected from the study of man'), and social relationships. Comparative psychology Lewes thinks is not a source of much information. This, he very characteristically explains, is not because man is wholly different from the animals, but because to the 'three great factors, Organism, External Medium, Heredity, which Human psychology has in common with Animal psychology,' it adds a fourth, namely, relation to a Social medium, with its product, the General Mind.

The idea that psychology ought to be a science was common to Lewes and Mill, but they differed in their idea of this science. Lewes definitely regarded it as a branch of biology. Mill inclined to regard it as a separate science united to the others in respect of method rather than matter. We have seen how Mill shared the tendency to make an advance from the position of his father's *Analysis*. In his *Logic* he gave an explicit statement of his position, contributing to this science what he contributed to all, clearer rules of procedure than were previously known. According to Mill there is room for a special science of the mind, because the feelings are inner states that have no known connection with the body. He admits that every mental state has a nervous state for its antecedent, but adds that we are 'wholly ignorant of the character of these nervous states.' The science of mind is made possible by the fact that 'there exist uniformities of succession among states of mind.' Beyond this Mill does not care to go, for he is chiefly concerned to arrive at his next point, the possibility of a science of character, Ethology. It is on the practical significance of the science that Mill concentrates his forces.

Lewes saw the weak point in Mill's position. He accuses Mill of not knowing enough physiology, says that he adopted the doctrine of the spiritualists without accepting the 'animating spirit,' and considers it a strange incongruity 'to regard the mind as a function of the organism, and yet suppose that some mental functions had no organic conditions.' To this attack Mill could have retorted that his idea of the method of psychology was not affected by his view of the Ego: but it must be admitted that in the main the attack was justified. The fact which most troubled Mill was the necessity of defining a science which began from sensations (so obviously liable to be claimed by the physiologists), and ended in processes which Mill was inclined to regard as almost, if not quite, independent of the organism. The same point troubled Spencer, and he, too, fell an easy victim to the criticism of Lewes.

Spencer was wholly concerned with the problem of finding a place for everything and putting everything in its place. To get over this difficulty about the sensations he created a sub-department of Aestho-physiology, a preparatory study leading to psychology, but not forming part of it. Having thus segregated the sphere of sensations, Spencer goes on to declare that Psychology is not only distinct from, but antithetically opposed to, all other sciences. His main reason for saying this is that the thoughts and feelings which constitute a consciousness, and are absolutely inaccessible to any but the possessor of that consciousness, cannot be classed with the existences with which the rest of the sciences deal. It is a little curious after this to find that Spencer thinks the odours which are inappreciable to man may have a distinct effect on the consciousness of a dog. Here Spencer feels able to transfer from a consciousness, which he alone could know, an effect (defined as unknowable) to another consciousness which, on these premises, could not be known at all. Clearly something requires correction.

Through all these disputes about the aim and method of psychology there began slowly to emerge a definite attitude of mind. This was largely due to the work of Charles Darwin. Though evolution and development were ideas as old as Thales, no scientific value could be given to them unless the processes of which they consisted were studied and formulated. To this inductive aspect of the subject Darwin applied himself; after 1859 no well-informed writer could ignore the fact that in every subject the genesis, as well as the static form, of the product must be considered. In the sciences of life there was a large mass of accumulated material dealing with organs and functions that seemed to exist together for no particular reason; lower levels of action remained when intellect had already supervened, and obsolete organs existed as a wanton challenge to all who believed that everything was created by one original omniscient act. Under the impulse of Darwin's work this accumulation of material was temporarily reduced to order. If, broadly speaking, it is possible to regard Nature as ceaselessly and infinitely productive; if at the same time the conditions of production are not the same as conditions of permanence, but every production is tentative, a kind of experiment which may or may not succeed, then the chaos of material may be viewed as a new kind of order, the dynamic order of perpetual production and selection.

The publication of the *Origin of Species* in 1859 is an event of peculiar interest to the psychologist; for it was not only a scientific achievement, it was also a spiritual crisis. It is notorious that in the land of its origin Darwinism seemed to many only a new name for atheism; it is enough merely to recall the old antitheses which furnished innumerable title-pages, such as creation and evolution, science and the faith. The intelligence that fastened on Darwinism as the chief of offences, was not misguided: other doctrines, notably the materialism of 1860, could be ignored; but the new mode of thought had come to stay, and with it accounts must be settled once for all. With the decrease of asperity on the one side and of exaggeration on the other, a new generation of writers began by assuming what their fathers disputed, and then proceeded to carry on the work of Darwin, both to amplify and to correct it. For the psychologist the gain lay chiefly in a fresh impulse to study origins and to take a genetic point of view. In consequence there was a movement toward a general biological treatment of mental functions, a renewed interest in animals, in children, and in the questions which concern environment taken as primarily social.

All these topics had already travelled far enough to reach the fringe of consciousness: Bain had shown no small appreciation of the possibilities inherent in psychology, while Spencer, J. S. Mill, and Lewes had almost grasped the meaning of comparative and social psychology. But Darwin (and with him Russell Wallace) was the real driving force, though Spencer's use of the evolutionary scheme had more general influence than any other production by reason of its comprehensiveness. Darwin's specific contributions to psychology were not large in quantity. To child psychology he contributed a specimen of his method in the study of the daily life of an infant: to animal psychology his most significant contribution was the treatment of instincts as modes of action dependent for their character on the progressive refinement of the organism and for their purposiveness on the fact that only actions which attain useful ends could be consistently employed by generations of creatures. To the study of emotions Darwin contributed the classical example of the method of expression. In his work on *The Expression of the Emotions in Man and Animals*, Darwin not only recorded facts by observing the appearance of animals when pleased or displeased, but also to a great extent inverted the common view of the subject; for he regarded the expressions as the organic side of emotions, and also as the relatively permanent element, since the organic structure is inherited, and can only be modified gradually. An emotion is therefore fundamentally a habit of the organism: consciousness is a comparatively insignificant element in a total state which includes a great variety of organic reactions; for anger, to take only one example, consists in bared teeth and bristling hair, quite as much as awareness of the opponent or the particular offence. The fact that emotional expression often contains movements that are apparently meaningless was explained by Darwin on the principle of 'serviceable associated habits'; the mode of expression was originally a serviceable action to attain an end, but the change of circumstances has modified the conditions, and so the original action has become a superfluous habit, linked by association to the feelings as they arise. Lastly, to the higher life of mind, the social and the moral, Darwin made a significant contribution in the *Descent of Man* (1871). The now famous chapters on the 'Comparison of the Mental Powers of Man and the Lower Animals' laid a strong and broad foundation for all the work which has subsequently developed our knowledge of animal societies, human societies, and of the relations between these in reference particularly to the part played by instinct (whether identical or analogous) in the collective life of human and sub-human species.

In speaking of Darwin we speak of evolution, but they are not altogether equivalent. The statement made above, that biological interests developed under the influence of Darwin, requires to be explained further. Heredity is the central problem, and in it the central question is whether or not successive generations inherit the modifications which are acquired by their predecessors. To this point Darwin gave little attention; the arguments for and against belong to the Lamarckists (e.g. Spencer, Wundt, and Cope), and their opponents. Herbert Spencer, for example, asserts that an instinct is inherited experience, assuming that the habits of the ancestors are inherited by the descendants in the form of organic structures and tendencies to action. Haeckel, realizing the difficulty of saying that a *habit* is hereditary, plunged further into speculation, and declared that the characteristic of all organic matter is reproduction, and reproduction is memory. Thus, the elements which successively combine to make organisms are 'souls' with an inherent tendency to do again what they did before. A similar view was expressed by Hering in 1870, when he published his essay *On Memory as a General Function of Organic Matter;* in the form given it by R. Semon (*Die Mneme*) and in the more readable work of Samuel Butler, this doctrine has obtained a vogue beyond its deserts. The use of the term 'Memory' in the phrase 'unconscious memory' is a poetic licence which has been a snare. The biologists did not, in fact, propose to explain memory, as normally understood: they were merely using a term to express the continuity of cell-structure or organism. Though Hering uses the term Memory (*Gedachtniss*), Semon more correctly employs a 'term of art,' *Mneme*, and rightly gives a new name to what he regarded as a new principle. None the less, for psychology, the outcome has been, and still is, a deplorable confusion. A book on Memory now starts with anything that can be regarded as 'after-effect of external circumstances,' continues with all forms of regular repetition (vegetable, animal, and organic 'rhythms'), proceeds to comprehend habits of all kinds, and ends with human memory in which appears as a sub-species the process of conscious association and recollection. This affords matter for contemplation. Nothing more significant for the history of thought can be quoted. In Plato or Augustine memory was the supremely spiritual element in man, because it alone was essentially continuous; whether linked with the transmigration of the Pythagoreans or the immortality of the Christians, memory was the name of the undying function which for ever perpetuated itself by summing up the past in its eternal present. In the modern exponent of science memory retains all this significance for the opposite reason; though we cease to speak of the soul, immortality remains in the matter that is never destroyed, and the energy that is never lost; though we turn away from Plato or Augustine and say their psychology was nothing but theology, we find that we have turned to another psychology which seems to be equally remote from the limited 'science of the human mind,' which rationalism once regarded as its symbol of enlightenment. Nothing in this sphere is finally settled: the evolution of doctrine, as Spencer said, is a part of the whole evolution: we shall have more to say later on the different departments whose origin in the genetic way of thinking has been noted here; but the ideas of evolution and of memory have been so closely related one to another that attention might well be directed at this point to a subject so attractive and so significant.

For the psychologist the natural focus of interest is the possibility of assigning to consciousness a definite part in the progress of animal life. It seems obvious that consciousness must have some 'survival value' on any theory; since it would be a singular perversion of thought to suppose that the acknowledged climax of all evolution was itself a superfluous accessory. The obscurity of the subject has been a deterrent, but the problems of instinct cannot be ignored and their solution has been looked for in a theory of 'functional selection' or 'organic selection,' which definitely employs mental powers as agencies. The co-operation of the physical and the psychic factors which this theory employs is explained by giving to the body a capacity for producing various movements, and to the intelligence a power of selecting, and so finally establishing, some modes of action in preference to others. Tendencies toward such an interpretation of life may be found in the earlier works of Bain and Spencer, who both described the formation of habits as a process of selection in which the movements attended by pain or lack of success were gradually eliminated. If in this or some similar manner pleasure, pain, and attention could be regarded as clearly operative in the whole process of evolution, the union of biological and psychological points of view might yield new insight into the whole study of life. Since the original suggestion (1896) of such a programme by Lloyd Morgan, J. M. Baldwin, and others, much has been done to utilize and extend these principles through the study of 'animal behaviour.'

D. New syntheses

I. WARD

We have now followed, with necessary brevity, the movements which occupied the interval between the first works of Bain and James Ward's article on Psychology published in the *Encyclopaedia Britannica* (1886). The comments which this at once evoked show that it was estimated as the beginning of a new attitude toward the problems of mind. The article clearly challenged the Associationists to show cause why they should continue to exist. No one wished to deny the value of the laws of Association as true for some aspects of consciousness and some of its connections; the question here put to the issue was whether 'association' should be regarded as the bedrock of all mental complexity and unity, or whether it was a minor affair dependent upon some larger and deeper conception of unity. Ward's article was a statement of what would be involved in such a conception of unity; it formulated and partly applied a scheme of psychology for which the terms 'continuity' and 'attention' were primary, and in which all the tendencies toward an emphasis on activity and on the priority of discrimination, already fostered by Bain, were developed so radically that it was useless to look upon this as anything but a new beginning.

The importance of the crisis was fittingly recognized. Bain gave a long account of the article in *Mind* (1886), and followed this up with an article 'On "Association" Controversies' in the next year. Nothing could have more historical interest than this direct conflict between the author of the new article and the vigorous thinker who was prepared to stand by the position he had taken thirty years before. In spite of his years—nearly three-score and ten—Bain was still a powerful debater; his trenchant style seemed to have gained in flexibility and grown richer in homely phrases that come like upland breezes through the chambered heat of controversy. To learn the meaning of this page of history we shall go back to these articles.

Bain does not stint his praise. 'The work,' he says, 'has the rare merit of being Psychology, and nothing but Psychology: it is nearly complete as regards fundamental problems, and the ultimate analysis of the distinctive properties of mind.' Again, after reviewing the detail, he says that 'when matters excluded by the narrow limits are filled in,' 'Mr. Ward will have produced a work entitled to a place among the masterpieces of the philosophy of the human mind.' The nature of this appreciation will be more intelligible if another point is recalled. In saying that Ward's article is 'nothing but Psychology,' we need not suppose that Bain has repented his own physiological matter. Ward's article succeeded the article by Mansel on 'Metaphysics,' which in the earlier editions of the *Encyclopaedia* supplied the needs of the time by dividing Metaphysics into Psychology and Ontology. No one had done more than Bain to upset that arrangement, and he might legitimately regard the independent status of psychology in this ninth edition of the *Encyclopaedia* as a tribute to his labours. Bain is thus seen to stand between psychology as an academic branch of metaphysics and psychology as an independent science; he is also seen to be the principal agent in putting psychology among the natural sciences; and, finally, in respect of Ward's article, he is seen to be the representative of a psychology which had fallen under the suspicion of being really in bondage to its own allies, the sciences of chemistry and physiology. This is, in epitome, the history of British psychology from 1855 to 1887.

Several influences, direct and indirect, enter into that intellectual current, which we are here regarding as finally arriving at the 'Psychology' of the *Encyclopaedia Britannica*. Green has already been mentioned, and equal or greater importance must be accorded to the *Principles of Logic* published in 1883 by Mr. F. H. Bradley. The ethical, logical, and metaphysical writings of Mr. Bradley, together with his critical articles on subjects like 'activity' (published in *Mind*) have exerted an influence on psychology, always in the direction of ideas opposed to Associationism. James had already begun, also in *Mind*, to stir the atmosphere and clear the air of academic hot-houses, while Wundt's work was great enough to produce an immediate effect far from its point of origin. In England Sully was already known as the author of important psychological works, which ripened and matured later. The recollection of these facts will help the reader to comprehend more exactly the relative importance of the article now to be discussed.

While Bain valued Ward's article as a sign of progress enfeebled by the tendency to go too far, Ward hardly saw how much Bain was conceding, and resented his criticism of the innovations. In

1859 Bain had himself been a daring innovator; he had begun the 'activism' that was to be at once the support and the destruction of his own school. This feature, which distinguished the 'Emotions and the Will' from the earlier work, had been the key to Bain's later writing: we find him speaking of 'the stream of consciousness,' of change as essential to all conscious experience, of discrimination as prior to association, of the will as fundamental and not derivative from ideas—in fact, almost all the modern machinery is implicit in Bain. Yet there was a further step which Bain would neither take nor allow others to take. What that step was we see best in Ward's article.

Psychology, according to the terms of this article, is concerned with certain phenomena which are not specifically 'inner' as opposed to 'outer,' nor 'mental' as opposed to 'material,' but are certain distinct characteristics of conscious individual life. These characteristics must be assigned to a subject or Ego. A sequence of 'states' has no inner unity and could not know itself; there is an agent as well as an action, and in addition to knowing, feeling, and doing we must admit *that which* knows, feels, and does. From this basis it follows that the most important characteristics of mental life are those which depend upon this agent, such as activity in the form of attention, reproduction of experiences, and the higher activities in general. If the Self or Ego is not to be some detached essence it must be equivalent to the total state of consciousness, regarded as the inner unity of self-knowledge. Every distinguishable element of the mental life is therefore a phase of its activity; it is no more separated from its phenomena than the moon is separated from its phases: the subject *is* the knowing, the feeling, and the doing in their own living unity. If this subject could be regarded as having its object in itself to begin with, nothing more would be needed; experience would then be simply the evolution of the subject; but this is not the case, and we have to deal with the fact that the material is largely given. This material consists of presentations, which are either sensory (sights, sounds, colours), or motor, the latter being equivalent to consciousness of efferent processes as means of producing effects in the outer world. The processes which constitute the life of consciousness are, in their simplest formulation, a presentation which induces attention, a feeling which marks the attitude of the subject in relation to the presentation, a voluntary direction of attention to motor presentations from which result changes in the field of consciousness.

The affinities of this doctrine are easily recognized. Kant's 'pure Ego' is the ancestor of this 'subject'; Fichte's way of developing the content of mind by a purely idealistic inner move-ment is avoided; Hegel's grasp of the fact that subject and object are not primary given distinctions is utilized, with the necessary amendment that for psychology the actual growth of the idea of a world is due to experiences in which we *react*, in which therefore the mode of action is determined by conditions which do not originate in our own consciousness. Bain could adjust himself to this outlook. He saw 'no insurmountable difficulty' in 'a series of states being aware of itself.' This bold assertion, which flatly denies the main contention of all the critics of 'Associationism,' is well made; for the idealist (notably T. H. Green) is much too ready to press home this difficulty of 'series.' From Locke onwards the British psychologists were not aiming to prove that any sequence results in knowledge; they were entirely concerned to show the fragmentary character of all experiences as given in the sequences of life; they were most of all concerned to prove that one could not retire within oneself and there find the whole mental furniture at home at one time. The restoration of the 'subject' looked to Bain like a return to the old obscurantism which defied analysis; he saw no advantage in the return to a concept which evaded definition and yielded nothing but specula-tive deductions, while he was not conscious of any intention on his own part to deny that the 'states' were states of something. It is convenient, he says, 'to have a something "in the chair," ' but it is hard to say what the chairman is to be. Some comfort is derived by Bain from noticing that Ward's 'subject' is to be taken with qualifications; for it is admitted that the mental life as a process is made up of presentations, and the subject as such is never presented. On these terms Bain is disposed to let it pass, so long as it is not made a 'nucleus and a hiding place of mysticism.'

Ward proceeds to treat of the unity of consciousness as a 'con-tinuance'; in other words, to deny that the essence of mental advance is 'the combination and recombination of various elemen-tary units.' On the contrary the whole process must be regarded as the gradual differentiation of a primary unity: mental chemistry must be abandoned. Bain retorts that the old method was right; 'our education from first to last takes principally the form of adding unit to unit.' Here we reach the heart of the whole matter; here the early education of Bain proves a 'prejudice,' which utterly blinds him to the real issue. For Bain, Mill, and Spencer never seem to have realized how entirely the concept of sensation had changed since they first learned the grammar of their science. It would be right to say that a word is made by adding one letter to another; it would be wrong to say that language had evolved from a chaos of letters into an ordered system of letters. While Bain thought in terms of anatomy and physiology, or Mill talked of chemistry, Ward was employing the notions of biology. From this science came the inspiration to treat the mind as an organism which grows by continuous differentiation, which needs only nutrition and assimilation, which presents ultimately a collection of 'parts' that develop in sustained relations and never change without involving a reciprocal change throughout the whole structure. The theory of language and the theory of society were also affected by this idea; in applying it to psychology Ward did not abandon science, he abandoned only those scientific formulae which were the framework of Bain's methods.

Bain is prepared to go a long way in making concessions, but he remains unenlightened on this point. To him the old idea of simple sensations seems fundamentally true. He admits that sensations once thought simple are really complex; but that is only a matter of degree. He cannot grasp the significance of treating sensation as a function, a living operation with an infinitely variable content. 'When the sensation is simple,' he declares, 'as the colour of gold, repetition merely deepens the impression on the memory.' In brief, Bain is prepared to change the elements of the mental life, but not to change his idea of that life; Spencer, too, was open to this charge, for he did even more to show how utterly the old material was discarded, and yet he clung to constructive methods that could only work if that material was still used.

Bain has now shown that he failed to understand Ward; from this point onwards his remarks, whether made to praise or blame, are consequently of inferior value. The rest of the exposition may be taken directly from Ward's article, which fully deserves to have the last word.

The position adopted by Ward tends to involve the rejection of physiological explanations. Accordingly Hamilton's assertion of latent mental modifications is supported against Mill's criticism that these modifications must be stated as dispositions of the nerves. Leibniz and Herbart are here followed in preference to the current British teaching. At the same time the Law of Relativity as stated by Hamilton and Bain is rejected; Wundt's position is also partially discarded; and the conclusion is reached that, while 'there is no unalterably fixed unit,' the 'mutual relations of impressions' is not everything.

Sensation and movement are treated by Ward as aspects of a continuous psychic life, their present differences being due to evolution. This treatment adopts the general principles of evolution, but rejects the physiological form given to the theory by Lewes and Spencer. While the latter attempted to derive the variety of sensations from 'some simple primordial presentation,' Ward conjectures that the original matrix was a general 'organic sensation' corresponding to the general physiological action of the various stimuli. In other words, primitive sensation must be conceived as undifferentiated, a condition in which seeing, hearing, tasting, smelling, and touching were all distinctly represented. This might be compared with Kant's idea of a primitive chaos (or 'manifold') of sensations as the antecedent of distinct knowledge. That this doctrine of Kant was in Ward's mind is shown by the reference to it which occurs in the next paragraph, on Perception. We are warned that the progressive differentiation of our senses does not go on alone; there is an accompanying integration by which the elementary presentations are continuously formed into complex groups. The 'presentation-continuum,' or mere transition from state to state, would be 'little better than the disconnected manifold for which Kant took it' if some other factor did not enter in and dominate the situation. That factor is subjective selection which emphasizes (by movement) one part of the total presentation and represses the rest.

This notion is open to criticism, but we shall not delay matters by raising problems. At this point we can see most clearly where and how the fundamental concept of activity is brought into action by Ward. We are asked to accept an original power of reaction which is not a physical but a psychic activity; it is not Bain's original idea of innate energy, but a totally different notion of pure spiritual agency. From this follows automatically the substitution of this agency with its selecting and assimilating processes for all that Bain and J. Mill described under the name or 'association.' The activism of the German school is now developed, and the theory gravitates toward the tradition of Leibniz and Herbart. Experience, which is the life of the mind, does not consist of parts added one to another, automatically. There is a given material and a synthesis, but the material does not furnish its own synthesis. Where then does this element, the form as distinct from the matter, come from? Ward replies that it comes from us, from the active organizing subject. This is announced as the signal merit of Kant, the recognition of a synthetic unifying agency, a primary apperceptive power. The modes of this activity are the (Kantian) categories, they are the laws which the mind brings to bear on its material. But these are not innate properties of the self; they are the gradually developing modes of its activity, and the order of their emergence can be observed: they are not transcendental principles of mind regarded universally, but organic principles of individual conscious existence. Time and space are the first of these organizing principles; unity, identity, resemblance, difference come next; the higher intellectual categories come latest (substance, cause, etc.). Though subtle, this analysis is not trivial. Psychology must deal with the nature of thought, and must therefore come in its systematic procedure to these factors. Ward took up a strong position in refusing to sacrifice them to Associationism, and his analysis was carried unflinchingly through its severest trial. It is a duty to the author not to shirk the task of grasping the difference between a logical and a psychological view of categories. For the logician categories are instruments of thought and forms of the relations between thoughts. For the psychologist they are activities, more akin to the typical forms of growth which biology describes, and capable of arrangement in reference to the stage at which they appear or the level at which they are active. In adopting the latter standpoint Ward preserved his fundamental thesis, the possibility of an independent psychology which should be neither physiology nor epistemology, and the Kantian nature of the exposition must not be allowed to obscure the real difference between Ward's psychology and Kant's epistemology.

Hume's distinction of the image from the idea, on the ground that the former is 'livelier,' is rejected in favour of a more direct analysis by which it is shown that the image does not differ from the idea in respect of intensity, but in its own character as being akin to the presentation-continuum. This means that images as such are not associated; they may contain connected elements (called, after Herbart, their complications), but only ideas are capable of true association. Images stand close to sensations, but do not involve feeling; as Bain puts it, 'they float in a level of their own.' Next comes the 'memory-after-image,' as described by Fechner. This introduces the 'memory-continuum,' a mental stratum overlying the 'presentation-continuum,' and involving retention and reproduction. Here we have all that Ward admits in the way of Association, namely, the control of the sequence by 'contiguity.' Association by similarity is rejected because, in this type of psychology, similarity cannot be an attribute of ideas; on the contrary, it must be an active recognition of the relation between a present and a former state of consciousness. The reproduction is achieved by other factors; the similarity is detected *after* the reproduction, being, in fact, due to subsequent comparison. The last point which can be mentioned here is the application of continuity to the subjects of time and space. In dealing with space, Ward introduced the term Extensity to denote pure quantity of space, as, e.g., the sensation of contact over an increased area when the hand is slowly thrust into water; for the rest his doctrine is based on Lotze's 'local sign' theory. Similarly, in relation to time, Ward favours the idea that succession as observed is the succession of emphasized points in the continuous tissue of consciousness. If we compare a 'crowded hour of glorious life' with an hour of dullness, the former seems in retrospect to be longer, though in experience it was shorter; this indicates that 'time, as psychically experienced duration, is primarily an intensive magnitude.' The perception of time is therefore different from the conception of time; the latter is a uniform scheme, but the former is an intensive experience depending on acts of attention which punctuate the 'presentation-continuum.'

After elaborating in the sphere of sensation and cognition what we might designate as a theory of the tissue of psychic experience, Ward proceeds to deal with feeling. Since feeling is coexistent with the other distinguishable types of function, it can be dealt with according as it accompanies each of these (sensation, complex states of sensation, and movement, the flow of ideas). Passing over the detail of this part we come to 'emotional and conative action.' The treatment of this was foreshadowed earlier when the author declared that activity is present from the first, and that it takes the form of selective movements. Primarily such movements may have been established by 'natural' selection, but 'purposive' selection began to take effect at a very early stage. While feelings are connected with movements, the emotions are to be described as total states of consciousness which involve forms of expression; the importance of the distinction being that the movements in the latter case are selected, purposive, and capable of reinforcing the emotion as a whole. Here the movements differ entirely from reflex movements; the movement does not account for the feeling, the feeling accounts for the movement. As the mind attains higher levels there is a gradual loosening of the bond between particular feelings and particular movements; the idea enters in and gives remote objects for our striving; the conative element is thus employed on the highest level of psychic life, and becomes desire and will. The coexistence of differentiation and integration is preserved to the end. For intellection is the process by which desire attains the means to its satisfaction. The flow of ideas becomes more developed and acquires a degree of synthesis through associations; desire prompts to 'a mental rehearsal of various possible courses of action'; the two lines of advance are united in the total psychosis of the mature mind. The analysis of intellectual activity is therefore achieved when we can distinguish the typical forms of its synthesis, which differs from associative synthesis in being purposely selective.

An article written for an Encyclopaedia is necessarily condensed; a further condensation might seem to be little short of mutilation. The end must justify the procedure, and the end here kept in view was to show how a new phase of psychological theory appeared in England. Its coming was clearly due in part to a better knowledge and fuller appreciation of German research and speculation. But it was no mere importation. The influence of Bain and Spencer is not to be overlooked. Ward broke new ground on one fundamental point—the idea that life and growth belong to the mind as truly as they belong to the body. The total impression, which we have aimed to reproduce in the account here given, is that of a process which must be described piecemeal but takes place always as a whole; it is an impression of organic unity, an impression of vital impulse ever extending its unity over a greater variety and complexity of action. To grasp this idea is more important than disputing details, for out of the idea comes inspiration.

2. STOUT

The philosophical outlook which gave a distinctive mark to Ward's *Psychology*, and was conspicuous by its absence in the more empirical attitude of Sully, has been again made prominent by G. F. Stout. The *Analytic Psychology* of 1896 was followed by the *Manual* in 1898, and the *Groundwork*, 1903. Each work has a degree of individuality and exhibits changes of thought, but in essential matters the Analytic Psychology is not superseded by the later (and briefer) expositions. A study of Herbart's Psychology (*Mind*, 1888) showed the preoccupations of the writer at that time, and the influence of Herbart was abiding. This influence, however, was not enough to make Professor Stout a Herbartian; he would be more correctly described as a follower of Ward if his independence did not justify the statement that his psychology is not to be treated as a mere reflection of any other theory. For his own part Professor Stout seems to acknowledge most indebtedness to Brentano.

In its broad outlines the *Analytic Psychology* is a study of the structure and processes of the mind. It is devoid of physiology, and so far aims to be 'pure' psychology. In this respect it is akin to Ward's article, and goes even further in the emphasis laid on activity. It is in a sense an introduction to the whole subject, for the genesis of the mental structure was the task first undertaken, but this genetic psychology presupposed ideas which seemed to require to be treated first; the genetic psychology was accordingly postponed until the analytic had been satisfactorily elaborated. The scope of the undertaking was therefore automatically limited. The first book deals with the elementary modes of consciousness and aims to fix their number and their nature; the second is devoted to the laws and modes of change. The principal achievement of the first volume was the restatement of the idea that consciousness has three fundamental modes, thinking, feeling, willing. While the idea was not new the establishment of it was original; against the Kantian view that these modes are ultimate because irreducible, the author argues that many other modes are equally irreducible; the distinction of modes must not be treated as a discrimination of irreducible contents, but as distinction of attitudes. The matter given to consciousness is the sum of presentations; to each presentation there is a possible reaction in one of three ways. If the presentation is referred to an object, and regarded only as significant, we are said to think; if we find ourselves in an attitude of liking or disliking, we have the volitional or conative mode; from this arises pleasure or pain. The striking points of this statement are the emphasis which falls on conation, a term derived from Aristotle through mediaeval Latin, and wholly saturated with the Aristotelian conception of striving or the biological notion of dynamic states; and, secondly, the way in which feeling is made an attribute of activity and secondary to it; pain is equivalent to hindrance, pleasure is the tone of unimpeded action. In reality then, only two modes are fundamental; we either think or will. But even this duality seems reducible, for both are processes of a vital kind and no more than aspects of vital action. The effort which is the essence of all life is an effort of self-maintenance, that striving which Spinoza called 'conatus,' and Avenarius elaborated in the doctrine of 'vital series.' Thought and will are operations by which the creature strives to regain its lost equilibrium. Their unity does not consist in the fact that will involves ideas or consistent thinking involves attention and will, though Green adopted this way of reducing plurality to unity. Stout, being a psychologist and not a dialectician, avoids that argument for ultimate identity; it is the underlying unity of the mental organism which he seeks to exhibit, and this really means that we cannot speak of thinking and willing, passive and active powers, but only of conscious activity—in other words, of thinking or conscious processes.

Thus the second book which deals with this mental activity as a unity is concerned with its complex forms: in their unity, that is to say, not the (mechanical) parts of our consciousness, but the (biological) development of its organic totality. Thought is the creature's way of satisfying its needs, including its need of thoughts; and therefore thinking is a kind of adaptation or invention by which the organism sustains its relations to the environment of circumstances. This is the description which can be given of mental life; it requires for its supplement an explanation of the ways in which the relations are sustained, and this genetic part is still awaited. In spite of this lack it is true to say that by its careful elaboration, its subtle but clear arguments, and its constructive breadth, the *Analytic Psychology* has been one of the most influential works produced in Great Britain during the last quarter of the nineteenth century. The later manuals mentioned above are well known and need not be described in detail.

3. JAMES

Of all the scientific works ever produced James's *Principles of Psychology* is most deserving to be called a 'phenomenon.' Though it did not appear until 1890, there had been preliminary instalments in periodicals, and many were anticipating eagerly the final publication. Its coming produced mixed feelings. There is a reassuring dignity about the march of systems; they tide themselves over the awkward places by sheer force of superiority; but already James had begun his opposition to systems and was determined to be systematically erratic. He announces that 'the reader will in vain seek for any closed system in the book; it is mainly a mass of descriptive details, running out into queries which only a metaphysics alive to the weight of her task can hope successfully to deal with.' Something may be allowed for the difference between a 'system' and a 'closed system': but no consistent thinking ever yet avoided the necessity of coherence and no one feels shocked at a reference to James's 'system of psychology.' We hear a more intimate confession when the author 'rejects both the associationist and the spiritualist theories,' and says 'in this strictly positivistic point of view consists the only feature of it for which I feel tempted to claim originality.' One reviewer described the author as an 'impressionist.' An instructive parallel might be drawn between Taine and James, not only in respect of their qualities as writers and the character of their interest in human life, but also as the two prominent exponents of anti-rationalistic methods. It is true that Taine was not fully emancipated; but it is also true that James was enslaved by excess of liberty.

For those who have not read all or part of the *Principles of Psychology*, a description of its rubrics would be worse than useless;

those who have read it know why such a proceeding is to be avoided. The author was primarily a man with medical training; his official positions were so many stations on the road from body to spirit. Born in 1842, James graduated in medicine at Harvard in 1870, became an instructor in physiology at Harvard, and later Assistant Professor of Comparative Anatomy and Physiology. In 1879–1880 he migrated from physiology to philosophy, and remained in that department till 1889, when he became Professor of Psychology (1889–1897); from 1897 to 1907 he was again officially Professor of Philosophy, retiring after that date from teaching in order to devote himself wholly to writing. At the end this psychologist was a philosopher, but the change was nominal; James himself did not change, and he was so far indifferent to formal distinctions as to be scarcely aware whether he was treating psychology philosophically or philosophy psychologically. Thus we are compelled to travel from the *Principles* to the *Pragmatism*, because, though not concerned here with philosophy, there is no dividing line at which one may reasonably stop.

Compared with the earlier American writers, James had distinct advantages. His intimate and practical acquaintance with the sciences of physiology and biology placed him in a position from which he could survey human action as a system of natural adjustment. Other factors of temperament and genius prevented him from dropping into a crass materialism. The result was a distinctively physiological psychology which claimed to be a statement of what actually happens in the course of one's conscious life. To avoid preliminary errors such as the atomistic 'elements' which make consciousness, and also to avoid fallacies due to preconceptions about the nature and purpose of life, a plunge into the 'stream of consciousness' must be made at the very beginning. This conception of life as the mere fact of living and of consciousness as the mere fact of being conscious is the means by which James struggled to get ever closer to reality. Introspection, with an almost mystical belief in the possibility of fusing what one knows and what one is, was the chief instrument, but its use was somewhat obscured by the elaborate physiological supplements. James did not belong to those who think all mental phenomena are 'epiphenomena' and therefore fully explained by pure 'cerebralism.' On the other hand, he seems to have been deeply impressed with Lotze's teaching about the difference between 'knowing' and 'knowing about' any phase of reality. In a certain way one only knows vision by seeing; but sciences are not immediate experiences, and a chapter on vision must describe the eye and its functions simply because the greater knowledge toward which men strive is attained by this particular circumnavigation. The reason why thoughts are explained with the help of physiological diagrams is that actual experience has no other way of rounding off its own development. To say that physiology throws no light on mental processes is very true; the fundamental error is in asking physiology to explain something which has previously been made inaccessible, instead of taking all facts as capable in some degree of being explained by all others.

As regards the introspection James was also able to point out where this method had been vitiated. The 'psychologist's fallacy' is the counterpart of the physiologist's fallacy. The latter sees in the brain both the organ which sustains consciousness and the consciousness which (after being separately recognized) is 'located' in that organ. The psychologist, having isolated an 'idea' as idea of something, proceeds to find in the original idea all the factors of which he is afterwards reflectively conscious. Hence the tendency to talk of 'parts' of an idea, as if a person's idea of a year contained 365 days, or his idea of a table had four legs. Introspection has often been condemned on this ground; Kant rejected it as being a perversion of true observation, since the object observed was altered by the observing. There is undoubtedly little chance of analysing a fit of anger while it lasts. But how do we get at anything? Space separates us from objects; time separates us from our past experiences. These are the conditions of all knowledge which have to be accepted. Some say 'we can never know ourselves': others complain that we can never know anything but ourselves. All this was for James essentially a talking about how to begin, instead of beginning—or rather instead of recognizing that one had already begun.

The *Principles*, not being a system, might be described as a critical survey of the possibilities of psychology. If James had no system, he had decided preferences, and a wealth of vituperative adjectives for all who came and were not chosen. The advantages of a non-scientific language are very limited; it is often difficult to guess the exact bearings of what is said upon what has been said, for James is given to translating instead of quoting the other employers of the Anglo-Saxon tongue. A readiness to let the reader 'drop the phrase' if he disliked it was no special advantage, and allowed many readers to think they agreed when they were only failing to discern their disagreement. But this is detail. The letter perishes, but the spirit lives. James was more subtle, more difficult to comprehend than most readers have thought. Particularly in his psychology, overshadowed as it is by an emotional passion for intuitive spontaneity, he becomes elusive. He talks physiology without intending to 'explain' consciousness, but only to make it more intelligible; he recognizes the machinery of association and the value of 'paths' in the brain, but warns the reader that this is subsidiary to the unitary 'flow of consciousness'; he believes emotion is nothing without the physical states usually regarded as merely 'accompanying it,' but does not mean that the strictly emotional part of the emotion (its felt significance, its inwardness) is really physical or physiological; the will he clearly regards as something to be talked round.

When all is said and done James remains the eminently readable psychologist. The interest which expressed itself in the *Principles* was not, strictly speaking, an interest in the mind, but an interest in men. Time only deepened that tendency. As a reviewer James was always prejudiced against any book that was 'dull'; he seems always on the verge of dropping all the emoluments of professorship and openly declaring that no one really explains anything; like the centipedes, we manage our instruments of progression best when we theorize least. In his later works James shows an increasing tendency to develop the 'voluntaristic philosophy.' In 1884 he had founded the American Society for Psychical Research. In 1886 he was much impressed with the ideals of subconsciousness, and at a later date declared:

'I cannot but think that the most important step forward that has occurred in psychology since I have been a student of that science is the discovery, first made in 1886, that, in certain subjects at least, there is not only the consciousness of the ordinary field with its visual centre and margin, but an addition thereto in the shape of a set of memories, thoughts, and feelings which are extra-marginal and outside the primary consciousness altogether, but yet must be classed as conscious facts of some sort, able to reveal their presence by unmistakable signs. I call this the most important step forward because, unlike the other advances which psychology has made, this discovery has revealed to us an entirely unsuspected peculiarity in the constitution of human nature. No other step forward which psychology has made can proffer any such claim as this.' (James, *Varieties*, p. 233. See Binet, *Alterations of Personality*.)

Though never mawkish, James was decidedly mystical, as perhaps every champion of the will to believe and every defender of an irreducible something called personality, must be mystical. Analysis is not compatible with that mood; it finds satisfaction in the contemplative study of unities, and with James it came to fruition in the study of experiences. The title of his Gifford Lectures, *Varieties of Religious Experience*, contains the two key-words of all his later thinking, variety and experience.

Here the psychologist and the philosopher were but two parts acted by one man. The psychologist named the varieties, studying them with the eye of a man used to diagnosis. The philosopher saw in experience a name for the total psychological process; life as a cosmic process being the sum of varieties and spontaneous expressions of power, whether considered widely as in biology or more specifically as in psychology. James made this study a great success because in it he had scope for the expansion of the idea expressed in the *Principles*: 'Once admit that the passing and evanescent [mental states, i.e.] are as real parts of the stream as the distinct and comparatively abiding; once allow that fringes and halos, . . . premonitions, awareness of direction, are thoughts *sui generis*, as much as articulate imaginings and proportions are; once restore, I say, the vague to its psychological rights, and the matter presents no further difficulty.' This was the real core of all the work James did. Around it grew his 'voluntarism,' his regard for 'fringes' and 'transitive states,' his dislike of associationism (as he stated it) and tendency to repudiate all analysis in order to keep unmarred the whole vitality of consciousness. This was the quality which ultimately made James appear so much at one with Bergson's *élan vital*.

Chapter Fifteen

TWENTIETH-CENTURY THEORIES

A. Introductory

The late Professor Brett's *History of Psychology* was published in 1921. To continue the story of the development of psychology with his erudition would not only be impossible without writing another volume of equal length; it would also be superfluous as there are many other excellent works describing recent trends in psychology.[1] All that is practicable in such a concluding chapter is to pick out the main trends of the first half of the twentieth century, to outline the important theories about man, and to show how they are reactions against or continuations of traditions of inquiry which have already been traced by Brett.[2]

The main stream of psychology in the first half of the twentieth century springs either from a reaction against certain elements in the observationalist tradition or from the increasing influence of other sciences and technology on the traditional inquiries into human nature. Behaviourism was a reaction against the method of introspection continued by the Introspectionists who were the direct heirs of the observationalist tradition. The Behaviourists, however, retained most of observationalism—the insistence on starting from certain sorts of 'data,' atomism, and associationism. Purposive psychology was a reaction against the intellectualism, sensationism, and associationism of the nineteenth-century tradition; yet it retained a certain degree of atomism. Gestalt psychology was a reaction against sensory atomism; yet its concentration on problems of perception and preoccupation with the data of psychology showed the influence of observationalism. Most of these reactions occurred because their exponents had been trained in other sciences. Darwinian biology and its derivative, animal psycho-

[1] See, for instance, R. Woodworth: *Contemporary Schools of Psychology* (Rev. Ed. 1948), J. C. Flugel: *100 Years of Psychology* (1933), E. G. Boring: *A History of Experimental Psychology* (1929), G. Murphy: *Historical Introduction to Modern Psychology* (1929), and O. Zangwill's article on 'Psychology' in *Chambers's Encyclopaedia* (1950) which gives a very good summary of twentieth-century experimental work.

[2] In writing such a brief summary the needs and interests of British and American students have been born particularly in mind. Many continental thinkers, such as Jaspers, Spranger, and Krüger in Germany, and Janet, Claparède, Pieron, and Sartre in France, would have featured large in a fourth volume of *Brett's History*. They have been omitted because their influence has been negligible on the development of psychology in Great Britain and America.

logy, was enormously important in its influence on Behaviourism and Purposive psychology; dynamics and physiology were important in their influence on Gestalt psychology. Above all, medicine made its contribution in its influence on Freudian psychology which orginated as a branch of medicine. Later on in the twentieth century social science began to exert an influence on the Freudian and purposive schools and to be welcomed by Gestalt psychology as a new ally. Industry and education, too, have played their part in widening our understanding of the behaviour of men.

The twentieth century has also witnessed a great reorientation of outlook in psychology in that the child has become more and more a centre of interest. This interest in the child is linked with the great advances in education and with the dawning realization made evident in the emphasis on conation, motivation, and the emotional determinants of adult behaviour, that the understanding of man's behaviour is impossible without the understanding of those irrational tendencies which are so obvious in the behaviour of children and which men carry with them into adult life. Finally the twentieth century has been characterized by a great amount of philosophical or second-order discussion on the status of psychology as a theoretical science and by a spate of recipes on how psychology should develop, recipes which have crystallized in the formation of 'schools' of psychology.

If, therefore, one had to pick out the main trends of psychology in the first half of the twentieth century one would mention the emphasis on conation, the substitution of stress on wholes or organization for atomistic analysis, the increasing realization of the importance of man's social environment as a determinant of his behaviour as an individual, the movement of the child into the centre of the stage, and the formation of 'schools' reflecting increased sensitivity toward methodological questions. We must now consider in more detail the development of these trends.

B. The observationalist tradition

I. INTROSPECTIONISM

The most striking continuation of the traditions of nineteenth-century psychology into the twentieth century is to be found in the various offshoots of observationalism. This philosophical account of the acquisition of knowledge had fostered the development of a science of mind in which the inquirer endeavoured to isolate simple sensory elements and to discover what the laws of their association might be. The tradition of Locke, Hume, Hartley, Bain, and Wundt was continued by the Introspectionist School of psychology and by various brands of associationism. Great importance was placed by the Introspectionists on the special techniques of observation necessary for a science of mind. Observers had to be trained to study mental contents as 'existences' rather than as 'meanings' in order to build up a comprehensive account of mental structure, an inventory of the mind. E. B. Titchener, an English pupil of Wundt who migrated to America, achieved fame for his insistence on this type of methodological purism. In his *Lectures on the Elementary Psychology of Feeling and Attention* (1908) the observationalist standpoint of the Introspectionists was made clear: 'We are agreed, I suppose,' he said, 'that scientific method may be summed up in the single word "observation"; the only way to work in science is to observe those phenomena which form the subject-matter of science.'[1] The Wurzburg School[2] under Külpe elaborated the methods of 'systematic experimental introspection' which involved both the performance of a task like remembering something, attending to something, or making a judgment, and retrospective reports on what the subject experienced in performing these operations. The experimenter, in other words, asked how as well as what his subject remembered.

The main theoretical importance of the innumerable experiments done by the Introspective School was to exhibit the inadequacy of the assumption of the observationalist tradition that all mental events were either sensations or images; for queer goings on were revealed which could not easily be fitted into either category. Marbe and G. E. Müller showed that the traditional account of judgment as the comparison of a present impression with a mental image was fictitious; instead mental states of readiness, hesitation, doubt, and such-like were stressed. As these could not be classed as sensations, images, or feelings they were named 'conscious attitudes.' Watt and Ach tackled association and showed that 'acts' of association were absent during the performance of a task; the organism seemed to be 'set' or to have a 'determining tendency' to react in certain ways on certain occasions. Similarly 'acts of will' were discovered to be mythical constructs, a more appropriate description being in terms of the exercise of 'determining tendencies.' These introspective findings were particularly interesting in that, though they were made by people nurtured in the observationalist tradition, they nevertheless undermined the observationalist epistemology. No longer could the mind be regarded as a receptacle for or collection of sense-data and images; no longer could the acquisition of knowledge be described as the passive colligation of these elements by laws of association. Instead the mind had to be regarded as a system of

[1] *Op. cit.*, p. 175.
[2] For an excellent account of the work done by this school see G. Humphrey: *Thinking*, 1951.

tendencies, attitudes, and expectations, and the acquisition of knowledge as the modification of these by contact with the social and physical
environments. The falsification of sensationism by those who were
brought up in it coincided historically with the development of other
systems by McDougall and Freud in which the mind as an active
system of innate and acquired tendencies took the place of the old
passive container of images. And later F. C. Bartlett, in his stimulating book on *Remembering* (1932), demonstrated with a wealth of
experimental material the detailed effect of attitudes and interests on
what is perceived and remembered. Perception and remembering are
now regarded as a process of selecting, grouping, and reconstructing.
The old picture of the mind as receiving, combining, and reproducing
has been finally abandoned.

2. BEHAVIOURISM AND ANIMAL PSYCHOLOGY

While Introspectionism continued to be almost equated with psychology a new field of study was making rapid strides whose influence
on the development of twentieth-century psychology has been very
great. The theory of evolution was, perhaps, the most decisive of all
the postulates of other sciences in its influence on psychology, in that
it occasioned the abandonment of any dogmatic separation of human
from animal modes of behaviour. The start of animal psychology was
one such offshoot of the realization that men are, after all, animals.
The very term 'behaviour,' which became so popular in psychology, is
itself a reflection of the change which gradually came over psychology
when the advance of biology drew attention away from the method of
introspection to the study of how people in fact behave in concrete
situations. In his *The Expression of the Emotions* (1872) Darwin himself
began with the movements which are similar in men and animals and
which constitute the common objective aspect of emotional states. In
his *Descent of Man* (1871) he applied the same method to the problem
of moral sentiments and postulated a gregarious instinct as the cement
of human relationships. These works provided a starting-point for the
study of animals and the respects in which they seemed to be similar
to men.

The result was that there was a developing tendency both to human-
ize animals and to brutalize men. The development of theories of
'instincts' in psychology and the great stress placed by Freud and
McDougall on the irrational determinants of behaviour exemplifies the
latter aspect of this tendency: the studies of learning and intelligence in
animals and the interest in herd phenomena or the social groupings of
animals exemplifies the former aspect, which found careful expression
at the beginning of the twentieth century in the work of Thorndike,
Pavlov, and the Behaviourists.

Thorndike was a student of James at Harvard University who was drawn towards the study of animal learning by the stimulating suggestions thrown out by Wundt in his *Lectures on Human and Animal Psychology* (1892). Wundt, as was to be expected, applied his principle of association of ideas to the phenomenon of animal learning. Thorndike attempted to demonstrate in more detail the satisfactoriness of this old explanation of learning on the part of human beings in the field of animal behaviour. We thus find in the work of Thorndike and in the work of the early Behaviourists the fusing of the old observationalist tradition with the new biological tradition stemming from Darwin. Thorndike's 'law of effect' was the result: 'any act which in a given situation produces satisfaction becomes associated with that situation, so that when the situation recurs the act is more likely than before to recur also.'[1] In other words means which prove successful in the solution of problems become 'stamped in' and the animal may be said to have learned how to solve a problem. In his 'law of exercise' he gave his own more detailed version, too, of the old principles of recency and frequency. Few would object to the first, at any rate, of these two laws as a statement of a necessary condition of learning; it is when they come to be regarded as sufficient conditions that uneasiness starts.

Pavlov was a Russian physiologist who got interested in animal learning as a result of the odd behaviour of dogs in experiments on digestion. He was examining gastric secretion and was surprised to notice secretion before the food arrived—e.g. at the sound of the food being brought in by the attendant. Pavlov concluded that experience in previous experiments must have 'conditioned' the dog to expect food before the food was actually presented. Visual and auditory cues thus came to serve as signals for food and Pavlov saw that these preparatory signals must play an important part in the adjustment of animals to their environments. He then proceeded to study salivation, which was more accessible to experimental analysis than gastric secretion. He built up under laboratory conditions what he called a 'conditioned reflex' by using a metronome as a signal for food. He also postulated a principle of 'reinforcement' by which he meant the 'stamping in' of the conditioned response when, after repeated trials, the stimulus of the metronome was always followed by the actual food. The similarity between this principle and Thorndike's 'law of effect' has often been noted.[2] Pavlov, however, came to his hypothesis quite independently of Thorndike and always expressed contempt for what went by the name

[1] E. Thorndike: *The Elements of Psychology*, p. 203.
[2] See R. Woodworth: *Contemporary Schools of Psychology* (Rev. Ed.), p. 50. It is important, however, to distinguish what was *learnt* in the two cases. In the classical conditioning experiments of Pavlov salivation, the learned 'response,' was not an action which was *instrumental* to obtaining food; in Thorndike's experiments the cats learned such instrumental acts.

of psychology. Pavlov did a great amount of empirical work elaborating and modifying his initial postulates as a result of comparing consequences deduced from them with actual observations, e.g. his work on inhibition of conditioned responses, on stimulus generalization and differentiation. A lot of this detailed work has now been incorporated in the more comprehensive works on learning by modern Behaviourists like Hull.

Thorndike and Pavlov worked on animals because they were interested in problems connected with animals. As animals cannot talk there was never any question of using introspective reports to confirm the hypotheses which they formulated about them. The steady progress which the animal psychologists seemed to be making provided a striking contrast to introspective psychology, which was occupied with controversies like that of 'imageless thought' which seemed difficult to settle experimentally—especially as it may well not have been an empirical question at all. Early Behaviourism, which emerged as a reaction against the rather abortive discussions of the Introspectionists, was a reflection of the progress made in animal psychology in comparison with the doldrums into which the study of human beings seemed to have been steered. The lasting contribution which the Behaviourists made to the study of human beings was to suggest that the actual behaviour of human beings should be studied rather than their introspective musings. The Behaviourists, to use Watson's own words, decided 'either to give up psychology or else make it a natural science.' Making psychology a natural science amounted in theory to confining their observations of human beings to visual observations of other people's behaviour to the exclusion of retrospective observations of their own. In fact the Behaviourists have worked almost entirely on rats.

Watson, significantly enough, was trained as a philosopher but switched to psychology later on. He set up one of the earliest laboratories for animal psychology and started in 1913 to launch polemics against the traditional studies of consciousness which he regarded as a relic of theological preoccupation with the soul. Later on (1924–1925), continuing the Darwinian tradition which started with the objective study of emotions, he did some valuable and original work on the emotional responses of babies in which he singled out fear, love, and rage as the only unlearned emotions. But early Behaviourism, though novel in its exaltation of animal psychology as the prototype of scientific psychology, was very much an heir of previous traditions. Watson himself, on account of his philosophical training, was an expounder of a new method rather than the inventor of a new theory. Just as Descartes had popularized and attempted to universalize the methods used by the mathematical physicists of his day, so also Watson popularized and attempted to universalize in psychology the methods of the new science which was carrying all before it—Darwinian biology. Watson's interests were, in other words, predominantly methodological, and like most philosophically trained people at the end of the nineteenth century, his picture of scientific method was thoroughly observationalist. The important thing that he had to say was that visual observation of how people actually behave is a much more reliable way of testing assumptions about human behaviour than reliance on introspective evidence. But he said it in such a way that the Behaviourists can almost be regarded as having derived their name from their determination to *start from* overt behaviour or visual data instead of from introspective data. Their difference of opinion with the introspectionists derived from their distrust of the data from which traditional psychologists had started. After all, they said, what are these externally unobservable goings-on which were referred to as mental contents? Are not these queer 'imageless thoughts' very insubstantial and impure data when compared with palpable data like rats or terrified babies? 'Today,' said Watson, 'the Behaviourist can safely throw out a real challenge to the subjective psychologists—show us that you have a possible method, indeed that you have a legitimate subject-matter.'[1] Similarly, Hunter, in advocating the merits of the new 'anthroponomy' which was to take the place of the old introspective psychology, was concerned mainly with defining an alternative *subject-matter*. 'Psychology,' he maintained, 'unlike the other sciences, has not found it possible to continue with the subject-matter bequeathed it by philosophy.'[2]

The early Behaviourists were not heirs of the observationalist tradition solely in the methodological conceptions which they shared with the Introspectionists. They were also atomistic and associationist in their theory. Like the Introspectionists, whom they attacked, they believed that the task of the scientist was to analyse the experimental data into atomistic units and then to find some general principles which determined the binding together and regular sequences of these units. The Introspectionists like Wundt had arrived at simple sensations whose links were explained by the principles of association. Watson arrived instead at simple stimulus-response units which were called reflexes. The connections between these units were built up by repeated experiences if they were not inherited. Learning and habit formation were explained by recourse to the Behaviouristic equivalent of Thorndike's law of exercise. Watson suggested that as a rat running a maze goes on running till it reaches the goal it must always run

---

[1] J. B. Watson: *Behaviourism*, p. 17.
[2] W. S. Hunter: 'The Psychological Study of Behaviour,' *Psych. Rev.* 1932, p. 7.

along the right path at least once. Therefore the right path must be run more often than any other path in a series of trials and the gradual elimination of other paths can be explained in an associationist manner in terms of frequency (part of what Thorndike meant by exercise). Thorndike himself pointed out the inadequacy of the law of exercise as a sufficient explanation, as rats often entered a blind alley a great number of times on the same trial. He maintained that the law of effect was indispensable for an adequate explanation. But the Behaviourists did not like it because of its connection with the mentalistic concept of 'satisfaction.' Watson later on began to introduce the notion of the conditioned response which he learnt from Pavlov, but he never recognized the importance of Pavlov's law of reinforcement nor the connection between it and Thorndike's law of effect. Thus Watson, in his main theoretical concepts, was very much in the old associationist tradition. He substituted 'behaviour' for 'consciousness' as his starting-point or subject-matter, analysed it into the Behaviouristic version of simple units, and postulated connections between the units built up in accordance with old associationist principles. His actual theory of behaviour became outmoded nearly as quickly as Descartes' theory of vortices, but his methodological advice, like Decartes', provided inspiration to many who followed him.

Of the later Behaviourists the two most famous are Tolman and Hull. It is hardly fair, however, to call either of them observationalists. Tolman shared Watson's concern to eliminate from psychology any statements that were visually untestable. But he departed from Watson's associationism, objected to Watson's atomistic, stimulus-response account of behaviour, and accepted the overwhelming importance of conation or purpose in the explanation of behaviour. He is better regarded as a methodological journeyman in the train of Purposive and Gestalt psychology rather than as an orthodox Behaviourist. He tried to state in a non-introspective terminology the assumptions put forward by people like McDougall, Freud, Thorndike, and the Gestalt psychologists. Though we find few new hypotheses in Tolman, his attempt to restate in Behaviouristic terminology the objectively testable hypotheses of other 'schools' of psychology represents the sensible part of Watson's polemics. There is, however, even in Tolman, a tendency shared by so many methodologically minded scientists to see in his particular recipe a panacea for the advance of science. This tendency is particularly marked in the later work of Hull, who explicitly abandoned the old observationalist account of scientific method but tended to see in Behaviouristic methodology combined with the establishment of a mathematico-deductive system the only road for scientific psychologists to tread. Hull preserved, to a certain extent, the associationist tradition of Watson and was very critical both of Gestalt psychology and of Purposive psychology. Nevertheless since both he and Tolman make great use of the concept of 'drive,' which turned out to be the objectively testable component of McDougall's more metaphysical concept of 'instinct,' it will be more convenient for expository, purposes to consider both their theories as variants of Purposive pyschology, or the school of psychology, deriving from McDougall, which makes the concept of goal-directed behaviour fundamental in explanation.

Another self-styled Behaviourist who made important contributions to psychology was Lashley. In his early work he even relegated introspection 'to a subordinate place as an example of the pathology of scientific method.'[1] However his methodological opinions were a second-order reflection of his passionate interest in the objectively observable manifestations of the functioning of the brain. His problem was the localization in the brain of functions like learning and remembering. Working with Franz on rats and other animals he discovered that the old theory of localization, so convenient for associationists and advocates of the conditioned response theory of learning, was untenable. He was led to formulate instead in 1929 the principles of equipotentiality and mass action. It seemed to be a fair generalization, which had been confirmed by experiments on animals, that one portion of the cortex was as good as another for learning a task and that the success of learning was a function of the total amount of cortex retained by the animal. Lashley, a pupil of Watson's, thus provided one of the most convincing refutations of explanations in terms of simple reflex arcs.

3. SKINNER'S OPERATIONISM

One of the more recent offshoots of observationalism in psychology is the operationist movement. It is difficult to be clear quite what operationism is because it is not always very clearly stated. Certainly all operationists are rationalistic in the sense that they maintain that unless scientists define their terms operationally they will not uncover Nature's secrets. But what does it mean to define a term 'operationally'? It could mean that hypotheses must be expressed in terms which render them testable by observation. This would be the view about the language of science which is parallel to the salutary part of the observationalist doctrine—that scientific hypotheses must be tested by observation. But operationism is misleading in exactly the same way as observationalism is misleading. And this is because operationism is an offshoot of observationalism. Just as it is salutary to say that observation is decisive in testing hypotheses but misleading to say that

---

[1] Quoted by C. Pratt: *The Logic of Modern Psychology*, p. 40.

scientists 'start from' observations, so also is it salutary to say that scientific terms are meaningful because there are concrete operations by means of which it can be determined whether or not a term is applicable or whether or not what is asserted in a sentence containing scientific terms is true or false, but misleading to say that scientists define terms by means of 'operations' or that terms 'stand for' operations. There is thus a wider and a narrower interpretation of 'operationism.' The wider doctrine is accepted by all scientists who make careful attempts to test hypotheses; the narrower doctrine is accepted only by those who assume an observationalist view of scientific method.

This movement in psychology was a reflection of the movement in physics epitomized in Bridgman's book *The Logic of Modern Physics*. There were a number of articles in the *Psychological Review* terminating in a symposium on 'Operationism in Psychology' in 1945 as well as a book called *The Logic of Modern Psychology* written by C. Pratt from an avowedly observationalist standpoint. The operationists tried to apply Bridgman's remark that 'The proper definition of a concept is not in terms of properties but in terms of actual operations'[1] to psychology. A typical expression of the view is that of Skinner: 'Operationism may be defined as the practice of talking about (1) one's observations, (2) the manipulational and calculational procedures involved in making them, (3) the logical and mathematical steps which intervene between earlier and later statements, and (4) nothing else.'[2]

Skinner's article in 1945, however, was merely the attempt to formulate explicitly a conception of scientific method which he had long espoused and which underpinned his main work, *The Behaviour of Organisms* (1938). For he shared completely the old observationalist conception of scientific method, that the job of the scientist was merely to find correlations between observations. Skinner not only eschewed recourse to hypothetical constructs; he even claimed, like Newton, that he made no use of hypotheses! Presumably he aimed, like Bacon, at replacing rash 'anticipations' of Nature by judicious 'interpretations,' though it is rather a puzzle to glean what would count as 'data' or 'observations' unless the research worker had criteria of relevance provided by a problem which is only a problem in the light of existing assumptions, and by 'anticipations' or hypotheses connected with the sort of thing which might constitute a solution. In fact Skinner came to his inquiries with a number of highly sophisticated assumptions provided for him by the Behaviourist tradition. However, he adopted the purely 'molar' approach and made no speculations about events

---

[1] P. Bridgman: *The Logic of Modern Physics*, p. 6.
[2] B. F. Skinner: 'The Operational Analysis of Psychological Terms,' *Psychological Review*, 1945, p. 270.

within the organism that might mediate between stimulus and response. His aim was simply to discover the laws of behaviour in the sense of functional relations between responses on the one hand and variations in the stimulus and experimental conditions on the other hand.

Skinner's major innovation in the Behaviourist tradition was linked with his introduction of the Skinner box. This enabled him to study instrumental conditioning in a much more controlled way than had been possible in Thorndike's puzzle box. The result was the formulation of his distinction between respondent and operant 'reflexes.' In a respondent reaction there is a known stimulus, such as the ticking of the metronome, with which a reaction like salivation can be correlated. In a respondent reaction, however, such as lever pressing, there are no known stimuli with which the response can be correlated in this way. There may, of course, be some form of internal stimulation, but such speculations were ruled out by Skinner's operational methodology. So operant responses can only be established as functions of experimental conditions such as food schedules. As behaviour consists largely of such operant responses, which are instrumental in obtaining a variety of goals, Skinner thought that the study of conditioned operants and their extinction must form the basic substance of a theory of behaviour. These laws of conditioning and extinction may one day be deducible from higher laws, but the scientist must proceed to such 'interpretations' in a Baconian manner; he must not, like Hull, develop a model of the internal workings of the organism by the use of hypothetical constructs and deduce consequences which can be experimentally tested.

Skinner's blend of Behaviourism and Operationism was thus one of the clearest examples of the continuation of the observationalist tradition into the twentieth-century. In respect of its conception both of the methods and of the language of science it imposes almost neurotic restrictions on what a scientist is permitted to do and say in order to remain respectable. Early Behaviourism, in forbidding reference to 'mind,' which is not publicly observable, was a rather banal application to psychology of the observationalist injunction not to go beyond the data. Skinner went further and ruled out the postulation of unobservable internal events of a physiological type to explain behaviour. Yet the most important imaginative advances in science have consisted precisely in the postulation of the unobserved to explain the observed—for instance in the atomic theory or in Galileo's postulation of the law of inertia.

Of course Skinner may well be right, but for other reasons, in decrying the attempt to deduce descriptions of behaviour from physiological postulates. Also the notion that mind is an explanatory concept of an unobservable sort may well be a misleading way of looking at the concept of mind. For how could we understand what behaviour is unless we understood the family of mental concepts connected with action such as 'purpose,' 'reason for action,' 'intention,' 'grasp of relevance,' and so on. Indeed in his distinction between operant and respondent reactions Skinner, again for other reasons, hit upon a distinction which is crucial for the understanding of human actions. Respondent reactions like salivation and eye-blinks, which can be dealt with reasonably well by classical conditioning theory, are indeed reactions which can be correlated with stimuli. But they are not, strictly speaking, actions; they are things that happen to us. When, however, we pass to Skinner's operants, to things done which are seen to be instrumental to an end, we are entering the sphere of action proper—and of mind. Such actions, at the human level at any rate, cannot either be described or explained in the same sort of way as the mere movements exhibited at the reflex level. For an action is not simply a series of bodily movements; such movements as are necessary to it are done for the sake of something. They are classed as belonging to an action because of their relevance to an end. We do not know what a person is doing for certain unless we know what he has in mind. The type of action it is depends on the end which the movements are seen as contributing to attain or bring about. It is thus difficult to see how Behaviourists can know what the action is which they are attempting to study without reference to what is commonly called 'consciousness.' And how even a beginning could be made in the study of cognitive performances such as perceiving, remembering, and thinking, which may involve no discernible overt movements, it is difficult to see. It is significant that Behaviourists have concentrated mainly on the study of simple motor skills. But even in that limited sphere Behaviourism is to be criticized not simply for its restrictive and outworn conception of scientific method; it is also to be criticized for having a very naïve and inadequate view of what constitutes behaviour.

C. *Reactions against the observationalist tradition*

I. PURPOSIVE PSYCHOLOGY

We have already seen how the Introspective School of psychology came to discover the inadequacy of the traditional picture of the mind as a passive container of sensations and images and to stress the importance of 'conscious attitudes' and 'determining tendencies.' These later Introspectionists served as a kind of fifth column within the crumbling defences of the old psychology. The major attack on the citadel was led by people who were trained outside in the fields of biology and physiology. The early Behaviourists and animal psychologists launched an attack on the methods of the old school but retained the concepts and principles of explanation in a disguised form. A more radical attack on the concepts and principles was led by McDougall. Sensationism, whether in the form of impressions and ideas or stimulus and response, together with associationism whether of ideas or of responses, was abandoned. In their place a system was built on the all-pervading concept of 'purpose.' McDougall, who was trained in biology and medicine, was not much influenced by any kind of methodological recipe. Indeed his lack of methodological precision rendered much of what he said untestable and even metaphysical. This defect in McDougall was remedied by Tolman, the Purposive Behaviourist, who tried to state many of McDougall's assumptions more precisely and to clear out the metaphysical lumber from McDougall's system. To do justice to Purposive psychology it is therefore convenient to outline McDougall's main postulates together with Tolman's emendations. They can be summarized as follows: (*a*) All behaviour is purposive. (*b*) There are certain innate goal-seeking tendencies. (This is the 'instinct' hypothesis.) (*c*) All behaviour is motivated by instincts either directly or indirectly through the formation of 'sentiments' and 'tastes.' (This is the 'instinct reduction' hypothesis.) Tolman accepted all these postulates with modifications. Let us consider them briefly in turn.

(*a*) *Purpose.*—McDougall was ambivalent in what he meant by 'purposive.' He veered between the subjective criterion of prevision of ends as a criterion, which made his speculations about animals untestable, and objective criteria for teleological chains of behaviour like persistence of activity until a goal is attained, docility relative to a goal, and so on. Tolman cut out the subjective criterion altogether and defined purposive behaviour in terms of readiness to persist through trial and error towards a goal and docility relative to a goal.

(*b*) *Instincts.*—McDougall maintained that the hormé or 'will to live' of an organism (cp. Spinoza's conatus, Freud's libido) was manifest in a number of specific behaviour-tendencies, the instincts. He defined an instinct as 'an inherited or innate psycho-physical disposition which determines its possessor to perceive or pay attention to objects of a certain class, to experience an emotional excitement of a particular quality upon perceiving such an object, and to act in a particular manner or at least to experience an impulse to such action.'[1] Instinctive activity was thus analysed into three phases—cognitive, affective, and conative. The affective aspect, or introspectable emotional quality, was regarded by McDougall as the distinguishing mark of the different instincts.

[1] W. McDougall: *Introduction to Social Psychology*, p. 25.

In his *Introduction to Social Psychology* in 1908 McDougall postulated seven major instincts, each of which 'conditions some one kind of emotional excitement whose quality is peculiar or specific to it.' They were escape (fear), repulsion (disgust), curiosity (wonder), pugnacity (anger), self-assertion (elation or positive self-feeling), self-abasement (subjection), and parental (tender emotion). There were also 'some other instincts of less well-defined emotional tendency,' including gregariousness, acquisition, construction, reproduction, and laughter, together with non-specific innate tendencies without specific emotional excitement such as sympathy, suggestibility, imitation, and play. Finally there were the minor instincts such as coughing, scratching, sneezing, and eliminating. In his *Energies of Men* in 1932 McDougall modified his early doctrine to meet a number of objections. He abandoned the word 'instinct' because of its confusion with the old biological concept of 'instinct' and instead he postulated eighteen 'propensities' and a great number of innate 'abilities' like standing, walking, swallowing, and speech. A 'propensity' was 'any part of the innate constitution whose nature and function is to generate upon occasion an active tendency.'[1] The same tendency may activate many different abilities. In the lower animals the abilities are much more closely 'geared to' the innate propensities. 'In the higher animals the setting free of abilities from their special service to particular propensities goes farther than in the higher birds.'[2] Abilities 'geared to' a propensity, the latter including a distinctive 'felt' character and a specific neurological structure, are the equivalent of the old instinct.

Tolman's modification of McDougall's position showed many of its deficiencies. In the first place McDougall made much of the 'felt' character of the different instincts as a criterion of distinction. The emotional core was for him the relatively unchanging aspect of an instinct. Yet, as he himself admitted, many of his instincts like constructiveness and gregariousness had no such introspectably recognizable characteristic, and also, as Tolman pointed out, 'raw feels' are difficult criteria for scientific purposes. Emotions cannot be separated from the type of context in which they occur and are to be defined by reference to end-states for which they are preparatory adjustments of an organic and kinaesthetic type.

Secondly, McDougall's teaching about the objects of instincts was so vague as to be almost irrefutable, especially as he admitted the great influence of learning in broadening the specificity of objects to which we are innately disposed to pay attention. Tolman tried to deal with this matter of cognitive prescription in more detail. He distinguished

---

[1] W. McDougall: *The Energies of Men* (1932), p. 64.
[2] *Ibid.*, pp. 76–7.

'goals' as end-states of physiological quiescence (e.g. hunger satiation) from 'means-objects' (e.g. food) encountered on the way to such end-states. In his treatment of 'means-objects' he postulated certain 'means-end readinesses' which are innate but docile relative to the success of the organism in getting to a goal via a means-object. Also in his account of 'behaviour-supports' he tried to escape the sensory atomism of stimulus-response psychology. 'A rat cannot "run down an alley" without an actual floor to put his feet against, actual walls to steer between, actual free space ahead to catapult into.'[1] These he called 'discriminanda' and 'manipulanda.' He then enlarged the concept of the 'means-end readiness' by incorporating in it the old law of redintegration—that the repetition of a stimulus corresponding to one part of a total means-end field tends to arouse an expectation of the whole complex. Thus the concept of the 'sign-Gestalt expectation' was developed which incorporated also Gestalt findings about the perceptual field. It was along these lines that Tolman attempted to build up a more adequate and less atomistic account of cognitive set and adjustment.

Thirdly, McDougall was very vague in his postulation of a physiological basis for his instincts, and, as Tolman pointed out, there is little evidence for it in the case of some of McDougall's instincts like curiosity, gregariousness, acquisitiveness, and constructiveness. Tolman therefore distinguished between first-order and second-order 'drives.' First-order drives, whether they be appetites or aversions, are linked antecedently with specific initial physiological excitements and consequently with specific states of physiological quiescence—e.g. food-hunger, sex-hunger, excretion hunger, rest-hunger, sensory-motor hunger, fright, and pugnacity. He regarded second-order drives like self-assertion, gregariousness, constructiveness, and so on, as much more hypothetical constructs. They seem to be attached usually to first-order drives and docile relative to them. Also, having no definite physiological basis, they are just as likely to be socially acquired as innate.

Finally, Tolman made an important contribution to the methodology of psychology by introducing the notion of the intervening variable. McDougall's instincts had a slight metaphysical glow around them. They seemed to resemble Aristotelian entelechies, to be dynamic mental atoms activating the mind or mental structures attached to physiological moorings. Tolman suggested that a 'drive' is a convenient scientific construct like 'habit' or 'force.' If, for instance, we speak of a 'hunger-drive' we are using a shorthand symbol for indicating the functional connection between antecedent conditions of, e.g., food-deprivation on the one hand (experimental or independent variables) and behaviour like eating food quickly on the other (behaviour or dependent variables). The investigation of a 'drive' thus involves

[1] E. Tolman: *Purposive Behaviour in Animals and Men* (1932), p. 85.

establishing a concomitant variation between antecedent variables such as heredity, age, and condition of food deprivation and the behaviour variables such as speed and manner of eating food. The 'intervening variable' is a shorthand device for postulating that under certain conditions an organism will tend to behave in certain ways because of certain antecedent conditions. In other words it is a dispositional statement about behaviour which incorporates a causal assumption; it does not refer to a mysterious entity in an organism, though there are, of course, organic processes intervening between the behaviour and antecedent variables which need further investigation.[1] Whether the concept of 'drive,' which acted as a bridge between mechanical and purposive theories, was a very fortunate one, is a further question.[2] But certainly the notion of the intervening variable was useful in that it encouraged theorizing without the taint of metaphysics and helped to pave the way for the later stress on the importance of theoretical constructs in psychology. It thus contributed to the freeing of psychology from the observationalist myth, shared by the early Behaviourists, that scientists must not go beyond what is observed. In fact the postulation of unobservables to explain the observed has been one of the most potent sources of scientific advance.

(c) *Instinct reduction.*—McDougall maintained that all human conduct is motivated either directly by instincts or indirectly by sentiments which he defined as 'an organized system of emotional tendencies centred about some object.'[3] McDougall gladly took over this doctrine of the organization of emotions from Shand. He used it to show how, by the formation of tastes and sentiments, the physical and social environments influence the native propensities. Love, hate, and respect were the main sentiments which determine our major goals; tastes determine our choice of means. Finally McDougall sketched very briefly how learning modifies the manner in which the propensities find expression by becoming directed towards objects which experience shows to be functionally equivalent. The 'core' of the propensity, however—its emotional tone—remains unchanged in the formation of sentiments but its cognitive and motor phases become decreasingly specific.

[1] But see 'On a distinction between hypothetical constructs and intervening variables,' by P. E. Meehl and K. MacCorquodale, in *Psychological Review*, vol. 55, 1948. The authors of the article point out that many psychologists fail to distinguish between 'intervening variables' which are properly to be regarded as nothing but ways of stating empirical laws correlating antecedent with behaviour variables and 'hypothetical constructs' which are not simply ways of stating empirical laws, but involve also the postulation of organic conditions, states, and processes which characterize the organism.

[2] For further discussion of the issues raised by 'drive' theories see R. S. Peters *The Concept of Motivation* (Rev. Ed. 1960).

[3] W. McDougall: *Introduction to Social Psychology* (24th ed. 1942), p. 105.

Tolman's war-cry was 'Rats, not men.' Nevertheless he believed that drives provide the primordial bases for behaviour. 'All the various specifications and elaborations of motivation, which appear in adult and experienced organisms, are to be conceived as but refinements, modifications, or elaborations built upon such more ultimate innate readinesses and demands.'[1] Tolman made no detailed attempt to work out a theory of sentiments to support this claim, though he included a chapter on 'personality mechanisms' in which he translated some Freudian hypotheses into behaviouristic language.[2]

No one can doubt that from the point of view of the development of psychological theory Purposive psychology constituted a tremendous advance on the old sensationism and associationism of the observationalist tradition. McDougall made a break with the dominant traditions of the past. He stimulated an immense amount of research. Like many who try to make a fresh start he attempted to explain too much in terms of his bright idea of instincts; often he expressed himself in such a vague and metaphysical manner that he could not easily be refuted—the cardinal scientific sin. But he stimulated many who tried to refute him. Science advances by the falsification of imaginative hypotheses; and if many of McDougall's assumptions have proved mistaken that is proof of the incentive he provided for others to put forward a better theory.

Perhaps McDougall's greatest mistake, from a philosophical point of view, was to translate a *conceptual* insight into genetic terms. Both McDougall and Tolman saw that the concept of 'purpose' is indispensable for the explanation of human behaviour and that it cannot be reduced to simpler terms—especially mechanical ones. But McDougall translated this conceptual insight into a genetic theory. He assumed that all behaviour is derivative from a finite number of innate purposive patterns. Furthermore, though McDougall abandoned the sensationism and associationism of the observationalist tradition, he still retained its atomism both in respect of his account of the mind and in respect of his attempt to explain social phenomena in terms of the innate equipment of atomic individuals. The instincts as dynamic mental atoms took the place of the old static impressions and ideas; individuals as organizations of innate behaviour tendencies took the place of individuals as passive containers of ideas. It was through the work of the Gestalt and Freudian Schools that this atomistic picture of the mind has become more and more to be outmoded and it was through the influence of the social sciences that nativistic theories of social organi-

---

[1] E. Tolman: *Op. cit.*, pp. 271–2.
[2] See also his later work, *Drives Towards War* (1942), in which he shows in more detail how basic biological drives become transformed by Freudian mechanisms.

zation have become increasingly difficult to defend. But before passing to a consideration of these developments it will be valuable to indicate in a cursory way a more recent blending of Purposive psychology with Behaviourism. For in the work of Hull, the modern Behaviourist, we have a very good example of the influence of Purposive psychology on a Behaviourist who, though retaining the methodological approach and associationist principles of Behaviourism, has nevertheless had to incorporate in his system McDougall's main postulates.

Hull, though fascinated by methodology, did not subscribe at all to the observationalist assumptions of the old Behaviourists. He tried to develop a hypothetico-deductive system, to quantify his hypotheses which he tried to test, to give operational criteria for his use of various constructs, and so on; there is no talk about starting from data or from measurements. He was a Behaviourist in method only in so far as he tested his hypotheses on rats and did not use introspective reports as evidence. He was in line with the old Behaviourist School, too, in his associationism. Nevertheless it can be briefly shown that McDougall's three main postulates find their counterparts in his *Principles of Behaviour*, published in 1943.

(a) *Purpose.*—Hull was rather chary of saying that all human and animal behaviour is purposive, though he admitted that a superficial study of the higher organisms shows that behaviour occurs in cycles initiated by a need and terminated by the reduction of a need. It is justifiable to speak of this end-state as a goal only for rough and ready purposes for the construction of a theory of very gross molar behaviour like Tolman's. But it won't do for exact science, in which, so he maintained, the psychological postulates of Tolman can be deduced from physiological postulates about stimulus-response connections. His basic assumption was a mixture of homeostasis and the theory of evolution. He quoted with approval Darwin's doctrine of survival. In order to survive organisms require optimal conditions of air, water, food, and so on, and the occasional presence and specialized reciprocal behaviour of a mate. When any of the commodities or conditions necessary for individual or species survival are lacking, or when they deviate materially from the optimum, a state of primary need is said to exist. These needs are reduced by exercise of the motor organs provided that their contractions occur in the right amounts, sequences, and combinations. Specialized receptors mediate the momentary states of the internal and external environment to the organism. Needs probably activate the proprioceptors. Neural impulses are set in motion by these two environments, and passed to the central ganglia of the nervous system, the brain acting as a kind of switchboard. The neural impulse reaches and activates the effector organ and after many unsuccessful trials the need is eliminated. A science of behaviour must isolate the laws according to which various combinations of stimulation, arising from a state of need on the one hand, and the state of the environment on the other, bring about the kind of behaviour characteristic of different organisms. His basic assumption is, therefore, a mixture of the traditional biology of Darwin and Herbert Spencer and of a more exact and more physiological rendering of associationist hypotheses—e.g. his first postulate of the 'stimulus trace' which is a generalization of Adrian's findings on the eye of an eel, and his second postulate of 'neural interaction' which develops Pavlov's finding that interaction takes place between activity in different cells of the cortex when they are simultaneously excited (cp. Köhler's 'field theory' of brain processes).[1] Thus Hull rather reluctantly admitted 'purpose' as a gross molar postulate but thought that it can eventually be derived from physiological postulates about the interaction between stimuli issuing from the external and the internal environment of the organism in its struggle to survive and preserve the species.

(b) *Instinct.*—Hull's basic motivational concept, like Tolman's, was that of the 'drive.' 'When a condition arises from which action on the part of the organism is a prerequisite to optimum probability of survival of either the individual or the species, a state of need is said to exist. Since need, either actual or potential, usually precedes or accompanies the action of an organism, the need is often said to motivate or drive the associated activity. Because of the motivational characteristic of needs they are regarded as producing primary animal drives.' Drives are intervening variables tied down to observable antecedent and consequent conditions—e.g. the amount of hunger-drive is a function of food-need measured by the number of hours of food privation and of the amount of energy expended in securing the food. Hull, in Darwinian fashion, classified the major drives on the basis of whether they promote survival of the individual organism or of the species. Amongst the former are hunger, thirst, need for air, need to avoid tissue injury (pain), need to maintain an optimal temperature, need to defecate and micturate, need for rest and for sleep, and the need for activity (after prolonged inaction); amongst the latter are those which lead to sexual intercourse and the need represented by nest-building and the care of the young.

Hull postulated inherited neural connections between receptors and effectors as a physiological basis of these drives. These make inherited behaviour tendencies possible which are not uniform or invariable. There are simple and constant behaviour tendencies where the role of chance is small in deciding which movements will be adaptive—e.g. need to micturate. But in complex situations such as those associated

---

[1] W. Köhler: *Dynamics in Psychology* (1940), p. 55.

with the need for food, water, or reproduction, the very variable factor of search intervenes as a preliminary.

Hull mentioned the initiating conditions in the organism which occasion the drives—lack of saliva in thirst, stomach contraction in hunger, and so on. But whereas Tolman only postulated such 'drives' in order to explain the *activation* of behaviour sequences, Hull used the notion of 'drive-reduction' to explain their *acquisition* as well, thereby fitting the phenomena of reinforcement into his theory. In this way Hull tried to provide a mechanical theory that would accommodate instrumental learning such as was studied by Thorndike and later by Skinner, into the framework of classical conditioning theory. He differed radically, too, from McDougall and Tolman in soft-pedalling any innate cognitive and motor prescription in instinctive behaviour. As a modern associationist he believed that the selection of means-objects can be explained by means of his postulate of stimulus-response association. His third postulate can thus be regarded as a summary of his version of the instinct hypothesis: 'Organisms at birth possess receptor-effector connections which, under combined stimulation and drive, have the potentiality of evoking a hierarchy of responses that either individually or in combination are more likely to terminate the need than would be a random selection from the reaction potentials resulting from other stimulus and drive combinations.'

(*c*) *Instinct reduction.*—Hull said that his book has been written 'on the assumption that all behaviour, individual and social, moral and immoral, normal and psychopathic, is generated from the same primary laws; and that the differences in the objective behavioural manifestations are due to the differing conditions under which habits are set up and function.'[1] We must therefore conclude that he thought that postulates about sentiment formation and so on can be deduced from his basic postulates once we know the more complicated conditions under which such habits are formed. But rats can't talk and their social environment is not very complex. The variables introduced by social traditions, speech, suggestion, writing, and perhaps telepathy are so formidable that Behaviourists have wisely stuck to rats and dogs. But it has yet to be shown that their findings, which deal mainly with the learning of simple motor skills, have much relevance to human learning where cognition and speech play a decisive role.

2. GESTALT PSYCHOLOGY

Gestalt psychology was a development of the dissatisfaction felt with the atomism and associationism of the observationalist tradition. Many had seen the problems of the unity, continuity, and organization

[1] C. Hull: *Principles of Behaviour* (1943), Preface, p. v.

of the perceptual field, but the Gestalt psychologists were the first to make the concept of organization the cornerstone of a psychological theory. In his epistemology Kant had spoken of a sensory manifold to replace Hume's 'loose and separate particulars'; in what we now call philosophical psychology Ward had postulated a 'presentational continuum,' and Stout had maintained that any specific sensation or image forms part of a total field in which spatio-temporal forms and other types of unity are as real and as ultimate ingredients as the items related. The Gestalt psychologists were not original in their basic conceptions so much as in the importance which they placed on the concept of organization and the wealth of experimental material with which they illustrated it. Their main contribution was to epistemology; but they illustrated their attack on the observationalist tradition in such detail that it often seemed as if they were making a major contribution to the psychology of perception.

Wertheimer's assault on sensory atomism began in 1912 with the revelation of the famous phi-phenomenon. The phenomenon of a motion picture was simplified in which a series of 'still' snapshots taken atomistically, when shown in rapid succession, reproduce on the screen the movements of figures off the screen, and the intervals of darkness, if rapid enough, are not seen because of retinal lag. Wertheimer showed that, if the interval between a shot of a vertical line and a slightly sloping line was made short enough, a single line moved from one position to another whereas if the interval was made too short the two lines appeared side by side without any discernible motion. The traditional view was that each stimulus gives rise to its own sensation and that, when we perceive, we integrate these sensory elements, making use of past experience. Thus it was thought that we must see the isolated elements and infer the motion. This was the only sort of explanation consistent with the Humean doctrine of the discrete and perishing existent. Wertheimer rejected this interpretation and maintained that we are always presented with a sensory field rather than with isolated sensations; in our perception of objects there are characteristics which do not belong to a single sensation. Wertheimer worked with Köhler and Koffka at Frankfurt and later founded the Berlin School before migrating to America.

It was, however, the Austrian School, led by Ehrenfels, who first spoke of a Gestalt or form quality which was present in a specific arrangement of stimuli. As early as 1890 Ehrenfels had experimented with sound. He maintained that a tune was a Gestalt which was inseparable from the various notes which made it up and which depended on the manner of arrangement of the notes. Yet the same tune could be recognized in a great variety of different auditory media. This fact can be demonstrated in visual as well as in auditory experience. It is often summed up in the saying that a whole is more than the sum of its parts. This is, as a matter of fact, an analytic statement defining one of the characteristics of 'wholes'; for we would not call something a 'whole' unless its constituents had a certain organization and if changes in one constituent involved no changes in others. Similarly we would not call something a case of 'perception' unless it involved organization, or seeing something as classified in some way. The Gestalt psychologists, however, did not make a stir in psychology by simply enunciating conceptual truths; rather they produced experimental evidence to show that we actually perceive wholes and do not just sense isolated elements. Ehrenfels and the Austrian School maintained that these Gestalt qualities were constructed by the perceiver out of the sensory data of tones and colours. He still retained, in a modified form, the distinction between sensation and perception. The Berlin School, however, disagreed with this interpretation of Gestalt findings; they claimed that even if stimuli reaching the sense-organs could be regarded as raw material, they are transformed into patterns by the nervous system and by the brain. So we are always confronted by an organized perceptual field which forms some kind of a whole.

The Gestalt psychologists perhaps stressed one important aspect of perception to the exclusion of others. Stout, for instance, while welcoming their emphasis on wholes, criticized them severely for disregarding the importance of past experience and mental set in the organization of the perceptual field. He himself maintained that in sense-perception both the sense-material and the form of unity are fundamental. The world as we see it is split up into a number of distinct things, which is only one of the many ways in which it might be split up. He distinguished the principles of grouping, sorting them out into objective and subjective determinants. The Berlin School, from the beginning, attacked this distinction and minimized the importance of the so-called subjective determinants like past experience, shifts of interest, and attention. They produced a wealth of experiments to exhibit the principles of organization of the perceptual field: the principles of nearness (grouping of things near together), quality (grouping of things qualitatively similar), closure (grouping of things enclosing a space), common destiny (grouping of things moving together), good continuation (grouping of things to make a symmetrical or simple figure), and good whole Gestalt or pregnance (grouping as good as conditions permit). Attempts were also made to show these various principles as subordinate to one principle as in the case of the old laws of association. Some advanced the claims of similarity or homogeneity (e.g. Musatti), others of pregnance (e.g. Koffka). Attention was also drawn to constancy phenomena like that of phenomenal regression in which a man walking away from an observer does not seem at first to be getting any smaller, his apparent size keeping much closer to his real size than to his perspective size.

The concept of organization began soon to be applied by pychologists to other fields. Köhler, in his theory of the isomorphism of physiological and mental structures, postulated a correspondence between the perceptual field and the physiological field of the brain and nervous system. 'A given visual field, for instance, is biologically represented by a certain distribution of processes in the occipital lobes of the brain; the correlates of other perceptual facts are located in various other lobes; and many psychological events are likely to concern the brain as a whole.'[1] But the converse, that every phase of brain activity is necessarily represented by corresponding phenomenal facts, is not necessarily true. The concept of a dynamic field which had been elaborated in physics, was applied to the brain. The cortex was pictured as an electrolyte in which organic tissue acted as a conductor for electric currents. If phenomenal fields were regarded as being the structural correlates of such electrical fields in the brain, then certain perceptual phenomena—e.g. figure ground characteristics and figural after-effects—could be deduced indirectly from already established generalizations about electric currents. The postulate of isomorphism would permit the deduction of hypotheses which could be tested by psychological techniques.

Another application of the concept of wholeness was to the field of learning. Köhler's war-time confinement to Teneriffe with his apes gave him ample time to collect material for exposing, in 1917, the deficiencies of associationist theories of learning—especially that of Thorndike. Köhler rejected both the trial and error explanation and the type of experimental apparatus that was fashionable. He regarded mazes and puzzle-boxes as just the sort of situation that would encourage trial and error rather than a more intelligent approach to problems. An obstacle to a goal should, of course, be provided, but the animal should be permitted to see the situation as a whole in order to solve the problem intelligently. Köhler's famous banana and stick experiments demonstrated the element of 'insight' in the solution of problems provided that the situation could be seen as an organized whole with the solution to a particular problem filling an otherwise empty gap. So too with chickens. In this case it was demonstrated that chickens trained to peck grain off light grey as opposed to dark grey, on being confronted with food on the original light grey and on a lighter grey still, will tend to peck off the latter. Reaction was to the field as a whole and not to isolated elements. This stress on the importance of wholes in learning and problem-solving had important educational consequences. In 1945 Wertheimer's book on *Productive Thinking* pointed out the relevance of

[1] W. Köhler: *Dynamics in Psychology* (1940), p. 40.

Gestalt principles to teaching and attacked the old emphasis on repetition and routine which derived from the associationist theory of learning.

In their early days the Gestalt psychologists tended to ignore questions of motivation, but, as the school developed, attempts were made to apply Gestalt principles to the field on which the Purposive psychologists had concentrated. Indeed, the principle of pregnance, when applied to motivation, looks very much like the postulate of Spinoza, Fechner, Herbert Spencer, Hull, and others that organisms tend to persist in their own being or to retain a constancy of form. In more recent times (1932) Cannon's principle of 'homeostasis'[1] would be a more precise statement of this principle of pregnance in the physiological field, and, as will be seen, Freud also made use of it in his account of motivation.

To Lewin, however, amongst Gestalt psychologists belongs the credit of being the first to apply systematically the concept of 'field' to motivation. The mind is viewed as a dynamic tension-system and behaviour is to be regarded as an attempt to relieve tensions and re-establish equilibrium. But the individual is part of a wider 'field'— his physical and social environment. Similar principles are necessary in order to understand this wider 'field' and the individual's behaviour within it. This wider 'field' is called by Lewin the 'life-space' which contains a person in his environment as it appears to him in view of his 'needs' and 'quasi-needs' (intentions). The objects in this 'field' have a positive or negative 'valence' which makes the 'field' one of attraction and repulsion or 'vectors' directed towards and away from various objects. A 'vector' tends to produce 'locomotion'—any sort of movement in the 'life-space' from actual physical movement to reflective drawing back in disgust at an imaginary episode. 'Locomotion' often encounters barriers either physical or social, which have varying degrees of strength. This new set of terms is then used by Lewin to show, for instance, that a child's behaviour towards a stranger in a room is in part a function of the child's distance from the stranger! Such startling revelations are not only redescribed in this 'field-theoretical' terminology; they are also illustrated by little diagrams. Topological representation, we are told, gives an explanation a self-evidence that it did not previously possess. In his first book, *A Dynamic Theory of Personality* (1935), Lewin combined some interesting methodological discussion (for instance on the difference between Aristotelian and Galilean methods of explanation) with a fair amount of empirical material. His concepts were used to describe experiments done on 'level of aspiration,' resumption of interrupted tasks, and substitute performances. In his later work, *Principles of Topological Psychology* (1936), he tried to develop an adequate system of mathematical con-

[1] See W. S. Cannon: *The Wisdom of the Body* (1932).

cepts for representing the 'life-space' of a person and for dealing with motives. He developed his own brand of topology for the former task and vector analysis for the latter. By means of these concepts he has succeeded in redescribing part of what most psychologists already knew about human behaviour in a way that emphasizes the importance of the environmental field of the person. He frequently castigated instinct theorists for neglecting environmental conditions and the momentary condition of the drive, while at the same time making use of their main assumptions in his account of 'needs' and 'tension-systems.' Those who have been thoroughly initiated into his conceptual system seem to have found it useful in suggesting novel types of experiment. But the uninitiated comment on the similarity of such empirical generalizations as emerge with those of the Freudian and Purposive Schools; the less charitably minded of them regard his systematization as an example of methodology run riot and of the substitution of methodological blue-prints for fertile hypotheses.

We may suggest tentatively that the main importance of the Gestalt work on motivation has not been to suggest a radically new theory but to insert a corrective into existing theories of motivation in which the old atomism of the observationalist tradition tended to persist. By stressing the wholeness of the individual mind or 'tension-system' and the inseparability of the person from his 'life-space,' the tendency to explain behaviour in terms of the atomistic instincts of isolated individuals was strenuously and effectively resisted. Of course McDougall was aware of the importance of the social environment and he also guarded himself against charges like 'atomism' by his principle of 'conative persistence and unity.'[1] But the effect of the doctrine of instincts has, in the main, been to encourage an atomistic approach to the mind and an over-individualistic approach to social phenomena. In the work of Freud, however, to which we now turn, there was remarkably little evidence of any of these characteristic inadequacies of the old tradition against which Gestalt psychology was such a welcome reaction.

D. The influence of technology

I. MEDICINE AND FREUDIAN PSYCHOLOGY

The late Professor Brett was wise to stress the particular importance of medicine to the understanding of human behaviour; for one of the major revolutions in psychological theory was accomplished by Sigmund Freud who was trained in medicine quite outside the academic schools of psychology. His initial interest had been in the more general

[1] See W. McDougall: *Energies of Men* (1932), pp. 119–22.

problems of human civilization and culture, but his conversion to Darwinism encouraged him to take up medicine. The story of his development is well known. He became interested in hypnosis as a result of studying under Charcot. He went into practice on his own account and came into contact with Breuer from whom in 1893 he learnt the method of 'abreaction' or getting the patient to talk about and relive in his imagination the troubles of his early life. Breuer got disturbed when his patients began, under this treatment, to transfer to him the loves and hates which they had felt for others; Freud was not a bit daunted but made due allowance for the part to be played by 'transference' in cure. He also developed out of talking it over the method of 'free association' which he substituted almost entirely for hypnosis; this method of letting the patient relax and state the first thing that came into his head led naturally on to the use of dreams. And so the now familiar psycho-analytic techniques developed as he worked at the practical task of trying to cure his patients. Some of Freud's greatest contributions to psychology lay in his development of these revolutionary techniques for discovering the forgotten incidents of people's early lives.

Now Freud was ostensibly a technologist. By that is meant that his professional concern was to cure his patients and to provide remedies for the discontents of civilization, discontents which seemed to him to be almost inevitable. This preoccupation with practical therapeutic problems involved using assumptions which seemed to work in so far as they helped to explain the genesis of various forms of maladjustments and to enable him to devise techniques for changing people's attitudes. These technological interests exerted, too, a considerable influence on his terminology. Models and dramatic language are useful in ramming home psychological insights to patients and to a wide public in a suffering civilization. Parents, nursery school teachers, mild neurotics, and social workers would not be touched by the mathematical constructs of Hull or the topological jargon of Lewin. His practical interests, too, did not encourage him to test his working assumptions in a deliberate manner; he tested them only indirectly as he discarded them when they did not work in his practical task.

But this emphasis on the technological aspect of Freud's work can be overdone. Woodworth, for instance, maintains that 'His life quest, we remember, was not so much to cure the neuroses as through the study of his patients to reach an understanding of the deep forces of human life, social as well as individual.'[1] And, obviously, if a technologist himself produces the theories which he uses, his interests are partly theoretical. Freud's prolific writings show his strong theoretical interests and his realization of the importance of his findings to psycho-

[1] R. Woodworth: *Contemporary Schools of Psychology* (Rev. Ed. 1948), p. 181.

logical theory. Considered as a theoretical scientist Freud appears a kind of Copernicus of psychology, responsible for a revolution in outlook. And like Copernicus, who was a Pythagorean in his metaphysical leaning, Freud mixed metaphysics with testable hypotheses. Schopenhauer peered wanly through some of his constructs. His work was the imaginative bulldozing of a pioneer in the jungle of human behaviour which uncovered many interesting phenomena for later investigators to follow up. In his adventurous surge forward he was always ready to remodel the tools of discovery (his 'basal concepts') or to take up new ones. For instance, in 1920 he developed the postulate of an innate aggressive urge, which he referred to rather picturesquely as Thanatos or the death-wish. He extended his doctrine of the libido to incorporate some of Jung's suggestions and expanded his conception of the ego-instincts to include Adler's contribution.

What, then, were his main theoretical postulates? They are very difficult to set out systematically as his work is essentially the product of a man on the spot rather than of a systematizer, consisting in a series of short books and articles dealing with a great variety of topics. His views changed on many crucial points; they vary in technical expression because they are addressed to so many different types of reader; metaphysical rumblings disturb his later works. Nevertheless it is possible to present Freud's system briefly, using the same main postulates as were assumed by McDougall and Tolman and in part by Hull.

(a) *Purpose.*—McDougall definitely regarded Freud as an ally who became obsessed with sex; for explanations in terms of desires, wishes, urges, and impulses are purposive explanations[1]—certainly in the broad sense of 'purpose' which is equivalent to 'goal directed.' Freud also had his own version of the familiar conatus of Spinoza, Rignano, Spencer, Tolman, Hull, and others. In his formulation of what he calls the 'pleasure-principle' Freud links his view with that of Fechner who postulated a tendency towards stability. Any given process originates in an unpleasant state of tension and determines for itself such a path that its ultimate issue coincides with a relaxation of this tension. Freud admits that what he calls the 'pleasure principle' is subservient to the function of rendering the psychic apparatus as a whole free from excitation or to keep the amount of excitation constant. Tensions and conflicts arise in the mind—especially in 'the unconscious'—and the behaviour which we adopt is an effort to preserve equilibrium. This avoidance of stimulation can operate at the level of the 'pure "pleasure" principle' or at the level of the 'reality principle' when concepts of logical consistency and causal connection are imposed on the disorderly wishes of the 'primary processes' of thought. Indeed Ernest Jones maintained that Freud's great discovery was not of 'the unconscious'

[1] See W. McDougall: *Outline of Abnormal Psychology* (5th ed. 1946), pp. 19, 20.

but of the fact that the primary and secondary processes worked according to quite different laws.[1]

(b) *Instincts.*—Freud's views about instincts, as expressed mainly in 1915 in his paper 'Instincts and their Vicissitudes,'[2] are rather sketchy. He was obviously much more interested in the 'vicissitudes' of instincts —especially the 'sexual' ones—than in their characteristics which he regarded as mainly a matter for biology and physiology. The main features of his treatment are his stress on physiological initiation, his denial of cognitive prescription, and the tremendous importance he gives to environmental conditioning.

He regards instincts as providing 'a stimulus to the mind' deriving from our internal physiological condition. For instance, the parched condition of the mucous membrane of the oesophagus or the contraction of the stomach provides a 'stimulus to the mind' which is radically different from an external stimulus. This is very similar to Hull's distinction between stimuli from the internal and external environments. He is like Hull, too, in calling a stimulus of instinctual origin a 'need.' The really important distinction between external and internal stimuli is that flight avails against the former but not against the latter; in fact Freud makes the most interesting suggestion that the common distinction between 'outer' and 'inner' derives from the fact that muscular action will avail against some stimuli but not against others. Freud distinguishes between the 'impetus' of an instinct, its 'aim,' 'object' and 'source.' The 'impetus' is 'its motor element, the amount of force or the measure of the demand upon energy which it represents.' He seems to be referring here to what Tolman and Hull call 'behaviour variables.' The 'aim' is the satisfaction of a need—Tolman's physiological quiescence and Hull's 'need-reduction.' The 'object' is that in or through which it can achieve its aim, the most variable thing about an instinct—Tolman's 'means-object.' The 'source' is the somatic process from which there results a 'stimulus to the mind'—Tolman's initiating physiological conditions. The parallel between Freud, Tolman, and Hull is most interesting, and is seldom mentioned by expositors. Freud denies the innate preparedness for certain sorts of means-objects stressed by McDougall and Tolman. Like Hull he believes that a means-object only comes to be associated with an instinct because it is found by experience to lead to satisfaction. For Freud this object may be a part of the subject's own body; it may change a great number of times; it may be the object of many instincts (Adler's 'confluence' of instincts). When an instinct becomes very closely attached to a particular object Freud calls it 'fixation.'

In his early work Freud proposed two main groups of instincts—

---

[1] See E. Jones; Sigmund Freud, *Life and Work* (1954), Vol. 1, p. 436.
[2] S. Freud: *Collected Papers*, Vol. IV, ch. iv.

the self-preservative and the sexual. This was partly his rendering of the traditional Darwinian classification (cp. Hull) and partly occasioned by study of the psycho-neuroses (hysteria and obsessions) in which the root of the trouble seemed to him to lie in conflicts between the claims of sexuality and self-preservation. Anyway Freud concentrated on the manifestations of sexuality and Adler later concentrated on the individual's 'will to power' or drives concerned with his own self-advancement. As has often been pointed out, Freud's use of the word 'sexual' is rather odd. He says that sexual instincts are numerous, emanate from different sources, act independently of each other, and later achieve synthesis in the function of reproduction. 'At their first appearance they support themselves upon the instincts of self-preservation, from which they gradually detach themselves; in their choice of object also they follow paths indicated by the ego-instincts.'[1] What, then, is the criterion for calling them 'sexual'? Consider the instincts of hunger and defecation. These, one would assume, are primarily self-preservative. But they become 'sexual' when satisfaction is derived from sucking or anal expulsion. This happens especially at certain periods—the famous oral and anal periods. It seems that when the 'aim' of the instinct becomes 'organ pleasure' rather than the terminating state of quiescence or need-reduction the instinct becomes 'sexual.' When, for instance, we enjoy sucking for its own sake and do not treat it just as a means to remove our hunger, then the instinct is 'sexual' rather than self-preservative. Woodworth suggests[2] that Freud was led to use this word 'sexual' in such a wide way because he was so greatly impressed by the difference between what was done spontaneously and with immediate pleasure and what was done as a necessary means to an end. All that was done with immediate pleasure was grouped together and called 'sexual' because sex activity is the clearest example of what is immediately pleasurable in terms of organ pleasure and because other organ-pleasures like sucking, being caressed, being cuddled, and so on, later become subservient to sex activity in the normal sense, when they take the form of kissing, petting, and being embraced. Later psycho-analysts like F. Alexander[3] have tended to restrict the use of 'sexual' to our more normal usage.

However there is a most important point wrapped up in Freud's doctrine of instincts and this odd use of the word 'sexual' that needs emphasizing. In Freud there is no atomism of instincts as there tends to be in McDougall. Freud pictures the mind of the very small child as a mass of very crudely differentiated urges which, through experi-

---

[1] S. Freud: *Op. cit.*, p. 69.

[2] R. Woodworth: *Contemporary Schools of Psychology* (Rev. Ed. 1948), pp. 160–1.

[3] See F. Alexander: *Fundamentals of Psycho-analysis* (English Ed. 1949), for modern restatement and modification of Freudian position.

ence, become associated with different objects. The child's mind cannot be clearly separated into different needs and satisfactions. Feeding at the breast satisfies more needs than that of hunger. In fact the hunger drive as clearly distinct from, e.g., the need for security is an atomistic abstraction. The all-embracing use of the word 'sexual' to characterize even activities clearly subservient to self-preservation is one way of bringing out this systematic interconnectedness of the outgoing needs of the child. This interpretation is reinforced by the fact that Freud later recast his original classification of instincts. The old ego and sex instincts became two classes of 'life-instincts' which were contrasted with the 'death-instincts.' The former motivate all activities bringing people into contact with each other, which are constructive and preservative; the latter, springing from an innate aggressive drive, motivate activities which are destructive to the self and to others. Our minds are in a constant tension of loves and hates; we can never love without hating or hate without loving. Conflicts within ourselves and with others are inevitable. Conflict is the driving force of change and development.

(c) *Instinct reduction.*—Freud's account of the 'vicissitudes' of instincts was his major contribution to psychological theory. His teaching about the characteristics of instincts was very similar to that of Hull and Tolman; but, whereas they were primarily interested in defining these characteristics more precisely by a detailed study of learning when rats found their way about a simple physical environment, Freud was interested in the 'vicissitudes' of drives when the child developed in a social environment. His hypotheses about the development and modification of instinctive drives are so numerous that it is quite impossible to do justice to them in what can only be a short and dogmatic summary. They come under four main groups— the doctrine of the 'wish,' the doctrine of 'the unconscious,' the hypotheses postulating the influence of the physical and social environments on 'wishes,' and the hypothesis that childhood wishes persist and that patterns of early solution to conflicts inevitable at certain periods of early life determine personality traits.

Freud's doctrine of the 'wish' is similar to McDougall's doctrine of 'sentiments.' He believed that all human behaviour is motivated by instinctive urges which appear, in consciousness, as 'wishes' centred round certain objects or states of affairs. 'Psycho-analysis,' to quote Freud's own words, 'grew on a narrowly restricted basis.' Many critics have maintained that at best the concept of 'the wish' could only explain 'abnormal' phenomena. This, however, is a very unilluminating contention. For, in the first place, the criterion by means of which the 'normal' is to be distinguished from the 'abnormal' is mainly a matter of law and of social acceptability. Secondly, dreams were amongst the first phenomena for which Freud gave an explanation, and there is nothing particularly 'abnormal' about dreaming.

A more helpful way of looking at the class of phenomena which Freud's theory actually explained is the suggestion that all the phenomena in some way represent fallings short of what we call actions or performances. There are at least three sub-divisions of this general class. There are, first of all, what Freud himself described as 'Certain inadequacies of our psychic functions' and 'certain performances which are apparently unintentional' of which he gave an explanation in his *Psychopathology of Everyday Life* (1904) and for which he gave clear-cut criteria.[1] Secondly, there are phenomena like dreams and visions which would not be classed as actions or performances at all. They are things that happen to us. Thirdly, there are things like obsessions and compulsions which have an exaggerated and distorted sort of point. They are, as it were, caricatures of actions. It is of interest to note that Freud himself in his paper called *The Claim of Psycho-analysis to Scientific Interest* (1913) tried to state explicitly the relevance of his theory to general psychology. He said:

'There are a large number of phenomena related to facial and other expressive movements and to speech, as well as many other processes of thought (both in normal and in sick people), which have hitherto escaped the notice of psychology because they have been regarded as no more than the results of organic disorder and of some abnormal failure in function of the mental apparatus. What I have in mind are "parapraxes" (slips of the tongue or pen, forgetfulness, etc.), haphazard actions and dreams in normal people, and convulsive attacks, deliria, visions and obsessive ideas or acts in neurotic subjects.'[2]

Freud claimed that he gave a psychological explanation for such phenomena, which was in terms of his concept of 'wish.' This was original; for previously such phenomena had been either regarded as due to chance, or explanation had been left either to physiology or to folk-lore. Of course Freud did not neglect actions and performances altogether; rather he gave the explanation of them which we all give, but couched it in terms of his theory of the ego and the secondary processes of thought. To quote Ernest Jones:

'Careful students have perceived that Freud's revolutionary contribution to psychology was not so much his demonstrating the existence of an unconscious, and perhaps not even his exploration of its content, as his proposition that there are two fundamentally different kinds of mental processes, which he termed primary and secondary respectively, together with his description of them. The laws applicable to the two

[1] See pp. 192–3 of 1914 Ernest Benn ed.
[2] S. Freud: *Collected Papers*, Vol. XIII, p. 166.

groups are so widely different that any description of the earlier one must call up a picture of the more bizarre types of insanity. There reigns in it a quite uninhibited flow towards the imaginary fulfilment of the wish that stirs it—the only thing that can. It is unchecked by any logical contradiction, any causal associations; it has no sense of either time or of external reality . . .'[1]

Freud postulated principles like those of displacement and emotive congruence to describe the operation of wishes and attempted to fit these into a strange mechanical theory which was really a translation of a physiological theory into the language of wishes and ideas—an impossible undertaking. However, whatever the correct sort of description for such goings-on which Freud called the primary processes, Freud saw clearly that they require a different sort of description from that which we give for processes explaining actions or performances. For we explain these in terms of the ends which people have in mind and their information about means to ends, which falls under rules of efficiency and appropriateness. To act or to perform a person must have a grasp of causal connexion, of time, external reality, and of logical contradictions. Such standards are the product of ages of convention, adaptation, and conscious experimentation. This inherited wisdom is handed on laboriously from generation to generation as what Freud called the secondary processes of thought begin to develop out of the autistic amalgam of the child's mind. A wish, to be transformed into a reason for acting, has to have logical and causal connections, together with standards of social correctness, imposed upon it, so that what is wished for, the objective, can be connected with acts that lead up to it. It is interesting to note that Aristotle, in his *Nichomachean Ethics*, distinguished 'wish' from 'choice' roughly along these lines. 'Wish,' he said, is only of the end, whereas 'choice' is of things that it is in our power to do. Plans and rules must be imposed on desire before we can be said to 'choose.' Freud himself did little to develop a theory of the growth of the ego and the secondary processes. This was left to later Freudians such as Hartmann, Erikson, and Rapaport.

'The unconscious' was regarded by Freud as being one of the main foundations of his theory. What exactly did Freud mean by 'the unconscious'? The criterion for the use of the word is fairly obvious; what is not obvious is what Freud calls the 'basis' of 'the unconscious' or his story about its genesis. Of course he speaks of it in an absurdly pictorial way as if it were a kind of compartment of something called 'the mind.' But he undoubtedly lighted upon some most interesting and important discoveries about human motivation which can be stated quite simply without recourse to primitive models of the mind.

[1] E. Jones: *Sigmund Freud, Life and Work*, Vol. I, p. 436.

In 1923 in *The Ego and the Id* Freud laid down the criterion for the use of the term 'unconscious.' He says that the term 'conscious' is used, to start with, purely descriptively—i.e. without implying any causal-genetic theory. Ideas pass in and out of 'consciousness' and leave 'traces.' But not all such 'traces' give rise to 'memories.' Thus the criterion of 'consciousness' is whether our previous experiences are retrospectively accessible to us via their hypothetical 'traces.' 'The unconscious,' therefore, comprises those 'ideas' which are not normally retrospectively accessible to us, 'traces' which give rise to no memories except under abnormal conditions like hypnosis or narcosis. The evidence for the existence of 'the unconscious' is that under such abnormal conditions we report memories which we cannot report under normal conditions. The 'ideas' or 'wishes' so 'repressed' are usually those of which we felt ashamed when they occurred. In other words the assumption is necessitated that 'very powerful mental processes or ideas exist . . . which can produce in the mind all the effects that ordinary ideas do (including effects that can in their turn become conscious as ideas) without themselves becoming conscious.'[1] A certain force is opposed to these ideas becoming conscious, and it can only be removed by psycho-analytic techniques. This is called 'resistance' and 'the state in which the ideas existed before being made conscious is called by us repression. . . .'[2] The theory of repression is the 'basis' of the concept of the unconscious. 'The repressed serves as a prototype of the unconscious.'[3] Thus inaccessibility to retrospection is the criterion of 'the unconscious' and 'repression' is a necessary antecedent condition of such inaccessibility. But Freud does not rest here in his account of 'the unconscious'; for we learn that there are certain tendencies in 'the id' of which we are not conscious.[4] Yet they have not been formed as the product of 'repression' though they behave very much like repressed material. The criterion of 'the unconscious' is maintained, but its 'basis' is denied as applying universally to all 'the unconscious.' There are further complications, too, which are introduced in his paper on 'The Unconscious.'[5] But enough has been said to indicate more or less what Freud meant by the term. It can be summarized as follows: Past experiences leave 'traces' which persist as causal determinants of behaviour. The 'traces' left by experiences in early childhood—especially those involving wishes of which we feel ashamed —are particularly important. Many such 'traces' do not give rise to memories. The past experiences, therefore, of which they are 'traces,' become inaccessible to normal retrospection though not to special

[1] S. Freud: *The Ego and the Id* (English Ed. 1927), p. 11.
[2] *Op. cit.*, p. 12.
[3] *Op. cit.*, p. 12.
[4] *Op. cit.*, pp. 26–8.
[5] S. Freud: 'The Unconscious,' *Collected Papers*, Vol. IV, pp. 109, 110.

retrospective techniques. The cause of this inaccessibility is usually repression.

Instincts and their derivative 'wishes' are modified by contact with the physical and social environments. Freud suggests hypotheses about the results of such transactions in his language of 'ego' and 'super-ego.' We are born with all kinds of undifferentiated instinctive urges (the 'id') which are not directed at birth towards any specific types of object. To say that we develop an 'ego' is to postulate that we learn by experience which means-objects tend to lead to satisfaction and which do not. We learn the limitations imposed upon the satisfaction of our wishes by our physical environment. In *The Ego and the Id*[1] Freud states explicitly that the 'ego' is that part of the 'id' which has been modified by the direct influence of the external world acting through our perceptual apparatus. In the 'ego' the 'reality principle' reigns instead of the 'pleasure principle' of the 'id.' The 'id' is biologically conditioned via the instincts; the 'ego' is environmentally conditioned via the perceptual apparatus, and controls voluntary movements. Freud's 'ego' is very similar to Bishop Butler's 'cool self-love.' To say that we have an 'ego' is a pictorial way of pointing out that we learn by experience to modify our impulsive conduct by reflection and calculation.

To say that we have a 'super-ego' is to suggest in an even more pictorial way that our behaviour is affected by the normative pressures of society—especially the early family situation. Other people adopt certain attitudes to us, expect certain things of us, prohibit certain courses of action; we 'introject' or take into ourselves these approving or disapproving attitudes. In the form of our conscience, sense of guilt, and so on, we come to internalize the standards expected of us, especially by parents, teachers, and other loved persons. Another aspect of this introjection of normative demands is the development of what Freud calls 'the ego-ideal.' This comes about through 'narcissism' or love turned inwards towards ourselves instead of outwards towards others. But it is not ourselves as we are that we love but a picture of ourselves modelled on our parents and admired persons in stories, films, and so on. Freud's 'ego-ideal' is very similar to McDougall's 'self-regarding sentiment' and Adler's 'guiding fiction.'

Freud's later preoccupation with aggression led him to incorporate even more components in the 'super-ego.' Often people who cannot deal with the external world turn their frustrated aggression inwards and take it out of themselves instead of other people or objects that prevent them doing what they want. The child is bound to be frustrated by his parents and is bound, to a certain extent, to direct some of his aggression inwards as he cannot prevail against his all-powerful parents. The 'super-ego' thus becomes even more exacting. Freud also maintained that the

[1] *Op. cit.*, pp. 28–30.

'sadism' of parents towards their children is often introjected as well as their disapproval.[1] The concept of the 'super-ego' is therefore complex. Basically it involves the use of a model to put forward many interesting and important conjectures about the influence of parents, teachers, and other admired persons, on the outgoing tendencies of the child, and the genesis of part of what we call 'conscience.' 'Conscience,' of course, can relate to a rational decision about what is in general right or wrong and to an individual's choice between conflicting duties in a particular situation, as well as to non-rational or irrational convictions and feelings of guilt. At best Freud's theory could explain conscience in the third sense.

Freud postulated many 'mechanisms' in describing how the transactions between the person and his environment take place. The inverse of 'introjection' is 'projection' or the attributing to the environment of unacceptable characteristics of our own personality. 'Identification' or attempting to model ourselves on others is very important in the formation of the 'ego-ideal.' In 'transference' we shift loves and hates for one person to another. 'Displacement' seems to describe a similar process but presupposes the inacceptability to the 'ego' of the original object of the emotion. These are some of the minor mechanisms. The major ones are ways of solving certain inevitable conflicts. To these we must now turn.

Freud believed firmly in the inevitability of conflicts between instinctive urges from the 'id' and the demands of the physical and social environment. Some of the minor mechanisms already mentioned, like projection and displacement, are ways of resolving such conflicts. Amongst the major mechanisms 'repression' is the most important, though it is difficult to discover what happens when we 'repress.' 'The essence of repression lies simply in the function of rejecting and keeping something out of consciousness.'[2] In this way pain is avoided. But though the 'ideational representation' of the instinct becomes retrospectively inaccessible, it persists and the instinct remains attached to it in 'the unconscious.' Ideas associated with the repressed idea are also repressed and 'the instinct-presentation continues to exist in the unconscious and organize itself further'[3]—like a fungus in the dark! The result of this growth is a 'complex.' The affective element of the 'idea' often emerges as anxiety or may trouble us in some other disguise. 'Repression' differs from 'inhibition' in not involving discriminative decision and from 'suppression' which involves conscious refraining from thinking about something for a time. It is compared by

[1] See J. C. Flugel: *Man, Morals, and Society* (1945) for an exposition of Freud's doctrine of the super-ego to which the editor is much indebted.

[2] S. Freud: 'Repression,' *Collected Papers*, Vol. IV, p. 86.

[3] *Op. cit.*, p. 87.

Freud to flight. We fly from our own libido in the same sort of way as we fly from an external stimulus. Picturesque, but does it tell us much more than that we are unable to face the implications of some of our loves and hates which then conveniently pass out of consciousness and wreak their revenge in 'the unconscious'?

'Unconscious conflicts' created by this process of 'repression' are resolved in many ways, or partially resolved. In 'conversion' we convert the repressed energy of basic drives into the functional symptoms of bodily disease. By getting ill we escape from a painful situation. 'Regression' is another device: by this we return to a more primitive way of dealing with a situation. When we 'sublimate' an instinctive urge we find a substitute goal which is satisfying and socially acceptable. 'Rationalization' is the invention of consciously acceptable motives to screen unacceptable motives. 'Reaction-formation' involves the adoption of behaviour diametrically opposed to that demanded by an 'unconscious wish'—e.g. the reformed drunkard who leads a campaign for total abstinence. We do not always, however, resort to one of these mechanisms for dealing with our unacceptable desires or 'wishes.' We may admit them and simply regretfully decide against satisfying them.

Freud not only made conflict and the method of resolving it fundamental in setting up certain styles of life; he also maintained that certain typical conflicts tend to arise at certain stages in the child's development and that the method of dealing with these conflicts exerts an enormous influence on later character. For him the child is indeed father of the man. At the oral stage the child inevitably comes up against the frustration of being weaned. His mother whom he loves must necessarily frustrate him. The growth of teeth provides him with tools for exercising aggression in the face of such frustration as the 'organ pleasures' connected with sucking and biting are threatened by his mother's weaning. How is the child to deal with this conflict between his love and his hate? He may just find other things to suck and bite— pipes, pencils, and nails. Or he may 'sublimate' his desire for 'organ-pleasure' by mouthing poetry or uttering scathing sarcasms. Or he may deal with it by 'reaction formation' and reject vehemently these sorts of pleasures like the man who will not eat certain sorts of food, will not kiss people, or who develops pedantic standards in speech. Some become 'fixated' at the sucking stage and continue passively through life accepting frustration as they accepted weaning. Others retain the aggression which they developed at this stage and retain their 'biting' or aggressive attitude towards all and sundry.

The frustration of weaning is followed by the frustration of potting. The child, so Freud maintained, enjoys the 'organ-pleasure' of bowel movement just as he enjoys sucking. Yet parents insist on his eliminating at certain times and certain places just as they insist on routine meals which are orally inferior to breast-feeding. The child's toilet tends to become the centre of interest and of conflict. The child comes to regard the retention of faeces as a way of exercising power over his mother, and its expulsion as a method of making her a gift. Freud insists on the tremendous symbolic importance of faeces. What the child does about them in relation to his parents exercises a determining influence on what he later does with his possessions in relation to others. Thus the child can merely continue his interest in faeces with lavatory stories and general humour at anything to do with the anus, which shows mild repression. He may 'sublimate' his love of faeces by taking up the plastic arts where the materials are socially acceptable substitutes for the beloved material of his childhood. He may develop a 'reaction formation' by developing ideas about the filthiness of faeces—usually learnt from his parents. Pedantry, parsimony, punctiliousness, petulance—all these are regarded by Freud as 'anal' traits or attitudes developed during a stage when regularity, so much stressed by parents in relation to the pot, is 'introjected.' Similarly, philanthropy is an 'anal' trait being derived from willingness to oblige the parents with a gift, and miserliness, also, which is derived from the habit of hoarding faeces in order to exert power over parents.

Interest in the breast and the pot gives way at about three years old to interest in the genitals. Masturbation, exhibitionism, and sexual curiosity begin and again come the conflicts with parents. There is no need to detail the obvious traits which develop—narcissistic cult of the body and later narcissistic self-stimulation in flirtations, unending gigglings at sex stories, 'sublimations' like acting or love-poetry, 'reaction-formations' like prudishness, and so on. The famous 'Oedipus-situation' usually occurs after the third or 'phallic' stage. The boy competes, as it were, with his father for love of his mother and how he deals with his conflict between his love and hate for his father is regarded by Freud as being of great importance. The latency period succeeds the phallic period and lasts till puberty when the sex-organs develop properly and when interest is centred on loved objects rather than on the self as was the case in the phallic period. The development of genital sexuality proper of course leads to conflicts in a society which prohibits early sexual intercourse. Many of the higher human endeavours are regarded by Freud as 'sublimations' of or 'reaction formations' against genital sexuality. In such conflict situations the adolescent or adult often 'regresses' and reverts to his method of dealing with one of the earlier frustrating situations. Indeed, if he has become 'fixated' at the phallic stage he is bound to be narcissistic in his sexual life, or if he has become 'fixated' at the anal stage he may well be unduly possessive.

These, then, are the main stages at which conflicts are almost inevitable. Freud produced masses of case-histories to support his general thesis that many infantile wishes persist and that the type of solution to conflicts occasioned by these wishes has a formative effect on character. Whether or not Freud put forward his hypotheses in a manner precise enough to make them testable is an open question. There has been, in more recent times, a considerable movement to salvage the testable assumptions from the mass of speculation which is to be found in Freud. Good examples of this are the work of Sears and of Dollard and Miller in their *Personality and Psycho-therapy* (1950), which had a behaviouristic orientation. J. F. Brown, too, in his *The Psycho-dynamics of Abnormal Behaviour* (1940) did much to restate Freud's theory in a more methodologically sophisticated manner and to relate it to 'field theory.'

If any justification is necessary for spending so much time on presenting Freud's theory as a whole it is to be found in its overwhelming importance and influence in twentieth-century psychology. It combines the purposivism of other theories with the stress on the unity or wholeness of the personality which purposive theories have often neglected. It has been illustrated by more empirical material than any other theory and is richer in causal-genetic hypotheses. In fact there are enough speculative hypotheses in Freud to keep a generation of psychologists going in the endeavour to state them precisely and to test them. The stress on 'the unconscious' and the importance given to early childhood experiences were revolutionary when we consider the theories in the field at the end of the nineteenth century. The only respects in which Freud was a child of the nineteenth century were his Darwinian approach, his vague metaphysical leanings derived from Schopenhauer, and his conception of 'ideas' as dynamic mental entities which he inherited from Herbart. In fact his picture of the mind as a system of 'ideas' or 'wishes' being pushed downwards and upwards was rather similar to Herbart's mental statics and dynamics in which ideas attract and repel each other and compete for the stage of consciousness. But no one can start afresh in building up a theory. When we look back on the development of Freudian psychology we are astounded by the novel hypotheses which he suggested while retaining much of the old terminology, as well as by the new terms which he invented for describing his discoveries. Before leaving the subject of Freudian psychology some mention should be made of Freud's famous followers who broke away from him in 1912 and started schools of their own.

Adler's 'Individual Psychology' agreed with Jung's 'Analytical Psychology' only in soft-pedalling the importance which Freud attributed to sex. Adler stressed the development of the ego-instincts as being themselves responsible for all kinds of nervous disorders quite irrespective of the influence of sexuality. He pictured individuals as concerned primarily with the assertion of themselves over others. His much popularized doctrine of the 'inferiority complex' was based on his hypothesis of 'organ inferiority.' Those who had some kind of organic defect were in a particularly poor position in relation to the struggle for power which was the universal characteristic of life. Just as Freud believed that the way in which people come to terms with the frustrations of potting or weaning are decisive in the formation of character traits, so also Adler believed that the way in which people deal with their 'organ inferiority' is decisive in determining their 'style of life.' Maybe the sufferer will convert his inferiority into superiority by diligence, maybe he will seek some other sphere where he can assert himself as a compensation, or maybe he will take refuge in disease or mental illness. As most people feel inferior in some kind of way, which may be quite mild compared with the obvious 'organ inferiority' of a small man like Mussolini or a stammerer like Demosthenes, this development of a 'style of life' based on the need to compensate for inferiority is a more or less universal phenomenon.

Adler, instead of developing Freud's doctrine of infantile sexuality, made some interesting suggestions about the kinds of social conditions in early life which will influence the 'style of life.' The 'family constellation' is one of the vital determinants. A second child, because of his physical inferiority to his elder brother or sister and because of the greater attention that is often paid to the elder, is likely to develop as a rebel, to resist authority and be for ever asserting himself in later life against substitutes for his elder brother. The first-born, on the other hand, is likely to develop a conservative attitude, to hang on to what he has got, and to expect respect and homage from others without doing much to deserve it by his own efforts.

After developing this Nietzschean doctrine of 'the will to power' in contradistinction to Freud's stress on sex, Adler then proceeded to develop his doctrine of 'social interest.' The child, although concerned primarily, like any other organism, with self-assertion, has a capacity for co-operation and friendliness which will develop if he is rightly treated in the early years. A middle road of give and take in social relationships must be worked out between the extremes of complete domination over children by their parents and complete domination of parents by their pampered children. An individual has to make three major adjustments—to society, to work, and to sex. The social adjustment is the first of these three and the 'style of life' worked out in early social relationships will persist in the later adjustments to work and sex.

As a matter of fact much of this is quite compatible with Freudian theory—especially in view of Freud's later emphasis on aggression. Allowance must be made for Freud's odd use of the word 'sexual'; his doctrine of the 'ego-ideal' can easily be equated with Adler's 'style of life' or 'guiding fiction.' Nevertheless Adler added some very important insights to Freud although he left out a great deal that was important—e.g. 'the unconscious,' the oral and anal stages, and the close connection between the instinctive urges of the small child. Perhaps Freud's later stress on aggression was in part due to Adler's revolt.

Jung differed from Freud in expanding the concepts of the 'libido' and the 'unconscious' and in stressing the importance of the exciting cause of a neurosis as well as of the predisposing cause. He used the term 'libido' in a broad sense which freed it of its close connection with sex. It was made to include all human drives, including Freud's sex and Adler's 'will to power.' Freud's later lumping together of the sex and ego instincts under the general concept of the 'life instincts' looks like a concession to Jung which paralleled his concession to Adler.

'The unconscious' of Freud is extended to include 'the collective unconscious' of the race. This contains the 'archetypes' of the human race as well as the instinctual urges of the 'id.' For Jung 'repression' is certainly not the basis of 'the unconscious.' 'The unconscious' is inherited and predisposes the individual to use certain sorts of basic concepts or 'archetypes' as well as to seek certain sorts of goals which are predetermined by the 'id.' There is, then, the 'personal unconscious' which is more or less equivalent to what Freud meant by 'the unconscious' when he said that its basis was 'repression.' Thus for Jung a dream about the patient's father might not be about his actual father at all but might instead be a symbolic rendering of the 'archetype' of power. Freudians, of course, replied that much of this interpretation was a way of avoiding the unacceptability of many more literal renderings of the contents of dreams. Much of Jung's later work, e.g. his lectures in 1938 on 'The Psychology of Religion,' is so mysterious as to be almost undiscussable.

Jung's less mystical departure from Freud was his stress on present problems as exciting causes of neuroses. He pointed out quite sensibly that many people are riddled with 'unconscious wishes' and 'complexes' but do not break down. They are lucky in not meeting a situation which calls forth more psychic energy than the individual, because of the energy being used in dealing with his conflicts, can muster. If they do meet such a situation, they may then, as Freud conjectured, regress to an earlier way of dealing with a frustrating situation. Therefore the present problem of the patient can often be vital both as indicative of his deep-seated trouble and as an avenue of temporary readjustment, if it can be removed.

Perhaps Jung is best known for his famous 'psychological types,' the 'introvert' and the 'extrovert,' or those whose interest is directed toward themselves and those whose interest is outgoing. The latter tend to take the world as they find it, the former to set up their own valuations and to wish that the world would conform to them. This dichotomy is based on attitudes. It is supplemented by the division on a functional basis into thinking, feeling, sensation, and intuition types. This gives Jung eight possible types of individuals. Thus an extroverted thinking type would deal in a matter of fact and logical way with the world as he found it, whereas an extroverted feeling type would go about the world feeling strongly about things and situations which he encountered. The trouble about a typology is that it is so rare to find an individual who fits any into one category. It is only useful in the development of a scientific theory if it is based upon some kind of causal-genetic assumption like the Linnaean classification on the basis of the possession of reproductive organs or the Freudian classification of anal and oral characters. Useful classifications, in other words, presuppose some kind of causal theory and have deductive consequences. Jung's classification incorporates no causal assumptions and looks very much like a classification on rather ill-defined and theoretically trivial similarities between people. Its relation to the Freudian type of classification is like calling a whale a fish because it swims in water in comparison with calling it a mammal because it possesses mammalian glands. Obvious similarities, though often *practically* useful, may turn out to be *theoretically* trivial. The theoretical importance of Jung's classification has yet to be established, though Eysenck has used the extrovert-introvert dichotomy extensively as a descriptive tool for personality testing.

2. CHILD PSYCHOLOGY AND INTELLIGENCE TESTS

The twentieth century in Europe has been characterized by a quite unprecedented interest in the problems and development of the child. This was partly the result of technological pressure from educationalists who had to implement various schemes for universal education introduced at the end of the nineteenth century, but, as in the case of Freudian psychology, theoretical interests were as influential as more practical requirements. The revolutionary influence was, of course, the theory of evolution. Just as Darwin shattered the picture of man as lord of creation and so paved the way for theories of instincts and irrational animal urges which men shared with the brutes, so also he stimulated interest in the development of the child as a field of biological study. The twentieth century has witnessed, as a result, the attempt of grown men to understand and come to terms with the animal and the child within them. Plato's picture of man as made up of a many-headed beast, a lion, and a man shows the intuitive realization which thinking people have usually had of the irrational components of the human constitution. But it was not till the twentieth century that the details of the child and beast within us were systematically studied. Men had tended before Darwin to set out the *differences* between men on the one hand and animals and children on the other; after Darwin the overwhelming tendency was to examine the similarities. And if, under the influence of theology, men had tended to say before Darwin: 'What a piece of work is man,' they now tend to say, under the influence of biology: 'How wonderful are children and the beasts of the field.' It is in this kind of way that the value-systems of man keep pace with scientific discoveries and enable men to endure life with fewer illusions about themselves.

Darwin himself made a start in developmental psychology by keeping a daily record of a child's activities. It was W. Preyer, however, who in 1881 first produced a book on the subject called *The Mind of the Child*. Ten years later, in 1891, Stanley Hall founded the Pedagogical Seminary in America and in 1893 Sully founded the British Association for Child Study. In 1896 Witmer founded at Philadelphia the first psychological clinic for maladjusted children.

Evolutionary theory postulated levels of development of the mind, the child's being half-way between the animal and the adult mind. Stanley Hall, in his great work on *Adolescence* in 1904, carried the evolutionary doctrine further. In his 'recapitulation' theory he conjectured that the child in its development to the adult recapitulates the evolution of the human race from the almost anthropoid level to the human. In play, for instance, the child develops to the hunting level of primitive man at about ten when he rushes round in gangs and plays at Red Indians. Then a kind of second birth develops in adolescence which marks the transition from primitive man to the more self-conscious level of civilized man. Karl Groos developed a different theory of play while retaining the same biological orientation. He believed that play was a kind of rehearsal for more adult activities and that those who played well would be more likely to survive in the struggle for existence than those who did not. These studies, together with Thorndike's experiments on animals, Freud's studies on hysteria, Havelock Ellis's start on studies in sex, and Stout's *Analytic Psychology* exhibit the predominantly biological orientation of the close of the nineteenth century.

Many educators before the twentieth century had advocated a more imaginative approach to the education of children. Rousseau's *Emile* is a classic in this respect with its emphasis on treating the child as a creature in his own right rather than as material to be moulded according to adult wishes. Similarly, Froebel in his *Education of Man* (1826) outlined his aim of educating children through their own self-activity which he put into practice in his kindergarten. The emphasis on letting children learn things for themselves and develop at their own pace was a departure from the tradition of Comenius and Locke, in which the mind of the child was conceived as a blank sheet on which the teacher had to imprint items of knowledge. The stress on the emotional life of man and on his instincts, urges, and attitudes which was introduced by those psychologists who adopted the biological approach to the study of man began gradually to reinforce the attack initiated by Rousseau and Froebel on the old intellectualistic conception of education which was part and parcel of the observationalist tradition. Instead of training, repetition, routine, and all other devices for helping the association of ideas and the filling up of the empty bucket of a mind, increasing emphasis came to be placed on winning the interest of the child, letting him develop his natural aptitudes, and letting him experiment with the materials of nature for himself. Play came to be regarded not as a wasted period in which the disgruntled teacher had to let his victim recuperate for the next dose of knowledge, but as an essential part of the school curriculum. In 1917 Caldwell Cook's *The Play Way* attempted to demonstrate that children could learn almost everything that was necessary as part of their play. T. P. Nunn's *Education: Its Data and First Principles* in 1920 was a landmark in bringing together the new purposive or 'hormic' psychology and the use of play as an educational method. A new attitude to the child came to be combined with an increasing insight into the development and motives of children.

The increased understanding of the motives of children made possible by the biological approach to their behaviour was enhanced by the brilliant speculations of Freud about the influence of early family life on children. The emergence of women in public life and the scientific world contributed also to producing a mass of child-studies. Amongst Freudian studies Flugel's *Psycho-analytic Study of the Family* in 1921 was followed by the work of Susan Isaacs (*Intellectual Growth in Young Children* in 1930 and *Social Development in Young Children* in 1933) and Melanie Klein (*The Psycho-analysis of Children* in 1932). The contribution of the Gestalt School came from Koffka in his *The Growth of the Mind* in 1925 and Watson's *Behaviourism* in 1924, with its celebrated behaviouristic studies of the emotions of infants, was another example of the universal interest in children. Studies not confined so rigidly to any particular psychological 'school' are those of Piaget (*The Language and Thought of the Child*, 1923; *The Child's Conception of the World*, 1926; *The Child's Conception of Causality*, 1930 and *The Moral Judgment of the Child* in 1932), in which he tried to distinguish the various stages in child-development. The transitions postulated, for instance, from autistic thinking, subservient entirely to wishes, to egocentric animism, or from acceptance of transcendentally given norms to reciprocity and autonomy in moral behaviour, are extremely interesting when considered in conjunction with Freudian theory and 'recapitulation' theories of the Stanley Hall type. There have been, too, other studies in child-development which have been influenced by the desire to work out a system of developmental tests for the various·stages of development. The work of Gesell, e.g. *The Mental Growth of the Pre-School Child* (1925), *Biographies of Child Development* (1939), etc., and of Charlotte Buhler, e.g. *From Birth to Maturity* (1935) and *Testing Children's Development from Birth to School Age* (1935) are good examples of this fusion of interest in child-development with the craze for devising various forms of test which is another typically twentieth-century phenomenon.

The origin of the intelligence test provides a very good example of the influence of technological pressure on psychology. In 1904 Binet was asked by the French Committee of Public Instruction to serve on a committee set up to deal with the problem of 'backward' children. In order to be able to distinguish between laziness and lack of ability Binet and Simon devised a series of graded tests. These tests were revised in 1908 and 1911. They aimed at measuring the 'mental age' of a child by fixing the norm for a child of a certain chronological age and measuring the performance of any child against what was normal for his chronological age. In this way a child's 'mental age' could be fixed at so many points above or below his chronological age. A furore of testing then began to break out amongst psychologists which was accelerated by the application of tests to two million recruits to the American army during the First World War. Tests were devised for special ability, vocational aptitudes, temperament, character, and so on. Also statistical procedures were developed by Pearson, Thurstone, Spearman, and others, for correlating the results of different tests. An experimenter might ask himself, for instance, whether there is any kind of correlation between backwardness and emotional instability. Given a way of testing both backwardness and emotional instability it could then be discovered whether there was any correlation between these two factors just as it could be discovered whether there is any correlation between a performance test like Kohs' blocks and a verbal test like those devised by Cattell.

Out of this development of tests and statistical methods the 'factor' school of psychology began to grow with Spearman of London University at its head. Spearman differed from other intelligence testers in trying to generalize the methods of factor analysis, which had a practical origin, to the field of general psychological theory. Thinking that this method of research was a way of mapping out the mind, he postulated, from the results of tests, a general factor of mental ability or mental energy (g) which varied in individuals together with a number of specific abilities (s). Thus, success in reading, for instance, could be regarded as dependent in part upon g and in part upon s or specific reading ability. Spearman tried to do for psychology what Newton did for physics, to find psychological laws from which facts of mental behaviour could be deduced. He formulated three noegenetic principles, three anoegenetic processes, and five quantitative principles.

His noegenetic principles were really an attack on associationist psychology via the gateway of relations. Starting from the postulate that 'any lived experience tends to evoke immediately a knower of its character and experiencer,' which is a restatement of Locke's 'ideas of sensation' and 'ideas of reflection,' he then passed to the education of relations—'the mentally presenting of any two characters tends to evoke a knowing of relation between them' and the eduction of correlates—'the mentally presenting of any character and relation tends to evoke a knowing of the correlative character.' These principles were really epistemology and logic in the guise of psychological laws. Had not Locke too postulated that knowledge arises through the noting of relations between our ideas? There are many philosophical objections to Spearman's principles even if we regard them as philosophical principles rather than empirical laws. For instance, apart from the more general objections to Cartesianism, it does seem as if his second and third principles draw attention to the cognition of logical relations only, the eduction of relations by considering the characteristics related being applicable only to necessary relations or those entailed by the nature of the characteristics in question. We can educe a relation like 'older than' by thinking about the characteristics of 'being a father' and 'being a son,' but we cannot, in the same way, educe the relation of 'hated by' which Freud suggested was a universal relation between sons and fathers.

The three anoegenetic processes of reproduction, disparition, and clearness variation were Spearman's way of contrasting the activity of the mind in noegenesis (which involves g) with the more automatic processes involved in memory, attention, and forgetting. Both in his account of these processes and in his three noegenetic principles Spearman seems to revert to a more mechanical and logical account of thinking—a revised associationism. Conation is not emphasized; yet without interest there is often no eduction of relations. Interest and other emotional factors influence enormously the direction of association and the variation in attention. Perhaps Spearman's early training under Wundt and Müller was in part responsible for this sort of approach.

In his five quantitative laws Spearman tried to fill in the background of his intellectualistic starting-point and to incorporate some of the findings of other psychologists. These were his laws of constancy of energy, retentivity, fatigue, conative control, and primordial potencies. Anyone familiar with the history of experiments on learning and problem solving can surmise what he meant by his first four principles; the last one, however, the law of 'primordial potencies,' sounds rather mysterious. All he meant was the effect on performance of physiological influences—heredity, age, drugs, and so on. A lot of work has been done in working out the relation between g on the one hand and heredity, sex, and race differences, health, brain injuries, drugs, climate, and other such variables on the other. This is the sort of empirical work in which the Spearman School is at home and which is of lasting value. Few would regard his mapping of the mind and neo-Cartesian principles as either interesting or important. But dissatisfaction with Spearman's general laws and principles should not be allowed to detract from the importance of his empirical research, which was his strong point, both in respect of his actual findings and in respect of the correlation techniques which he helped to devise. These have proved most useful in dealing with problems of all kinds where some kind of concomitant variation between factors is sought. The discovery of concomitant variations is the beginning of the establishment of scientific laws or relations of functional dependence between variables. Even if Spearman's own laws were rather dubious he nevertheless helped to establish a technique which may well facilitate the discovery of psychological laws—the Mecca of many methodologically conscious psychologists.

The empirical work involved in testing need not be closely tied to any such theory of cognition. Indeed, a great deal of the detailed research since Spearman has been directed to the refinement of tests, to be used as technical tools, in education, industry, and the armed forces. In analysing test results statistically and consequently making inferences about the nature of human cognition, the chief successors to Thurstone and Spearman have been Burt[1] and Vernon.[2]

The statistical approach of the Spearman School has been applied also to the measurement of personality traits, attitudes, and values. The work of Eysenck,[3] for example, is directed towards the diagnosis of personality clusters by relatively objective testing, particularly towards describing the characteristics of neurotic personality types. Other psychologists, at the same time, have approached the attempt to assess personality more from the theoretically-derived standpoint of the psycho-analysts, and have constructed techniques, so-called 'projective tests,' which resemble miniature clinical situations. That both approaches

[1] C. Burt: *The Factors of the Mind* (1940).
[2] P. E. Vernon: *The Structure of Human Abilities* (1950).
[3] H. Eysenck: *Dimensions of Personality* (1947).

have much to offer, both to the assessment of individuals and to the identification of personality types, can be seen in large-scale investigations in which both approaches have been used, as in Murray's *Explorations in Personality* and in *The Authoritarian Personality* by Adorno, Frenkel-Brunswik, Levinson, and Sandford.

E. The influence of other sciences

I. BIOLOGY AND PHYSIOLOGY

It is almost superfluous for a separate section to be written on the influence of biology and physiology on twentieth-century psychology. Their influence—especially that of biology—has been seen in nearly all the theories with which we have dealt. The biology of Darwin in which most of the early twentieth-century psychologists have been nurtured had both a general effect in the reorientation of the approach to man and a specific effect in the carrying over of certain concepts and generalizations. The main general influence derived from the theory of evolution and the accompanying realization that men were animals. This, as has been mentioned before, encouraged the exploration of the similarities between men and animals, the actual study of animals as part of psychology, and the attempt by the Behaviourists to apply the methods successful in the study of animals to the study of man. When man could no longer be regarded as 'trailing clouds of glory' or as weighed down with original sin it became natural to suggest that he was motivated by more or less the same kind of impulses as were animals. In other words the *same sort of explanation* was sought for the behaviour of men as for the behaviour of animals. Animals are not manifestly motivated by the pursuit of truth, beauty, or eternal life; it therefore became plausible to suggest that these higher levels of desire were reducible to basic urges in disguise. Without a proper understanding of the tremendous impact of biology on the minds of thinking people the psychology of Freud, of McDougall, and of the Behaviourists, together with the onslaught on the old intellectualism and sensationism of the observationalist tradition, is incomprehensible. It was not till the middle twenties of the twentieth century that the swing away from a predominantly biological orientation began and the influence of the social sciences was felt. Psychologists became increasingly aware that men were very different from animals, not because they had a soul which animals did not have, but because they had a very complex social environment. They began to appreciate the large element of truth in Marx's saying that it is not the consciousness of man that determines his existence, but his social existence that determines his consciousness.

The influence of biology can also be seen in particular hypotheses and concepts which came into psychology. There was, for instance, the working assumption of so many psychologists that organisms tend to act in ways which preserve their equilibrium—their behaviour is 'purposive' or goal-directed in the sense that certain characteristic states of quiescence can be viewed as terminating points in behaviour cycles. The notions of self-preservation and race preservation are frequently used—especially as a way of classifying 'instincts' or 'drives,' another biological concept. The heredity and environment argument in biology was transferred to psychology in the discussions of innate behaviour tendencies, and in studies like that of Galton on identical twins. In brief, psychology during the early twentieth century became one of the biological sciences.

The gradual realization of the continuity of human and animal life made it more and more difficult to maintain a Cartesian dichotomy between body and mind. This made the findings of physiologists even more relevant to psychology. A great deal of the physiology of the twentieth century has been a continuation of the work done by the school at Leipsig founded by Wundt, and influenced particularly by Helmholtz. It has been concerned mainly with peripheral and proprioceptive sensation, perception of form and colour, and, largely due to the influence of investigators like Hughlings Jackson, Henry Head, Charles Sherrington, and E. D. Adrian, with further analysis of reflexes and localization of function. In their work on the peripheral senses the early experimental psychologists discovered sensitive posts of four kinds in the skin—for touch, pain, warmth, and cold, although it had often been suggested that subjects may be able to distinguish more than these four basic qualities. The influence of Johannes Müller's Law of Specific Energies was such that it was assumed that each sensation would be mediated by a particular kind of receptor. This seems now not to be the case. It also appears that sense-spots do not correspond to isolated nerve endings. The confusion was exemplified by the prevalence of the association between the Krause end-organ and sensations of cold; but it has been shown that the Krause organ has in fact a very limited distribution.[1] However, evidence has continued to support the hypothesis that the several modalities are represented discretely up to the level of the thalamus.

Continuation of the investigation of form perception has presented many puzzles. The work of the micro-physiologists (especially Hartline and Granit, who have shown that many receptors in the retina are optimally excited when a stimulus *ceases*), suggests that the camera is a

[1] For a review of later work on the subject see the chapter 'Somesthesis' in S. Stevens's *Handbook of Experimental Psychology* (1951); for the earlier work see E. Boring: *Sensation and Perception in the History of Experimental Psychology* (1942).

most inadequate model for the eye. Theory is in such a state of flux that it is now difficult to understand how a straight line can ever be perceived as such. A theory which has carried some weight suggests that learning is involved together with eye-movements. Research into the mechanisms of colour-vision has been largely guided by prevalent theories. Histology has so far failed to reveal several kinds of receptor which might be responsible for discriminating colours, but there is evidence for the separate representation of colour at the thalamic level of the brain. Theories deriving from the original Young–Helmholtz and Hering proposals have inspired much of the work. Granit has proposed a two-system theory, based on his experiments using micro-electrode techniques, which has had considerable influence.[1]

Refined micro-electrode techniques have also been used in investigating the nature of the nervous impulse. Facts which have proved important to psychology are: the existence of a physiological threshold, the discontinuity of nervous impulses, the relationship between intensity of stimulation and frequency of impulses, and the phenomenon of neural adaptation. E. D. Adrian has been a pioneer in this field.[2] In 1875 Hughlings Jackson suggested that functions in the nervous system were arranged hierarchically, and that if a higher level should cease to act, there would be 'release phenomena' and behaviour would regress. This concept, but applied to levels of behaviour, had considerable vogue both with clinicians and theoreticians. Because, however, of the over-simplifications which it involved, it had only very general application. Another neurological theory which has had even greater influence has been that of Sir Henry Head. His concept of 'body-schema' has been adapted particularly by Sir F. C. Bartlett in his theory of perception and remembering.[3]

Physiological psychology, however, has not been a simple continuation of the work of the last century. It has also stimulated and been stimulated by twentieth-century theories of behaviour. Attempts have been made to integrate the findings of Freud, for instance, with physiological discoveries, an integration which Freud himself hoped for,[4] and which has already found application in psycho-somatic medicine. But it is not just Freudian theory that has benefited greatly from cross-fertilization with physiological findings. Other theories have been both influenced and inspired by the development of physiology. Particularly interesting are those theorists like Hull and Köhler who hope that psychological postulates will eventually be deducible from physiological theory. Hull starts explicitly from physiological postulates and Köhler suggests that

[1] See R. Granit: *Receptors and Sensory Perception* (1955).
[2] E. D. Adrian: *The Basis of Sensation* (1928).
[3] F. C. Bartlett: *Remembering* (1932).
[4] See, for instance, S. Freud: 'Instincts and their Vicissitudes,' *Collected Papers*, Vol. IV, p. 64.

psychological laws will eventually be deducible from a physiological theory of brain processes, there being an isomorphism of the psychological with the physiological field.[1] This postulate of isomorphism is, as a matter of fact, highly speculative. During the twentieth century, following from the clinical observations of Broca, and the experiments of Fritsch and Hitzig in 1870, there has been a continuous search for the function of the various parts of the cerebral cortex. The early work on the motor, sensory, visual, auditory, gustatory, and olfactory cortices has been consolidated and additional information obtained. It is now clear that it is normal for there to be two or three projection areas for any one modality, one possibly being concerned with involuntary reflexes. Near one-to-one relationships between motor cortex and muscles, and between retina and visual cortex are known to exist. This does not mean that the principle of isomorphism is to be accepted in its entirety. In fact the nature of the visual cortex suggests that the principle over-simplifies the dynamics, while the discovery of continuously changing electrical activity as shown in the electro-encephalograph records suggests that the comparatively static conditions necessary for the existence of isomorphic processes do not obtain. On the other hand, the atomistic analysis of perception into occurrences in individual neurones has thrown no light on field organizations which can be demonstrated in perception. It is necessary to postulate some kind of neural interaction to explain such phenomena, as suggested, for instance, by Hull.

Although the Gestalt school of psychology and field theories have postulated neural traces as the basis of learning and remembering, there has been little physiological research inspired by these theories and the principle of isomorphism remains relatively unconfirmed. The learning theories, on the other hand, which derive from the conditioned reflex hypothesis, have given rise to much research designed to discover the neural basis of learning. This research has fallen into three classes: investigation of reflexes, of the cortical basis of learning, and of the physiological basis of drives. Research on reflexes has shown that a simple connectionism as proposed by Pavlov and the early theorists is no longer tenable, partly because of the advances that have been made in the analysis of the reflex. The work of Lorente de No, in particular, has shown that reflex connections are more complicated than was supposed. Pavlov's concept of irradiation has also had to be abandoned.

Secondly, Lashley's work on the 'search for the engramme' has been, perhaps, the most outstanding research during the twentieth century into the cortical basis of learning.[2] His influence has been very

---

[1] See C. Hull: *Principles of Behaviour* (1943), and W. Köhler: *The Place of Value in a World of Facts* (1938) and *Dynamics in Psychology* (1940).

[2] K. Lashley: *Brain Mechanisms and Intelligence* (1929).

great—especially his discovery of mass action in the rat's cortex, necessitating the abandonment of simple connection and trace theories. His work agrees best with the dynamic theory of brain function suggested by Flourens during the last century. There is also support for the aggregation theory of Munk (1909), and 'localization' theory can be said to combine these two approaches.[1] It appears that in man primary projection and association areas exist together with areas of much less specific function—for instance, the frontal areas which behave more or less in a mass-action fashion. It still remains difficult to decide whether memories are retained in some localized form or whether they are represented by more dynamic systems, one theory suggesting a compromise between these two possibilities.[2]

The third class of investigations connected with learning theories has been into the physiological basis of drives. It having been established that many drives have relatively simple physiological bases,[3] argument became centred around whether drives were activated peripherally or centrally. Cannon's theory of homeostasis,[4] deriving from Bernard, which sought to explain motivation in terms of disequilibrium within the system, gave great impetus to research in this field. Richter in particular has shown how changes in bodily chemistry will alter the pattern of behaviour. Accumulating research indicates that behaviour may be initiated by changes in the internal environment; but the termination of the behaviour is a different matter. An animal stops eating long before its blood sugar level is restored. Indeed, the act of swallowing appears to be adequate to stop hunger-driven behaviour, at least for a time.

Cannon is also famous for his work on the physiological changes in emotion. In the last century it was frequently suggested that the viscera were the seat of the emotions. Bichat (1771–1802) was one of the earliest to express this view which culminated in the James–Lange theory of emotions. Sherrington, Cannon, and Bard are the best-known figures in research prompted by this theory. Much of the work has been of limited value because animals were used whose subjective emotional experiences were inaccessible to observation. Although the main tenets of the theory have not been conclusively falsified, Cannon thought it necessary to propose a modified theory in which the importance of the hypothalamus in emotion is stressed. Whatever new evidence is produced, it still appears that changes mediated by the autonomic nervous system are important physiological concomitants of feelings. Little advance has been made in the analysis of the pleasant emotions.

[1] See J. F. Fulton: *Physiology of the Nervous System* (1938).
[2] D. Hebb: *The Organization of Behaviour* (1949).
[3] C. T. Morgan: *Physiological Psychology* (1943).
[4] W. Cannon: *The Wisdom of the Body* (1932).

To date the development of physiology has been considered in so far as it has constituted a continuation of the experimental psychology of the nineteenth century and in so far as it has been stimulated by and has exerted an influence on theories of learning, perception, and motivation. Many of the important developments, however, have come from clinical research. At the beginning of the century three major areas of the brain were known as 'silent areas' because no result was obtained when they were stimulated directly with electricity. Clinical research has now led to many discoveries. Sir Henry Head was the first to discover the importance of the occipito-parietal regions, when symbols are being used. His research on the aphasias in particular has had great influence, not only on future research, but also on psychological theories of language and conduct.[1] It is now clear that the occipito-parietal regions are of the greatest importance in processes which are usually called intellectual. The function of the other 'silent areas,' the frontal and the temporal lobes, are not yet, however, clearly understood. Experimental work on monkeys and clinical evidence from man have yielded conflicting clues. Most common symptoms from temporal lobe lesions are auditory and speech defects, epileptic seizures, smell and taste hallucinations, and dreamy states. The use of frontal lobotomy in humans, first reported by Moniz in 1936 following Jacobsen's work with monkeys, has resulted in a wealth of clinical evidence regarding the function of these areas. Despite this, it has proved difficult to describe the changes in the patient which tend to occur. At the beginning of the century it was thought that, since the frontal lobes are large in men compared with lower animals, their function must be predominantly intellectual. But, in fact, intellectual deterioration after lobotomy seems slight, an inability to synthesize being the most outstanding result. Personality changes are characterized by a reduction in anxiety and a consequent devil-may-care attitude. In a high proportion of cases there is a reversion after a period to the original personality organization, so that this approach has still yielded inconclusive evidence on the function of these large areas.[2] The general problem has been suggested in the course of this reasearch of 'why is there so much cortex which seems to be useless?' Half the cortex may be removed, so it seems, with little impairment of intellectual functions. Wiener has suggested that man has evolved in such a way that there is now too much grey matter for the connecting fibres to cope with.

Clinical work has also led to the modification of the view, common in the 1920s, that differences in personality could be explained in terms of difference in the system of endocrine glands. Subsequent research has shown that, in the first place, if the endocrine system is

[1] H. Head: *Aphasia and Kindred Disorders of Speech* (1926).
[2] G. Rylander: *Personality Changes after Operations on the Frontal Lobes* (1939).

tampered with, it tends to revert to its initial state. In the second place it now appears that the system as a whole is more under the control of the nervous system than was formerly supposed. However, some successful attempts have been made to classify people in terms of objective physiological criteria, and the relationship between such physiological classifications and psychological classifications seems quite well established. Some attempts have been made to apply the techniques of factor analysis to results obtained from measurements of autonomic activity, and so to arrive at personality types. Better known is the physical typology devised by Sheldon, and deriving from Kretschmer, in which correlations are found with temperamental types.

Psychiatry has provided interesting material which helps to integrate the approaches of the psycho-analyst and those of the physiologist. In psycho-somatic medicine it has been found that many disorders in the autonomic nervous system may be relieved both by medicine and by psychotherapy. Physiological aspects of the neuroses are already better understood than those of the psychoses. Although the genetics of the psychoses appear fairly simple, and certain physical methods of treatment are sometimes effective, there has so far been no overwhelming evidence for any of the physiological hypotheses that have been suggested.[1]

Finally it is worth mentioning a development which may be considered to fall within the scope of physiological psychology. The nervous system has two important functions, those of control and of communication. These functions are possessed by many other systems, by certain machines, for instance—especially guided missiles and calculating machines. Techniques which have been evolved for dealing with these machines are therefore claimed to be suitable for analysing some of the functions of the nervous system. These techniques are the concern of cybernetics, of which Wiener's book may be taken to be definitive.[2] There is also a journal devoted to mathematical methods of analysing nervous function.[3]

In conclusion, it might be said that at the turn of the century there appears to have been abundant faith that physiological aspects of behaviour would relate in simple ways to phenomena which had previously been thought the proper subject-matter of psychology. Subsequent work in physiology indicates that the relations are not so simple. In particular the more peripheral processes of the nervous system are more complex than was imagined, and, if anything, physiological explanations of sensation and perception seem more puzzling and confusing than ever. On the other hand, new relationships have

[1] J. McV. Hunt: *Personality and the Behaviour Disorders* (1944).
[2] N. Wiener: *Cybernetics* (1948).
[3] *Journal of Mathematical Bio-physics*.

been found between the more molar aspects of nervous organization and the dynamics of personality. Much has been done on the physiological basis of drives and emotions and attempts have been made to integrate both theories of learning and theories of personality with the findings of physiological research.

These developments show how far psychologists have travelled from Descartes' picture of 'the ghost in the machine,' to quote a recent caricature of his theory.[1] But they express only one trend in twentieth-century psychology. Another trend, as exemplified by Weiss who in 1925 described psychology as a bio-social science, or by Wheeler who in 1929 started his *Science of Psychology* with the social organism and ended up with the senses and nervous system, is to substitute a predominantly social orientation for a physiological or biological one. To this relatively novel trend we must now turn.

2. THE SOCIAL SCIENCES

The nineteenth century marked the beginning of systematic studies in social science. Hegel's doctrine of the 'objective mind' which was manifest in laws, customs, and institutions encouraged an increasing interest in social phenomena. Marx's studies in social history and his theory about the economic determinants of individual behaviour and value systems were not an isolated phenomenon; they were paralleled by Galton's studies of the faculties of natives, by the social science of Comte, Mill, and Herbert Spencer, and Tylor's inquiries into primitive culture.

Broadly speaking it could be said that the first reaction of psychologists to the accumulating researches of social scientists was to attempt explanations of them in terms of the invariable characteristics of individuals. In fact ever since Aristotle's conception of man as 'by nature' a social and political animal it had usually been assumed that social organization was a reflection of man's needs and requirements. Hume, who was one of the first to set himself up self-consciously as a social scientist, had conjectured that society was rooted in man's physical infirmity in conjunction with his multifarious wants, his sexual instincts, and his innate sympathy for others. His *Treatise on Human Nature* was an attempt to give an objective, value-free, explanation of human society and its moral conventions, from a psychological point of view. Similarly Hobbes, in his *Leviathan*, had attempted to deduce man's social and political behaviour from basic psychological postulates about self-preservation which were themselves presumed to be deducible from physical postulates about matter in motion. This had been the normal approach to social phenomena, though there had

[1] G. Ryle: *The Concept of Mind* (1949).

been exceptions like Montesquieu who had attempted to explain variations in conduct by variations in climate. Thus there was nothing very novel in the psychological approach to social phenomena which became so popular at the end of the nineteenth century and which lasted for the first quarter of the twentieth. Wundt, for instance, wrote three volumes on *Folk-Psychology* in which he used a psychological starting-point to interpret and elucidate ethnological and historical material. In 1895 Le Bon produced his celebrated study on *The Psychology of the Crowd*, in which he used psychological analysis to elucidate historical facts. The root of his sort of interpretation was to be found in the notion of the 'herd-instinct' which had been used by animal psychologists. Galton, in his essay on *Gregarious and Slavish Instincts*, put this point of view in a nutshell when he said: 'I shall endeavour to prove that the slavish attitudes in man are a direct consequence of his gregarious nature, which itself is a result of the conditions both of his primeval barbarism and of the forms of his subsequent civilization.'[1] Trotter, later on in 1919, in his *Instincts of the Herd in Peace and War* achieved fame for his 'gregarious instinct' which he ranked with sex, self-preservation, and nutrition, as playing a fundamental part in the behaviour of men.

The psychologists, however, who became deeply committed to this type of nativistic explanation of social phenomena were McDougall and Freud. In his *Introduction to Social Psychology* in 1908 McDougall provided just the sort of exciting and over-simplified interpretation of social phenomena which was likely to be welcomed by biologically trained investigators who were more and more turning to the investigation of different societies. McDougall maintained that men are born with similar instinctive tendencies and that society is explicable in terms of them. This sort of explanation won wide acceptance until Freudian theory began to diminish the popularity of McDougall's doctrine, especially in the United States. This led to the replacement of one nativistic type of explanation by another. In his *Totem and Taboo* (1913) Freud compared certain neurotic mechanisms, as revealed by psycho-analysis, with savage institutions like exogamy, taboo, magic, and totemism. He tried to show that a taboo presupposes the ambivalent attitudes of love and hate and that a taboo, for instance, on a king is a large scale reflection of the ambivalent attitude to the father. Similarly, he tried to show that the two great taboos on eating a totem animal and on endogamous marriage reflect the omnipresent desire to kill and eat the father and to marry the mother—the Oedipus situation. Freud viewed social organization as a system of restraints which had evolved to repress the basic instincts of men. If these had been allowed to develop without check, they would have made social organization

[1] Quoted by Brett: *History of Psychology*, Vol. III, p. 294.

and hence human survival impossible. Taboos, for instance, on endo-
gamy are constraints which have evolved to protect the race against the
universal desire to marry the mother. This is a much more ingenious
type of explanation than that of McDougall with its multitude of
distinct instincts to explain different types of behaviour; but it still
presupposes invariable and innate desires on the part of men.

In contrast to this nativistic type of explanation the theory is much
more popular now that social organization, conventions, institutions,
and so on, depend much more on cultural, economic, geographic, and
climatic conditions than on any innate psychological dispositions.
Indeed, though it would be admitted that there are some innate tendencies, rather like the 'drives' postulated by Hull and Tolman which
have a definite physiological basis, it would be maintained that a great
number of the so-called instincts like gregariousness, acquisitiveness,
constructiveness, aggressiveness, curiosity, and so on, are socially
determined. Klineberg, for instance, reviewing the work that has been
done on this subject in 1940 in his *Social Psychology*, came to the conclusion that the only motives which are absolutely dependable, have a
definite physiological basis, and admit of no exceptions in the human
race are thirst, hunger, the need for rest and sleep, the elimination of
waste products from the body, and similar other organic requirements;
also activity drives and 'esthetic' drives. He maintained that sex, post-
maternal behaviour, and possibly also self-preservation have a definite
physiological basis, are found in all societies, but admit of exceptions
in the case of individuals. Social factors, however, not only determine
the manner of their expression (as in the case of the first group) but
also in certain circumstances cause them not to appear. Aggressiveness,
flight, and probably self-assertiveness form a third group of motives
having an indirect physiological basis, occurring with great frequency
in the human race but admitting of exceptions both in groups and in
individuals. Finally, amongst motives having no known physiological
basis, but occurring with some frequency either because of social
factors common to the majority of human communities, or as a means
to the satisfaction of practical interests, the means then becoming the
end, he places gregariousness, the paternal motive, the pre-maternal
motive, the filial motive, acquisitiveness, and self-submission.[1] But
this sort of compromise between the instinctivists and the environ-
mentalists was only possible because of the great amount of work
that had been done by field-workers in detailed studies of the folk-ways
and institutions of different societies. This led to a swing of the pendulum in the opposite direction of environmentalism. For a time
explanations in terms of instincts became outmoded. Their place was
taken by explanation in terms of social conditioning—the reverse of

[1] O. Klineberg: *Social Psychology*, pp. 160–2.

the former tendency. They were attempts to explain psychological facts in terms of sociological generalization rather than social facts in terms of psychological generalizations.

The environmentalist movement began long before people attempted to refute McDougall and Freud. Plato was a thoroughgoing environmentalist, maintaining that although men may have differences in innate ability, how and whether they use it is a matter of education and social conditioning. He placed enormous importance on the social environment of man—not just direct instructions but the subtle indirect influences of ways of behaving and social traditions. He stressed the great plasticity of human beings. Hume, Burke, and Rousseau combined a theory of human instincts with an insight into the overwhelming influence of social traditions on human beings. They attacked the attempts by Hobbes, Locke, Macchiavelli, and others to explain society as a by-product of the wants, needs, and decisions of individuals. With Hegel, Marx, and Comte sociological determinism began to be developed with a wealth of historical examples. The concepts of the class, the nation, and the collective began to take precedence over the concept of the individual. Indeed, the individual tended to be regarded as a resultant of social and economic forces; his beliefs and attitudes were determined by his economic class or by the type of social organization in which he was nurtured. This way of thinking, together with the empirical data collected about other societies (i.e. the combination of sociological determinism with an outburst of historical and anthropological studies), began to exert its influence on the concepts of explanation of academic psychologists. In 1890 Gabriel Tarde published a book on *The Laws of Imitation*, in which he attempted to distinguish and exemplify the different forms of social interaction. As a result of many years' service as a jurist he had become convinced that criminal behaviour was the product of social factors far more than of individual endowment. Men are by nature infinitely suggestible if they are anything 'by nature.' The criminal is usually the man who has been brought up amongst criminals, the gentleman the man who has been brought up amongst people who accept and practice the required conventional standards. Tarde's work, however, in which desire and imitation were the key concepts, was a transitional work—a bridge between the old associationism of the nineteenth century and the purposivism and stress on social conditioning of the twentieth.

The real landmark in the development of social psychology proper was Charles Cooley's *Human Nature and the Social Order*, which was published in 1902. This book has had an enormous influence in America, which is the home of modern social psychology. Its main theme was that human personality is a social product and that most of our beliefs and attitudes are socially acquired. The 'social order' thus determines

individual personality. In 1908 E. A. Ross put forward the outlines of
the sort of view that was later to act as a corrective to McDougall's
Introduction to Social Psychology, but which was temporarily laid
aside in favour of the more biological approach of McDougall. To
quote Brett: 'Professor E. A. Ross writes on social psychology in the
manner of the sociologist. Social psychology, as he conceives it, "studies
the psychic planes and currents that come into existence among men
in consequence of their association." He adds that "the individuality
each has received from the hand of Nature is largely effaced, and we
find people gathered into great planes of uniformity." The subsequent
chapters elaborate topics such as suggestibility, the crowd, the mob
mind, custom, fashion, conventionality, and public opinion. We leave
the reader to discover how much of this is properly psychology; at any
rate the hypothesis of a kind of innate individuality, which is ultimately
effaced, seems best suited to end in a description of human automata.
Some writers do actually reach that conclusion!'[1] Brett obviously did
not much like this particular twentieth-century trend! But we might now
reply that what we call 'individuality' can only develop in a society and
it is difficult to see what could be *meant* by 'individuality' without one.

The best known of the attacks on McDougall from the point of view
of social psychology was that of Bernard in his *Instinct: a Study in
Social Psychology* in 1924. He tried to show that many of McDougall's
so-called instincts were not invariable patterns of behaviour in all
cultures but depended upon the particular sort of social environment
in which the individual was nurtured. The social environment rather
than the innate equipment of man provides his goals except those
which have a strictly physiological basis. A wealth of anthropological
material has since Bernard's time demonstrated the correctness of his
general line of attack. Books like Ruth Benedict's *Patterns of Culture* in
1934, R. Linton's *The Study of Man* in 1936, and Margaret Mead's
works on Samoa and New Guinea (1928 and 1930) have amply illustrated this trend. Murphy and Newcomb's *Experimental Social Psychology* was published in 1931, and in 1947 Newcomb and Hartley, in their
Readings in Social Psychology, collected a mass of experimental material
'to present illustrative selections of the ways in which the influence of
social conditions upon psychological processes have been studied.'
This invaluable collection of extracts included not only the kind of
material on leadership, group decisions, social class, propaganda,
prejudice, public opinion, which is usually associated with 'social
psychology.' It also included a lot of material which demonstrated the
invasion of 'general psychology' by 'social 'psychology.' For instance,
Sherif's famous work on perception was included in which he tried,
by his auto-kinetic experiments, to demonstrate the effect on the

[1] G. Brett: *History of Psychology*, Vol. III, p. 295.

perception of the individual of a 'frame of reference' which is socially acquired.[1] F. C. Bartlett's work on the social factors operative in recall was included together with a great deal of other material showing the importance of social factors in motivation, frustration, and learning. This illustrates the modern trend. The recent textbook on social psychology by Krech and Crutchfield,[2] for instance, devotes a great amount of space to perception and the social factors which influence it in the building up of 'attitudes' and 'beliefs.' Not only theories of motivation but also theories of perception and learning are becoming increasingly affected by stress on social conditioning and the social situation. In the realm of explanatory theory, in which we are most interested in tracing the development of twentieth-century trends, this sort of material has made it impossible to defend a full-blown theory of instincts like McDougall's. The tendency nowadays, as exemplified by the citation of Klineberg, is to combine a theory of 'drives,' or universal and dependable motives having a definite physiological basis, with a modified form of environmentalism. In this way two of the main twentieth-century trends, purposivism and stress on social conditioning, can be combined. T. H. Newcomb's recent *Social Psychology* (1950) is a good example of this integration of 'drive' psychology with anthropological and sociological material.

There has, similarly, been a reaction against Freudian concepts which has been occasioned by the influence of social science. Malinowski was one of the first anthropologists to take the Freudian theory, as set forth in *Totem and Taboo*, seriously enough to advance detailed refutations of it on certain points. He tried to show that the Oedipus complex is not something that any boy is bound to develop but is rather a product of the interaction between the growing boy and the parental pressures which are usual in a patrilineal family organization. The Trobriand islanders have a matrilineal form of organization and the natural father is regarded as the friend and companion of the son. The authoritative duties of fatherhood are undertaken by the mother's eldest brother; he is also the model of manhood to his nephew and leaves him his most important possessions. Similarly weaning takes place much later at the child's wish and without much conflict. Sex-repression is not at all severe and shows itself mainly in the taboo between brother and sister who are never allowed to be intimate with each other. The result of this different family set-up is the absence of the Oedipus situation as Freud understood it. 'In the Oedipus complex, there is the repressed desire to kill the father and marry the mother, while in the matrilineal society of the Trobriands the wish is

[1] M. Sherif: *An Outline of Social Psychology* (1948).
[2] D. Krech and R. Crutchfield: *Theory and Problems of Social Psychology* (1948).

to marry the sister and kill the maternal uncle.'[1] This type of criticism could be put in an extreme form by saying that Freud took as universal human characteristics the behaviour patterns and dominant repressions of the middle class in nineteenth-century Vienna. What is of lasting value in his view is his insight into the importance of the early social environment—especially that of the family—on the growing child. But he was rather insular in his conception of the family. Like most scientific generalizations—e.g. Galileo, Kepler, etc.—it has been refuted by being shown to hold not universally but only under certain conditions. It is now being replaced by wider generalizations about the influence of the early social environment on the child and can be regarded as a deduction from a wider generalization which is exemplified in middle-class Vienna as well as in the Trobriand Islands.

A 'Neo-Freudian' who has suggested that psycho-analysis should have a social rather than a biological orientation is Fromm. In his *Fear of Freedom* (1942), for instance, he attempted to show the interaction between psychological and sociological factors and to supplement the psycho-analytic interpretation of certain political and religious attitudes by a sociological theory of the economic determinants of social change taken from writers like Marx and Tawney. This attempt to work out the interrelation of the insights of Marx and Freud is most suggestive and is a welcome change after the over-simplified theories of both. It is also characteristic of the twentieth-century trend away from the tendency to interpret social phenomena exclusively in psychological terms.

Another Freudian with a social rather than a biological orientation is Kardiner. In *The Individual and his Society* (1939) and *The Psychological Frontiers of Society* (1945) he explored the possibility of linking social anthropology with Freudian psychology. He raised the questions whether a trait like aggressiveness, if found frequently in a culture, is part of the basic 'personality structure' of this particular culture rather than a universal human trait. The suggestion is that there is a basic level of biological needs which issue in drives—e.g. for food and drink. Superimposed upon this basis each culture has a 'basic personality structure' which is the sort of orientation of beliefs and attitudes which is compatible with a given system of social institutions and traditions—e.g. the basic personality differences between a middle-class Viennese and a Trobriand islander. Over and above this is the 'character' of the individual which is the specific orientation of a specific individual to the social norms defining his culture. Kardiner was interested in showing how this 'basic personality structure' is a function of the methods of child-rearing within a given culture which are themselves dependent upon the general system of social norms.

[1] B. Malinowski: *Sex and Repression in Savage Society* (1937), p. 81.

These examples are sufficient to show the way in which social science has made its influence felt on psychoanalysis. It is only fair to Freud, however, to say that he was well aware of the differences between cultures and that his great importance lay in demonstrating the modification of instinctive drives when they came up against normative pressures. No man was more conscious of the common saying that all psychology is social psychology. His explicit words on this subject will serve to illustrate his own attitude and to summarize the insight of this twentieth-century trend: 'The contrast between Individual Psychology or Social or Group Psychology which at first glance may seem to be full of significance, loses a great deal of its sharpness when it is examined more closely. It is true that Individual Psychology is concerned with the individual man and explores the paths by which he finds satisfaction for his instincts; but only rarely and under certain exceptional conditions is Individual Psychology in a position to disregard the relation of this individual to others. In the individual's mental life someone else is invariably involved, as a model, as an object, as a helper, as an opponent, and so from the very first Individual Psychology is at the same time Social Psychology as well—in this extended but entirely justified sense of the words.'[1] Freud started off with a predominantly biological orientation. But he came to see more and more the infinite plasticity of human beings and the determining influence of their social relationships.

F. Psychology as a theoretical science?

If the nineteenth century marked the self-consciousness or coming of age of psychology, the early twentieth century was characterized by vociferous intimations of the correct career upon which the new adult science should embark. These wranglings are usually referred to as the rise of 'schools.' Woodworth defines a 'school' as 'a group of psychologists who put forward a certain system of ideas designed to point the way that all must follow if psychology is ever to be made a genuine, productive science of both theoretical and practical value.'[2] It is tempting to suggest that the rise of these 'schools' is not explicable just in terms of the different interests and theoretical explanations of the psychologists in question. No doubt the Introspectionists and Gestalt psychologists were mainly interested in perception and cognition, the Behaviourists and animal psychologists in motor activity and learning, the Purposive School and Freudians in motivation. But such understandable differences in interest were surely only partly the cause of the almost fanatical fission of psychology into different 'schools.'

[1] S. Freud: *Group Psychology and the Analysis of the Ego* (1922), pp. 1–2.
[2] R. Woodworth: *Contemporary Schools of Psychology* (Rev. Ed. 1948), p. 3.

Was not there also lurking at the back of the mind of most of the early twentieth-century psychologists the old rationalistic assumption which has been referred to as dogmatic methodism? Does not this well-worn philosophical prejudice about the necessity of following the right method account for much of the wrangling and dissension amongst different 'schools' of psychology?

This claim has been illustrated with reference to those 'schools' who carried on the observationalist tradition—the Introspectionists and Behaviourists who argued about the proper 'data' of psychology and the operationists who saw in operational definition of terms the key to progress in psychology. The Gestalt psychologists were also, to a certain extent, because of their concern with perception, tarred with the same brush. There are long homilies in Koffka's *Principles of Gestalt Psychology* (1935) about the necessity of starting from the 'behavioural' rather than the 'geographical' environment;[1] Köhler constantly emphasizes the point that psychology must start from 'direct experience' which is quite different from what the old sensationists took it to be. They make the point that their experiential starting-point distinguishes them from other 'schools' like the Behaviourists as well as the explanatory concepts which they employ.

There are also other methodological recipes leading to different schools which have not been mentioned. One of the more interesting of these is the school of Allport which puts great emphasis on individual differences and which concludes that psychology should be an 'idiographic' rather than a 'nomothetic' inquiry. 'Somewhere in the interstices of its nomothetic laws psychology has lost the human person as we know him in everyday life. To rescue him and to reinstate him as a psychological datum in his own right is the avowed purpose of the psychology of personality.'[2] Generalizations are to be based on the behaviour of the individual, not upon human behaviour in general. Every trait is *unique*. In view of the frequency of this type of methodological advice we would expect most of Allport's book to be devoted to the study of concrete individual personalities, their life-histories and social contexts. But instead we find an attack on McDougall's 'nomothetic' assumptions (instincts) and a substitution of Allport's own nomothetic assumptions! He calls them 'drives,' 'organic segmental tensions,' 'traits,' and 'attitudes.' He maintains that the purposes of different people are too numerous and too diverse to be traced to a few primal motives. 'Theoretically all adult purposes can be traced back to these seed-forms in infancy. But as the individual matures the bond is broken. The tie is historical, not functional.'[3] Whatever drives,

[1] K. Koffka: *Principles of Gestalt Psychology* (1935), pp. 27–35.
[2] G. W. Allport: *Personality* (1937), p. 558.
[3] *Op. cit.*, p. 321.

drives now. But really McDougall's 'taste' and 'sentiments' are very similar to Allport's 'traits' and 'attitudes.' Allport, however, puts great stress on the present determinants of behaviour—the physical and social environments and the present state of the organism. 'What motivates each person is not some element common to all individuals, but his own particular pattern of tensions.' How, then, do these unique traits of each individual have motivating power? His solution is, of course, a 'nomothetic' solution—the Gestalt principle of 'closure' or drive towards a position of greater pregnance, our old friend the tendency towards equilibrium used by Freud, Spinoza, Herbert Spencer, Fechner, and countless others. Once an activity is undertaken it tends to acquire a certain attraction in itself. Unfinished tasks occasion discomfort, which is removed by 'closing the gap.' McDougall's principle of conative unity and his doctrine of tastes appear in a more up-to-date dress.

Allport's book was therefore a kind of methodological prolegomenon to psychology proper—the study of individual personalities and the 'functionally autonomous' traits from which, together with a detailed description of environmental conditions, behaviour of an individual can be predicted in a given case. What Allport did not bring out sufficiently is that the kind of psychology he envisaged exemplifies a difference in interest rather than the absence of nomothetic assumptions. His idiographic psychology was another name for history or biography. He wanted to know why particular people in concrete social settings do what they do. In order to explain particular events he had to use general or 'nomothetic' assumptions, just as the historian does.[1] No explanation is possible without recourse to general assumptions. There is no reason why psychologists like Allport should not follow the example of the 'understanding' psychologists like Dilthey[2] who maintained, for quite different reasons, that psychology together with the social studies should be 'descriptive' rather than 'explanatory' and should be classed with biography, autobiography, and history. But it should be realized that the difference between psychologists who are interested in setting up hypotheses and testing them and others who are interested in explaining the particular actions of particular people is a difference in interest only. Both types of inquiry presupposes each other and there is really no more reason for Allport to quarrel for methodological reasons with 'nomothetic' psychologists than there is for an historian like Tawney to quarrel with a sociologist like Max Weber, or a social-psychologist like Fromm.

While some psychologists like Allport deprecate the attempt to set up psychological laws, others like Lewin and Hull were fascinated by the

[1] See back ch. i, section 3.
[2] See H. A. Hodges: *William Dilthey* (1944), chs. 2, 3 and 5.

project. And it could be reasonably argued that this has to be done if psychology is to develop as a theoretical science. For, by definition, theoretical science consists in consciously setting up hypotheses, deducing consequences from them, and comparing the deduced consequences with actual observations. Yet the stock insult which is hurled at psychologists is that they have produced no causal laws. 'A string of raw facts,' said James, 'a little gossip and wrangle about opinions; a little classification and generalization on the mere descriptive level . . . but not a single law in the sense in which physics shows us laws, not a single proposition from which any consequences can be causally deduced. . . . This is no science, it is only the hope of science.'[1] There has been a considerable advance in psychology since 1892 when James uttered these celebrated remarks; but the criticism which he raises is still often heard. What lies behind it?

The problem of psychological laws is in part a matter of verbal decision. What are we going to call a 'law'? It is possible to make a rough and ready distinction between general assumptions, working assumptions, and laws. General assumptions are those which we *use* in ordinary life, in history, and in our technological activities without being much interested whether or not they hold universally. Working assumptions are hypotheses which we consciously set up to test in a piece of research and which act as fact finders. Laws are working assumptions which have been rigorously tested by conscious attempts at falsification and which express functional relationships between variables. This may seem rather a rigorous prescription for the use of the word 'law' but it is the one which is most in accordance with scientific usage. Now psychologists certainly have general assumptions; they also have many working assumptions, some of which, like the various forms of the principle of pregnance, are accepted by many different psychologists belonging to different 'schools.' But it is very doubtful whether they have many laws in the sense of statements expressing functional relationships which hold universally, and which have been rigorously tested. And, incidentally, there are very few sciences which have laws in this sense. It is, furthermore, absurd to deny that psychology is 'scientific' because it has not laws in this sense. Such a prescription would rule out practically all sciences except physics, chemistry, and astronomy. All that is required for an inquiry to be a theoretical science is that conscious attempts should be made to overthrow hypotheses. 'By their fruits ye shall know them' is an absurd prescription in this context.

What particular reasons are there, then, why so many seem to be derisive at the prospect of psychology producing laws? One of the commonest objections is that made by the Allport School. They main-

[1] W. James: *Psychology: A Briefer Course* (1892), p. 468.

tain that individuals are unique and that no general assumptions about them could ever hold universally. This, it seems, is an objection which can be quickly disposed of. It is obvious that there are respects in which everything is different from everything else. No two peas are completely alike; every pea and every rabbit is a mass of 'individual differences.' But this did not seem to worry Mendel any more than it worried biologists and physiologists. The planets are quite different; yet Kepler and Newton got on all right. The importance of individual differences depends upon the questions to be asked about peas, rabbits, and planets. Psychology differs from genetics only in degree. All human beings get thirsty and hungry, need to eliminate, need shelter and rest; all human beings learn, remember, solve problems, forget, and have mothers. To test general assumptions about human beings one only has to be able to say 'if under conditions xyz factor A is varied then factor B will vary also, and if factor A is not varied then factor B will not vary either,' and surely it can be said of *any* human being that if he is deprived of food for three days he will salivate when presented with a food stimulus, or that if he is completely deprived of security during his early childhood he will develop certain forms of character disorder. This is the typical form of scientific prediction. Objectors to psychology often muddle prediction with prophecy and ridicule psychologists because they cannot prophesy whether a boy will choose an academic career or whether a politician will break a promise. But such objectors seldom realize that astronomy is almost the only science which can make such long term unconditional predictions,[1] and that this possibility is connected with the special nature of the solar system as a relatively closed system. Our meteorologists are not derided because they cannot predict for a long time ahead the particular type of weather in a particular place. And physicists are not expected to forecast whether the 12.30 to Liverpool Street will be five minutes late or to explain why a boulder rolling down a slope got wedged twenty yards from the bottom. Yet psychologists are often accused of being pseudo-scientists because they cannot make analogous prophecies. A scientific law asserts a functional relation between variables; it is not a Revelation of Destiny.

There are, however, at least two good reasons why the production of psychological laws is likely to be difficult. In the first place the sort of behaviour which we would like to have explained—e.g. cruelty to children—can be regarded as a function of *at least* four distinct types of variable—hereditary endowment, past training (leaving 'traces'), present stimuli (social as well as physical), and initiating physiological conditions. If we could devise experimental set-ups or, better still,

---

[1] This point about astronomy and the distinction between prophecy and prediction I owe to Karl Popper. Ed.

'real-life situations,' in which one variable could be varied at a time, we might have a good chance of getting some sort of a functional relationship. But this has only been done in the limited fields of perception, reflex-action, learning, remembering, and simple problems of primary motivation. In testing the Weber–Fechner law or in establishing simple laws of learning, factors like hereditary endowment and past training can be treated more or less (but not entirely[1]) as empirical constants or, as in the case of rats, they can be rigidly controlled by selective breeding and training. Also control over stimulus variables is possible. But these fields are not as exciting as the fields of criminal behaviour, sexual abnormalities, megalomaniac tendencies, and so on. These behaviour patterns depend far more on hereditary endowment and on past training than on present stimulus variables or initiating physiological conditions. A kleptomaniac will steal in practically any physical or social environment, even if he is hungry, thirsty, or sexually excited. How can we devise experiments to test hypotheses about the hereditary and training factors which have determined this anti-social trait? Have conscious attempts been made to falsify an assumption like the Freudian hypothesis that both avarice and philanthropy are caused by anal eroticism in infancy? If not, how could it be conclusively tested?

This can be summarized by saying that in cases where there is a correlation between behaviour and antecedent stimulus items it is relatively easy to formulate and test hypotheses of functional dependence—e.g. perception, learning. But in complex forms of behaviour, where the relevant antecedent variables are either hereditary endowment or past training, correlation between behaviour and antecedent stimulus items is practically nil and it is very difficult to formulate precisely or to test hypotheses of functional dependence between behaviour and the antecedent variables of past experience or hereditary endowment.

The second sort of difficulty is moral rather than technical. Recourse is often had to 'intervening variables' like 'traces' by means of which past experience is presumed to influence present behaviour via the brain and nervous system. Now variations of brain tissue and nerve connections are very difficult to observe. The difficulty is not just a technical one; there is also a moral objection to experimenting on people's brains. We only square it with our consciences in cases like pre-frontal leucotomy when our interests are technological—i.e. we want to cure the sufferer of something. We object to extirpation experiments in the interests of theoretical science just as we would object to purposely inducing a diseased liver in a healthy person. Yet experiments on animals cannot tell us many of the things which we want to

---

[1] See, for instance, Krech and Crutchfield: *Theory and Problems of Social Psychology* (1948), ch. iii.

know about the brain-processes of human beings. This sort of objection applies also to all forms of experimental conditioning under controlled social conditions which might be of interest to psycho-analysts. As parents we would not, in an experimental way, smack our children soundly every time they had an accident in order to provide evidence for psycho-analysts. Yet without deliberate control of situations and the deliberate variation of one variable at a time it is very difficult to establish precise functional relationships. The practice of psychologists reflects this limitation upon the types of experiment that are morally allowable. On the one hand we find methodologically competent psychologists, full of anxiety about being scientifically respectable, sticking mainly to rats and asking relatively simple questions about them. On the other hand we find technologists like psycho-analysts *using* vaguely expressed assumptions in their attempts to cure individuals and to devise educational and reformative institutions. The criticism of the former class of people is that it is difficult to see how sticking to rats is going to help us to explain the more complicated behaviour of human beings who can talk and whose environment is predominantly social; the criticism of the latter is not so much that technological pressure has forced them to develop working assumptions about the determinants of more complex behaviour-patterns, but that they have made few conscious and sustained attempts to *overthrow* the assumptions which they use. Work along these lines has been summarized by Sears in his *Survey of Objective Studies of Psychoanalytic Concepts* in 1943; but such work is only just beginning.[1]

Nevertheless, in spite of these difficulties, many assumptions put forward about the more complex forms of behaviour have been falsified. This has been partly due to the counter-examples produced by historians and social scientists to the over-simplified assumptions of people like Freud and McDougall and partly to the progress made by technologists in their own fields. Freud himself discarded many of the assumptions which he started with because of the counter-examples which his practical work provided. *Using* assumptions for practical purposes is an indirect way of testing them as has been demonstrated in the case of planners who have had to discard certain assumptions produced by economists. The trouble, of course, about an indirect test like a successful cure of a patient is that the variables are often unknown and always difficult to control. A cure might fail in psycho-analysis; but one would be chary of saying straight away that the assumptions used by the analyst were falsified, because the situation is so complex.[2]

[1] See, for instance, J. F. Brown: *The Psycho-dynamics of Abnormal Behaviour* (1940), ch. xxii.
[2] For fuller discussion of this problem see the editor's *Cure, Cause, and Motive Analysis*, April 1950.

Failure might be due either to the inadequacy of his theoretical assumptions about the causes of maladjustment, or to his failure as an historian or detective with this particular patient in tracking down the particular incidents in the patient's past which occasioned the repression of unacceptable 'wishes,' or to the inadequacy of his assumptions about attitude-changing (e.g. about 'identification,' 'transference,' 'abreaction,' and so on), or to the analyst himself being a poor technologist in the sense of lacking himself the necessary knack or personality to effect changes of attitude in his patient. Christian scientists often cure people of physical ailments; but we would be chary of saying that such cures act as confirmations of their assumptions. Indeed we would probably say that the cure was effected in spite of rather than because of their theoretical assumptions.

Psychologists nowadays are asked to tender advice about the improvement of conditions in industry, about bringing up children and educational curricula; they are consulted by magistrates, community organizations, the armed forces, public corporations, and parsons. The question is not whether they or the people who consult them should have general assumptions about the causes of various types of behaviour; they cannot avoid having them. The question is rather whether the assumptions which they use should be more or less adequate. This can only be discovered by consciously constructing test situations where the nature of the assumption in question permits it and by indulging in small-scale pilot technological experiments where moral or technical objections prevent a direct test. In other words, educational, industrial, and medical psychology would benefit greatly by the development of a more theoretical and experimental attitude on the part of many practitioners. Technology always goes hand in hand with theoretical science but is not a substitute for it. In the case of Freud we have a very good example of a technologist with very strong theoretical interests; it is a pity that some of his followers do not take after him in this respect.

This understandable and laudable endeavour to develop laws in psychology has often been confused with the rather different ambition of developing an all-inclusive theory of human behaviour. Hence the pining for the coming of psychology's Galileo long before the time when psychology has any well-established laws which might be deduced from such a theory. Indeed it might be said that the period of the 'schools' of psychology represents a climax in this conception of psychology. For Lewin, Hull, McDougall, Tolman, and perhaps Freud in his early physiologizing had this ambition in common. But those who conceive the role of the psychologist in this light seldom reflect on the glaring disparities which exist between the types of thing to be explained.

There are, first of all, what we call human actions. We cannot begin to understand what these are, or to recognize particular cases of them, unless we have a grasp of a whole family of concepts, such as was sketched by Aristotle, like 'reason,' 'purpose,' 'desire,' 'means to an end,' 'intention,' and so on. We assume that a man has certain 'ends' together with information about means that are efficient and socially appropriate for attaining them, and that he will take the means required, other things being equal. Any explanation of actions must, logically speaking, be couched in terms such as these. McDougall, it has been argued, saw that 'purpose' was a fundamental and irreducible concept for understanding and explaining human behaviour; but he was misled by this conceptual insight into thinking that all behaviour must therefore be compounded out of a finite number of built-in purposes.[1] It is significant that much of the criticism of his theory came in the first place from anthropology. For, surely, given that the concept of 'purpose,' together with that of 'rule-following,' is taken as logically irreducible in explaining human actions, it is largely a matter of anthropological and historical investigation to discover what content, in terms of particular goals and rules, is to be given to this formal explanatory schema in different societies.[2]

Tolman, too, assumed the irreducibility of 'purpose' but tried to translate this family of concepts into a bizarre behaviouristic jargon. He was, however, more interested than McDougall in what might be called human performances such as perceiving, remembering, learning, and judging. Such performances are unintelligible unless we understand the criteria which are written into the concepts which describe them. For to perceive is to see something that is there, to remember is to be right about the past, to know is to have good grounds for what we assert, to learn is to get something right or to improve. In dealing with such performances Tolman borrowed considerably from Gestalt psychology, another of the recent 'schools.' But the Gestalt psychologists themselves, in developing their theories of perception, were not altogether clear about what they were explaining. The question which Koffka posed, 'Why do things look as they do?', obviously requires a very different *sort* of answer from the problems posed by illusions or distortions of perception.[3] It is considerations such as these which lead many to regard Gestalt psychology as having contributed more to epistemology than to empirical psychology.

The mention of illusions and distortions introduces a whole range of human phenomena which require a very different type of explanation from that given for actions and performances. Attention has

---

[1] See *supra* pp. 707.
[2] See R. S. Peters: *The Concept of Motivation* (1958), ch. I.
[3] See D. W. Hamlyn: *The Psychology of Perception* (1957).

already been drawn to the sort of phenomena which Freud's theory explained—lapses from actions and performances, things like dreams and visions which do not rank as actions or performances at all, and things like obsessions and compulsions which are more or less caricatures of actions and performances. Whether Freud was right in thinking that an explanation can be given of such phenomena in terms of a concept such as that of 'wish' rather than in physiological terms is a further question. But certainly they require a very different *sort* of explanation. So also do things like salivation and eye-lid blinks dealt with by conditioning theory. For, *prima facie* at any rate, these are not things done by someone for the sake of something, to come up to some standard. As Ryle put it: 'The classification and diagnosis of exhibitions of our mental impotences requires specialized research methods. The explanation of the exhibitions of our mental competences often requires nothing but ordinary good sense, or it may require the specialized methods of economists, scholars, strategists, and examiners.'[1]

The point is that explanations both in terms of 'ordinary good sense' and as given by specialists such as economists, historians, strategists, anthropologists, and so on, all presuppose the basic explanatory model of a man taking means to an end in accordance with rules. Physiological explanations might do for salivation or slips of the tongue; but they will not do for actions and performances since descriptions containing man-imposed standards and criteria could not be deduced from descriptions merely of bodily movements, or from any theory which was couched only in such naturalistic terms, e.g. a mechanical one.

The word 'explanation,' of course, is ambiguous; for some would regard the discovery of necessary conditions of actions and performances as going a long way towards explaining them. Much of physiological psychology, together with the study of the mechanisms underlying perceiving, remembering, thinking, and a great variety of motor performances falls into this category. The trouble starts when ambitious theorists, such as Hull, think that such a physiological theory will eventually be able to explain human actions and performances in the sense of developing a theory of 'colourless movements' from which descriptions of behaviour could eventually be *deduced*. This seems to be a logically outrageous programme; for though movements might be predicted from a theory couched in terms of 'colourless movements,' actions and performances could not be unless the predictor already had the family of concepts necessary to recognize the movements of the body as parts of human actions or performances. Similarly, given that actions and performances could already be recognized and classified, it might be possible to correlate these with movements of the brain,

[1] G. Ryle: *The Concept of Mind* (1949), p. 326.

and from a physiological theory to predict actions and performances indirectly by means of such correlations. But such predictions would presuppose the ability to handle the family of concepts connected with action which occupy a different logical status from those connected with mere movements. The descriptions of actions and performances could never be *deduced* from the physiological theory alone.

The study of what Ryle calls our 'mental impotences' and of the necessary conditions of action does not exhaust the different types of questions to be answered by psychologists. There are also genetic questions to do with how individual purposes, traits, and abilities are acquired, and how individual differences develop within the same society. There are also questions about maturation levels for different skills and performances such as Piaget studied. This is the field of learning theory, social psychology, and of genetic studies. The existence of 'schools' of psychology bears witness as much to a genuine interest in answering quite different questions about human behaviour as to the mistaken belief that scientific studies are made by people who adopt the right sort of method and that there is only one proper way of developing psychology. This disastrous delusion has been encouraged by the belief, so prominent in the first fifty years of the twentieth century, that there could be one all-inclusive psychological theory. Does not the yearning for a deductive system in psychology as abstract and as all-embracing as that of physics spring from the Cartesian assumption that there are two realms, that of matter and that of mind, and that each must have its own very abstract laws as Spinoza suggested? Physics achieves its abstractness and generality by confining itself to asking questions about the most general characteristics of bodies— their motion, shape, and so on—including human beings. Psychology confines itself to a specific class of objects and asks far less abstract and very different types of questions about them. Can it be that in the welter of modern talk about psychological theory we can see evidence of the persistence of the old rationalist tradition?

G. Conclusion

It has been shown, in this final chapter, that despite the setting up of different 'schools' of psychology in the early twentieth century, certain very general trends are discernible which survive the methodological wrangles. The observationalist tradition was continued by the Introspectionists and, with minor modifications, by the Behaviourists. We then have the development of the concept of purpose in various forms by McDougall and Freud. This reaction against the old observationalist tradition was supplemented by the Gestalt movement which was a revolt against sensory atomism. The stress on 'field' and organization was then supplemented by the increasing influence of social science on the early purposive theories. Behaviourism has continued but, in the work of Tolman and Hull, it too has been strongly influenced by the concepts of purpose and of organization. The emphasis on purpose, organization, and social conditioning, together with an increased interest in children and in methodological questions connected with the status of psychology, are the trends which distinguish twentieth-century psychology from that of the nineteenth century. The similarities rather than the differences between the different 'schools' have been stressed in order to bring out these trends. The existence of 'schools' has been due as much to the influence of the old rationalist trust in method as to divergences in interest and explanatory concepts. There are signs, however, that the old almost fanatical fissions are beginning to close up. Modern Behaviourists are much milder in their methodological strictures of others; they are even beginning to do something about testing some Freudian assumptions, and have incorporated a lot of purposive psychology into their systems. In the work of Lewin and J. F. Brown a rapprochement is evident between Gestalt and Freudian psychology. Bartlett's social psychology and research on remembering show a subtle blend of Gestalt concepts, introspectionism, purposivism, and the influence of social science. These are welcome signs. For methodology is no substitute for speculation and methodological wrangles have tended to cause psychologists to ignore the important contributions to theoretical understanding made by other schools and to shroud the similarities between different working assumptions. The cross-fertilization of different theories—e.g. Freudian with Marxist theory—is one of the most common causes for the development of new theories. Speculation is the life-blood of science; too much methodological purism may tend to dry it up. The day soon may dawn when psychologists will tackle the problems that interest them, whether scientific or technological or historical, in their own way, combining imagination in formulating hypotheses with ingenuity and thoroughness in testing them. And they may forbear to write those tedious introductory chapters, so common in textbooks of the first forty years of the twentieth century, in which they maintained that their way of doing psychology was the only scientifically respectable one. One bright idea which is testable is worth a whole book of advice on how to make psychology scientific.

'Some of the major disasters of mankind have been produced by the narrowness of men with a good methodology. . . . To set limits to speculation is treason to the future.'[1]

[1] A. N. Whitehead: *The Function of Reason* (1929), pp. 8 and 30.

LIST OF MAJOR OMITTED SECTIONS

VOLUME I

PART I

THE CHARACTER OF PRIMITIVE THOUGHT

Chapter I
  Sec. 1. Characteristics of primitive thought.
  Sec. 2. Origin of psychology from personal interests. Interest in the living produces theories of feelings and faculties. Interest in the dead gives rise to ideas of the soul as distinct from the body.

SCIENTIFIC VIEWS AND RELIGIOUS BELIEFS

Chapter II
  Sec. 1. Development of scientific from general observation: science and animism.

THE PSYCHOLOGY OF THE ATOMISTS

Chapter IV
  Sec. 4. Materialism in Diogenes of Apollonia.

THE PLATONIC VIEW OF MAN (I)

Chapter VII
  Sec. 1. Plato: his ideal and his relation to previous writers; his interest in science.

THE PLATONIC VIEW OF MAN (III)

Chapter IX
  Sec. 3. Platonism after Plato: Speusippus and Xenocrates.

PSYCHOLOGICAL THEORIES AFTER ARISTOTLE

Chapter XIV
  Sec. 1. The Peripapetics: Theophrastus and naturalism.
  Sec. 2. Eudemus and the theological trend.
  Sec. 3. Complex views of Aristoxenus and Dichaearchus.
  Sec. 4. Strato: further development of a naturalistic theory.

THE STOIC THEORY OF MAN

Chapter XV

Sec. 6. Stoic classification of emotions. Stoic ideal.

PROGRESS OF THEORY IN THE LAST CENTURY B.C.

Chapter XVII

Sec. 1. General tendency of thought in the Academy: Arcesilas.

Sec. 2. Carneades.

Sec. 3. Modifications of Stoicism: Panaetius: Posidonius.

Sec. 4. Critolaus the Peripapetic.

Sec. 5. Eclecticism in Andronicus of Rhodes.

Sec. 6. Cicero.

THE IDEA OF THE SOUL IN SOME EASTERN WRITINGS

Chapter XVIII

Sec. 1. Indian writings: (i) Classification, (ii) Vedantic psychology, (iii) Sankhya doctrine, (iv) Nyava and Vaiseshika, (v) Buddhist theory.

Sec. 2. Egyptian beliefs.

Sec. 3. Persian beliefs.

Sec. 4. Later beliefs derived from Eastern sources. Mithraism: Hermetic writings.

PART II

THE UNION OF GREEK AND HEBREW THEORIES

Chapter II

Sec. 8. Philo's doctrine of Divine power and daemons; the Logos: the generic powers: virtue and vision of God.

THE ECLECTIC WRITERS OF THE FIRST CENTURY A.D.

Chapter III

Sec. 1. Eclectic writers: Eudorus, Arius Didymus, Ammonius: changes in traditional doctrine.

Sec. 2. Plutarch: his dualism: mystical tendenceis: interest in science of revelations.

PROGRESS OF THE CHRISTIAN DOCTRINE IN THE
ALEXANDRIAN SCHOOLS (1)

Chapter V

Sec. 1. Attitude of the Apologists: Justin Martyr: Athenagoras: Tatian.

MEDICAL INFLUENCES FROM ERASISTRATUS TO GALEN

Chapter VII

Sec. 1. Erasistratus and Herophilus: beginning of a theory of nerves.

THE NEO-PLATONIC IDEA OF MAN

Chapter VIII

Sec. 2. Metaphysical basis: idea of the One and its forms: the scale of Being: consequences of this theory: opposition to materialism.

ECCLESIASTICAL WRITERS FROM TERTULLIAN TO NEMESIUS

Chapter IX

Sec. 1. Tertullian's views on the soul.

Sec. 2. Lactantius: his dualism: details of his theory.

Sec. 3. Gregory of Nyssa: man's place in the cosmos: spiritualistic theory of the soul.

Sec. 4. Gregory of Nyssa (cont.): theory of conduct: the affections: uses Stoicism: on sin.

Sec. 5. Nemesius: general characteristics: soul incorporeal: relation to Aristotle and others: soul and body: parts of the soul: emphasis on activity and consciousness: his eclecticism.

VOLUME II

PART I

THE INFLUENCE OF THEOLOGY

Chapter I

Sec. 3. Origin of the soul.

SCHOLARSHIP AND TRADITION

Chapter II

Sec. 1. The Commentators (except Alexander).

Sec. 2. Other literary influences.

PROGRESS OF DOCTRINES IN FIFTH AND SIXTH CENTURIES
Chapter III
Sec. 2. Christian writers: Claudianus, Cassiodorus.
Sec. 3. Christian writers: the Eastern line.

THE ARABIAN TEACHERS
Chapter IV
Sec. 1. Arabian literature and politics.
Sec. 2. Al-Farabi and the Brethren of Purity.

PART II

THE GROUNDWORK OF MEDIAEVAL DOCTRINES
Chapter I
Sec. 2. Physiology and psychology.
Sec. 6. Immortality of soul.
Sec. 7. Matter and form.

THE BEGINNINGS OF MEDIAEVAL PSYCHOLOGY
Chapter II
Sec. 2. The tenth century: Arab influence.
Sec. 4. Richard of St. Victor. Isaac of Stella: Alcher.

THE THIRTEENTH CENTURY
Chapter III
Sec. 1. Literary activity: the translators.
        Gundissalinus: William of Auvergne.
Sec. 5. Problems of love: the individual and society.

THE SIXTEENTH CENTURY
Chapter V
Sec. 7. Melanchthon.
Sec. 8. Part of influence of new movement on theories of education.
Sec. 5. The Marburg School.

PART III

EXPANSION OF PSYCHOLOGY IN THE SEVENTEENTH CENTURY
Chapter IV
Sec. 1. Educational reformers: Comenius to Locke.
Sec. 2. Literary expression of the new views: Bacon: Overbury:
        the drama: oratory: Pascal: the 'maxims.'

PART IV

CONTINENTAL EMPIRICISM

Chapter II
Sec. 3. The Italian School.

THE BEGINNINGS OF GERMAN PSYCHOLOGY

Chapter III
Sec. 3. The empirical tendency.
Sec. 5. Tiedemann.

INFLUENCE AND APPLICATIONS OF PSYCHOLOGY

Chapter IV
Sec. 1. Enthusiasm (Ethics and Religion).

VOLUME III

PART I

THE TRANSITION IN BRITAIN AND FRANCE

Chapter I
Sec. 1. The Scottish School.
Sec. 4. From Scotland to France.

THE TRANSITION IN GERMANY

Chapter II
Sec. 1. Fichte, Schelling, Hegel.
Sec. 2. Fries.

THE TRANSITION IN GERMANY (CONTINUED)

Chapter III
Sec. 2. The conflict of ideas.
Sec. 4. Minor phases.

PART II

GENERAL SCIENTIFIC TENDENCIES

Chapter I
Sec. 6. Some general considerations.

FROM FECHNER TO WUNDT

Chapter II
Sec. 3. Stumpf: G. E. Müller.

REPRESENTATIVE TYPES OF THEORY

Chapter III

Sec. 5. Biological tendencies: Jodl.

THE PROGRESS OF PSYCHOLOGY: GENERAL SURVEY

Chapter V

Sec. 2. Italian writers.
Sec. 3. Psychology in America. (Until W. James.)
    Appendix: A geographical survey.

THE SCOPE OF MODERN PSYCHOLOGY

Chapter VI

Sec. 1. Developments in method.

    (a) The question of measurements.
    (b) Psychometry.
    (c) Time.
    (d) Experimental treatment of thought.
    (e) Applied psychology.

Sec. 2. Social psychology.
Sec. 3. Child psychology.
Sec. 4. Animal psychology.
Sec. 5. Psycho-analysis.
Sec. 6. Criminal psychology.

BIBLIOGRAPHY

BIBLIOGRAPHY FOR STUDENTS

Students will find that most of the important passages from the major figures in the history of psychology are included in the work by Benjamin Rand called *The Classical Psychologists* (Constable & Co., 1912). In addition students may find the following brief bibliography a help in their reading. Publishers or dates are only included where it is anticipated that difficulty will be encountered in tracing the work in question.

PART I

TEXTS

Aristotle: *De Anima* (for Pre-Socratic theories as well as for Aristotle's own theory).

Plato: *Phaedo, Theatetus, Republic* IV, VI, IX, X, and *Timaeus*.

M. C. Nahm: *Selections from Early Greek Philosophers* (New York).

T. V. Smith: *Philosophers Speak for Themselves—Thales to St. Augustine* (University of Chicago).

COMMENTARIES

J. Burnet: *Early Greek Philosophy*.

J. Burnet: *Greek Philosophy: Thales to Plato*.

W. K. Guthrie: *The Greek Philosophers from Thales to Aristotle*.

G. Grube: *Plato's Thought*.

F. M. Cornford: *Plato's Theory of Knowledge*.

F. M. Cornford: *Plato's Cosmology*.

W. D. Ross: *Plato's Theory of Ideas*.

W. D. Ross: *Aristotle*.

W. Jaeger: *Aristotle*.

J. Beare: *Greek Theories of Elementary Cognition from Alcmaeon to Aristotle*.

R. Onians: *Origins of European Thought*.

D. Hamlyn: *Sensation and Perception*.

PART II

TEXTS

Diogenes Laertius: *Lives and Opinions of Eminent Philosophers* (Ed. Loheb). Book VII on *Stoics* and Book X on *Epicureans*.

Lucretius: *De Rerum Natura* (Ed. Loheb), Book III.

W. J. Oates: *The Stoic and Epicurean Philosophers.*
Plotinus: *Enneades* (Ed. Loheb), Books VII–IX.
St. Augustine: *Confessions* and *On the Trinity*, Book X.
St. Thomas Aquinas: *Selected Writings* (Everyman Ed.).
Roger Bacon: *Opus Maius* (Trans. Philadelphia, 1928).
R. McKeon: *Selections from Mediaeval Philosophers.*
E. Cassirer: *The Renaissance Philosophy of Man.*
Macchiavelli: *The Prince.*
Montaigne: *Essays.*

COMMENTARIES

E. Bevan: *Stoics and Sceptics.*
E. Zeller: *Stoics, Epicureans, and Sceptics.*
E. Caird: *The Evolution of Theology in the Early Greek Philosophers.*
C. Bailey: *The Greek Atomists and Epicureans.*
W. R. Inge: *The Philosophy of Plotinus.*
T. Whittaker: *The Neo-Platonists.*
J. Maritain, E. Gilson, and others: *A Monument to St. Augustine* (Sheed and Ward, 1934).
D. Saliba: *Étude sur la métaphysique d'Avicenne* (Paris, 1927).
Carra de Vaux: *Avicenne* (Paris, 1900).
E. Renan: *Averroes et l'Averroisme* (Paris, 1861).
C. J. Webb: *John of Salisbury.*
A. C. Pegis: *St. Thomas and the Problem of the Soul* (Toronto, 1934).
C. M. O'Donnell: *The Psychology of St. Bonaventura and St. Thomas Aquinas* (Washington, 1937).
W. B. Monahan: *The Psychology of St. Thomas Aquinas.*
J. H. Bridges: *The Life and Work of Roger Bacon.*
H. O. Taylor: *The Mediaeval Mind.*
H. de Wulf: *History of Mediaeval Philosophy.*
E. Gilson: *Philosophy in the Middle Ages.*
F. Copleston, S.J.: *History of Philosophy*, Vol. II.
O. Lottin: *Psychologie et morale aux XIIe et XIIIe siècles.* Tome 1. Problèmes de psychologie.
J. B. Banborough: *The Little World of Man* (Renaissance psychological theory).
D. W. Hamlyn: *Sensation and Perception.*
J. Wynn Reeves: *Body and Mind in Western Thought* (Penguin Ed.).

PART III

TEXTS

F. Bacon: *Novum Organum.*
R. Descartes · *Discourse on Method.*

R. Descartes: *The Passions of the Soul.*

T. Hobbes: *Leviathan*, Part I.

B. Spinoza: *Ethics*, Parts II and III.

G. Leibniz: *Monadology, New Essays*, and *A New System of Nature and of the Communication of Substances.*

J. Locke: *Essay Concerning the Human Understanding*, Books 1 and 2.

G. Berkeley: *A New Theory of Vision.*

D. Hume: *Treatise on Human Nature*, Parts I and II.

D. Hartley: *Observation of Man, His Frame, His Duty, and His Expectations.*

J. Butler: *Sermons on Human Nature*, 1, 2, 3, 11.

T. Reid: *Essays on the Intellectual Powers of Man.*

T. Brown: *Lectures on the Philosophy of the Human Mind.*

James Mill: *Analysis of the Phenomena of the Human Mind.*

A. Bain: *The Senses and the Intellect.*

E. de Condillac: *Treatise on Sensations.*

C. Bonnet: *Analytical Essay on the Faculties of the Soul.*

F. Maine de Biran: *Essay upon the Foundations of Psychology.*

W. Wundt: *Principles of Physiological Psychology.*

W. Wundt: *Outlines of Psychology.*

COMMENTARIES

E. Boring: *History of Experimental Psychology.*

E. Boring: *Sensation and Perception in the History of Experimental Psychology.*

D. Hamlyn: *Sensation and Perception.*

H. C. Warren: *History of Associationist Psychology.*

N. Smith: *Studies in the Cartesian Philosophy.*

S. Mellone: *The Dawn of Modern Thought: Descartes, Spinoza, Leibniz.*

E. Boyce-Gibson: *The Philosophy of Descartes.*

S. Hampshire: *Spinoza* (Penguin Ed.).

R. S. Peters: *Hobbes* (Penguin Ed.).

G. J. Warnock: *Berkeley* (Penguin Ed.).

R. L. Saw: *Leibniz* (Penguin Ed.).

B. Russell: *The Philosophy of Leibniz.*

G. Croom-Robertson: *Hobbes.*

C. Morris: *Locke, Berkeley, and Hume.*

D. J. O'Connor: *John Locke* (Penguin Ed.).

A. H. Basson: *Hume* (Penguin Ed.)

J. Passmore: *Hume's Intentions.*

A. Seth: *Scottish Philosophy.*

E. A. Burtt: *The Metaphysical Foundations of Modern Science.*

B. Willey: *The Seventeenth Century Background.*

A. N. Whitehead: *Science and the Modern World*, Chapters I–VI.

H. Hoffding: *History of Modern Philosophy*.
E. Bréhier: *Histoire de la Philosophie*.

PART IV

TEXTS

I. Kant: *Critique of Judgement*, Part II.
J. Herbart: *A Text-book in Psychology*.
F. Beneke: *A Textbook of Psychology as Natural Science*.
G. Fechner: *Elements of Psycho-physics*.
H. von Helmholtz: *A Manual of Physiological Optics*.
E. Hering: *Theory of Light Sensation*.
R. Lotze: *Outlines of Psychology*.
H. Spencer: *The Principles of Psychology*.
J. Ward: *Psychological Principles*.
G. Stout: *Analytical Psychology*.
G. Stout: *Manual of Psychology*.
W. James: *Principles of Psychology*.

COMMENTARIES

G. Murphy: *Historical Introduction to Modern Psychology*.
J. C. Flugel: *A Hundred Years of Psychology*.
J. Passmore: *A Hundred Years of Philosophy*.
E. Boring: *History of Experimental Psychology*.
E. Boring: *Sensation and Perception in the History of Experimental Psychology*.
D. W. Hamlyn: *Sensation and Perception*.
W. B. Pillsbury: *History of Psychology*.
A. Zillboorg: *History of Medical Psychology*.
A. Roback: *History of American Psychology*.

Texts and commentaries for the final chapter on 'Twentieth-Century Theories' are referred to either in the text or in footnotes. For background to the methodological commentary in this chapter and in the edition generally students can consult:

S. Stebbing: *A Modern Introduction to Logic*, Part II.
J. O. Wisdom: *Foundations of Inference in Natural Science*, Part I.
S. E. Toulmin: *The Philosophy of Science*.
A. N. Whitehead: *The Function of Reason*.
K. R. Popper: *The Open Society and Its Enemies*, Vol. II, Chapter 25.
R. S. Peters: *The Concept of Motivation*.

For methodological problems arising in modern psychology students are advised to study *The Psychological Review*, *Mind*, and *Proceedings of the Aristotelian Society*—especially symposia in Supplementary Vols. XIV, XX, XXI, XXIII, XXVI.

INDEX

Abelard, P., 226, 271, 272
Ach, N., 693
Adelard of Bath, 271, 301
Adler, A., 717, 718, 719, 724, 728–30
Adorno, T. W., 737
Adrian, E. D., 709, 738, 739
Albertus Magnus (Albert the Great),
  262, 263, 280–4, 301, 303
Alcmaeon, 52–4, 110
Alcuin, 267
Alexander of Aphrodisias, 234–5, 245,
  312
Alexander of Hales, 262, 278–80, 311
Alexander, F., 719
Alhazen, 250–5, 297, 302, 303, 410
Alkindi, 244–6
Allport, G. W., 752–5
Anaxagoras, 43, 45–7, 54
Anaximander, 40
Anaximenes, 39, 40, 54, 113
Anselm, 367
Aquinas, T.: see Thomas Aquinas, St.
Aristippus, 66–8, 164
Aristotle, 33, 34, 55, 75, 83, 94–139,
  143, 144, 145, 146, 147, 148, 152,
  153, 154, 157, 163, 164, 179, 193,
  194, 199, 200, 202, 204, 205, 206,
  210, 212, 225, 226, 227, 231, 233,
  234, 235, 238, 240, 242, 243, 245,
  246, 247, 248, 249, 250, 251, 252,
  254, 259, 260, 264, 271, 276, 279,
  281, 282, 283, 284, 285, 287, 289,
  290, 294, 312, 313, 314, 321, 322,
  323, 328, 339, 362, 365, 366, 371,
  372, 378, 385, 396, 409, 412, 415,
  422, 431, 433, 434, 440, 444, 449,
  453, 458, 465, 473, 553, 557, 561,
  564, 565, 576, 577, 579, 583, 584,
  601, 602, 640, 664, 685, 722, 744,
  759
Aristoxenus, 206
Arnauld, A., 407
Asclepiades, 195–6, 199
Athenaeus, 196–7, 198
Aubrey, J., 380
Augustine, St., 31, 143, 144, 145, 181,
  190, 214–25, 226, 228, 229, 230,
  231, 232, 239, 260, 271, 273, 274,
  278, 282, 286, 293, 309, 310, 318,
  325, 354, 365, 388, 389, 392, 473,
  492, 673, 674
Avenarius, R., 514–16, 685
Averroes (Ibn Roshd), 226, 255–7, 312
Avicebron, 279
Avicenna (Ibn Sina), 246–50, 279

Bacon, F., 25, 26, 290, 319, 321, 331,
  335–6, 339, 349–54, 355, 374,
  380, 384, 392, 467, 490, 700
Bacon, R., 251, 289, 290, 293, 301–3,
  311, 317
Bain, A., 352, 456–65, 499, 500, 604,
  660, 665, 666, 671, 675–81, 683,
  692
Baldwin, J. M., 675
Bard, P., 741
Bartlett, F. C., 694, 739, 749, 762
Bastian, C., 621, 624
Beaunis, H., 500, 503
Bell, C., 625, 633
Benedict, R., 748
Beneke, F. E., 336, 456, 533, 534,
  563–74, 606
Bergson, H., 493, 496, 501, 502, 690
Berkeley, G., 357, 410, 420, 423–9,
  467, 471, 485, 612
Bernard, C., 626, 667, 741
Bernard, L. L., 748
Bernoulli, D., 340
Bernstein, J., 589
Bichat, M. F. X., 474, 493, 495, 575,
  616, 617, 618, 741
Binet, A., 502–4, 535, 734
Boccaccio, 306
Boerhaave, H., 346, 438, 522, 614
Boethius, 271, 275
Bonaventura, St., 263, 289, 291, 292,
  293
Bonnet, C., 469, 478–81, 482, 483,
  484, 485, 490, 613, 616, 617,
  656
Borelli, G. A., 348
Boring, E. G., 691 (footnote), 738
  (footnote)
Bouillaud, J. B., 620, 621
Bradley, F. H., 676
Brentano, F., 601–4
Breuer, J., 716
Bridgman, P. W., 700
Broca, P., 621, 622, 740
Brown, J. F., 534 (footnote), 728, 757
  (footnote), 762
Brown, T., 444, 447, 449, 450, 451,
  452, 461
Bruno, G., 267
Buffon, G. L., 468, 525, 526, 613, 617
Buhler, C., 734
Buridan, J., 296–7
Burke, E., 747
Burt, C., 736
Butler, J., 724

Cabanis, P. J. G., 469, 472-8, 489, 490, 492, 493, 495, 496, 497, 498, 575
Campanella, T., 318, 321, 351
Cannon, W. B., 714, 741
Cardanus, J., 319, 322
Carus, C. G., 620
Cattell, J. McK., 734
Charcot, J. M., 441, 502, 621, 622, 651, 716
Chrysippus, 150, 155, 157, 171, 196, 201, 227
Cicero, 144, 152, 153, 163, 371, 374, 473
Claparède, E., 691 (footnote)
Cleanthes, 151
Clement of Alexandria, 144, 145, 184-91, 192, 225, 229
Comenius, J. A., 733
Comte, A., 498, 601, 666, 744, 747
Condillac, E. B. de, 321, 444, 448, 462, 466, 468-73, 474, 475, 476, 477, 479, 480, 482, 483, 487, 489, 492, 494, 495, 496, 497, 525, 526, 527, 557
Condorcet, M. J. de C., 474
Constantinus Africanus, 270, 271
Cook, C., 733
Cooley, C., 747
Copernicus, N., 51, 337, 338, 380, 717
Cournot, A. A., 493
Cousin, V., 494
Croom-Robertson, G., 431, 464
Crutchfield, R., 749, 756 (footnote)
Cudworth, R., 386, 419, 453

Dante Alighieri, 291, 306
Darwin, C., 36, 353, 456, 460, 526, 529, 611, 648, 651, 660, 661, 670-4, 694, 695, 708, 709, 731, 732, 737
Darwin, E., 447, 450
David of Dinant, 279
Dax, M., 621
Democritus, 38, 47-51, 54, 83, 102, 111, 113, 161, 165, 377
Descartes, R., 69, 190, 223, 237, 274, 288, 335-6, 339, 340, 341, 342, 343, 344, 346, 347, 348, 353, 354-6, 357, 358, 359-70, 371, 372, 373, 374, 375, 376, 377, 387, 388, 394, 395, 396-9, 400, 405, 407, 415, 417, 418, 419, 420, 421, 429, 433, 434, 437, 444, 458, 467, 472, 473, 475, 483, 491, 509, 522, 525, 526, 537, 538, 583, 615, 625, 668, 696, 698, 744
Destutt de Tracy, A., 495, 496
Diderot, D., 466-7, 468, 474, 526
Dilly, A., 376

Dilthey, W., 753
Diogenes of Apollonia, 54, 113
Diogenes Laertius, 156
Dumont, L., 650
Duns Scotus, 267, 289, 293-5, 297

Ebbinghaus, H., 516-18
Eckhart, (Meister) J., 273, 289, 290, 292-3, 543
Ehrenfels, C. von, 711, 712
Ellis, H., 732
Empedocles, 37, 42-5, 48, 54, 102, 110, 111, 287
Epictetus, 157, 371
Epicurus, 42, 145, 158-65, 206, 259, 377, 378
Erasmus, D., 326, 327
Erikson, E., 722
Eriugena, J. S., 267-9
Esquirol, J., 497
Euclid, 380
Euripides, 145
Eysenck, H., 731, 736

Fabricius, H., 315
Fechner, G. T., 506, 508, 534, 535, 542, 548, 580-91, 601, 602, 646, 682, 714, 717, 753
Féré, C. S., 502, 651, 655
Fichte, J. G., 566, 593, 641, 678
Flechsig, P., 624, 625
Flourens, P. J. M., 495, 619, 620, 623, 625, 741
Flugel, J. C., 691 (footnote), 725 (footnote), 733
Fortlage, K., 647
Fouillée, A., 501
Fox, G., 290
Francis, St., of Assisi, 226, 291
Franz, S. I., 699
Frenkel-Brunswik, E., 737
Freud, S., 34, 535, 694, 698, 703, 714, 715-28, 729, 730, 732, 733, 735, 737, 739, 745, 747, 749, 750, 751, 753, 757, 758, 760, 761
Fries, J. F., 544, 545, 546, 564
Fritsch, G., 622, 623, 740
Froebel, F., 732, 733
Fromm, E., 750, 753
Fulton, J. F., 741 (footnote)

Galen, C., 31, 196, 197-204, 243, 246, 252, 255, 271, 287, 315, 316, 323, 328, 371, 473, 620
Galileo, G., 51, 95, 307, 335, 337, 338, 348, 349, 351, 352, 353, 355, 356, 380, 381, 535, 701, 750, 758
Gall, F. J., 490, 616, 618, 619, 620, 621
Galton, F., 738, 744, 745
Garnier, A., 492

Gassendi, P., 377-8, 385, 418
George, L., 636, 647
Gerson, J. C., 289, 292
Gesell, A. L., 734
Gesner, C., 304
Geulincx, A., 387, 388
Glisson, F., 344, 613
Goethe, J. W., 617, 634, 639, 640, 642, 643
Goltz, F., 623
Gorgias, 63-4, 67
Granit, R., 738, 739
Green, T. H., 559, 667, 676, 678, 685
Greene, G., 145
Gregory of Nyssa, 238
Groos, K., 732
Grosseteste, R., 293, 301

Hale, M., 375
Hall, M., 625, 628
Hall, S., 732, 734
Haller, A., 340, 344, 347, 348, 613, 614, 616, 617, 632
Hamilton, W., 352, 392, 444, 447-9, 492, 597, 619, 661, 666, 680
Hamlyn, D. W., 759 (footnote)
Hartley, D., 347, 352, 436-43, 444, 447, 448, 449, 450, 453, 457, 461, 462, 484, 615, 692
Hartley, E. L., 748
Hartman, H., 722
Hartmann, K. R. E. von, 578-80, 582, 648, 722
Harvey, W., 315-16, 341, 342, 359, 380
Head, H., 632, 738, 739, 742
Hebb, D., 741 (footnote)
Hegel, G. W. F., 241, 257, 449, 580, 581, 582, 593, 604, 633, 641, 678, 744, 747
Helmholtz, H. de, 251, 255, 592, 623, 633, 635, 638, 640, 641, 642, 643, 644, 645, 646, 665, 738, 739
Helmont, J. B. van, 342-4, 348
Helvetius, C. A., 468, 522-4, 569
Henry of Ghent, 293-4, 302
Heraclitus, 37, 40, 43, 50, 56, 62, 128, 147, 583
Herbart, J. F., 255, 413, 420, 456, 504, 533-4, 542, 545-63, 564, 565, 566, 569, 571, 580, 581, 590, 594, 596, 597, 599, 600, 604, 607, 608, 620, 635, 636, 647, 648, 653, 680, 681, 682, 684, 728
Hering, E., 590, 612, 632, 638, 639, 640, 642, 673, 739
Hilary of Poitiers, 238
Hippocrates, 31, 54-9, 197, 317, 322, 473, 475
Hitzig, E., 622, 623, 740

Hobbes, T., 96, 103, 104, 321, 355, 374, 377, 378-86, 395, 396, 405, 407, 412, 417, 422, 440, 490, 520, 569, 744, 747
Hodges, H. A., 753 (footnote)
Horace, 145
Horwicz, A., 602, 631, 646, 648-50, 653
Huarte, J., 327
Hugh of St. Victor, 272-8, 292
Hull, C., 104, 698, 701, 708-10, 714, 716, 717, 718, 720, 739, 740, 746, 753, 758, 760, 762
Hume, D., 26, 33, 34, 61, 69, 336, 339, 352, 353, 357, 420, 423, 429-36, 440, 444, 447, 449, 450, 453, 457, 466, 485, 487, 519, 520, 521, 533, 536, 538, 559, 561, 574, 579, 605, 681, 692, 711, 744, 747
Humphrey, G., 693 (footnote)
Hundt, M., 304
Hunt, J. McV., 743 (footnote)
Hunter, W. S., 697
Huschke, E., 620
Hutcheson, F., 536
Huxley, T. H., 522, 661, 667

Ibn Roshd: see Averroes
Ibn Sina: see Avicenna
Isaacs, S., 733

Jackson, H., 621, 623, 627, 738, 739
Jacobsen, C. F., 742
James, W., 398, 513, 588, 589, 600, 611, 622, 639, 645, 651, 652, 654, 676, 686-90, 695, 754
Janet, P., 501, 691 (footnote)
Jaspers, K., 691 (footnote)
Jenkin, T., 525
Jesus, 30, 143, 144
John of Salisbury, 267, 269-72, 378
Jones, Ernest, 717, 718 (footnote), 721, 722 (footnote)
Jouffroy, T., 492
Jung, C. G., 717, 730-1
Jurin, J., 612
Juvenal, D. J., 145

Kant, I., 33, 143, 165, 257, 263, 287, 288, 293, 309, 367, 400, 411, 448, 486, 490, 533, 534, 535-45, 546, 547, 554, 557, 558, 561, 564, 574, 577, 585, 586, 593, 599, 600, 603, 604, 608, 617, 633, 634, 636, 637, 653, 678, 680, 681, 685, 688, 711
Kardiner, A., 750
Kelvin, Lord, 34
Kepler, J., 51, 337, 338, 339, 340, 352, 355, 750, 755

Klein, M., 733
Klineberg, O., 746, 749
Koffka, K., 733, 752, 759
Köhler, W., 709, 739, 752
Krech, D., 749, 756 (footnote)
Kretschmer, E., 743
Krueger, F., 691 (footnote)
Külpe, O., 516, 518–19, 639

Lactantius, 215, 232, 374
Laelius Peregrinus, 330
Lamarck, J. B., 495, 575
La Mettrie, J. O. de, 346, 521, 522, 525, 614
Lange, C. G., 651, 652, 741
La Rochefoucauld, F. de, 521, 523
Laromiguière, P., 489, 495
Lashley, K., 699, 740
Laurentius, 316
Laycock, T., 663, 664
Le Bon, G., 501, 745
Legallois, J. J., 625
Lehmann, A., 655
Leibniz, G. W., 34, 155, 292, 311, 347, 387, 406–16, 437, 438, 449, 471, 482, 483, 485, 487, 488, 489, 490, 491, 495, 510, 525, 535, 536, 542, 551, 557, 574, 586, 608, 680, 681
Lemnius, L., 305–6
Leonardo da Vinci, 289, 290, 307, 328
Leroy, C. G., 526, 527, 528, 529
Levinson, D. J., 737
Lewes, G. H., 498, 619, 649, 650, 661, 666–74, 680
Lewin, K., 336, 714, 716, 753, 758, 762
Linton, R., 748
Lipps, T., 518, 569, 590, 604–9, 639
Livy, 307, 499
Lloyd-Morgan, C., 674
Locke, J., 26, 31, 34, 61, 69, 326, 327, 336, 339, 352, 353, 357, 407, 411, 413, 414, 417–23, 425, 426, 428, 429, 430, 431, 440, 445, 450, 452, 457, 466, 468, 470, 471, 473, 474, 485, 489, 491, 495, 504, 512, 524, 535, 536, 537, 562, 569, 631, 678, 692, 733, 735, 747
Lorente de No, R., 740
Lotze, R. H., 533, 534, 547, 563, 589, 591–600, 604, 635, 636, 637, 638, 639, 641, 647, 682, 687
Lucretius, 159, 160, 163, 259
Luther, M., 318

Macchiavelli, N., 289, 306–7, 335, 374, 385, 395, 747
MacCorquodale, K., 706 (footnote)

McDougall, W., 145, 361, 535, 630, 639, 694, 698, 699, 703–8, 710, 715, 717, 718, 720, 724, 737, 745, 746, 747, 748, 752, 753, 757, 758, 759
Mach, E., 514–16
Maimonides, 405
Maine de Biran, M. F., P. G. de, 459, 472, 474, 488–93, 495, 496, 499, 501, 504
Malebranche, N. de, 341, 388–94, 407, 425, 426, 438, 472, 492
Malinowski, B., 749, 750 (footnote)
Mamertus Claudianus, 238
Manderville, B. de, 528
Mansel, H. L., 449, 676
Marbe, K., 693
Marcus Aurelius, 145, 157
Marie, P., 622
Mariotte, E., 340
Martineau, J., 459, 460–2, 463, 464
Marx, K., 737, 744, 747, 750
Maudsley, H., 602, 664
Mayow, J., 346
Mead, M., 748
Meehl, P. E., 706 (footnote)
Meissner, G., 638
Melanchthon, P. S., 328
Mendel, G., 755
Mesmer, F. A., 474
Meynert, T., 624
Mill, James, 436, 447, 449–55, 456, 457, 458, 459, 461, 463, 679, 681
Mill, J. S., 234, 352, 447, 451, 454, 456, 459, 460, 461, 462, 472, 498, 499, 502, 661, 666–74, 744
Mondino de' Luzzi, 315
Moniz, E., 742
Montaigne, M. E. de, 289, 307–11, 349, 393, 473, 525
Montesquieu, C. de S., 524, 745
More, H., 373, 386
Morgan, C. T., 741 (footnote)
Moses, 180, 185, 194, 318, 375
Mosso, A., 651, 655
Müller, G. E., 456, 590, 591, 594, 639, 665, 693, 735
Müller, J., 625, 626, 632, 633, 634, 635, 637, 641, 738
Munk, H., 622, 623, 741
Munsterberg, H., 516, 657–60
Murphy, G., 691 (footnote), 748
Murray, H. A., 737
Musatti, C. L., 712
Myers, C. S., 588

Nahlowsky, J. W., 647–8
Neuhus, 328, 332
Newcomb, T. H., 748, 749

Newton, I., 340, 356, 407, 431, 437–8, 440, 457, 466, 612, 613, 634, 700, 735, 755
Nietzsche, F., 579
Nunn, T. P., 733

Ockham: see William of Ockham
Origen, 191–5, 225

Paracelsus, T. B. von, 317–18, 342, 343, 374, 375
Pardies, I. G., 376
Parmenides, 41–2, 47
Pascal, B., 521, 580
Paul, St., 30, 144, 181–4, 185, 229
Pavlov, I. P., 357, 694–6, 698, 709, 740
Pearson, K., 734
Pelagius, 230
Perrault, C., 347
Pestalozzi, H., 491
Peters, R. S., 706 (footnote), 759 (footnote)
Petrarch, 306
Peyrere, I. de la, 375
Philo, 143, 168, 170, 171–80, 184, 185, 186, 189, 190, 191, 342, 394
Philolaus, 54
Piaget, J., 733, 761
Piderit, T., 651
Pieron, H., 691 (footnote)
Pinel, P., 474, 497
Plato, 31, 33, 51, 62, 69–93, 94, 97, 106, 109, 110, 111 112, 122, 126, 128, 129, 138, 143, 146, 154, 164, 171, 175, 179, 184, 185, 186, 188, 190, 191, 199, 201, 204, 205, 212, 213, 219, 220, 225, 227, 230, 231, 232, 235, 239, 240, 242, 245, 271, 279, 281, 284, 286, 292, 307, 318, 338, 355, 356, 365, 366, 385, 400, 409, 428, 433, 453, 454, 473, 489, 520, 539, 557, 558, 562, 577, 581, 582, 596, 673, 674, 731, 747
Plattner, E., 564, 612
Plotinus, 145, 168, 204–14, 219, 224, 225, 227, 237, 240, 241, 243, 255, 427, 583, 595, 596, 661
Plutarch, 238, 309, 473, 525
Pomponazzi, P., 311–14
Popper, K. R., 29 (footnote), 349 (footnote), 755 (footnote)
Porphyry, 235–7, 309, 374
Posidonius, 192
Pratt, C., 699 (footnote), 700
Preyer, W., 732
Priestley, J., 436, 443, 613, 617
Prochaska, G., 615, 616
Proclus, 237–41, 252, 581

Protagoras, 60–3, 66, 67, 69, 70, 123, 290
Proust, M., 145
Ptolemy, 251, 252, 337
Purkinje, J. E., 626, 640
Pythagoras, 51, 581

Rapaport, D., 722
Regius, H., 376
Reid, T., 443–6, 447, 450, 453, 457, 485, 496, 504, 574, 586
Reimarus, H. S., 526–9
Ribot, T. A., 297, 396, 399, 496, 499, 500, 529, 560, 577, 590
Richter, C. P., 741
Rignano, E., 717
Rondeletius, 316
Rorarius, 374, 525
Ross, E. A., 748
Rousseau, J. J., 327, 468, 472, 478, 491, 521, 564, 732, 733, 747
Rylander, G., 742 (footnote)
Ryle, G., 103, 744 (footnote), 760, 761

Sandford, R. N., 737
Sartre, J. P., 145, 691 (footnote)
Scalinger, J. C., 322, 328
Schelling, F. W. J., 415, 575, 580, 581, 663
Scherffer, C., 613
Schleiermacher, F. E. D., 543, 564
Schopenhauer, A., 459, 501, 545, 575–8, 579, 581, 582, 618, 648, 717, 728
Sears, R. R., 728, 757
Semon, R., 673
Seneca, 144, 371, 396
Sergi, G., 652
Servetus, M., 315
Shaftesbury, Earl of, 519
Shand, A. F., 706
Sheldon, W. H., 743
Sherif, M., 748, 749 (footnote)
Sherrington, C., 628, 738, 741
Simon, T., 504, 734
Skinner, B. F., 700, 701, 702
Smith, A., 519, 520
Smith, R., 612
Socrates, 60, 61, 62, 64–6, 69, 70, 189, 290, 370
Spearman, C., 734–6
Spencer, H., 164, 256 (footnote), 405, 408, 456, 459, 460, 498, 499, 501, 522, 627, 650, 651, 660–6, 670, 673, 674, 679, 680, 683, 709, 714, 717, 744, 753
Spinoza, B. de, 31, 34, 357, 358, 394–406, 412, 434, 585, 586, 703, 714, 717, 753, 761
Spranger, E., 691 (footnote)

Stahl, G. E., 347–9, 495, 613
Stensen, N. (Steno), 346, 348
Stevens, S., 738 (footnote)
Stewart, D., 444, 445–6, 447, 451
Stout, G. F., 145, 611, 639
Stumpf, C., 639
Sully, J., 676, 684, 732
Swedenborg, E., 537, 616

Tacitus, 145, 473
Taine, H., 472, 488, 492, 494–500, 502, 686
Talbot, W. H. F., 638
Tarde, G., 501, 747
Tawney, R. H., 750, 753
Telesius, B., 319–21, 328, 349, 350
Tertullian, 195, 238
Tetens, J. N., 293, 481–8, 564
Thales, 39, 40, 83, 670
Theophrastus, 322
Theresa, St., 297–300
Thomas Aquinas, St., 31, 181, 226, 257, 280–8, 293, 300, 312, 431, 526, 601
Thorndike, E. L., 694–6, 697, 698, 701, 732
Thucydides, 145, 307, 380, 385
Thurstone, L. L., 734, 736
Titchener, E. B., 357, 518, 693
Tolman, E. C., 698, 703–6, 707, 708, 717, 720, 746, 758, 759, 762
Trembley, A., 478, 617
Trotter, W. D., 745
Trousseau, A., 621, 622
Turgot, A. R. J., 473, 474
Tylor, E. B., 744

Unzer, J. A., 615

Vanini, L., 375
Varolius, C., 316
Vauvenargues, L. C. de, 521
Venturi, G. B., 612, 613
Vernon, P. E., 736 (footnote)
Vesalius, A., 315, 359
Vieussens, R., 346
Villanova, A. de, 316–17

Virchow, R., 628, 632
Vives, J. L., 31, 323–30, 378
Volkmann, W. F., 563, 589, 638
Voltaire, F. M. A., 466, 468, 471, 474, 524

Waitz, T., 563, 635, 636, 637
Waller, A. V., 627, 628
Wallis, J., 379
Ward, J., 336, 456, 457, 569, 589, 611, 639, 675–84, 711
Watson, J. B., 357, 696–9, 733
Watt, H., 336, 693
Weber, E. H., 255, 506–7, 534, 548, 586, 587, 588, 591, 594, 602, 632, 634, 635, 636, 637, 646
Weber, M., 753
Weiss, A. P., 744
Wernicke, K., 621, 622
Wertheimer, M., 711, 713
Wheatstone, C., 638
Wheeler, R., 744
Whitehead, A. N., 35, 762 (footnote)
Whytt, R., 615
Wiener, N., 742, 743
William of Conches, 269–71
William of Moerbeke, 301, 302
William of Ockham, 289, 293, 295–6
Willis, T., 344–6, 428, 429, 525
Witelo, 251, 255, 289, 302–3
Witmer, L., 732
Wolff, C., 406, 413–16, 487, 533, 535, 536, 617
Woodworth, R., 691 (footnote), 695 (footnote), 716, 719, 751
Wundt, W., 357, 493, 504–13, 514, 518, 519, 580, 590, 591, 601, 604, 605, 633, 639, 649, 651, 653, 654, 655, 656, 657, 673, 676, 680, 692, 693, 695, 697, 735, 738, 745
Wünsch, J., 613

Young, T., 613, 640, 641, 643, 739

Zangwill, O., 691 (footnote)
Zeno, 151, 156, 157, 371
Ziehen, T., 655–7, 658

THE M.I.T. PRESS PAPERBACK SERIES

1 **Computers and the World of the Future** edited by Martin Greenberger

2 **Experiencing Architecture** by Steen Eiler Rasmussen

3 **The Universe** by Otto Struve

4 **Word and Object** by Willard Van Orman Quine

5 **Language, Thought, and Reality** by Benjamin Lee Whorf

6 **The Learner's Russian-English Dictionary** by B. A. Lapidus and S. V. Shevtsova

7 **The Learner's English-Russian Dictionary** by S. Folomkina and H. Weiser

8 **Megalopolis** by Jean Gottmann

9 **Time Series** by Norbert Wiener

10 **Lectures on Ordinary Differential Equations** by Witold Hurewicz

11 **The Image of the City** by Kevin Lynch

12 **The Sino-Soviet Rift** by William E. Griffith

13 **Beyond the Melting Pot** by Nathan Glazer and Daniel Patrick Moynihan

14 **A History of Western Technology** by Friedrich Klemm

15 **The Dawn of Astronomy** by Norman Lockyer

16 **Information Theory** by Gordon Raisbeck

17 **The Tao of Science** by R. G. H. Siu

18 **A History of Civil Engineering** by Hans Straub

19 **Ex-Prodigy** by Norbert Wiener

20 **I Am a Mathematician** by Norbert Wiener

21 **The New Architecture and the Bauhaus** by Walter Gropius

22 **A History of Mechanical Engineering** by Aubrey F. Burstall

23 **Garden Cities of To-Morrow** by Ebenezer Howard

24 **Brett's History of Psychology** edited by R. S. Peters

25 **Cybernetics** by Norbert Wiener

26 **Biological Order** by Andre Lwoff

27 **Nine Soviet Portraits** by Raymond A. Bauer

28 **Reflexes of the Brain** by I. Sechenov

29 **Thought and Language** by L. S. Vygotsky

30 **Chinese Communist Society: The Family and the Village** by C. K. Yang

31 **The City: Its Growth, Its Decay, Its Future** by Eliel Saarinen

32 **Scientists as Writers** edited by James Harrison

33 **Candidates, Issues, and Strategies: A Computer Simulation of the 1960 and 1964 Presidential Elections** by I. de S. Pool, R. P. Abelson, and S. L. Popkin

34 **Nationalism and Social Communication** by Karl W. Deutsch

35 **What Science Knows About Life: An Exploration of Life Sources** by Heinz Woltereck

36 **Enzymes** by J. B. S. Haldane

37 **Universals of Language** edited by Joseph H. Greenberg

38 **The Psycho-Biology of Language: An Introduction to Dynamic Philology** by George Kingsley Zipf

39 **The Nature of Metals** by Bruce A. Rogers

40 **Mechanics, Molecular Physics, Heat, and Sound** by R. A. Millikan, D. Roller, and E. C. Watson

41 **North American Trees** by Richard J. Preston, Jr.

42 **God and Golem, Inc.** by Norbert Wiener

43 **The Architecture of H. H. Richardson and His Times** by Henry-Russell Hitchcock

44 **Toward New Towns for America** by Clarence Stein

45 **Man's Struggle for Shelter in an Urbanizing World** by Charles Abrams

46 **Science and Economic Development** by Richard L. Meier

47 **Human Learning** by Edward Thorndike

48 **Pirotechnia** by Vannoccio Biringuccio

49 **A Theory of Natural Philosophy** by Roger Joseph Boscovich

50 **Bacterial Metabolism** by Marjory Stephenson

51 **Generalized Harmonic Analysis** and **Tauberian Theorems** by Norbert Wiener

52 **Nonlinear Problems in Random Theory** by Norbert Wiener

53 **The Historian and the City** edited by Oscar Handlin and John Burchard

54 **Planning for a Nation of Cities** edited by Sam Bass Warner, Jr.

55 **Silence** by John Cage

56 **New Directions in the Study of Language** edited by Eric H. Lenneberg

57 **Prelude to Chemistry** by John Read

58 **The Origins of Invention** by Otis T. Mason

59 **Style in Language** edited by Thomas A. Sebeok

60 **World Revolutionary Elites** edited by Harold D. Lasswell and Daniel Lerner

61 **The Classical Language of Architecture** by John Summerson

62 **China Under Mao** edited by Roderick MacFarquhar

63 **London: The Unique City** by Steen Eiler Rasmussen

64 **The Search for the Real** by Hans Hofmann

65 **The Social Function of Science** by J. D. Bernal

66 **The Character of Physical Law** by Richard Feynman

67 **No Peace for Asia** by Harold R. Isaacs

68 **The Moynihan Report and the Politics of Controversy** by Lee Rainwater and William L. Yancey

69 **Communism in Europe**, Vol. I, edited by William E. Griffith

70 **Communism in Europe**, Vol. II, edited by William E. Griffith

71 **The Rise and Fall of Project Camelot** edited by Irving L. Horowitz